THE AFRICAN
BACKGROUND OUTLINED

OR

Handbook for the Study of the Negro

BY

CARTER G. WOODSON

NEGRO UNIVERSITIES PRESS

NEW YORK

Reprinted in 1968
by Negro Universities Press
A DIVISION OF GREENWOOD PUBLISHING CORP.
New York

Library of Congress Catalogue Card Number: 68-55922

Reprinted from a copy in the collections of
The New York Public Library
Astor, Lenox and Tilden Foundations;

Printed in the United States of America

PREFACE

THIS elementary treatment of the African background of the Negro, together with brief outlines for the study of the race in the modern world, is intended to stimulate greater interest in this field. Hitherto most Europeans and practically all Americans have regarded the Negro merely as an undesirable—an undeveloped person constituting a problem in not being able to keep pace with others. The facts herein presented will show that the Negro has achieved much in various spheres, and to know the possibilities of the race a scientific appraisal of its past is necessary. The author considers the Negro as human—responding very much as others do to the same stimuli, advancing when free to go forward and lagging behind when hindered by obstacles not encountered by others.

To the large majority of persons the facts herein set forth may seem striking. To those who have given serious attention to Africa, the treatment will be purely elementary. The author has not even undertaken to direct attention to all works on Africa, for the large majority of such productions are too biased and unscientific to merit such attention. It is hoped that the simple and direct method, the illustrations by maps and the detailed outlines with accompanying bibliographical notes will so facilitate the effort as to create a general interest in the study of the Negro.

The African background is only slightly documented, but the work is very clear as to the main treatments on which the author has depended. Thanks are due A. Fayard and Company, of Paris, for the privilege of adapting one map of Jacques Weulersse's *L'Afrique Noire;* to the Librairie Delgrave, of the same city, for making similar use of several maps in J. L. Monod's *Histoire de l'Afrique Occidentale Française.* Mr. Rayford Logan assisted in reading the proof.

CARTER G. WOODSON.

Washington, D. C.
February, 1936

CONTENTS

PART I

MAPS

PART I

CHAPTER I

INFORMANTS ON AFRICA

DIFFICULT indeed is the past of Africa. Some investigators have learned sufficient about it to consider the continent as the cradle of humanity while others have discarded its history as an uninteresting field. The unfortunate thing is that the Negroes themselves of the early times left no written records except a few rare works in Arabic dating no further back than the sixteenth century, and some of these are legendary and self-contradictory. Traditions among the natives are rich, but they go back only a few centuries. Yet what we do know of Africa is both interesting and valuable. To these facts science will doubtless add other information as we approach the study of the Africans with objectivity. Most of the productions on Africa now available are worthless.

We first learn of Africa from the ancients of other continents who early worked out written languages. These ancients reached this stage before the development of the systems of writing among the Vai, among the natives of the Cameroon, or among those of Dahomey. The Orientals who are supposed to have had early contacts with Africa before the rise of Islam are the Chinese coming across the Indian Ocean, the Persians and Arabs approaching by way of Yemen, and the Hebrews entering the continent by way of Suez and the Red Sea. These people left only occasional references to the shores of Africa and made guesses as to the interior which they had never seen. From the Chinese have come practically nothing about that area, and not much more from the Persians and Arabs of ancient times. The writers of the books of the Bible sometimes mentioned the people of Africa, but they reflected merely the traditional ideas of an unknown land. Yet in spite of this lack of documentation the all but universal belief in the infallibility of the Bible has

3

forced most writers on Africa to take these observations into account.

The ancient Greeks and Romans who knew less about Africa and had the least contact with that continent wrote most about it. The Greeks hardly ventured beyond the northern shore and apparently made no effort to reach the interior. Learning of the land through Negroes who came out of the interior into the Mediterranean or from Asiatics who had invaded that region, Greek writers, with Homer as the most conspicuous, referred to the land of the blacks. Æschylus mentioned the Ethiopians as coming from Africa, and Hesiod, Mimnermus, Euripides, and Appolonius also took notice of these blacks. Herodotus, the most celebrated historian of ancient times, recorded what he had heard about that land and estimated its natives as a great people.[1] Strabo, Pliny, and Heliodorus likewise noted the presence of these black people in the Mediterranean world. Other early sources help only a little in referring chiefly to Northern Africa; and they are "drowned in an amalgam of impossibilities or obscurities from which it is extremely difficult to obtain any light."[2] The contact of the black Africans with the Greeks is portrayed, however, in the works of Greek art throughout the duration of the nation—in outstanding sculptures and paintings and in decorative art on masks, cups, pitchers, jugs, vases, terra cottas, and on such jewelry as necklaces, rings, bracelets, and talismans.

These Africans are portrayed more frequently in the art of the ancient Greeks than any other people with whom the latter had contacts. The Ethiopians are mentioned as coming into the Greek World as soldiers on two occasions. They came with the invading army of Xerxes in 480 B.C., and evidence from the excavations of Sir Arthur Evans in Crete shows that the blacks had already influenced Minoan culture.[3] They are portrayed as actors and as favorites among the rich and at the courts of rulers.

---

[1] *Iliad,* I, pp. 423-424; XXIII, pp. 205-207; *Odyssey,* I, pp. 22-24; IV, p. 84; V, pp. 282-283; X, pp. 190-192; and the *Argonautica* of Appolonius Rhodeus, III, p. 1190 f.

[2] Maurice Delafosse, *Negroes of Africa, History and Culture,* translated by F. Fligelman (Washington, D. C., 1931), p. 28.

[3] See G. W. Parker's "The African Origin of the Grecian Civilization," in *The Journal of Negro History,* II, pp. 334-344.

The Africans were not mainly slaves in ancient Greece, as Grace H. Beardsley tries to make it appear from a distortion of valuable facts published in her book, *The Negro in the Greek and Roman Civilization.*

Homer speaks of the Ethiopians as a "blameless, most just folk whom the gods themselves visit and partake of their feasts." Herodotus said they were the tallest, the most beautiful and long-lived of the human race. "Yet," says Lady Lugard, "while they are described as the most powerful, the most just, and the most beautiful of the human race they are constantly spoken of as black, and there seems to be no other conclusion to be drawn than that at that remote period of history the leading race of the Western World was a black race." [4]

These observers, others say, however, doubtless exaggerated the culture of the Ethiopians in regarding them as idyllic beings and their country as a terrestrial paradise. A few, going to the other extreme, have later pictured them as brutes of the land of darkness. Some writers, like Gobineau, refer to the Africans as "big children"; another circle of Europeans designate these natives as "backward," and still others refer to them as "retarded." [5] "Primitive" is another such designation, but science does not know people as "primitive."

The Romans who held the northern shore of Africa from the first to the seventh century left practically no records of the interior. They had, however, a little more opportunity than the Greeks to know Africa and brought it into their literature as did Terence, Vergil, and Ovid. Roman sculptors and painters did not fail to incorporate into their designs conceptions of that continent and its people.[6] Since the Romans were a conquering people subordinating and enslaving the natives of other lands, however, they, as a rule, referred to the African in rather contemptuous fashion [7] as they did to the Thracians, Angles, and the like whom they sold in the market as slaves.[8]

[4] Lady Lugard, *op. cit.*, p. 221.
[5] Delafosse, *op. cit.*, XXIX.
[6] Beardsley, *op. cit.*, Chapter XII.
[7] *De Senectute*, p. 6; *Juvenal*, V, pp. 54-55; *Florus*, IV, p. 7; *Martial*, III, pp. 36, 39, VII, p. 87; Riese's *Antologica Latina*, I, No. 9, pp. 353, 354.
[8] G. H. Beardsley, *The Negro in the Greek and Roman Civilization;*

The slave status was not the lot of all Africans in Rome. The monuments of Rome show the Africans in all spheres into

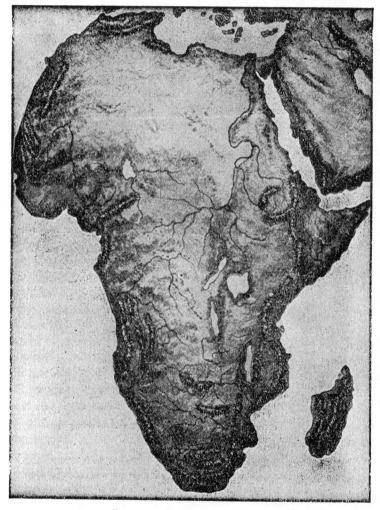

PHYSICAL FEATURES OF AFRICA

which other foreigners went. As other slaves increased, however, so did those from Africa; and as the empire became more and more an agency of oppression and exploitation of the outer

world African slaves along with other slaves were gradually
debased. Yet the extent to which the African figured in Roman
painting and sculpture refutes the biased conclusion that Negroes
were merely slaves functioning as menials and clowns as Grace
H. Beardsley's American race prejudice read into her work tries
to prove when the very facts which she has collected refute her
theory.

Most European writers taking up the interior of Africa, moreover, resort to conjecture to show migration from Caucasianized
centers to prove that foreign influence was the stimulus to the
culture discovered in West and Central Africa. Egypt, described
as a white man's land, is given as the first guess, but this is
rejected by several, although Lady Lugard contends that prior
to the coming of Cambyses of Persia to conquer Egypt in 527 B.C.
that empire must have influenced the natives of the interior.[9]
Then Berber Africa, once influenced by Romans who conquered
it, organized it as provinces, and Christianized it, is considered
only to be likewise rejected by Delafosse. Unlike Lady Lugard,
Delafosse does not get much light from these sources and looks to
Phœnicia as an explanation of the culture in Negroland.[10]

Delafosse believes that the Negroes of the prehistoric period occupied even the areas on which they are not found today. Homer,
the first of the Greeks to refer to the Ethiopians, considered the
Ethiopians as separated into two divisions, which Europeans of
today try to distinguish as "white Africa" and "black Africa."
Later other Greek writers referred to these two divisions as one
east of the Nile and the other west from the Nile to the
Atlantic. Evidently there had been much migration from Asia
into Africa which had resulted in mixed breeds near the East
Coast but had not affected very much the interior. Only a few
dared then to penetrate the hinterland.

Waves of such migrations are supposed to have swept over
the northern shore of Africa, at different times the home of
various ancient peoples. The one drove the other down the
slopes into the desert to become nomads of various bloods and

André Berthelot, *L'Afrique Saharienne et Soudanaise, ce qu'en ont connu
les anciens* (Paris, 1927).

[9] Lady Lugard, *A Tropical Dependency* (London, 1912), p. 95.
[10] Delafosse, *op. cit.,* p. 32.

traditions—Toucouleurs, Tuaregs, Kabyls, Amozighs of the west, the Tibbos, the Berdoas-Berbers, mulattoes, mixed breeds.[11]   The first inhabitants of Africa below the Sahara were dwarfs or pygmies lighter in color and slighter in build than the generality of Negroes, those with no traces of European or Asiatic blood. From what place these little Negroes came, these theorists say, no one knows.   Most writers speak of a movement from west to east.   Some go so far as to say that the Negroes came from a now submerged land in Oceania towards the limits of the Indian Ocean, sometimes referred to as *Lemuria.*   This may account for the Negroid elements in Australia, Papua, the Philippines, and the Melanesian islands.   The supposed Negroes who came into Africa have been referred to as nomads or semi-nomads, while others consider them a sedentary people, cultivators of the soil, who because of other movements or pressure from without had to dislodge the African aborigines called Negrillos.[12]

The Negrillos, it is said, were differentiated from Negroes of the usual type by the more disproportionate relation of the respective dimensions of the head, the trunk, and the limbs.   When Hanno, the Carthaginian general, explored Africa as far as Sherbro in the sixth century B.C. he discovered a people of small stature whom he called the "gorii."   The Persian, Sataspe, found there the following century little men of the same type probably as far south as did Hanno.[13]   According to Herodotus (450 B.C.) some young Nasimonians inhabiting Syrte, between Tripolitania and Cyrenaica, crossed the desert and found a plain of trees separated by marshes from a city watered by the great river containing crocodiles, the inhabitants little men of dark color of a stature below medium.   They were said to have bows and arrows and rode in chariots armed with scythes.   Evidently they had discovered the use of iron.   Georges Hardy imagined these

[11] Since the days of Herodotus the history of North Africa has been treated in extenso by other writers.   Among these works are E. Mercier's *Histoire de l'Afrique Septentrionale depuis les temps les plus reculés jusqu'à la conquête française* (3 vols), (Paris, 1888-1891); Ch. André Julien's *Histoire de l'Afrique du Nord* (Paris, 1931); and Stéphane Gsell's *Histoire Ancienne de l'Afrique du Nord* (8 vols.), (Paris, 1928-1930).

[12] Delafosse, *op. cit.,* pp. 13-18; Dr. Pantrin, "Les Negrillos du Centre African" in *L'Anthropologie,* vols. XXII and XXIII (Paris, 1911-1912).

[13] Delafosse, *op. cit.,* p. 25.

aborigines to be dwellers in trees, fishermen, and hunters.[14] This has been referred to as the region now known as the Niger or the Chad. The Hottentots and Bushmen are considered the descendants of these little Negroes.

"Then came the first Negroes, who reached the African continent by the South-East," says Delafosse. "They also must have been nomads or semi-nomads and hunters, principally because they were in a period of migration and were looking for territories in which to establish themselves, being obliged, in the course of their continual displacements, to nourish themselves with game; but they had almost certainly a tendency to be sedentary and to cultivate the soil as soon as they found favorable ground and could install themselves upon it. It is probable that they practiced the industry of polishing stone, be it that they had imported it or that they had later borrowed it from the autochthones of the north during the time that they had been in contact with them, or finally, that they had perfected the processes of the Negrillos. They must have possessed fairly pronounced artistic aptitudes and a strong religious impregnation. Perhaps it is to them that one must attribute the stone monuments that have been discovered in various regions of Negro Africa, monuments which have so much puzzled Africanists and whose origin remains a mystery, such as the edifices of Zimbabwe in Rhodesia and those raised stones and carved rocks of Gambia in which traces of a sun cult are considered to be revealed. They probably spoke languages employing prefixes, in which the names of various categories of beings or objects were divided into distinct grammatical classes.[15]

"According to all probability, the Negrillos of the epoch anterior to the coming of the Negroes into Africa were hunters and fishermen, living in a semi-nomadic state suitable to people given exclusively to hunting and fishing. Their customs were probably similar to those of the Negrillos who still exist at the present hour and, doubtless, like these, they spoke languages which were half isolating, half agglutinating, characterized, from

[14] Georges Hardy, *Histoire d'Afrique* (Paris, 1930), p. 2.
[15] Delafosse, *op. cit.*, p. 13.

the phonetic point of view, by the phenomenon of 'Clicks' [16] and by the employment of musical tones. The great trees of the forest, grottoes of the mountains, rock shelters, huts of branches or of bark, lake dwellings constructed on piles might have served them, according to the region, for more or less temporary habitations. Perhaps they were given to the industry of chipping or of polishing stones, and it might be proper to attribute to them the hatchets, arrowheads, scrapers and numerous instruments of stone that are found nearly everywhere in contemporary Negro Africa and which the present Negroes, who are ignorant of their origin, consider as stones fallen from the skies and as material traces left by the thunder. It is possible again without being permitted the formulation of definitive affirmations, that the Negrillos knew only chipped stone, while their prehistoric neighbors of North Africa had already arrived at the art of polished stone." [17]

Various migrations, all agree, have moved the interior of Africa. The first one, according to Delafosse, must have been of people of the type of the Bantu and drove the little Negroes into the swamps. Then was unfurled over Africa a second invasion of the same origin and in the same direction, but made up of slightly different elements. "If we admit," says Delafosse, "that the new arrivals reached the African continent at about the same localities as those who had preceded them, that is to say, on the East Coast and about as high up as the Comoro Islands, we are led to think that they found the best lands already occupied by the first immigrants. Thus the newcomers found themselves constrained to push further toward the north and toward the west and to settle among the Negrillos, remaining there in possession of the soil, demanding of them a hospitality which probably was not refused: hence the tradition, reported above, of the Negrillos being regarded by the Negroes of the Sudan and of Guinea as the real masters of the land. They chose their domicile by preference in the uncovered regions, well watered and easily cultivated, situated between the Equator and the Sahara, absorbing the few

[16] A "click" is a sound produced by the play of the organs of speech accompanied by an *inspiration* of air instead of an expiration.
[17] Delafosse, *op. cit.*, p. 12.

Bantu elements which were already settled there or pushing them back towards the northeast (Kordofan) or towards the north-west (the Cameroons, the Gulf of Benin, the Ivory Coast, the Grain Coast, the Rivières du Sud, Gambia and Casamance), where today we still find, here and there, languages, such as certain dialects of the Kordofan, for example the *Diola* of Gambia and the Casamance, which are closely related to the Bantu type.[18]

"This second wave must have mixed with the Negrillo much more so than did the first Negro immigrants and little by little became assimilated with them, at the same time that they per-fected the technical processes of the autochthones and of the *Bantu,* developing agriculture, introducing a rudiment of cattle and poultry raising, domesticating the guinea-fowl, importing or generalizing the practice of making fire and its utilization for the cooking of food, inventing the working of iron and the making of pottery. Their languages must have possessed the same system of classifying names as those of the *Bantu,* but proceeding by means of suffixes instead of employing prefixes. From the linguistic point of view as well as from the anthro-pological, both the Negro and the Negrillo elements, in all places where they became fused, very certainly reacted upon one an-other in variable proportions, according as one or the other pre-dominated. Of these unequal fusions were probably born the often profound differences that we note today between the vari-ous populations of Guinea and a part of the Sudan, such as the differences between their languages." [19]

Those to the north, according to the same writer, had contact probably with the Mediterranean race from the central Sahara onwards, Lybia and Egypt. Mixed breeds resulted as the Bishari, Somali, Galla, Danakil, Sidama, of more white blood than black; and the Masai, Nuba, Tubu, Kanuri, Hausa, Songhay, Sarakolle, Tukulors, Wolofs, of more black blood than white. Those toward the south, with the exception of certain islets of Negrillos, have remained pure after an original infusion of foreign blood. These are the Bantu. To the north of the Equator, in the southern part of the Sudan and along the Gulf of Guinea are those more

[18] Delafosse, *op. cit.,* p. 15.
[19] *Ibid.,* pp. 15-16.

or less mixed with the Negrillos called the Negroes of Guinea. Farthest to the north the Negroes mixing with Negrillos and with the Mediterranean race, formed the type called the Sudanese. The passage from one of these primordial types to the other takes places by such graduation as to be imperceptible, thus giving intermediate types.

It has been believed by some writers like W. E. B. DuBois, who by 1915 when he wrote *The Negro* had digested the works in this field, that primitive men dispersed from some ill-defined center in Southern Asia and went in two directions. The "long-headed and flattened-hair follicled Negro" directed his course, it is said, toward the south into Africa where members of this race exist today after undergoing ethnic changes. At the same time the other branch of the human race going northward became the broad-headed and straight-haired Mongolian. Between these two branches, these theorists say, developed a third or intermediate type with hair and cranial measurement uniting some of the features of each. Various other stocks, they tell us, have developed by the variations of environment and the intermingling of these three types. At the time of advancing this theory so-called scientists were not only tracing human migrations but were busily engaged in making cranial measurements to figure out from the space thus determined how much brain a race had or how much this capacity permitted it to have.[20]

The same authorities have thought that the Negro branch of the primitive race went eastward to Burma and the Sea Islands and then proceeded through Mesopotamia into Europe and left among the people their curly hair, dark complexion, as a distinguishing mark of the Jew, Syrian, Assyrians, and Southern Europeans. The early Mediterraneans commonly called Pelasgians, Cretans, Minoans, Tyrrhenians and Estrucans were mixed breeds of African blood. "Recent discoveries made in the vicinity of the principality of Monaco, and others in Italy and western France," says Sir Harry H. Johnston, "would seem to reveal the actual fact that many thousand years ago a negroid race had penetrated through Italy into France, leaving traces at the present

[20] This foolhardy theory has given place to another equally untenable in degrading psychology by the groundless claims of recently devised tests and measurements.

day in the physiognomy of the peoples of southern Italy, Sicily, Sardinia, and western France, and even in the western parts of the United Kingdom of Great Britain and Ireland. There are even at the present day some examples of the Keltiberian peoples of western Scotland, southern and western Wales, southern and western Ireland, of distinctly negroid aspect, and in whose ancestry there is no indication whatever of any connection with the West Indies or with modern Africa. Still more marked is this feature in the peoples of southern and western France and of the other parts of the Mediterranean previously mentioned." [21]

The aborigines of Africa, however, are not considered as representative of the extreme type thus classified today. The primitive Negro was a reddish brown type with a round skull like the Mongolian as one finds the skulls of Pygmies and Bushmen.[22] This Negro reached Africa, it was believed, about fifty thousand years ago and took possession of the region about Lake Chad and the Great Lakes. The next migration to Africa, we are informed, was about twenty thousand years later and was of mixed breeds with Negroid characteristics resulting from amalgamation with black men in other parts. These were of a lighter color and straighter hair. From these developed the race around the Mediterranean embracing stocks from Southern Europe, Western Asia and Northern Africa. To these mulattoes or mixed breeds belong the Egyptians, the Berbers and the people of Modern Africa above the equator. In "Negro Africa" three outstanding types are noted: "the lighter and smaller primitive stock, the larger forest Negro in the center and on the West Coast, and the tall, black Nilotic Negro in the eastern Sudan." [23]

The African of the lighter color grew still lighter with straighter hair, as other migrations to Africa facilitated more interbreeding while the Negro in the equatorial forest tended to become a bigger and blacker stock. Africa, then, has all sorts of racial types as "transitions between absolute Caucasian and absolute Negroes" when "no such absolute types ever existed on either side." [24] In the Philippines, it is observed, the Malay varies

[21] *Contemporary Review*, August, 1911.
[22] *L'Anthropologie.*
[23] Du Bois, W. E. B., *The Negro* (New York, 1915), p. 24.
[24] *Ibid.,* pp. 23-24.

between the light brown of sharp features and the flat-nosed, thick-lipped, woolly-haired man whom scientists contend is not Negro in the African sense; the Caucasian varies from the type of blue-eyed blonde to that of the kinky-haired, thick-lipped, and prognathic-jawed Australian whom scientists do not consider a Negro. While these stocks came from a common ancestor they have remingled their blood to produce a world of mulattoes. As a result of such interbreeding, according to this theory, there is no such thing as race. Africa is really the land of mixed-breeds or mulattoes.

The earliest records refer to Negroes in the Nile Valley as proceeding from the interior and intermingling with Semites to furnish the basis for the culture of Ethiopia and Egypt. The Negroes extended their sway from the Nile to Guinea where developed a culture later merged with conflicting cultures of Europeans and Asiatics in the center of the Sudan. Under other influences, centering around Zimbabwe and extending throughout South Africa developed a Negro culture. These migrations set in motion certain central tribes which moved southeastwardly gathering sufficient momentum and numbers to constitute a great stock calling themselves the Bantu. They overran and settled South Africa and influenced the natives toward the north as far as the Equator.

Endeavoring to explain the origin of the various South African stocks called the Bantu, S. M. Molema, an educated African, says in his *The Bantu,* "How the section of the Negroes south of the equator and known as the Bantu actually arose will always be a difficult question to answer. That they are sprung from Negroes seems beyond question. They are said to have sprung from the mingling of Negro blood with that of the Hamites of North Africa and also the Semites of North and East Africa—that is, in short, the Bantu are a hybrid race—Negroes modified by considerable infusions of Caucasian blood. That, of course, is quite easily possible and readily understood; what forms the difficulty is the complete and abrupt separation of the Bantus from other Negroes in language, and also the striking homogeneity of all the Bantu languages as opposed to the astounding diversity of the

Negro languages. For, consider, the Negroes north of the Equator are very uniform in their physical appearances, but speak languages as different as English is from German. Even between conterminous tribes, the slightest linguistic resemblance cannot be made out. In fact, it is stated on good authority that in one district of several villages, each village may be found speaking its own language totally unrelated to that spoken in another village." [25] In his long study of these languages, however, Maurice Delafosse claimed there is a unity. [26]

"Contrast with this the position south of the equator down to the most southerly point of Africa," says Molema. "Here the inhabitants are all black also, but they show great diversity in their physical appearance. In language, however, there is a remarkable uniformity. You may hear the same words occurring in most of the languages. When the languages are considered on a grammatical basis, their uniform construction and syntactical agreement becomes even more striking. It appears, in fact, as if all those people had sprung from one common stock. Their language is neither Hamitic nor Negro nor a cross of the two, in words or syntax. [27]

"Until better information about the birth of the nation can be adduced, however," continues Molema, "it may for the present be taken that the Bantu reached Central Africa in the shape of their Negro ancestors somewhere about 30,000 years ago. After 20,000 years or so, they gradually mixed their blood with the Hamites who had penetrated from North Africa as far south as Southern Sudan, Abyssinia, and Somaliland. After the conquest of North Africa by the Arabs about 6,000 years ago, these gradually filtered southward by land on the steps of the Hamites, while by sea they reached the east coast of Africa and probably mixed their blood about 3,000 years ago with the Negroes (destined to be Bantus) to a greater extent than did the Hamites before them.

[25] This is well brought out in H. H. Johnston's two volumes entitled *A Comparative Study of the Bantu and Semi-Bantu Languages.*
[26] Maurice Delafosse, "Sur l'Unité des Langues Négro-Africaines" in the *Revue d'Ethnographie et des Traditions Populaires,* 1920.
[27] S. M. Molema, *The Bantu, Past and Present* (Edinburgh, 1920), pp. 5-6.

This is a hypothesis. It is enough to explain the hypothetical infusion of Sabæan blood in the Bantu.[28]

"From this equatorial region the huge, seething mass of humanity began a southward migration on a broad front but separate lines—now rushing forward with impetuosity, now advancing more slowly, and now halting but never receding. The advance was necessarily slow, and it was probably only a few decades before Christ that the Zambesi was crossed, and about the fifteenth or sixteenth century the Limpopo was reached." [29]

All this, however, is theory. What we do not know about the people in Africa will fill many volumes. At best we still know little of the so-called "primitive" man, for science has made only a beginning in penetrating this sphere. The Aryan theory of the evolution of culture from the preeminent Asiatics who in migrating covered both Europe and Africa with new ideas has been generally rejected by thinkers of our day. The thought that the long-headed Nordics came southward to civilize the rest of the world has also been abandoned as unscientific.

Coming to the Middle Ages, we are not much better off with respect to information about Africa, although we do get a little light from the productions of Mussulman geographers, and historians of Spain, Barbary, Egypt, and Arabia; and from certain works later reedited in Arabic by the Sudanese.[30] The Mohammedan slave traders, touching the country here and there in the east for exploitation, gave merely occasional glimpses into the life of that continent, for they were primarily concerned with commerce on the Indian Ocean, on the Red Sea, and on the Eastern Mediterranean. Later Arabs traveling farther into the interior began to record more valuable, although imperfect, information. The first one of prominence was Ibn-Haukal, of Bagdad, who spent twenty-eight years traveling in Mohammedanized countries. Among the lands which he visited were the Sahara and Northern Sudan. He became acquainted with the Niger which he confused with the Nile. He thought it ran from west to east into Egypt. In the tenth century he visited Kumbi (Ghana) and Howdaghost and returned to Morocco. In his book

[28] *Ibid.*, p. 6.
[29] Molema, *op. cit.*, p. 6.
[30] Delafosse, *op. cit.*, p. 28.

entitled *Routes and Kingdoms* his knowledge of the country is set forth.[31]

The next informant was El-Bekri, an Arabian geographer,

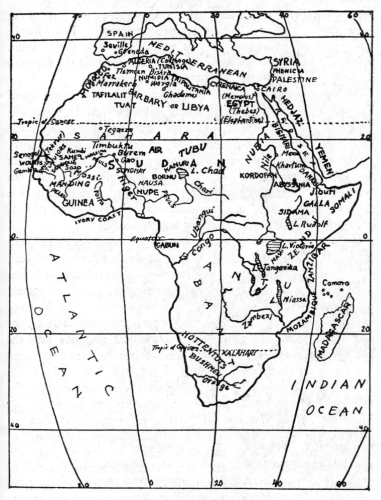

AFRICA AS FOREIGNERS FOUND IT

born in Spain about 1030. In his work on Africa he described two Niles, one running to the east and the other to the west.

[31] J. L. Monod, *Histoire de l'Afrique Occidentale Française*, pp. 15-17.

He doubtless had in mind the Niger and the Senegal. From his work we learn much more about Kumbi (Ghana) and the capital of the empire. Next we are informed by Edrisi, of the family of the Edrisites, a man born at Ceuta and exiled from his country. We learn from his work, composed in Sicily, a summary of what was known about Africa in the twelfth century. In the thirteenth century, Yakut, a native of Persia, brought out a dictionary of geography in which he showed that the Niger and the Nile were two distinct streams; but Ibn-Said, living at the time of the destruction of Kumbi (Ghana), and Aboulfeda, a geographer of Damascus, apparently ignored this distinction. They confused the Niger, the Chad, and the Nile under the same name of Nile. About this time, too, El-Gharnati published an account of the Almoravide movement into Africa and the Islamization of the Sudan.[32]

From the other Arabs and Persians taking up Africa we obtain more reliable information. In the fourteenth century, Ibn-Batuta, a geographer, born at Tangier in 1302, visited Egypt, Arabia, Persia, India, and China, and, returning, traveled from 1352 to 1353 through Spain and certain parts of the African interior known as Walata, Melle, Timbuctoo, and Gao. His account, although showing an Islam bias, is regarded as valuable. Ibn-Khaldun, born in Tunis in 1332, wrote a history of the Berbers in which he gave an account of these mixed-breeds who invaded Negroland when forced to find new homes. Hassan-Ibn Mohammed, called Leo the African, born in Granada in 1483, traveled through North Africa and about 1507 visited Walata, Jenne, Timbuctoo, Gao, Kano, and Agadez. Abderrahman Es-Sadi and Mahmoud Kati, black Sudanese, gave the world still more information in the *Tarikh Es-Soudan*[33] and the *Tarikh El-Fettach*.[34] These authors, although Mohammedan partisans, approving what appealed to them and denouncing the ways of the natives who resisted Islam, nevertheless confirm the leading

[32] Monod, *op. cit.*, p. 53.

[33] Es-Sadi, *Tarikh Es-Soudan*, Chapter I (Translation by Houdas, Paris, 1898-1900).

[34] Kati, *Tarikh El-Fettach* (Translation by Houdas and Delafosse, Paris, 1913), Chapter I.

facts set forth by their predecessors in history and thus constituted themselves the most informing of the writers on the Sudan
for the Middle Ages.[35]

[35] Monod, *op. cit.*, pp. 53-64; and A. O. Stafford's "The Tarikh Es-Soudan"
in the *Journal of Negro History*, II, pp. 139-146.

CHAPTER II

ETHIOPIA AND EGYPT

"Many facts," contends Delafosse, "corroborate the hypothesis which tends to relate the first formation of the Sudanese populations known as Negroid to an epoch far more remote than that which is generally assigned to it and to attribute to the prehistoric peoples who preceded the Egyptians, the Libyan Berbers and the Semites in North Africa, the influence which has often been accorded to these latter. It does not follow that the role of the Egyptians, the Libyan Berbers and the Semites has been of no consequence in the definitive constitution of certain Negroid peoples labeled, the one as Chamites or Hamites, the other as Sudanese. But if this role cannot be denied in the development of the civilization of such peoples, or in a certain measure regarding the evolution of their languages, it seems very likely that it has been much less important, from the physiological point of view, than the role played by the most ancient populations of whom, after all, it must be remembered, we know almost nothing except that they already existed before the epoch of the first Egyptian dynasty." [1]

Carvings on African monuments in Northeast Africa are further enlightening. The zodiac was found there on one. Records of the conquests of Meroe by Rameses the Great of Egypt show that it was a country of luxuries and splendor with tributary states of which Thebes was one. Women were armed and lived on equality with men. They had a government by a priest-caste. Gau, Champollion, and others have said, "In Nubia and Ethiopia stupendous, numerous, and primeval monuments proclaim so loudly a civilization contemporary to, aye, earlier than that of Egypt, that it may be conjectured with the greatest confidence that the arts, sciences and religion descended from Nubia to the

[1] Delafosse, *Negroes of Africa*, pp. 18-19.

lower country of Misraim [Egypt] ; that civilization descended the Nile, built Memphis, and finally, sometime later, wrested by colonization the Delta from the sea." [2]

"In general," Delafosse warns, "we have a tendency to place much too near to us facts whose dates are not known to us and to put into periods with whose history we are approximately familiar, events which generally have preceded these periods by many centuries or even by many thousands of years and which, moreover, have required several centuries or even several millenniums for their integral development. This tendency may be noticed in many authors who deal with the formation of countries or peoples, and it is necessary to react against such an unfortunate habit." [3]

African civilization, like others, this author might have added, may have been influenced by an influx from Asia, but before that time Africans had demonstrated their gifts. Africans by themselves have developed systems of writing, that of the Vai of Guinea and that of the Bamoun or Bamon of the Central Cameroons. Before any Asiatic or European invasions the Africans had clay houses with openings, decorated pottery, metallurgy, and cultivated land. In the interior of Africa the first European and Asiatic observers found among the natives the horse, the art of equitation, the use of the bit, stirrup, and saddle. They had learned the use of textiles, could weave, and sew. They had become acquainted with copper and bronze, had learned to work in gold and had developed iron. Some of the later observers, like biased Europeans and Americans of our time, have tried to prove that these ideas were borrowed, but they themselves, after spinning out their legends and theories, have had to admit that their assertions are only conjectures. They have no more proof that what the Africans at that time knew was borrowed from foreigners than that the latter have borrowed such ideas from the blacks of the interior.

Social institutions like representative democracy, trial by jury, and other contributions have been accredited to ancient Africans

[2] Lady Lugard, *A Tropical Dependency,* pp. 220-221; M. Delafosse, *Haut-Senegal-Niger* (Soudan Français), Paris, 1912, volume I.

[3] M. Delafosse, *Negroes of Africa,* p. 19.

by authorities like Herodotus, Diodorus, Josephus, Volney, Erman, Pritchard, Von Luschan, Champollion, Roselinin, Petrie, Sayce, Maspero and other scholars. All recognized scientists support the claim that the use of iron in the interior of Africa dates from time immemorial. Volney and others contend that these Africans first named the stars. The conception of the four elements and their relations to the cosmos, according to Egyptologists, came from the Milesian school, some of whom traveled in Egypt and Ethiopia. The double spiral motif copied in the Greek Minoan culture has been traced to Africa. The idea of the unity of God, accredited as a contribution of the Jews, was an African idea. The Jews, as the Bible itself proves, were polytheists until their captivity and enslavement in Egypt influenced by Ethiopia. While under the yoke in Africa they learned *Jahweh* whom they called *Jehovah* by mistake and worked out a revolution from polytheism to monotheism when they emerged from their captivity and returned to Judea. The God of Abraham, the God of Isaac, and the God of Jacob, in contradistinction to other gods of the Jews, were carefully differentiated throughout the Old Testament.[4]

Egypt, the land of Negroid mixed breeds, became the connecting link between black Africa of the Nile and the other parts of the ancient world. Phœnicians, Greeks, Romans, and Carthaginians had with certain blacks just below the Sahara a caravan trade in ivory, gold, cloth, precious stones, and slaves. Negroes served in their armies and infused their blood into the veins of their people. Black men followed the fortunes of Hannibal. Mulatto kings like Masinissa and Jugurtha served on thrones in North Africa. Negro people marched with the Mohammedans through North Africa and settled with them in Portugal and Spain. Negroes who served in the armies of the followers of the Prophet facilitated the fusion of the Mohammedan culture with that of the natives in laying the foundation for the culture of the Upper Sudan of today. Kingdoms like Ghana, however, had already developed in Africa, but because of pressure from without they failed to endure as large empires.[5]

[4] *L'Anthropologie*, 1901; and Gsell, *Histoire Ancienne de l'Afrique du Nord*, Vol. IV: *La civilization carthaginoise*.

[5] Du Bois, *op. cit.*, pp. 100-102.

Ethiopia, the forerunner of Egypt, was a promising kingdom at an early period. Ethiopia was the land of the black-faced, the land of fairies and gods, so fascinating to the Greeks that they adopted as one of their heroes the black Memnon, King of Ethiopia. The wars of Egypt, Persia, Rome and Byzantium stifled Ethiopia, however, in ancient times. Another effort at state building showed promise in the southeast, but the Bantu tribes nipped this in the bud only to assure the rise of small kingdoms which did not long endure. An attempt to develop later the states of Benin and Yoruba was made; but the Bantu became active to the contrary and the Sudanese stimulated with Mohammedanism crushed this in its incipiency in the interest of their imperialism. And when there arose the greatest of empires in Africa they perished because the forest natives pressed upon them from the south in wars for slaves, and the routes through which trade with Africa and the Mediterranean was carried on were closed in the sixteenth century by Moors expelled from Europe and cut off from the Orient by the Seljukian Turks.[6] The slave trade with the Europeans on the coast, then, became the only commercial outlet. After the slave trade had done its work came the partition of the continent by Europeans. Yet the past of this continent is all but fascinating.

"When the history of Negroland comes to be written in detail," says Lady Lugard, "it may be found that the kingdoms lying toward the eastern end of the Sudan were the home of races who inspired, rather than of races who received, the traditions of civilization associated for us with the name of ancient Egypt. For they cover on either side of the Upper Nile, between the latitudes of ten degrees and seventeen degrees, territories in which are found monuments more ancient than the oldest Egyptian monuments. If this should prove to be the case, and the civilized world be forced to recognize in a black people the fount of its original enlightenment, it may happen that we shall have to revise entirely our view of the black races, and regard those who now exist as the decadent representatives of an almost forgotten era, rather than as the embryonic possibility of an era yet to come."[7]

[6] The story of Africa here becomes mainly Oriental in connecting it with movements which led to the Crusades.

[7] Lady Lugard, op. cit., pp. 17-18.

Going into the details of the history of the first of these empires, however, Delafosse would say that Semites in Abyssinia did the same there as the Carthaginians had done elsewhere in Africa. These Semites, he says, had the name of Ben Israel. "Should we relate them," says he, "to the Hebrews whom Joseph, son of Israel, brought to Egypt, and who did not all return to the Holy Land with Moses, a certain number on the contrary, making their way toward the West? Should we see in them the remains of those Hyksos mentioned in the Egyptian annals who, after all, were perhaps not distinct from the Hebrews of Joseph? Should they be identified with the Jews who, as a consequence of religious quarrels, emigrated from Tripolitana toward the end of the first century of our era in the direction of Air and toward the beginning of the following century in that of Tuat and who afterwards did not leave any real historical traces of their passage? Should we admit several successive migrations, the first of which goes back to the epoch of Moses and the dispersion of the Hyksos, that is, to about sixteen centuries B.C., and the last of which are as recent as the first centuries of the Christian era?"[8]

Delafosse admits, however, that this is all conjecture. If the Hebrews came to Abyssinia they appeared upon the scene in small numbers after another Oriental culture had taken distinct form. It cannot be denied, of course, that Northeast Africa has been a melting pot. The word Abyssinia comes from the word of Arabic, *Hebech* which means a melange of families. Abyssinian history, however, is distinctly African by its natural isolation—situated on a mountainous plateau inaccessible by way of streams, especially during the dry season. The country had intercourse with Asiatics from across the Red Sea in Yemen, which was once a dependency of Ethiopia. That ancient land was visited by others but by infiltration rather than by migration; they are, therefore, one people but of various bloods—Berber, Negro, Peul, Arabic, and the like, the type varying with the regions but after all a fusion of races which Americans would segregate for being black Negroes.[9]

---

[8] Delafosse, *Negroes of Africa*, pp. 37-38.
[9] The European idea of designating a man as a Negro only when he

Christianity reached Abyssinia in the fourth century after Buddhist missionaries had prepared the way and in time to be able to withstand the advance of Islam. The Monophysite schism in the time of Justinian upset things. Then Abyssinia, they say, turned from Europe to the Arabs for its influence after that period. Yet the country was not altogether a borrower. Abyssinia dominated its neighbors the Galla, Danakil, Somali, and beyond the Red Sea a large part of Yemen.[10] Antar, an Arabized African, the son of a black woman, became a military leader and one of the great pre-Islamic poets of Arabia. We are informed that one of the great poets at the court of Haroun [11] al Raschid was black. With these lands arose the great commerce of a rich, invincible, and feared Ethiopian empire which eventually brought Egypt under its control.

The civilization of the Nile started among the blacks of Ethiopia and passed on to influence the mixed breeds of Egypt, which later came under Asiatic influences.[12] In Book III of Diodorus Siculus it is said, "The Ethiopians conceive themselves to be of greater antiquity than any other nation; and it is probable that born under the sun's path its warmth may have ripened them earlier than other men. They suppose themselves also to be the inventors of divine worship, of festivals of solemn assemblies, of sacrifices, and every religious practice. They affirm that the Egyptians are one of their colonies." [13] The Egyptians, too, asserted that their civilization came from the black tribes to the south, and "at the earliest period in which human remains have been recovered Egypt and Lower Nubia appear to have formed culturally and racially one land." [14]

Among the later Egyptians developed octoroons, quadroons, samboes and blacks, the same types which developed as a result

has one hundred per cent Negro blood must be borne in mind as a contrast to the American attitude of considering a man white only when he has one hundred per cent white blood.

[10] Du Bois, *op. cit.,* p. 43.

[11] See A. O. Stafford's "Antar, the Arabian Negro Warrior, Poet and Hero" in *The Journal of Negro History,* I, pp. 151-162.

[12] Flinders Petrie, *History of Egypt,* I, pp. 52, 237.

[13] Herodotus, *History* (translation of Larcher, revised by Personneaux), Paris, 1883.

[14] Petrie, *op. cit.,* II, p. 337.

of race admixture in America. Berbers, Semites, and Negroes went into this melting pot to make up what we call the Egyptians who led the world in government, industry, science, architecture, literature, and art. In the early period, the predynastic epoch, however, Egypt was mainly Negroid.[15] Their outstanding monuments like the Sphinx at Gizeh, the Sphinxes of Tanis, the statue from the Fayum, that of the Esquiline at Rome, the Colossi of Bubastis, are of Negroids or black men. These monuments show high cheek bones, flat massive noses, both in one plane, firm projecting lips, and thick hair, with an austere and almost savage expression of power.[16] The statues of Rahotep and Nefert, of Khafra, Amenemhat I and III, Usertesen I, Tahutmes III, Queen Mutema, and Rameses II show distinctly Negroid features. Ancient writers considered the early Egyptians as Negroes. Herodotus referred in two places to them as "black and curly-haired," and Æschylus describes them as of black complexion. Immigration brought a change in color, but here black rulers figured just as conspicuously as those of other bloods. We learn that about 2500 before Christ Ra Nehesi, a full-blooded Negro, sat on the throne of the Pharaohs. The mulatto King Aahmes appears later in the role of redeeming Egypt from barbarian pressure; and his queen Nefertari, "the most venerated figure in Egyptian history" was a black woman of great beauty.[17]

When Egypt began to decline after the world wars of Rameses II and Asiatics had overrun the Lower Nile the interest passed to Ethiopia. This land was known to the Egyptians as the land of Kush, in the remote part of which was said to be Punt, the cradle of Ethiopian culture. In soil and natural facilities Egypt had the advantage of Ethiopia and could more easily resist the inroads of natives who when captured were lost in that crucible of cultures. At the same time Ethiopia, more exposed to such incursions, admitted still larger numbers of wild tribes while losing much of its advanced population to Egypt. Egyptians, however, made little effort to subdue Ethiopia until an independent native culture developed there during the middle empire around

[15] *Harvard African Studies*, I.
[16] Du Bois, *op. cit.*, p. 34.
[17] *Ibid.*, pp. 35-36.

Nepata and Meroe. There flourished a bustling trade in gold, ivory, precious stones, skins, wood, and works of handicraft, which attracted the Pharaohs. Pressed by the Semitic Hyksos the Egyptians took refuge in Ethiopia. The Pharaohs moved their capital to Thebes and from that vantage point regained control of Lower Egypt.[18]

Under the new empire Ethiopia was gradually incorporated into Egypt. The Pharaohs sent armies to subdue Ethiopia, and their sons later styled themselves under the title of the "Royal son of Kush," comparable with that of Prince of Wales. What armies could not do to bring Ethiopia under the influence of Egypt was done by her culture. From Nepata as their capital the Egyptian dynasty dethroned by Sehsheng I, the Libyan usurper, expanded the Ethiopian kingdom to the north and ruled Egypt for a hundred years. These black kings were known as Kashta the Kushite, Shabaka, Tarharqa and Tanutamen. The sons of these kings ruled Egypt just as the sons of kings of Egypt had been designated to rule Ethiopia. To the new order of things Ethiopians brought the worship of native gods of the interior, the female succession in the kingdom, and the election of kings from competing royal pretenders.[19]

In this dependent position, then, Egypt could not repel attacks upon its borders, and fell a prey to the Assyrians and then to the Persians. The culture of Egypt passed on to influence the future of Tunis, Tripoli, Algeria, and Morocco on the northern shore. Ethiopia remained independent, however, thanks to its natural handicaps and to the courage of such kings as Aspeluta Horsiatef and Nastosenen, who fought the warlike tribes on the south and repelled the Persians. The capital at that time was removed from Nepata to Meroe although for religious traditions the kings were crowned at the former seat of government. Greek culture was introduced under King Arg-Amen, and a new Ethiopian alphabet was worked out. At Meroe ruled the Candaces at the time of the international high standing of the country.

[18] C. Peters, *Im Goldland des Altertums, Forschungen zwischen Zambesi und Sabi* (Berlin, 1902).

[19] One should bear in mind that most writers on Africa, biased as a rule, consider these practices as African merely because they did not find these conditions obtaining elsewhere.

There runs a legend of a visit of Alexander the Great to Candace the Queen of Meroe, who would not permit him to enter Ethiopia. She warned him not to scorn her people because they were black, for they were whiter in soul than his white folk. Ludolphus wrote in the seventeenth century that the Abyssinians "are generally black which (color) they most admire." [20]

Ethiopia, however, was not beyond the reach of its enemies. Emperor Diocletian of Rome invited the barbarous Nubians to invade the country. These newcomers gave their name to Northern Ethiopia. Then came to Ethiopia Semites with an infusion of Negro blood. The legendary history of Abyssinia says that they are the descendants of the offspring resulting from the visit of the Queen of Sheba to Solomon about 1000 B.C. This legend probably results from the known influx of Semites and the beginning of the Axumite kingdom with a capital of the name Axum. Byzantine influence began to appear in Ethiopia in the fourth century, for in 330 A.D. St. Athanasius of Alexandria consecrated Fromentius as Bishop of Ethiopia. The country was mainly Christian by the reign of King Caleb who became a sort of defender of the faith in that area. Judith, a Jewish princess, later usurped the Axumite throne, and the Abyssinians were expelled from Arabia. Then ensued a period when Ethiopia was encompassed by the enemies of their religion.[21] The last Christian king remained only in story. However, the great achievements of Prester John in fiction would indicate more significant results.

The Nubians were converted to Christianity in the sixth century and they developed a new capital at Dongola. These Nubians held back the Mohammedans from the Nile for two centuries. The Fung Kingdom of wild tribes rushing from the Sudan into the Nile region diverted the Mohammedan hordes by declaring themselves of that faith and became the next dominant power in that area. Islam then circumscribed Abyssinia and cut it off from the rest of the continent. During the thirteenth, fourteenth,

---

[20] Du Bois, op. cit., p. 42; La Comtesse de Jumilhac, Ethiopie Moderne (Paris, 1933), p. 160.
[21] Du Bois, op. cit., p. 43.

fifteenth and sixteenth centuries the Egyptian Sudan saw a number of kingdoms ruled by Arab, Berber, and black kings.[22]

It is difficult to say what was going on in Abyssinia in its isolated state. The records were destroyed by fire in the tenth century. When the Portuguese reached the country in the seventeenth century it was learned that the Axumite kingdom had fallen, and out of it had come a number of smaller states. These held in check the Mameluke beys in Egypt and the Turks until the nineteenth century when the Sudan was incorporated into Egypt. Ethiopia during these years had been kept so far down by conquests and wars that she made little impression on the world except through her slave trade.[23] The modern history of Ethiopia begins with the coronation of Theodore as king in Axum, the holy city, in 1855.[23a] When England came into Egypt after the building of the Suez Canal a Sudanese Negro, Mohammed Ahmad or Mahdi, proclaiming a holy war, kept Egypt and England out of the Sudan for sixteen years. Control passed to the Europeans in 1898. The Italians, taking up the designs of England on Abyssinia, undertook to reduce Menelik to the status of a vassal, but he put an end to their schemes by a crushing defeat in the battle of Adowa, March 1, 1896. This victory made Abyssinia an independent nation.[24]

For centuries, however, ever since the days of the Romans, North Africa, although influenced by Ethiopia through Egypt, had become a European sphere of influence after domination by Islam from about 750 to the fall of the Barbary States. The first factor of consequence in this part of the drama was the Moors who carried civilization to Spain. Through them Africa influenced Europe.[25]

The African dominion in Spain was overthrown in 1142. The

---

[22] Es-Sadi, *Tarikh Es-Soudan.*
[23] W. S. Harris, *Highlands of Ethiopia* (London, 1844), p. 38.
[23a] F. E. Work, *Ethiopia a Pawn in European Diplomacy* (New York, 1935), p. 7.
[24] Lord Noel Buxton in the *London Times,* 1931.
[25] Among the fruits transplanted by the Moors to Spain was the peach from Negroland, not from Persia, for Strabo says the Persians found it there where it was cultivated by the Ethiopians. It may have been introduced to Africa and India. During the rule of the Arabs in Spain intercourse between Negroland and Spain was maintained.

Almohades conquered the country in 1147. When driven out of
Spain they went to Africa as an influence. Here also, before the
date of Ibn Batuta's visit, we are brought into touch in the year
1338 with the political life of the Negro kingdom of Manding
(Melle). Mansa Musa, or Gonga Musa, a black sovereign, of
whom elsewhere we shall hear more, and the seat of whose empire
was in the territory now known as the Bend of the Niger, sent an
embassy on the occasion of the conquest of Tlemcen by the Meri-
nites to congratulate their sovereign, who was his nearest white
neighbor. His embassy was accompanied by an interpreter from
Massina in the Upper Niger, where the Fulani had then a principal seat of occupation. Abou el Hacen—the king so warmly
praised a few years later by Ibn Batuta—received them very cor-
dially, and sent back by their hands a very handsome present to
the black Mansa Musa. Although there were wars between the
Berbers and blacks, there were no such conflicts between the
Spanish Arabs and the blacks with whom they traded. When expelled from Europe, however, the Spanish Arabs reversed this
policy and devastated Negroland.[26]

[26] Lady Lugard, *op. cit.,* pp. 291-295.

CHAPTER III

KUMBI [1]

Kumbi, or Ghana, as it was called by foreigners who first discovered it, was the first of the states below the Sahara to become known. The country was once called Ghanata, or Walata, and the principal town was later designated as Aiwalatin. Its founding, some say, dates back as far as the fourth century A.D. Others believe that Kumbi (Ghana) was founded as early as 700 B.C. since before 300 A.D. as many as forty-four kings had ruled in that land. We are told by biased Mohammedans trying to make a good case for their sect, that certain "white" kings once reigned there before the Hegira, but no one has ever produced any proof for such an assertion. The Arabs found the black Sarakolle in possession of Kumbi (Ghana), and the Berbers of the more northerly desert towns paid tribute to them. What really happened was that these so-called "whites" ruled the small Semitic settlements just below the Sahara before Kumbi or Ghana expanded and absorbed them as a part of the black empire. These

[1] In the treatment of these African kingdoms of the other parts of Africa we shall use, as far as possible, the names given them by the Africans themselves rather than the names by which they were known to foreigners. It is here taken for granted that a country, like an individual, is the best judge of its own name. The author is following the same rule with respect to titles which the rulers of these kingdoms and empires bore. While occasionally the titles of *king* and *emperor* are used for clearness, or rather to convey to Americans and Europeans as far as possible the meaning of these designations, it must not be believed that the complete significance of these terms is thereby translated. The meaning of these to the African is merely approximate when we use the terms more familiar to us.

In a study of this sort the ready adoption of so-called parallelisms is often dangerous. One thereby leaves the impression that the Africans were trying to imitate the European or Asiatic kingship and the like when the blacks of that continent had never heard of the institutions of the lands so far away. On the contrary, the foreigners had heard more about the Africans and had learned more about the culture than the latter had learned concerning the Asiatics and Europeans.

foreigners never ruled that empire. There was no empire of the name at the time mentioned in their legends. The Semites in the Sudan never had a real kingdom much less an empire. They were usually subject to the blacks to the south of them, and they were all but blacks themselves—mixed breeds, not whites.

To say that these "whites" founded and ruled Kumbi (Ghana), moreover, is the worst sort of intellectual dishonesty.[2] Such a claim is about as near the truth as if we would say that the Dutch were the founders of the republic of the United States because they settled and ruled for a number of years New Amsterdam which, changed to New York, became the first capital of the United States. Instead of contributing to the rise of kingdoms and empires of the blacks these interlopers, as the same writers admit throughout their narratives, were mainly nomads who became the chief factor in the undoing of Africa as it had developed under the blacks. Had it not been for these adventurers and the Mohammedans with their holy wars some of these African kingdoms and empires would be intact today.[3]

Kumbi (Ghana), we are told, was not at first an organization as stable as that of Egypt or Abyssinia. It was a region of men camping on plains. They made their way into this region not by an uninterrupted pushing or pressure, but by mutual adjustments, tribal fights, rivals among nomads, agreements of nomads with settlers. During the most ancient times there was no real domination except momentary and without historical significance. The social order, however, finally emerged. Then came the art of excavation, of masonry in wells, the cultivation of wheat, millet, and cotton, houses and fortresses of stone replacing temporary shelter, herds enriched with cattle, sheep and goats. Artisans manufacturing stuffs multiplied; implements and arms abounded.

The elements tended to group under powerful hands the commercial points in contact with foreigners in the desert, the watered places, the salt routes, and the gold routes. Real empires bringing together diverse races under one domination opening up from the Atlantic coast in a line of eastern fractures arose upon the banks

[2] For a brief statement of such theories see J. L. Monod's *Histoire de l'Afrique Occidentale Française*, pp. 54 to 55.

[3] Delafosse all but takes this position in his *Negroes of Africa* on pages 84 and 85, with respect to Juder and the horde he led into the Sudan.

of the Senegal, the Niger, and Chad. Kumbi (Ghana) was one of them. These were organizations with politics and instruments of power: a regularly supplied treasury, administrative hierarchy, armed tribunals, and marine. One observer found the population agricultural or pastoral, scattered in the plains, but "large towns and cities on the banks of streams or near watered places, settled in their family squares, cut with narrow streets, shaded with tall trees, the green of which sparkled on the desert, surrounded by full grown fields of millet, huts like anthills, certainly animated by that marvelous gayety which is characteristic of Negroes and constitutes the best gage of their vitality." [4]

Kumbi (Ghana) at first did not have precise boundaries. These were determined by the degree of force Kumbi could exert or by the resistance of her neighbors. It stretched over a vast plain from Timbuctoo to the Atlantic. Around the states which belonged to the governing race grouped others of a secondary order, tributaries, vassals or simply allies, which in times of crises became centers of small empires themselves or massed themselves together with or to neighboring political units. [5]

These states were not arrested hordes in the act of invasion. These units became actual states whose organization was not at all uniform. In Kumbi, for example, the distinction was clear between the vassal kingdoms and those called the domains of the crown. This territory was divided into provinces, the governors of which were at the same time great dignitaries of the empire—intendants, leaders of the infantry, commanders of cavalry, keepers of the royal tombs. These with ministers, equally specialized, formed an imperial council. Governors and ministers were chosen by inheritance among the old aristocratic families who, like the imperial family, had their courts and their vassals. [6]

Kumbi (Ghana) may be considered the type of Sudanese state. It was feudal and devoted especially to the arts of peace.

[4] Lady Lugard, *A Tropical Dependency*, p. 38.
[5] As to the exact boundaries of Ghana in ancient time, however, we know very little.
[6] While writers on Africa thus inform us as to inheritance they are not always clear as to whether or not the rule of primogeniture obtained according to the foreign custom in contradistinction to that of descent through the son of the sister of the defunct.

War was allowed but for a short while and on condition that the
diverse parties find a real interest in common. Should any state
try to make an occupation of war it would be necessary for the
central power to fortify itself and become actually imperial. Towards the tenth century Kumbi and its allies expanded beyond the
Sudanese region but peacefully. No long wars followed in this
effort. Agriculture and commerce had the preference. The people
of Kumbi adhered to their native religion and did not proclaim
holy wars as a pretext for conquest as was the custom of so many
kingdoms under the influence of Islam.[7]

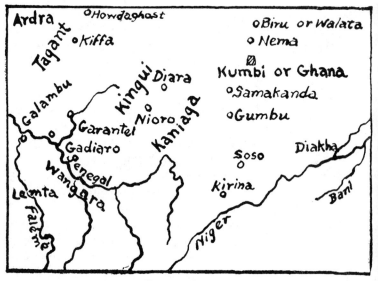

KUMBI (GHANA)

Kumbi, the capital, the name of which is mentioned as Ghana
for the first time, it seems, in the *Golden Prairies* of Masudi, who
died in 956, was visited in the second half of the tenth century by
the celebrated Arab geographer Ibn-Haukal,[8] and by El Bekri
who gave a fairly detailed description of it in the following century. It was called Ghana only by the foreigners and notably the

[7] The fanaticism of the Mohammedans developed later.
[8] Ibn-Haukal, *Description de l'Afrique* (Slane Translation) in *Journal
Asiatique*, Paris, 1842.

Arabs, who made it known by this name in Europe and Asia. "This was not its name but, as Bekri expressly says and as Sudanese traditions confirm, one of the titles borne by the sovereign, who was further designated by that of *Kaya-Maga* or simply *maga* or *magan* (the master) or again by that of *tunka* (the prince). The city itself was known to the inhabitants under the name of Kumbi-Kumbi (the butte or tumulus), by which even today its site is pointed out. It is situated between Gumbu and Walata, about a hundred kilometers to the north-north-east of the first of these localities, in a region of the Hodh which the Moors call *Howker* or *Howkar* (a geographical term common to many sub-Saharan regions). The Mandingo and the Bambara call it *Bagana* or *Mara,* the Kassonke *Bakhunu,* and the Sarakolle *Wagadu.* It extends in a general fashion to the north and to the north-east of Gumbu." [9]

From 961 to 971, a hundred years before El Bekri's writing on Africa, a black prince, Tin Yeroutan ruled Kumbi (Ghana). He had subdued the neighboring Berbers settled in the desert north of the Sudan from the Atlantic to the Sahara. More than twenty black kings acknowledged his rule and paid him tribute. It required two months to cross his kingdom. He was able to put in the field 100,000 men mounted on camels. When the neighboring Berber prince asked for help against a black neighbor Tin Yeroutan sent 50,000 men to assist him.[10]

In 1067 Kumbi (Ghana) is still the principal black kingdom with Tenkamenin as king. He had succeeded his maternal uncle Beci. Succession among the blacks went to the son of the king's sister. The town of Kumbi (Ghana) was composed of two settlements, one Mohammedan and the other African. The king was African and lived in the native quarter. For political reasons his advisers were Mohammedans, but the people as a rule remained loyal to their local religion. In Mussulman town there were twelve mosques, schools, centers of learning, a meeting place for

---

[9] The word *mara* means a region without permanent water courses but provided with ponds; the Mandingo word *baga-na,* which became *bakhu-nu* in certain dialects and the Sarakolle word *waga-du* both signify "a country of herds, region of cattle raising." See El Bekri, *Description de l'Afrique Septentrionale* (Slane Translation), Paris, 1859.

[10] Delafosse, *op. cit.,* pp. 42-43.

merchants, a resort for the learned in the Koran, the rich, and the pious of other nations, Egypt, Angila, Fezzan, Ghadames, Tuat, Draa, Sidjilmessa, Susu, and Bitu.[11]

The emperor, according to El Edrisi, lived in a well built castle thoroughly fortified, decorated inside with sculptures and pictures, and having glass windows. The buildings of the royal and well-to-do were of stone and acacia wood while the people lived in their typically conical African huts. The people wore robes of cotton, silk or brocade, according to their means. The royal town was surrounded by groves jealously guarded, which were sacred to the worship of the gods in native temples under their own priests. There stood also the royal prison and the tombs of the tunkas.[12]

Tenkamenin ruled over a vast empire. The country was wealthy, the soil fertile, and crops were produced twice a year. Gold was abundant. Nuggets went to the king and gold dust to the people. Salt in one part was so scarce, however, as to sell for its weight in gold. Tenkamenin could put in the field an army of 200,000 men, of whom more than 40,000 were armed with bows and arrows.[13]

The dependencies of Kumbi were many. Prominent among them was Sama with its capital at Samakanda. This was a country of archers skilled in fighting with poisoned arrows. Their king was succeeded by his son in contradistinction to the custom in Kumbi. Another dependency was Garantel to the West of Koniakary. The Garantel country was noted for its numerous elephants and giraffes. The people fed on millet, fish, and camel's milk, and wore woolen clothing. While they were not Mohammedans they were hospitable to foreigners who frequently crossed the country. Still another of the dependencies was Gadiaro or Gundiuru, a fortified town with much frequented markets probably because it was near the Senegal, not far from the Kayes. Gadiaro was an entrepôt for the gold from Wangara and to this point were drawn merchants from Ghana and Morocco. Upon the banks of the Senegal near the confluence of the Falémé with this stream was another such subordinate state, Galam with its capital at Galambu. South

[11] Lady Lugard, *op. cit.*, p. 49.
[12] El Edrisi, *Description de l'Afrique et de l'Espagne* (Slane Translation), Paris, 1859.
[13] Lady Lugard, *op. cit.*, p. 50.

of this state was Lemlem where the people of Tekrur, of Gadiaro and of Kumbi came to capture slaves.[14]

Under the reign of the dynasty Sisse, who Masudi and other Arab authors insist were Negroes, the state of Kumbi attained its apogee. According to Bekri, Yakut [15] and Ibn-Khaldun,[16] its power made itself felt from the ninth century "over the Zenaga or Sanhaja Berbers (Lemtuna, Goddala or Jeddala, Messufa, Lemta, etc.) who had shortly before pushed their southern advance-guards as far as the Hodh and into what is now Mauritania; Howdaghost, the capital of these Berbers, situated doubtless to the south-west and not far from Tichit, was vassal to the Negro king of Ghana and paid tribute to him; an attempt at independence on the part of the chief of the Lemtuna led, about 990, to an expedition of the tunka of Ghana (Kumbi), who captured Howdaghost and reaffirmed his authority over the sedentary Berbers and over the 'veiled Zenaga' of the desert, as several Arab authors express themselves." [17]

"On the South," says Delafosse, "the dependencies of Ghana (Kumbi) stretched to the other side of the Senegal river and as far as the gold mines of the Falémé and of the Bambuk, whose product fed the treasury of the Sisse and served to operate fruitful exchanges with Moroccan caravans coming from Tafilalit and from the Dara; they extended even as far as Manding, on the upper Niger. Towards the east, the limits of the empire reached nearly to the region of the lakes situated to the west of Timbuctoo. To the North, its influence was felt in the very heart of the Sahara, and its renown had penetrated as far as Cairo and Bagdad." [18]

Situated on the way frequented by people of the Mediterranean and the Wangara, the gold country, Kumbi (Ghana) was a rendezvous for African, Arab, and Berber merchants from North

---

[14] Monod, *op. cit.*, pp. 58-59.

[15] Yakout, *Geographisches Wörterbuch*, Leipzig, 1866-1870.

[16] *Prolégiomènes Historiques* (Slane Translation), Paris, 1868; and same author, *Histoire des Berbères* (Slane Translation), Alger, 1852-1856.

[17] Delafosse, *op. cit.*, pp. 47-48. See also W. D. Cooley, *The Negroland of the Arabs*, London, 1841; H. Barth, *Travels and Discoveries in North and Central Africa*, 1855.

[18] Delafosse, *op. cit.*, p. 48. At first Africa attracted Mohammedans as a desirable field for proselyting, but the much-talked-of wealth became later the attraction to Islam.

Africa. The route of the Maghrebiens was from Diara or Sid-jilmessa, in the Tafilet Oasis, to the south of Morocco. Their caravans of several hundred camels made the painful trip across the Sahara. They arrived at Kumbi-Kumbi with textiles, totonal salt, dates, figs, cowries, brass, blue pearls, bracelets, and rings. Salt, still worth its weight in gold, came also from Aulil and also gray amber. There was a busy market for wheat, fruit, sugar, and dried raisins from Mohammedan countries. Honey came from Negro settlements below the Sahara. Copper and dress stuff were also in demand in Kumbi. These were exchanged for gold from Wangara (Gangorary, Bambuk, and Falémé) and for amber, rubber, ivory, and slaves sold as far away as Cairo and Bagdad which recognized the splendor of Kumbi (Ghana). The tunka or emperor collected a tax on both exports and imports. All the gold nuggets belonged to him. He had one of more than thirty pounds to which he attached the rein of his horse. Gold dust alone served as the medium of exchange. Meat was abundant, but there was little wheat, dourra (millet) being used instead. Sheep and cattle appeared upon thousands of hills. Gardens and date groves surrounded the towns. The people were rich and in comfort.[19]

The empire was really worthy of the name. The ruler was called tunka or magha, maghan or kaya maghan (the master of the gold or the master of the territories). He was called also Ghana (war chief) and foreigners gave this name to his empire and to his capital. Later in the development of these parts Berber as well as black kings sat on the throne of Ghana, but it remained a black empire in spite of the interchange and the acceptance of the Mohammedan faith. The foreign element was absorbed by the black through race admixture.

The emperor was greatly venerated by all. Only he and his heir had the right to don magnificent attire. He was decorated with a gold collar and bracelets. He wore several bonnets placed around his turban. His subjects wore only plain woolens and cotton stuffs, but these men with shaved heads and women with bobbed hair did not fail to attract attention. The natives saluted the emperor by prostrating themselves before him and covering

[19] Monod, *op. cit.*, pp. 55-56.

their head with dust, as was customary in African kingdoms and empires; but the Mussulmans only clapped their hands as indicating their respect in the tunka's presence. When the ruler or tunka died he was succeeded not by his son but, according to the African custom, by the son of his sister, to be sure that the successor might be of royal blood.[20]

So great was the African love of justice here that the administration of it was not entrusted to the lieutenants of the tunka. He administered justice himself. Seated under a large pavilion or in a tent, he suffered the people to come unto him. Round him there were ten caparisoned horses held by the servants with bucklers and swords pointed with gold. The sons of the vassals clothed with expensive attire and with their hair plaited and decorated with golden jewels stood around the tunka. The ministers and the chief of the town sat in front of the ruler. Dogs decorated with collars and golden or silver bells guarded the entrance to the tent. The hearing opened with beating of long drums made from the trunks of hollow trees. The ordeal of poison was imposed upon the accused who refused to acknowledge their guilt. Every morning, followed by his officers, the emperor on horseback made a tour of his capital. He heard the complaints of the people and adjusted them immediately. He resumed his tour in the evening, but no one could approach him in official capacity at that hour.[21]

When the emperor died the court built a canopy of wood on the place of his tomb. Under the dome was set up a platform covered with carpet and pillows which received the dead body. Around the body were placed the arms, the ornaments, and the utensils which he used during his life. There were heaped up foods and drinks under guard of the servants who had to be entombed with their master. With mats and cloth was closed the tomb which the people assembled covered over with earth. Thus was formed a mound, around which was dug a ditch. From time to time food and drink were brought to the dead, and victims were offered in sacrifice.[22]

Evidences of the splendor of Kumbi (Ghana) are not wanting.

[20] This sort of inheritance determined often the control of property in Africa.

[21] Monod, *op. cit.*, p. 57.

[22] *Ibid.*, p. 57.

The explorer, Bonnel de Mézières, who visited and excavated this locality in 1914, found there the vestiges of a great city corresponding to that described by Bekri, with ruins of hewn stone constructions, sometimes sculptured. Trying to account for the passing of this civilization, this and other investigators discovered an explanation not altogether in the hordes which swept into Africa for economic exploitation and religious propaganda but also in the change in the climatic conditions. "The region where Kumbi (Ghana) was built," says Maurice Delafosse, "is now very arid. In truth it rains here every year, but there are no rivers; and, except at a few points where pools or sheets of not very deep subterranean water exist, the vegetation, although fairly thick in spots, is reduced to thin pasturage, gum-trees and other spiny bushes. The region contains no village and is traversed only by nomadic Moors and hunters of the Nemadi or Nimadi tribe. But very numerous and extended traces of former habitations and burial places which turn up at every instant, show that the country was formerly inhabited, in part at least, by sedentary peoples, and lead us to suppose that it was better watered than it is today and more suitable for tillage. Besides, Bekri speaks of vast and prosperous fields which extended to the east of Ghana and local traditions are unanimous in attributing the decline of the kingdom and the dispersion of its inhabitants to the drying up of the Wagadu and consequent famine. It is probable that these circumstances had much more influence on the end of the empire of Ghana than the successive pillages to which the city was subjected by the Almoravides in 1076, by the king of Soso, Sumanguru Kannte, in 1203, and finally by the king of the Mandingo, Sundiata Keita, toward 1240. A populous city and a flourishing state survived pillage and defeat, but could not resist lack of water and nourishment." [23]

"At that distant epoch when they lent themselves to tillage and a sedentary life," adds Delafosse, "the Bagana or Wagadu and most of the sub-Saharan districts which we unite today under the name of Hodh in the East and Mauritania in the West, must have been inhabited by the Negroes, more or less mixed with Negrillos and North African aborigines of lighter color. These Negroes formed an ensemble, fairly disparate perhaps in certain aspects,

[23] Delafosse, op. cit., pp. 43-44.

which Moorish traditions generally designated by the term *Bafur;*
from them have doubtless gone forth, by ramification, the Songhay
or Songai toward the East, the Serers toward the West and, toward the Center, a great people called *Gangara* (Gangari in the
singular) by the Moors, *Wangara* by Arab authors and writers of
Timbuctoo, and comprising in our day, as its principal divisions,
the Mandingo properly speaking or the Malinke, the Bambara
and the Jula.[24]

"It is in this region and among these *Bafur,* doubtless already
ramified," continues Delafosse, "that immigrants of the Semitic
race probably settled." These immigrants probably included at
the same time farmers and shepherds. "However considerable
their number," says this writer further, "it was certainly very inferior to that of the Negroes in the midst of whom they settled.
There must have been, from the very beginning, a number of
unions between the whites and the blacks and of these unions were
born, it seems, two very important populations, each of which in
turn was to play a rôle of the first order in the history of the
western and central Sudan and in the development of its civilization.[25]

"Even at Ghana, in the Wagadu, in the Massina and at still other
places, the union of the Semites, for the most part sedentary, with
the Wangara, who were considerably more numerous than the
former, probably engendered the people who give themselves the
name of *Sarakolle,* that is to say, 'white men,' in memory of one
of their ancestors. They are called by several Sudanese tribes
Soninke, by the Moors Assuanik; the Bambara denominate them
Mara-ka or *Mar'-ka* (people of the Mara or Wagadu) and the
Arab authors and the Songhay of Timbuktu designate them by the
term *Wakore.* These people spoke a language closely related to
that of the Wangara; it became the customary language of Ghana
(Kumbi-Kumbi) and is still today that of the Sarakolle of the
Sahel and of Senegal, of the sedentary inhabitants of the black
race called Azer or Ahl-Massine (people of the Massina), of certain oases such as Tichit, and finally of some tribes who have either
adopted the errant habits of their Moorish neighbors or conserved

[24] Delafosse, *op. cit.,* pp. 44-45.
[25] *Ibid.,* p. 45. Here "white" means a black person with even a little
Caucasian blood.

those of their Semitic ancestors, for example, the Guirganke shepherds and also, it is believed, of the Nemadi hunters.[26]

"To the West of Ghana, in the region of the Termes pastures, the mixture of the nomadic Semites with the Serers and especially the long cohabitation of these Semites in the midst of the Serers must have given birth to the Fulani or Fulbe people, who speak a language quite near to that of the Serers and who later swarmed toward the Massina and, on the other side, toward the Tagant and the Futa-Toro, afterwards to send forth groups to the south-west into the Futa-Jallon, to the east and to the south-east in the bend of the Niger, to Hausaland, Adamawa and other countries bordering on Lake Chad." [27]

[26] Delafosse, *op. cit.,* p. 46.
[27] *Ibid.,* pp. 46-47.

CHAPTER IV

SMALLER KINGDOMS FROM THE RUINS OF KUMBI

AFTER the decline of Kumbi, or Ghana, because of the attacks of enemies from without and the drought which made its future precarious, several smaller kingdoms developed independently. These maintained that status until taken over by the Manding (Melle) or Songhay which came upon the scene respectively as the largest political units of the following centuries.[1] Kumbi availed nothing against the local princes when in the middle of the thirteenth century it constituted nothing more than a small state at Howkar which Sun Diata Keita destroyed in 1240.

The larger states had to reckon too with such settlements as Tekrur (Toucouleur), Silla, Massina, and with prosperous towns on the Niger like Ras-el-ma, Tirca, and Kagho or Kaugha. These with an abundance of gold dust from nearby mines were centers of commerce frequented by foreign black merchants whom El-Bekri calls the Nughamarta, the chief agents in carrying this article abroad. Borgu and Mossi, moreover, had maintained their sovereignty from a period of considerable antiquity. Nupe, likewise independent, was well known to Byzantium prior to the coming of the Mohammedans because of the trade relations established between this kingdom and the Greek Empire which some writers say taught the former certain kinds of work in bronze and glass.[2]

The most important of these little kingdoms which asserted thus their independence of the tunka of Kumbi were Diara, Soso, and Galam. Diara, which still exists under modified form to the northeast of Nioro in the French Sudan, was the principal town of Kaniaga founded in the thirteenth century by the Sarakolle dynasty of Niakhate whose princes used the title of *manna-magham* or

---

[1] These kingdoms are succinctly described in J. L. Monod's *Histoire de l'Afrique Occidentale Française,* pp. 61-80.

[2] Delafosse, *Negroes of Africa,* p. 36.

manna. In the thirteenth century the king became rich by the commerce established with foreigners and could raise and support armies large enough to maintain his position and enlarge his state by taking over the southern provinces of the declining Kumbi. He thus made himself the master of Tekrur. These Niakhate, however, did not know how to continue in power. In their commercial operations they made the impression of being wicked and cruel. They became odious to their subjects who under the leadership of the Diawara contrived to unite their forces and drive them from the country by 1270.

The Diawara were the descendants of a legendary hunter of unknown origin named Daman Guile. European writers say he came from the East, but this claim is purely legendary. He probably sojourned in Manding (Melle) about the time of Soun Diata and later reached Kingui in the time of the Niakhate of whom he became the friend. Far and wide he was known as a ruler of consequence. His sons who succeeded him, however, did not sustain the same friendly relations with those sons of the neighboring ruler, and they dethroned him. Fie Mamadu Diawara, son of Daman Guile, was the first of his line to rule at Diara and at Kingui under the title of *faren.* He perished in an expedition against the Silatigui of Futa and was succeeded about 1300 by his son Silla Makhan Diawara, distinguished by ruling forty years and by having had thirty-seven children, fifteen of whom were boys. He had troubles with the Peuhls who under Diawando du Kingui founded Nioro. At this time Kaniaga was taken over by (Manding) Melle. Silla was succeeded by his oldest son, Daman Diawara, in 1340. His successors were known by the less significant title of *sagone.* One of his younger brothers, Daba, became the chief of the Dabora clan. These two developed into hostile leaders who from 1340 to 1754 kept up family quarrels and thus involved the other Diawara clans and weakened the nation. Although the kingdom endured in some form for five centuries it never grew into a great state. It became the vassal of Manding near the fourteenth century and next that of the Songhay in the sixteenth century. In the seventeenth century its power had about ceased to be, and the Bamabara-Masasi incorporated it into Kaniaga.

The kingdom of Soso, or Susu, south of Ghana, in the direction of Bamako, developed next around a village bearing that name, This place had served as the capital of Sarakolle district, which had earlier belonged to Kumbi (Ghana). A tunka of Kumbi had sent one of his lieutenants, Gumate Fane, to govern Soso as a province. He was the father of the clan of the Sarakolle of Diarisso who in 1076 established their independence of Kumbi. From 1076 to 1180 seven princes of this line ruled in that land. The first of these princes, Kambine, descendant of Gumate Fane, was ruling in 1076 when the town of Kumbi was taken by the Almoravides. He declared his independence and established the kingdom of Soso. The last of this dynasty had nine sons who warred among themselves for the ascendancy. Availing himself of the opportunity offered by these discords, Diara Kannte, a general of Bambara, took possession of the country and drove out the Diarisso. The dynasty of Kannte of the caste of smiths next governed the country from 1180 to 1235. Of these Sumanguru, adding to his influence by passing for a sorcerer, was the most illustrious. An able general, he greatly extended his kingdom and brought it to its highest level between 1200 and 1235. He was powerful enough to take Kumbi (Ghana) itself in 1203 and make a vassal of the tunka. In 1224 the rich Mohammedans of Kumbi (Ghana) in order to escape from the pagan domination of the Soso fled toward the north under Sheik Ismail who had increased his prestige by making the pious pilgrimage to Mecca. They established a settlement at Biru which later, under the name Walata, succeeded the city of Kumbi (Ghana) as the commercial metropolis of the Western Sudan. This could work out at that time because Sumanguru had turned his attention toward conquests in the south. After killing off nine of its princes he subdued the Manding (Melle), but Sun-Diata Keita, the twelfth of this line, rallied the forces of the Manding, and in a battle about 1235 defeated and killed Sumanguru by a *ruse de guerre*. Thus Soso came to the end of its course as an independent power, of which we are to hear again.

Out of the Sarakolle disputes at Wagadu emerged another kingdom called Galam or Gadiaga. One of the families scattering from that point under Alikassa Sempre settled at the confluence of the Senegal and the Faléme where they founded the town of Galambu while other chiefs of clans founded Yaressi or Diarressi, and Silla on the right bank of the Senegal. According to the legend, Ali-kassa Sempre, acquiring power as a sorcerer, contrived to have himself elected as the king of the settlements. This was the beginning of Galam or Gadiaga which included such provinces as Goye, Kamera, Guidmakha, and later Diomboko, with Galambu as its capital. This kingdom, however, had only periods of independence. It was almost always the vassal of either Tekrur, Kumbi (Ghana), Kaniaga, or Manding (Melle). At the death of one of the successors, Mari-Kassa Bakili, the four provinces became autonomous. The most significant fact in the history of this country from the modern point of view is that it was the proprietor of the gold mines of Bambuk and later it was the door of access to the Senegal.

The Kingdom of the Tekrur (Toucouleur, Tukulor) or Senegalese Futa was the next to develop from the disintegration of Ghana. This grew out of settlements attached later to Futa on the left bank of the Senegal, Dimar, Lao, Bossea, Damga, Toro and others, all of various stocks and hence called Toucouleurs. These people were Sérères (Serers), Woloffs, Mandingoes, Sarakolles, and Peuhls. The capital was the island of Morfil. The Berbers in the country who settled at Tagant to the north did not molest these Toucouleurs, but they later forced them to the left bank of the Senegal. Among the towns later subjected to them was Sengan or Senegana from which was derived Senegal. Europeans have seized upon the legend that the first settlers of these parts were Semites who established themselves in the country about 870, and that these formed the group now called the Peuhls who held such local sway for 130 years. They were called Dya-Ogo after their first chief. It is contended that, following these Semites, the Manna, a black dynasty came into power. The evidence, however, tends to confirm that the invaders after maintaining themselves in restricted quarters toward the north were absorbed as others had been by the blacks who constituted an expanding empire of which the Semitic settlements were only an inconspicuous and troublesome part. This fact is supported by the other observation that the Manna were none other than the Niakhate representatives of the kings of Diara who, ruling the district from the

Tagant to the Senegal, took possession of Futa as a mere province.[3]

Ouar Diabi or Ouar-Ndiage, sometimes called Abu-Dardai, was the most celebrated of the kings in control of these Semitic mixed breeds. He was converted to Islam and obliged his family to conform before the time of his death in 1040. His successors were ardent Mohammedans who allied themselves with the Almoravides, the destroyers of civilization in West Africa. His son, equally ardent, came to the aid of Yahia-ben-Omar against the Goddala in 1056. Another line of kings called the Tondyon succeeded the Manna. These were evidently native Serers of Dya-Ogo mixture, hostile to the Manna and the Niakhate. The Manding (Melle), after annexing the kingdom of Niakhate, used the people of Tondyon to destroy that part of Futa subjected to the Niakhate.

The new conquerors governed through what they called a *faren* after 1270. He had under him representatives to rule the provinces. It was under the reign of the Tondyon, about 1350, that a descendant of Manna Ouar-Diabi or Abu-Dardi, known as Ndiadiane Ndiaye, left Futa and established the settlement which became the kingdom of the Woloffs. The situation became further complicated when a larger number of the Peuhls from Termes coming from Tagant joined them about 1450; and finally under the conqueror Koli about 1450 they took Tekrur and with the assistance of blacks recruited from Gambia established the dynasty called Denianke which endured until 1776. From 1776 to 1881, the Tukulor blacks, after getting rid of the Peuhl supremacy, introduced Mohammedanism as a state religion. The ancient religion then ceased to be, and a sort of elective theocratic monarchy took its place and was the order of the day until it was annexed to the Senegal by the French in 1881.

There was also during these years another important settlement founded by nomadic Berbers who probably came from Southern Morocco in the third or fourth century before Christ, as already noted above. They comprised the four tribes known in history as the Lemtuna, Goddola, Lemta, and Messufa. They scattered with

[3] Both Delafosse and Monod, while trying to be broad, cannot get rid of the bias shown in thinking of all advanced ideas and movements in Africa as importations from Caucasian centers. Lady Lugard shows still more of this bias. If they do not find "white" men on the ground they search for some tradition or legend to give that race credit for all progress in Africa.

their flocks in Tiris, Adrar, and Tagant. The first center which they developed was Azgui in Adrar to the northwest of Atar; but Howdaghost, founded in the seventh century B.C. off Walata, between Kiffa and Tichit, to the east of Tagant, became the center of sufficient importance as to become the capital of a small country in the beginning of the ninth century A.D. Their first chief was Wayaktine. Then came Tilagagguine. For a hundred years prior to this time some of these people had been making incursions into the region of Hodh, but in the ninth century Howdaghost became the vassal of the black kingdom of Kumbi (Ghana) after developing under their chief Tiloutane to the extent of having an army of a hundred thousand Meharistes of sufficient force to impose their rule upon as many as twenty-five black chiefs. These very vassals combined to kill off Tiloutane's successors, and the Tunka of Kumbi (Ghana) extended his authority over the land of the veiled Zenaga. Tin Yeroutan who ruled over these people from 920 to 940 tried to regain their power, but his successors could not hold the people together, and the efforts to maintain the independence of the Tunka of Kumbi (Ghana) ultimately failed. In spite of all such upheavals Howdaghost, which in our time has disappeared, was in the tenth century a center of agriculture, industry, and commerce. By the caravan trade this city-state connected North Africa with the land of the blacks among whom these Berbers lost their authority as well as their color.

In this connection developed a small kingdom of the destructive Almoravides. The founder or first prince was Tarsina, a Lemtuna chief, who became the ruler of Howdaghost about 1020 and extended his sway over the Berbers of that area. He was probably the first of his stock in that quarter to embrace Islam, and he increased his prestige by becoming a sort of champion of this faith after making a pious pilgrimage to Mecca. He then undertook a holy war to subjugate the blacks, but he was killed in the effort. The chief or king thereafter was chosen from among several tribes. Kahia succeeded Tarsina, and he was followed about 1035 by his son Ibrahim who also made the pilgrimage to Mecca. On his return Yahia brought with him to convert the natives a distinguished and scholarly Mohammedan, Abdallah-ben-Yassine, but he did not make much headway at it among the Goddala who were first approached. Then he and his followers went into a monastery for secret communing and spiritual preparation. About 1040 they built a hermitage near the mouth of the Senegal where princes and chiefs converted to Islam came to be instructed. They were called Al-Morabetin or Marabouts, and we derive therefrom the word Almoravides. When he had grouped about 2,000 or more adepts he began to proclaim holy wars to convert the Berbers and the blacks by force. Accept the crescent or die was the motto. When Yahia ben Ibrahim died Yahia ben Omar, a descendant of Tilagagguine became chief of the Zenaga and also the commander of their holy forces. They then overcame all the dependencies of Kumbi (Ghana) and the area of West Sahara. They next massacred and pillaged Howdaghost under the pretext that it paid tribute to the Tunka of Kumbi (Ghana), a black prince. The garrison of Almoravides of Sidjilmessa had just been massacred by the Moroccans who reoccupied Tafilalit and Dara. Abdallah-ben-Yassine retook these places and began the campaign which dominated Morocco and extended to Spain.

The Holy war was then carried into Adrar. Yahia-ben-Omar, however, had the opposition of the Goddala who did not like his being chosen king from some other tribe. He had to deal with them; and the Goddala, aided by the Tukulors, defeated the Lemtuna in a battle in which Yahia was slain. Abubekr-ben-Omar succeeded his brother, and Abdallah-ben-Yassine, killed in an expedition in 1058, left Abubekr in supreme command of temporal and spiritual forces. The kingdom, however, could not be sustained. It was divided.

Abubekr left his cousin to take charge of things in Morocco to give him time to stop the revolt in the south. His cousin, however, then built up an empire of his own in the north; and, threatened with war from the south, appeased Abubekr with gifts. He directed himself especially to the Tunka of Kumbi (Ghana) from 1061 to 1076 with a merciless war by which the country was conquered. This was the apogee of the Almoravides, for soon thereafter Abubekr was killed with a poisoned arrow, and the kingdom went down. At the same time Yusuf in Spain and Morocco was rising. In 1063 he founded Marakech. He took Fez in 1069, entered Spain a little later, and fought Alphonso VI of

Castille. He entered Seville in 1086. In 1090 the Almoravide empire of the north extended from the Ebro to the Sahara and from the Atlantic to Algeria. Yusuf had himself proclaimed commander of the believers, a title which he did not enjoy very long, for he died in 1106. His empire, although vast, was not well organized and passed away as rapidly as it arose. The Moslems remained, however, to constitute mixed breeds of a new destiny in the Sudan.

The Mohammedans' religion, unlike the ephemeral kingdoms which it made possible with cruel and sanguinary holy wars led by fanatics, however, left a more lasting impression on the blacks than did their state building. The Mohammedans made converts of the Tukulors, the Sarakolle, and indirectly the Diula and the Songhay, who spread this faith in Africa during subsequent years. A disciple of Abdallah-ben-Yassine, the legendary Abu-Dardai, without doubt the same as the King Ouar-Diabi or Ouar Ndiaye, became the great preacher of Islam to the Tekrur as noted above. He converted first the princes, and the blacks of the Tekrur became the most ardent allies of the Almoravides to the aid of whom they sent large armies. The Sarakolle,[4] neighbors of the Tukulors resisted Islam as long as they had control of the Hodh. Once conquered, however, they accepted the faith and became the most earnest propagators of this religion wherever there were colonies in Sahel, Senegal, and Masina. The Diulas were converted by the Sarakolles who were merchants going to practically all parts of the Sudan as far as the equatorial forests. From the eleventh century they had on the Gulf of Guinea trading posts which were centers of the faith of Islam. Another preacher or prophet, the father of Yahia and Abubekr-ben-Omar, probably went to Manding (Melle) and converted the King Baramenda-Keita and induced him to make the pious pilgrimage to Mecca, about 1050. About this time it is certain that Dia Kossai of the Songhay accepted Islam in the midst of pagan subjects.

All the people of these countries, however, did not become Mohammedans, and they are not so even as a majority today. The princes of these countries for snobbishness or for political reasons accepted the faith; and sometimes they did so in order to increase

[4] J. H. Saint-Père, *Les Sarakollé du Guidimakha* (Paris, 1925).

their prestige abroad, sometimes in order to escape the horrors of a holy war: not often because of conviction, for the people as a majority continued with their native religion. Certain settlements resisted Islam even when it meant a dear cost in blood. Some chose exile rather than submit to the new faith. The Serers, established in the Hodh and in the west of Mauritania at that time, were among the first offered either Mohammed or the sword, and they fought it out to the point that they had to leave their abodes and invade the lands to the south. They crossed the Senegal and took flight into Futa-Toro. From there they pushed on as far as the Sine. The Peuhls from Termes and Tagant who had long lived with the Serers moved with them into Futa-Toro, where they long resisted Islam. In the same way the Bambara, the Mossi, and many others have resisted Islam even to the present time.

CHAPTER V

THE MANDING

MANDING, or Melle, extended from Bamako on the Upper Niger as far as Siguiri. In this area were the famous gold mines of Bure, almost as rich as those of Bambuk. To the empire belonged also the mountainous regions from the two arms of the Senegal, the Bakoy and the Bafing, Gangaran, Bambuk, and the Gambia. The people who inhabited this area were of Wangara origin. The capital of Manding was first at Dieriba, or Jeliba, upon the right bank of the Niger, at the confluence and on the left bank of the Sankarani. The capital was evidently moved later from this place to Niani upon the left bank of the Sankarani off Siguiri near the village of the same name which exists today.

The first kings of Manding were the Keitas. We do not know much about their history because the Arabs who recorded the first accounts were primarily interested in that part of the history in which the Mussulman element participated. Most of these foreign accounts start with Islamization of the country thus described. These people of Manding were not Mohammedans, and through these annalists we hear only of those who opposed or espoused that faith. It is said that these early kings greatly increased their power by passing as skillful and dangerous sorcerers. This ruse of the dynasty of Manding, however, is not an exception in African history, for many others thus gained ascendancy. These rulers bore the title *mansa*, and took wives from among the Konte or Konde or Kone family. The *affairs* of early Manding, then, were mainly in the hands of these two families.[1]

About the middle of the eleventh century Baramendana Keita

---

[1] Lugard, *A Tropical Dependency*, chapter on Melle; Monod, *Histoire de l'Afrique Occidentale Française*, pp. 80-93; Delafosse, *Negroes of Africa*, pp. 59-66, 74-76; same author, *Haut-Sénégal-Niger (Soudan Français)*, Paris, 1912, 3 volumes.

was the ruler of Manding. The events of his reign attracted the attention of Arabs, Persians and other Orientals because he was the first to embrace Islam. The tradition is that a drought had set upon the country, and ruin seemed inevitable. Inasmuch as Africans believed in the possibility of making rain, and sometimes had a special functionary for this task, this king was induced by a Berber, Lemtuna Omar, father of Yahia and Abubekr, chiefs of the Almoravides, to accept Islam in order to bring rain; and the much desired rain happened to come at that time. Considering this striking evidence of the power of Islam, Baramendana declared himself an adherent of this faith, and made a pious pil-

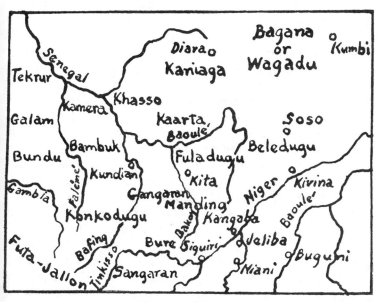

MANDING (MELLE)

grimage to Mecca. This, however, was more of a political gesture than anything else because the subjects of the ruler remained true to their native religion. With Islam as an aid, however, the kings freed themselves from Kumbi (Ghana) and formed with their neighbors other alliances which increased the prestige and power of Manding (Melle). Bure with its gold mines equal to those of

Bambuk contributed much also to this same richness and grandeur.[2]

Following Baramendana came two other kings in the twelfth century. Hamama and Dyigui-Bilali, of whom we know very little probably because they did nothing to impress the chroniclers of their time although they might have been just as great as their predecessors. We do not learn of another ruler until we come to Musa, called Allakoi, who reigned from 1200 to 1218. He was noted mainly for his devotion to Islam and for making a pilgrimage to Mecca. He had become rich through the gold mines of Bure and could easily afford such an expensive tour. His people, however, continued with their own religion as they had under his predecessors.

Nare Famaga, son of Musa, held the throne from 1218 to 1230. He had trouble because the gold mines of Bure had awakened the covetousness of his neighbors. The king of the Soso, Sumanguru Kannte, who already exercised a sort of overlordship over the Keita, annexed Manding in 1224. He had the eleven sound sons of the Keita assassinated to destroy the last vestige of Manding independence. Fortunately or unfortunately, however, he left alive a sickly son Sun-Diata, or Mari-Diata, who happened to regain vigor. He developed into a great warrior and a hard ruler. His subjects feared rather than loved him; but during his reign from 1230 to 1255 he attained distinction as a great king of Manding (Melle) in becoming more than the equal of Sumanguru.

Aided by his uncle, Danguina-Konte, the chief of the Sangaran, Sun-Diata put a large army in the field. The chief of Labe soon had to submit and supplied Sun-Diata with additional forces. Juma, an aid of the king, took possession of the Bambara region between the Niger and the Baule about Buguni. He next conquered Kita and southern Beledugu. In 1235 at the head of a large army Sun-Diata marched against Sumanguru and defeated and killed him in battle. Soso then became the vassal of Manding (Melle) over which it had once ruled. Going toward the north with his conquests the conqueror subdued Kumbi (Ghana) which had been a dependency of Soso since 1203. He pillaged the city, set fire to it, and destroyed it root and branch.

[2] Mungo Park, *Travels in the Interior of Africa* (*1795-1797*); Barth, *Travels and Discoveries in North and Central Africa;* Es-Sadi, *op. cit.;* and Mahmoud Kati, *Tarikh El-Fettach.*

These conquests made the empire of Manding (Melle) immense. It then controlled in addition to the Manding Beledugu, Diaka, Bagana or Wagadu, and Kaarta or Kaniaga. In the meantime the chief aid of Sun-Diata occupied Gangaran, Bambuk, Bundu and imposed the sovereignty of Manding (Melle) upon the area as far as Tekrur, Wolof, and Gambia. Manding (Melle) had then placed itself in the position of leadership in Africa once enjoyed by Kumbi (Ghana).

Having accomplished all this, Sun-Diata reposed at Niani, the new capital of his empire while his generals further extended these conquests. The greatest of these generals, Amari-Sonko, took possession of Gangaran, Bambuk, and Bundu. He extended his conquests as far as Tekrur and towards Gambia and put in authority over these new possessions officers who established small kingdoms as vassals of the Manding. During the reign of Mansa-Ule, the successor of Sun-Diata, Amari-Sonko, commissioned Sane Niango Tarore, his assistant, to organize the kingdom of Gangaran embracing the territory bordered by the Bafing, the Bakoy and the Tinkisso. A little later another such general Siriman Keita, a relative of the Mansa of Manding (Melle), took possession of Konko-dugu to the south of Bambuk and established with Deku as the capital a vassal kingdom over which the Keita retained their power until the nineteenth century. Still another officer Musa Sisoko established the kingdom of Bambugu or Bambuk between the Falémé and Bafing; but when Musa Sisoko died near the end of the thirteenth century his seventeen sons partitioned the provinces among themselves under the suzerainty of the eldest, Kamakan-Jita. The Sisoko continued in power with the title of Siratigui, sometimes as vassals of Manding (Melle), and sometimes more or less independent. The rulers had introduced Islam, but when the Marabouts, the propagators of this new faith of Islam, desired about 1540 to take possession of the gold mines of the country, the natives massacred them and returned to their primitive religion. In 1550 the Portuguese who likewise desired to take possession of these mines settled in the country. They rapidly died from tropical diseases. Others were eliminated by self-extermination in warring among themselves, and the native blacks massacred those who survived the other misfortunes.

On the whole, however, the reign of Sun-Diata was characterized by order and progress. He watched over the administration of the states, insisting on peace and security. He encouraged agriculture, trade, and industry. He introduced the cultivation of cotton and weaving. He rendered prosperous not only his own country, but that bordering upon his kingdom. He died in 1255 as a result of a wound received in the midst of a great celebration or by being drowned near Niani. Thus passed one of the greatest rulers of Manding. The people still sing his praises. Often he is the object of a religious cult, and sacrifices are offered him near the place where he passed away.

Sun-Diata was succeeded by Mansa-Ule (1255-1270). He was known for his pilgrimage to Mecca and for the extension of his country westward toward the gold regions of Bambuk and the Falémé. He annexed by conquests both Bundu and a part of the Basin of the Gambia. Ule was succeeded by his brother Wati, who ruled from 1270 to 1275. Next came Kalifa for a few months, and then Abubakari, a nephew of Sun-Diata, who held out from 1275 to 1285 without making any particular impress upon his time. The dynasty was then suspended for fifteen years by a usurper, a serf named Sakura. This was not an unfortunate change, however, for the usurper extended the conquests of his predecessors as far as Jenne and Massina and subdued Diara with its Tekrur dependencies. Sakura established commercial connections with Morocco and Mauritania and thus further stimulated the progress of the country. On his return from a pious pilgrimage to Mecca, however, he was killed for his gold by certain Danakil near Jibuti. His body having been dried was returned to Melle, and his people did him the great honor of entombing his remains among the Keitas of Manding (Melle). The Keita, Gau, Mamadu, and Abubakari II who reigned from 1300 to 1307 did not leave brilliant records.

Mansa Musa or Gonga Musa was the next to rule the Manding. He has been eulogized by Mohammedan historians for his justice, enlightenment, and holiness. He completed the conquests which Sakura had begun and gave Manding a grand and glorious reign. He maintained friendly relations with the rulers to the north and especially with the kings of Morocco, the Barbary states, and even with Egypt. In 1324-1325 he made a celebrated pilgrimage to

Mecca. He had a caravan of not less than 60,000 persons, part of whom were a military escort. The baggage was conveyed by camels and 12,000 slaves dressed in tunics of brocade or Persian silk. "When he rode five hundred of them marched before him, each carrying a staff of pure gold, which weighed sixty-two ounces. The caravan was accompanied by all essential luxuries, excellent cooks, choice eatables and drinks. The king carried with him more than a million sterling of gold dust in eighty camel loads of 200 pounds each. With this he paid his expenses, lavished gifts upon friends and places, and built mosques." Mansa Musa went first indirectly to various parts of his kingdom doubtless for the effect of it on his subjects. Then he proceeded to Tuat and from there to Egypt and finally to Mecca and Medina. He returned by the eastern route of Ghadmes, bringing back with him Abu Ishak or Ibrahim Es-Sahel, the Spanish poet and architect. This co-worker directed the building of mosques and palaces both in the Manding and in Timbuctoo which the Manding overthrew in 1336 after a conflict with the Sultan of Mossi who sacked the town in 1330. Mansa Musa, as pointed out above, exchanged gifts with other princes, notably with Abu El-Hacen who ruled Morocco and had conquered Tlemcen. Timbuctoo became a center of much learning under this, the greatest of the black kings, Mansa Musa, "a pious and equitable prince, unequalled for virtue or uprightness." He reigned for twenty-five years.[3]

Ibn Batuta, who had been at rest from travel at the court of Abu El-Hacen in Morocco-Televiscan, was attracted to the black kingdom of Manding on hearing of the hospitality shown foreigners.[4] He visited Manding in 1352 within ten or fifteen years after the death of Mansa Musa who had been succeeded by his son to reign only four years. Under this weakling Manding declined. He could not protect his empire, for Nassegue, Naba of Yatenga, pillaged Timbuctoo in 1333. This son also permitted the two hostages from the royal family of Gao to escape. The succession had passed to his uncle Mansa Suleiman, a brother of Mansa Musa. He reigned twenty-four years and gave lustre to his line.[5]

Ibn Batuta found the country peaceful and prosperous, with an

---

[3] Lugard, *op. cit.*, pp. 122-123.
[4] Ibn Batouta, *Voyage dans le Soudan* (Slane Translation).
[5] *Ibid.*, p. 39.

abundance of food, fruits, spices, salt, beads, aromatic gums, cattle, corn, and cotton.   European goods were welcomed there and were paid for in gold, cotton, slaves, ivory, skins, and kola nuts.   Gold was abundant.   There was a Berber quarter in the towns, although the people had adopted outwardly Mohammedanism and the emperor had made a pious pilgrimage to Mecca.   Nupe was considered one of the important towns of the Sudan.   The king received his ministers and subordinates who showed much servility, reminding one of the customs among the Aztecs in Mexico about that same time.   At some places Ibn Batuta was not received with much respect, probably because of the low level to which so many of his " 'white' people there had descended under the domination of the blacks." [6]

"It is evident from what he says that the Berbers, though Mussulmans, and observing all the religious customs of their faith, studying jurisprudence and theology, and devoting a considerable portion of their time to learning the Koran by heart, had to a very great extent assimilated themselves to the customs of the blacks. The domestic privacy of the Moslem was not observed, and they had adopted the native habit of tracing their genealogy in the female line through a maternal uncle.   The inheritance, as with the native royal dynasties in pre-Mohammedan days, went to the son of a sister.   This was a practice which, though it is known to be common in Negroland, Batuta says that he had never seen, except amongst pagan Indians in Malabar." [7]

The empire was divided into provinces, each under a "ferba," or farba, a viceroy of the sovereign, while each town had its "mochrif" or inspector "who was responsible to the viceroy for the maintenance of order, the suppression of crime, and presumably for the collection of taxes."   It seems, however, that co-equal with the "ferba" or having somewhat similar power were the "koi," doubtless native kings, semi-independent.   The "koi" had probably increased and thus may have contributed to the disruption of the empire.[8]

The finances of the Manding were flourishing in the fourteenth century.   Taxes consisted of royalties on minerals and on foreign

[6] Lugard, op. cit., p. 130.
[7] Ibid., p. 131.
[8] Monod, op. cit., p. 89; and Lugard, op. cit., p. 142.

goods. Mansa Suleiman was said to be avaricious with respect to taxes, but this is not borne out by others. The judicial system was conspicuous with judges black and Berber-black, and there was much study of law. In the government there was a separation of powers. Cases referred to the sovereign were sent to the proper tribunal.

The system was a success, for Ibn Batuta says that occurrences of acts of injustice were rare. "Of all people," says he, "the blacks are those who most detest injustice. Their sultan never forgives any one who has been guilty of it." This traveler refers also to the "complete and general safety which is enjoyed in the country. Neither those who travel nor those who remain at home have anything to fear from brigands, thieves, or violent persons." [9] Evidently this was a tribute to the African rather than to the influence of Islam, for in other Mohammedanized countries travelers as a rule expressed an eternal dread of the brigands and pirates which rendered communication with them dangerous.

The official church at this time was the orthodox Mohammedan. There were mosques with salaried readers and teachers and cathedral mosques in Melle, Timbuctoo and Gao. Schools flourished in many towns. The people's assiduity was praised, for children were punished for not learning the Koran. Wherever the Arabian travelers did not find these conditions obtaining they branded the people as heathen and denounced their rulers as profligate. [10]

The army, an organized military force, consisted of cavalry and infantry armed with bows and arrows, swords and long and short spears. These forces were divided into units, each under a captain or commandant. When the commander was appointed he was raised up on a shield as did the people with their leaders and kings in Northern Europe. Larger groups were brought under generals or military leaders of whom there were two in chief, one commanding the army of the south and the other that of the north. The authority of the Manding was respected to the south by such kingdoms as the Mossi, Borgu, Nupe, all which maintained their independence. Manding extended into the desert as far as Teguidda. It trenched also upon Gober and Hausa. Because of this military

[9] Lugard, *op. cit.*, p. 144.
[10] The way in which they referred to the unorthodox Sonni Ali is a striking case in evidence.

prowess Jenne found it advisable to pay tribute to the Manding. The African had lived in peace. Converted to Islam, then given to the enslavement of men for laborers around their harems and soldiers in their armies, the people of Manding freely raided their neighbors for slaves. The pagans had no rights which they should respect. Slaves, however, were not persecuted except in raiding.

Black governors ruled in those parts, and Berber and black lived on perfect equality. A black governor was "called one of the best and most generous of men." Says Lady Lugard, "In the cordial expression of the respect and sympathy awakened in his mind by friendly intercourse with this and other black dignitaries of the kingdom of Manding, it becomes clear how greatly Ibn Batuta had modified his opinion with regard to the inhabitants of the Sudan since he first crossed the frontier at Aiwalatin." He considered Gao or Gago, the capital of Songhay, "one of the finest cities of the blacks." [11] He seems to regard it higher than Timbuctoo, which, it is said, was founded by Arabs.

Mansa Suleiman ruled for twenty-four years. He was succeeded in 1359 by a ruler who remained in power only one year. He was dethroned by a "vicious tyrant" during whose reign of fourteen years the country began to decline. This was Mari Diata II. He spent money recklessly in folly and debauchery and sold the famous nugget of thirty pounds of gold so jealously guarded by his royal predecessors. He finally developed a sleeping· sickness of which he died in 1374.

From 1374 to 1387 ruled Musa II, a weak and indolent man. The actual exercise of power, however, was in the hands of his chief minister called Diata, who with a considerable military force waged war against the Sultan Omar ben Idris in Bornu. He utterly failed, however, in his operations against Teguidda which refused to pay the required tribute and maintained its independence of Manding. Of Maghan II, Santigui, and Maghan III, who sat on the throne from about 1387 to 1390 little has been recorded. The decline of the empire was still more evident during the first decades of the fifteenth century under Musa III and Musa-Ule II. Governors of the provinces failed to respect these weak emperors and refused to pay the taxes which they levied. Not only

[11] Ibn Batuta, *op. cit.;* Lady Lugard, *op. cit.,* p. 150.

were the parts of the empire breaking away from the trunk, but enemies began to invade its domain. The Tuareg chief Akil took Timbuctoo and Walata in 1435. Songhay, which had declared its independence of Melle in 1335 actually freed itself from that sovereignty by wars from 1465 to 1473. In 1400 the Mossi king, Bonga, overran Massina as far as Debo, and in 1480 Nassere, another Mossi king of Yatenga, sacked Walata. Reduced to an extremity, Mansa Mamadu, on the throne from 1481 to 1496, demanded of John II of Portugal protection from his enemies. That country had already established trading posts along the coast.

The empire of Manding was dying hard, however, for according to Leo the African, who traveled there in the beginning of the fifteenth century, much of it was still intact. The capital had 6,000 families. Industry was kept alive by numbers of mechanics and artisans. Merchants there were prosperous. The Mohammedan religion was practiced, and schools of influence were maintained. However, Leo the African could observe that the neighbors of Manding were making inroads, and in the beginning of the sixteenth century the frontiers of the empire had been reduced to what they were when Sun-Diata ascended the throne.[12]

Mamadu II, who ruled from 1530 to 1535, was unable to prevent the dismemberment of his empire in the west. Tekrur, already independent, threatened Bambuk. Manding again asked help of Portugal when Koli Tenguela began to invade the imperial provinces of Gambia while on the way to conquer Futa-Toro. In 1545, too, David, the brother of the Askia of Gao, took Melle and pillaged it, violating even the palace of the emperor. Disregarding the weak Mamadu III, Moroccans entered Timbuctoo in 1592. From 1600 to 1670 Manding was threatened with the rapidly increasing prestige of permanently developed kingdoms of Segu and Kaarta. In 1670, Mama Maghan, the last of the emperors, failing in the effort to resist the attack of the Bambara Kulabili of Segu, took flight to Kangaba, where the ruler of Manding became again the chief of a province as had been his ancestor Sun-Diata four centuries before. His descendants to this day exercise the same local authority under French rule. Thus with the exception of an interregnum of fifteen years this dynasty has ruled in that quarter from time immemorial, certainly since the eleventh century.

[12] Leo Africanus, *The History and Description of Africa*.

CHAPTER VI

THE SONGHAY EMPIRE

THE Songhay empire of a little later development than Kumbi (Ghana) or Manding (Melle), had three well-connected dynasties covering about a thousand years. The first of these lines had thirty-one kings between 700 and 1335. This empire showed such splendor that Lady Lugard, like most foreigners,[1] regarded it as having come under Egyptian influence just as Felix Du Bois does in his *Timbuctoo the Mysterious*.[2] The latter thought that the Songhay people themselves were of Egyptian origin, but Delafosse who was the best informed European on Africa in his day, while believing in Egyptian influence, shows conclusively that the Songhay were Negroes with little or no other infusion of blood. The Songhay language, to most European writers, gives proof of Nilotic influences, and so do the architecture and art. Strange legends are recited to show this culture as having migrated from Egypt which, considered a land of white men, is regarded as the civilizing force in West Africa.

Here as elsewhere, however, these biased writers run into conjecture. They have no proof for their assertions, but in spite of themselves they must protest against accrediting to Negroes unreservedly such unusual achievements. Any Egyptologist who has compared the art and architecture of Egypt with those of the Songhay clearly sees a striking difference between the two. While the art of Egypt shows a uniformity or a unity that of the Sudan, although creditable, does not disclose any such general pattern.[3] The scientific study of Africa rather shows that the early culture of Egypt was borrowed from the hinterland of Africa; and, while in

[1] Lugard, *A Tropical Dependency*, Chapter XVIII.
[2] Felix Du Bois, *Timbuctoo the Mysterious*, pp. 89-121. Consult also P. A. Talbot's *The People of Southern Nigeria*, Oxford, 1926.
[3] Jean Caport, *Les origines de la civilisation égyptienne*, Brussels, 1914.

contact with the outer world Egypt modified its culture, that from which she borrowed in the interior remained isolated and therefore changed little as in the case of Songhay.[4]

The Songhay empire had its beginning in ancient times on an island in the Niger between Ansongo and the rapids of Labezenga. Probably fifteen or sixteen centuries ago lived there a number of black people in villages, the chief one of which was called Kukia. These people consisted of two outstanding clans, the Gabbi who cultivated the fields, and the Sorko who restricted themselves to fishing. The latter incurred the ill will of the other clan by pillaging its farms. The Gabbi, with the assistance of Arabs or Berber immigrants, it is said, finally drove the Sorko toward the north

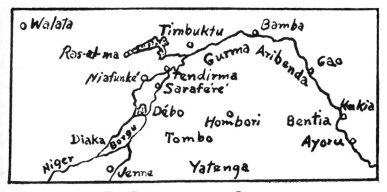

THE BEGINNINGS OF THE SONGHAY

about the year 800 A.D., and established the dynasty of the Dia who continued in power under thirty-one princes until 1335 with their capital at Kukia. Of the first fourteen little is known. The participation of Arabs and Berbers in these beginnings, however, has no support in fact. It is purely a legendary Mohammedan story embellished by biased Europeans.[5]

The known history begins with Dia Kenken, the fourteenth ruler, who died in 1009. Dia Kossai, who succeeded him extended his territory north and dislodged the Sorko. Under their leaders, Faran and Fono, the Sorko had established Gao and Bamba about

[4] *L'Anthropologie;* Maurice Delafosse, *Haut-Sénégal-Niger* (*Soudan Français*).
[5] Monod, *Histoire de l'Afrique Occidentale Française*, pp. 93-96.

690. The Sorko then migrated and settled on the Debo near the Sarakolle and after further extending their sway founded their capital Farem-Koirà (Sarafére). In the meantime the Dia of Gao were building a kingdom of considerable extent during the reign of seventeen succeeding princes, the last one of whom Dia Bada passed out in 1335. Dia Kossai was the first to accept Islam.[6]

These rulers made Gao a city of as much importance as any in this region of Africa had ever become. Commerce flourished to the extent that a foreign quarter had to be provided for the large number of Arabs and Berbers who came there to trade. The merchants had commercial connections with Ghadames and Wargla, by way of Tadmekket (Es-suk) a Berber and Mussulman settlement to the north and northwest of Kidal. Added to these advantages were the copper mines of Teguidda. The money current was salt from the Sahara.[7]

The sovereign reigned in splendor according to well-established rules. His repasts were announced by the beating of drums. He could be approached only by prostrating oneself before him, and he had to be saluted by striking the elbow on the ground and covering oneself with dust. The election of a new sovereign offered occasion for great rejoicing and feasting. The one thus chosen received the seal, a sword and a copy of the Koran. Outwardly the prince was a Mussulman, but the people continued with their local religion. Yet this kingdom was at that time sufficiently developed to withstand the rising power of Manding (Melle) as mentioned above. In 1325 Sagamandia, a general of Manding, took Gao and made it subject to Manding; but Gonga Mussa unknowingly worked indirectly the undoing of this conquest when returning from his pilgrimage to Mecca he took as hostages the two sons of Dia Assibai mentioned above. Trusted by the Gonga Musa and his successor to conduct occasional raids, the elder son profited by the occasion to learn the roads and to deposit arms at strategic points preparatory to flight from Manding.

In 1335 these youths escaped to Gao; and Ali Kolon, the elder,

---

[6] This, however, does not mean that the whole country was Islamized at that time. The ruler and his court had merely embraced that faith. The people had to be forced to accept it.

[7] Es-Sadi, *Tarikh Es-Soudan*, Chapter I; Mahmoud Kati, *Tarikh El-Fettach*, Chapters I and II.

with the intention of restoring the independence of Gao, made himself king with the title of *Sonni* or *Chi;* but this was not a new dynasty, for the same family was at that time merely serving under another name. The Sonni ruled the land from 1335 to 1493. Yet of the nineteen kings who served during this period we do not know very much until we reach Sonni Ali, the eighteenth of that line and next to the last of his family to be thus honored. Sonni Ali liberated his country from Manding (Melle) which had held Gao as a vassal state.

Sonni Ali ascended the throne of the Songhay in 1464 at the time the Sudan was in a chaotic condition. He was a born soldier, and the world around afforded him opportunity for his art. He did not concentrate on Manding. He included in his objectives all her foes, the whole empire which was being torn to pieces by them. He first constructed a river fleet and took possession of both banks of the Niger. In this way he marched upon Timbuctoo, and in the second attack took it in 1468. The wealthy and "learned" there opposed him and, therefore, suffered massacre or exile. Some "learned and wealthy" escaped with what they could to Aiwalatin while others returned later to enjoy the new régime. Thus Timbuctoo had suffered already in being sacked by the ruler of Mossi before it was possessed by Mansa Musa, in the interest of Manding which dominated the city from 1325 to 1433. The Tuaregs had held it since 1434.[8]

Sonni Ali finally encouraged "learning" at both Gao and Timbuctoo, after destroying the opposition of the "scholars," [9] the hostility of whom was fanatically Mohammedan rather than political. He said, "Without learning life would have neither pleasure nor savour"; and says the historian, "If he injured some, he did great good to many, and loaded them with favor." Sonni Ali was not an orthodox Mohammedan. With him it was more of a political gesture. He was a native African to the manner born. He prayed,

[8] The Mohammedans who recorded these things showed a religious bias in exaggerating this persecution because the objects of it were of their faith.

[9] An idea of the native language may be obtained from Ardant du Picq's *La Langue Songhay, Dialecte Dyerma* (Paris, 1933). The same author treats these particular people in his *Une Population Africaine, les Dyerma* (Paris, 1933).

but it was, "You know my sentiments." The Mohammedan annalists, of course, tried to detract from this ruler because he was not of their faith. These writers without any proof branded him a libertine, a tyrant, and fitful despot. He was supposed to have been restrained much by his unusually efficient prime minister Mohammed Abu Bekr El-Ture, a pure-blooded black of the Sarakolle.[10] Sonni Ali had great regard for Mohammed's counsels.[11]

This prime minister was born on the island of Neni, a little below Sinder in the Niger. He first made his reputation as one of the greatest generals in the army of Sonni Ali, but he ranked still higher as a statesman "of liberal principles and large views, naturally humane, and disposed to temper justice with mercy, more than usually cultivated, active, wise, and firm." [12] He came of good stock. His father was a man universally respected. His mother was a woman of remarkable piety, who brought up her children with care. Leo Africanus refers characteristically to a brother of the prime minister as "black in color but most beautiful in mind and condition." [13]   The prime minister took no part in luxuries or loose living.

The friendship of the ruler and his prime minister continued without being broken during thirty years. Lady Lugard says, "The minister would seem to have had the rare power of understanding the strength and weakness of the character with which he had to deal. He appreciated the genius of Sonni Ali and entered upon his great designs. His constant care was to assist him in carrying them out. At the same time he endeavored to save both him and the country from the consequences of madness with which in this case genius seems to have been closely allied." [14]   The minister often stood between the ruler and culprits condemned to death and hid them until his ardor cooled off. He thus risked his own life at times, but the people knew that he was pleading their cause, and they offered prayer that God might sustain him, for the ruler could with a word end his life. Thus was the conflict between militarism

---

[10] The customs of the *Sarakollé du Guidimakha* are set forth by J. H. Saint-Père in a work bearing this title, Paris, 1925.

[11] Lugard, *A Tropical Dependency*, p. 171.

[12] Lugard, *op. cit.*, p. 171.

[13] Leo Africanus, *History and Description of Africa.*

[14] Lugard, *op. cit.*, p. 172.

and statesmanship well illustrated. The genius of the sword and the genius of the mind united.

Sonni Ali's next conquest was Jenne about 1427. This town had resisted no less than eighty-nine sieges from Manding and by not a few was regarded as invincible. It cost Sonni Ali a siege of seven years, seven months, and seven days, but he finally brought Jenne to terms. On entering the town, Sonni Ali feasted and married the widow of the recently deceased ruler. As an evidence of his liberal attitude toward Jenne, moreover, he permitted her son N'So Mana to rule Jenne as his vassal. Jenne, then, after four hundred years of separation became again subject to the Songhay.

Sonni Ali next overran most of Massina and established there the government of Dirma under Dirma-Koi, as a vassal of Sonni Ali at Tendirma. In 1477 the Naba of Yatenga, however, ravaged Massina and pillaged Walata, and to protect this city from such raids Sonni Ali undertook to connect it with Ras-el-Ma with a canal, but he did not accomplish this task. He had too many other frontiers to defend. He had to fight the Nasere at Debo in 1483, and could not pursue them farther than Yatenga because of the necessity to combat soon thereafter the Tombo or Dogon or Habe. He had to fight and subdue Borgu in the east. In 1492 Sonni Ali was drowned in the Niger while returning from an expedition against the Fulani of Gurma. During his day, however, he had built up an empire which extended from Dendi to Mopti along the Niger, upon a large part of the loop and the left bank of the West Niger, and the lake region as far as Walata was a dependency of Gao. This extension of territory placed the Songhay in a position to dispute the supremacy of the Manding in that part of Africa.

Before his death Sonni Ali had become known in Europe, especially among the Portuguese operating on the coast of Africa. The Portuguese had taken to Lisbon a certain prince of the Wolofs of the black branch of the Fulani. He was received there with royal honors by the king and queen with whom he had audiences. These Europeans who had thought the Mossi were the most powerful in the Sudan had been granted a trading station at Hoden or Wadan. Sonni Ali put the glory of the Mossi to an end in 1483, and the Portuguese had to deal with him to reach those parts; but he did not disturb the pagans of the Gold Coast. The

Benins at the mouth of the Niger were the most advanced of these natives. They had made an impression with their fine art in metals, especially in bronze.[15]

Mohammed Abu Bekr, the great prime minister, secured the throne after overthrowing the successor of Sonni Ali, his son, Sonni Bakari, who contrived to rule only a year. Mohammed assumed the title of Askia, the usurper. He had to fight to hold his throne, for a minority favored the son of Sonni Ali and took flight with him to set up a small kingdom in the region south of Gao. Dependencies took occasion also to separate from the empire, but Askia Mohammed subdued them and organized the conquests of Sonni Ali.

Next Mohammed made a pilgrimage to Mecca to secure the sanction of the Crescent. He did not go with the train which marked the pilgrimage of Mansa Musa. Three hundred thousand pieces of gold was the most striking thing in the caravan. He went "not with barbaric splendor but with piety and in quest of knowledge."[16] The religious and scholarly accompanied him. He made helpful contacts, acquaintances, and friendships which endured. Among the subjects arresting his special attention the annalist noted "everything that concerned the government and administration of peoples; principles of taxation, and especially land tax and the tithe or tribute to be taken from newly conquered peoples; verification and inspection of weights and measures, regulation of trade, laws of inheritance, laws for the suppression of fraud, customs duties; laws for the suppression of immorality, and measures to be taken for the introduction of better manners among the people."[17]

A writer dwells at length on his bowing to the Caliph in Egypt, his resigning the throne of Songhay, and accepting it of the Caliph as an investiture. The European princes had been doing this under the Pope; and inasmuch as the Pope had just divided the world between Spain and Portugal by the Tordesillas treaty in 1494 it may be that this pilgrimage, this "rapprochement," was an effort to unite the Moslems against Christians in order to dispute their

[15] Felix von Luschan, *Die Altertümer von Benin;* Pitts Rivers, *The Antique Works of Art of Benin.*

[16] Lugard, *op. cit.,* p. 183.

[17] *Ibid.,* p. 184.

control of the world. Later Spain was cut off from Africa, and the Barbary States in driving Christians from the northern shore, closed that gateway to that continent. Because of the pagan natives and the swamps on the West Coast, moreover, foreigners could not penetrate that way, and Moslem Africa was shut up to the world. If this coronation of Askia Mohammed by the Caliph had any such significance as that herein mentioned, then, it availed little.[18]

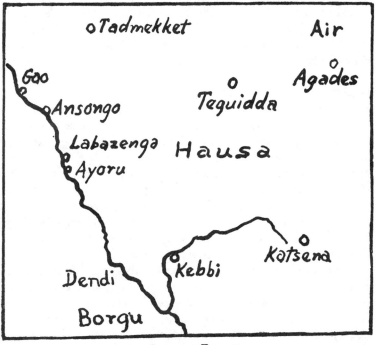

THE SONGHAY EXPANDED

On his return from Mecca Askia Mohammed undertook to accomplish what he saw was necessary for the glory of the empire even before he made this pilgrimage. In this effort he had the aid of an able lieutenant, Ali Folen, who served Askia the Great just as the latter had functioned under Sonni Ali. In this he was fortunate, for the emperor had to deal with risings on every hand in states left in semi-independence under their *koi*. Askia Mo-

18 Lugard, *op. cit.*, pp. 185-187.

hammed first made war on the Mossi of Yatenga. He did not exactly subdue the country, but he weakened it and carried away with him a large number of children whom he converted to Islam. Proceeding next to take advantage of the decaying Manding (Mellestine) empire, Askia Mohammed annexed Bagana and a part of the kingdom of Diara (Kaniaga) in 1498. He sent an expedition into the Tekrur as far as Galam in 1506. Rushing next into the insurrectionary provinces of the Sahel, the forces of Songhay defeated and killed Tinguella, the chief of the Peuhls of Termes in 1512. Going to the south of Gao, Askia Mohammed subdued the small kingdom built up by his fleeing opponent, Sonni Bakari, whom he had dethroned in Songhay. Extending his efforts as far as Borgu among the Bariba, he took with much loss in his own ranks a number of captives.

Proceeding, then, toward the east, the conqueror endeavored to subdue the Hausa region, but although he took Katsena, invaded Air, took Agadez and forced the Tuaregs to pay a large war levy, he was less successful in that quarter than elsewhere. The Kanta or king of Kebbi, who had assisted him in taking some of this territory revolted because he did not receive what he considered his just share of the booty, and he made Kebbi independent of Songhay. The empire, however, was still immense. It extended from Bornu to Lake Chad, to the Atlantic, and to the mountains which divided the uplands of the interior from the jungle coast.

Askia the Great, learning early to rule wisely and efficiently, was just as successful in administration as in conquest. He divided his possessions into several parts and placed in charge of each carefully chosen governors called *fari*. These, however, were more ministers from the emperor's court than actual magistrates. Under these functionaries served the chiefs called the *koi* who administered affairs in the provinces and the large cities. The scheme of government under which all these had to operate was minutely detailed in order to secure the greatest efficiency with the least expenditure of energy. The army to maintain the empire, of course, was likewise efficiently organized and controlled. The troops consigned to labor were recruited from among prisoners and slaves. Farmers, artisans and merchants could apply themselves in the army in keeping with their occupations. The army thus organized was apportioned among the provinces to protect their frontiers, but a well disciplined and strong guard was retained to protect the emperor.

These states as provinces were in quasi-independence. The emperor appointed just people to administer the affairs of state. He had regard for the law, but he did not codify it. In the case of injustice one could appeal to the governor of his province and from him to Askia the Great, because he loved justice and hated iniquity. The law was Mohammedan, and the teaching of the Koran was thought sufficient to clarify matters. The emperor required reports on markets, unification of weights and measures, and inspection of sales. Banking and credit systems were improved. Commerce was chiefly in the hands of Arabs, but black traveling merchants were numerous. Commercial intercourse and luxury brought the softening of manners. There was much gaiety, we are told; dancing and looseness could not be stopped; the emperor had been loose himself from the Western point of view. Yet there was much learning. Sankore around a mosque by that name was a popular school. There, it is said, great scientists and surgeons performed such delicate operations as that for cataract which baffle medical skill today.

A pious Mussulman himself, Askia the Great took counsel of these leaders of the new faith by whom he was surrounded. He himself underwent instruction that he might more successfully promote this religion. He made of Gao, Walata, and especially of Jenne and Timbuctoo, Mussulman centers of importance with widely famed schools. These cities not only attracted the people of that empire but foreigners from distant parts desiring to be educated in the tenets of Islam. Askia the Great extended these centers his special protection that they might be at ease and make a contribution to knowledge in the literature which they produced in the Arabic language.

Gao and Timbuctoo stood not only as centers of learning but also of trade and industry. Both were markets frequented by traders from Asia and Europe mingling with black men who also knew how to drive a bargain. Caravans brought goods from Europe and salt from Sahara to be exchanged for gold dust and slaves. The profitable trade with the Sudan became proverbial. Against the itch of the camel, it was said, use tar; against poverty, make a voyage to the Sudan. In all probability the riches of the Sudan were exaggerated, but men of that time were looking for inviting places as outlets for adventure. The Sudan thus became such an attraction that both Europeans and Asiatics fixed covetous eyes upon it.

Askia the Great, thus served his country nobly. While Sonni Ali had attracted much attention to himself as a remarkable conqueror, Askia the Great had made the world know the greatness and glory not of himself but of the Songhay. In spite of his eminence, however, this distinguished emperor was not allowed to die on the throne. He was dethroned by his eldest son, Askia Musa, who reigned only three years. At his death the throne was usurped by a nephew, Mohammed Benkan, the son of the Great Askia's favorite brother. He humiliated the Great Askia and was punished by being dethroned by Ismail another son of the noted ruler. These saw the beginning of the trouble with Morocco about the salt mines of Sahara. Ismail reigned only two years. He was succeeded by his brother Ishak, a cruel prince, who after a reign of ten years was succeeded by another brother Askia Daouad or David, the most distinguished of all Great Askia's sons. He reigned from 1548 to 1582; and did much to reform the court and subdue the provinces, but it was too late. After him the brilliant period of Sudan history ends. Mohammed III and Mohammed Bani did not live up to the record of reform set by David; and Issihak II was the last of the line to rule from Gao.

Stability, however, had been shown by long reigns and long lives of the people and the rulers. Kingdoms had lasted as long as Greece, Rome, and Britain. Industrial life was based on slavery in a mild form far removed from the system of bondage later developed in America. A few were rich, and many poor. Education was encouraged but along lines not emphasized today because of our interest in things practical rather than in the spiritual and philosophical.

Trouble had developed from Morocco as noted above. The Sultan there wanted the ruler of Songhay to give him the salt mine of Tegazza. This he refused to do. Next we hear of plots resulting in the murder of the Songhay Governor of Tegazza. This so interrupted the salt trade there that another mine had to be opened elsewhere. This disturbance resulted in foreign interference. This was aggravated, too, by trouble within. All outlying dependencies had to be reconquered or subdued—Manding (Melle), Mossi, Borgu, Bussa, Gurma, Hausa, Katsena, and the Fulani of Massina. This the successors to the Songhay throne could not do; and the invasion from the north was thereby made an easy task. The Moorish conquest thus facilitated marked another epoch in Africa to which we shall again refer.

CHAPTER VII

MOSSI STATES COMBINED AS AN EMPIRE

In Dagomba had developed a family which gave rise to several states on the Gold Coast near the confluence of the Volta Blanche and the Rouge rivers.[1] Little is known of the founder of this royal branch except the legend that he was the son of an exiled Malinke king by a princess carried astray into the same forest by an excited horse. This son was called Widiraogo. He subdued the natives of those wilds and established the kingdom around Tenkodogo which became known as Dagomba. At the death of the founder in the eleventh century his possessions became the nucleus of smaller states ruled by his three sons.

Zungurana, the eldest, had the west; but when he died his son Ubri merged his part of the country with that of Tenkodogo. He founded also the kingdom of Ubri-Tenga which became the state of Wagadugu. The capital was Ubritenga. Other provinces, Busuma, Belusa, Yako, Kipirsi, Gurunsi, and Nankana were later annexed. The empire was next called Mossi or Morho of the south and the ruler bore the title of *naba* or *morho-naba*. Thirty kings followed Ubri, the first fifteen of whom had no fixed capital. It was the ninth *naba*, Niandeffo, who in the beginning of the fourteenth century founded Wagadugu, but the sixteenth *naba* made it his capital. The twentieth *naba* abolished the custom forbidding the *naba* to leave the capital and thus allowed him an opportunity for conquest. The French took the country from the thirtieth *naba*, Bokari Kutu (1890-1896).[2]

Rau, the son next to the eldest, inherited the territory to the

---

[1] See Monod, *Histoire de l'Afrique Occidentale Française*, pp. 104-112; Delafosse, *Negroes of Africa*, pp. 67-72; same author, *Haut-Sénégal-Niger* (*Soudan Français*).

[2] These people among others are treated in Louis Tauxier's *Le Noir du Soudan*, Paris, 1912; and also in the same author's *Nouvelle Notes sur le Mossi et le Gourounsi*, Paris, 1924.

northwest around Zandoma which became the Mossi state to the
north under the name of this city.   This state became a vassal of
Tenkodogo and then that of Wagadugu.   Ya-Diaga, his grandson,
however, succeeded in retaining the ancestral amulets which con-
ferred authority.   In this way he contrived to conquer Zandoma
which he expanded to form the state of Yatenga with a capital at

THE MOSSI STATES

Gursi.   When he died he possessed Zandoma, Rizian, and Gurai.
The establishment of the Mossi state then was a *fait accompli*.

Following Ya-Diaga, came forty rulers of Yatenga, most of whom
were not so distinguished.[3]   Naba Nassegue (1320-1340) pillaged
Timbuctoo the year after the death of Mansa Musa.   Buga (1380-
1410) liberated his country from the vassalage of Wagadugu.

[3] These people and their history are treated among other things in
L. Tauxier's *Le Noir du Yatenga*, Paris, 1917, pp. 48-129.

Nasere (1475-1500), the greatest military leader of all this line, conducted expeditions into Massina and Bagana. He sacked Walata in 1480 when Sonni Ali was in power. In 1498 he drove back from his frontier an army of Askia the Great who had declared a holy war on Yatenga. From 1754-1787 ruled Kango, a cruel prince known as a skillful magician. After living on friendly terms with the Bambara he became involved in trouble with them and alienated that nation. The French took over the country from Baogo (1885-1895).

Diaba-Lompo, the third son, inherited the possessions to the east around Yungu which became the Gurmanche state or Gurma. These rulers were called the M'Baro or emperors of Gurma, of whom there were twenty-four following Diaba-Lompo. This state became the vassal of Tenkodogo and then of Wagadugu. Labi Diedo expanded the empire, but died of an arrow shot in the air and falling into his eye. Tukurmu was a cruel prince. He would put to death persons on mere suspicion as he did his wives. Yendable, the fifteenth of this line, waged war on Sansane Mango and brought back much booty. Batchande received the French in 1895.

Thus in the northern part of the Volta basin, the West, and East Niger developed during the eleventh and twelfth centuries these three states with sufficient cohesion to withstand the attacks and nominal conquests of Melle and Songhay and bordering kingdoms down to the time when they were taken over by the French in the nineteenth century.[4] They were enabled thus to survive by building from within and staying within their own borders rather than making excursions abroad to pillage their neighbors. These kings stayed at home, too, because there was a tradition of permitting the people to pillage the capital when the sovereign was absent. If any army had to be sent abroad it was placed under the command of a lieutenant of the emperor. While such a commander might not serve the army as efficiently as the emperor would, the loss in conquests was compensated for in the good results obtained from close administration.

The Mossi states of common origin had practically the same organization. Considered together, the three original kingdoms

---

[4] Lady Lugard, *A Tropical Dependency*, pp. 165, 175, 178, 192.

with two others are known in history as the Empire of Wagadugu. As in many empires, even in those of today, one of the kingdoms constituting Wagadugu belonged personally to the emperor as his own domain which he kept under direct control; and the others were ruled as annexed parts of the empire. Through his lieutenants the emperor administered the states of Tenkodogo, Busuma, Belusa and Yako. For local administrative purposes each state was divided into provinces, each province into cantons, and each canton into villages. The administrative staffs of the divisions and subdivisions were very much alike with the exception the larger the unit the larger the staff.

The emperors selected were descendants of the Ubri, chosen from one family. All the states recognized the authority of the *morho-naba,* and aided each other mutually and reciprocally under the direction of the emperor and his sixteen ministers through whom he governed. The first five of these ministers were the governors of the five states constituting the empire, and they served as a council of state. These ministers had such functions as intendant, *maître des pages,* the chief of the eunuchs, the commander of the infantry, the commander of the cavalry, and the keeper of the royal tombs. The others were in the order of precedence, the grand commander of the army, the commander of the imperial guard, the most high priest of the local religion, the master of rites and sacrifices, the chief of the servants and his associate, that of the musicians, of butchers, and of the *palefreniers,* the collector of taxes, and the syndic of the Mussulmans. These positions were handed down or passed from sire to son. The vassals of the emperor and their subvassals, like the emperor himself, had their smaller courts of dignitaries and ministers.

These vassals exercised unusual powers within their respective jurisdictions. They could levy taxes, exact gifts of their subjects, and impose the penalty of capital punishment. The chiefs of cantons and the subchiefs of the villages were mainly concerned with matters of local administration. Along with the chief of the village served also the religious chief or priest who was the master of the soil. He not only looked after purely religious matters, but he stood as the champion of the people's right to the land as guaranteed by custom before the country was overrun by foreigners.

The emperor was surrounded by a large number of pages, pale-freniers, guards, and servants charged with rigidly defined and worked out tasks. Their life was ordered according to a minutely detailed rule. Everything done was indicated by airs from flutes or the beating of drums. Every morning the *morho-naba,* or emperor, received his ministers to learn the state of the country and to devise means for its welfare and prosperity. On approaching the emperor each minister would prostrate himself before the ruler, touching the ground with his forehead, striking the soil with his elbows, and covering his head with dust. Then these lieutenants took up with their sovereign the matters of state decided upon as the order of the day. Should certain affairs require an inquiry or the hearing of testimony the longer time necessary for their solution was allowed. It was customary for the emperor to hold such meetings in the evening to deal with matters of public order and criminal justice. The inquiries which he made and the procedure in hearing the matter brought to his attention showed all the beginnings of trial by jury. Doubtless here the Africans anticipated the Nordics in the development of our jury system, as contends Professor Nathaniel Cantor, of the University of Buffalo.

In this procedure, however, the emperor was governed by custom which had the force of law. If he made a procession through his capital in the daytime, he went on horseback accompanied by his entire court. Servants drove the horse, held the stirrups, and carried the sword and the large umbrella to protect the emperor from rays of the sun. Drums would beat, griots chant, to bring about throughout the city a cessation of activities. At night the emperor would go out disguised, accompanied by one page only. He would proceed through the quarters of the capital incognito and enter homes in order to inform himself as to what was being said or done. At fixed periods or on specified dates he would repair to designated places on the borders of the capital to offer sacrifices that he might be preserved from all misfortune.

These traditions made sacred by time prescribed also the manner of living for the wives of the emperor, the sort of education to give his children and the rights they should exercise. When the emperor died he had to be buried according to customary rites, but the ceremony involved more pomp and display than was usual for others. Sacrifices of importance were required, and the voluntary offering up of human victims, somewhat like that of the Japanese, was permitted.

At the end of such royal funerals the properly constituted authorities arranged for the election of a successor to the emperor. The three grand commanders of the army and the keeper of the royal tombs would hold a private and secret meeting and elect a successor from the Ubri family. The new *morho-naba* would choose a new name. As such he would be proclaimed to the public which would confirm the election by their cries of approval. During the required interregnum of a year between the death of the emperor and the coronation of his successor the country was subject to complete freedom like that of the Hebrew year of jubilee. Prisons were thrown open, criminals were not punished, and debts were not collected. Every one conducted himself as he desired without the fear of punishment; and thus license rather than liberty reigned until the new sovereign was chosen and accepted by the people.

While there was an actual concentration of power in the emperor, the important vassals of this sovereign were monarchs themselves. They reached their positions by customs and laws very much like those by which the accession of the emperor was determined, and in their own sphere they were similarly powerful to the extent that they did not infringe upon the prerogatives of the emperor. While there was no standing army the social and economic order so operated as to enable the rulers to call in mass on the spur of the moment all able-bodied men to defend the realm. The cantons were under chiefs and villages under subchiefs who with the local priest functioned in these smaller divisions according to the customs of the aborigines of the country.

This organization of an empire, incontestably Negro, as it will appear to any one well informed on African affairs, resembles very much that of other states herein mentioned. Although these Mossi fought against and refused to admit dominant influence, this was apparently the African pattern of government which dominated the political thought of practically all organizers of government in ancient and medieval Africa, whether natives, mixed breeds or invading foreigners. This, then, is the strongest argument in favor of the large contribution of the Negro to government. It is at the same time an argument equally strong against the unscientific assertions of foreign writers who have tried to give immigrants into Africa credit for bringing the African such ideas. It is clear, moreover, that instead of greatly influencing what the African did during these early years the Africans at first determined the course of foreigners when settled on that continent.

Near the Mossi states, developed somewhat in more or less backward condition, were the people of the Tombola country. These people were the Tombo, or Dogon, or Habé. They occupied a region along the Bani to Hombori between the zone of inundation of the Niger to the west and the sandy half-desert to the east. On a slope of the elevated district are found villages almost like nests of eagles. They are of interest because they are primitive people who maintained their independence until the coming of the French, although attacked by the Askias, the Pashas of Timbuctoo, the Peuhls, and the Tukulors.

These natives, however, have never constituted a homogenous state. Each canton is a little kingdom. The chief of the state is elected by the patriarchs according to the promptings of the spirits. After election must intervene a year before the son of the *hogon* rules. When the *hogon* is finally installed he is placed apart from others in a sort of asylum where have accumulated the unusual objects consecrated to worship or representing the talismans of the dead Hogons. The insignia are a red mitre and a trident serving as a baton of authority. The *hogon's* person is sacred. He may be approached only with great ceremony. One cannot speak directly to him. His life, regulated by fixed rules, is complicated. The *hogon,* however, can levy upon the people to maintain his court. This consists of his son as the first lieutenant, the minister serving as an intermediary of the king, and a third minister in charge of worship.

To the north of Mossi also developed the kingdom of Liptako. It extends to the northeast in the circle of the Dori. It ends in a fertile spot beyond which begins the half desert zone in the bend of the Niger. The Deforo, who are of the same stock as the Dogon, formerly lived there. The chiefs of the Deforo ruled there until the end of the sixteenth century. The Gurmanche took the country about this time, and held it from about 1590 to 1690. The last of the line was Diari who had a quarrel with the Peuhls of Liptako under their chief, Ibrahima Saidu. He conquered the country; and his line held it until about 1800.

These Peuhls came from Massina. They belonged to the same group of Peuhls who had migrated and established colonies on the Niger and in the Hausa country. They drove the Gurmanche to the south, held back the Songhay approaching from the east, stopped the Tuaregs coming from the north, and suppressed the revolt of a slave who had raised an army of some worth. Ibrahima died after ruling thirty years. Under Salihu and Ibrahima Hamma, his successors, there was trouble from the Mossi and Tuareg inroads, but they contrived to defend the country. The next ruler was Seku, who permitted his lieutenant, Hammadu-Aisata, to take over the government, and he ruled from 1779 to 1783. Then came Abubakari and next Hamma-Tua, who were the last to rule Liptako. About 1800 Ousman-dan-Fodio, the Tukulor leader, put an end to this kingdom.

CHAPTER VIII

AFNO STATES

THE Afno (Hausa) people were of remote antiquity, but their early history is somewhat mythological. Their records were destroyed by conquerors under Sultan Bello. This happened to both Hausa and Bornu. These countries are different, however, in that the Bornu population is a mixture of blacks with invading Berbers while Afno (Hausa) is wholly black. The Afno (Hausa) district extends from the West Niger to Chad over a fertile region constituting the Eastern Sudan, included mainly today in what is known as the English Nigeria. The Hausa, too, have the tradition of having come from the East, and writers of Europe have unduly enlarged upon this conjecture which has no scientific basis or significance for these all but perfectly black people.[1]

These Afno or Hausa people had seven original states—Biram, Gober, Kano, Rano, Zaria, Katsena, Daura, the last six of which, according to a legend, were said to be the result of the marriage of Biram, the father, with Diggera, the mother. They had six children who became the progenitors of other states. Then there were seven illegitimate children who founded seven illegitimate states, Zanfara, Kebbi, Nupe, Gwari, Yauri, Yoruba, and Kororofa. This legend probably developed from the fact that these first named evolved early and independently and later attached the others.

The government of these states was that of a confederacy, for these powers were independent units somewhat like Tyre and Sidon. At times they were at war and then at peace. To combat a common foe, however, they had to unite. The states were nominally united also by the native religion of the worship of a goddess ruling at Zaria as a queen. This state was later conquered by Kano which was ruled by a king. He paid the queen Almena, or Almina, much deference and had her supported by special taxes. At this

---

[1] Monod, *op. cit.*, pp. 116-117; Delafosse, *op. cit.*, pp. 104-109.

time, according to Sultan Bello, Katsena was the center of the Afno (Hausa) state, and was noted for its industry and learning. The state of Gober on the edge of the northern desert, a frontier area, became the most warlike. Zaria, the most southern, extended its power over non-Afno territory. Kano played the leading rôle.

The first king of Kano was Daud, or David, who reigned about the tenth century before the invasion from the west which carried Mohammedanism through the Sudan. Afno people held to native customs until the immigration of Wankore or Wangara. Mohammedanism came in from Melle about the middle of the thirteenth century. It was accepted in Kano at that time by its King Yahaya. The native religion, however, struggled with Mohammedanism for years, but the former gradually yielded ground.

Kano entered into closer relations with Bornu, the king of which had to take refuge in that country because of rebellious subjects about 1430. Later the relations of these sovereigns were strained. Both were ambitious to extend their territory in the same area. There were in that region a number of petty states which the larger powers longed to annex peacefully if they could or by war if necessary. War followed, and because of the fine showing made by Bornu, states were ceded to the latter.

The immigration of Fulani when Manding (Melle) was declining about the time of the rule of Yakub, or Jacob, brought other troubles but stimulated trade without. Under their Kano king, Mohammed Rimpa, Islam spread. He built the walls of Kano with seven gates and a palace for himself. His aides, following his modern idea, built palaces for themselves. He divided the territory into nine provinces and made Kano one of the recognized native powers.

The kings of these states respected the law-abiding tendencies of Africans. The rulers, therefore, were not absolute. Matters were settled by courts, and the people through their representatives assembled participated in the enactment of laws. Then came a decline through unsuccessful wars under a succession of weak kings. Ahmadu Kesoke, probably the most illustrious of the line, followed Rimpa in the sixteenth century.

This was the summit of Kano greatness. Songhay then conquered the country. Local affairs, however, were not disturbed by the intervention of the conqueror, but wars and convulsions within brought Kano to grief especially the Katsena and Kororofa conflicts.   Kororofa in spite of rude tribes in the mountains had in the meantime developed as a state of importance by exploiting there gold, tin, lead, silver, antimony, and iron and the industries of weaving and dyeing.   Following Kororofa came the rise of other states which disputed the claims of Kano.   The first of these was Zaria, the most extensive of the Hausa states at one time but later annexed by Kano.   Katsena, Zanfara, and Gober respectively attained ascendancy later.

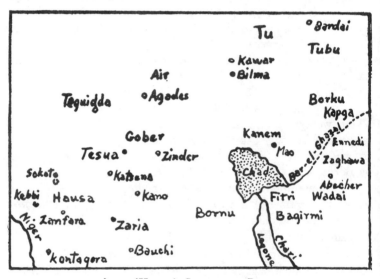

AFNO (HAUSA) STATES AND BORNU

Katsena, Barth discovered to be a great town, the leading city of this part of native Africa.   Katsena had also, he tells us, figs, melons, pomegranates, and limes; and until the destruction of the vines at the period of the Fulani conquest, grapes were plentiful. In addition to these evidences of agriculture, the rich pasturage was dotted with vast herds of cattle and goats, while the park-like scenery, diversified by native woods formed, he says, one of the finest landscapes he had ever seen in his life.   Among the woods the shea butter tree of commerce and the tamarind tree were re-markable.

The administration was efficient, and there were evidences of law, learning, religion, and refined language. Katsena was a sort of university town. In Katsena the Hausa language attained its greatest richness and served to convey to less advanced states a higher culture than that of their ancient epoch. Hausa is more extensively spoken than any other native tongue in West Africa. With a knowledge of Hausa, Bantu, and Arabic one would not need an interpreter in any part of Africa.[2]

About 1500, according to Monod, the most promising political organization in the Afno or Hausa region emerged as the kingdom of Kebbi. The ruler called *kanta* had taken possession of Kano, Gober, and Zanfara, and had made others respect his authority as far as Agades and even to the west in Bornu around Chad. Disturbed by this ascendancy of his neighbor, the ruler of Bornu attacked the *kanta* of Kebbi, but was driven back and followed by the ruler of that country. The latter on his return home, however, was defeated and killed by his own rising subjects in Katsena in 1513. His successor by making an alliance with Askia Mohammed reconquered Katsena and extended their conquests as far as Aïr, in the east. They also subdued Agades and made it a dependency of Songhay. Inasmuch as Askia Mohammed took most of the booty of this campaign, the *kanta* of Kebbi broke the alliance with him, and in 1517 defeated the army of Gao sent to subdue Kebbi. The authority of the kingdom was reestablished not only over Katsena but over the neighboring states of Hausa. At the end of the first century of the rule, about 1600, these states united, Gober, Zanfara, and Aïr and made themselves independent of Kebbi. Thus they remained for two centuries until they were taken over by Ousman-dan-Fodio about 1800.

BORNU

The people of Bornu, being mixed breeds, were different from the Afno (Hausa) in language and descent. The Afno are generally good-looking, with regular and pleasant features and graceful figures. The Bornuese have generally a broad-faced, heavy-boned physiognomy, which, especially in their women, is said

---

[2] Lugard, *op. cit.*, p. 264; Homburger, L., *Les préfixes nominaux dans les parlers peul, haoussa et bantous* (Paris, 1929), pp. iii-vii.

to be far from pleasing. The original inhabitants were called the "So," of Teda origin, and their first king was a Negro named Sefu who founded the dynasty of that name and had his capital at Njimi near Mao in Kanem. This country extended from Lake Chad as far as Fezzan and to the Lybian desert in the sandy region dotted with oases and comprising the districts north of the Wadai. To Bornu later were attached Kawar, Tibesti (Tu) and Borku. Dugu or Dugua of the Teda dynasty was ruling the land in the ninth century.[3] It is thought that under Ume, one of the founder's successors near the end of the eleventh century, Mohammedanism, the factor in the undoing of the Teda kingdom, was introduced. This meant the infiltration of Mohammedan Arabs and race admixture.

At the end of the twelfth century the Teda dynasty was overthrown by Tsilim or Salmama who reigned from 1194 to 1220 with the title of *mai*. His successors, however, had to combat the Teda who for two centuries fought to regain the throne. This struggle to retain possession was especially the task of Dunama who ruled from 1220 to 1259 and of Ibrahim who had to fight also the Bulula tribe from 1288 to 1304. These Mussulmans on the throne, however, were black.

Of some of these parts we have interesting accounts. Abel el-Hakem (870), one of our informers as to control of Africa, did not know much about the Sudan. El Bekri did in 1067. The founder and first governor of Bornu, he says, was black. "It seems contrary to modern ideas," says Lady Lugard, a biased European, "that white people should under any circumstances consent to be ruled by blacks, but it will seem that in the history of the Western Soudan this objection was not universally felt. Instances are common, especially in the western portions of the territory of the Soudan, of Berbers paying tribute to black sovereigns. The Fulani, who counted themselves a white race, were constantly subject to black rulers, and it is related of the black women of one of the kingdoms of the Soudan, that when their monarch was overthrown by a contemporary Berber king, they, 'too proud to allow themselves to fall into the hands of white men,' preferred to commit suicide."[4]

---

[3] Monod, *op. cit.*, pp. 118-121; Delafosse, *Negroes of Africa*, pp. 109-113.
[4] Lugard, *op. cit.*, p. 87.

Black and white mingled in that area. We note a famous black poet from Kanem at the court of El Mansour, one of the Almohade sovereigns of Spain, and Ibn Khaldun found the situation of race admixture about the same in the thirteenth cer.tury. This was regarded, however, as a brilliant period. Before the twelfth century it is said that the kings were light-complexioned, of Berber origin; but from the beginning of the twelfth century it is distinctly mentioned that they were black.[5]

In the year 1352-53 Ibn Batuta found King Idris (1352-1376) on the throne of Bornu. The people still had on their hands the war of the dethroned dynasty, but there was an active trade in slaves, eunuchs, and yellow cotton cloth. The celebrated copper mines of Takedda were then in operation. The Bulala, or Bulula, had continued to fight the empire of Kanem and to weaken its power. Omar (1394-1398) had to abandon the old capital Njimi, or Jima, and fix the royal residence at Bornu. Bornu then began to interfere with the Hausa states. At one time the kings had to seek assistance and shelter of Kano of the Hausa. This led to an acquaintance which enabled Bornu to conquer Kano. Wars, however, with victory first on one side and then on the other, followed; but final success crowned the efforts of Bornu.

At this time the brilliant Bornu prince, Ali Ghajideni, who ruled more than a quarter of a century (1472-1504), was on the throne. He was somewhat on the order of Sonni Ali, his contemporary. He reduced his conquests to order and fixed his capital at Gasaro west of Chad. He had to contend next with the *kanta* of Kebbi, and in trying to take possession of the capital of Surani he was defeated near Katsena. The rise of Askia Mohammed, moreover, had changed the course of things there.

Idris II (1504-1526) who succeeded Ali Ghajideni was a great warrior. He subdued the Bulula and annexed Kanem again. He was the contemporary of Leo the African who visited his kingdom and, while leaving some useful information as to its status at that time, confused the name of Idris with that of a predecessor called Abran.

From Ali Ghajideni in 1472 to Idris III, or Alaoma, who died in 1603, Bornu was under kings of vision. The empire was reor-

[5] *Ibid.*, p. 271.

ganized in the fifteenth century by the former. His successors expanded it, and Idris Alaoma reorganized and consolidated the heterogeneous mass of states. Idris conquered the states of Hausa, the province of Kano, but the city of Kano itself remained independent. He then turned upon the Berbers of the desert and next the natives of the thick forests. All turbulent elements, savages and nomads obeyed his will.

One of these black kings was found making gun powder about the time of Queen Elizabeth of England. There was a prosperous development toward higher standards. Government was less despotic than that of Songhay. A council of twelve held the principal offices. The monarchy was elective, but troubles from wars forced upon the country the hereditary line from father to son. The country was divided into districts with governors. Queen mothers, like that of King Idris, were very great and influential.

By 1583 the empire of Bornu had acquired the reputation of being irrepressible in the Sudan. It had attained the status of the Songhay. This was eight years before the coming of the destroying Moors. Idris Alaoma was killed in battle in the year 1603. His successors were too weak to hold the frontiers of the empire intact. The Bulula retook Kanem, but they were soon driven therefrom by the Tunjur coming from Wadai. The Tunjur established a capital at Mao and held the Kanem for two centuries but had to pay tribute to Bornu. Bornu at that time extended to the east over Kanem as far as Fitri, to the north over all the Teda country, to the west over Kano, Zinder, Air, and to the south from Chad as far as the Middle Logone. The empire was recognized as far as the Nile and the Mediterranean.

CHAPTER IX

THE SELF-EXTERMINATING KINGDOMS

To complicate matters further for the Negro kingdoms and empires of West Africa and the Sudan there had been coming as nomads a Semitic, Arabic element gradually infiltrating into these parts from the settlements which they had established on the southern fringe of the Sahara.[1] Some of these have already been noticed. There were two groups of these Arabs, the Kunta led by a conqueror Okba in the seventh century. They settled stationary at Tuat, and in the fifteenth century scattered over the country north of Timbuctoo in the Mabruk region. The other group of Arabs were the Beni-Hassan, ardent Mussulman adherents who claimed descent from the Great Prophet. They left Yemen about the eleventh century to spread over North Africa. In the thirteenth century they were in Morocco. In the fourteenth and fifteenth centuries they took over Adrar. In the sixteenth century they had entered Hodh and touched the banks of the Senegal. In this long-drawn-out process they mixed their blood with the blacks and imposed upon them and the Berbers the Mohammedan religion. These Arabs constitute today the military caste among the Moors of Mauritania and Hodh.[2]

Matters for both West Africa and the Sudan were still further complicated by another development. Following the Great Askia, the emperors permitted the Songhay to decline under this foreign pressure. Hausa and Bornu next after developing under Ali and Idris III had their day and likewise declined in facing the interlopers from the north. The countries far off had heard much about the splendor of these African kingdoms and especially with respect to the fabled wealth. Morocco, the nearest neighbor of the

[1] Monod, *Histoire de l'Afrique Occidentale Française,* pp. 121-126; Delafosse, *Negroes of Africa,* pp. 49-54; Lugard, *A Tropical Dependency;* and Hardy, *Histoire de la Colonisation Française,* pp. 41-62.

[2] Delafosse, *op. cit.,* p. 82.

Sudan, yielded to its covetous desires for the possession of that region. Knowing that salt mined at Tegazza supplied the Sudan and that it was worth its weight in gold to these people, Morocco picked a quarrel in trying to take possession of this area. In 1345 the Sultan of Morocco had asked Askia to turn over these mines, but the latter at that time was powerful enough to reply by sending a thousand Tuaregs to seize Dara in Southern Morocco. Under Askia David about 1578, however, the Sultan Ahmed-el-Mansour succeeded in renting these mines by the year for 10,000 pieces of gold. This step having been made, the Moroccan ruler availed himself of the opportunity to send a delegation of spies apparently to offer condolences to Askia. Through these he learned that the military forces of Songhay were weak, and he immediately sent a detachment of 20,000 men into Tegazza. Although decimated by the ravages of the climate, they took the place with 200 fusiliers. To secure salt thereafter the Sudanese had to open other mines at Taodeni.

Salt, however, was merely a pretext. The Sultan of Morocco wanted the gold of that region. An army of 3,000, then, was dispatched against the Sudan for this purpose; and, although reduced fifty per cent by privations by the time they reached the Niger, their small number of men armed with modern weapons defeated and put to flight the Gao army of 30,000 fantassins and 12,000 cavaliers. The antiquated weapons of the African natives could not avail much against the modern firearms of the invaders. On October 12, 1591, Askia Issihak, abandoned by his family and his lieutenants, fled to the bend of the Niger where he was massacred by the King of Gurma. Juder, the leader of the invaders, took Gao, but because the Mohammedanized Timbuctoo was more to his liking he settled there.

The invaders, however, had not conquered the country as a whole. They had merely destroyed the center of authority. Another Askia had escaped to set up a new Songhay kingdom south of Gao, and continued the opposition to the invaders who ruled from Timbuctoo by *pachas* named by the Sultan of Morocco. The followers of Juder, however, did take possession of the banks of the river from Gao to Jenne. Mixing their blood there with that of the blacks, they produced a caste of warriors called the Armas who dwelt in that district for two centuries, although they actually controlled those parts only sixty years. A nominal *askia* of the North ruled along with the *pacha* of Timbuctoo. Under the *pacha* were *caids* who in effective and brutal fashion administered smaller divisions like Timbuctoo, Jenne, Bamba, and Gao mainly at the dictation of a venal army.

Up to about 1660 the *pachas* were regularly named from Morocco, and there were twenty-one who first served apparently efficiently, but trouble developed when the *caids* began to quarrel among themselves about their respective portions of the plunder. Civil war followed. It soon came to pass that these factional leaders recognized no authority above themselves and ceased to send to Morocco any of the revenue collected. Mainly from among these soldiers mixing with native women were the *pachas* later chosen. As mulattoes they constituted a sort of noble caste. They unfortunately broke up into still smaller factions, the most warlike of which named the *pachas* from its army. A hundred and twenty-eight thus came and went between 1660 and 1750. After 1660 these interlopers thus held out by paying tribute to the black Bambara king of Segu who made the law to the south, or on "condition of pouring forth heavy contributions to the Tuareg Ulmidden (Oulmidden) who ruled in the north and who did not abstain from pillaging Timbuctoo each time hunger pressed them." [3]

The natives were then pillaged and crushed beneath a load of impoverishing levies. Famine ensued, and disease followed thereupon; desolation marked the spots where once had flourished promising Negro kingdoms and empires. The whole course of the Niger was given up to anarchy, insecurity, debauchery, persecution, pillage, and famine. This is what Juder brought to the Sudan in that army of religious fanatics, of low degraded Mussulmans together with some of the lowest type of Spaniards, who, renouncing the Christian religion, had joined the Mohammedans to pillage Negroland. They were unrestrained, cupidous, debauched, cruel, rapacious, and race-hating. They took away or destroyed the wealth of the Sudan and brought no good to the country. They could not thus last forever, however, for they soon

[3] Delafosse, *op. cit.*, p. 85.

began to lose ground, and the *pachas* came and went at the dictation first of the Tuaregs, next of the Peuhls of Massina, and finally of the Bambara of Segu. About 1770 the Tuaregs took Gao and pillaged Timbuctoo. By 1780 every trace of the Moroccan authority had disappeared. It had lasted long enough, however, to destroy much of the foundation laid by Manding (Melle) and Songhay. "The intervention of this scum of Europe," says Delafosse, "was one of the saddest blows that had been given to Sudanese civilization." [4]

Some of the Negro kingdoms survived in modified and reduced form the Moroccan invasion and the ravages of the Moslem slave trade made possible by their holy wars; and there sprang up smaller kingdoms from nuclei of later development in West Africa and the Sudan. These, however, were not to expand to the extent of those of yore, for the Europeans were already knocking at the door of Africa to afflict it with a more extensive and still more cruel Christian slave trade and to pave the way for the actual dispossession of the natives and the exploitation of their country according to inhumane methods considered just in the modern world.

The first state which we should mention here is the kingdom of the Bambara. These people are a branch of one of the most ancient stocks of Africa, the Wangara. One of their most ancient families is called the Kulubali, founded by two brothers fleeing from an enemy. One called himself Baramangolo and the other Niangolo. At the beginning of the seventeenth century the Bambara had covered the territory between the Niger and Bani, and the Kulubali clan was under a chief called Kaladian, a descendant of Baramangolo. He had his capital at Markaduguba, once included in Manding (Melle), later controlled by Jenne, and still later by the invading Moroccans. At the death of Kaladian in 1620 came Noteme. Finally by the next forty years the country had been ruled successively by Danfasari and Soma, who endeavored to make the empire independent, but this was actually accomplished by the son of Kaladian, Mamari, who bore the title Biton Kulubali.[5]

Biton did this by the organization of a powerful army. He built up also a formidable navy of fishermen on the Niger. He fortified

[4] *Ibid.*, p. 85.
[5] Monod, *op. cit.*, pp. 126-132.

Segu, his capital, with a thick wall and a strong fortress. Between 1660 and 1710, then, he gave his country its most prosperous rule and is remembered as the shining light there after a prolonged darkness. The Mansa of Manding (Melle) laid siege to Segu in 1666, but had to abandon the idea and come to terms with Nyamina as their frontier. Biton next conquered all the Bambara provinces on the right bank of the Niger, and imposed his authority on Bagana, Massina, and Timbuctoo. He divided the kingdom into sixty districts and administered its affairs efficiently. Those who would not yield he treated despotically and cruelly as in the case of the Kulubali Masasi who escaped north and established at Nioro, the other faction of the family which has perpetually waged war on the branch ruling at Segu.

From 1711 to 1736 ruled a number of weaker rulers. Denkoro succeeded Bakari, another son of Biton, who could rule only a few months. Denkoro might have succeeded better than he did if he had inherited the organizing ability of Biton rather than merely his traits of despotism and cruelty. He was soon assassinated and replaced by his brother Ali who, for becoming a Mohammedan, reigned only a fortnight. The Tondion assassinated him and dispersed the family. While in control from 1736 to 1750 the Tondion made the mistake of dividing the people into two factions, one supporting the infantry and the other the cavalry. The best the Tondion could do, then, was to maintain themselves by murder; and finally, an old chief of the Tondion, a follower of the Kulubali, N'Golo or Molo Diara, took over the kingdom and controlled it for thirty-seven years.

The dynasty of the Diara supplanted at Segu that of the Kulubali after an interregnum of fourteen years. N'Glo Diara attacked Yatenga in 1760 and led another expedition against that country in 1787 in the midst of which he died. Monson Diara, his successor ruling from 1787 to 1808, had to fight his brother Nienekoro five years before he could establish his authority. Monson also waged a bloody war upon Kaarta in 1796 and ravaged Timbuctoo in 1803 because it refused to pay him the usual tribute. From 1808 to 1861 when the country was taken over by the Europeans nine other kings of this line ruled without much lustre upon the country. Under Da Diara from 1818 to 1827 the most significant event was that Massina made itself independent of Segu. About 1810 the Peuhls were placed under the suzerainty of the Marabout Seku Hamadu of the Bari family, and he took Jenne and Timbuctoo from Segu. Finally the rulers of Segu and Massina had to make peace and unite against the rising power on the horizon, El-Hadj-Omar, but they fought him in vain. Ali, the last of this line, was put to flight in 1862 and slain by order of this rising star in Africa.

As already noted above, the branch of the Kulubali, claiming descent from Niangolo migrated to the left bank of the Niger about the middle of the seventeenth century and settled at Nyamina. From that point they went to the region between Murdia and the Baule on the borders of Kaarta and built a capital which they called Sunsana or Suntian in honor of their leader Sunsa.

Masa, who ruled from 1670 to 1690, succeeded Sunsa. Under him the tribe prospered as a result of strict regulations one of which was that his numerous children should not intermarry with the Masasi. The Masasi made incursions into the territory of their neighbors and compelled them to fear them and seek their friendship. Masa extended his territory west to the Senegal and annexed provinces of the declining Manding (Mellestine) Empire. These possessions he organized as the kingdom of Kaarta, which later was strong enough to defy the Diawara of Diara, and the Kulubali of Segu. Bemba or Beni Fale and his brother Folokoro, on the throne from 1690 to 1709, next held sway; but the latter enraged the king of Segu by a raid in his country in which he took one of the daughters of Biton. The aggrieved ruler attacked the Masasi, put Folokoro to death, and with the exception of four destroyed the rest of that royal line.

Thus weakened these members of the royal family remained (1709-1759) in quietude in preparation for the deliverance of their country. Under Sieba-Mana they built their capital in the west at Guemu, and entering the quarrels of Diawara between Sagone and Dabo as a pretext, Sieba-Mana annexed the kingdom of Diara or Kaniaga. Masa Bakari, the brother of Sieba, waged war in the east against Nyamina, took sixty villages, and had himself recognized as the ruler of the tribes of the Diawara. Kaarta, Kingui, Bakunu, Guidiume, and Diafunu were annexed to this rising kingdom. Deni or Dembabo, who held the throne ten years and his successor, Sirabo, who ruled nine, extended these conquests. They demonstrated their prowess further by fighting the Khasso and pillaging Koniakari, its capital. It was Besekoro (1789-1802) who received Mungo Park. This king kept up a continuous war against Monson of Segu who finally invaded Kaarta and destroyed Guemu.

The country had reached its zenith but it was not yet declining. For some time feats of rulers still attracted attention. Teguen Koro (1802-1811) subdued the Kagoro; and Sakaba, his successor, attracted attention by his raids. Musa or Kurabo (1815-1818) took Koniakari, and drove Demba Sega the king of Khasso, into Bundu. Bodian Moriba (1818-1835) moved the capital to Yelimane and made peace with Demba Sega who was permitted to return to Khasso. Gran and Kandian Mamadi or Mamari Kandian (1833-1854) next held the throne, but in 1846 the latter moved the capital to Nioro. He also defeated decisively the Diawara of Diara who had refused to pay him tribute. In triumph, however, he soon faced defeat from another quarter. In 1854, El-Hadj-Omar, the Tukulor leader, after taking Koniakari and Yelimane, conquered Nioro and executed all members of the royal family.

Certain Peuhls, a people of Semitic origin mixing their blood with that of the African, have already been noted. About 1400 a leader of this stock, Maga Diallo, led some of this element from Termes to Diaka or West Massina. There they established settlements which they ruled in a way for four centuries, sometimes independent and sometimes subordinate to the black Africans. At first Maga Diallo had to obtain from the Sarakolle the permit to settle in Diaka which was a dependency of Manding. He settled as a residence at Kebbi north of Dia on the shore of Lake Massina. The successors of Maga Diallo ruled under the Mansa of Manding, and later we find Sonni Ali attacking the country to dispossess Manding (Melle) of it. In 1477 the Naba of Yatenga pillaged this country and did the same for Walata three years later. Askia of Songhay took Massina in 1499 after a four years' war. From 1510 to 1670 the Peuhls of Massina weakened themselves by their protracted quarrels of hostile factions among them. Massina was unable then to succeed in the various efforts to free itself from the Songhay during the second half of the seventeenth century. Next they had to contend against the *pachas* of Timbuctoo with similar results because of their internal strife. After 1670 Massina came under the Bambara of Segu during the reign of Biton. These rulers who had been not higher than governors of a dependent province were brought to an end with the passing of control of Hamadi Dikko in 1810. From that time until 1862 Massina was a state of much consequence.[6]

The power then went to the Bari clan, Mohammedans, whereas the Dallo and their subjects adhered to the native animism. The one was hostile to the other. As a result of a quarrel between them, Hamadi Dikko asked aid of his suzerain Da Diara, king of Segu. An army was sent; and Hamadu Lobbo's son, Seku Hamadu, long an ardent teacher and propagator of Islam, proclaimed a holy war against the native animists, defeated his enemies, and made himself the head of a new dynasty with the title Amiru. He then extended his power over all Massina from Jenne to Timbuctoo, where he established a garrison. He founded Hamdallahi as his capital in 1815. He then divided the state into provinces and established in each a local administration under a governor, a *caid,* and a commander of the military force. He raised an income by taxing the herds, the harvests, and gold, Deriving a good treasury therefrom, he made Massina a place to be reckoned with. Hamadu Seku, the successor of his father, could not maintain this power. Timbuctoo became independent. This ruler resigned in favor of his son in 1852, but the horrors of another holy war overtook his country. El-Hadj-Omar took Segu in 1861, and Hamdallahi in 1862, when he put to death this last one of the Peuhl dynasty.

[6] In Monod, *op. cit.,* pp. 132 to 135, there is a different opinion.

CHAPTER X

EUROPEANS ON THE COAST OF AFRICA

WE hear of the ancients trying to touch Africa, but during most of the early Middle Ages they are inactive in this sphere. We learn no more about Africa until we reach the Mohammedan invasion of the seventh and eighth centuries. Then came Arabs, Persians, Hindoos, and probably Chinese on the East Coast of Africa.[1] On the West Coast, however, such invaders from Europe do not appear until the thirteenth or fourteenth century. We learn that the Genoese adventurers touched the Canaries, the Isles of Fortune, by 1275, and advanced as far as the mouth of the Senegal by 1292. The Normans in their wanderings reached the Canaries in 1330, Guinea in 1339, doubled Cape Verde in 1364, and founded by 1365 a factory called Petit Dieppe in honor of the city from which these traders came. French merchants, associated to exploit further this trade, sent other ships to the Gold Coast in 1365, 1380, 1381, 1383, and 1402; but although they built there a factory, La Mine, these adventurers without the support of their home government accomplished nothing of great note. France was not then the leader in European commerce.[2]

The Portuguese accomplished the task which others had attempted. They conquered the Canaries in 1341 without much result. In 1346 Jac Ferrer coasted along Morocco, doubled Cape Bojador and reached the Rio de Oro; but during the reign of

[1] Jerome Dowd, "The African Slave Trade" in the *Journal of Negro History,* II, pp. 1-20.

[2] This aspect of European History is succinctly stated in J. L. Monod's *Histoire de l'Afrique Occidentale Française* (Paris, 1931), pp. 144-192; also in Sir Charles Lucas's *The Partition of Africa* (Oxford, 1922), passim; and in P. D. Rinchon's *La Traite et l'Esclavage des Congolais par les Européens* (Brussels, 1929); Gaston Martin's *Nantes au XVIII Siècle; L'Ere des Négriers* (Paris, 1931); Georges Hardy's *Histoire de la Colonisation Française* (Paris, 1931); E. L. Guernier's *L'Afrique Champ d'Expansion de l'Europe* (Paris, 1933).

John I of Portugal these explorations were further developed under the inspiration of his fourth son, Henry. He sent expeditions to the Madeiras and the Azores in 1419 and 1432 respectively. In 1445 he directed his ships to the coast of Africa where they entered the Bay of Arguin, built a fort, and established relations with the Moors of the coast. Under Dennis Fernandez the Portuguese next discovered Senegal and Cape Verde. In 1442 Gonçalvez introduced African slavery into Portugal. In 1455 Cada Mosto in the service of Prince Henry brought back from this point gold dust and other slaves. He stimulated further interest with the information he received of Timbuctoo, Tegazza, Budamel, Cape Verde, Dakar, Rufisque, Casamance, Gambia, and the people called Wolofs. However, he did not learn sufficient of the interior to know that the Senegal and the Gambia are not branches of the same stream and that the Nile and the Niger are not one and the same.

The Portuguese reached Sierra Leone in 1462, and with 6,000 men, debarked in 1471, they built the fort San Jorge d'El Mina. Near the end of that century they were establishing trading posts in what is now the Senegal. Still earlier they had attempted to take over the gold mines of Bambuk; but, as related above, because of the climate, the Africans in opposition, and differences among themselves which resulted in their self-extermination, the enterprise came to nought. These Europeans, however, were in touch with the kings of the Sudan by 1431. The Portuguese were more fortunate in 1534 when the ambassadors of Portugal sent to Manding (Melle) were received by Mamadu II, of the decaying empire, who implored help from Portugal against the attacks of Koli Tenguella, Salatigui du Futa-Toro. The Portuguese were further stimulated by their navigation and exploration in other parts under Diogo Cam who in 1486 ventured a thousand miles beyond the Equator and saw the Hottentots; under Bartholomew Diaz who in 1487-1488 doubled the Cape of Good Hope; under Vasco da Gama who in 1498 pushed as far as Mozambique and the East Indies; and under Magellan, one of whose ships completed the tour around the world, although he perished on the Island of Cebu in the Philippines. All these voyages engaged in the trade of slaves, ivory, and gold dust for cloth, rum, and the like.

These settlements, however, meant little at that time when there was no such a system as international law; and, on the contrary, the nations encouraged privateering. The French were blocked in their designs by such raids along the coast in the fifteenth century. The Spaniards and the Portuguese held the power on the seas during the sixteenth century and had had the Pope divide the outlying world between them by the Treaty of Tordesillas in 1494. Francis I failed in his opposition to Charles V of Spain even though the latter tried to enlist in his cause the Non-Christian Sultan of Morocco and privateers from France did much to retaliate. The French claimed, however, that their trade was more honorable, for when they captured a slaver of the Spanish or Portuguese they set the victims free. The Dutch finally supplanted the Portuguese along the coast at Cape Verde and Goree, but France was to have a share later.

It soon became necessary to organize this trade under the protection of commercial companies controlled by nations rather than leave it in the hands of associating merchants. This had been urged in France. Henry IV and Louis XIII saw the necessity for it and endeavored to act thereupon, but Sully under the influence of the Dutch did not favor it; and the policy of commercial expansion built upon a real French navy as worked out by Richelieu and Colbert had not then developed. England, under Elizabeth, then, comes upon the scene to claim her share of the plunder made possible by the adventurers sent out from Europe, and Philip II even after uniting Portugal to Spain on the passing of the last of the Portuguese dynasty lost his opportunity, by the defeat of his "invincible" armada in 1588, of preventing the English from participating in the new trade.

The English had tried to get a foothold on Africa as early as 1481. William Hawkins touched the continent in 1530, 1531 and 1532; and his son, the famous John Hawkins, a bolder adventurer, began his operations there in 1562. The English finally established themselves in Gambia in 1618. The Dutch appeared there in 1595 to dispute the claims of other nations, made an indentation on Goree in 1617, and established a fort on the Gold Coast in 1624. With national states thus concerned these smaller associations became large corporations organized with universal connections. These promoters began even at that early date to see the feasibility of mercantilism, of bringing to Europe the raw materials of the new lands and of selling back to these belated peoples their manufactured glassware and shoddy goods at a price sufficiently high to keep a favorable balance of trade on the side of the European states. This was the beginning of what we today call economic imperialism.

With the names of these corporations we need not concern ourselves here. Almost every European state had a West Indian Company and an East Indian Company, indicating by their names the connecting points in their trade in gold dust and slaves in Africa, the disposition of these bondmen to exploit the New World, and the spices of the Far East to be brought to Europe in larger quantities. Facing unexpected difficulties from piratical war among themselves and opposition from the natives in Africa, only a few of these large companies succeeded; most of the smaller ones proved to be visionary enterprises. Those which had some measure of success developed into actual governments with trading posts as headquarters gradually becoming settlements for which the corporation under charters from the home country provided an administrative force for commercial colonies.

As to Africa itself many changes were made in the carrying out of this program. France without a navy could not protect itself in Africa, although she was among the first to touch the shores commercially and had established herself in the Senegal with such settlements as St. Louis on the island of N'Dar in 1643. Goree was taken by the Dutch in 1677, although France, as a result of the rising of the natives under the Bourba of Sine, the Tegne of Baol, and the Damel of Cayor against the Dutch, recovered most of this coast in 1679 by the treaty of Nimwegen. The English got the lion's share of this slave traffic through the Asiento in the Peace of Utrecht in 1713 which closed the War of the Spanish Succession. The French had made strenuous efforts through the directors of the reorganized Senegal Company to establish themselves there, but they lost the results from such efforts in having to cede all in Africa except Goree as provided in the Treaty of 1763 closing the Seven Years' War. St. Louis and the rest of the French territory in Africa went to England. Taking sides with America in its struggle for independence in the Revolution from 1778 to the end of the conflict, France carried the war into Africa and conquered most of the territory which had been lost in the previous struggle. She was then in a position to renew and enforce its claims there when the nations made peace in 1783. France was thereby assured the possession of Arguin, Portendick, St. Louis, Goree, and Galam, while the Fort of St. James and Gambia went to England. Both nations were to have the right to frequent the coast of Guinea.

The new governors of the coast settlements sought to extend their authority into the interior by visiting and making treaties with the native rulers especially with the King of Barre in Gambia, the Damel of Cayor, the King of the Brakna, and the Almamy of Kussa, but this effort was somewhat paralyzed in 1786 when Rubault, charged with the mission of restoring the fort Saint Joseph, was slain in Galam by the slaves he had taken. These possessions emerging as the Senegal of our day were taken again by the English during the French Revolution which had worked the abolition of slavery in 1794. The system was restored by the British, who in spite of the defense made by the French Governor Blanchot in enduring a very long siege finally secured control of the country in 1809 by taking St. Louis. The English held the country until it was restored to France in 1817. From this time until 1854 France in Africa did little more than to learn from her many mistakes and misfortunes how to emerge from disorder into a systematized effort under colonization as developed under Raffenel and Faidherbe. In the meantime the efforts of England were to mature peacefully into the colonization of Sierra Leone [3] and the penetration of the interior from lower points on the West Coast.

In this story the reader must not miss the main cause of the difficulties of the European colonizationists. They had for the first obstacle the difficulty of making the natives believe that the presence of such adventurers on their shores augured well for the success and well-being of the aborigines. When the Europeans secured from one African people the right to settle or trade they easily alienated other Africans by their plundering and oppression; and it was always a simple matter for one of these European agents to

[3] The colonial policies of these European powers are well summarized in Marcel Du Bois's *Systèmes Coloniaux et Peuples Colonisateurs*, Paris, 1895, *passim*,

bring the natives to the position of revoking the privileges granted and of transferring the same to another foreign master of the same type. The natives, of course, in thus changing their policy were merely trying to find the easiest way out of their difficulties, a problem which they have not yet solved.[4]

Prominent among the natives thus concerned were the people of the ancient state of the Wolofs who influenced those of Walo, Cayor, Baol, and Sine.[5] Among the Wolofs were mixed in numerous Serers (Sererés). The Wolofs were brought under the authority of their powerful neighbor, the Tekrur to the northwest, but near the middle of the fourteenth century the Wolofs under the leadership of N'Diadiane N'Diaye threw off this dependence. At the close of the fifteenth century or the beginning of the sixteenth, a conspirator, supported by the Lebu, weakened the state in an effort to gain the throne, although he failed and the Lebu had to escape to the south of Cayor. This area was relieved by the emigration of the Mandingoes from that point toward the Gambia, which left open that part of the Lebu as far as Cape Verde.

Biram Dieme Cumba, the next ruler of the Wolofs, crushed out such internal strife, and united his possessions. His success was apparently made easier by his noble wife, a princess widely admired for her beauty. She was the mother of two sons, Lat Samba Buri Dieleme and Guirane Buri Dieleme, who succeeded their father on the throne. In the eighteenth century the Danki sat on the throne of the Wolofs, but did not seem to add much to its prestige, for under them Cayor established its independence. Ali Buri was the *bur* or king of the Wolofs in 1889 when the French took control by a treaty of protectorate.

The Cayor, referred to above, dependents of the Wolofs, were among the first natives reached by the French who tried to take over the coast of Rufisque at Joal. The French found their effort

[4] The literature of these explorations and conquests with respect to France is summarized in A. Roland Lebel's *L'Afrique Occidentale dans la Litterature Française,* Paris, 1925, pp. 1-120. See also Lebel's *Histoire de la Litterature Coloniale en France,* Paris, 1931, pp. 23-24; E. L. Guernier's *L'Afrique Champ d'Expansion de l'Europe,* Paris, 1933, pp. 74-84 and 273-278.

[5] J. Bourgeau, "Coutume successorale des Sérères du Sine et du Saloum," in *Outre-Mer,* Quatrième Année, Mars, 1932, pp. 3-8.

frequently undone until they could deal with Amadi N'Gone Sobel, who made Cayor independent of the Wolofs. From him the French obtained in 1763 the cession of all Cape Verde from the Cape des Mamelles as far as Cape Bernard, including the towns of Dakar and Ben. This was renewed by another treaty in 1765. From 1791 to 1810 under Amadi N'Gone N'Della Cumba his hordes were permitted to pillage the Lebu of Diander and Cape Verde to the extent that they declared their independence and set up a government called the Republic of the Lebu with a theocracy based on the Koran.

Birma Fatma Tiup who ruled the Cayor for the next twenty-eight years had to wage incessant wars with the Lebu; and Dial Diop, his successor had to recognize their independence in 1812. With the Lebu the Europeans treated. These wars were taken advantage of by Europeans who encouraged them to secure captives for slavery in America to exploit the mines and plantations. It was because the King of Cayor participated too freely in these wars which became pillaging expeditions that the smaller chiefs under their best military forces united against the Cayor and made the Lebu Republic possible. It was practically a French possession in 1815.

The Futa-Toro played a part here also. They developed from the Tukulors, vassals of Manding (Melle) through the exercise of authority by the Diawara of Diara, later passing under the suzerainty of Songhay. Chafing under the yoke of the Diara, Tenguella proclaimed a holy war of freedom only to be defeated and killed by the brother of Askia the Great. In vengeance of this adopted father's death, Koli Tenguella took the warpath and with a number of Peuhls and Mandingoes conquered the Wolofs and put their king to death. He next invaded Futa, subjugated the states of Kaniaga and of the Wolof, Cayor and Walo, and thus made uneasy the emperor of Manding (Melle), Mamadu II, who implored the assistance of Portugal.

The successors of this conqueror were called Silatigui or Salatigui of the Denianke caste or the Deniankobe. Others were called Koliabe. With these Peuhls of Futa and those of Senegal the Europeans had to deal. They had to pay these people tribute to deal in their country, from 1586 to 1776. Next we observe from

1776 to 1881 the emergence of a theocratic monarchy of the Mussulman type as a result of the holy war of conquest started by the marabout Abdulkader Torodo against the Peuhls who were not Mohammedans. He conquered Sule-Bubon, the last king of the Denianke and destroyed the Koli dynasty. The authority under the new kingdom rested with the marabouts under the almamy.

CHAPTER XI

THE LAST STAND IN WEST AFRICA

AFTER many efforts against the natives along the coast and annoying international conflicts growing out of commercial rivalry the Europeans still found themselves outside of the interior of Africa. As late as 1850 the French had only Algeria, the Senegal, and some strategic points on the coast. England had permanently occupied the Cape and was disputing with France the control of Egypt. Faidherbe as a conqueror of the coastal native kingdoms bordering the Senegal and as an efficient administrator from 1854 to 1865 laid there a foundation upon which he and his successors based later a campaign of extension into the interior. Up to this time the real interior was unknown to Europeans in spite of the records made by a number of more or less serious travelers and explorers. Among these were Houghton in 1791, Mungo Park in 1795 and 1805, Dorchard in 1818, Meslay in 1819, Mollien the same year, Clapperton and Denham in 1824, Lander in 1830, Gordon Laing in 1826, René Caillé in 1827, Duranton in 1828, Raffenel in 1843 and 1846, Panet in 1850, and Barth in the same year.[1] Livingstone's exploration of Africa after 1870 opened it up to Europeans as a new field of exploitation. Before this could be done, however, they had to contend with two other imperial efforts of ambitious natives converted to Islam. The policy of these African leaders was to free the country by holy wars, attacking the natives who would not submit and finally combating the Europeans who saw in such efforts the possible ruin of their colonial enterprises.[1a]

The first of these leaders of the new day was El-Hadj Omar, already mentioned above as the nemesis of several West African

[1] For bibliography see Delafosse, *Negroes of Africa*, pp. 72, 102-103, and 140.

[1a] Monod, *Histoire de l'Afrique Occidentale Française*, pp. 227-236, 244-253.

kingdoms. Omar Saidu Tal, as he was originally known, was born at Aloar, near Podor in Futa Toro about 1797. He was a man of Negro blood, although his father was a Mussulman and thoroughly instructed his son in the faith of the Prophet. About 1820 Omar made a pious pilgrimage to Mecca where he remained until 1838. There he was initiated into the Mussulman Brotherhood of the Tijania and invested with the title of Khalif. Returning to Africa with these titles, Omar became a figure of great prestige. He easily attracted disciples and trained these to become lieutenants who later followed him in his enterprises. Omar first settled at Futa-Jallon and next at Dinguiray. From 1850 to 1854 Omar, starting from Dinguiray, the capital of his first conquests, overran the region of Bure and Bambuk as far as the Senegal and pushed on to Nioro where, as stated above, he executed the last Bambara Masasi king of Kaarta. Because of the assistance given the Bambara of Kingui by the French under Paul Holle and Faidherbe the Tukulor forces failed in the siege of Medina in 1857 and had to return to Nioro in 1859.

Leaving as governor of Nioro, a former slave, Mustafa, Omar proceeded toward Segu in 1859. He took possession of Merkoia and Damfa and put to death a number of opposing Bambara. He next seized Nyamina and Sandsanding and struck such terror to the hearts of the conquered that Ali, the King of Segu, and Hamadu-Hamadu, the King of Massina, decided it wise to unite their forces against the conqueror; but to no purpose was this last effort, for the Tukulor army defeated the allies near Sansanding on the Niger, put to flight these united forces, and entered Segu in triumph on March 10, 1861. A second effort of Hamadu-Hamadu to dislodge the Tukulor with an army of 40,000 was likewise unsuccessful. The taking of Segu produced a great consternation throughout the Sudan.

Omar organized Segu along theocratic lines and imposed upon the people the regulations of everyday life required by the Koran. They had to shave their heads and pray five times a day according to teachings of Mohammed. They could no longer take alcoholics, and dared not eat the flesh of dogs, horses, or dead animals. The chief builder, Samba N'Diaye, fortified Segu and built there a royal palace. He had constructed also a *réduit* to conceal such valuable treasures as gold, cowries, salt, and powder.

From 1862 to 1868 Omar conquered the territory between Segu and Hamdallahi. Leaving his son Ahmadu in authority at Segu in 1862, Omar proceeded toward Massina with an army of 30,000 Sofas or *talibés*. He defeated first the army hurled against him by Ba Lobbo and a second army of 50,000 Peuhls at Tiaewal that same year led by Hamadu-Hamadu. Omar, then, entered Hamdallahi the capital of the country and decapitated the king. Frightened by such appalling news, the chiefs of Massina readily submitted to the hero of the hour.

The conqueror next took Timbuctoo, but could only pillage it because of the difficulty of holding the place when the Kunta, the masters of Timbuctoo, had allied themselves with the Peuhls of Massina and had laid siege to Hamdallahi. This was a severe blow to Omar, for his success lay mainly in operations in the field. He was more of a man of action than a strategist in close quarters. As the siege lasted eight months the city was reduced to famine; and Omar, in trying to escape under cover of a fire set to the capital, perished in a grotto in 1864.

The empire which he had founded was considerable. It extended from Massina to the Falémé and from the Tinkisso to the Sahel. This expansion had been effected between 1848 and 1864. The empire soon went to pieces, however, for lack of solidification. Omar had left in each of these kingdoms a relative to rule while he was going forth to other conquests. In one kingdom, as noted above, a faithful slave had been thus exalted. These local rulers became jealous of one another and failed to cooperate.

When Omar passed out of the picture Ahmadu, who had been settled as king of Segu claimed the imperial authority. The people in the capital of Segu itself tolerated Ahmadu, but in the remote parts they arose against him. Revolts became incessant. Taxes could not be collected, peace could not be maintained, and the frontiers could not be defended even when the ruler tried such terror-striking methods as that of beheading his opponents. Sansanding proved to be invincible. The Bambaras kept up a guerrilla warfare and pillaged the country as far as Segu until they were checked in 1865 by a victory of the Tukulors. This amounted to little, however, when the relatives of Omar left in control of the various parts of the empire began to war among themselves and failed to give the empire the support necessary to maintain it. Kaarta and Massina finally broke away, and by 1887 the disintegration of the Tukulor Empire was complete.

During these years the people, both the Mussulman and the unconverted, had combined to throw off the heavy yoke which, we are told, the selfish heirs of Omar imposed, but only to fall into the hands of another conqueror. This gave the French further excuse to take over the country in the interest of "general peace." Omar was played up before the African and European public as a bloody despot, and his successors were portrayed in still darker colors. The French, of course, were "humanitarians" trying to deliver the land from oppression and maintain peace. Archinard, the next aggressive conqueror after Faidherbe, rapidly gained ground in this quarter. They gradually eliminated the much detested Ahmadu by strengthening the arm of his enemies and fiercely attacking his forces themselves. The French took Segu April 6, 1890, and on January 1, 1891 carried Bandiagara, the Tukulor capital of Massina.

The French had to face another obstacle, however, before they could possess the Sudan and control the Niger. This was Samori, or Samory, who built up all but suddenly another empire in West Africa. Samori was of slave ancestry. He was born about 1835 at Sanankoro. His father, Lafia Ture, and his mother, Massokono Kamara, were Mandingoes. They were engaged in business as colporteurs and taught Samori this trade. When Samori was twenty, warriors from Konia raided his home and carried his mother away as a captive to their chief Sori-Ibrahima. Samori out of love for his mother appealed to this rich marabout for her freedom, but the ruler replied by enslaving Samori also. Accompanying this king on his military expeditions, however, Samori made the reputation of a great soldier upon whom Sori thought he might well learn to depend. Sori desired to make Samori the chief of his forces, but the latter was satisfied as a reward to be permitted to return home with his mother to Sanankoro. He resumed there his former business, but at the same time paid more attention to preparations for war than to his occupation.[2]

[2] André Mevil, *Samory* (Paris, 1889) ; Gilbert D'Alem, *Madame Samory, Roman Soudain* (Paris, 1924).

THE WASULU EMPIRE

Samori next entered the service of Bitiki-Suane, king of Torongo. In this capacity he soon became the head of these forces and recognized by the soldiers as their only chief so easily did he gain the ascendancy over their minds. Samori, then, easily supplanted Bitiki as King of Torongo. With the prestige of such a position he went forth to war to make this kingdom the center of an African empire. Samori had his first important battle with Famadu, the chief of Kanadugu, whom he defeated and beheaded. Bisandugu and all Kanadugu fell at Samori's feet. The echo from this victory was enormous in Konian. Rising at that time against the conqueror's former chief, Sori-Ibrahima, Konian was easily taken by Samori who defeated and slew the two brothers of Sori-Ibrahima sent against him. This enabled Samori to choose Sanankoro as the capital of the new empire. Samori then subdued the chief of Kankan. With the exception of Keniera to the north all Wasulu was in his hands, and for this reason his possessions were called the Wasulu Empire. Sori-Ibrahima, disturbed at this alarming advance of his foe, decided to take the field against Samori; but he, too, was defeated. Samori would not behead him as he had done in the case of the other leaders whom he had defeated, but he condemned Sori-Ibrahima to pray for the success of the Wasulu arms. With this increased prestige Samori took the title of Emir of Moumenin, Commander of the Believers.

Samori next proceeded toward the Niger. He crossed that stream and took Sangaran to the south of the Tinkisso. He then entered Kangaba, the former capital of Manding (Melle); and, going toward the Bakoy, he threatened Niagasola. The French then entered the war, as they say, for they faced the loss of prestige in failing to defend the natives who had come under their protection, and they were in danger of being bottled up, if Samori took the Bakoy. Well might they take precaution, for Samori's forces cut to pieces the first French troops sent against him. They stopped Samori's conquests in 1881, however, and for the next sixteen years they contrived with superior forces to defeat him here and there and compelled him to sign treaties which gradually diminished his territory and impaired his influence. Samori charged the French with a violation of these agreements in encouraging his subjects to rise, and twice took the offensive against them only to be finally defeated. In the last effort Samori was turned by the French away from Sierra Leone where he had hope of securing provisions; they cut him off from Liberia to which he tried to repair; and they finally captured him on the Ivory Coast. He was deported to Gabun with his son Sarankieni Mori. He died at Niole on the Ogowe in 1900 at the age of sixty-five. In spite of his unfortunate end, however, the griots still sing the praises of their hero.[3]

With Samori thus eliminated the French prepared to extend their territory farther toward the Niger and into the Sudan. They had another impediment in Mamadu Lamine, a Sarakolle marabout, who dreamed of imitating El-Hadj-Omar and Samori. He gained influence and riches by making the pious pilgrimage to Mecca and studying thoroughly the principles of the faith. Returning to the Sudan, he traversed Massina in safety; but he was stopped in Segu where the king was not disposed to assist him in thus building up another theocratic state and imprisoned him. Escaping from prison, Mamadu Lamine rushed to the Upper Senegal where he secured numerous partisans. He took a number of important places by surprise and naturally encountered the French. First checked, he contrived to extricate himself by satisfactory promises, but when he took Senudebu after reducing Guidimaka, Goye, and Gadiaga the French proceeded against him to block his effort toward the Gambia. In this campaign he was killed.

The next impediment was in the rise of the Senufo kingdom of Kenedugu or of Sikaso under a mixed breed, Tapri Taraore. The first of this line succeeded in imposing his authority on or having himself accepted as the ruler of the Sienerhe of Kenedugu about the beginning of the nineteenth century. About 1860 Masa Daula organized a permanent army, expanded the territory, and moved the capital from Finkolo to Bugula. Killed in an expedition toward the east, he was succeeded by his eldest son, Molo Taraore about 1870; but because of unsatisfactory rule he had to face a violent revolt led by Fafa, one of his subjects, by whom after being for some time successful in maintaining his position with the aid of the king of Segu, Molo was killed. Tieba, his brother who succeeded him, moved the seat of government to

[3] Monod, *op. cit.*, pp. 244-250.

Sikasso, but he also had to contend with the revolt led by Fafa and had to rely on the Tukulor aid in the person of their military leader Yahia. He made some advancement in subduing small neighboring states, but he had to undergo a seven-year siege of his capital by Samori, although Binger, the French commander, was on the spot to combat the native leader.

Tieba then sought the friendship of the French. He dreamed of an empire like that of Samori, and after disposing of Fafa, he made an alliance with Simogo Kone, chief of Konseguela. Tieba took Kinian, most of Minianka, and then Tiere. This was the summit of the kingdom's greatness. Tieba died in 1893; and it was not long before the French found themselves in a quarrel with Babemba, his brother, who succeeded him under French protection. Desirous of extending the empire further, he made an expedition to the south against the will of the French. Trying to free himself from their influence, he encroached upon the Samori states. He insulted the French officials, had the French resident stripped, and invaded French territory in Africa. The French, therefore, entered the field against him and took Sikasso in 1898.

CHAPTER XII

SMALLER STATES WHICH ENDURED

OTHER native African kingdoms endured for years during this same period. Following the coastal zone from the mouth of the Senegal appear the three kingdoms of the Wolofs remarkable for their organization. The kingdom of Walo was ruled by a *brac,* the Wolof, by a *bur,* and the Cayor by a *damel.* All these though small, were remarkable for their organization. Then there was to the south of these the Baol of Wolof and Serer extraction ruled by a *tegne;* and the Serer kingdom of Sine, which, before being upset by conquest, had done much to develop agriculture. Next there were scattering backward tribes mixed with Fulani and Mandingo people along the West Coast—the Diola of the lower Gambia and of the Casamance, the Balant, the Banyoun, the Bissago, the Papel, and the Biafada of Portuguese Guinea; the Nalu, the Landuman, and the Baga of lower French Guinea; the Timme, the Bulom of Sierra Leone; the Tiapi, the Bassari, the Koniagui to the north of the Futa-Jallon; and the Kisi and the Golo to the north and west of Liberia. These areas as a hunting ground for human beings supplied most of the slaves for the European colonies. Peoples related to the Mandingo, the Suso or Soso, the Mande of Sierra Leone [1] and the Vai of both Sierra Leone and Liberia, assisted in pushing toward the ocean the tribes mentioned above. The most progressive of these people were the Soso, certain Fulani Sarakolle, Tukulors from the Futa-Toro, and Mandingo from the upper Senegal, who formed a nation of some promise. The Vai, however, must be given credit for developing a written language toward the end of the eighteenth century. [2]

In this region, as already indicated, developed Sierra Leone and Liberia. The former grew from the idea of providing an asylum

---

[1] See 100.

[2] Delafosse, *Negroes of Africa*, pp. 94-97, 98-108, 267-268; G. W. Ellis, *Negro Culture in West Africa*, New York, 1914, pp. 247-255.

for slaves liberated chiefly by the decision of Lord Mansfield in 1772 and by the efforts of Clarkson and his coworkers who labored for the abolition of the traffic in human flesh. Numbers of Negroes had made their way to England when thus set free. The need for such a colony developed from the need for an asylum to which the English might deport their "poor black." Prior to this enterprise the English had only a few trading posts along the coast.

This effort was to make of Africa also an asylum for slaves who had come to England in order to enjoy such freedom from their United States masters from whom they escaped to the British during the American Revolution. There were brought also Maroons, who, after defying Jamaica authorities from their mountain strongholds in that island had been transported first to Nova Scotia and from there for a brighter future to this point in Africa. With the support of the abolition movement in England the effort assumed the phase of founding a colony in 1787 when 400 of the first of such settlers arrived at what is now Freetown. Soon thereafter followed others led by Thomas Peters, a loyalist who deserted to the British during the war for American independence and had served Sir Henry Clinton as sergeant. In 1790 the promoters of the undertaking organized the St. George's Bay Association and prayed for a charter to "colonize a small part of the coast of Africa to introduce civilization among the natives, and to cultivate the soil by means of free labor." At the same time these petitioners abjured all concern whatever in the odious traffic of human bodies and bound themselves neither to deal in slaves, nor to allow any slave trade in the territory. The Association, incorporated in 1790 as the Sierra Leone Company, exercised control until the Crown took over its rights in 1808. The colony did not pay as was expected, but the general emancipation of the slaves in the British Empire in 1833 supplied a larger number of colonists and assured its future, although England did not penetrate the hinterland until 1896.[3]

Liberia, established to carry out the policy of the American Colonization Society of deporting the free Negroes from the United States, was settled on the African coast below Sierra Leone

[3] Walter L. Edwin's "Notes on the Nomolis of Sherbroland" in *The Journal of Negro History*, II, pp. 160-163.

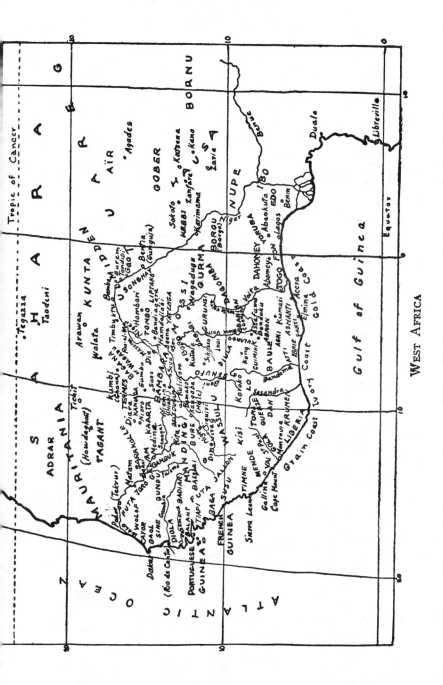

WEST AFRICA

in 1821.[4] As in the case of its predecessor, Liberia had a hard struggle and had to seek recruits to inject new life in what for a number of years seemed to be a failing enterprise. A new day dawned in 1841 when the colony came under the control of a Negro governor, J. J. Roberts, a native of Petersburg, Virginia, who replaced the last white functionary. The country was reorganized as a republic, and it declared its independence in 1847. Roberts was elected the first president. The future of Liberia was assured by recognition by France and England; but the United States, under proslavery control during those years, failed to treat with Liberia as an independent nation until 1862.

Since the Civil War the United States, the very country which delayed in recognizing Liberia as a member of the family of nations, has nevertheless been a sort of beneficent force in safeguarding the independence of the country. Pushing forward rapidly with their program of partitioning of Africa, European nations have not only tried to infringe upon Liberian territory, but have devised schemes for the dismemberment of the nation. Equally as much trouble has come also from European commercial enterprises with ramifications in Africa. They have advanced sums of money on terms disastrous to the republic by taking advantage of its weakness when at its extremity. The unsound economic policy of Liberian administrations, too, has contributed to this undesirable development. Up to the present the republic has stood the test largely because one power will not consent to the other's undoing of that land. When one thinks of the little help which the nations have given Liberia while others have been endeavoring to destroy the nation he must concede that Liberia with all of its shortcomings has been a success.

Other less progressive tribes with little political organization are found to the southeast of Futa-Jallon near the dense forests, even primitive and cannibalistic. Among these are the Toma, the Guerze or Pessy, the Manon, the Dan or Mbe, the Tura, the Lo or Guro, the Muin or Mona, the Ngan and the Gbin. In the dense

---

[4] R. C. F. Maugham, *The Republic of Liberia,* New York, 1919; and H. N. Sherwood's "The Formation of the American Colonization Society" and "Paul Cuffee" in *The Journal of Negro History,* I, pp. 209-228, and VIII, pp. 153-229.

forest from the St. Paul River to beyond Sasandra are tribes still less advanced. Of those of this order near the coast the Krumen have become known to Europeans as efficient workmen on their ships. East of the Krumen are remarkable intellectually developed tribes, surprising all by their meticulous bodily cleanliness and etiquette. The Baule, the Agni, the Zema or Appolonians noted for their clever merchants; the Abron, noted for their well organized government; the Fanti, exploited as laborers especially by the English; and the Ashanti with their well constituted kingdom enduring from 1700 to 1895, appear also in this area. Much credit for the glory of Ashanti is due to their famous king Osai Tutu Kwamina and to Primpeh.[5] The Ashanti vanquished the tribes between their country and the coast and defeated the British under Sir Charles McCarthy in 1821. The spirit of resistance was such that the English did not make much of an inroad into the country until 1874 and did not actually conquer it until 1895. Kumasi, the Ashanti capital, was sacked in 1900; and Primpeh, who was exiled in 1925, was permitted to return to the Gold Coast to die in 1931.

Going eastward, one finds other interesting tribes, "gifted from the intellectual, artistic and political point of view."[6]   Among these are the Ewe of the lower Togo, the Mina and Fon or Jeji of lower Dahomey, the Yoruba of Nago of modern tendencies, the Benin or Edo, noted for their industrial arts and fine work in bronze, and the Nupe of Southern Nigeria.

Of Dahomey which developed in this area, Delafosse says, "Every one in France knows about the kingdom of Dahomey which, founded before the sixteenth century, with Abomey as its capital, was annexed by the French in 1894 at the end of a famous campaign. The kings of Dahomey were great warriors and slave traders and became celebrated for their human sacrifices, but on the other hand it must be said that they had known how to organize their state and their army and administer their kingdom in a fashion which did them honor; it must also be added that the talents of the Dahomeans as farmers and artisans, joined to their

[5] Casely Hayford, *Gold Coast Native Institutions* (London, 1903), pp. 19-31; R. S. Rattray, *Ashanti Law and Constitution* (Oxford and the Clarendon Press, 1929).
[6] Delafosse, *op. cit.*, p. 99.

undeniable intellectual capacities, place them among the first ranks of the Negro peoples of Africa." [6a]

Along the coast where now stands the present Dahomey there were several undeveloped tribes which may be dignified with the name of petty kingdoms, some of which have already been noted above. In the interior were three more important nuclei of natives known as Ardra or Allada, Kana, and Nago. It seems that the Adja tribe gained the ascendancy here at an early period and in the seventeenth century the kingdom of Ardra emerged from bloody conflicts as the leading state of that area. Family disputes led to further dispersion and the settlement of two factions which gave rise to the two kingdoms of Abomey and of Porto Novo. The Portuguese were soon upon the scene to complicate matters, and the Dutch did not long delay in playing their rôle in this theatre of the slave trade.

Dahomey with its capital Abomey, however, emerged about 1650 or 1680 with the present area as a result of the conquests and organization of Dako, the first real king, and such successors as Wegbaja, Akaba, Agaja, Tegbesu, Kpengla, and Agonglo. The last mentioned was so unworthy that he was poisoned. Adanzan, his successor, did not make much of a contribution to the progress of his country, but Ghezo undertook to do what his predecessor had neglected, although he could not prevent Porto Novo from gaining its independence. The Dahomans, demonstrated however, not only their capacity for government but for the most dashing military manœuvres observed during that time. The French were in relation with the Dahomans as early as 1842, made a treaty of amity with them in 1851, and took over in 1863 as a protectorate Porto Novo which had maintained a nominal independence of Dahomey. After several interventions the French penetrated Dahomey in 1894 as a result of their operations against the warring King Glele and his son, Behanzin. With better trained and more efficiently equipped forces thrown into the conflict the French under the dashing Senegalese mulatto General Dodds finally won the day in 1894. With Dahomey, of course, followed adjacent territory under the control of the French. [7]

[6a] *Ibid.*, pp. 99-100.

[7] Henri Labouret, and Paul Rivet, *Le Royaume d'Arda et son Evangelisation au XVII Siècle* (Paris, 1929) ; A. Le Herisse, *L'Ancien Royaume du*

Another important kingdom in this part of Africa should be noted because of its having been very much modernized. This is Yoruba, divided into several autonomous cities without tendencies toward the imperial. These states today are provided with legislative assemblies and "sometimes with journals—official and private —edited in English. The capital of one of these states is Abeokuta, an extremely populous and very industrious city." Leo Frobenius believed that "the technical summit of that civilization was reached in the terra-cotta industry, and that the most important achievements in art were not expressed in stone, but in fine clay baked in the furnace." This investigator found, too, that hollow casting was thoroughly known and practiced by these people, that iron was mainly used for decoration, that, whatever their purpose, they kept their glass beads in stoneware urns, within their own locality, and that they manufactured both earthen and glassware. He observed also that the art of weaving was highly developed among the Yorubans, "that the stone monuments show some dexterity in handling and are so far instructive, but in other respects evidence a cultural condition insufficiently matured to grasp the utility of stone monumental material; and, above all, that the then great and significant idea of the universe as imaged in the Templum was current in those days."

Of another kingdom with a line of twenty-three kings dating from the ninth century we may agree in saying that "as for Benin it was formed, without doubt, since the fifteenth century and perhaps since a more remote epoch, a powerful and redoubtable state, where the industrial arts and notably the art of bronze working and that of ivory have flourished in a remarkable fashion; certain bronzes of Benin of the fifteenth and sixteenth centuries, that may be seen today in the museums of Holland, Germany and England and in private collections, are worthy rivals of analogous products of several renowned civilizations." [8] Having in mind especially

---

Dahomey, Moeurs, Religion, Histoire (Paris, 1911); Alexandre L. d'Albega, *La France au Dahomey* (Paris, 1895); *Le Dahomey* (Société d'Editions Géographiques, Maritimes et Coloniales (Paris, 1931); Victor Nicolas, *L'Expédition du Dahomey en 1890* (Paris, 1892); Delafosse, "Les Agni," *Anthropologie*, 1893, pp. 403-445.

[8] Delafosse, *op. cit.*, p. 100; see also Felix von Luschan, *Die Altertumer von Benin* (Berlin, 1912), and Pitt Rivers, *The Antique Works of Art of Benin* (London, 1912).

the art of Benin, Felix von Luschan considered it "of extraordinary significance that by the sixteenth and seventeenth centuries a local and monumental art had been learned in Benin which in many respects equaled European art and developed a technique of the very highest accomplishment." [9]

In the bend of the Niger appeared other tribes which must be noted in passing, although they have shown little political organization. These include the Tombo or Habe, the Samo, the Fulse, the Nioniose, the Kipirsi, the Nuruma, the Sisala, and the Gurunsi. To these may be added the Dagari, the Birifo or Birifor, the Gbanian or Gonga, the Dagomba, the Nankana, the Bobo, the Lobi,[10] the Dian, the Kulango, and the Sumba. Yet although lacking in political organization beyond the family unit they are as a rule marvelous farmers, and the "attachment to the land seems to be the only solid and fecund institution in their chaotic society." [11]

Throughout the region of San and Kutiala on the right bank of the Bani as far as that of Bonduku and the elbow of the Black Volta are the Senufo or Siena people. Among these are the Jula who at Sikasso and Kong have developed small states of considerable "cohesion and vitality." "The iron industry and that of pottery, as well as agriculture and the art of music have attained among certain Senufo a development which merits attention." [12]

In the central and eastern Sudan the Hausa states first claim attention. Toward 1600 tendencies toward disintegration of the kingdom of the Kebbi began to appear as noted above. Difficulties had arisen also between the Fulani shepherds of Gober and their Hausa patrons. Availing himself of this situation, the sheik Ousman the Torodo or Ousman-dan-Fodio, raised an invincible army, and in 1801 preached a holy war which resulted in the conquest and the Islamization of the Hausa states and the founding of a new kingdom with Sokoto as the capital. To this empire this conqueror soon added Nupe, Kebbi, and Liptako. Ousman undertook to subdue Bornu also, but he was driven out by the Kanemi

---

[9] Delafosse, *op. cit.*, p. 101.

[10] For an extensive treatment of the Lobi see Henri Labouret's *Les Tribus du Rameau Lobi* (Paris, 1931).

[11] Delafosse, *op. cit.*, p. 101.

[12] Delafosse, *op. cit.*, p. 102.

in 1810. The conquests of this warring Negro, however, entitle him to front rank as a military leader.

When Ousman died in 1815 his son Mohammed Bello, a poor warrior, had difficulty in maintaining his empire. Zanfara, Gober, Katsena, and Kebbi rebelled as did also the Tuareg of Air and Damerghu, aided by the Kanemi, the Wadai, and the Bagirmi. Although hardly able to hold his empire intact, Mohammed Bello distinguished himself in another field. He composed in Arabic a number of poems and religious and historical works. He believed in justice and exercised a system of inspection of his lieutenants. Mohammed Bello died in 1837.

His brother Atiku, who succeeded him and reigned until 1843, alienated some of his subjects by proscribing all such amusements as dancing and music, and Gober and Katsenà arose again in protest against the abuses of the princes who had been stationed over them as governors. Ali, the son of Mohammed Bello, who reigned from 1843 to 1855, had to contend also with frequent uprisings of his subjects in Gober and Kebbi, who would not accept Islam. He was followed by five Tukulor kings who did not have the ability to rule successfully an empire which was never well organized, and it rapidly disintegrated. It came to an end in 1904 when Sir Frederick Lugard occupied Sokoto.

Bornu comes next in the course toward the interior of the Sudan. Properly described, however, this area east of Hausa and on both sides of Lake Chad is called Bornu in the west and Kanem in the east. Bornu, as we have learned above, reached its highest level under Idris III, but after his reign the petty states began to assert themselves and the Tunjur got control. The Tukulor Ousman-dan-Fodio attacked the country in 1808 but was repulsed by "the Kanemi" after he had caused the dispersion of leaders under Mai Ahmed near Gassaro in a successful battle. This Ahmed and his followers served the country thereafter as puppet kings while the authority was almost entirely in the hands of "the Kanemi" and the members of his family. New life was injected into the situation when sheik Omar, son of "the Kanemi," had himself proclaimed Sultan of Bornu with his residence at Kukawa, or Kuka, the capital of a new dynasty which he founded. Troubles came in 1893 when the adventurer Rabah defeated and killed Hashem, Omar's successor, destroyed Kuka, and transferred the capital to Dikoa. The new ruler, however, was soon vanquished thereafter by the French under Major Lamy in 1900, "and Abubekr Guerbei, a nephew of Hashem, was recognized by the English as Sultan of Bornu, which became a British protectorate."

South of the Kanem is the kingdom of Bagirmi, supposedly established by a hunter sometimes known as Bernim-Besse and elsewhere as Dokkengue. He built Massenya, the capital, about 1513. He was succeeded by his son Malo; and Malo's son, Abdallah, who succeeded him, introduced Islam about 1602. The ninth ruler of this line, Borkumanda-Tadele was a warrior of varying fortune. While he was twice victorious over Wadai, the country had been so weakened that his successor Alawine went down before the onslaughts of the emperor of Bornu and became his vassal about 1741. His successor, Mohammed Alamine (1741-1784), shook off the tutelage of Bornu, but Abderrahman Gaurrang (1784-1806), the next to ascend the throne, succumbed to the Wadai who thereafter directed the affairs of Bagirmi as that of a vassalage under his son. Still another son of the last king Ousman Borkumanda (1807-1846) endeavored to free Bagirmi of the tutelage; but the forces arrayed were unequal to the task. He was defeated at Lederi in 1824, when conducting an expedition against Bornu. Abdelkader (1846-1858) failed in an attempt to become independent. Another effort of Bagirmi against the Wadai by Abu-Sekkine in 1871 was only temporarily successful. His son Borkumanda alienated his subjects by cruelty, and his successor was driven by Rabah in 1897 to accept French protectorship.

Thus passed Bagirmi which was swayed perpetually between the rule of Bornu and Wadai. Wadai, settled with a few Arabs and mainly Negroes of the Maba, Tama, Massalit, Mimi, Kuka, Bulala, and Rougna tribes, however, was much to be feared by the Mohammedans. With their capital first at Kadama black kings of the Tunjur, hostile to Islam, ruled Wadai. About 1615 it is said that Jameh or Saleh, a native of the country, converted to Mohammedanism, proselyted a portion of the population; and Abdelkerim, his son, with an army of Arabs and Islamized Negroes, proclaimed himself Sultan of the Wadai, dethroned the Tunjur prince, and established a kingdom with a capital at Wara; but he had to pay tribute to the Darfur. His successors after further

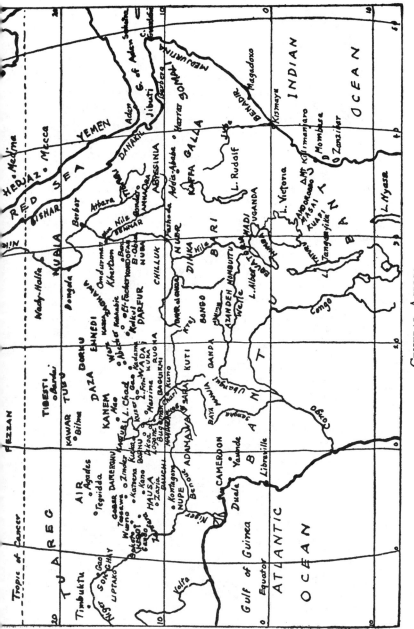

CENTRAL AFRICA

fortifying themselves with the propagation of Mohammedan-ism finally contrived to defeat the Darfur. Later Wadai under another aggressive ruler extended its influence over a part of Kanem. Cruel and weak kings, from 1803 to 1835, invited the invasion of the Wadai land by the Darfur who placed on the throne of the Wadai Mohammed-Cherif (1835-1858) in the position of their vassal. He enjoyed great prestige and developed the power to defeat the Sultan of Bornu and force him to pay the tribute of 8,000 thalers. This conqueror was succeeded by Ali who restored order and encouraged very much the commerce between that country and the Mediterranean. King Yussef, his successor, permitted the Bagirmi to regain their independence. Various princes, including Rabah (1894), then arose and invaded the land, and the suzerainty once accepted of the Wadai passed to France in 1894. France, after taking the sides of various kings who entered the conflict, took over the country in 1912.[13]

The Darfur and the Kordofan of this Negro area, like the Wadai, were once dominated by the ambitious Tunjur. A Mussul-man, Soloun-Sliman, in the sixteenth century secured control and brought about a turning point in the history of this kingdom. He had his capital at Bir-Nabak, but Omar-Lele, his fourth successor, who overcame the king of the Wadai, transplanted the seat of government to Kabkabie, before 1700. Then followed Abubekr, Abderrahmin I, and next Teherab, who introduced the Mohammedan culture; and finally came Abderrahmin II, who established his capital at Tendelty, or El-Facher, from which he treated with Napoleon when the latter was campaigning in Egypt. Under Mohammed-Fadel (1800-1840) the Kordofan threw its allegiance to the Darfur but was immediately conquered by the Egyptians. His second successor, Haroun, was defeated in combat with the Egyptians. The Darfur was incorporated into the Egyptian Sudan in 1874, and thus it remained in spite of a revolt of Haroun, the last of that line, who was killed in action in 1879.

The Kordofan or Kordofal lies between the Darfur and Sennar. The country is inhabited by Negroes speaking different languages,

---

[13] These facts are given in brief in Julien Migret's *Afrique Equatoriale Française* (Paris, 1931), pp. 99-117; and Maurice Abadie's *Afrique Centrale: La Colonie du Niger* (Paris, 1927), pp. 95-110, as well as in Delafosse's *Negroes of Africa*, pp. 104-129.

some of which resemble the Bantu. From the real Nuba, of South Kordofan (elsewhere confused in speaking of Africa) came the Mussulman Nuba led by Mussabba, their chief who conquered the whole country which was annexed to the Darfur under Teherab and Islamized. Under the régime a *magdum* or governor was stationed at Bara; but, as already noted above, the Kordofan was conquered by the Egyptian *defterdar* Mohammed-Bey, who chose El-Obeid as the seat of government.

Throughout the history of these kingdoms during the last quarter of the nineteenth century runs the adventure of Rabah and the Mahdist movement. The occasion of the rise of Rabah was the revolt against the Egyptian government of Haroun, the dethroned Sultan of the Darfur in 1875. The development of the new act in this drama starts with Zobeir Pasha, an Arab named governor of Bahr-el-Ghazal in 1875. Summoned from his post to confer with officials in Cairo, he left his son Suleiman in charge. This son was "betrayed to Gordon-Pasha by the Dongola people, enemies of the Jaaline," the Arab tribe to which Suleiman belonged. Believing in the hostility of the Gordon-Pasha, the son took sides against the Egyptian government in favor of the revolt of Haroun, the dethroned Sultan of the Darfur. Gessi-Pasha sent against him decisively defeated Suleiman. His chief lieutenant was Rabah, the son of a Negro woman, the wet nurse of Zobeir-Pasha, who appeared in the new effort for liberation.

At the overthrow of Suleiman, Rabah fled with the remnants of his master's army and began his conquests to the northwest of the Bahr-el-Ghazal (1878). Going west, he subdued the Banda in 1879, defeated the Kuti in 1883, and installed Senussi there as Sultan in 1890. "In 1892 he attacked the Bagirmi and in 1893 seized Bougoman, which at that time replaced Massenya as the capital. The same year he attacked Hashem, sultan of Bornu, vanquished and put him to death (December, 1893). Then he marched on the Gober, where Abubekr, nephew and successor of Hashem, had taken refuge. Stopped by the army of the emperor of Sokoto, he turned against the little States to the South of the Chad, took Gulfei from the Busso, Kusseri from the Mandara, Logone from the Kotoko, and again invaded the Bagirmi in 1898." He "set fire to Massenya, pursued the *mbang* near to Kuno, there, with 8,000 men, clashed with some thirty militiamen commanded

by the administrator Bretonnet (July 18, 1899) and did not finish
with this handful of brave men till after eight hours of combat.
On April 22, 1900, he was beaten at Kusseri by Major Lamy and
killed at the end of the battle, which also cost the life of his conqueror." [13a]   Thus ended an adventure which lasted twenty-two
years.[14]

Mahdiism, like the adventure of Rabah, was a development of
Sudanese Negroes. The beginning of it came when Mohammed-
Ahmen of Dongola, fresh from a victory over Rachid-Bey, governor of Fashoda, proclaimed himself *mahdi,* a sort of prophet or
deliverer inspired by the Great Prophet as this fanatic understood
it. Encouraged by his first success, he defeated a detachment of
Egyptian troops in 1882, conquered all the Kordofan by 1883,
annihilated the entire army of 10,000 of Hicks-Pasha at Chekan
the same year, forced the surrender of Slatin-Pasha as governor of
Bahr-el-Ghazal in 1884, took Khartoum in 1885, and put Gordon-
Pasha to death. Thus in five years the *mahdi* had made himself
the master of four-fifths of the Egyptian Sudan.[15]

The *Mahdi* died of typhoid fever shortly afterward at Omdurman, his capital. Abdullah, from the cowherders of the Baggara
tribe of crossbreeds of Arabs and Negroes, was designated as the
successor. Disconnecting himself from the relatives and com-
patriots of the *madhi* and surrounding himself with Darfur people,
Abdullah sent against Abyssinia a formidable army which took
the city of Gondar and killed the negus John in 1888. His cohorts
overran Equatoria in 1892. His power soon began to decline
thereafter, however, for Dongola, Berber, Fashoda, and Omdurman fell into the hands of the Anglo-Egyptian troops, and Abdullah was killed by these forces in Kordofan in 1899.

The Islamization and Christianization of West, South, and Central Africa, as we have observed, resulted then in the undoing of
the African economic, social and political order. In East Africa,
in Abyssinia, Christianized at an earlier period, there was sufficient
force to maintain the independence in spite of these evils which

[13a] Quotations from Delafosse, *Negroes of Africa,* p. 123.
[14] Max Oppenheim's *Rabeh und das Tchadsgebiet,* Berlin, 1902, *passim;*
and E. Gentil's *La Chute de l'Empire de Rabah,* Paris, 1902.
[15] Philipp Daryl, *Lettres de Gordan à Sa Sœur écrites du Soudan,*
Paris, 1886.

worked so disastrously elsewhere. Abyssinia, or Ethiopia, not only civilized ancient Egypt but exerted a salutary influence on both sides of the Red Sea. When Mohammed was born in 570 Yemen was subject to Ethiopia. She sent an army of 40,000 men against Mecca. The *negus* "Prete-John" of this country also enjoyed an unusual renown throughout the Middle Ages, and Abyssinian influence tended to civilize the natives near her borders. This influence can be observed in the Bishari or Beja to the north, in the Danakil or Afar to the east, among the Somali to the southeast, and the Galla or Oromo to the south. Some of these tribes, like the Galla farmers and shepherds, a great power in the tenth century, and migratory in the fourteenth and fifteenth centuries, were for a long time bitter enemies of the negus of Abyssinia, but were finally absorbed by that empire. The tribe supplying the rulers of Abyssinia is the Amharic, which, without disclaiming its Negro blood, contends that it resulted from the Semitic origin of the visit of the Queen of Sheba to Solomon. The country is a feudal state with the Coptic religion in ascendancy, and the people have undergone some modernization under foreign influences intended to effect the partition of the land among Europeans.

Far away in various directions from Abyssinia, however, were Sudanese tribes which failed to come under such beneficent influences. Even Mohammedanism and modern Christianity with all their military support have failed to make great inroads among them. They have, therefore, remained in their native state following their customs of yore. These tribes are such as the Gbari, Munchi, Batta, Fali, Mbum, Baya, Manjia, Banda, Azendeh, or Niam-Niam,[16] Sara, Kenga, Gaberi, Bulala, Kuka, Bongo, Krej, Rougna, Dinka, Nuer, Shillook, Bari, Madi, Mombuttu, Wandorobo, Kuafi, Humba, Taturu, and Masai.

[16] C. R. Lagie, "Les Azande oú Niam-Niam," *L'Ethnographie,* 1928, pp. 230-232.

CHAPTER XIII

AFRICA BELOW THE EQUATOR

IN lower Africa continued the Bantu among whom the passion for lucre and the thirst for power which account for the rise of kingdoms and empires elsewhere have not developed to the extent that these motives dominated the Sudanese. Their country too, is handicapped by impediments to any such ambitious political effort. For lack of communication across impenetrable swamps, exceedingly high plateaus, and rivers unnavigable from the ocean, close association for political organization has been difficult. Yet we have reason for believing in the existence of very ancient kingdoms in this area, although we have few sources. Neither Greek geographers, Arabic chroniclers, nor Semitic traditions abound with much about Southern Africa. That part of Africa below the equator, it has often been said, was probably about what it is today—with no actual state organization but dense forests, with some federation of tribes otherwise detached, and with no larger units than that of villages.[1] This, however, is largely conjecture. We must learn these people of the interior better and study their traditions further before we can speak of them with authority.[2]

The Bushmen or Hottentots, who must have been the ancient inhabitants of land around the Great Lakes in Africa, had some political organization. Negroes expanding from the north, after undergoing admixture with Jews, Arabs or Persians, pushed these primitive types toward the south in promoting their trade in ivory, gold, skins, gums, beasts, birds, and slaves. There was evidence

[1] Robert Pimienta, *L'Ancienne Colonie Allemande de Sud-Ouest Africain* (Paris, 1926); Carl Seyfert, *Totengebraüche and Todesvorstellungen bei den Zentral-Afrikanischen Pygmäen de Buschmännern und Hottentoten* (*Archiv. fur Anthropologie*, Vol. XII, fas. 3 (Brunswick, 1913), pp. 184-219.

[2] Delafosse, *Negroes of Africa,* Chapter VI; M. Plancquaert, *Les Jaga et les Bayaka* (Brussels, 1932).

at the same time of the movement of the Bantu toward the south. These migrations caused the admixture of the Bushmen or Hottentots with the Bantu in certain parts, and forced certain of these aborigines into restricted quarters where they are found today. "In those places the resulting stocks settled down; they cultivated the soil, exploited the gold supply, and quarried valuable stone for buildings and fortifications."

The Hottentots must have engaged in state organization at an early period and probably a thousand years before Christ evolved an interesting social and economic order. They left cut quartz, pits, underground passages, processes of irrigation, stone buildings, huge fortifications as discovered in the Kalahari desert in Rhodesia. In Toroa or what is called Butua, a kingdom ruled by a *burrow,* were found interesting ruins, a square fortress, of well dressed stone of a large size "without any lime showing the joinings, the walls of which are over twenty-five hands thick, but the height is not so great compared to the thickness. And above the gateway of that edifice is an inscription which some Moorish (Arab) traders who were there could not read, nor say what writing it was. All these structures the people of this country call Symbaoe (Zimbabwe) which with them means a court, for every place where Benomotapa stays is so called." [3] At Niekerk, it is said, were found nine or ten halls of thirty to fifty fortified concentric walls with a village at the top, enclosing forts, citadels, workshops, and kraals. At various places were discovered useful iron implements, adorned pottery, and trinkets worked out of bronze, copper, tin, silver and zinc. A flourishing gold market existed there.

This civilization, however, decayed and passed away. How and why we do not know. It has been thought that about the end of the sixteenth century the migration of tribes less civilized upset the social order and caused such uncertainty as to bring the people to the point of wandering from place to place rather than to remain in their permanent abodes. The bones of the soldiers left upon the battlefield where conflicts took place and the ruins of deserted cities and fortifications indicate that such was the later history of the nations which had once existed in these parts prior to the coming of that "strange people never before seen there, who,

[3] Du Bois, *The Negro,* p. 82.

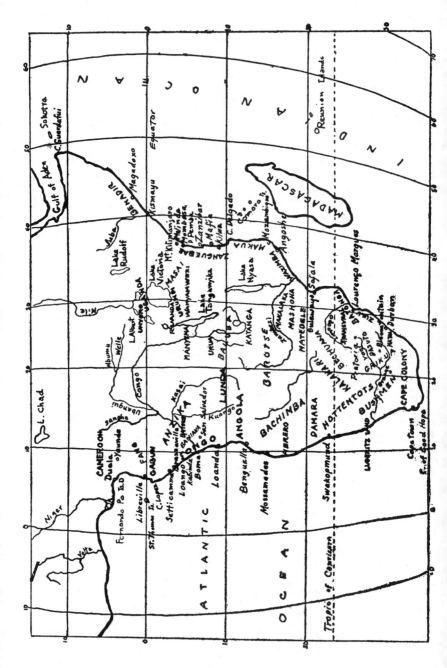

leaving their own country, traversed a great part of this Ethiopia like a scourge of God, destroying every living thing they came across." [4]

In these parts at a later period have been kingdoms worthy of notice. Such were the kingdoms of Loango or of the Brama between Cape Lopez and the mouth of the Congo. Such also was the empire of the Congo dating from the fourteenth century. The rulers of this country extended their control as far as Setti-Camma in the north and Benguella to the south and to Kasai and upper Zambesi in the east. In the sixteenth century the empire declined so as to be restricted to Cabinda in the north, Loanda in the south, and Kuango in the east. The seat of government was at Banza, later changed to San Salvador.[5] The son of the Negro Emperor Mfumu who was converted to Christianity was taken to Portugal; and, thus educated there, he reached the priesthood and served as the maker of a Catholic kingdom south of the valley of the Congo. This has endured for three centuries.

Other organizations in South Africa also deserve attention. Not far from where Brazzaville now stands was the capital of the Ansika or Anikana of the Bateke and the Bayaka [6] people occupying the area to the east of the Loango and at the northeast of the Congo. Their king was called *makoko*. These people were warlike and were much feared in the sixteenth century because of their exaggerated cannibalistic tendencies.

South from the empire of the Congo developed the Mataman, a kingdom with a capital near what is now Mosammedes. The inhabitants were the Bachimba, Herero, Damara, and Hottentots. What we have heard of the past of this country is mainly legendary. Investigation now in progress in this area may further inform us.

Another state, the kingdom of Bechuana occupied the present area of the Union of South Africa. The Bechuana, traders, artisans, cultivators of the soil, and builders of towns, some of the most advanced of these people, exercised feudal authority over

[4] Du Bois, *op. cit.,* p. 83. See also Theal's *Record of South Africa,* Vol. VII, "Ethiopia Oriental" by Dos Santos.

[5] George Bruel, *L'Afrique Equatoriale Française,* pp. 1-29; Rinchon P. Doudonne, *La Traite et l'Esclavage des Congolais par les Européens,* pp. 1-97; R. P. Van Wing, *Etudes Bakongo* (Brussels, 1921).

[6] M. Plancquaert, *Les Jaga et les Bayaka du Kwango* (Bruxelles, 1932).

the Basuto, the Zulu, and a part of the Hottentots and Bushmen. There sprang up also between the Lourenço-Marques Bay and that of Sofala the Monomotapa before the tenth century, extending their sway over the Matebele, the Makalaka, the Matongo and the Mashona. These people had much trouble from incursions of a warlike nation west of Sofala and for that reason did not develop their kingdom to the level to which it might have otherwise gone. With these were allied other city states carrying on among themselves an extensive commerce. This trade was probably not only between Asia and East Africa but doubtless with certain countries of West Africa also; and it extended as far as India, China, and Malaysia. This was later disorganized, of course, by Christians from Portugal.[7]

At an earlier period, however, in the tenth century, we learn from Masudi, an Arabic writer who visited the east coast of Africa about that time, that the Bantu had a well organized kingdom under the ruler bearing the title of *waklimi*. With an army of thirty thousand men he had brought under his control most of the tribes of the north. The country was apparently in peace and prosperity. The inhabitants were cultivating the soil, producing gold, silver, and iron, and supplying skins of animals and ivory, as the important commodities of their commerce.

Several other peoples of this area are known to Europeans as dependents of sultanates established by Arabs of Muskat and Persians from Shiraz and Bushire, with commercial concourse of Hindus from Bombay and Malabar. These were not exactly states, but rather outposts for recruiting slaves and thus contributed to the decay of native African culture. Zanzibar means the country of slaves.

At this time, during the seventeenth century, Asiatics were touching the coast of Africa in large numbers. It is said that the first of these adventurers to reach the shore of East Africa was Zaide, great-grandson of Ali, nephew and son-in-law of Mohammed, who was banished from the court as a heretic. Leading with him thousands of people, he settled upon these shores where they mingled with the blacks to constitute a new order of mixed-breed traders called the Emoxaidi. Other Arabs, hearing of this successful adventure, settled the towns of Magadosho and Brava

[7] Delafosse, *op. cit.*

and drove the Emoxaidi into the interior. Later adventurers from Magodosho made a settlement at Sofola to control the gold trade. Persians came later and settled at Kilwa about the beginning of the eleventh century. At this place in 1330 Ibn Batuta found a flourishing trade in ivory and gold. The city had developed with considerable success having numerous mosques and palaces built of stone and lime. There were attractive homes with gardens, showing excellent masonry and beautiful decorations. Portuguese came some years later after Vasco da Gama had doubled the Cape of Good Hope in 1497 and gave this development another trend.

In the interior was the kingdom of Lounda to the east of the empire of the Congo, astride the valleys of the Kasai and the Zambezi. Between Lounda and the Monomotapa, on the middle Zambezi, stood the kingdom of the Barotse, and to the north of this state that of the Katanga. Still farther north to the west of Lake Tanganyika was the kingdom of Urua or Baluba near that of the Manyema. Wissman appraised these people as "a nation of thinkers." Batemen considered those whom he met "thoroughly and unimpeachably honest, brave to foolhardiness, and faithful to each other and to their superiors. Calemba, their ruler, Bateman believed would "amongst any people be a remarkable and in many respects a magnificent man."

To the east of Tanganyika was found that well-known "empire" of the *muene-muezi* or Wanyamwezi with the Ruanda and Urundi as vassals. Then to the north of Lake Victoria developed the Uganda with the Unyoro as vassals. The people of Uganda trace their kings four centuries back.[8] The first ruler was called Kuntu. Stanley found upon their throne a very able ruler called Mutesa. He was succeeded by Mioanga in 1884.

Tradition would have it that under their chief, who resembled very much the Norman, William the Conqueror, who defeated the Angles and Saxons at Hastings in 1066, the people of Uganda came into their glory. The name of this hero was Muganda. It is said that he came with a pack of hounds, a woman, a spear and a shield to the Katanga Valley. He was an expert in hunting,

[8] A. A. Goldenweiser, *Early Civilization*, chapter on Uganda. Robert Stigler, *Ethnographische und Anthropologische Mittellungen über einige wenig bekannte Volkstämme Ugandas.* (Extract from the *Mittellungen der Anthropologische Gesellschaft* in Wien, 1923.)

and he easily attracted a following that soon crowned him as their chief. From these as a nucleus he built up a powerful state. This was the beginning of the kingdom of Uganda probably about the fourteenth century. The successors of Muganda extended his conquests, developed the wealth of the country, and maintained its prestige for five centuries.

The government of Uganda was well organized. The king ruled with the assistance of a prime minister, several princes, a chief butler, chief baker, and commander of the army and navy. The feudal lords, acknowledging their allegiance to the king, assisted him in bringing into action 25,000 men accompanied by an additional number of armed women and children. Mutesa who was king of Uganda in 1862 when the country had been somewhat Islamized admitted both Catholics and Protestants. These hostile forces plunged that area into a religious conflict. This finally resulted in the death of an English bishop in 1885 under Muganda, Mutesa's successor, who believed that missionaries were forerunners of conquest. This actually took place when the English made it a protectorate in 1894.[9]

High tribute has been paid also to the Kaffir-Zulus who developed in the South. They impressed Europeans especially with their "habit of manipulating men in their numerous campaigns." "Their strategy in war and diplomacy in politics," says a writer, "would do credit to any race; and some of their military leaders have been not inaptly compared to Cæsar. In 1852, when Sir George Cathcart invaded Basutoland, his army was led into a trap by the simple stratagem of the native leader, Moshesh, of exposing an immense herd of cattle in a position on the Berea mountain where their capture appeared easy. The British army was surprised, defeated and forced to retreat." Moshesh had thus measured arms with the Dutch four times. He is still remembered for his kindness, his attractive personality, which enabled him to weld his people into a nation.[10]

About this time developed another military chieftain who made himself felt in Europe. This was Tshaka (Chaka), doubtless the most illustrious chief of the Zulus. Restless as a youth, he had difficulty in finding people who saw the world from his point of

[9] H. H. Johnston's *Uganda Protectorate.*
[10] James W. Johnson's *Native African Races and Culture,* p. 13.

view. He left his own native tribe; and, after wandering to find a place which might appeal to him, he established himself among people who supported him in his aspiration to become master of the world about him. Tall, erect, fine-looking and commanding in his bearing, he easily impressed men as a leader. Resorting to force as his chief weapon, he waged war upon opposing tribes, annihilating them upon the spot or driving them from their habitations. In twenty-five years, says Molema, a Christianized native, he destroyed a million souls to make himself master of Natal.

Throughout South Africa he was feared by Europeans and natives. "There has probably never been," says one, "a more perfect system of discipline than that by which Chief Tshaka ruled his army and kingdom. At a review an order might be given in the most unexpected manner which meant death to hundreds. If the regiment hesitated or dared to remonstrate, so perfect was the discipline and so great the jealousy that another was ready to cut them down. A warrior returning home from battle without his arms was put to death without trial. A general returning unsuccessful in the main purpose of his expedition shared the same fate. Whoever displeased the king was immediately executed. The traditional courts practically ceased to exist so far as the will and action of the tyrant was concerned.[11]

Much farther north were developments of consequence in later years. The disorganized state of the Congo region as a result of the Arabic slave trade invited the intervention of Europe, which culminated in the organization of the Congo Free State. Stanley opened this unknown area to the European world and organized in 1878 an international committee for the further study of the region. Undertaking the task as a philanthropic effort to facilitate communication with this hinterland, Stanley endeavored in 1881 to build a road beyond the falls to connect the navigable waters, and by 1884 he had secured the cooperation of the majority of the chiefs in that region in this much desired enterprise. The country then underwent organization as a modern state. The Congo Free State was recognized by the United States, and in 1885 Leopold II of Belgium was chosen as king. In carrying out this program the Congo Free State found it necessary to overthrow the king

[11] Du Bois, op. cit., pp. 98-99.

of the Kantanga country which precipitated a revolt that could not be subdued until 1893.

The bright future for the Congo, however, even after the slave trade had been checked, did not come, for the Europeans themselves under Leopold's régime introduced other practices which were more horrible than those of the Arabs. They ignored the customs of the tribes, upset their social order, abrogated their tribal laws, confiscated their land, apportioned natives among European exploiters as slaves to develop the ivory and rubber industry, and when certain ones rebelled or refused to serve as ordered they were ruthlessly murdered. The civilized world, then, threw up its hands in holy horror; and the very name of Leopold II became anathema. An international protest forced the transfer of the Congo Free State from private hands into the possession of the Belgian Government which has removed some of these abuses.

We have heard much of the results of the European's reaching Africa and of the Islamization and Christianization of the natives. Up to the present, however, Africa has been neither Islamized nor Christianized. There is not a single tribe on the continent which has been thoroughly brought under these influences. The natives as a majority still follow their own customs as they did in the days of old. The first foreigners, Mohammedan and Christian, coming into Africa sought that land not for its evangelization but for gold and slaves; and they restricted themselves largely to the coast until 1870 when Livingstone opened up the interior to the outside world. Since that time the interior of Africa has been subdued by European adventurers and apportioned among European nations, but they have not as yet uprooted the civilization of the natives.[12] The story of Africa, then, runs into present-day developments.

[12] *De la colonization française*, pp. 131-291; Camille Guy, *L'Afrique Occidentale Française*, pp. 79-110.

CHAPTER XIV

THE PARTITION OF AFRICA—ECONOMIC IMPERIALISM

In keeping with the European policy of satisfying their greed for material things the powers of that continent have been scrambling for African possessions from time immemorial; and they are still thus engaged since Liberia and Abyssinia are left as two independent areas from which the aggressors will not lift their eyes. This story is told herein in fragmentary form in the preceding chapters. A mere summary of the present status of the European occupation of Africa, then, is all that is required at the conclusion of this brief treatment of the African background. The details are given in various books setting forth the progress of the intrusion of the European nations and justifyng the methods by which they have exterminated some of the natives while exploiting others. J. S. Keltie, Sir Harry H. Johnston, Sir Charles Lucas, Jean Darcy, E. L. Guernier, H. A. Gibbons, and N. D. Harris have treated this European expansion in brief fashion while others dealing in detail with special problems have enlarged upon the colonial enterprise of their respective countries.

Here we are primarily concerned with the present bounds of the nations in Africa after this long colonial rivalry. Yet the present status can be easily grasped only by seeing the picture of Europe in Africa at certain important epochs while bearing in mind the changes during recent years. As noted above, Spain and Portugal opened the drama in 1494 with the Treaty of Tordesillas which divided the outlying world between them. A turning point was reached in 1578 when King Sebastian of Portugal was defeated at Kasr-al-Kabir; a new factor entered in 1588 with the grant of a royal charter to British merchants to trade in Senegambia; Napoleon Bonaparte stirred Africa somewhat when he landed in Egypt in 1798; but England attained an objective in the cession of the Cape of Good Hope to that country as a result of the conqueror's failures in 1814.

European nations began to take seriously territorial expansion into Africa more than a century and a half ago, but there was so much upheaval both in Europe and Africa prior to the close of the nineteenth century that definite lines could not be decided upon as settled. Foreign possessions easily changed hands according to the fortunes of war. At the end of 1815 the situation was very much as it was in the beginning of the European occupation. France had the Senegal, the island of Réunion and standing ground in Madagascar and the English the Gambia, the Cape, St. Helena, Ascension, Mauritius, Seychelles, and Rodrigues. No Europeans except the Portuguese then had a foothold there from the mouth of the Niger to the Cape; and there were no permanent settlements except Sierra Leone under the British and Liberia of "Philanthropic" American origin. The Spanish held Ceuta and Melilla on the Moroccan coast, the Canaries and Fernando Po and Annsbon; the Portuguese a part of Guinea, Angola, Mozambique, Madeira, Cape Verde Islands, Azores, St. Thomas and Principe islands. The Dutch and the Danes at that time had no territory except on the Gold Coast.

Territorial changes in Africa continued. In 1817 France recovered her possessions lost during the Napoleonic wars and became sufficiently aggressive by 1830 to undertake the conquest of Algeria and to make a settlement on the Gabun River in 1845. France later acquired Assinie and Porto Novo. By a Franco-British agreement of 1857 the rights of these two nations were more definitely recognized in the areas in which they had been merely trading. Departing from the suggestion that the English should withdraw from the Gold Coast, the English tended to become the sole masters there after 1865. The Danes had been eliminated by purchase in 1850 and the Dutch went in similar fashion in 1872. Some Baptist missionaries settled Victoria, Ambar Bay, on the Cameroon coast about that time. The Spaniards obtained some indefinite holdings on the Corisco Bay and the Muni River. The French, going toward the south, established a settlement on the Gabun River about 1842 and Ogove a generation later. In South Africa the trek of 1836 resulted in the settlement of Natal and the two Boer republics. Cape Colony was extended by annexing Basutoland and Griqualand West, with Diamond Fields.

On the East Coast the territory above Natal except Delagoa Bay was conceded to Portugal by 1875. The French purchased Obock on Tajoura Bay in 1862, although it did not occupy it until a generation later. After securing the right to Aden in 1839 the English sought the support of the natives in keeping other nations out. The French finished by 1847 the conquest of Algeria. The Suez Canal by a purchase of the majority of the shares of the corporation passed to Great Britain in 1875. These two last-mentioned events together with the Spanish isolated holdings indicated the ultimate European control of North Africa just as the developments in South Africa had pointed toward such colonial development. The interior however was not actually penetrated until the explorations of Livingstone, begun in 1840 and completed after his death in 1873 by others inspired by his example. The interior was claimed by different nations, but no definite boundaries had been established in this opening up of Africa.

As early as 1891, however, the European nations began to refer to well-defined possessions as agreed in the Berlin Conference of 1885. With the exception of Morocco, Liberia, and Abyssinia overshadowed by the claims of an Italian protectorate, all accessible Africa was dominated by some foreign influence. Turkey claimed Tripoli as its province; the Sudan had temporarily made itself independent of Egypt; parts of the Sahara and innermost central regions still remained unclaimed by the European conquerors. Egypt had not at that time been thoroughly appropriated, but events as early as 1891 indicated that England would dominate affairs in that country. Great Britain, France, Portugal, and Spain, which prior to 1880 had established themselves on African soil, had immensely increased their domain by 1891; Germany and Italy, new powers in Africa, had by this time gained extensive possessions there, the former in Southwest Africa, in Togoland, in the Cameroon, and in East Africa; the latter in Eritrea and Somaliland. The Belgians had established themselves in the Congo.

While the two new powers were entering the African theater others already there were not inactive. France conquered Dahomey in 1893, and the next year expanded from Dahomey to Timbuctoo when the British declared a protectorate over Uganda. In 1895 France pushed on to the upper Ubangui territory and toward the Nile. The Italians who undertook to occupy the Tigre province in 1895 were defeated by Menelik in the battle of Adowa in 1896 which made Abyssinia independent. In 1897 the German protectorate of East Africa became a German colony when the French about the same time occupied Niki and Busa. The European situation was clarified somewhat in 1898 by the Anglo-French Convention with respect to boundaries and spheres of influence. In 1899 when France agreed to withdraw from the Nile Valley and Great Britain and the Khedive reached an agreement concerning the Sudan war broke out with the Boers who by the treaty of 1902 lost their possessions to become merged with the British colonists now organized as the South African Union. In the meantime France was busy conquering the Lake Chad kingdoms. In 1901 the British Crown assumed control over the territories administered by the Royal Niger Company and declared a protectorate over Northern Nigeria.

The Europeans, however, did not cease immediately to have trouble with the natives. The Herero tribes arose in 1903 against the cruel German rule in Southwest Africa, and in 1904 the Namaqua tribes joined the Herero in this war for freedom and independence. While the British, Italian, and Abyssinian forces were reducing to submission the Mullah of Somaliland there took place another uprising of the natives against their oppressors in German East Africa. The Mullah resumed hostilities in 1909. The year before this the Belgian Government, excoriated for atrocities in the Congo, assumed the sovereignty over the Congo Free State. Other European nations were gradually extending their conquests, reducing the natives to order, and securing their economic interests. In 1911 the French and Germans reached an agreement with respect to Morocco and French Equatorial Africa. That same year Italy invaded Tripoli in a war on Turkey and the following year forced the latter to concede its sovereignty over Tripoli and Cyrenaica in the Treaty of Ouchy (Lausanne). France recognized also at the same time a Spanish protectorate over the Rif country in Morocco. In 1914 the British reoccupied Somaliland and secured the recognition of Egypt as a British Protectorate independent of Turkey.

Great Britain had secured its control of Egypt by stopping the

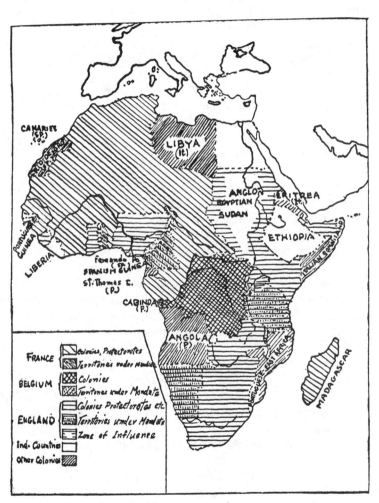

THE PARTITION OF AFRICA

eastward extension of France through the Sudan to the Nile, fixing their boundary line between Wadai and Darfur and at the same time barring the expansion of the Germans from the Cameroons into the Nile basin. The Germans, however, had stopped the British from advancing from the south to the north. In South and West Africa other changes were noted. British East Africa and Uganda had become protectorates under the Crown. In South Africa as a result of the Boer War Great Britain had expanded along the East Coast up to the Portuguese boundary. On the West Coast the French and Spanish had reached an agreement on Spanish Guinea and the protectorate of Rio de Oro.

Higher up France tended to consolidate her coast line claims. After defeating and appropriating Dahomey, she closed up the gap between the Gold Coast and Liberia, secured complete control of the Upper and Middle Niger, and expanded her territory behind Lake Chad from the Mediterranean to the Congo. Next by the trading of minor claims France brought England to the position of approving her conquest of Morocco in cooperation with Spain in return for giving England a free hand in Egypt in 1904; and, although temporarily blocked by German diplomacy, France ultimately succeeded, thanks to the support of other European powers, when she finally gained a free hand in Morocco. From this deal Spain received very little. Germany, however, had to be paid in exacting from France in exchange for 7,000 square miles 107,000 square miles of French Congo to extend the German Cameroon. The Germans thereby gained access to the Congo just as they had by a treaty with England in 1890 reached the Zambesi.

Germany had designs on North Africa, but she had to content herself with expansion into Central Africa. The designs of that nation on Tripoli came to nought in 1911 when the Italians by war preempted that area as already noted above. England, France, and Italy, left alone to contend for Abyssinia, finally declared a truce in a troublesome rivalry in agreeing in 1906 that Abyssinia should remain intact unless these three powers agreed jointly to infringe upon its integrity and independence. This practically ended the scramble until the upheaval of 1914. As a result of the World War a new map of Africa was made.

The chief difference made by the upheaval of the World War was the elimination of Germany from Africa by the Peace Conference of Versailles. After the retrocession to France of what she had ceded to Germany in the Cameroon in 1911 this African possession and Togoland were divided into British and French mandate zones. German East Africa became a British mandate with the designation as Tanganyika Territory and the two provinces of Ruanda-Urundi became a mandate of the Belgian Government. All these were designated by the treaty as areas to be administered as "B" mandates in which the nations as guardians must "respect the rights and safeguard the native population" while maintaining nevertheless the "open door." German Southwest Africa was annexed to the South African Union in a veiled manner as a "C" mandate which permitted its incorporation into that country.

Roughly speaking, then, we refer to France as the dominant influence in North Africa, in the Sudan, and on the West Coast; to the Belgians as the main factor in the Congo region; to the British as the lord of South Africa, and to the Portuguese with divided interests on the East and West Coast; but there are many exceptions to these general statements. Africa is a large continent, and the nations have sliced off here and there whatever they could bring the others to agree to, and at whatever time they found such aggression convenient. Of the dominant powers in Africa today France is the only one with a large area of contiguous territory. The nominal possession by Great Britain of the Union of South Africa, may be regarded as an exception in this case. Since most of these nations have territories in various parts of Africa the situation becomes decidedly different from what it would be if their African colonies were delimited as their areas are in Europe. The area inhabited by one African tribe, for example, may be divided among two or three European powers.

The exclusion of Germany from Africa, moreover, has not helped very much to change this significant aspect of the European occupation. This reduction of the number of European powers dominant in Africa, it should be noted, has been viewed from an unexpected angle. Some observers consider this change as fortunate for the natives inasmuch as these Teutons were terribly hard taskmasters; but to the extent that the number of European nations occupying territory in Africa is reduced, to that extent the way is open for increase in abuses by those remaining. Where there are several European powers bidding for the control of natives of the same areas or settled in possessions encircled by other Europeans the one serves as a check on abuses which might be inflicted upon the natives.

This same possibility of abuses is determined, too, by the colonial policy or the method of colonization—whether Europeans are settled among the natives to live side by side with them or whether the natives are to be left to continue on their lands chiefly unmolested except being under the supervision of the European through whom the natives must find an outlet to the outer world. In some areas the natives have been permitted to proceed very much as they did before the conquest except to pay taxes and dispose of their raw materials through the channels of the conqueror. In other cases the natives have been dispossessed as in South Africa by driving them from their lands and debasing to meniality and drudgery those remaining among the colonists who by law appropriate to themselves the higher pursuits of labor.

For another reason the elimination of Germany from Africa has been regarded as a blessing to the Europeans. The Germans, although hard taskmasters, nevertheless made the natives conscious of their worth in training them unduly for military purposes. To have Germany of such military tendencies still in Africa the natives under them might develop such knowledge of modern warfare as to threaten the position of the Europeans on that continent. Enough of this happened during the World War, for the British, ever distrustful of those whom they have oppressed, viewed with some alarm the employment during the World War of 475,000 French native troops, the vast majority of whom were Africans. "When the horrors of the war are staled in men's minds," says Sir Charles Lucas, "it may be not only that some European power, despot or nation, will use African legions to reduce the world, but also the Africans themselves may envisage their future along military and crusading lines." [1]

Doubtless for this reason the League of Nations multiplied the number of "non-African civilized nations who are responsible for Africa, and the mandates contain express provisions against the militarizing of the natives in the mandated territories. In Southwest Africa where the natives are crushed under the South African Union wheel of oppression it was provided that in the former German territory taken over there should be no military training

[1] Sir Charles Lucas, *The Partition of Africa* (Oxford, 1932), p. 198.

of natives otherwise than for purposes of internal police and the local defense of territory. It was further provided in that now British area that no military or naval forces shall be established or fortifications erected in the said territory.

Voicing further the sentiment of a good many of the English, Sir Charles Lucas was very much concerned about the effect the World War had on these natives. He says, "It cannot be doubted that the War tended to equalize the relations between white and coloured. Natives of Africa were taken far afield in Africa and, in many thousands, overseas out of Africa; they saw white men fighting white men, and they were called upon to fight white men by the side of white men. Their eyes and minds must have been opened, and they must be asking questions which never occurred to them before, and revising their estimates of white men. Incidentally they have been given more opportunities than could ever have come to most of them of comparing the kinds of white men. They will no doubt still follow the guidance of the white men whom they know and trust, but it will be a more reasoned following, made cautious and sophisticated by a knowledge of good and evil. It has been the same all the world over. The War has been no respecter of colour and in so far has worked for racial equality. Its effect in the dependent continent, in spite of its dependence remaining outwardly as before the War, must have been profound." [2]

The effects of these recent changes in the interest of economic imperialism in Africa may be further considered from the point of view of the home country. In the first place, the domination of the so-called weaker peoples has tended to make home governments drift from democracy toward autocracy. The increasing burden of defending the frontiers of these distant domains and of making them profitable to the few has tremendously increased taxation imposed upon the many. These empires require large appropriations for surveys, for subduing the rising natives, for subsidizing colonial administrations unable to balance their budgets, for financing secret diplomacy, and for providing armaments in competition with rival powers. Such diversion of wealth has precluded the possibility of much-needed improvements in Europe. This very sort of policy caused the American colonies to strike

[2] *Ibid.,* p. 201.

for independence in 1776 and enlisted sympathy for the revolution among the thinking classes of Great Britain.

On the other hand, the imperialists point out certain counter-balancing benefits to the home country. From Africa Europeans obtain diamonds, gold, rubber, cotton, and numerous other products required in supplying the modern world with necessities and luxuries. Africa, moreover, in the proportion as it becomes modernized offers a market for the European manufactured goods, although this has been a slow process except in the South African countries to which Europeans have shown an inclination to go. The scholarly element in Europe would point out as advantages the use of Africa as a training camp for officials in the public service. This supplies experience in colonial administration which heretofore has been mainly political theory. Natural and applied sciences have found in Africa a profitable field for the study of its plants, animals, and minerals while students of cultural anthropology have enriched their knowledge by the study of the natives.

With respect to the natives themselves not so much may be said as to the benefits which have resulted from economic imperialism. They have been the last factor in the equation to be given consideration, and when thought of they have usually been listed among the resources of the country rather than as human beings requiring philanthropic aid. In Africa primarily for private gain, the European has imposed upon the natives forced labor, heavy taxes, and brutal punishments. While drafting the natives to fight their own wars both in Africa and Europe, the Europeans have deprived these Africans of the best lands; and, in South Africa, the European descendants have barred the natives from higher pursuits secured by law exclusively to white men. The lower type of Europeans usually settled in Africa, moreover, bring more vices than virtues of their race and descend easily to lower levels with alcohol and venereal diseases, which have worked havoc among the natives.

As an offset to these evils, however, Europeans emphasize the blessing from the break-up of tribal wars, barbarous rites, and primitive practices. The Europeans note also in their favor the stamping out of tropical diseases, the abolition of slavery, the security of property, the development of facilities of communication, and the introduction of new articles of food. The Europeans, in their own defense, however, fail to note that some of these things like the improvement of railways and waterways have led to the destruction of the social order of the natives while no effort is being made to introduce European culture; and slavery continues in the forced labor system of those who claim the credit for abolishing it. The tribal wars, too, are hardly worse than those waged by the Europeans themselves at home or those which for selfish reasons the Europeans stir up among the natives.

The Europeans claim, however, that much improvement in recent years has been shown as a result of greater interest in the natives. This tendency, they say, is especially in those parts where the climate indicates that Europeans will never settle in large numbers. But these benefits have not followed, not even from the Permanent Mandates Commission of the League of Nations. The natives in that area are actually worse off now than they were before. The powers in control have the right to exploit those parts without assuming the burden of providing for the natives out of their own treasury, as was formerly done prior to the World War. The much-talked-of provisions for health, education, and the improvement of justice have not yet been generally observed. Where some improvement in education has been made it has assumed the aspect of giving the natives such safeguarded practical training as will make them useful in producing wealth for the European. To this the all but "saintly" missionaries have given their approval in the name of God.

Whatever the Europeans may do for the natives or against them, then, their case is not hopeless. The native African himself cannot but profit by the universal drama in which he plays even an inconspicuous part. Says H. L. Hoskins, "The very reaction of European methods on the native, whether wild Tuareg or lowly Hottentot, tends to make him more capable of maintaining and improving his position. Education is not necessarily formal, and African peoples have been learning apace the secrets of European superiority. Formal education will but accelerate the lessening of the gulf between the white man and the man of color. The World War, in which the African native and the European often fought side by side, considerably disillusioned the former by giving him bases of comparison, hence its tendency has been to equalize the relations of the two. These developments will not necessarily make for future peace between the peoples of Europe and those of Africa, but in time they will certainly affect the character of European control." [8]

Some recent developments in Africa may have justified these fears. The natives have grown restless under restrictions as to labor. Strikes intended to remove the differences between the wages given natives and those paid Europeans and to remove the barriers between white and colored labor have become frequent. Natives, moreover, have been more receptive to the appeals of prophets heralding a new day as those inspired by the divine to lead the people into a promised land. Several cases of actual defiance of government, too, have shown how far these natives may go in trying to right their wrongs by force. A few Europeans are thinking of the natives, then, as persons to be reckoned with rather than as things thought of in connection with the exploitation possibilities of the country. Sympathetic Europeans advise cooperation as a substitute for exploitation. Into the new scheme of things, then, the World War introduced a new factor in Africa. The force which this new factor will exhibit will depend upon how well by training or contact the natives may learn from the interlopers to surpass them at their own game.

[8] Halford Lancaster Hoskins' *European Imperialism in Africa* (New York, 1930), p. 105.

CHAPTER XV

AFRICAN CULTURE

AFRICANS have made a living just as other people similarly circumstanced. Many are fishermen and hunters, but the usual story about the nomad in Africa has been much exaggerated with respect to the natives. What these writers say about nomads applies mainly to those so-called white foreigners who have wandered through Africa from time immemorial, destroying the culture found without developing a better pattern of life for those thus dispossessed. As a rule the African has shown attachment to the soil, and he has made an impression tilling it. In many cases in which the Africans have been portrayed as running behind time in other respects they have nevertheless been noted as tillers of the soil.[1]

Even today the European exploiters of the continent complain that many of these so-called white African elements from Asia are worthless in the economic development of the country. About as far as they go toward manual labor is to pasture their flocks. They undertake to subsist by scheming and fleecing the industrious natives. And yet these same Europeans thus complaining refer in the next breath to this element of fanatically religious parasites as having introduced a higher culture in Africa, when the facts in the case support the conclusion that they destroyed the advanced culture of African nations.

In the African collectivism, like that of the ancient village community, labor is required as a rule. Everybody is supposed to work, and everybody has the right to enjoy the fruits of the common labor. There can be neither any extremely rich nor any extremely poor. Capitalism and pauperism, then, are eliminated. Individualism is given no place by the dominant collectivism underlying this communistic or socialistic system. Private property, as a rule, is allowed in things other than land, and such effects may

[1] Blyden, E. W., *African Life and Customs,* pp. 51-52.

be inherited. The soil, however, belongs nominally to the collectivity allotted it for cultivation. A family thus occupying the land may permit others to share it with them, but no one can transfer the title to land, since it is regarded as belonging to the divinities. They must be consulted by the priest or patriarch in all serious transactions with respect to land.[2]

While most African natives were tillers of the soil, many of them were driven to something else by immigrations of nomads. In only a few cases can it be established that any considerable number of an African tribe depend altogether on hunting and fishing. Among the Africans these were largely collateral efforts toward making a living. In certain parts, of course, the natural endowment of the country was such that cattle raising became the chief occupation. Africans have never been known as naturally lazy people in the sense in which we have viewed the North American Indians and other belated peoples. The African as a majority are industrious for the reason that their social order requires labor of all members of the group. They are so organized as to eliminate drones. The Bambara, for example, do not consider one a working man unless he is devoted in some way to the use of the axe or hoe.[3]

Numbers of tribes, too, have been observed as workers in various metals. Certain investigators have referred to the Africans as the great metal workers of the ancient world. They first discovered iron and developed far in the industrial arts. The Africans learned to use iron so much earlier than others that anthropologists consider the Negroes of Africa as having passed from the stone to the iron age without experiencing a bronze age through which other people groped in the ancient world. The trade of the blacksmith was found all over Africa from north to south and from east to west. Along with the blacksmith went also the weaver, the worker in wood, the ivory carver, and the goldsmith.[4] African industry has not grown into such enterprise as that of modern nations, but the foundation was laid, and the way

[2] *Ibid.*, pp. 34-38. Consult also Gordon B. Hancock's "Three Elements of African Culture" in the *Journal of Negro History*, VIII, pp. 284-300.

[3] L'Abbé Jos. Henry, *Les Bambara, leur vie psychique, éthique, sociale, religieuse* (Paris, 1910), p. 5.

[4] Franz Boas, *The Mind of Primitive Man*, pp. 270-271; and Delafosse, *Negroes of Africa*, pp. 158-160, 254, 260.

was pointed in these directions. Had Africa been helped rather than hindered from without her story might have been decidedly different.

In science and things practical the African accomplished much worthy of attention. The African medicine man had a knowledge of *materia medica* from which the scientists of modern nations are beginning to find new treatments for diseases which have hitherto baffled our most distinguished physicians. The Hottentots knew sufficient chemistry to concoct poisons for their arrows and also antidotes for such drugs. The application of chemistry to embalming and the development of geometry to facilitate the location and measurement of irrigated land along the Nile were other important contributions of Africans. The Hottentots before they heard of Europeans and Asiatics had developed a complete system of counting on the decimal basis to facilitate accounting for their numerous cattle on a thousand plains. The Baganda people carried this system of calculation a little further in having words for every multiple of ten up to twenty millions.[5]

In their communistic order of things where we could not expect much large state-building political organization has nevertheless evolved. The family is the unit, but the grown-up family becomes a clan, and several clans a tribe or nation. The king of a nation does not rule with absolute sway in all parts of the continent. The king, far from being the despot commonly thought of, is usually a limited monarch. As a rule he has no such power as Mussolini, Hitler or Roosevelt. The position of the African king is often hereditary through brothers on the mother's side or through the uncle and his sister's sons. Sometimes the council of elders choose the king, and for proper cause remove him.[6]

The king's power, however, is real. He is the chief magistrate,

[5] James W. Johnson's *Native African Races and Culture*, pp. 20, 21. See also Ben N. Azikiwe's "Nigerian Political Institutions" in *The Journal of Negro History*, XIV, pp. 328-340; Robert Stigler, "Ethnographische und Anthropologische Mitteilungen über einige wenig bekannte Volkstämme Ugandas," "Extract" from the *Mitteilungen der Anthropologische Gesellsch.*, Wien, 1923.

[6] This social order is discussed thoroughly by Delafosse in his *Negroes of Africa*, pp. 172 to 213, by E. W. Blyden in his *African Life and Customs*, and by Casely Hayford in his *Gold Coast Native Institutions*.

the general in time of war, the supreme judge within the jurisdiction, and, nominally at least, the "most high priest." In action the king is surrounded by courtiers, and he maintains himself with much pomp. His affairs are transacted by a number of subordinates like stoolbearers, swordbearers, criers, butlers, huntsmen, farmers, and "physicians." Ever present also is the body-guard of the king assisted further by other military bodies to maintain the peace. Most of the wars result from disturbing the peace by interfering with national institutions. Africans do not wage war because of any particular fondness for such a performance.[7]

In the "village community" which is the basis of the African life, all males of the same blood dwell together. When a young man takes a wife he brings her to his family circle, and when a daughter marries she goes to the clan of her husband. An African nation, then, is held together by ties of blood. Most marriages are arranged for the youth rather than by them. Gifts are required by families whose daughters are desired, but these when given are not considered as actual purchase of the wives but as a guarantee of protection against ill-treatment.

Some tribes are monogamous, and others are polygamous. Polygamy does not obtain throughout Africa, and it is not general in tribes where it is supposed to be practiced. Where polygamy is practiced it is of necessity restricted to the rich and official classes since others cannot afford to defray the expense involved in taking care of more than one wife. In this respect the custom is much better than secret polygamy in Europe and America. The rule is that every woman should be attached to some man, and that all should bear children.[8] Sexual profligacy, then, is rare. Bachelors and spinsters are not desired in this social order and are considered a disgrace to any community.

Children in Africa are carefully educated. Boys are brought under the instruction of carefully selected old men, and girls under wise and discreet matrons. The boys and girls are instructed in the physiology and hygiene with reference to motherhood and fatherhood inasmuch as every one is expected to produce offspring. In addition, boys are taught to do everything

---

[7] Hayford, *op. cit.*, pp. 85-92.

[8] Blyden, *op. cit.*, pp. 83-84; P. P. Marchal, *La Condition de la Femme Indigène,* Lyon, 1930.

in which their fathers engage. They must look after the young goats, and learn hunting, fishing, and agriculture. Later the boys may be called upon to tend larger animals and to herd cattle. At the completion of their education or at a specified age boys must be circumcised in some of these tribes. Circumcision, however, is not observed there everywhere.

The girls of the same "age class" must begin with the study of household administration which consists of supplying water, cleaning the home, pounding grain, and preparing food. The course terminates with a ceremony of dancing with the faces painted with bewildering colors. In parts where girls undergo an operation as boys do circumcision other ceremonies are staged on such occasions in the villages. In many tribes where girls are thus treated the boys do not undergo circumcision.[9]

Africans have a highly developed moral sense. However, they are often dubbed liars by foreigners who expect Africans to put these enemies on the right road and figure out accurately distances and locations when such knowledge furnishes the key to conquest and the destruction of the African social order. The African considers an untruth a sin. Any one disturbing the property of another, moreover, becomes a criminal subject to the severe penalty of a fine, imprisonment, or death. Locks and safes are unnecessary in that land, except where it has been contaminated by foreigners. The patterns of morality of the Hebrews and certain Africans, the Kaffirs, for example, are strikingly coincident. Among these particular Africans "theft is punished by restitution and fine; injured cattle, by death or fine; false witness, by a heavy fine; adultery, by fine or death; rape, by fine or death; poisoning or witchcraft, by death and confiscation of property; murder, by death or fine; treason or desertion from the tribe, by death or confiscation."[10]

The African emphasized especially moral training. He taught that there are three great friends in this world, courage, sense, and insight. The African, then, made a high estimate of wisdom. He said, "A man of wisdom is better off than a stupid man with any amount of charm and superstition." "No man puts new cloth

[9] Delafosse, *op. cit.*, pp. 210, 212, 218-233, 269.
[10] *Atlanta University Studies, Select Discussions of the Race Problem,* quotation from Franz Boas.

into an old garment." "Nobody is twice a dunce." "Remember that all flowers of a tree do not bear fruit." "A man may be born to wealth, but wisdom comes from length of days."

To teach one to choose desirable company the African said, "The butterfly that brushes against thorns will tear its wings." "He who goes with the wolf will soon learn to howl." In all man's contact with his fellows he should be careful, for "familiarity breeds contempt, but distance secures respect." The young man should learn also to distinguish the gold from the dross, for "he who marries a beauty marries trouble." "Quick loving a woman means quick not loving a woman." In other words, do not marry in haste and repent at leisure. "Regret causes an aching which is worse than pain. After a foolish act comes remorse." "Remorse weeps tears of blood and gives the echo of what is lost forever."

The African believed in courage and emphasized it in the teaching of the youth. He said, "Be courageous if you would be true." "Truth and courage go together." "Boasting is not courage." "He who boasts much cannot do much," "Boasting at home is not valor; parade is not battle; when war comes the brave will be known." [11]

In emphasizing the importance of knowledge the African taught that one should proceed in the natural way, beginning first with himself. "Know thyself better than he who speaks of thee. Not to know is bad, not to wish to know is worse." "Lack of knowledge is darker than night." "Men despise what they do not understand." "An ignorant man is always a slave." "Whoever works without knowledge works uselessly."

The African believed that "property is the prop of life" that "he who has no house has no voice in society," and he emphasized that "trade is not something imaginary or descriptive, but something real and profitable." Yet, the African developed collectivism rather than the dominating individualism of our social order. He believed in a sort of equality which the unusual wealth

[11] These proverbs, words of wisdom, have been collected and published in C. G. Woodson's *African Myths* (Washington, D. C., 1928). Some of these appear also in Maurice Delafosse's *L'Ame Nègre* (Paris, 1922); other proverbs or a different arrangement of them appear in A. O. Stafford's "Mind of the African as Reflected in his Proverbs" in *The Journal of Negro History*, I, pp. 42-48.

of an individual should not upset. He said, "Birth does not differ from birth. As the free man was born so was the slave." "The laborer is always in the sun, the landowner always in the shade." "To love the king is not bad, but to have the king love you is better." "It is better to be poor and live long than rich and die young."

Man, however, must be industrious. To emphasize work and the preparation for it the African said, "A person prepared beforehand is better than after reflection." "The day on which one starts is not the time to commence one's preparation." "He who waits for a chance may wait for a year." "You cannot kill game by looking at it." Time, then, must not be wasted. "The coming year is not out of sight, let us be up and doing." "Today is the elder brother of tomorrow, and the heavy dew is the elder brother of rain." "A fruitful woman is the enemy of the barren, and an industrious man is the foe of the lazy." Be industrious, then, for "beg help and you meet with refusals; ask for alms and you meet with misers."

To emphasize the proper appreciation for children the African insisted that "there is no wealth without children." He said further, "If you love the children of others you will love your own better." To direct children in the right way the African taught "the duty of children to our elders, not elders to children." "Disobedience is the father of insolence." Children of all stations should be polite to every one, for "bowing to a dwarf will not prevent one from standing erect again," "I have forgotten your name is better than I know thee not."

The African made a distinction between character and reputation. He said, "Every man's character is good in his own eyes." "A man's disposition is like a mark in a stone, no one can efface it." "Wherever a man goes to dwell his character goes with him." "Ordinary people are as common as grass, but good people are dearer than the eye."

The African emphasized also the necessity for patience. "A matter dealt with gently is sure to prosper, but a matter dealt with violently causes vexation." "If one knows thee not or a blind man scolds thee, do not get angry." "Anger does nobody good, but patience is the father of kindness." "Anger draws arrows from the quiver, but good words draw kolanuts from the bag." "A counsellor who understands proverbs soon settles difficult matters." "Ashes fly back in the face of him that throws them." "Wrangling is the father of fighting." "He who forgives ends the quarrel." "Patience is the best of qualities; he who possesses it has all things." "At the bottom of patience there is heaven."

Students of African life are almost unanimous in saying that the Africans are "the most just of all the people of the world." That of all things to be detested the Africans hate injustice most. These advanced Africans doubtless take this position because they believe that "he who injures another brings injury upon himself." They say also that evil deeds shall be made known because the "sun is a king of torches." Believing as they do that one should not take snap judgment, the Africans thus remind us, "You condemn on hearsay evidence alone, your sins increase." "Lies however numerous will be caught when it rises up. The voice of truth is easily known."

To inculcate an appreciation for love the African always cautions the youth against hate. "When a person hates you he will beat your animals." "Hate the evil which a man does, but do not hate the man himself." "If you love yourself others will hate you; if you humble yourself others will love you." "There is no medicine for hate." "He is a heathen who bears malice."

With the thought of the one who cautioned us to remove the beam from our own eye before we see the mote in our brother's eye, the African said, "Do not repair another man's fence until you have seen to your own." "Faults are like a hill; you stand on your own and you talk about those of other people." "My badness is more manifest than my goodness; you look up my goodness in the room, and you sell my badness in the market."

CHAPTER XVI

RELIGION AND ART

In religion the Africans are far from thinking in common. As among other peoples foreign creeds have made inroads. Up to the present Islam has been the most effective of the imported faiths. The followers of the Prophet have been more successful than the Christians who try to make the Negro feel that he is an inferior and should be content with exploitation by their "co-working" interlopers. The Mohammedans, on the contrary, accept the Negro as a social equal and try to make the Africans feel that their race is recognized in the Koran which contains a chapter inscribed to a Negro. It is taught that Mohammed was in part descended from a Negro and had a Negro as his confidant in Arabia, that on one occasion Negroes slew a rival of Mohammed, and that the Great Prophet greatly admired the celebrated Arabized Negro poet and warrior who delivered his country from the throes of its enemies and composed beautiful verse which made him the father of Arabian poetry and the messenger of a new thought to a war-ridden world.[1]

Nothing, however, has been the subject of more misunderstanding than the religion of the African. Missionaries and travelers who have studied religious theories try to fit into their terminology various expositions of phenomena which they have not observed long enough to understand, as pointed out by Emil Torday in his "Dualism in the Bantu Religion." In the first place, natives considering foreigners as interlopers, never readily express themselves for fear that the disclosure of any real truth may result in injury to the tribe. The rule among the natives, then, is to tell the investigator not what he thinks but what he does not think. One frequently finds books on certain African natives depicting their

[1] George W. Ellis, *Negro Culture in West Africa*, New York, 1914, pp. 109-110.

religion as monotheism, polytheism, or dynamism when other works on the selfsame African tribes present these manifestations as some other religious phenomena. A European who first observed the Hottentots, for example, wrote home that they had no religion at all because he did not find on the surface a priesthood, houses of worship, and ritualistic observances. Probably in the expositions of Captain R. S. Rattray, Emil Torday, Maurice Delafosse, Georges Hardy, and Henri Labouret, who have spent sufficient time among these natives at least to penetrate these mysteries, if not to understand them thoroughly, we come nearer to a real picture of the African religious mind, although these gentlemen because of their imperfections do not agree on certain important points.[2]

---

[2] In religion we are confused with respect to Africa. Most of the comments on the religion of the African have been made by Christians and Mohammedans who decry what they call an unreasonable animism. Yet the religion of the African is just as reasonable as theirs. All religion is belief in what we know to be impossible. In other words, such comments are not scientific. They are not written with objectivity.

This bias with respect to religion of the African is summarized in numerous works. Among these may be noted N. Stam, "The Bahanga," in the *Publications of the Catholic Anthropological Conference*, I, 1929 (Washington, D. C.); "Dualism in Western Bantu Religion and Social Organization" in the *Journal of the Royal Anthropological Institute of Great Britain and Ireland*; M. Prouteaux, "Notes sur certains rites magico-religieux de la Haute Côte d'Ivoire," in *L'Anthropologie*, 1918-1919, pp. 37-52; Amaury Tabbot, *Life in Southern Nigeria;* Carl Seyffert, "Totengebraüche und Todesverstellungen bei den Zentralafrikanischen Pygmäen den Buschmännern und Hottentotten" in *Archiv fur Anthropologie*, XII, 1913; E. Torday, "Fetischisme, l'Idolatrie et la Sorcellerie des Bantous Occidentaux," in *L'Anthropologie*, 1929; J. Henry, *L'Ame d'un peuple africain: les Bambara* (Munster, 1910); R. E. Dennett, *Nigerian Studies of the Religious and Political System of the Yoruba* (London, 1910); Mgr. Le Roy, *La Religion des primitifs* (Paris, 1911); M. Delafosse, "Souffle vital et esprit dynamique chez les populations indigènes du Soudan Occidental" in *Comptes-rendus des séances de l'Institut Français d'Anthropologie*, supplement to *L'Anthropologie*, No. 5; H. Labouret, "La terre dans les rapports avec les croyances religieuses chez les populations du cercle de Gaoua" in *L'Annuaire et mémoires du Comité d'études historiques et scientifiques de l'Afrique Occidentale française* (Gorée, 1916); A. Werner, *The Natives of British Central Africa* (London, 1906); N. W. Thomas, *Anthropological Report on the Ibo-Speaking Peoples of Nigeria* (London, 1913 and 1914); the same author, *Anthropological Report on Sierra Leone* (London, 1916); C. R. Lagie, "Les Azande ou Niam Niam," *L'Ethnographie*, 1928, pp. 230-232. To these may be added similar works of Ch. Monteil, L. Tauxier, Ad. Cureau, and H. H. Johnston.

Taking up especially the African's religion and his philosophy of life,[3] Delafosse says, in referring to West Africa, the most advanced part of the so-called Dark Continent, "The African Negroes believe that every animated being encloses within itself, in addition to its body, two immaterial principles. One, a sort of breath or vital fluid, has no other rôle than to animate the material part and to communicate life and movement to it; it is a principle without an individuality or personality of its own, which is eternal in the sense that it is anterior to the body that it animates for the time being and will survive it to go and animate another, and so on until the end of time. Like matter, it is infinitely divisible and can dissociate itself into various elements each of which suffices alone or combined with another element coming from elsewhere, to animate a given body. When a man dies, it is that the vital breath has abandoned its carnal envelope in order immediately to create a new life either in a human or animal fœtus in gestation or in a germinating plant. Of course, this sort of fluid, without personality, without intelligence, without will, that may be compared to an electric current, is not the object of any cult. It is, if you will, a spirit, but only in the etymological sense of the word (*spiritus* 'breath').[4]

"The second principle is very different: born with the body which harbors it and at the same time, it constitutes the veritable personality of the being to whom it communicates its thought, its will and the force to act; the vital breath permits the members of a man or an animal to move, it permits the sap of a tree to circulate in its veins, but this movement and this circulation cannot be accomplished if they are not ordered by the spirit. If it happens that one day the control of the vital breath escapes from the spirit and that, as a consequence, this breath leaves its envelope and death follows, it is because another spirit which is stronger has neutralized the first: that is why all death is attributed by the

[3] A striking case of the failure to understand the African's philosophy of life is set forth in Mamby Sidibé's "A Propos de la Gaieté du Noir d'Afrique" in *Outre-Mer*, Vol. III, No. 1, March, 1931, pp. 5-22; and Vol. VI, No. 4, December, 1932, pp. 244-257. For a slightly different point of view read Georges Hardy's "De la Gaieté chez les Noirs d'Afrique" in *Outre-Mer*, Vol. II, No. 1, January, 1930, pp. 37-40.

[4] The quotations, the one on this page and others following, are from Delafosse's *Negroes of Africa*, pp. 220-229.

Negroes not to material causes, which for them are only secondary and immediate causes, but to the psychic influence of an evil-minded spirit, the only real and first cause of death.

"After the decease of a being, only his spirit lives, and it lives such as it was during the lifetime of this being with the same personality, the same character, the same affections and the same hatreds. Only it no longer has the vital breath to command nor the carnal envelope limiting its fancy; and so it becomes even more powerful, being no longer hampered in its action by the necessity for directing the life of the body and for guiding itself, in a way, by the vital breath. Also, it is then deified; and it is here that we must find the origin of the cult of the dead, or of the manes of ancestors.

"If every animate being—man, animal or plant—possesses the two principles of which we have just spoken," continues Dela-fosse, "inanimate beings—the defunct, dead animals or plants, solid minerals, liquids or gases—are naturally deprived of the vital breath, which has no importance whatever from the religious point of view, but each one is endowed with an individual spirit, intelligent and active, all the more efficient and redoubtable, as I have just said, because it does not have to occupy itself with the inert body which is only its material representation and to which it is not bound by the obligation to control the play of the absent vital breath. This body, moreover, can disintegrate, as is the case with corpses, and the spirit is not held to make of it, its constant dwelling place."

"Whether it is the spirit of a deceased person or of a mountain, a block of stone, a gulf, a river, the heavens, the rain, the wind, the land and especially a particular piece of land, the parcel of ground one inhabits and from which one gains a living, for the Negroes it is always the same kind of spirit, it is always a principle that is invisible but which sees everything, which takes account of all, is sensitive, can be offended unintentionally, equally irascible and capable of causing hard expiation for even involuntary offenses that have been done to it, but feeble and vain as man who created it in his own image, letting itself be moved and cajoled by prayers and offerings or influenced by propitiatory sacrifices."

From this point of view differs somewhat Henri Labouret, a successor in many of the enterprises engaged in by M. Delafosse during his life. Labouret says, "At times the notion of soul has been difficult to define and it is not easy to know what it is for the Africans. Certain observers even suppose that this concept does not even exist among the individuals arbitrarily called primitive; others assure us, on the contrary, that every Negro believes himself to possess several of them whose appellations are no better known than their rôle.[5]

"For M. Delafosse, the *nia* seems to be a kind of soul and this word would signify exactly 'personal life'; it is born at the moment that the human being or animal is conceived, it exists equally in every tree, every stone, every natural phenomenon. The *nia* of animated beings continues to exist after their death and becomes a redoubtable power, whose wrath one seeks to avoid by offerings. Thus the cult rendered everywhere to the dead would be explained.

"Besides this, there is in living beings another essential principle, the *dia,* a sort of vital breath, an impersonal fluid, without thought, without will, without independent force, but whose presence is necessary in order that life be manifested within the body.

"These explanations do not seem to be in accord with the ideas of the natives such as one can discern them by the light of their own declarations and the linguistic facts. First of all, the Mandingo, far from imagining the *dia* (or better *dya*) as an impersonal fluid, without thought and without will, consider it as an immaterial double of the individual, animating the body of the latter and sometimes abandoning the envelope which serves it as an habitual dwelling-place in order to run about on adventures, especially during sleep, which supposes intelligence and will. It is then often a prey to witchcraft, to the enterprise and the violence of sorcerers, who can capture it, wound it, kill it and eat it. In this case the body soon dies. Let us note that we are not dealing here with the actions and reactions of what certain authors call the 'dream-soul,' that is to say, of a special category of souls, but indeed with the same principle of *dia* or *dya* of which we have been speaking.

"I do not think that this word can be connected, as M. Delafosse assures us, with the monosyllabic root *di* signifying at the

---

[5] The quotations, the one on this page and those on the following are from Henri Labouret's INTRODUCTION to Delafosse's *Negroes of Africa.*

same time: to be gentle, easy, agreeable, and also gentleness, facility, pleasure, when to this same root is added the suffix *ya,* a current usage in Mandingo for the formation of certain qualitative substantives, thus permitting the reading *diya* and not *dia.* Now the term in question is certainly *dia* or rather *dya* pronounced with an occlusive, deep-toned media-palatal consonant. In the mind of the natives here considered, it applies to an element susceptible of emotion, and from all evidence, without the concourse of what M. Delafosse calls *nia.* Numerous expressions prove this: *dya geleya,* to reassure, calm, soothe the *dya; dya uli, dya sira, dya tike,* all synonymous, indicating the action of frightening the *dya.*

"As for the *nia* or *nya* there are strong presumptions for believing that it could never be given the sense of 'soul or personal life.' The Mandingo, in fact, employ a special term, fairly different, for expressing this double idea which is *ni.*

"The conception of these natives and the greater part of those observed by me during the years that I spent in West Africa seems to be the following: the human being is composed of a carnal body, serving as an envelope to a fluidlike body, transforming itself after death into a specter which is able to inhabit the country of the dead or else reincarnate itself in a new-born person.

"Is this saying that the *nia* described by M. Delafosse as a dangerous force does not exist? The term is inexact in form, but the notion is proved by observation."

"Let us remark that in the first place, one should not speak of *mia* but of *gnama.* M. Delafosse had, at first, admitted the latter reading in his works; he then considered that '*niama,* a dynamic and efficient spirit, can be the spirit of a genie, an ancestor, a sacred object, an animal, a mountain, a stone.' Later, led on by the apparent analogy of the roots *nia* and *ni,* he abandoned the term *niama* or *gnama* to adopt *nia* and gave to it the explanation reported above.

"The Mandingo natives themselves employ the word *gnama* to designate not a personal fluid but a special force, something efficient and in any case evil, which is neither general nor universal, but, on the contrary, peculiar to certain individuals, certain animals, certain places, certain objects, certain gods, the approximate list of which could be drawn up. I may add that in numerous

African languages there exist, from all evidence, terms corresponding to the Mandingo *niama* or *gnama* and covering the same idea. To my mind, these terms cannot be connected with the notion of soul."

Referring especially to the religion of the Negro, which is manifested in various ways, especially in art, Georges Hardy says (in his *"L'Art Nègre, l'Art Animiste des Noirs d'Afrique*),[6] that many errors have been made in trying to picture the soul of the Negro in these widely differing manifestations so easily misunderstood by those who cannot see beyond these things. While these manifestations change from place to place and the religious organizations appear diversified the ensemble of these beliefs and relations of different religious elements among them remains essentially the same. Conspicuous in this doctrine appears the belief in one unique God, who created everything which exists but who after finishing this task ceased to concern himself with human affairs. He is an inaccessible God without any image of him left in the minds of the natives; with a name, however, which is not confused with that of other supernatural forces. They ascribe to him no character or fixed attribute. They say nothing about his sojourn or his occupations. Everything about him seems extremely vague. They admit the existence of the creator but they do not concern themselves about him since he does not concern himself about them.

"Everything in nature is animated, but these spirits are not divinities. They are emanations from a superior divinity. Along with this spirit or dynamic principle these animated beings enclose a principle or a vital breath the animation of man, of animals, of all plants, but which has no connection with that which it animates. It passes from one body to the other, and it is in this sense that it is eternal. It is of interest, then, only in proportion as it assures the duration of the individual life."

With respect to the far beyond the ideas of the African natives vary in their details. Notable is the absence of any idea of reward or punishment beyond this life. The spirits in which they believe manifest themselves as good or evil according to the attitude of

---

[6] In addition to Georges Hardy's *L'Art Nègre* see also his treatment of the same theme in his "L'Ame Africaine" in *La Revue des Vivants,* Quatrième Année, No. 1, Janvier, 1930, pp. 102-111.

man toward these spirits. The practices of which these spirits are the object may be reduced to a small number: the worship of ancestors, the belief in "genies," interpretations of their will and the like. They involve a series of long and complicated operations necessitating a special initiation. This is the rôle of the special class of individuals, a clergy: magicians, sorcerers, "feticheurs," constituting frequently religious associations, secret societies, performing ceremonies according to rigorously defined rules.

"This ensemble of beliefs is clearly reflected in the different productions of Negro art. The essential characteristics of this art are: an ever alert sensibility, an easy motivation, an aptitude peculiar to self-abnegation, capacity for enthusiasm, and joyous tendency toward unselfish creation."

The most striking thing of all in the soul of the black is its mobility, the "inconsistency of impressions, sentiments, whims; the absence of a real sense of the true," says Georges Hardy. The idea does not happen to take form. By reason of all the circumstances under which it has been developed, the art of the blacks of Africa is an *art refoulé*. It has almost taken refuge in religion. Artistic production itself, instead of tempting individuals who feel that they are gifted, has developed in the closed and scorned castes of artisans. And as Hardy has further said, "It is inevitable that an art thus become an *art refugié,* held to the protection of the fashion and caprice of multitudes, retain a strong unity in spite of the diversities of the people and their physical environment; it lives by traditions and ritualistic forms; it maintains by agreement or by force the accord between the artist and the public; it rebels against introducing something new, secured in the narrow bounds of the racial soul."

One is carrying things too far toward documentation to try to trace schools or even centers of this art, Hardy believes. This African art is restricted to three categories: the symbolism of the open plain characterized by the important place which Islam occupies in it; the realism of the forest of the heart of Africa; and finally an embryo of "art libre," as in that of Benin and its neighbors.[7] In thus characterizing this esthetic expression as different

[7] *La Revue des Vivants,* January, 1930, "L'Ame Africaine," pp. 102-111; see also Georges Hardy's *L'Art Nègre,* Paris, 1927, *passim.*

from other manifestations elsewhere, however, there is no thought of depreciation.

In art the Negro has reached a high level.[8] The achievements of Africa in this sphere have been so convincing that scientists have had to revise their estimates of the cultural contributions of the native of this continent. Yet some phases of art in Africa do not show full development. Art in architecture has not been well expressed in the anthill-like homes of the African; and with the exception of the figures of Sherbro, the megaliths of Gambia, the ruins of great constructions at Zimbabwe in Southern Rhodesia and the palaces of a few kings elsewhere we do not see much evidence of its development in native Africa.[9] No effort is made here to estimate the progress in architecture after the influence of Islam which gave unusual stimulus in this direction especially in the building of mosques.

[8] On African art there are numerous works, most of which are merely unscientific attempts to prove that what the Africans have achieved in this sphere has been borrowed. Some of these are the following: Daniel Real, "Notes sur l'Art Dahoméen," *L'Anthropologie,* 1920, pp. 369-392; S. P. Impey's *Origin of the Bushmen and Rock Painting of South Africa* (Cape Town, 1926) ; D. H. Neel, "Statuettes en Pierre et en Argile de l'Afrique Occidentale," *L'Anthropologie,* 1913, pp. 418-443; H. Clouzot and A. Level, *L'Art Nègre et l'art océanien;* J. Maes and H. Lavachery, *L'Art Nègre* (Paris, 1930) ; J. Maes, *La Psychologie de l'Art Nègre* (Wien, 1926) ; the same author, "Le Xylophone des Bakuba" in *Man,* XII, 1912; the same author, *Figuerines commemoratives et allégoriques du Congo-Belge* (Leipzig, 1928) ; Hugo Obermaier, *Buschmannkunst, Felsmalereien aus Sudwestafrika* (Berlin, 1930) ; Martin Heydrich, "Afrikanische Orna-mentik," *Internationales Archiv. fur Ethnographie,* Supplement to XXII, 1911; M. C. Burkitt, *South Africa's Past in Stone and Paint* (Cambridge, 1928) ; D. F. Bleek, *Rock Paintings in South Africa from Parts of the East-ern Province and Orange Free State* (London, 1930) ; M. A. Goodwin and C. Van Riet Lowe, "The Stone Age Culture of South Africa," *Annals of the South African Museum,* XXVII, 1929; Melville Jones, "On the Implement bearing Deposits of Tuangs and Tiger Kloof in the Cape Town Provinces of South Africa," *The Journal of the Royal Anthropological Institute,* 1920; Gaston Murray and Sophie Getzowa, "Les Lèvres des Femmes Djinges," *L'Anthropologie,* 1923; H. Gaden and R. Verneau "Stations et Sepultures Néolithiques au Territoire Militaire du Tchad," *L'Anthropologie,* 1920; E. R. Collins and Reginald Smith, "Stone Imple-ments of South Africa," *Journal of the Royal Anthropological Society;* XLV, pp. 79-92; D. L. Peringuey, "The Bushman as a Paléolithic Man," *Extracts from the Transactions of the Royal Society of South Africa,* V, December, 1915.

[9] Waterlot, E. M., *Les Bas-Reliefs des Batiments Royaux d'Abomey* (Paris, 1926), *passim.*

Yet while painting and monumental statues in Africa have not been frequently met with, other manifestations of art are abundant. In the case of small sculptures in stone, wood, and ivory or modeling in wax, clay or metals African art ranks high.[10]   In these particular manifestations the Negroes, according to Delafosse, "have shown themselves to be ingenious workers, powerfully helped by a high inspiration, a sharp sense of detail and a very profound conception of the form to be given to their ideas.[11]   In recent times foreign art has entered Africa, but it has been shown that "Negro art appears more perfect in the measure that it is more purely Negro." "Indeed," says Delafosse, "it cannot be contested that the funeral statuettes, the sacred masks, the carved seats, the vases, the knick-knacks of bronze or copper, the gold and silver jewelry made in the northern region of the Sudan and in the Europeanized centers are very inferior to the productions of the same order of the tribes of Guinea, of Dahomey, of the Congo, and of the Great Lakes."

In music the achievements of the Negroes are not to be despised. Certain anthropologists assert that the Africans were the first to use stringed instruments.   The instruments are xylophones, violins, guitars, zithers, harps, flutes, flageolets. Of all these the xylophone is the most extensively used.   Delafosse says, "Many xylophone

[10] The observations on Negro art are numerous.   The following will assist the student from various points of view: J. P. Johnson's *Prehistoric Period in South Africa* (London, 1912) ; S. P. Impey's *Origin of the Bushmen and the Rock Painting in South Africa,* Cape Town, 1926; I. Schapera's "Some Stylistic Affinities of Bushman Art," *Journal of Science,* Vol. XXIII, pp. 504-515; A. J. Goodwin's "Caspian Affinities of South Africa. Stone Age Culture," *Journal of Science,* XXII, pp. 428-436; R. Verneard's "La Parenté des Négroides Européens des Boschmans," *L'Anthropologie,* 1925, pp. 234-265.   For West Africa consult among others Daniel Real's "L'Art Dahoméen," *L'Anthropologie,* 1920, pp. 369-392.   Read also D. W. Neel's "Statuettes en Pierre et en Argile de l'Afrique Occidentale," *L'Anthropologie,* 1913; Fr. De Zeltner's "Les Gravures Rupestre de L'Air," *L'Anthropologie,* 1913, pp. 171-184; and Oswald Mengheim's "Die Tumbakultur und der Westafrikanische Kulturkreise," *Anthropos,* XX, 1925, pp. 516-557.   From the point of view of ornamentation consult Alexander Yunger's *Kleidung und Umwelt in Afrika, Eine Anthropologische Studie, zugleich ein Beitrag zur Frage nach den Grundsprinzipien der Fracht,* Leipzig, 1926; and Martin Heydrick's "Afrikanische Ornamentik, Beitrage zur Erforschung der Primativen Ornamentik und zur Geschichte der Forschung" (*Internationales Archiv. fur Ethnographie,* Supplement au Volume XXII, 1911.

[11] Delafosse, *op. cit.,* p. 254.

players are real virtuosos. Sometimes they are associated in groups, one of them improvising the recitative and the others taking up the refrain or the leitmotif, each doing his own part. The harpists, too, obtain very harmonious effects."

Africa also has a literature, in spite of the fact that there is nothing approaching a common language. In the northern two-thirds of the continent are found about a hundred different languages. In the remaining third to the south the Bantu language with certain variations prevails. Writers have said that African literature is altogether oral, but some of it is written. Of course, the popular oral literature has the dominating place in African life and it is interesting. Professional story-tellers, belonging to a class called "griots," learn to recite historical romances and the genealogies of the distinguished families. Each one of them is a veritable encyclopædia often called in to decide matters of history, law, or liturgy. The "griots," then, are the libraries of oral literature.[12]

There is such written literature as has developed since the coming of Islam by adapting the Arabic to the use of the natives. In other cases the natives have developed their own alphabet as the Vai on the frontier of Liberia and Sierra Leone and the Bamom or Bamoun of the Cameroons who have been using their own written language for more than a century. Dahomey has recently worked out a written language. Of the works of the natives who have produced creditable treatises in the languages of foreigners who have settled in Africa we can make mention here of only a few. The most outstanding of these is the *Tarikh-es Soudan,* the first history of the country, written by Es-Sadi, a native African, a black man; and the *Tarikh-El-Fettach* written by Kati, also a black Sudanese.

---

[12] A. Depuis-Yakouba, *Les Gow ou Chasseurs du Niger,* Légendes songais de la région de Timbuctou (Paris, 1911) ; René Trautman, *La Littérature populaire à la Côte des Esclaves, contes proverbes, devinettes;* Henri Gaden, *Proverbes et Maximes, peuls et toucouleurs tradiuts, expliqués et annotés;* G. G. Woodson, *African Myths* (Washington, D. C., 1928) ; Roland Lebel, *Le Livre du Pays Noir* (Paris 1927) ; the same author, *Histoire de la, Littérature Coloniale en France,* Paris, 1931; the same author, "Les Poètes de l'Afrique Noire," *Outre Mer,* Vol. I, No. 3, September, 1929, pp. 366-374; Fr. De Zeltner, *Contes du Sénégal* (Paris, 1913) ; C. Monteil, *Contes Soudanais* (Paris, 1905) ; Siré Abbas-Soh, *Chroniques du Fouta Sénégalais* (Paris, 1913) ; Blaise Cendrars, *Anthologie Nègre* (Paris, 1927).

CHAPTER XVII

AFRICAN SURVIVALS IN AMERICA

THE African background of the Negro offers an explanation for much which we find today among the Negroes of the United States. Subordinated to a ruling class of another race, the Negro with his imported culture could not escape transformation in this new atmosphere of prohibitions and social repression; but he who can find in the American Negro today only the survival of an African temperament, who sees no connection between the Americanized branch and its African forbears is an unfortunately uninformed individual with respect to the findings of history, ethnology, anthropology, and archæology. The fact that we have had university professors to advertise such ignorance in the schoolroom and in print shows how badly off we are for a scholarly attitude to supplant this bias with respect to the African background of the race.

The imported Negroes' experience in government, of course, had no influence on politics in this country except in the indirect way of making the Negro a law-abiding citizen. The Negro in Africa had been accustomed to strict tribal control under chiefs and kings who had to be obeyed. To this ideal the American Negro has consistently conformed. With the exception of infractions of law resulting from impoverishment and so-called offenses considered virtues elsewhere, Negroes are far from being a criminal element. Brought into a new country and still more rigidly controlled by superior force than formerly, the Negroes thus situated never developed toward vulcanism as have done the European settlers who have come in this country as a result of social and political upheavals in which they had participated. While the latter came seeking an asylum from wrongs which they had suffered they readily afflicted others with the evils from which they had tried to escape. The Negroes, on the other hand, have never resorted to force except in self-defense or self-preservation from evils which their uprisings were intended to correct. In freedom the Negro has still lived up to this ideal of being a law-abiding citizen. He does not throw bombs; he does not start riots; he does not engage in lynching; and he has never assassinated a high public functionary or tried to overthrow the government.

This law-abiding may be accounted for, too, in the African's love of justice. Most of the observers of governments developed in Africa are all but unanimous in speaking of administration of justice as a most important concern, for of all things which the African detests most it is injustice. The kings and emperors herein recorded would intrust many other affairs of importance to their lieutenants, but these rulers personally supervised the administration of justice in order to be sure that no one might be dealt with unjustly. The African would not excuse an individual for treating another unjustly. It might seem strange, then, that people who have loved justice are today doomed to suffer more injustice than any other people in the world.

The customary reference to the American Negro as a criminal element is mere bias which no scientific investigator takes seriously. The records show that so-called crimes of Negroes such as socializing with women, frequenting places of amusement, crossing certain residential lines, going into desirable places, taking something to eat when all but starved, would pass as matters of duty and necessity in other countries. Investigation further shows that in cases of altercation between members of different races the Negro is charged with the offense although he may not be the aggressor. In spite of the libellous and slanderous attitude of traducers of the race they present no facts to uproot the eloquent truth that the Negro in Africa, removed from such outside interference as that of the Mohammedan and Christian interlopers, is a peaceful and law-abiding individual and that tradition has been preserved in the Negro in America.

Certain aspects of the African social order may still be observed here. The emphasis placed by the Negroes on secret societies in Africa has survived here not to evade or cover up anything undesirable or to take advantage of those not thus connected, but to provide for the community certain facilities for social outlet which could not be otherwise afforded. The Negro was not permitted to continue his African secret functions here, but he finally found acceptable substitutes in taking up those of the Europeans and modifying them to meet his demands. While those in Africa, just as these taken up by the Negroes in America may have been the occasion for the parade of things secret, revealed only to the chosen members who adorn themselves with expensive regalia, these organizations had more serious functions. It must be admitted, too, that the Negro in the regalia of the Orient is more at home and shows up to better effect as an Oriental than the European.

These orders in Africa conformed to the requirements of meeting a social need felt in Africa; and so have they developed in America. While they bear in some cases the same names as those of the whites or, if under different names, have some of the same ritualistic basis they serve the Negroes in a way different from the manner in which similar organizations function among whites. Among the Negroes secret societies are more social than convivial. They are sometimes even more economic than social. Drawing upon the African Negro's penchant for burial pomp, many Negro secret societies have been developed mainly around the idea of taking care of the sick and burying the dead; and from this as a nucleus these orders have become mainly insurance companies. In so doing they have followed the example set by the True Reformers, organized and promoted by W. W. Browne, an enterprising Methodist minister of Richmond, Virginia, about fifty years ago. Most of the large Negro insurance companies may be traced to such beginnings. The secret society aspect of Negro life in America has been so much further developed among the Negroes than among others that judges handling cases arising in this sphere seek the opinion and assistance of Negro attorneys who are so much better informed thereupon than white lawyers.

In language this migration of culture cannot register such claims. The Negro African language was lost here for the two reasons that the imported Negroes were compelled to learn the language of their enslavers, and Africans brought from various places speaking different tongues did not find themselves always in contact with fellow members of the same stock. In spite of this, however, certain African words were retained and today constitute good English. These are such as *tobacco, yam, goober, canoe, banjo,* and *buckra.* The use made by the Negro of the English even when correctly spoken, however, shows picturesque, verbose, and colorful influences which are distinctly African.

On the folk literature of America, moreover, the African slave had a tremendous influence. The Negro brought to America the most active and productive imagination of all the elements contributing to the founding of America. The rich African folklore of which we hear so much today from all persons who have long observed the natives on that continent was translated here into English; and much of the folklore which we think of today as the productions of Americanized Europeans consists of myths and fables handed down by Africans. The "Brer Rabbit" stories by Joel Chandler Harris show what remarkable literary treasures we have permitted to be lost to the world. A general collection of the valuable fragments of this literature would demonstrate conclusively how much this country is thus indebted to the African Negro.

The industry of the Negro in the United States may be partly explained as an African survival. The Negro is born a worker. In the African social order work is well organized. Everybody is supposed to make some contribution to the production of food and clothing necessary for the whole community. This is religiously carried out in all African communities. There were few drones in Africa until the Arab and Persian traders settled there to make their living by taking advantage of the tillers of the soil, until the Semitic nomads who drove their flocks from place to place and lived by ravaging the lands of the Africans, or until the Spanish-Moors under Juder, that mischievous horde, the scum of the earth, reached West Africa, and destroyed its social order. Thereafter many Africans had to resort to pillaging after being dispossessed of their lands.

The Africans brought to the United States did not have to be made to work as did the unprofitable white indentured servants and the untractable Indians who could not live up to the tempo set by the exploiters of the New World. The imported Africans felled the trees, drained the swamps, plowed the soil, and cultivated the staple of the country. This new factor thus laid the foundation for the wealth of a large area of the United States; and the industry of the race is still a factor in that part of the country.

From the imported African's religion and philosophy of life, most elements of interest have passed out as a result of his Europeanization. For example, until a few generations ago, the "conjure doctor" the survival in America of the African "witch doctor" was still to be seen working tricks which brought disease and death to some and health and life to others. The undue emphasis on ghosts, the return of spirits from departed bodies, and the filial faith in the intervention of the supernatural were the survivals of the African's belief in animism. Likewise in the African secret societies may be found an explanation of the Obean practices in the West Indies, the folkways of all but un-Europeanized Negroes in the backwoods of British Guiana and such cults as we still see today in South Carolina and New Orleans. The Negro has undergone Europeanization, but at the same time has tried to hold on to some things African which he has been reluctant to let go. Not in all cases have these things been commendable, but in most instances they have served to preserve what is best in a past culture.

The religion of the Negro in America today, although labeled as of European production, is still to some extent African. The Christianization of the Negro was an easy task, a much easier one for the Negro than for the European pagans, because Christianity is an Oriental cult and the Negro has an Oriental mind. The Negro brought to America did not have to be convinced that there is a supreme being. His African ancestors have always held this position. It is said, too, that the Jews in captivity in Egypt learned from Africans the unity of God. The so-called African animism and Judaism had much in common. Their ideas of creation and the dualism of good and evil are about the same. It would seem that the Hebrew ideas are variants in more intelligent form of those of Africa or that those of Africa are variants of those of Judea; but we are rather inclined to think that the parallelism is due to the fact that people under the same circumstances, though widely separated, will respond in similar fashion to the same stimuli.

The manner in which religion was administered in Africa, by the chief or by a high priest cooperating with the chief of the tribe, may have had something to do with the religious sects to which the Negroes in America have taken a liking. We often say that Negroes took over the religion of their masters, which is partly true; but there were some faiths of their masters and friends which they preferred to others. For example, some of the best friends of the Negroes were Quakers, Puritans, Catholics, and Presbyterians, and some of their masters belonged to these churches; but the Negroes went in large numbers into the Baptist churches because the mode of worship thus presented resembled more nearly that democracy in religion to which they had been accustomed in Africa. One half of the Negroes in the United States belonging to the church today are Baptists. The Methodists who count the next largest proportion may have also had certain features which to the Negroes seemed somewhat African. The extent to which Negro Baptist and Methodist churches of today differ from those of white Americans similarly labeled is due mainly to the survival of African traditions.

The spiritual experience of the Negro in Africa finds another survival in the thought of "old men for wisdom and young men for war." The old women who as matrons had charge of the age classes or societies for girls and old men who likewise functioned among the boys survived in America as the advisors in Negro communities. He or she was the one to whom they went first before they called the doctor, the lawyer, or the minister. This advisor knew the best remedies, could settle the worst disputes, and could give the best spiritual advice. As such in America this Negro figure gained the ascendancy over the minds of white persons as well as over those of Negroes. There was no quarrel in a family, no dispute in a church, no feud in a community for which this wise counsellor could not offer a solution. The home of this peculiar friend was crowded sometimes with people of both races. One leaving found the other coming; and no one left without feeling that he had been benefited by that spiritual presence and wise words. The person who thus functioned was oftener a woman than a man, for the tender sympathy and loving-kindness in the woman generally gave ascendancy to one of the female sex. However, many Negro communities had such seers of both sexes. And strange to say, too, for such services there was no charge. Why make your fellowman pay for assisting him in a time of need? That would be unjust.

Such interest as this in humanity would be a natural development from the African community based upon the idea of having all things in common. No one in that social order is extremely rich and no one extremely poor. No one suffers for anything which the community affords. There we may find also an explanation of the generosity of the Negroes of today. They are generous to a fault. While all but in the bread line they will give a part of what they have to help others. Children cast off as orphans must be provided for; illegitimate offspring, human beings in spite of their parent's misfortune, must be cared for; the burdens of the unfortunate in the struggle of life must be borne by others even when otherwise encumbered. God made them as He made others, and they are entitled to the consideration due human beings. No man must live for himself. The human race can fulfil its mission only by observing the principle of living for others. Africans built their social order on these principles, and they are still dominant even among the impecunious Negroes in America.

Sentiment, it is evident, plays a large part in the life of the Negro in Africa, and this must be taken into account in understanding the background of the present-day Negro. The Negro is naturally emotional and can become easily moved. This emotion is expressed in dance, in mimicry, in music, in art, in painting and sculpture. The plantation dances were original with the imported African slave. The European landlord had never seen such before. The Negroes' ideas of the theatre in Africa in the use of masks and the like found expression on the plantation in the minstrels popular before the Civil War and staged throughout the country as one of the greatest theatrical attractions about fifty years ago. The spirituals were expressions of the reaction of Africans to his lot in the New World. The Negro in America has not yet had the chance to develop in the fine arts. He has been forced into the education mold of practical things intended for those who are otherwise gifted.

From the same emotion comes the explanation of the oratory of the Negro. The experience of the race shows the development of the orator as a necessity. The newspaper and other printed matter have supplanted the orator among others, but not so among the Negroes even in America. Students of Africa often note how eloquently the natives can speak and how they can move their followers. In America we have seen the same among those who as spokesmen for people largely illiterate have had to move them by the spoken word. Yet they have not had to study the art of oratory. They were orators by nature, for that unusual emotion made them thus effective. "They had eyes that tears can on a sudden fill and lips to smile before the tears are gone."

PART II

CHAPTER XVIII

THE AFRICAN BACKGROUND OUTLINED

SUMMARIZING then, we may say that the African Negro, like the exterminated Mesopotamian, Greek and Roman, deserves a high place in history. No other race has achieved so much with such a little help from without as has the Negro. No other element of our population has risen to such heights in spite of so many handicaps. While there have been few agencies to help the Negroes in Africa or abroad, there have been hordes to impede their progress. In spite of all difficulties, however, the annals of this race read like beautiful romances of a people in an heroic age. The people of today detest and oppress the Negroes because they have not learned to appreciate the capacities of their neighbors of African blood.

The natives of Ethiopia first felt the impulse and produced in ancient times an advanced civilization which they passed on to predynastic Negro Egypt. The latter, overrun by migrating elements from Asia, became a melting pot with its people later becoming mulattoes classified as Negroid. While inland Ethiopia enjoyed a natural protection by its peculiar environment, Egypt, the child of Ethiopia, in the channel of world culture movements, advanced beyond its mother country and once dominated it; but the racial aspects of Ethiopia never changed to the extent to which the Negroid peoples were absorbed in Egypt and throughout North Africa. This region along the Mediterranean became the land of blacks mixed with Berbers, Jews, and Arabs.

While difficult of access for Africans the Mediterranean historians record at least infrequent contact with that continent throughout the ages. The natives in West Africa and the Sudan had a desire for the commodities brought to the shores of North America, and the Mediterranean adventurers were always anxious to tap the resources of gold in the so-called "Dark Continent." Although the trips of caravans across the desert required from forty to sixty days the fabulous rewards, which became storied, were sufficient inducement to make the painful journey across the Sahara or to brave the high seas beyond the Pillars of Hercules down the West Coast of Africa. In this way sufficient knowledge of the interior was acquired to invite the penetration of Africa on a systematic scale by Mohammedanized Asiatics. These pushed the ancient Berbers from North Africa over its slopes, across the Sahara, and down into the Sudan in the furtherance of Islam or in their quest for slaves and precious metals. Christian traders and exploiters followed in the fifteenth and sixteenth centuries to organize the slave trade along the coast, to subdue the natives, and to take possession of their continent.

We are naturally concerned, then, with the picture of the Africans prior to this upheaval. We are anxious to know what they had achieved before they were thus subdued or exterminated. These foreigners were greatly surprised to learn that the Africans had shown remarkable capacity for trade, industry, and political organization. Under Africans Kumbi (Ghana) had developed as an empire with a line of conquering and organizing princes called the *tunka,* Mansa Musa had brought the Manding (Melle) to its apogee of still greater leadership in West Africa, Sonni Ali and Askia Mohammed had made of the Songhay an empire equal in splendor to those which had sprung up in Asia and Europe. The Mossi under the same stimulus, but temporarily more fortunate than its predecessors, resisted foreign influence and built up a remarkable imperial organization incontestably African.

Briefly told, the early history of Africa is very much like that of any other continent. Just as we have learned that the Japanese, Chinese, Hindu, Assyrian, and Babylonian empires developed in Asia, and just as we have likewise surveyed the rise of Carthage, Greece and Rome, so we find their parallels in Kumbi, Manding, Songhay, and Mossi. Their history shows a social and political order which maintained the peace, provided for the public welfare, and promoted human progress. The people were healthy, industrious, happy, and long-lived. Their kingdoms and empires endured as long as the most successful of ancient and modern times.

These African kingdoms and empires, however, were of a still longer duration than were those of Europe, considered with respect to the earlier political order which developed in Asia. Carthage,

Greece, and Rome followed Mesopotamia, and so did these empires and kingdoms of Africa apparently follow in chronological order those of ancient Europe. While we speak of the ancient period as ending in Europe about the year 500 A.D., we observe that the ancient African kingdoms and empires dating from a remote period did not come to an end until Europeans were emerging from the chaos of the Middle Ages and began to produce similar disorder in Africa.

Yet, although the contemporaneous aspect is lacking, the development in ancient or medieval Africa all but parallels that of the other continents. The evolution of the family as the first unit and then that of the clan which, merged with others, made up the tribe or nation in Africa is very much like that of a similar development in early Greece and Rome, even though one was in a hot climate and the other in a temperate region. Out of this social order came feudalism in Africa just as it did elsewhere. People subjected to the same stimuli respond very much alike in spite of race or temporary influences.

In the larger organizations of kingdoms and empires in Africa we see a system of government strikingly resembling that of earlier organizations in Asia and Europe. The kings ruled with the assistance of the elders and the feudal assemblies of the people through their representatives. These rulers had a cabinet consisting of a group of ministers with carefully defined duties, and they maintained a court of the sub-vassals who ruled the smaller states or kingdoms constituting the African empires. The organization of their armies and the means of supplying the treasury by taxation did not differ widely from such methods which we observe throughout Europe and parts of Asia. This is no argument, however, that the Negroes borrowed these ideas from these people, for we have no evidence to support any such theories. We do have, however, abundant evidence of Africans carrying their ideas into the Mediterranean world to influence the course of affairs in Carthage, Greece, and Rome.

While we observe here several points of resemblance between the African political organizations and those elsewhere, we cannot fail to note also certain differences. Although the African idea of property in the ancient world was somewhat on the order of that of the village community, almost everywhere at that time, the law or custom of inheritance differed from this rule in some parts of that continent. Instead of the law of primogeniture we have the heir of the king or the heir of the chief of the family, clan, or nation, designated sometimes as the son of the sister of the defunct. This was to make sure that the heir would be one of the same tribe to which the defunct belonged. Among Africans, too, as is well brought out in the case of the Baganda people of Uganda, who have been regarded as having had the most highly developed political organization of primitive peoples, woman reached a higher status than she occupied in the ancient world in either Asia or Europe. Although among these African people a woman is not permitted to ascend the throne, next to the king the most exalted persons of the realm are his sister and his mother.

Certain other contributions among these African people, moreover, may be pointed out as exceptional achievements due to the initiative of Africans. While we find in Africa only a few evidences of such architecture as developed at the centers of civilization in Asia and Europe, we do discover remains of an advanced art on a high level. This art, the remains of which have recently been discovered and evaluated, is now supplying a new motif for such endeavors in European centers where art has reached the point of stagnation. The peculiar contribution of the Negro to art, however, is his mastery of sculptural design by which he uses art to give tone to the thing designed and to derive tone from it.

This art, too, as observed by such thinkers as Georges Hardy, can be understood only by an appreciation of the Negro's sense of religion. The two are so interwoven in the life of the race that efforts of those who, misunderstanding Africa, try to separate these manifestations, always result in wrong conclusions. This sense of religion in the Negro, therefore, is considered a contribution because it is more highly developed among the members of this race than among others. The explanation is found in the deep feeling or unusual emotion of the Negro which expresses itself with spontaneity in music, dancing, drama, folk lore, poetry, and oratory.

The Negro's philosophy of life, too, is expressed in his local literature. It is observed by persons who have lived among Africans long enough to study them from within that they thereby show considerable development of mind. In these literary productions, as crude as they may appear sometimes, there is an element of wisdom which doubtless accounts in part for the social, political, and economic order which foreigners first found in Africa. Some of these ideas, of course, would seem very much like the principles advanced by centers of thought outside of Africa, but in certain respects they show characteristics peculiar to that continent or to those people. We are undoubtedly justified in thinking of the African as having a philosophy of his own. What we now know of the African's mind indicates that a further scientific study of these people will reveal a system of thought of which we have long believed the African incapable.

The people of Africa, like those of other parts of the world, have achieved certain things which are all but earmarked as African. It is considered exceptional to point to just one outstanding achievement for which a nation may be given sole credit. We are wont to think of the Chinese as giving the world the mariner's compass, printing, and gunpowder; of the Hindus as developing a peculiar philosophy; of the Mesopotamians as exhibiting the best in architecture and government; of the Jews as teaching the unity of God and producing the Bible; and of the Phœnicians as inventing the alphabet and spreading civilization. In the same way we may list similar achievements to the credit of the Africans. Africa first developed trial by jury as a means of assuring justice to every man in keeping with the idea of loving justice and hating iniquity. Negroes in Africa first discovered iron and with it developed the industrial arts. Africans first learned to use stringed instruments to find a new means of expression for their deep emotion. Africans first domesticated the sheep, goat, and cow. Before Africans ever knew of the system of writing and printing in Europe the Vai tribe and the natives of the Cameroons produced written languages; and in our day the people of Dahomey have worked out an interesting system of writing of their own.

In the passing of Africa into foreign hands, moreover, the natives were not indifferent observers. On the contrary, they bravely defended their soil. At first the Africans followed the policy of the Romans in gradually incorporating into their kingdoms and empires the Berbers, Peuhls, Arabs, and Jews just as the Romans absorbed the Vandals, Huns, Goths, Franks, Jutes, Angles and Saxons. However, when this policy proved inadequate to deal with these hordes increased by large numbers of Moors and fanatical

Mohammedans equipped with modern weapons, the lines of the African empires yielded and suffered destruction just as Rome did. In the course of time came a reorganization of certain areas on a different basis under the control of the natives weakened by the mongrel classes which had resulted; but this political organization did not have the time to develop the power of former days before the Europeans appeared upon the West Coast with their exhausting slave trade and their agencies established to penetrate the interior and dispossess the Africans.

Still it can be said, however, that the African, reluctant to the last to yield further ground, made a creditable fight in the last stand for his native soil. The Ashanti in defense of their native land vanquished the submissive tribes between their country and the coast and defeated the British under Sir Charles McCarty in 1821. The spirit of resistance was such that the English could not make much of an inroad in the country until 1874 and did not actually conquer it until 1895. The kings of Dahomey, keeping up a fight against the French from 1842, out-manœuvered these European detachments, annihilated several of their expeditionary forces, and did not give up the struggle until they were overpowered by a more efficiently equipped army under the dashing Senegalese General Dodds in 1894.

El-Hadj Omar, a Tukulor Negro converted to Islam, which he believed should be the nucleus of a new political organization, likewise stood his ground. He arrayed himself against Europeans and their unconverted sympathizers, conquered three powerful states in eight years, and with them established an empire. Samori, a Mandingo warrior, of Wassulu, rushed into the Eastern Soudan, reduced three countries, attacked the British on the Gold Coast in 1897, outwitted the French, and for eighteen years maintained the Wassulu empire. Mamadu-Lamine, inspired by the heroic deeds of El-Hadj Omar and Samori, organized an army in 1885, fought the French and their allies on the Falémé and the Gambia, and for two years hammered away unsuccessfully at their strongholds in Africa.

Rabah, another fighter of this order, declared a holy war and defied the English in the Eastern Soudan. He took Kuti in 1883, vanquished Harshem of Bornu in 1893, defeated a French detachment under Bretonnet in 1899, and thus for eight years kept the enemy on the watch until he went down to death under superior forces in a battle at Kusseri in 1900. Mahdi, another warrior of religious fanaticism, likewise showed his mettle in taking the war-path in 1881. He defeated Rachid-Bey, governor of Fashoda, vanquished an Egyptian army in 1882, forced the surrender of Bahr-el-Ghazal in 1884, seized Omdurman in 1885, entered Khartoum a few days later, and put to death Gordon-Pasha as a public enemy in Africa. At the end of five years he had conquered four-fifths of the Egyptian Sudan.

In South Africa the same sort of opposition was encountered among the natives who disputed every inch of the ground gained by the Europeans in dispossessing them of their lands. The Kaffir-Zulus especially led this fight. "Their strategy in war and diplomacy, and politics," says a writer, "would do credit to any race; and some of their military leaders have been not inaptly compared to Cæsar." Moshesh, one of these chieftains, is still remembered for measuring arms with the Dutch and for the stratagem by which he defeated the British on Berea Mountain. Chaka, probably the most celebrated of these warriors, became widely known for the dashing figure into which he developed in these wars for his native land. "There has probably never been," says McDonald, "a more perfect system of discipline than that by which Chaka ruled his army and kingdom."

This African background of the Negro offers an explanation for many things observed today among the Negroes of America. The African, subjected to the strict control of chiefs, kings and emperors, had the tradition of being law-abiding. To this ideal the Negro has lived up consistently. With the exceptions of those charged with infractions of the law resulting from impoverishment and social repression, the Negroes constitute the most law-abiding element of our population. Because of the African's keen sense of justice he could not develop otherwise abroad. The Negro does not throw bombs; he does not start riots; he does not engage in lynching; he does not burn men at the stake. The American Negro has never assassinated a public functionary or tried to overthrow his government. Haiti, which is often cited as evidence to the contrary, has not had any more revolutions than there have been in France, to which the former owes its beginning.

In other ways African traditions have survived in America. The Negro has retained only a few words of his native tongue like *canoe, banjo, yam, goober, tobacco,* and *buckra;* but his productive imagination has preserved here a wealth of folklore. The African secret societies account for the Negro's penchant for such in this country, and fortunately he has used them as nuclei for business enterprises to stimulate the economic progress of the race. The African religion, having much in common with that of the Hebrews, facilitated the Negro's acceptance of Christianity. The village community life in Africa, requiring the production of food and the enjoyment of the harvest in common, accounts for the American Negro's generosity. He will give even when apparently he has nothing; for, according to the civilization of his ancestors, no member of the social order must suffer when others have plenty. Since everybody must be cared for everybody must work. There must be in the group no drones fleecing their fellows for a livelihood. Everybody must use the axe or the hoe. Except where the Negro has been brought under other influences in the cities he has lived up to this tradition. The Negro is still one of the most industrious elements in the United States.[1]

[1] For an introductory course on the Negro in Africa the student may use solely the chapters of this work constituting Part I together with a few important references like Maurice Delafosse's *Negroes of Africa,* the author's *Negro in Our History,* and W. E. B. Du Bois's *The Negro.* These chapters are herein given for the benefit of those who have no access to large libraries in which works on the Negro in Africa may be consulted. This brief treatment is intended also for those who may not master foreign languages sufficiently to learn from such works many important facts of Negro history which cannot be otherwise obtained. In this case the outline while followed will be merely a guide for the development of the thought on Africa—to help in presenting to the mind that entire history as a continuous panorama.

For teachers and advanced students of more mature minds and in touch with the best libraries, however, the outline of the course herein given should not only serve as a guide, but the references under the headings and subheadings should be carried out. The latest and best authorities on the various aspects are herein cited, and an effort has been made to distinguish between the biased and the scientific, between the reliable and the unreliable authorities. The reader will make a mistake in regarding these citations as lists of works to attest the erudition of the author. These bibliographical notes suggest plans and projects which must be thoroughly carried out in the advanced study of this African background.

I. AFRICA AS AN UNKNOWN LAND

II. PREHISTORIC AFRICA ABOUT 500 B.C.

1. This isolation is made clear by the study of almost any relief map of Africa showing the high plateau formation, the rivers made unnavigable by rapids or falls, and the coast without inlets. The sandy waste of the Sahara running through the northern half of the continent tells its own story of handicapping the development of that continent. This is merely a problem of geographic influence.

2. A brief reference to the authorities is found in C. G. Woodson's *Negro in Our History*, chapter i. This is further discussed in M. Delafosse's *Negroes of Africa*, pp. 21-29 and 73-74; the same author's *Haut-Sénégal-Niger, Soudan Français*, II, pp. 1-22; J. L. Monod's *Histoire de l'Afrique Occidentale Française*, pp. 52-54.

3. The particular point in such information is that the same man who writes a book on Africa in which he refers to as white every African who may not have one hundred per cent Negro blood classifies and segregates as Negro in America every one of African descent who has even one per cent of Negro blood. What most of them say about Negroes, then, is without any particular meaning or scientific value. See pages 1 to 19 of Part I. Read also Woodson's *Negro in Our History*, pp. 1-9 inclusive.

4. These are set forth in the references given above, but should be summarized under such headings as race hate, religious prejudice, snobbishness, unscientific study, traditional attitudes, exploitation of weaker races, and economic imperialism.

5. See Maurice Delafosse's *Negroes of Africa*, chapter i; J. L. Monod's *Histoire de l'Afrique Occidentale Française*, pp. 1-51; and Georges Hardy's *Vue Générale de l'Histoire d'Afrique*, pp. 1-4.

6. While many informants on Africa cannot be considered seriously when consciously trying to make a case for or against some element of the population these same authors may be taken seriously for the evidences as to the past unconsciously given. Wherein one differs from the other in matters of opinion the reader must consider the facts only and reach his own conclusions. The accounts interwoven with legends and unreasonable traditions offer no help whatever. For this reason only general trends and turning points in early African history are actually known. The scientific study of Africa has hardly had a beginning. Some Europeans like Maurice Delafosse, L. Tauxier, D. Westermann, Henri Labouret, J. P. Johnson, John Roscoe, R. S. Rattray, Emil Torday, David Randall-Maciver, and George

II. PREHISTORIC AFRICA TO ABOUT 500 B.C.—*Continued*

7. PEOPLES OF AFRICA, NEGRILLOS, NEGROES, BUSH-
   MEN, HOTTENTOTS, AND BANTU
8. STONE AGE
9. IRON AGE
10. DOMESTICATION OF ANIMALS AND PLANTS
11. AFRICAN LANGUAGE

Greenfield have addressed themselves to this task, but they do not always show the scientific attitude. Greek historians, Arab geographers, early travelers, and explorers from Europe and Asia left accounts of the coast. The interior was unknown. See Part I, chapter i.

7. These facts are presented in Part I of this volume; but for extended treatments consult the following: Herodotus, *History*, Translation of Larcher revised by Personneaux (*Paris*, 1883); E. Mercier, *Histoire de l'Afrique Septentrionale depuis les temps les plus reculés jusqu'à la conquête française* (Paris, 1888-91); Karl Peters, *Im Goldland des Altertums, Forschungen Zwischen Zambesi und Sabi* (Berlin, 1902); Dr. Poutrin, "Contribution à l'étude des Négrilles (type brachycéphale)," *L'Anthropologie*, XXI (Paris, 1910); same author, "Les Négrilles du centre Africain (type sousdolicocéphale)," *ibid.*, XXII and XXIII (Paris, 1911-1912); Dr. Jouénne, "Les monuments mégalithiques du Sénégal," in *Annaire et Mémoires du Comité d'études historiques et scientifiques de l'Afrique Occidentale Française* (Gorée, 1916-1917), and *Bulletin du Comité d'Études*, etc. (Paris, 1918). same author, "Les roches gravées du Sénégal," *Ibid.* (1920).

8. See J. P. Johnson's *The Stone Implements of South Africa*, and his *Prehistoric Period in South Africa*. Consult also Oswald Mengheim's "Die Tumbakultur und der Westafrikanische Kulturkreis," *Anthropos*, XX, 1925; pp. 516-557. This work contains interesting and valuable facts, but the author misuses them, a reviewer has said, in reaching wrong conclusions. See also I. Schapera's "Some Stylistic Affinities of Bushmen Art," in *The South African Journal of Science*, XXII, pp. 504-515. Schapera believes that the Bushmen borrowed from North Africa, and so does A. J. H. Goodwin in his "Caspian Affinities of South Africa," the same volume, pp. 428-436.

9. This is briefly discussed in Franz Boas's *Mind of Primitive Man*, p. 268; in Delafosse's *Negroes of Africa*, pp. 36, 102, and 154-155.

10. See Delafosse's *Negroes of Africa*, pp. 15-16; J. L. Monod's *Histoire de l'Afrique Occidentale Française*, page 14; *Select Discussions of the Race Problems, Atlanta University Publications*, pp. 83-85, 92.

11. Consult Delafosse's *Negroes of Africa*, pp. 12, 13, 15, 16, 19, 33, 34, 39, 197, 212, 234, 267-268, 273-274, 280. See also his *Vocabulaires Comparatifs de plus de soixante langues ou dialects parlés à la Côte d'Ivoire et dans les régions limitrophes* (Paris 1904); Sir Harry H. Johnston's *A Compara-

II. PREHISTORIC AFRICA TO ABOUT 500 B.C.—*Continued*

12. EARLY SCIENCE AND ART

III. ETHIOPIA AND EGYPT

13. ETHIOPIA AND EARLY INFLUENCE IN EGYPT
14. EGYPT IN ASCENDANCY IN NORTHEAST AFRICA

tive Study of the Bantu and Semi-Bantu Languages, two volumes (Oxford, 1919); F. Fligelman's *The Richness of African Negro Languages* (Paris, 1932); Alice Werner's *The Language Families of Africa* (London, 1925); and the numerous grammars and dictionaries of African languages therein cited.

12. The art of the Negro is succinctly presented in Delafosse's *Negroes of Africa,* chapter xiv; and in C. G. Woodson's *The Negro in Our History,* sixth edition, chapter xxxv. A detailed treatment of African art is found in Guillaume and Munro's *Primitive Negro Sculpture* (New York, 1926); Carl Einstein's *Afrikanische Plastik* (Leipzig); the same author's *Negerplastic* (München, 1920); Felix von Luschan's *Die Altertümer von Benin* (Berlin, 1912); Pitt Rivers's *Antique Works of Art from Benin* (London, 1900); Georges Hardy's *L'Art Nègre* (Paris, 1927). For early science in Africa see *Select Discussions of Race Problem,* etc., pp. 83-85.

13. The books treating Ethiopia or its successor, Abyssinia, are too numerous to mention. The time spent in perusing most of them would be lost inasmuch as they are not scientific. What these works actually say is fairly well summarized in Delafosse's *Negroes of Africa,* pp. xxx, 21, 25, 124-128, and 215. W. E. B. Du Bois discusses the same facts in *The Negro,* chapter ii. Other facts and opinions may be obtained from *A New History of Ethiopia,* by Job Ludophus (London, 1682); *Highlands of Ethiopia,* by S. Harris (London, 1844); *The Portuguese Expedition to Abyssinia,* by R. S. Whiteway; "Les Migrations des Ethiopiens," by R. Verneau, *l'Anthropologie* (Paris, 1890); *Ethiopie Méridionale,* by Jules Borelli (Paris, 1890); *Beitrage Zur Ethnographic und Anthropologie der Somali, Galla und Harrari,* by Ph. Paulitschke (Leipzig, 1886); *Second Interim Report on the Excavations at Meroe in Ethiopia,* by I J. Gastang; *Excavations,* II, *Annals of Archæology and Anthropology* (Liverpool, 1911).

14. The references given above deal with Egypt also, but for further treatment consult Du Bois's *The Negro,* chapter iii, Delafosse's *Negroes of Africa,* pp. 16, 24, 29, 33, 36, 38, 73, and 120-136. Bruce's *Voyages aux Sources du Nil et en Abyssinie pendant les années, 1763 à 1772 (Castera Translation)* gives some facts of early Egyptian history. Also Denham, Clapperton and Oudney's *Travels and Discoveries in the North and Central Parts of Africa;* Flinders Petrie's *History of Egypt;* and J. H. Breasted's *Egypt.* Most of these last-mentioned authors, however, show the usual bias. They classify as white every progressive African who has not one hundred per cent Negro blood. See also *Les Origines de la civilizations égyptienne,* by Jean Capart (Paris, 1914).

IV. CONTACTS WITH ASIA AND EUROPE

15. The Extent of Foreign Influence—Jews, Cretans, Sicilians
16. The Negro as an Enduring Factor in North-east Africa
17. The North African Melting Pot
18. Ethiopians in Yemen
19. The Greeks in North Africa

15. Consult the authorities on Egypt and Ethiopia cited above. See also M. Delafosse's "Les Hamites de l'Afrique Orientale d'après les travaux les plus récents," *L'Anthropologie*, Paris, 1894. In this article the author summarizes the opinions of those who would not give the real Negro credit for much achieved in Africa. See also the same author's "Sur Les Traces Probables de Civilization Egyptienne et d'Hommes de Race Blanche à la Côte d'Ivoire," *L'Anthropologie*, 1900. This is mainly legendary and traditional. Consult *Ethiopie Moderne* by the Comtesse de Jumilhac and the histories of Egypt given under 14.

16. This is largely a problem of ethnology and ethnography. Were the Negroes in North Africa absorbed or did they absorb others? Such works as Guillam's *Voyage à la Côte Orientale d'Afrique* (Paris, 1846-1848) and the same author's *Documents sur l'histoire, la géographie, et le commerce de l'Afrique Orientale* (Paris, 1848) should be perused. See Job Ludolphus's *New History of Ethiopia* (London, 1682), and W. S. Harris's *Highlands of Ethiopia* (London, 1844). All scientific treatments of the races of North and East Africa will supply helpful facts. Consult also pictures, paintings and monuments of these people.

17. The factors in the remaking of North Africa from the earliest period down to the present time are discussed in C. A. Julien's *Histoire de l'Afrique du Nord* (Paris, 1931). For a detailed treatment one should consult Stéphane Gsell's eight volumes of *Histoire Ancienne de l'Afrique du Nord*. Consult R. Verneau's "La Prétendue Parenté des Négroïdes Européens et des Boschmans," *L'Anthropologie*, 1925; J. Matiegka's "Negroid Hair in Central Europe," *L'Anthropologie*, VIII, 1929, pp. 108-118.

18. See R. Verneau's "Les Migrations des Ethiopiens," *L'Anthropologie*, Paris, 1899, and Delafosse's *Negroes of Africa*, pp. 125-127. Study carefully also the map of Africa with respect to other parts.

19. These facts are set forth in references already given with respect to informants on Africa and foreign influences there. The *History of Herodotus* (Larcher Translation) is the best source. Delafosse has summarized this in his *Haut-Sénégal-Niger*, II, pp. 4, 6, in connection with other claims of foreign invasions. Monod has done the same in his *Histoire de l'Afrique Occidentale Française*, pp. 39-40. The trade, the main reason for such contact, however, should be the chief point here as emphasized in Lady Lugard's *Tropical Dependency*, pp. 3-13.

IV. CONTACTS WITH ASIA AND EUROPE—*Continued*

V. THE EMPIRE OF KUMBI-KUMBI (GHANA)

20. See Delafosse's *Negroes of Africa*, pp. 8-9, 25, 32-36; also Monod's *Histoire de l'Afrique Occidentale Française*, pp. 38-39. These authors summarize what is said by many others already cited.

21. In the work of Delafosse just cited, on pages 39-41, and in that of Monod mentioned with it above, pages 28-29, the same sort of summary is given with respect to the contacts of Africans and Romans.

22. The contact of the Mohammedans with Africans was a long-drawn-out process traced through numerous sources. Es-Sadi's *Tarikh Es-Soudan* (Houdas's Translation, Paris, 1898) and Mahmoud Kati's *Tarikh El-Fettach* (Houdas's and Delafosse's Translation, 1913) give the story from the Mohammedanized natives' point of view. E. W. Blyden's *Islam, Christianity and the Negro* is stimulating. George W. Ellis's *Negro Culture in West Africa* (New York, 1914), on pp. 67, 85, 95, 97, 99, 100, 105, 108, 113, 122, 125, 126, 128 refers to the movement. Briefer and more succinct treatments may be consulted. From the usual European point of view one will find Delafosse's *Negroes of Africa* adequate, especially pp. 85, 93, 106, 109, 112, 127, 214, and 265. See also Monod's *Histoire*, pp. 77-80.

23. See Delafosse's *Negroes of Africa*, pp. 42, 44, 48-54, 56, 61; and Monod's *Histoire*, pp. 73-77. This particular aspect takes up a considerable part of Lady Lugard's *Tropical Dependency*.

24. For the biased attitude with respect to Kumbi-Kumbi (Ghana) read the chapter on this country in Lady Lugard's *A Tropical Dependency*. For a little less biased account see Delafosse's *Negroes of Africa*, pp. 42-54, 144-145, 269-270; and Monod's *Histoire*, pp. 54-61. See also Delafosse's *Haut-Sénégal-Niger, Soudan Français*, II, pp. 20-59. The African himself has not yet told his own story in modern language. That the foreigners who have written thereupon have not said the last word is evident from the fact that they disagree; and the one attacks the other, as the works herein cited show.

25. The most picturesque and, at the same time, biased presentation of the Kumbi-Kumbi (Ghana) political organization is found in the work of Lady Lugard, cited above, pp. 110-116. The other writers cited herein, Delafosse and Monod, approach the task with more objectivity. The works of Arab travelers give incomplete descriptions because of imperfect observations and inevitable confusion of places, persons, and periods. Delafosse and

V. THE EMPIRE OF KUMBI-KUMBI (GHANA)—*Continued*

VI. SMALLER KINGDOMS FROM THE RUINS OF KUMBI-KUMBI (GHANA)

Monod have endeavored to eliminate most of their inconsistent and self-contradictory accounts.

26. Consult the references given in 24. See also W. E. B. Du Bois, *The Negro*, pp. 50-52. The eleventh chapter of Lady Lugard's *Tropical Dependency* is devoted altogether to "The Trade of Ghana."

27. These first steps either as a result of the author's imagination or of additional data are set forth in the account of Kumbi-Kumbi (Ghana) given in Lady Lugard's *Tropical Dependency*. The same is traced also by Delafosse, depending mainly on the accounts of the annalists and travelers from Asia herein noted.

28. See Monod's *Histoire*, pp. 56-57; and Delafosse's *Negroes of Africa*, pp. 42-43.

29. Monod's *Histoire*, pp. 55-58; and Delafosse's *Negroes of Africa*, pp. 47-48.

30. The works of Travelers from Arabia are the best sources here. See *Ibn Haukal Description de l'Afrique;* Bekri's *Description de l'Afrique Septentrionale;* Edrissi's *Description de l'Afrique et de l'Espagne;* Yakut's *Geographisches Wörterbuch;* Ibn Batuta's *Voyage dans le Soudan;* and Ibn Khaldun's *Prolégiomènes historiques.*

31. These smaller states are briefly treated in Monod's *Histoire*, pp. 61 to 77; and in Delafosse's *Negroes of Africa*, pp. 54-56. In the case of Monod's *Histoire* it must be noted that this author is mainly concerned with the smaller settlements of so-called "whites" in Africa, and he devotes more space thereto than to the kingdoms and empires of the natives who dominated these infiltrating elements. Here the European bias of the author is apparent, sometimes even to the point of becoming self-contradictory. Detailed accounts of these nations and cities have been produced by persons chiefly concerned with local studies. See the bibliography in Delafosse's *Negroes of Africa*, chapter iii.

32. In addition to what is said about Soso in the reference in 31, consult Delafosse's *Haut-Sénégal-Niger*, I, pp. 228, 261, 265, 268; II, pp. 27, 55, 56, 155, 158, 162-170; and III, p. 180.

VI. SMALLER KINGDOMS FROM THE RUINS OF KUMBI-KUMBI (GHANA)—*Continued*

VII. THE RISE OF THE MANDING EMPIRE (MELLE)

33. Consult Delafosse's *Haut-Sénégal-Niger*, I, pp. 165, 226, 227, 228, 253, 262, 265, 267, 277, 289, 319, 320, 322; II, pp. 27, 41, 55, 91, 165, 207, 214, 301, 307, 354, 355, 358, 359, 383, 384, 385, 389, 400, 401, 402.

34. Delafosse's *Negroes of Africa*, p. 17; his *Haut-Sénégal-Niger*, I, p. 119, and Monod's *Histoire* pp. 66-70.

35. Delafosse, *Negroes of Africa*, pp. 49-54; Monod's *Histoire*, pp. 70-77; Lugard's *A Tropical Dependency*, pp. 107-112.

36. Delafosse's *Negroes of Africa*, pp. 32-33, 48-54, 90-92, 104-108, 120-122; Monod's *Histoire*, pp. 77-80; and Lugard's *Tropical Dependency*, pp. 106-116.

37. See Delafosse's *Negroes of Africa*, pp. 59-67, 74-76; Monod's *Histoire*, pp. 80-93; Lugard's *Tropical Dependency*, pp. 117-152. For a more extensive account consult Delafosse's *Haut-Sénégal-Niger*, II, pp. 173 to 219.

38. This is treated in the references above. However, it should be noted that Monod in his *Histoire* carefully treats by epochs the rule of the Keitas as distinguished from the subsequent period of the Mansas. The achievements under Sun-Diata, Sakura, and Gonga Musa respectively are given in detailed fashion as herein outlined.

39. All the authors herein quoted enlarge upon the organization of the Manding empire, but the best exposition is found in Delafosse's *Haut-Sénégal-Niger*, II, pp. 197-201. Delafosse leans heavily, however, on Ibn Batuta's account, which is not generally accessible.

40. The best accounts of the economic conditions are given by travelers like Ibn Batuta (*Description*, etc.), Ibn Khaldun (*Description*, etc.), and Leo Africanus (*Travels*); but for a brief statement based upon these sources the references given in 37 will suffice.

41. Islamization here may be traced in the references already given; but it must be noted that while it had about the same effect in the long run in

VII. THE RISE OF THE MANDING EMPIRE (MELLE)
—*Continued*

VIII. THE RISE OF THE SONGHAY EMPIRE

one place as it had in another, its influence on political developments was not the same everywhere because it was not introduced throughout Africa at the same time. While some of the African natives accepted Islam others opposed the faith of the Prophet. Because of a later introduction in some places it was uprooted by Europeans before it became generally accepted.

42. Here it is necessary to note the policies of Gonga Musa in contrast to those of his successors. Yet the personal element must not be over-emphasized. The external conditions obtaining during his reign must be compared with those obtaining under his successors. Most of the writers herein quoted failed to observe these differences. The student must see many things at the same time.

43. Approached in the manner suggested above, it becomes easy to account for the decline of the Manding. What is said in the *Tarikh Es-Soudan* and the *Tarikh El-Fettach* may be taken seriously with the reservation that these writers, although black natives, were Mohammedan partisans; and so were most travelers herein referred to. Very little of this so-called African history is of local record. Most of it is foreign narrative made to order.

44. The entire story of this empire is told by Lady Lugard in a biased but romantic fashion in the chapter on the Songhay in *A Tropical Dependency*. The same history is presented in a more expository fashion by Delafosse in his *Haut-Sénégal-Niger, Soudan Français,* pp. 60-121. A briefer statement is given in the same author's *Negroes of Africa*, pp. 74-88; and in Monod's *Histoire*, pp. 93-104.

45. The Songhay empire in its beginning and as a dependency is discussed in the works cited in the note above and in those referring to the Manding Empire. The student, however, should observe the bias running through these productions. Where the authors failed to find any facts to support the claims of European influence or Asiatic origin they invariably fell back on legends to make it appear that the credit for these foundations of a desirable political and social order belongs to some imaginary "white" element of whom they failed to find any trace in Africa. This bias must be kept in mind throughout this study.

46. Sonni Ali, the conqueror, is likewise treated by these biased writers. The estimate of this man should be based on what he actually did and not upon what his traducers said about him. The lustre of Sonni Ali is sometimes dimmed by the Mohammedan writers because he did not particularly

VIII. THE RISE OF THE SONGHAY EMPIRE—*Continued*

47. ASKIA MOHAMMED AS A STATESMAN
48. GAO, TIMBUCTOO, AND JENNE, CITY-STATES
49. THE IMPERIAL ADMINISTRATION
50. WEALTH AND SPLENDOR
51. LEARNING AND RELIGION

espouse their religion, and European writers, taking their cue from them, have perpetuated this traditional attitude toward a great ruler.

47. Askia Mohammed should be contrasted with Sonni Ali as Augustus was with Cæsar. The one as a warrior conquered the then neighboring lands, and the other as a statesman held the lines thus established and organized the empire. Askia Mohammed was not as stern and fiery as Sonni Ali; and as the successor of the conqueror he did not need to be so. Sonni Ali made Askia Mohammed possible. The career of Askia Mohammed has been put in story form by Miss Gollock in *Eminent Africans*. Delafosse pays him high tribute as a statesman while carefully noting that he was a black man. His record is found in all creditable works on West Africa.

48. Gao, Timbuctoo, and Jenne deserve special mention as city-states themselves. It should be borne in mind, however, that Timbuctoo was never the capital of the Songhay empire. Gao had that distinction. It has been said that Timbuctoo was begun as trading post by Semites or Arabs; but it is clear that when the Songhay expanded over that area and took over the place it was not of much consequence. It was Askia Mohammed who rebuilt Timbuctoo and beautified it with imposing mosques and palaces. The description of it is given in European fashion by Felix DuBois in his *Timbuctoo the Mysterious*. Accounts of Jenne and Timbuctoo may be found in Monod's *Histoire*, pages 136 to 145. Lady Lugard says much about Gao, Jenne and Timbuctoo in her characteristic fashion, but everything she says should not be taken seriously.

49. The administration of the Songhay Empire is outlined in the sources herein given. The task at this juncture, however, is to compare this plan of government with that observed in Kumbi-Kumbi (Ghana) and in the Manding. Did one show an improvement over the other? Did one learn from the other? This administration, too, should be compared with that of Assyria or Rome.

50. The best sources for the wealth and splendor of the Songhay are the works of Ibn Khaldun, Leo the African, Bekri, Edrissi, Ibn Haukal, Es-Sadi and Mahmud Kati. Since these are not available in small libraries some students can do no more than to use with discretion the other accounts herein cited.

51. The stimulus given to learning by Askia Mohammed after the so-called scholarly class had been discouraged by Sonni Ali is already presented in sources cited. However, the main task here is to understand what was considered an educated man in those days or the difference between learning at that time and learning of today. A comparison of the educated man of Africa with the educated man of Europe or Asia at that time will facilitate

VIII. THE RISE OF THE SONGHAY EMPIRE—*Continued*

IX. THE MOSSI STATES IN ASCENDANCY

the understanding of the African civilization. Was Africa behind the procession?

52. The decline of the Songhay under the successors of Askia Mohammed is given in the characteristic fashion by Lady Lugard in the chapter on the Songhay, but the story is given in a more satisfactory manner by Delafosse as referred to above. Felix DuBois, in his *Timbuctoo the Mysterious,* yields to his emotions in telling the same part of this story. Compare the decline of Rome with that of the Songhay. Were the causes of decline the same?

53. The fall of the Songhay for reasons already observed should be studied mainly from the point of view of its consequences. What was the effect of this collapse of the political and social order on the people of West Africa? On the Sudan? How did it influence the course of trade, industry, religion, and learning? In what way was Europe thereby influenced?

54. The best brief statement of the rise and development of the Mossi States is found in Monod's *Histoire,* pp. 104 to 112. Additional facts and more extended treatment are given in Delafosse's *Haut-Sénégal-Niger, Soudan Français, II,* chapter iv. The account in Delafosse's *Negroes of Africa,* pp. 67 to 72, is inadequate. Various aspects of the Mossi people have been discussed in detail by Louis Tauxier in his *Le Noir du Soudan* (Paris, 1912); *Le Noir de Yatenga* (Paris, 1917), *Études Soudanaises* (Paris, 1925), *Les Nègres Gouro et Gagou* (Paris, 1924), *Le Noir du Bondoukou* (Paris, 1921; and *Nouvelles Notes sur les Mossi et Gourounsi* (Paris, 1931).

55. The rôle played by a family in the rise of these states may be compared with the history of other nations thus developed in Europe and Asia. A sort of unity in political organization may be considered apparent.

56. Likewise one may study the relations of the first three kingdoms which formed the nucleus of the Mossi Empire. The wise policies of one, and the mistakes or misfortunes of the others may lead to an understanding of their virtues and shortcomings; and these when compared with developments elsewhere may seem but natural rather than exceptions in the case of Africa, as biased misinformants often say.

57. The merging of the three kingdoms together with two others added to form an empire should be contrasted with the methods employed in build-

IX. THE MOSSI STATES IN ASCENDANCY—*Continued*

ing other empires in Africa and with the development of political organization in Asia and Europe. The factors contributing to the ascendancy of one of these kingdoms emerging with an overlordship over the others should be carefully noted.

58. In the explanation of matters already noted will be clarified certain traditions of the Mossi. Resisting foreign influences longer than others in Africa and holding on to the best in their past, the Mossi demonstrated what Africans without help can do. Yet the parallels noted between their institutions and those of their neighbors demonstrate how little resulted from the so-called contributions of foreigners to state building in Africa. The foreign element blocked the progress of political organization in Africa and contributed to the destruction of the states already developed.

59. The comparison may be carried further in the examination of the plan of government which the Mossi followed. While some of the provisions seem strange and undesirable today, the Mossi surpassed most other states in the matter of administering justice. Other powers might be delegated to lieutenants, but so great was the desire to give every man justice that the emperor himself supervised this particular department of the government. Among the Mossi there was the custom of a jury service.

60. The Mossi Empire, more successful than others in duration, requires special study. What were the traditions or customs of the people which contributed to its success? Were the Mossi people informed as to the pitfalls of others and determined to avoid them? Or was the course of things worked out altogether in keeping with the customs of the country? These questions are not answered in the sources herein cited, but Monod in his *Histoire*, p. 112, attempts an explanation. Some help may be obtained also from Louis Tauxier's *Nouvelles Notes sur le Mossi et le Gourounsi* (Paris, 1931), chapters i and ii. It will be better, however, for the student to study the matter thoroughly and decide for himself.

61. The infringement upon the Mossi was as natural as that upon any other state in that part of Africa. The matter of concern here is how the Mossi met the aggressor or what the attacking hordes found here and did not find elsewhere. The time of these attacks in contradistinction to invasion in other parts may facilitate the understanding of this situation. The location of the Mossi with respect to the attacking forces will prove to be further helpful in grasping the full picture of the participants in this African drama.

62. It is remarkable that in reduced form the Mossi state still exists. What is the title of the present ruler? To what European power is this kingdom subject? What authority does the ruler of the modern Mossi

IX. THE MOSSI STATES IN ASCENDANCY—*Continued*

X. THE AFNO (HAUSA) STATES AND BORNU

exercise under his foreign overlord? What is the area of the present terri-tory thus administered?

63. The hisory of the Afno (Hausa) States is summarized in Monod's *Histoire*, pp. 116-118. Delafosse in his *Negroes of Africa*, pp. 104-109, gives the same story with a few more ramifications. The same author gives parts of the story here and there in his general treatment of the *Haut-Sénégal-Niger (Soudan Français)*. What Lady Lugard says about this country in *A Tropical Dependency* needs to be checked with data from the more recent studies. The origin of these states is accounted for mainly in legendary fashion. A study of the remains of antiquity there, however, may furnish a clue to the understanding of the early history of the Afno people. Investi-gators have found sufficient evidence to support the conclusion that the origin belongs to the remote past. While these states did not grow into large empires they have continued to exist for many centuries.

64. The peculiar customs of these people, their situation with respect to the outer world, or the economic foundations of their social order—some such influences account for the lack of bonds of union sufficiently strong for the cohesion discovered elsewhere. Yet in spite of the lack of unification these units did have at times sufficient in common to support a confederation. What was the nature of this central government? What powers did it exercise? What powers were delegated to or reserved by the members of the confederation?

65. What was the rôle of the Kantas of Kebbi? What difference in the situation did their efforts make? Account for their successes. Were they on the right way to imperial organization? Why did they fail to attain it? Monod in his *Histoire* emphasizes especially the work of the Kantas.

66. The defense of Hausa, like that of other states below the status of the imperial domains, requires explanation. While this country could not compare with its powerful neighbors it often contrived to defend its frontiers. Is the explanation of this to be found in the Afno people or in the policies of their hostile neighbors? Does Islam constitute a factor here?

67. Out of a study of the history of the entire Sudan will come an explanation of the ultimate independence of the Afno people. While some authors try to set off the story of these states by itself it can be understood only by comprehending the whole theatre in which these organizations played their part. Delafosse undertakes to do this in his *Haut-Sénégal-Niger, Soudan Français*, in treating these particular states along with others, but he fails to make this clear.

X. THE AFNO (HAUSA) STATES AND BORNU—*Continued*

68. How Bornu Differed from the Afno (Hausa) States
69. The Organization of Bornu under the Tedas
70. Bornu under the Kanembu Dynasty
71. The Work of Idris Aloama
72. The Successors of Idris Aloama

XI. THE DESTRUCTION OF AFRICAN KINGDOMS AND EMPIRES

73. The Covetousness of Foreigners

68. It is well to note that while the Afno (Hausa) and the Bornu were contiguous and subjected to all but the same natural environment they differed greatly in other respects. One of the most striking differences was the racial composition of the people. The one was chiefly a native population and the other had an infusion of foreign blood. Did the racial difference make a difference in the course things took in that region? The account of Lugard in chapters on Hausa and Bornu in *A Tropical Dependency* raises this question. The story as given by Monod in his *Histoire*, pp. 118 to 120, and by Delafosse in his *Negroes of Africa*, pp. 105 to 114, fails to clear up this matter. It is advisable, however, to read the entire second volume of Delafosse's *Haut-Sénégal-Niger, Soudan Français*.

69. The study of the organization of Bornu under the Tedas may offer further opportunity for the comparison of these nuclei of states. The sources for this particular line of rulers, however, are meager; and it is not advisable to posit anything on legends and traditions.

70. For the events transpiring under the Kanembu dynasty we have more reliable accounts from the authors herein cited. Consult also C. H. Robinson's *Hausaland* (London, 1896); and R. C. Slatin-Pacha's *Fire and Sword in the Soudan* (translated by F. R. Wingate, 5th edition, London, 1897).

71. The work of Idris Aloama comes as a sort of climax of supreme effort at state-building in Bornu; but the fact that his efforts did not have the success of men of such ability elsewhere must be accounted for in a thorough examination of his career. The sources already noted supply what information has been made available. It seems that he was a great man without the great success of less efficient men elsewhere. Account for this.

72. Likewise the weakness or inefficiency of the successors of Idris Aloama must be determined. These rulers evidently had some virtues. Was the explanation in the rulers themselves or in the times during which they served? The mere noting that a king or emperor failed does not do him justice. Islam had long been in the picture. Had the Europeans complicated matters?

73. The accounts of the raids of covetous foreigners and the immigrations and migrations resulting from the pressure from European and Asiatic centers are much more numerous than those dealing with the ancient natives of Africa. In fact, the works of Ibn Batuta, Ibn Khaldun, Ibn Haukal,

XI. THE DESTRUCTION OF AFRICAN KINGDOMS AND EMPIRES—*Continued*

74. Immigrations and Migrations
   a. Berbers
   b. Peuhls
   c. Arabs
   d. Moroccans
   e. Agents of Islam, Almoravides, Prophets with Holy Wars
   f. Dislocation of African Tribes
75. The Resulting Race Admixture

Bekri, Yakut, and Edrissi deal primarily with these migrants and immigrants with whom these travelers themselves were identified. These informants knew more about these movements than about other matters. Of the details we need not be concerned, but it should be noted that the first of these interlopers in Africa were the weaker or the less desirable elements dislodged by their superiors in North Africa, Asia, or Europe, and forced to seek asylum elsewhere. A large number of them were nomads who undertook to live on the country by pillaging Africans attached to the soil and living in peace and comfort.

74. In some cases, probably like that of the Berbers and Peuhls, the process was one of infiltration, gradually entering the area below the Sahara without disturbing the peace of the Africans and occupying the unsettled, sparsely populated fringe on the southern edge of that desert. But in the case of the Arabs, the Moroccans, and the prophets of Islam like the Almoravides, the country was often destroyed root and branch to secure slaves and soldiers or to impose upon the natives the faith of the Prophet. This story is well told throughout Delafosse's *Negroes of Africa,* but it is not made clear in Monod's adaptation of Delafosse's work in the *Histoire de l'Afrique Occidental Française.* Monod is inclined to think of Islam as a blessing as well as an evil, although he does say (on p. 126) the Moroccan *pachas* of Timbuctoo gave a death blow to Sudanese civilization. Delafosse's more elaborate account in the second volume of his *Haut-Sénégal-Niger* is a more satisfactory source. Islam is treated throughout this work.

75. The inevitable result of such immigrations or migrations was race admixture. These people had religious prejudice but no race hate. Miscegenation ensued naturally, especially after the blacks began to accept Islam. The extent of this race admixture is best determined by a study of the present-day mixed breeds of that region. Outnumbered by the blacks, these foreigners were easily absorbed while leaving the Africans about as black as they were before. The Europeans writing on Africa confuse matters by referring to these all but perfectly black people as being "white" because a small percentage of white blood has been lost among them. In the United States they would be thought of only as Negroes and dealt with unceremoniously.

XI. THE DESTRUCTION OF AFRICAN KINGDOMS AND EMPIRES—*Continued*

76. AFRICAN NATIVES DIVIDED BY RELIGION
77. THE HORRORS OF WAR FOR SLAVES

XII. SURVIVALS IN AFRICA

78. THE PASHAS OF TIMBUCTOO
79. THE RISE OF THE BAMBARA KINGDOM OF SEGU

76. Another result from these movements was a division of opinion in matters of religion. Some Negroes of Africa readily accepted Islam and fought in their holy wars for the propagation of the faith, as told by Delafosse in his *Negroes of Africa* (pp. 32-33, 90-92, 104-108, 214-220), while others fearlessly opposed it. This, of course, broke the ties which had once been strong bonds of union in Africa. The religious question, further complicated by the introduction of Christianity, is still a handicap to Africa.

77. The Mohammedans, uniting religion and slavery, sought human beings in Africa. The Christian slave traders following in their footsteps did the same sort of man-hunting to secure cheap labor for the mines and plantations in America. Both Mohammedans and Christians stirred up wars among the natives for this purpose. The Mohammedan slave trade, however, has been purposely exaggerated. The number of slaves thus carried away captive may be estimated by the number of Negroes or their descendants as mixed breeds in Mohammedan countries. Considered with the evidences of such in the Western Hemisphere there can be no comparison of the two traffics. The extent of the traffic in the Orient has been discussed by J. H. Johnston as "The Mohammedan Slave Trade" in the thirteenth volume, pages 478 to 491, of the *Journal of Negro History*. The American or European slave trade may be traced in numerous sources with which the student is already familiar, such as John R. Spears's *The American Slave Trade,* T. K. Ingram's *History of Slavery and Serfdom,* T. F. Buxton's *The African Slave Trade,* Thomas Clarkson's *History of the Abolition of the African Slave Trade,* and W. E. B. Du Bois's *The Suppression of the African Slave Trade.*

78. Survivals of the destroying period may be summarized under settlements of the invaders themselves. Some of these endured in spite of the fact that they were self-exterminating. The Berbers or Lybians pressed down on the natives and the Peuhls upon the Berbers. Then came Moroccans to upset all. Finally came organized Islam with prophets proclaiming holy wars on all who would not believe. The *pashas* of Timbuctoo in spite of the undesirable crowd which they represented contrived to exist for a century or more by paying tribute first to one and then to another army sent by an overpowering nation to pillage that city. Gao and Jenne, however, were not so successful. Why? At one time these three cities were of about equal splendor.

79. Certain forces working toward the cohesion of states, moreover, still endured. The rise of the Bambara Kingdom of Segu may be thus accounted for. The story is briefly told in Monod's *Histoire,* pp. 126-129; in Delafosse's *Negroes of Africa,* pp. 88-91. In the last-named author's *Haut-Sénégal-Niger, Soudan Français,* II, chapter xi, the details are given. In

XII.　SURVIVALS IN AFRICA—*Continued*

XIII.　EUROPEAN COMMERCIAL EXPANSION INTO AFRICA

this source is the extensive account of the Tukulor conqueror, El-Hadj Omar, with numerous ramifications.

80. The student will hardly fail to see the rise of Biton Kulubali as a great conqueror somewhat on the order of Sonni Ali, but one must bear in mind that the story of his predecessors is not yet known. What foundation they left for him to build on or what he owed to their genius is not known to writers of modern nations. We simply know that part of the history which happens to be recorded by the original annalists relying upon the authorities herein cited.

81. The successors of Biton Kulubali did not live up to the tempo of their predecessor. Here, however, the situation from the international point of view must be noted to discover the actual causes of the decline within or without the kingdom. In the brief treatment given by most writers these successors are disposed of too dogmatically. In Delafosse's *Haut-Sénégal-Niger*, cited above, a better grasp of the situation is possible.

82. The rise of the kingdom of Bambara of the Masasi is given in Monod's *Histoire*, pp. 130-132. In Delafosse's *Negroes of Africa* the sketch is too brief to be useful. Resort is necessary then to his larger work *Haut-Sénégal-Niger, Soudan Français*, II, chapter xi, and to Ch. Monteil's *Bambara*, passim.

83. The work of the Masa was the impulse to efficiency and cohesion which made the new kingdom possible. The sources are the same as those given in 82. It should be noted, however, that this kingdom, branching from another in the seventeenth century, endured almost to the present. To account for this longevity is the problem for the student.

84. It is also a problem to figure out how a political organization thus launched with vitality declined in new hands and fell before the conqueror. Was this kingdom as well preserved as others of that area? Or did it suffer the common fate of all before the overpowering hordes? The work of Ch. Monteil is our best answer to these queries; but he writes only from the European point of view and leaves untold much which he, as a member of a nation participating in the downfall, could not say.

85. The Crusades connect closely with Africa. One of these expeditions was directed chiefly to that continent. From the point of view of being

XIII. EUROPEAN COMMERCIAL EXPANSION INTO AFRICA—*Continued*

86. AFRICA AND THE RENAISSANCE

87. EXPLORERS WITH NEW METHODS LOOKING FOR NEW ROUTES AND NEW COMMODITIES

88. THE DREAM OF WEALTH FROM GOLD DUST AND SLAVES

directed against the Seljukian Turks who were finding their way to Africa these movements as a whole are significant. As a result of the spread of Islam by these agencies the gateways for others to Africa were closed and its progress was thereby impeded. This is fully accounted for by Lady Lugard (*Tropical Dependency,* pp. 296-321) and others treating the civilizations in Africa likewise note this effect. See also Du Bois's *The Negro,* pp. 57-58.

86. The movements affecting Europe during the thirteenth, fourteenth and fifteenth centuries, commonly known as the Renaissance, had no beginning among African peoples who had such a little contact with the outer world. Indirectly, however, through contact with points along the northern shore, Africa even in the interior had some knowledge of what was revolutionizing the world. One of the conspicuous events of the Renaissance was the commercial expansion for which Africa with the exception of America proved to be the most important field. This story of men in quest of new routes, new commodities and new methods of commerce is told in every history of Europe. For the African angle of it, however, the best accounts are the *Cambridge Modern History* (*North Africa*), Stone's *Reformation and Renaissance,* and C. A. Julien's *Histoire de l'Afrique du Nord;* but these show only general trends which in affecting the whole world indirectly concerned North Africa.

87. The knowledge gained by the Crusades stimulated travel and trade. Africa became also an object of exploration. Cut off by the attitude of the Barbary States under the Turks, Europeans could touch the continent only on the West Coast. From points there they began their trading. See T. F. Buxton's *The African Slave Trade* (London, 1816); Thomas Clarkson's *History of the Abolition of the African Slave Trade* (London, 1808); and Carlton J. H. Hayes's *Political and Social History of Modern Europe* (New York, 1919), I, pp. 17-19, 43-49, 62-69.

88. The stimulus to active trading was the desire to become rich with little effort. This is noted in all histories dealing with the commercial revolution. The records left by the Arabian travelers and authors herein cited present vividly exactly what the uninformed thought of Africa. The point to be noted, however, is that in spite of some disillusionment these ideas persisted, and the outside world today thinks of Africa as a rich land. This part of the story is told in an all but popular vein by Sir Charles Lucas in his *Partition of Africa* and Lady Lugard in *A Tropical Dependency* (pp. 322-355). Many other authors may be consulted, but few of them deal with the interior of Africa, for little of it was then known.

XIII. EUROPEAN COMMERCIAL EXPANSION INTO AFRICA—*Continued*

89. EUROPEANS STIR UP TRIBAL WARS TO SECURE CAPTIVES AS SLAVES
90. THE INTERNATIONAL CONFLICTS
91. FINAL SETTLEMENTS ALONG THE WEST COAST
92. THE OPERATIONS OF COMMERCIAL CORPORATIONS

XIV. THE LAST STAND IN WEST AFRICA

93. ISLAM ALLIED WITH NATIVE AFRICANS

89. The Africans, as the sources quoted will show, were peacefully attached to the soil, but Asiatics and later Europeans divided them on the question of religion, cheated them in exchanging gewgaws for gold dust and slaves, and encouraged them to engage in raids and pillaging to obtain these attractive commodities brought to the coast.   This story is told by three volumes of the original records themselves compiled by Elizabeth Donnan as *Documents Illustrative of the Slave Trade;* and by Ruth A. Fisher's *Records of the African Companies.*

90. The international conflicts in which slavery was a prominent factor would include almost all European wars up to the nineteenth century but mainly from 1689 to 1763. This conflict is well interpreted by Carlton J. H. Hayes in his first volume of *A Social and Political History of Modern Europe* (New York, 1919). Many other European and American historians may be consulted, but their works show little connection with Africa. The treaties closing these wars show how conspicuous Africa was in those conflicts.

91. The settlements finally brought under permanent control of various European nations and remaining mainly so until the close of the World War may be traced in Delafosse's *Negroes of Africa*, passim. The maps in this volume help to illuminate the narrative. Charles Lucas's *Partition of Africa* is also serviceable. Monod's *Histoire* is informing primarily with respect to France.

92. For a statement of the commercial companies see Donnan, *op. cit.* Consult also the second volume of Channing's *History of the United States,* John R. Spear's *The American Slave Trade,* and George F. Zook's *Royal Adventurers Trading into Africa.* Any creditable work on the African slave trade covers this ground.

93. Islam and the Negro is well covered from the philosophical point of view by E. W. Blyden in his *Islam, Christianity, and the Negro* (London, 1888). George W. Ellis's *Negro Culture in West Africa* (New York, 1914) makes a few references to this situation under the caption "Islamic Faith among the Vais." Delafosse, in his *Negroes of Africa*, treats the same briefly also under the caption "Islamization," on pp. 32-33, 41, 48, 57, 67, 71, 90-92, 104-108, 110, 113, 115, and 214-215. It will be noted that Islam after becoming established in Africa fought European invaders.

XIV. THE LAST STAND IN WEST AFRICA—*Continued*
    94. THE TUKULOR EMPIRE OF EL-HADJ OMAR
    95. SAMORI, THE FOUNDER OF THE WASULU EMPIRE
    96. MAMADU LAMINE AS A DIE-HARD LEADER
    97. THE PENETRATION OF THE SUDAN
    98. THE PASSING OF GUINEA AND THE GOLD COAST

XV. SMALLER KINGDOMS WHICH ENDURED
    99. REORGANIZATION OF LOCAL UNITS ON A SMALLER
        SCALE

94. The stand taken by the Negro against the European occupation is neglected by European writing on Africa. Delafosse comes nearer than the others in treating especially the rise of El Hadj Omar in *Negroes of Africa*, pp. 90-93. Elsewhere in his volume, although he says less about other African patriots than about the one just mentioned, the author does concede that it was commendable for them thus to defend their soil. As a rule, European writers refer to these warriors in the most scathing terms. They are branded as cruel, despotic, and tyrannical because they would not yield their native soil without a struggle. See Monod's *Histoire*, pp. 229-253, 256-315. Consult also Delafosse's *Haut-Sénégal-Niger*, II, pp. 380-418.

95. Samori is mentioned to be commended or condemned in all the references to European writers given under the heading above, but he is given a slightly more sympathetic treatment by A. Mevil in his *Samory* (Paris, 1899). Gilbert d'Alem has covered this romantically in his *Madame Samory* (Paris, 1924). These writers, however, tend to follow what is said about Samori by Binger. The "griots" of the Sudan still sing of Samori as a hero.

96. The rise and fall of Mamadu Lamine is related briefly by Monod in his *Histoire*, pp. 250-253. This warrior is mentioned also by others as a conqueror who took the field against the French. While this patriot did not last long his career shows how difficult it was to make the Africans yield their ground without a fight.

97. The elimination of these warriors from their native sphere made the march of the Europeans to the Niger and to the Sudan possible. The similar annihilation of patriots of this order in South Africa cleared the routes there to the interior. The difficulty involved in this conquest can be estimated only by considering the long time intervening between the beginning of these conquests and the final success of the European invaders. It required a century.

98. The loss of ground at these strategic points in the interior rendered the occupation of Guinea easy. All fighting for the native soil did not cease altogether, but there was no organization strong enough to make any headway against the Europeans with modern arms. The Mohammedans after destroying what the natives had produced in Africa had finally merged with them to combat the European, but it was a futile effort. They had too much to build between the period of devastation and the reconstruction necessary to combat the enemy equipped for modern warfare.

99. The smaller kingdoms which took form and as such endured for some time present an aspect of things as they probably existed in West and

XV. SMALLER KINGDOMS WHICH ENDURED—*Continued*

Central Africa before the days of their larger kingdoms and empires. Of this earlier period, however, we have only traditional and legendary accounts. A number of independent and sometimes troublesome small states appeared upon the scene. Since it was impossible for so many to maintain an administrative force for an area of scant resources some of these, learning from the Asiatic interlopers and nomads, resorted to pillaging. Monod briefly refers to these states while treating *in extenso* the French in his *Histoire* from page 250 to the end of his volume. Delafosse in his *Negroes of Africa* does the same in Chapters IV and V. For more extended treatment consult the bibliographies given at the end of the chapters of Delafosse's work just cited.

100. It is well to note here, however, that some of these countries like Liberia and Sierra Leone developed for different reasons, and others like Dahomey, Ashanti, and Benin had contrived to exist without becoming wholly incorporated into the fallen empires.

Of Liberia we have ample information in the records of its founder, the American Colonization Society, and in such books as Alexander's *History of Colonization,* Frederick Starr's *Liberia* and R. C. F. Maugham's *The Liberian Republic* (New York, 1919). It will be advisable to consult also *The Journal of Negro History,* I, pp. 272-301, 318-338; II, pp. 209-228; V, pp. 437-447; VIII, pp. 153-229.

The story of Sierra Leone is likewise given in general treatments on Africa. The account of its beginning is told in detail in almost any history of Sierra Leone. Consult F. W. B. Thompson's *Sierra Leone in History and Tradition;* Thomas J. Aldridge's *A Transformed Colony: Sierra Leone* (London, 1910); H. O. Newland's *Sierra Leone* (London, 1916); N. W. Thomas's *Anthropological Report on Sierra Leone,* in three parts (London, 1910-1916); *Sierra Leone Studies* (Freetown, 1918-1925); and Delafosse's *Negroes of Africa,* pp. 95-96.

101. The history of Dahomey is given in numerous volumes but practically all of them from the point of view of the biased conqueror. Delafosse in his writings has endeavored to be liberal. With this exception European writers generally misrepresent this land of achievement as a backward, primitive, brutal, and murderous region. For some of these accounts see L. and G. L. Brunet's *Dahomey et Dépendances* (Paris, 1901); Édouard Foà's *Dahomey* (Paris, 1895); and G. A. F. O. François's *Notre Colonie du Dahomey* (Paris, 1906). The story of the real Dahomey is yet to be written in a modern language. See Delafosse's *Negroes of Africa,* pp. 99-100.

102. In addition to Delafosse (*Negroes of Africa,* 70, 98) Captain R. S. Rattray (*Ashanti,* Oxford, 1923), in his "Arts and Crafts of the Ashanti," *Journal of African Society,* XXIII, 265; and *Ashanti Law and Constitution,* Oxford, 1929) also found some virtue in the despised Ashanti. They

XV. SMALLER KINGDOMS WHICH ENDURED—*Continued*

XVI. AFRICA BELOW THE EQUATOR

were really some of the most progressive people of their day. See also Casely Hayford's *Gold Coast Native Institution* (London, 1903), pp. 11-26.

103. A. B. Ellis's *Yoruba-Speaking Peoples of the Slave Coast* (London, 1894), is informing with respect to Yoruba. See also W. L. Hansberry's "The Material Culture of Ancient Nigeria" (*Journal of Negro History*, VI, pp. 261-295).

104. The Art of Benin has been described in detail by Pitt Rivers in his *Antique Works of Art of Benin* (London, 1913); and by Felix Von Luschan in his *Die Altertümer von Benin* (Berlin, 1913).

105. The subsequent history of Hausa and Bornu states is treated by Delafosse in the fifth chapter of *Negroes of Africa*. More extended treatment is found in the second volume of the same author's *Haut-Sénégal-Niger*. What Lady Lugard says is inadequate and confusing.

106. In the same chapter of the work of Delafosse referred to above are treated these four kingdoms. Most works on the Sudan deal with them briefly. Consult C. H. Robinson's *Hausaland* (London, 1896); R. C. Slatin-Pacha's *Fire and Sword in the Soudan* (translated by F. R. Wingate, London, 1897); and A. Schulte's *Sultanate of Bornu* (translated by P. A. Benton, London, 1913).

107. Of the Bushmen and Hottentots much worthless material is available. The only thing we actually know about them is what we find among them today. There are the theories that they are the remnant of the primitive type of man. Some say that the Hottentots are a crossbreed type resulting from the admixture of the Bantu with Bushmen. Legends and traditions lead the student astray in a mass of self-contradictions. All comprehensive accounts of South Africa, however, mention these people. See Delafosse's *Negroes of Africa*, pp. 14, 27, 133, 139 and 159. Consult G. Hardy's *Histoire de l'Afrique*, pp. 1-4; also W. E. B. Du Bois's *The Negro*, pp. 22, 79, 80, 93, 109. For general information read G. M. Theal's *The Beginnings of South African History* (London, 1889), and his *History of South Africa* (London, 1902). Read thoroughly S. M. Molema's *The Bantu* (Edinburgh, 1920), and George W. Stow's *The Native Races of South Africa* (London, 1910).

108. The Bantu people are also a mystery. The theories as to their coming into Africa from some strange land and the race to which they actually belong (because they are not exactly black) will fill many worth-

XVI. AFRICA BELOW THE EQUATOR—*Continued*

XVII. LESS DELIMITED KINGDOMS

less volumes. Their case is briefly stated by W. E. B. Du Bois in the second and eighth chapters of his *The Negro*, and by S. M. Molema in his *The Bantu* (Edinburgh, 1920).

109. These same sources are sufficient to support the claim of a lack of political organization from the European's point of view. Yet it must be remembered that in their way these units have been sufficiently well organized to exist there longer than those of certain peoples of Asia and Europe.

110. This story is told by Proyart in his *Histoire de Loango et Kakongo et autres royaumes d'Afrique* (Paris, 1776).

111. Van Wing in his history of the Congo Kingdom, cited above, gives a fulsome account. Also A. Bastian in his *Ein Besuch in San Salvador der Hauptstadt des Königreichs Congo* (Bremen, 1859).

112. Of the smaller South African kingdoms still less is known. References are made to them in the sources herein mentioned. Delafosse does the same in his *Negroes of Africa*, Chapter VI.

113. Consult R. N. Hall's *Great Zimbabwe, Mashonaland, Rhodesia* (London, 1905), and Charles Bullock's *Mashona Laws and Customs* (Salisbury, Rhodesia, 1913).

114. Consult Delafosse's *Negroes of Africa*, pages 130 to 140; J. A. Farrer's *Zululand* (London, 1879); Henri Junod's *Condition of the Natives of Southeast Africa in the Sixteenth Century* (Capetown, 1914); James Young Gibson's *The Story of the Zulus* (London, 1911); T. B. Jenkinson's *Amazulu, the Zulus* (London, 1882).

115. Consult A. Wilmot's *Monomotapa* (London, 1896).

116. The only useful brief statement of these kingdoms is found in sixth chapter of Delafosse's *Negroes of Africa*; and a brief statement of what is now known is about as valuable as a long digest of the guesses and theories based on these ancient kingdoms. We know little about them except what is yielded by legends and traditions. Some reference is made to these kingdoms in H. H. Johnston's *British Central Africa*, and G. M. Theal's *Beginnings of South African History*.

117. See Delafosse's *Negroes of Africa*, p. 137.

XVII. LESS DELIMITED KINGDOMS—*Continued*

XVIII. THE PARTITION OF AFRICA

118. *Ibid.,* 137.

119. *Ibid.,* p. 137, also Pierre Colle's *Les Baluba* (Bruxelles, 1913).

120. Delafosse's op. cit., p. 138.

121. *Ibid.,* page 138.

122. *Ibid.,* pp. 138, 139, 145, 215. Consult also John Roscoe's *The Bagesu and Other Tribes of the Uganda Protectorate* (Cambridge, 1924); J. F. Cunningham's *Uganda and its Peoples* (London, 1905); A. A. Goldenweiser's *Early Civilization,* chapter on the Baganda (New York, 1922); and H. H. Johnston's *Uganda Protectorate* (London, 1902).

123. Works treating the partition of Africa are too numerous to be mentioned here inasmuch as our problem is merely to make a brief survey of the Europeanization of that continent. For details in the study of the partition of Africa one should consult such bibliographies as *Bibliographie d'Histoire Coloniale* (Paris, 1932), *Bibliography of South Africa,* two volumes (London, 1934), and the *Bibliography of the Negro* by Monroe N. Work (New York, 1928).

It will be necessary also for the advanced study of this aspect of history to supplement what is set forth in these particular bibliographies because of their inadequacy. In the case of the *Bibliographie d'Histoire Coloniale* the works listed are selected primarily from those which approve the colonial policies of the various European nations now occupying Africa. Few works to the contrary are given. In the case of the bibliography dealing primarily with the South African Union almost everything of importance pertaining to the government such as the laws, reports, proceedings, ordinances, and memorials, may be found as well as books and periodicals, but this work, too, does not include many productions which do not support the European or the South African Union points of view. In the case of Monroe N. Work's *Bibliography* these objections do not hold, but unfortunately the author failed to learn of and to include in his various lists numerous informing works which bear upon the Negro in Africa but do not have such titles.

The following works are sufficient for the average student: J. H. Rose, *The Development of the European Nations, 1870-1900,* II (1905); *Histoire générale,* XII, chapter xxvi, *Le partage de l'Afrique, 1870-1900,* by R. de Caix de St. Aymour; Sir Edward Hertslet, *The Map of Africa by Treaty,* 3d edition, completed to 1908, 3 vols. (1909): H. H. Johnston, *A History of*

XVIII.　THE PARTITION OF AFRICA—*Continued*

124. SPANISH AFRICA
125. ITALIAN AFRICA

the Colonization of Africa by Alien Races, (1913); J. S. Keltie, *The Partition of Africa* (1895); Sir Charles Lucas, *The Partition and Colonization of Africa* (1922); Jean Darcy, *Cent Années de Rivalité Coloniale* (1907); H. A. Gibbons, *The New Map of Africa* (1918); N. D. Harris, *Europe and Africa* (1927).

For Africa since the War one should consult the following in addition to the works of Lucas, Gibbons and Harris: P. E. Lewin, *Germans in Africa* (1915), G. L. Beer, *African Colonial Problems;* Raymond Leslie Buell, *Native Problem in Africa;* Rayford W. Logan "The Operation of the Mandate System in Africa," *Journal of Negro History,* Volume XIII, pp. 423-477.

With respect to Portugal itself one will find the following useful: Fortuanto de Almeida, *Portugal e as colonias Portuguesas;* Jules Mees, *Henri le Navigateur et l'Académie Portugaise de Sagres;* Sophus Ruge, *Historia da Epoca dos descobrimentos pelo;* Marechal Gomes Da Costa, *Descobrimentos e Conquistas;* Kurt Krause, *Os portugueses na Abissinia;* and Charles de Lannoy, *Histoire de l'Expansion Coloniale des Peuples Européens;* Gabriel Pereira, *Diogo Gomes.*

124. Spain in Africa during recent years is treated in the works which deal with North Africa inasmuch as Spain with the exception of a slice of Guinea has not very much of a foothold beyond that point. The earliest efforts of Spain in colonization are treated in the histories of Saco, Oviedo, and Herrera. These, however, concern largely the New World since Africa at that time was merely a hunting ground for slaves. With the works touching the various aspects of Spanish colonization in Latin-America, although bearing to some extent upon Africa, we are not much concerned. Most of these are given in the *Bibliographie d'Histoire Coloniale* referred to above. For our purposes here it is sufficient to refer to a few general works like H. H. Johnston's *History of the Colonization of Africa by Alien Races,* J. S. Keltie's *The Partition of Africa,* E. L. Guernier's *L'Afrique Champ d'Expansion de L'Europe,* and Sir Charles Lucas's *Partition of Africa.*

125. Modern Italy in Africa is a development later than that of other European powers and it is not so extensive. The chief possessions of Italy are in North Africa and in Northeast Africa, that is, in Eritrea, Tripoli, and Somaliland. This is dealt with in sufficient detail in the works cited above as general treatments of the European colonization of Africa. Italian relations with Abyssinia especially are treated in almost any history of that country. A brief statement of Italy in Africa is given in P. E. Lewin's "German and Italian Interest in Africa" in *Foreign Affairs,* V, pp. 472-481. The earlier period is treated in André J. J. A. Pellenc's *Les Italiens en Afrique* (Paris, 1897); E. Bassi *La zona d'influenza* (Rome, 1921); E. Cucinotta, *La costituzione sociale Somala* (Rome, 1921); C. Zoli, *La conquista del Fezzan* (Rome, 1921); F. Bianchi, *Colonizzazione e credito*

XVIII. THE PARTITION OF AFRICA—*Continued*
126. FRENCH AFRICA

agrario nella Libia (Vicenza, 1922); F. Geraci, *Lettere dalla Tripolitania* (Piacenza, 1922); A. Pollera, *La Donna in Etiopia* (Rome, 1922); C. Tumelei, *La Questione tunisia e l'Italia* (Bologna, 1922); P. D'Agostino Orsini di Camerota, *Espansionismo Italiano odiérno* (Salerno, 1923); the same author, *La nostra economia coloniale* (Salerno, 1923); C. Zoli, *La battaglia di Adua* (Rome, 1923); G. Capra, *L'Africa centro-australe e l'emigrazione italiana* (Torino, 1924); G. Jaja, *L'avvenire economico dell'Angola* (Rome, 1924); A. Palumbo, *Il problema transahariano ai confini occidentali della nostra colonia libica* (Rome, 1924); F. Serra, *Italia e Senussia in Cirenaica* (Turin, 1924); G. Stefanin, *I Possedimenti italiani in Africa* (Florence, 1924); R. Onor, *La Somalia Italiana* (Turin, 1925); F. Bertonelli, *Il problema coloniale Italiano; cenni storici* (Florence, 1926); G. Bertoni, *La Somalia Italiana e la sua valorizazione* (Naples, 1926); R. Cantalupo, *Il fascimo e la coscienza coloniale* (Rome, 1926); V. M. Castellani, *La questione di Tangeri* (Rome, 1926); C. Cesari, *L'Africa orientale italiana ed i suoi precedenti storici* (Rome, 1926); G. Gibello-Socco, *Colonie d'Italia e colonie ex-germaniche d'Africa* (Milan, 1926); C. Manfroni, *La rinascita della Tripolitania* (Rome, 1926); G. Masturzi, *La Colonia Eritrea* (Florence, 1926); F. Meriano, *La questione di Giarabub* (Bologna, 1926); G. Borghetti, *Le Colonie italiane* (Bologna, 1927); G. Caraci, *La Spagna al Marocco* (Rome, 1927); E. De Agostini, *Notizie sulla regione di Cufra (el Cafra)* (Bengasi, 1927); E. Manzini, *Origini, vicende, natura dei sistemi coloniali europei* (Rome, 1927); M. D. Maroni, *Le Colonie italiane* (Milan, 1927); A. Rocchi, *Colonie d'Italia* (Milano, 1927); F. Virgili, *Le Colonie italiane, nella storia presente e nel loro avvenire* (Milan, 1927); L. Federzoni, *Rinascita dell'Africa Romana* (Rome, 1928); E. Cerulli, *Etiopia occidentale* (Rome, 1929); C. Conti-Rossini, *L'Abissinia* (Rome, 1929); D. D'Orazio, *Riverberi d'Africa* (1929); M. Grosso, *Cronologia della Somalia Italiana* (Rome, 1929); G. Stefanini, *I possedimenti Italiani in Africa* (Florence, 1929); U. Bassi, *Note sur diritti dell' Italia in Africa* (Modena, 1930); L. Battistelli, *Africa Italiana* (Florence, 1930); F. Bertonelli, *I Confini fra la Libia e l'Africa equatoriale francese* (Rome, 1930); L. Federgoni, *Vecchia e nuova politica coloniale: l'Eritrea* (Milan, 1930); A. Giaccardi, *Le Rivendicazioni Italiane in Africa durante il Conflitto Mondiale* (Rome, 1930); R. Graziani, *La situazione cirenaica* (Bengasi, 1930); R. Martinelli, *Sud: rapporto di un viaggio in Eritrea ed in Etiopia* (Florence, 1930).

126. With respect to French Africa we find numerous books. Among these publications in French should be noted first those which appeared from the press of the Société d'Editions Géographiques, Maritimes et Coloniales in connection with the "Exposition Coloniale Internationale de 1931." While these productions are primarily intended to portray the economic conditions of these colonies they give information on the natives in showing the extent to which their continent has been modernized. It should be noted, too, that in 1927 this same press brought out an interesting work, *L'Afrique Centrale: La Colonie du Niger*, by Maurice Abadie, with an

XVIII. THE PARTITION OF AFRICA—*Continued*

127. BRITISH AFRICA
128. THE DUTCH IN AFRICA
129. BELGIUM IN AFRICA

introduction by Maurice Delafosse. These later productions of mainly commercial value are *Le Niger, Le Sénégal, Le Soudan, La Côte d'Ivoire, La Mauritaine, La Haute-Volta, La Guinée, Le Dahomey,* and *La Circonscription de Darkar et Dépendances.* Two of these works of this society are more informing with respect to the natives and more nearly scientific than the others. They are *L'Afrique occidentale française,* by Robert Delavignette, and *L'Afrique équatoriale française,* by Julien Maigret, both of 1931. For a brief statement of this, however, one should consult E. L. Guernier's *L'Afrique Champ d'Expansion de L'Europe,* Georges Hardy's *Géographie de la France Exterieure,* the same author's *Histoire de la colonisation française,* his *Nos Grands Problemes Coloniaux; L. L. C.* Faidherbe's *Le Sénégal;* W. M. Sloane's *Greater France in Africa;* Georges Bruel's *L'Afrique équatoriale française;* M. Delafosse's *Les Frontières de la Côte d'Ivoire, de la Côte D'Or et du Soudan,* and his *Haut Sénégal-Niger.*

127. In the case of British Africa we find their efforts briefly treated in E. L. Guernier's *L'Afrique Champ d'Expansion de L'Europe;* in Sir Charles Lucas's *Partition of Africa* (1922); Sir Harry H. Johnston's *History of the Colonization of Africa by Alien Races;* in the same author's *Opening Up of Africa;* and in J. S. Keltie's *The Partition of Africa.* The bibliographies of the *Statesmen's Year Book* will also be helpful. One will find likewise interesting articles in the *Encyclopaedia Britannica* bearing on colonization. This may be further extended by the other works in the bibliographies referred to under Number 1. For the history one should consult G. M. Theal's *History of South Africa* and *The Beginnings of South Africa.* Likewise special histories dealing with the other colonies of the British in South Africa may be consulted, but they are too numerous to concern us here.

128. The story of the Dutch in Africa belongs to a period in the remote past. This country has no outstanding possessions there at the present time. What has been said about the other colonies will be adequate treatment of the present status of the Dutch in this sphere. The most important of this history would be that of the Boer Republic which as a result of war in that area has become a part of the South African Union. The histories bearing upon South Africa referred to above cover adequately the efforts of the Dutch in this quarter. Consult G. M. Theal's *History of the Boers in South Africa.*

129. The story of Belgium in Africa is likewise told in sources already cited. It is given from the point of view of Belgians themselves in a semi-official publication called *Notre Colonie.* The same is given in some detail in Louis Franck's *Congo Belge* (Brussels, 1928). Other helpful works have already been cited under X. The books in which the colonial policy of Belgium has been attacked are given above.

XVIII. THE PARTITION OF AFRICA—*Continued*

 130 THE GERMANS IN AFRICA

 131. MANDATED AFRICA—AFTER THE WORLD WAR

XIX. AFRICAN CULTURE

 132. METHODS OF MAKING A LIVING

  (a) FISHING

  (b) HUNTING

  (c) AGRICULTURE

  (d) CATTLE-RAISING

  (e) COMMERCE

  (f) INDUSTRY

130. The Germans, eliminated from Africa as a result of the World War, do not concern us so much here, but the facts of importance are set forth in P. E. Lewin's *Germans and Africa* (1915), Robert Pimenta's *L'Ancienne Colonie Allemande de Sud-ouest Africain* (Paris, 1920); and in H. C. O'Neil's *The War in Africa and in the Far East*. Consult also Rayford W. Logan's "German Acquisition of Southwest Africa," *Journal of Negro History*, XVIII, pp. 369-395. For extended treatment read Leo Frobenius, *Das Sterbende Afrika* (Munich, 1923); Hanemann, *Wirtschaftliche und politische Verhaeltnisse in Deutsch-Südwest-Afrika* (Berlin, 1904); Kurt Hassert, *Deutschlands Kolonien* (Leipzig, 1910); Adolf Heilborn, *Die deutschen Kolonien* (Leipzig, 1906); *Koloniale Studien, Hans-Meyer Festschrift zum 70. Geburtstag dargebracht von seinen Freunden, Verehrern und Schulern* (Berlin, 1928); O. Kobner, *Einführung in die Kolonialpolitik* (Iena, 1908); A. Leue, *Die Besiedlungsfaehighkeit Deutschostafrikas, Ein Beitrag zur Auswanderungsfrage* (Leipzig, 1904); Wilh. Mensching, *Farbige und Weisse Rassen, Kolonial-und Kulturfragen* (Wernigerode, 1930); Hans Meyer, *Das deutsche Kolonialreich* (Leipzig, 1922); Paul Samassa, *Die Besiedlung Deutsch-Ostafrikas* (Leipzig, 1909); Kurd Schwabe, *Mit Schwert und Pflug in Deutsch-Sudwest-Africa* (Berlin, 1904); A. Seidel, *Deutschlands Kolonien* (Berlin, 1902); K. Martin and H. Siemer, *Die Zukunft der Deutschen im Ausland* (Hamburg, 1921); Paul Sprigade und Max Moisel, *Deutsch-Sudwest-Afrika* (Berlin); A. Zimmermann, *Die Kolonialreiche der Grossmaechte, 1871-1916* (Berlin, 1916).

131. As to the Mandataries one will find reports of the League of Nations helpful, but these do not give all the facts. The same may be said of Sir Frederick Lugard's *The Dual Mandate in British Tropical Africa*. Read Rayford W. Logan's "The Operation of the Mandate System in Africa," *The Journal of Negro History*, XIII, pp. 423-477. Consult also R. L. Buell's *The Native Problem in Africa*, the same author's *International Relations*, Moon's *Imperialism and World Politics*, and the *Minutes of the Permanent Mandates Commission*.

132. On African culture the works are too numerous to mention. The worthwhile ones, however, are few. Most books dealing with the life and

XIX. AFRICAN CULTURE—*Continued*

133. SOCIAL AND POLITICAL INSTITUTIONS
  (a) SOCIAL CLASSES
  (b) CASTES—SMITHS, HUNTERS, ETC.
  (c) SECRET SOCIETIES
  (d) GOVERNMENT
  (e) FEUDALISM
  (f) FREEDOM AND SLAVERY
  (g) MARRIAGE AND THE POSITION OF WOMEN
  (h) HOME AND PRIVATE LIFE
  (i) RELIGION AND MORALS
  (j) SCIENCE AND EDUCATION
  (k) LITERATURE AND ART
  (l) AMUSEMENTS

XX. AFRICAN SURVIVALS IN AMERICA

134. IDEAS OF GOVERNMENT AS BEING LAW-ABIDING

customs of African natives are written by persons who have not lived among them long enough to understand what they observed. Maurice Delafosse, Georges Hardy, Louis Tauxier, and Henri Labouret, in spite of their French bias, have done this task better than others in their country; and so have John Roscoe, Emil Torday, R. S. Rattray, and George Greenfield in the English language, despite their Nordic slant. The works of the authors already cited herein should be consulted in the study of African culture. A useful summary from a partly sympathetic point of view is found in Delafosse's *Negroes of Africa,* pages 141 to 281. Articles now appearing in *Africa* throw some light on these matters. This is a magazine published quarterly in London by the International Institute of African Languages and Cultures.

133. In the references given above are found discussions of the culture of only the outstanding African peoples. Not all have been investigated. From what is said the student can picture for himself what the Africans were and how they have become what we now find them to be. S. M. Molema's *Bantu* and Casely Hayford's *Gold Coast Native Institutions* give the picture from the native African's point of view; and, in a manner, E. W. Blyden's *African Life and Customs* serves the same purpose.

134. As to African survivals in America there is little to which the student may be referred. The Negro in the United States has never been scientifically studied. He has been considered as one imitating the white man after disconnecting himself altogether from what he left in Africa. R. E. Park, E. B. Reuter, and their disciples boldly take the position that

XX. AFRICAN SURVIVALS IN AMERICA—*Continued*

135. PENCHANT FOR SECRET SOCIETIES
136. FEW AFRICAN WORDS REMAIN
137. INDUSTRY PRESERVED, ART IN WORKMANSHIP
138. MUCH OF AFRICAN PHILOSOPHY IN AMERICAN FOLKLORE AND PROVERBS

the African retained nothing brought from Africa but his temperament. This is mere dogma, for these gentlemen cannot explain away the facts to the contrary. Yet, it depends upon what they mean by "temperament," for temperament is what often serves as a peculiar characteristic of culture. What they say about the Negro may be said about any other Americanized element in the United States. In other words, after these misinformants have said what they imagine, they have actually said nothing according to science.

The Negro as a law-abiding citizen, for example, is living up to an African tradition. He has always had regard for law. His tribal life in Africa was based on this principle. Literature on crime, however, runs to the contrary, for the very race-hating people who force the Negro down to crime levels daily produce magazine articles, addresses, and books to support the claim of what they themselves have done and charge it to the account of the Negro.

135. Here the student should compare the make-up and procedure of African secret orders with those of Negroes in America. W. W. Browne's efforts with the True Reformers, the rise of the Galilean Fishermen, the careers of the Mosaics, the work of the St. Luke and the like should be studied. We are not concerned here with the secret societies of whites which Negroes have taken over. The attention here is directed to those original with the Negro. Consult A. E. Bush, *History of the Mosaic Templars of America* (Little Rock, 1924) ; W. H. Gibson, *History of the United Brothers of Friendship and the Sisters of the Mysterious Ten* (Louisville, 1897) ; W. T. Thom, *The True Reformers* (Washington, 1902) ; W. P. Dabney, *Maggie L. Walker, Her Life and Deeds* (Richmond, 1929).

136. These few African words, although limited in number, have a significant history which should be traced. A word does not simply happen to be used. Its history explains many other things. Consult E. R. Embree's *Brown America* (New York, 1931), pp. 10-13.

137. The industry of the Negro should be compared with that of the other laboring elements tried by the Europeans in the New World. When others proved unequal to the requirements of labor in this country the Negroes were imported, and they supplied the demand. What was there in the Negro that did not exist in the others? The skill of the early Negro mechanics now observed in many colonial structures in the South will give some traces of African industrial art.

138. A comparison of African folklore with that of the Negroes in America will bring out this point without much difficulty. Almost any of the works of the best authorities on Africa herein cited contain considerable folklore. The productions of the American Folklore Society give abundant

XX. AFRICAN SURVIVALS IN AMERICA—*Continued*

139. SPIRITUAL LIFE IN AFRICA ENDURES IN THE CHURCH
140. AFRICAN IDEA OF JUSTICE STILL DOMINANT
141. GENEROSITY DUE TO CUSTOMS IN AFRICA
142. AFRICAN ART CARRIED OVER IN THE DANCE, DRAMA, AND MUSIC

materials from the Negroes on this side of the Atlantic. Blaise Cendrars' *Anthologie Nègre* is especially helpful for Africa. Likewise the other works cited in this volume under African literature. See C. G. Woodson's *African Myths.*

139. The study of religious phenomena in the Negro Church of today will explain much observed among African tribes. Most writings on the Negro Church, however, are purely narrative or statistical and never touch these reactions which require scientific study.

140. A special study should be made of the administration of justice in the well-developed African kingdoms. The special rôle of the king or emperor in the administration of justice should be noted.

141. The custom of generous distribution in the African social order should be studied from the point of view of its origin and influence in the development of the African character. The works of Molema, Hayford, and Blyden are specially helpful here.

142. The penchant of the Negro for the stage and his success thereon which has caused many to refer to him as "a natural born actor" should be projected against the African background. However, with the exception of discussing the dance and the work of the "griots" or professional story-tellers, the idea of the theatre among African Negroes has not been studied. Here, then, the student treads upon practically virgin soil.

CHAPTER XIX

THE NEGRO IN EUROPEAN MIND

THE first notice taken of the Negro by the European resulted from curiosity. The Pelasgians, Cretans, and Etruscans of the Mediterranean world, coming into contact with Africans for the first time, found them most interesting. Their black or bluish color struck these early Mediterraneans as being desirable. The most ancient Greeks from whom we learn the first recorded impressions of the Africans considered them a remarkably beautiful people who held their feasts among the Gods. Subsequent Greek literature supports this favorable impression which the Mediterranean aborigines had of the early African blacks. Not only in Homer and Herodotus but also in Æschylus we find complimentary references reflecting the later impression of the Greeks. In none of their literature so far examined do we find a very different attitude. The later contacts of the Greeks as a colonizing people, a thing which often changes a nation's attitude, does not show much departure from this point of view. This may be due in part to the Greek colonization methods which did not embrace the exploitation which territorial expansion later manifested.

The painting and sculpture of the Greeks support also the inevitable conclusion deduced from a perusal of the Greek literature. Paintings found on the walls of caves of ancient Greece treat the Negro as a welcome factor in the Mediterranean. The frescoes unearthed in the Temple of Minos in Crete would indicate not only that the African figured in the ancient Mediterranean on a parity with others but that the African had so mixed his blood with that of some of these early dwellers that their features were distinctly Negroid. Many of them had curly hair, full lips, and African facial outlines. Several authorities have taken this to mean that the early Mediterraneans were what we in America designate today as colored people, the inevitable result of a melting pot.

The sculptures of the Greeks of a later period frequently featured the African Negro. In representations of world elements was included the black man. Negroes brought into the Mediterranean were kept as mascots and favorites by circles of men and women. It was a mark of aristocracy to have around an African with color and features differing from those of the Greeks. Amulets, charms, and small statuettes of blacks, then, were prized as works of art. That these early sculptures were often of an hilarious, festive, or popular order supports the conclusion that Negroes among these Greeks were not reduced to the status of meniality or drudgery. Probably the present dominant esthetic manifestation of the African, frequently referred to as the expression of his unusual emotion, was so apparent in the life of the Negro at that time that he thus first impressed the outer world with his spirituality.

When we leave the Greeks, however, and take up the Roman's attitude toward the Negro we do not find among the latter the same tendencies. While the Romans of the ancient world did not show what we today call race prejudice, this attitude did manifest itself as that of the superior toward the subordinate. The Romans were a conquering people, and they brought captives from Africa as they did from other parts and enslaved them. Just as the Romans referred with contempt to the Angles and Saxons whom they captured and sold as slaves in the markets of Rome so did they treat the Negroes. In their literature there are not as many references to the blacks as we find in that of the Greeks, and these are not so complimentary, as shown by the biased G. H. Beardsley in her *The Negro in Greek and Roman Civilization*.

In the sculpture of the Romans the dominant motive was the glorification of the republic or the empire and the men who made Rome. Little thought was given to international forces. The Romans' methods of colonization, moreover, did not bring them into peaceful contact with Africans. The story of the famous generals, returning home indued with the spoils of their conquest, pictured the Negro driven along with others under the yoke. Such close relations as had existed between ancient Greece and Ethiopia did not develop between that country and Rome. While the Greek literature and art tell us of the greatness of these people beyond the land of sand and sunshine, the Romans, having had little or no contact with ancient Africans, not even with Egypt until it began to lose its Negroid aspects, saw the Africans from a different point of view.

During the Middle Ages when most ties were broken it is difficult to determine from promiscuous records with scant mention of the Negro exactly what was the attitude of any large number of people of that day. The barbarians of the north who during that period destroyed the civilization of Rome and set the world back for at least a thousand years were not sufficiently enlightened to give an intelligent response to anything. The modern nations which these tribes projected in the embryonic state could not be expected to have universal points of view at that early stage of localism and individualism.

However, in the church which conquered the minds of Europe just as Rome had brought nations under its political sway one does find attitudes toward all the constituents of the universal social order. In the first place, the fathers of the church had to develop a literature for religious propaganda. Conspicuous in that literature was the claim that God is not a respecter of persons and that he had sent His son to die for all men. While special thought of the Negro was not dominant this liberal doctrine was made clear in the preachments of all fathers of the Church like Tertullian, Cyprian, Augustine, Ambrose, Albertus Magnus, and Thomas Aquinas. In the proportion as the Church extended its jurisdiction over Europe this claim gradually grew upon the minds of its barbarian adherents.

The idea of universal brotherhood, too, was registered by the artists most of whom in the later Middle Ages and the beginning of the Renaissance made their way to fame by embodying in art the thought of the Christian Church. In the "Adoration of the Magi," at the "Feast in Cana," in the "Resurrection of the Dead," and in the "General Judgment" all races had to be pictured; and the Negro was there, not as some one brought in for necessity, but as a member of the human family. And probably for this reason the few Negroes first carried to Europe by ships engaged in the commerce of the Renaissance period were not made beasts of burden. They were given above all things the opportunity to be enlightened and Christianized. The effort of Portugal is a case in evidence of such good will toward the African.

The policy thus established doubtless tended to soften also the attitude of the hardened enslavers who later plundered the shores of Africa for human souls to be transported as serfs to the New World. These were to be debased lower to the status of slaves required for cheap labor on the plantations and mines in America. There was a general objection to any brutalization of the African; and European sovereigns like Queen Isabella and Charles V of Spain consented to the importation of slaves into their colonies only on the condition that every effort should be made to Christianize them either before being taken to America or to provide for their evangelization immediately after importation.

The French slave code also thus provided. In fact, most of the Catholic adventurers in America felt this a duty, inasmuch as the chief argument in justification of slavery was that the African would have the opportunity to embrace the Christian religion. During these early years, too, it was not believed that the bondage of the Negro would be any more than that of the contemporary indentured servant white man. There was an unwritten law in Christendom that one could not hold a Christian as a slave. It was a condition to which were subjected only infidels captured in holy wars. Conversion, then, automatically worked manumission. To make slavery permanent, therefore, the religious hierarchy, both Catholic and Protestant, had to reverse themselves and make an exception against the Negro. Although he might embrace the Christian faith it would not in his case be a passport to freedom.

Thereafter the Negro was differently portrayed in both literature and art. This was especially true of England. The modern world became accustomed to him in a subordinate position, and while there does not appear to be any understanding to this effect among artists and writers of the later years they seldom show the Negro in a favorable light. In those days, it must be noted, however, it was unpopular to depict any of the lower elements of the social order as having virtues worthy of imitation. Every trait worth while was found in the royalty, and the world had to undergo several revolutions before the bourgeois or the commoner could be staged as an ideal man. The Negro, of course, when enslaved had still less opportunity to be seen and understood as a desirable human being.

While literature and art of that day had little commendatory of the Negro, there was no tendency to attack the race unduly just as there was none to idealize it. The Negro became a non-entity. When we reach the intellectual revolution of the seventeenth century we hear again of the liberal attitude toward the Negro in theories as to the natural right of all men to be free. This thought, however, was blighted by the commercial and the industrial revolution (1750-1835) before universal emancipation could be effected, but we see and hear more of the Negro. Slavery, ceasing to be accidental, had become the great adjunct to producing raw materials, especially cotton, which when manufactured to supply increasing needs became the basis for fabulous wealth on both sides of the Atlantic. Becoming a cruel system which reduced the Negro slaves to mere machines, the institution received the attention of writers who either denounced or approved it. Occasionally an artist endeavored to portray the contentment of the slave or, on the contrary, using art for another sort of propaganda, would paint the bondman as enduring the horrors of an intolerable institution.

Because of the domination of the element of propaganda, however, neither these first artists nor writers advocating liberty stood in front rank. It was only in later years that the terrible evils of both the trade and slavery itself enlisted the efforts of the best writers in European countries. It would have made such producers unpopular among those upon whom they had to depend for a livelihood, if they had attacked this foundation of so many fortunes. An important inspiration to the more liberalizing efforts of Europeans, however, was the talent exhibited by those Africans who, educated on that continent, had given the same response to the highest ideals expected of persons of the so-called advanced races.

Portugal, the first to come into contact with Africans in large numbers, found them a people differing widely from Europeans, but mentioned them in its literature as having the possibilities and capacities of other people. The Portuguese converted the Congo empire into the Catholic kingdom of San Salvador by Christianizing the heir to the throne and educating him in Portugal in the fifteenth century. The dominant figure in Africa from 1364 to 1580, Portugal received so many of its natives that the provinces of Estramadura, Alemtejo and Algrave were almost entirely black; and at one time, it is said, the blacks outnumbered the Latins in

Lisbon. In the poetry and fiction of that day Negroes were thus noted to the extent that they were recognized socially, and they were incorporated into that population as any other natural infusion of new blood. The sculptures and paintings of these Iberians likewise accorded with what had impressed itself on the public mind, and this reflection of the thought of that day mirrored the Negro as a member of the human family. The enslavement of the Negro was not at first considered a thing unusual, for men of all races were found in the same condition; and especially since the world was not far removed from the time when slavery or serfdom was the normal condition of two-thirds or three-fourths of the people in the ancient world.

Spain, bringing in its wake the Dutch kingdom which it once controlled, showed still more thought of the Negro in its literature and art. Large numbers of black persons infiltrated into the Moors who brought them later into Spain and made the Negro an element to be taken into account. At one time there were so many Negroes in Seville that the authorities provided for their local self-government under their own executive, Juan de Valladolid. In the writings of the earliest times, the Negro found his place also as a hero. Andres de Claramonte, a seventeenth-century Spanish dramatist, we are told, produced *El Valiente Negro en Flandes* to show the sterling qualities of the race. Juan Latino, a poet of Negro blood, was there himself to tell his own story, which in our time has been embellished by Marin-Ocete.[1] Juan de Pareja, elevated from

[1] "A vast number of tributes were paid by contemporary men of letters to Don John of Austria; but among them none is more curious than a Latin poem in two books, containing seventeen or eighteen hundred hexameters, the work of a Negro, who had been brought as an infant from Africa, and who by his learning rose to be Professor of Latin and Greek in the school attached to the cathedral of Granada. He is the same person noticed by Cervantes as "el Negro Juan Latino," in a poem prefixed to the Don Quixote. His volume of Latin verses on the birth of Ferdinand, the son of Philip II., on Pope Pius V., on Don John of Austria, and on the city of Granada, making above a hundred and sixty pages in small quarto, printed at Granada in 1573, is not only one of the rarest books in the world, but is one of the most remarkable illustrations of the intellectual faculties and possible accomplishments of the African race. The author himself says he was brought to Spain from Ethiopia, and was, until his emancipation, a slave to the grandson of the famous Gonsalvo de Cordova. His Latin verse is respectable, and, from his singular success as a scholar, he was commonly called Joannes Latinus, a *sobriquet* under which he is frequently mentioned. He

servitude to be the companion of Velásquez, became a painter as well as the subject of an impressive portrait by the great artist. Sebastian Gomez, a painter of note adopted by and developed under Murillo, did not have to portray his race because he could not

was respectably married to a lady of Granada, who fell in love with him, as Eloisa did with Abelard, while he was teaching her; and after his death, which occurred later than 1573, his wife and children erected a monument to his memory in the church of Sta. Ana, in that city, inscribing it with an epitaph, in which he is styled 'Filius Aethiopum, prolesque nigerrima patrum.' (Antonio, Bib. Nov., Tom. 1. p. 716. Don Quixote, ed. Clemencin, Tom. L. p. lx, note.) Andreas Schottus in his 'Hispaniae Bibliotheca sive de Academiis et Bibliothecis,' (1608) speaking of the city of Granada, says: 'Hic Joannes Latinus Aethiops, (res prodigiosa) nostra tempestate rhetoricam per multos annos publice docuit, juventutemque institui, et poema edidit in victoriam Joannis Austriaci navalem.' p. 29.

"There is a play entitled 'Juan Latino' by Diego Ximenez de Encisco, in the second volume of the 'Comedias Escogidas,' (Madrid, 1652) which gives a full sketch of him. In the first act he is a slave of the Duke of Sesa, ill enough treated, kicked about and cuffed. In the second, he is tutor to Doña Ana de Carlobal, sister to an ecclesiastic of rank, and makes love to her through his Spanish verses, and in other ways after the Spanish fashion. In the third, he rises to distinction; obtains his chair in the University; and, favored by Don John of Austria, is enfranchised by the Duke of Sesa, who, however, manumits him very reluctantly, on the ground that it is his great glory to hold so distinguished a man as his property. Addressing Don John, Juan Latino is made to say, (f. 57) in the fervor of his gratitude:

> Yo prometo a vuestra Alteza,
> Que he de quitar a la Fama
> Una pluma con que escriva
> Sus memorables hazanas.
> Y, como muchos poemas
> Toman nombre del que cantan,
> Llamare Austriada mi libro,
> Pues canta Don Juan de Austria.

"This promise, of course, was made by the poet half a century or more after it had been fulfilled.

"It may not be amiss here to add, that another Negro is celebrated in a play, written with skill in good Castilian, and claiming, at the end, to be founded in fact. It is called 'El Valiente Negro en Flandes," by Andres de Claramonte, actor and playwright, and is found in Tom. XXXI., 1638, of the collection of Comedias printed at Barcelona and Saragossa. The Negro in question, however, was not, like Juan Latino, a native African, but was a slave born in Merida, and was distinguished only as a soldier, serving with great honor under the Duke of Alva, and enjoying the favor of that severe general."—George Ticknor, *History of Spanish Literature*, II, pp. 582-583.

Consult also Rudolph Schevill's *The Dramatic Art of Lope de Vega*, Berkeley, 1918, pp. 207, 305-310.

have but been heartened by the liberal treatment of the Negro by the Spanish painters. In the sculpture of Spain, too, there was no bias to exclude the Negro, not even on the ground that he did not figure among the royalty to which most artists had to go for their subjects. Goya's works are evidence of this attitude.

In the productions of the seventeenth-century writers of Spain like Cervantes, Lope de Vega, and Calderon, the Negro is just as prominent as we find him in the literatures of other countries where persons of this blood were found in considerable numbers. Negroes as musicians and dancers were brought into various comedies on the Spanish stage, and some of these writers devoted entire plays to the African Negro. Yet the presence of the Negro in Spain was considered as a matter of fact. The Negro was not a problem there. In the histories of that day accordingly there is no extensive treatment of this element as such; for persons of color were readily absorbed by the Spanish population.

In the eighteenth century and the still more modern literature the Negro appears infrequently and incidentally. He is still no problem to writers and artists. He must not be painted as a saint or branded as a devil. He is merely a human being, and when referred to he is limned with all the shortcomings as well as with the virtues which belong to man. Some saw him from one point of view while others painted a different picture. Alarcon, Valdés, Caballero, Valera, Galdós, and Echagaray bear out this attitude in their productions. Spanish artists of this later period conformed themselves accordingly.

Italy, at first a battleground for the emerging modern nations, did not have sufficient contact with the distant outer world to think much of the Negro. The Church, the dominant influence during this period, maintained generally its former attitude in literature and art although it did not militantly attack slavery. Italian painters of the time took notice of the Negro as a part of the human family. Thus did Paolo Varonese in placing a Negro in his "Repast at the Home of Simon, the Pharisee," Benedetto Grillandajo in having Simon the Cyrene, a black man, bear the cross of "Christ Marching to Calvary," Paolo Caliari dil Pasto in showing a Negro at the "Wedding Feast in Cana," Guido Reni in picturing a Negro dwarf in the "Abduction of Helen," and Nicolas Poussin, a

Frenchman under Italian influence, in his "Adoration of the Magi."

So far as Italy at that time impressed the world it was mainly through its highly developed urban centers which became city-states. In 1459 there were as many as 3,000 Negroes in Venice.[2] While the *Merchant of Venice* gives a fair picture of the attitude toward the Jew, *Othello* makes out a different case for the attitude toward the Negro in these centers of a new emerging culture along the Adriatic and the Mediterranean. Othello was taken from Giraldi Cinthio's novel appearing in a collection of short stories of the sixteenth century. Papini introduced to Italy the Negro poet Danko or Sancho in his volume *Stroricature*.

In Italian, too, we note references to the Negro of a more recent date. This was natural to all European countries coming into closer contact with Africa in the nineteenth century. Arrigo Boito published *L'Alfier nero* in the *Novelle e Riveste drammatiche* through Ricciardi in Naples. This story appeared originally in 1868 in a review of Milan, *Il Politecnico,* together with *Iberia* under the title "Un paio di novelle" in *La Strenna Italiana pel 1868,* published by Ripamonti-Carpano of Milan.

Of the thought of Italy with respect to the Negro we do not have much more of literary value until we find that country with an increasing interest in Africa after 1891. Ferdinando Martini brought out in 1925 *Nell'Africa Italiana,* published first in 1891 as a literary book of travel. C. Anti produced in 1921 *Scultura negra.* In 1922 U. Antonielli published *La Terra e la Vita* in which the Negro is mentioned. In *Cuore,* an interesting story by De Amicis, the Negro is also given extensive notice. In 1929 Orio Vergani brought out a rather fantastic novel, *Io, povero negro.* Some Italian painters, following those of other countries, have yielded to the recent influence of African art.

France with fewer Negroes than Spain or Portugal in the early modern era has consistently shown a most favorable attitude toward black people. The Negro character is mentioned in the *Chanson de Roland.* A large number of blacks were portrayed as having participated in the feats of the hero. The *chanson de geste,* however, does not teem with such references to black people as do the ver-

[2] P. D. Rinchon, *La traite et l'Esclavage des congolais par les Europeens.* p. 28.

sions of the Knights of the Round Table and Holy Grail. The thought of the black man appears again in 1759 when Voltaire brought out his *Candide* in which the abolition of slavery was shown as desirable.

In contact with Africa itself for exploitation and colonization, the French writers of this bent became more realistic. The *Correspondance* of the Chevalier de Boufflers and his fiancée, Mme. de Sabran, 1778 to 1788, shows the better side of the Negroes of Senegal. We are given a picture of Africa in Bernadin de Saint-Pierre's *Paul et Virginie,* which appeared in 1788. Of the writings of Abbé Grégoire on slavery, and the letters and speeches of Robespierre, Mirabeau, Lafayette and Napoleon with such allusions we are familiar. The public has probably taken little notice, however, of the interesting references of De Tocqueville and Chateaubriand to the Negro. Victor Hugo, the next writer of importance to manifest such interest, produced in 1821 *Bug-Jargal,* an echo from San Domingo. Lamartine's dramatic poem, *Toussaint Louverture,* shows the same interest. The artist, Thomas Coutre, in "Romans of the Decadence" and Ferdinand Victor Delacroix in his "Death of Sardanapalus," showed the same liberal-mindedness of the French painter. Le Nain, an artist of later years, manifested similar tendencies. Of Manet and Renoir nearer our day, however, not so much with respect to the Negro can be recorded.

In the further development of French thought the place of the Negro became still more conspicuous. In *Ourika,* a novel by the Duchess of Duras in 1824 appeared the Negro as an aspirant for consideration as a man. *Atar-Gull* by Eugene Scribe in 1831 presented the Negro in a tale of vengeance and the spirit of evil. *Toussaint le Maître* by Anthony Thouret in 1834 followed the same model. Gustave Beaumont introduced in France the abolition question by *Marie* in 1835. In the *Chevalier de Saint Georges* in 1838 Roger de Beauvoir showed a Negro winning the affections of a countess by liberality. In 1843 Frederic Soulié advocated the maintenance of slavery in *Le Bananier.* Mery in *Floride,* in 1844 had Negroes appear as supernumeraries. Four years later, however, Alexander Dumas, père, a mulatto himself, published *Georges* a story of the struggle and triumph of a mulatto.

Thus the situation was until about thirty years later we reach a period of more frequent productions bearing on the Negro. Gustave Aymar who had traveled extensively produced such works as *Les Vaudoux, L'Œil Gris, Le Commandant Delgres,* and *Une Goutte de Sang Noir.* Next in 1881 we hear of Pierre Loti's *Roman d'un Spahi.* Productions of the sort then became more numerous. Works of travelers abounded, but since they have a right to lie we need mention only one or two like Jules Verne and General Baratier who had some literary merit. What Ampère, Merimée, Gautier, Daudet, Laboulaye, Maupassant, France, Bourget, and Gide noted of the Negro is projected also in this picture.

Probably as a result of the rise of France as a more aggressive colonizing power in Africa the works bearing on the Negro became more numerous than ever before, beginning about 1900. One or more productions of the sort appeared every year.[3] An epoch of still greater interest in the Negro was reached after the World War.[4] Of these writers André Demaison was the most conspicuous. Following him, came a number of authors who frequently supplied the public with works dealing with the African at home and abroad.[5] As a result of the interest of the French in African art

[3] Among these authors were Vigne d'Octon, Jean Hess, E. M. de Vogue, G. Bergeret, Charles Valois, P. Zaccone, Vast-Ricouard, Alieus de la Prée, P. Feval, R. Gineste, Pol Prille, G. Grandidier, J. Charles Roux, Ernest Psichari, and Paul Adam. Among the numerous others were A. Dupuis-Yakouba, C. Monteil, and Franz de Zeltner who published collections of folklore.

[4] Of the more literary production of this period there were such works as Pièrre Benoit's *Atlantide,* Jean Marville's collection of poems in prose, *La Chanson de Kou-Singa* appearing in 1920, René Maran's Goncourt Prize work, *Batouala* in 1921 and his *Djouma, chien de chasse* in 1927, Jerome and Jean Tharaud's *La randonnée de Samba-Diouf,* Paul Jourdy's *Le sculpteur de lumière* in 1923, Gaston Joseph's *Koffi* that same year, Alfred Chaumel's *Aminata, femme noire* in 1923, Charles Regismanset's *La Faya sur le Niger* also in 1923, and several novels by André Demaison entitled *Diato, Roman de l'homme noir qui eut trois femmes et en mourut, La femme et l'homme nu, La reine de l'ombre, Les Oiseaux de'ébène, Diaeli, Tropique,* and, *D'Autres Bêtes qu'on appelle sauvages* in 1923, 1924, 1925, 1931, 1933, and 1934 respectively.

[5] Among these authors are Gilbert d'Alem, J. F. Boeuf, L. Charbonneau, Michel Perron, and Delhaise-Arnould. Some of these works have been analyzed by Roland Lebel in his *L'Afrique Occidentale dans la literature française.* The same idea of treating in fiction the customs of the natives is carried further by René Trautmann in his *Tu y reviendra,* and his *La littérature populaire a la côte des esclaves;* by Georges Poulet in his *Author*

about this time, too, painters and sculptors began to choose Negro subjects more frequently especially in decorative art. R. R. Nivelt in the "Head of a Senegalese Woman," René Riot in "Requiescant" and Gurdjan in his "Head of a Negro" showed this attitude. The tendency toward African influence is still more pronounced in Matisse and Soutine because of their increasing interest in African Art.

Germany, farther removed from the African scene than the Mediterranean powers, recorded little about the Negro. We know of the favorable attitude of the Holy Roman Empire toward Angelo Soliman, brought into the country mainly as a curiosity. He was given the opportunity to learn military tactics and distinguished himself in the service of the Holy Roman Emperor. Some differences arose between the two about the German woman whom Soliman married, but whether this was race prejudice or some other objection is not made clear. After this misunderstanding, however, a reconciliation followed.

It is well to note, however, that in later years, Germany welcomed Anton Wilhelm Amo, an African, and after educating him invited him to serve as a professor of philosophy at the University of Wittenberg. Negroes in minor rôles figured later in the life of that country. Of the subsequent attitude in Germany we hear little more until we come to such travelers as Johann Schoepf, Gottfried Duden, Frederich Schlegel and Bernard Von Sachsen-Weimar, who gave to the German public their impressions of the Negro in other countries. Among German artists the Negro does not play any conspicuous part, but in the histories of the time he was naturally mentioned in very voluminous productions mainly as a traditional nonentity but apparently without prejudice. However, it should be noted that for some reason certain Germans have manifested a deep interest in Haiti and Santo Domingo. In 1826 F. Phillippi published *Geschichte des Freistaates von Santo Domingo,* in 1846 Wilhelm Jordan brought out his *Geschichte der Insel Haiti,* and in 1856 H. Handelmann published also a *Geschichte der Insel*

---

d'une femme sous les tropiques; by Claude Bréton in his *Bilali ou la vengeance du lion*; by Julien Maigret in *Tam-Tam*; by Alfred Cazes in his *Le Niger sentimental*; by Prevaudeau in *Nahi, femme de blanc*; by Francois Valdi in *La femme-antilope*; by Jean d'Esme in *Le soleil d'Ethiopie*; by Jane Valriant in *La Randonnée Soudanaise de Suzanne Davenel.*

Haiti. Recently we have noted Erwin Rusch's *Die Revolution von Saint Domingue.* McLean's *Uncle Tom's Cabin in Germany* (New York, 1910) shows another interest of these people at the time this narrative was moving other parts of Europe.

Productions of a literary order, however, came from German writers who had some serious thought with respect to the Negro and his condition in the modern world. Among such writers were Charles Sealsfield, Frederick Gerstacker, and Barthold Auerbach who expressed themselves on slavery. Gerstacker gave this question the dignity of real literature in bringing out in 1844 his *Streifund Jagdzüge durch die Vereinigten Staaten.* Sealsfield did likewise in 1846 in publishing his *Lebensbilder aus der Westlichen Hemisphaere.* In 1856 *Wolfseden* was produced as a story of a planter whose mother turns out to be partly Negro and is himself almost enslaved. Theodore Storm wrote in 1857 his *Von Jenseits des Meeres,* the struggle of a mulatto girl. Adelbert Heinrich Baudissin, with less literary merit, published in 1869 *Peter Tutt: Zustande in Amerika,* a work of fiction portraying conditions in the United States at that time.[6] In 1869 Berthold Auerbach brought out *Das Landhaus am Rhein,* the story of a German who served among the Americans first as a slavetrader and then as a Confederate soldier. Baldwin Molhausen struck the note of the Negro in *Das Hundertguldenblatt* and *Der Piratenlieutenant* in 1870, in *Die Kinder des Sträflings* and *Nord und Sud* in 1876, in *Wildes Blut* in 1885, in *Die Familie Melville* in 1889, and in *Welche von Beiden?* in 1897. In 1873 appeared Adolf Schirmer's novel, *Die Sklavenbarone; oder Weiss und Schwarz,* although written at a much earlier date.

The post-Civil War literature abroad which, like that on this side, first portrayed the freedman in the new day, expressed about the only thought the Germans gave the Negro until that nation became a colonial power in Africa. Thereafter Germany tended to show in its literature the attitude of other Europeans exploiting that continent. These productions, however, dealt mainly with the political, industrial, and economic aspects of the African continent. The German's scholarly treatments bearing upon the natives of Africa are chiefly ethnographic and anthropological.

More recently, however, other productions of the Germans have been noted. In 1917 appeared Johannes Emonts' *Der Zauberer der*

[6] Consult the work bearing this title.

Bahiri, and in 1926 Marc R. Breyne's *Die Zukunft von Sudafrika;* but these were not literary productions. Hanna Meuter attracted some attention on both sides of the Atlantic in 1927 with the publication of *Der Neue Neger in Amerikanischen Literatur* in the *Kölner Vierteljahrshefte für Soziologie.* The publishing in the German language in 1932 of an anthology of American Negro verse under the title *Amerika singe auch ich* by this author and Paul Therstappen showed the drift of the mind of an increasing number of the German population before it became committed to the anti-racial policy of the recent régime. At present it seems that the German liberalism resulting from the World War upheaval has been generally crushed.

Russia, of later development and never a colonizing nation in Africa, had still less reason to give thought to the Negro. Abram Hannibal, the grandfather of Pushkin, was taken to Russia mainly out of curiosity as the "Negro of Peter the Great." His career shows no thought of being assigned to a subordinate position in the public mind. He and his son, the father of Pushkin, educated as an engineer in France, were rather great favorites at the Russian court. Pushkin never finished a tale in which he referred to his grandfather as an Arab; but, as stated by Professor Clarence A. Manning, of Columbia, there is abundant evidence that he was a Negro.[7] Tolstoy made few if any references to the Negro, although he favored the abolitionists in the Civil War because in his opinion they were trying to destroy the old order in America. N. Gumilev, who visited Africa before the World War, made some comments on Liberia, but he was not very complimentary of what he observed there.

Since the revolution in Russia by which the old régime was destroyed unusual interest has been expressed in Negroes in all sorts of productions. The black people have been taken into consideration as the oppressed which the new social order must try to relieve. In 1919 appeared Vl. Markov's *Iskusstvo Negrov,* a study of Negro sculpture. In 1926 came S. Ginzburg's *Dzhaz-band i Sovremennaya Muzyka,* a work on jazz music. About the same time ap-

[7] Clarence A. Manning, "Aleksandr of Sergieevich Pushkin" in the *South Atlantic Quarterly,* XXX, pp. 76-88, January, 1926; D. S. Mirsky, *Pushkin,* New York, 1926; and Alexander Nazaror, "Russia's Greatest Poet and the Soviets." (*Lit. Digest,* Int. Bk. R. N., 1924: pp. 864-5).

peared N. N. Breshko-Breshkovski's *Demon Pustyni,* a novel with
one of the characters a Negro. In 1927 followed V. Mayakovski's
Black and White, a poem on the Negro. In 1930 a translation of
Du Bose Heywood's *Porgy,* by V. A. Dilevsky reached the public.
In 1932 appeared V. Tan Bogoraz's *Lyudi i nravy v Amerike* which
contains chapters on the Negro theatre, and on Langston Hughes.
In 1933 came Yu Anisimov's *Afrika v Amerike,* which was an
Antologiya poezii amerikanskikh negrov, an anthology of Amer-
ican Negro poetry. In 1934 followed R. Magidov's *Negry Poyut,
Antologiya Negrityanskoi Poezii,* another such anthology. Walter
White's *Fire in the Flint,* an exposé of lynching in the United
States, has been translated into the Russian language and exten-
sively circulated in that country.

Of the Dutch with their much diminished contacts after being
displaced as the leader on the high seas we know very little.
Negroes taken over or received by Dutch traders were given the
same opportunity as others of this status. Slavery as developed
by the Dutch in their colonial domain does not show more evil aspects than those observed elsewhere, although for some reason
Dutch slave-traders are thought of as the worst in the world. For
example, Diaguillo, a Havana slave, who escaped from the
Spanish to a Dutch ship, became a favorite captain of a vessel himself and left an impression on the high seas as a corsair. J. E. J.
Captein, taken to Holland by a slaver that captured him in West
Africa, was educated in Holland and honored there for his knowledge of the classics, theology, and philosophy.

In its attitudes, Belgium, although with various extractions, has
tended to follow the course of most Latins. In the early sixteenth
century Antwerp had a thriving international commerce like that of
Venice and tended to deal with men and nations in the same way.
Things developed to the contrary when Amsterdam, London, Hamburg, and Frankfort surpassed Antwerp in its own sphere and became the centers for the popular money-lenders and speculators.
Belgium, not yet evolved as a nation because of the wars with
Spain, did not have a place in the public mind until the end of the
seventeenth century; and even after it was recognized as an independent state in 1831, the country was too small and isolated to
figure in international affairs except as to maintain the balance of
power in Europe. The most continuous contact with Africans and

their continent came with the occupation of the Congo by a Belgian company under Leopold II when the whole civilized world had to throw up its arms in holy horror at the atrocities committed there in the exploitation of the rubber industry. These malefactors, however, did not represent the people of their country. In their every day life, in their literature, and in their art the Belgians have maintained chiefly the attitude of the Latins. The distinguished literary men and artists of Belgium belong to the liberal minded class. Peter Paul Rubens brings the Negro into his "Diogenes Seeking a Man," the "Adoration of the Magi," and the "Triumph of Religion." Likewise Jacob Jordaens paints a Negro figure in his "Jesus Driving the Venders from the Temple," and the Negro is not one of these money-mongers.

In Denmark, however, more thought was given to the race as a result of the Negro population of its possessions. In that country arose a group of ardent abolitionists who in cooperation with Thomas H. Clarkson, of England, expressed their views in their writings. Only occasionally, however, has the Negro been mentioned in their literature. One thought of the race is given by Karl Kyersmerer's *Negere som Digtere* (Negroes as Poets) which appeared as a translation in the *Crisis* in August, 1925. The history of the Danish West Indies, the Virgin Islands purchased by the United States, also occasionally found a place in Danish thought. The Danes did not prove to be such terrible taskmasters there as the ruling class became on some other islands. The frequent insurrections in the Virgin Islands which at times assumed large proportions show either the disinclination or the inability of Denmark to reduce the Negroes of these parts to the usually low beast-of-burden status.

In the earliest references to the Negro in English literature and art we find the Negro treated more as a curiosity than as some one to be detested or shunned. Approaching the matter without prejudice, "Negroes" were portrayed as participants in the "Quest of the Holy Grail" and in "King Arthur and his Knights of the Round Table." It should be noted, however, that the English during their early years used the word Moor [8] or Saracen interchangeably with that of the black man.

[8] See C. G. Woodson's "Some Attitudes in English Literature," *The Journal of Negro History*, XX, pp. 27-85.

In later British literature we find that the Negro was referred to both favorably and unfavorably. While there easily develops in the mind of the Nordic an attitude of snobbishness or superiority over other races the number of Negroes in England was never sufficient to bring to that country the race question as it has existed elsewhere in all its intensity. However, at one time some one did express alarm when the number of Negroes in London reached twenty thousand. There were, moreover, statesmen who, like Chatham and Nelson, believed that the slave trade was essential to the commercial expansion of England. But there were among the common people, those who had the thought of this inscription on a Liverpool jug found in the Municipal Museum at Hull: "Health to the Sick, Honor to the Brave, Success to the Lover, and Freedom to the Slave."

In both poetry and fiction this sentiment was found, and the Negro when thus treated was not infrequently presented as a man of virtue. Shakespeare himself refers to the Negro in various ways in certain of his works. He presents Othello as incontestably a native of Africa. It is clear that he was thought of as a Negro, for he says in reference to Desdemona, "Her name that was as fresh as Dian's visage is now begrim'd and black as mine own face." Shakespeare had a special interest in the Negro himself doubtless for the reason that he once had a popular Negro mistress on account of whom his relations were strained with his rival in her affections, the Earl of Southampton. Several of his sonnets were based upon his relations with this woman of color.

In the development of an attitude toward slavery, of course, certain people of England led by Clarkson, Sharp, Buxton, Wilberforce and Lushington, reflected that of the most distinguished advocates of freedom on both sides of the Atlantic. The question, however, had been discussed by Daniel Defoe and Horace Walpole in their works. Carlyle who did not seem to favor instant emancipation notwithstanding advocated freedom by purchase; but Pope, Cowper, Shelley, Tennyson, Thomson, Wordsworth, Browning and Byron all reflected a liberal attitude toward the blacks. Although debased by slavery the Negroes were nevertheless thought of as persons. The English public reflected an attitude in becoming interested in the poetical works of Phillis Wheatley, in the rise of

Toussaint Louverture, in the agitation for the abolition of slavery in the West Indies, and in the appearance of *Uncle Tom's Cabin.* Thomas Hughes, a man of letters, by his interest in the abolition of slavery showed the deep concern of the highly literary men with respect to the future of the Negro. It is with literary production with a Negro slant rather than with the anti-slavery efforts here, however, that we are chiefly concerned.

Some of these productions thereby produced may be interesting. There were numerous books on travel and adventure teeming with such thought. Aphra Behn's *Oroonoko,* a realistic novel appearing in 1678 and its adaptation to the stage by Southerne made a deep impression in England. In 1798 appeared an interesting account of *Devotion of a Negro Guide and Friend, Yahomey* by George Cumberland, and about 1800 the *African Widow,* the purpose of which was to arouse interest in the home established for the poor blacks and Indians. Much sympathy was aroused for the Negro by the contribution in 1826 by the Reverend Leigh Richmond entitled *The Negro Servant in the Annals of the Poor,* and by Selwyn's *Negro Boy* the same year. In 1830 W. Naish produced *The Negro Slave,* a tale addressed to the women of Great Britain. Edwin L. Sabin published a novel, *Rio Bravo,* dealing with the Mexican War in its bearing upon slavery. In 1854 Mrs. William Noy Wilkins appeared with a production entitled *The Slave Son.* The introduction of a West Indian heiress, a naive character in Thackeray's *Vanity Fair,* aroused some interest in the Negro. *Black Ivory,* a tale of adventure of slaves of East Africa, by R. M. Ballantyne in 1873, also evoked comment. Lady Burton's edition of her husband's *Arabian Nights* (1886-87) in which was emphasized the rôle of King Shahryar and his brother and the tale of the ensorcelled prince received a little notice. *Reverend John Greedy* by Grant Allen, which appeared in 1889 among *Strange Stories* in the *Cornhill Magazine* attracted more attention. During these years British Art as expressed by Reynolds, Gainsborough and Turner, however, was not so mindful of the Negro.

The Negro was introduced to the British public and to the other parts of the English-speaking world especially by the productions of travelers in America. These run from the time of Andrew Burnbay down to Viscount James Bryce. Of those giving fulsome accounts of their observations when traveling in America we need mention here only a few.   While Sir Charles Lyell put his impressions of this country into such literary form that we study it in our schools even today Charles Dickens displeased us very much by what he had to say about Americans.   Harriet Martineau wrote especially on the Negro as would an abolitionist.   Giving a picture of the United States after the Civil War, however, there were few productions of the sort more impressive than David Macrae's *The Americans at Home,* Robert Somer's *Southern States Since the War,* and Sir George Campbell's *White and Black.*   A number of other travelers published their observations on America, but because of too many misrepresentations and inadequate statements their works are considered neither literary nor informing.

In later authors who have referred to the Negro in some way we find the popular attitude reflected in both ways, for and against the Negro.   Among these works may be noted Allen McCauley's (Charlotte Stuart's) *Black Mary* (1901), Henry Cottrell Rowland's *In Shadow* (1902), Francis Bancroft's *Of Like Passions* (1907), John Masefield's *Multitude and Solitude* (1909), E. Temple Thurston's *The Guardian Resurrection* (1911), Sir H. Hesketh Bell's *Love in Black* (1911), Maxwell Laurie's *The Black Blanket* (1921), Sarah Gertrude Millen's *God's Stepchildren* (1924), and George Bernard Shaw's *The Adventures of a Black Girl in Her Search for God* (1932).   H. G. Wells among others has been broad enough to treat the Negro as a person entitled to the consideration shown other elements of the social order.

In other European states there has been such a little contact with Africans or their descendants that their attitudes in this respect are not well defined.   The Scandinavian countries are practically neutral on this point.   Switzerland, an international center, does not have to assume any such attitude.   Poland, of a precarious existence, has not had time to deal with such matters.   Austria, until recently, followed the fortunes of Germany.   Hungary, Servia, Roumania, Bulgaria and other Balkan states have had little reason to be thus concerned.   For these reasons an introductory treatment of this field is impracticable.   Only by research and careful presentation can one of a mature mind deal wtih the problems herein presented.

I. FIRST NOTICE TAKEN OF THE NEGRO BY THE MEDITERRANEANS

1. Pelasgians, Cretans, Etruscans
2. Greek Writers—Homer, Æschylus, and Herodotus
3. The Thought of Ancient Writers of a Later Period
4. Greek Art—Painting and Sculpture
5. Unearthed Ruins of Antiquity
6. In Greek Colonies

II. THE ATTITUDE OF THE ROMANS

7. The Negro in the Roman Empire

1. A brief statement of these early contacts of peoples of color in the Mediterranean world is set forth in George Wells Parker's "The African Origin of the Grecian Civilization" in *The Journal of Negro History*, II, pp. 334-344. See also the *History* by Herodotus (translation of Larcher, revised by Personneaux, Paris, 1883; and the translation by G. Rawlinson, New York); and G. H. Beardsley's *The Negro in the Greek and Roman Civilization*, chapter I (Baltimore, 1929).

2. See Munroe N. Work's "The Passing Tradition and the African Civilization" in *The Journal of Negro History*, I, pp. 34-41; Lady Lugard's *Tropical Dependency*, pp. 10, 12, 221; and M. Delafosse's *Negroes of Africa*, chapter I.

3. Consult George Wells Parker, *loc. cit.* in *The Journal of Negro History*, II, pp. 339-340. See also the *Works* of Æschylus (Translation by E. H. Plumtree, New York, 1868); and Beardsley's work cited above, chapters I and XI.

4. This attitude can be determined only by examining Greek painting and sculpture. Some idea may be obtained from reproductions of these works. Consult G. H. Beardsley's *The Negro in the Greek and Roman Civilization*. Bear in mind, however, that she injects her American anti-racial bias into almost every sentence of this work in which she undertakes interpretation. She misuses valuable facts.

5. See *The Journal of Negro History*, II, pp. 334-344. Consult also the works of Schlieman and Sir Arthur Evans's *The Palace of Minos*, I, pp. 302, 310, 312, 321, 526, 757.

6. Works of art found in the outer Greek world, in their colonies, show that some thought was taken of those Africans known to them. Consult Beardsley's *The Negro in the Greek and Roman Civilization*, the part dealing with the Hellenistic civilization, pp. 82-110.

7. The map of the Roman Empire in its golden age will show how much of Africa was therein included. Most African Negroes were below the Sahara, but from time immemorial they were crossing the Sahara for con-

II. THE ATTITUDE OF THE ROMANS—*Continued*

8. TREATMENT OF AFRICAN CAPTIVES
9. ROMAN CITIZENSHIP AND FREEDOM WITH RESPECT TO THE AFRICAN PROVINCE
10. LATIN AUTHORS—TERENCE, VERGIL, OVID, CICERO, JUVENAL, AND MARTIAL
11. ROMAN ART—PAINTING AND SCULPTURE
12. EXCAVATIONS IN THE ROMAN AREA

tacts with the mixed breeds along the Mediterranean. It is now known that the Sahara is more of a desert today than centuries ago, and travel across it was not so difficult at that time. Because of the changing complexion of the people in this part of the Mediterranean melting pot, however, it is impossible to figure out exactly how many Negroes were actually brought under the control of the Roman African province. The ruins and sculptures of the empire give evidence of a considerable number. The historians support this conclusion.

8. Africans, like others subdued by the Romans, were treated as captives. There is no record of cruel treatment being accorded persons on the basis of their color. A captive was a captive; a slave was a slave whether he was a Thracian, a Syrian, or an African. The early Romans, following the policy of the Greeks, treated the African blacks with more consideration than they did others of foreign shores. Imperialism, however, changed this attitude. See Hutton Webster's *Early European History* (Boston, 1920) pp. 268-270, 436, 463; and E. S. Bouchier's *Life and Letters in Roman Africa* (Oxford, 1913). Scores of other works of this sort may serve here the same general purpose.

9. Consult almost any recognized treatment on the organization of the Roman Empire. See Webster, *op. cit.,* pp. 155, 177, 179, 187, 297, 204, 206, 215; W. T. Arnold's *Roman System of Political Administration, passim;* and Lady Lugard's *A Tropical Dependency* (London, 1905), pp. 13-14.

10. A number of references to the Negro in Roman literature are set forth in G. H. Beardsley's *The Negro in the Greek and Roman Civilization.* This author, however, has not collected all such data; she noted only those which appealed to her. Further information may be obtained by consulting the works of the Roman writers whom the author quotes.

11. In the same way that Mrs. Beardsley treated the references mentioned above she has noted instances of Negroes in Greek and Roman works of art. This study should be carried further by the actual examination of these works by students thus concerned. This particular author is concerned mainly with those cases in support of her point of view which shows an ever present anti-racial bias.

12. Excavations in the outer parts of the Roman Empire rather than in Italy itself more clearly reflect the attitude of the Romans toward the people in the provinces than the books written about it fifteen centuries

III. ATTITUDES DURING THE MIDDLE AGES

later. Unfortunately, however, students on the American side of the Atlantic have few opportunities for such investigation; and American historians who have had such access fail to record the whole truth. In most large American museums there are a few art works based upon the African in the Mediterranean. European museums teem with such relics.

13. Almost any standard history of Europe during the Middle Ages will give a detailed account of conditions obtaining during this period as a result of the break-up of the Roman Empire. Chapter XIII of Hutton Webster's *Early European History*, Chapters I to XII of Lynn Thorndike's *History of Medieval Europe* or E. Emerton's *Introduction to the Middle Ages* will suffice.

14. During this turmoil nothing could be considered permanently established or well-defined. The changing order of evolving states becomes apparent to one reading the works referred to under 13. It appears as a period of transition through a slow reconstruction from the chaos of a dark age. Instead of reaching out to the outlying world like Africa the new states in the making had more than they could do in trying to administer efficiently the area which had at one time been brought under the civilizing influences of Greece and Rome. This left Africa as a field for Asiatic exploitation.

15. The northern European tribes had knowledge only of what was immediately in sight. They had no well defined notions even of the Roman world before them. They had to be absorbed or assimilated to civilized standards before they could bestir themselves in other directions. What survived in Rome was sufficiently satisfying to them for years to come. These barbarians had no immediate dreams for further conquests.

16. The Vandals went to Africa not to conquer that continent, as the sources cited will show, but in order to reach Rome more easily than by direct invasion from the north. There was nothing particularly attractive to them in North Africa except what they believed the Romans had there. The contact of the Vandals with the Berbers and blacks of North Africa, however, made possible the introduction of an additional number of Africans to Rome. The later struggle of Justinian with the Vandals in Africa is well discussed by Lynn Thorndike in the twelfth chapter of his *History of Medieval Europe*. More elaborate accounts may be found in E. S. Bouchier's *Roman Africa*, pp. 105-111; and in Charles André Julien's *Histoire de l'Afrique du Nord*, pp. 288-308.

III. ATTITUDES DURING THE MIDDLE AGES—*Continued*

    17. ISLAM IN NORTH AFRICA AND EUROPE
    18. SPANISH, MOORS, AND ARABS ON THE WEST COAST

IV. THE POSITION OF THE EARLY CHURCH

    19. THE APPEAL TO ALL MEN
    20. AN IDEA OF UNIVERSAL BROTHERHOOD
    21. THE DOCTRINE OF THE CHURCH ACCORDING TO THE FATHERS
    22. THE CONCEPTION OF RELIGIOUS ARTISTS

17. Islam in North Africa may be traced in almost any useful history of the promotion of that religion. Thorndike briefly treats it in the tenth chapter and on pages 178 to 180 and 182 to 190 of his work cited above; and so does Webster in his work on pages 375-379. A more extensive account is given in the Cambridge *Medieval History*, II, chapter x, "Mohamet and Islam," by A. A. Bevan.

18. The Spanish, Moors and Arabs who penetrated the interior of Africa after plying along the West Coast for years, have their story told all but throughout "The African Background" of this work. These facts are briefly stated on pages 381 to 383 of the second volume of M. Delafosse's *Haut-Sénégal-Niger*. The treatment of these forces at a later period is also given on pages 81 to 88 of the same author's *Negroes of Africa* and on pages 140 to 142 of J. L. Monod's *Histoire de l'Afrique Occidentale Française*.

19. The message of the early church to the war-ridden world has been related by thousands of witnesses. For a concise statement, however, the student will find adequate the sixth chapter of Lynn Thorndike's *History of Medieval Europe*. The New Testament itself is the best source, but men promulgated their interpretations of the Scriptures rather than the principles therein set forth.

20. In the sources cited above the idea of the brotherhood of man is made clear as a dominant teaching of Christianity. However, thousands of works dealing with this aspect of church doctrine may be consulted. G. P. Fisher's *Beginnings of Christianity* (New York, 1878), and T. J. Shahan's *The Beginning of Christianity* (New York, 1903) are helpful. Many other works of this order will serve the same purpose.

21. The actual teachings of the Church Fathers may be studied in English translation in two works entitled *The Anti-Nicene Fathers* and *The Nicene and Post-Nicene Fathers*. These, however, have been confused by commentaries thereupon.

22. An examination of the works of the painters and sculptors of Christian bent or satisfactory reproductions of them is necessary to understand these artists' attitude toward universal brotherhood and the equality of man before God. Study especially the paintings portraying the "Adoration of the Magi," the "Wedding Feast at Cana," and the "General Judgment." Consult the *Cambridge Medieval History*, I, 598-613.

IV. THE POSITION OF THE EARLY CHURCH—*Continued*

V. THE NORMANS FOLLOWED BY THE PORTUGUESE IN CONTACT WITH NEGROES

23. Various histories of Egypt and Ethiopia may be consulted. In most of such works the Christianization of these countries occupies some space. Church histories dealing with missionary enterprise *in extenso* cover this topic fully. It is referred to also in general works like W. E. B. Du Bois's *The Negro* on pp. 42, 128 and 129; and in M. Delafosse's *Negroes of Africa*, pp. 40, 48, 112, 125-126. The student should consult the fifth chapter of *Ethiopie Moderne* by the Comtesse de Jumilhac, and also the second volume of the *History of Egypt* by Flinders Petrie.

24. Consult E. Hatch's *Organization of the Early Christian Churches* (1881) ; G. Ulhom's *Conflict of Christianity with Heathensim*, (New York, 1879) ; and A. Carr's *The Church and the Roman Empire.*

25. See Duruy's *History of the Crusades*, Chapter XX. Consult also *Translations and Reprints of the University of Pennsylvania*, I, Nos. 2 and 4, and III, No. 1.

26. Here the student will find little bearing directly on the Negro. He should know, however, that the schism which resulted in the Reformation or the Protestant revolt weakened the Church as a world force and delayed the evangelization of Africa. The various branches of the Church which thereby resulted may have long delayed the evangelization of Africa. This delay made possible more extensive inroads by the Mohammedans in Africa. When the Europeans were busy warring among themselves Asia was left free to give attention to Africa. Islam advanced far in the meantime with the slave trade in Africa, and both Catholic and Protestants later yielded to the national states demanding Christian approval of the human traffic to fill their coffers. A strong and undivided Church controlling rather than being controlled by national states would have had less reason for such a compromise.

27. The Normans, unlike the other tribes who never ventured into Africa far from the northern shore, explored the West Coast of that continent. They were the first Europeans to undertake this task, although they were later supplanted by the more aggressive Portuguese. It is well known that the Normans were the greatest sea rovers of their day, and it is not surprising that they ventured so far from Europe as early as the beginning

V. THE NORMANS FOLLOWED BY THE PORTU-GUESE IN CONTACT WITH NEGROES—*Continued*

28. As Adventurers along the West African Coast: Prince Henry and Da Gama

29. The Negro in the Portuguese Colonial Empire

30. Efforts to Christianize the Natives—the Kingdom of the Congo

31. The Importation of Negroes into Portugal

of the fourteenth century. The best brief account of these operations along the West Coast of Africa is found in J. L. Monod's *Histoire de l'Afrique Occidentale Française*, pp. 147-150. For more extensive information C. H. Haskins' studies of the Normans should be read. These later contacts concern us elsewhere in this treatment.

28. The early efforts of the Portuguese in Africa are briefly discussed by M. Delafosse in his *Negroes of Africa*, on pp. 67, 74, 76, 136, 138, and 139; by W. E. B. Du Bois in his *The Negro* on pp. 17, 18, 44, 71, 75; and by J. L. Monod in his *Histoire de L'Afrique Occidentale Française* on pp. 156 to 157. More extensive treatments are C. R. Beazley's *Prince Henry, the Navigator*, in "Heroes of the Nation" Series (1897); J. P. Oliveira Martin's *The Golden Age of Prince Henry, the Navigator*, (translated with notes and additions by J. J. Abraham and W. E. Reynolds, 1914); and K. G. Jayne's *Vasco da Gama and his Successors* (1910).

29. The sources given above supply adequate information as to the territory included in the empire conceded the Portuguese as a result of their explorations and granted by the Treaty of Tordesillas. That the large number of Negroes thus claimed as subjects of Portugal were not always thus influenced goes without question, especially since Portugal was later annexed to Spain; and, although subsequently made independent, Portugal did not regain her lead in exploration and commercial enterprise. Some Portuguese contacts and influences along the coast, however, must be noted as significant. In the meantime many Africans were taken to Portugal and absorbed there by that nation as social equals. See C. G. Woodson's "Attitudes in the Iberian Peninsula," *Journal of Negro History*, XX, pp. 190-243.

30. For the Christianization of the natives of the Congo kingdom consult Angel Marvaud's *Le Portugal et ses colonies;* Charles Edward Chapman's *Colonial Hispanic America* under "Brazil"; G. M. Theal's *History and Ethnography of Africa South of the Zambesi*, I, *The Portuguese in South Africa from 1505 to 1700* (1907); and Van Wing's *Etudes Bakongo* (Brussels, 1922). See also for further treatment A. Bastian's *Ein Besuch in San-Salvador, der Haupstadt des Königreichs Congo* (Bremen, 1859); and Gio Cavazzi de Montecuccolo's *Istorica discrizione de tre regni Congo, Matamba e Angola* (Bologna, 1687).

31. Use the references given under 30 and consult *The Journal of Negro History*, XIX, pp. 120-121; W. E. B. Du Bois's *The Negro*, pp. 74-75; and P. D. Rinchon's *La Traite et l'Esclavage des Congolais par les Européens* (1929); pp. 46-70.

V. THE NORMANS FOLLOWED BY THE PORTU-GUESE IN CONTACT WITH NEGROES—*Continued*

32. NEGROES CARRIED TO PORTUGUESE COLONIES
33. THE PORTUGUESE TREATMENT OF SLAVES
34. THE NEGRO AS PRESENTED IN PORTUGUESE LITERA-TURE AND ART
35. THE RECENT PORTUGUESE ATTITUDE

VI. THE ATTITUDE OF THE SPANIARDS

36. NEGROES IN MEDIEVAL SPAIN

32. Almost any history of Brazil, the outstanding Portuguese colony of that day, contains the facts as to the importation of African slaves by the Portuguese and by the Dutch there. The latter had more or less control of Brazil from 1624 to 1654, after which an uprising of Portuguese restored Brazil to their home country. Consult, however, Angel Marvaud's *Le Portugal et ses Colonies* (1912), H. M. Stephens's *Portugal* (1891); P. D. Rinchon's *La Traite et l'Esclavage des Congolais par les Européens* (1929); and C. G. Woodson's "Attitudes in the Iberian Peninsula," *Journal of Negro History,* XX, pp. 190-243

33. The treatment of the slaves, as the references herein given will show, is often referred to as that of the Latin in contradistinction to that of the Teuton. From what the student has already read he should be able to make the comparison himself. However, several of these authors do this task for the reader. Consult *The Journal of Negro History,* Volume III, pp. 31-32, and C. E. Chapman's *Colonial Hispanic America,* pp. 81, 84. Bear in mind, however, that Chapman writes from the point of view of the Nordic.

34. Here as elsewhere in the use of works of art as historical evidence the student himself must see the productions of these masters or accepted reproductions of them. This is a difficult problem for those who have had no opportunity to travel in Europe. In the case of Portuguese literature the task is apparently easy, but most of it must be read in the original. Not much Portuguese literature has been translated into English. The Negro, however, is occasionally mentioned therein. See C. G. Woodson's "Attitudes in the Iberian Peninsula," *Journal of Negro History,* XX, pp. 190-243.

35. In modern times, the Portuguese, shorn of some of their colonies and reduced to a third rate power, have not influenced the world very much in art and literature. With the exception of the notices taken of the Negroes in their African colonies, the race has ceased to be concerned with those people except as an element of population which when Christianized and modernized should be treated as other men. Consult E. L. Guernier's *L'Afrique Champ d'Expansion de l'Europe* (Paris, 1933), and Woodson, *op. cit., passim.*

36. The Negro in Medieval Spain is extensively treated in the sources cited on pp. 222-224. The main point is to connect here the thought therein expressed in order to give a broader picture of Spain in all its aspects.

VI. THE ATTITUDE OF THE SPANIARDS—*Continued*

37. The Negro Policy of Spanish Sovereigns—Ex-
    ploration and Colonization
38. The Negro in the Spanish Colonial Empire
39. The Attitude of the Spanish Clergy—Azurara
    and Bartolemé de las Casas
40. The Negro in Spanish Literature and Art
    during the Sixteenth and Seventeenth
    Centuries

37. The policies of the Spanish sovereigns are set forth in these same sources, especially in the work of Sir Arthur Helps. Consult also, however, C. G. Woodson, *Education of the Negro Prior to 1861*, pp. 19-20; E. G. Bourne, *Spain in America*, p. 241; Herrera, *Historia General*, dec. iv, libro ii; dec. v, libro ii; dec. vii, libro iv; and P. D. Rinchon, *La Traite et l'Esclavage des Congolais par les Européens* (Paris, 1929). The Negro with the Spanish explorers has received treatment from various points of view in the following: Woodson's *Negro in Our History*, pp. 59-60; *Journal of Negro History*, VI, pp. 183-189. Almost any comprehensive work treating Spain in America deals in some way with this question.

38. The best brief statement of the status of the Negroes among the Spaniards is in C. E. Chapman's *Colonial Hispanic America*, pp. 6, 27-28, 108, 116, 119-10, 123-124, 147, 154, 166, 172, 188, 189, 194, 206, 209-210, 235, 239, 253, 294, 298. Chapman, however, is biased. He has the attitude of the Nordic and makes his interpretations *ex parte*. See also Clarence H. Haring's *Trade and Navigation between Spain and the Indies*, in the "Harvard University Economic Studies;" Justin Winsor's *Narrative and Critical History*, II; Mary Wilhelmine Williams' "The Treatment of Negro Slaves in the Brazilian Empire" in *The Journal of Negro History*, XV, pp. 315-336; H. B. Alexander's "Brazilian and United States Slavery Compared," the same magazine, VII, pp. 349-364; and Bernard Moses's *The Establishment of Spanish Rule in America*, passim.

39. Consult C. E. Chapman's *Colonial Hispanic America*, pp. 26, 27, 53, 112-114, 119, 152. Advanced study may necessitate the examination of Azurara's lamentation in *The Journal of Negro History*, XX, pp. 190-243; and the *Brevissima relación de la destruyción de las Indias, Historia general de las Indias*, and *Historia apologetica de las Indias*—both by Bartolomé de las Casas himself.

40. The available histories of Spanish literature are too brief to give the facts desired here. Consult *Comedia famosa de Juan Latino*, by Diego Ximenez de Enciso in the second part of *Comedias escogidas de las mejores de Espana* (Madrid, 1652). Read also *El Negro, Juan Latino*. This is a critical biographical effort by Antonio Marin-Ocete, of Granada (Granada, 1925). Professor V. B. Spratlin's article on the Negro in Spain in the *Crisis*, November, 1928, is also informing. Consult the works of Cervantes, Lope de Vega, and Calderón.

VI. THE ATTITUDE OF THE SPANIARDS—*Continued*

VII. THE FRENCH AND THE NEGRO

41. The thought of the eighteenth century is expressed in the last mentioned reference above, but the works of the following should be consulted: J. Fitzmaurice-Kelley, *Cambridge Readings in Spanish Literature*; H. Thomas, *Spanish and Portuguese Romances of Chivalry*; G. Le Strange, *Spanish Ballads*.

42. The change of attitude, if any, will appear in the works produced during this period. The important productions to be noted are chiefly those of Valdés, Galdós, Valera, Echagary, Moratín, and Alarcón.

43. Here again the works themselves must be studied. Examine those appearing at the present time. Periodical literature will assist in clarifying matters. See *The Journal of Negro History*, XX, pp. 240-243.

44. The attitude of France in the sixteenth century is portrayed as favorable to liberty in J. L. Monod's *Histoire de l'Afrique Occidentale Française*, p. 156. He gives as evidence thereof, the refusal of the Norman Corsairs to engage in the slave traffic on the West African coast and the freeing of captives by the Parlement of Bordeaux in 1571, proclaiming that "France, the mother of liberty, does not permit slavery." This thought is not elaborated by this author.

45. Whatever the early attitude was the French later entered upon the same trade as did others in their commercial expansion and colonial development. From a universal point of view this settled policy is given in the sixth chapter of the second volume of Carlton J. H. Hayes' *A Political and Social History of Modern Europe*. For details as to Negro slaves and mulattoes in this empire one must read works like A. J. Sargent's *Economic Policy of Colbert;* Pierre Clement's *Lettres, Instructions, et mémoires de Colbert* (1861-1873); Gaston Martin's *L'Ere des Négriers* (Paris, 1931); Georges Hardy's *Histoire de la Colonisation Française* (Paris, 1931), and E. L. Guernier's *L'Afrique Champ d'Expansion de l'Europe* (Paris, 1933).

46. The French slave code is digested in several of the works just mentioned above, but the actual *Code Noir* (Paris, 1745) should be examined. The decrees of the Spanish sovereigns first supplied the basis for the regula-

VII. THE FRENCH AND THE NEGRO—*Continued*

tion of Spanish slaves. The Barbadian slave code, one of the first to influence the English slaveholding plantations, was copied extensively along the Atlantic.

47. Fernand Masse in his "Negro Race in French Literature" in the *Journal of Negro History*, XVIII, p. 227, speaks of a new interest created in Africa by the correspondence, 1778-1788, of the Governor of Senegal, the Chevalier de Boufflers, with Madame de Sabran. This writer failed to note also that in 1725 Marivaux, interested in leveling the social order, aroused some of such interest in the publication of his *Ile des Esclaves*. In this he expressed the idea of the equality of all men. The works of Bernadin Saint-Pierre, following Aphra Behn, opened up a new field of realism in thus picturing Africa as beautiful. In 1759 Voltaire expressed a thought of the African in his *Candide*. Consult W. Mercer Cook's *Le Noir* (New York, 1934).

48. Here it is necessary to determine the extent to which the theories of Rousseau and Montesquieu took into account the Negro of that time. This may be best understood by noting at the same time the extent to which the Negro figured in the theories of Blackstone, Locke, Milton, Moore, Hobbes, and Filmer. The works themselves should be studied after learning the trend of their thought from a treatment like the *History of Political Theory* by W. A. Dunning.

49. Of the abolition movement in France several writers have written. Consult T. H. Clarkson's *History of the Abolition of the African Slave Trade by the British Parliament*, II, pp. 123-145. *The Journal of Negro History*, I, pp. 404-405, 408-426, 428-432; II, pp. 164-174; XIX, pp. 365-367; Woodson's *The Negro in Our History*, p. 133; Abbé Grégoire's *De la littérature des Nègres;* and J. P. Brissot de Warville's *New Travels in the United States of America* (London, 1794), I, pp. 220-223. Dr. Anna J. Cooper has treated this in an unpublished thesis submitted for the doctorate at La Sorbonne.

50. Consult *The Journal of Negro History*, pp. 225-245; and XIX, pp. 118-136; and W. Mercer Cook's *Le Noir* (New York, 1934). Consult also the works of the authors herein referred to, such as Victor Hugo, Daudet, Anatole France and the like.

VII. THE FRENCH AND THE NEGRO—*Continued*

51. THE NEGRO IN NINETEENTH CENTURY FRENCH
    LITERATURE
52. FRENCH LITERATURE AND THE NEGRO SINCE THE
    WORLD WAR
53. FRENCH ART AND THE NEGRO

VIII. THE BELGIAN POSITION

54. THE COMMERCIAL ATTITUDE OF CITY-STATES
55. NO PARTICULAR THOUGHT DURING EARLY
    STRUGGLES
56. POLICY IN ITS AFRICAN COLONIZATION

51. Use the references cited under 50. See also W. Mercer Cook's "Edouard Lefebre de Laboulaye and the Negro" in *The Journal of Negro History*, XVIII, pp. 246-255; Gustav Lanson's *Histoire de la Littérature Française* (Paris, 1923); Roland Lebel's *L'Afrique Occidentale dans la Littérature Française* (Paris, 1925); and the same author's *Histoire de la Littérature Coloniale en France* (Paris, 1931).

52. Consult the article on "French Literature since the World War" by René Maran in *The Encyclopedia Britannica*, the last edition. See also "The Negro Race in French Literature" by Fernand Masse in *The Journal of Negro History*, XVIII, July issue, 1933; Roland Lebel's *L'Afrique Occidentale dans la Littérature Française* (Paris, 1925) and his *Histoire de la Littérature Coloniale en France* (Paris, 1931).

53. Consult these works of art themselves. See pp. 1-32 of the African background herein sketched. Read thoroughly A. C. Barnes' "The Evolution of Contemporary Painting" in *The Journal of the Barnes Foundation*, II, pp. 18-27. See sketches of Manet, Picasso, Modigliani and Matisse in *La Rousse, Grand Dictionnaire Universel du Dix-neuvième Siècle;* and Guillaume and Munro's *Primitive Negro Sculpture* (New York, 1926), chapter IV.

54. In almost any account of European city-states Antwerp appears as a typical center of what Belgium was in those days of commercial expansion. See Carlton J. H. Hayes' *A Social and Political History of Modern Europe*, New York, 1919, I, pp. 66, 93, 95, 96; *Cambridge Modern History*, II (1904) chapter xix, III (1905) chapters vi and vii; and P. J. Blok's *History of the People of the Netherlands*.

55. Consult the authorities cited under 54. In addition the student should use also J. L. Motley's *Rise of the Dutch Republic* chiefly for its fine dramatization; but one should bear in mind that he is chiefly concerned with the Protestant Dutch and the account is biased and prejudiced with respect to the Spaniards.

56. Consult *Histoire Générale*, XII, chapter xxvi, *Le Partage de L'Afrique, 1870-1900;* H. H. Johnston's *A History of the Colonization of*

VIII. THE BELGIAN POSITION—*Continued*

57. THE ATTITUDE IN LITERATURE
58. THE LIBERALISM OF ARTISTS
59. THE PRESENT ATTITUDE

IX. THE ATTITUDE OF MODERN ITALY

60. CONTACTS BY COMMERCE OF CITY-STATES—ALESSANDRO DE MEDICI
61. ATTITUDE AS REFLECTED IN OTHELLO

Africa by Alien Races (1913) ; J. S. Keltie's *The Partition of Africa;* and L. Franck's *Congo Belge,* two volumes.

The literature on the Belgian atrocities in the Congo is abundant. The files of the Negro newspapers will serve as an adequate index. Consult also E. D. Morrell's *The Congo Slave State* (Liverpool, 1903), *The Future of the Congo* (London, 1909), *Great Britain and the Congo* (London, 1909), *King Leopold's Rule in Africa* (London, 1904), *A Memorial on Native Rights* (London, 1909), *The New African Slavery* (London, 1904), *The Treatment of Women and Children in the Congo State* (Liverpool, 1904) ; Frederick Starr's *The Truth about the Congo* (Chicago, 1907) ; *The Case Against the Congo Free State* (London, 1903) ; *Affairs in the Congo* (State Department, Washington, D. C., 1909) ; *Congo Conference,* and *Message of the President of the United States transmitting a Report of the Secretary of State Relative to the Affairs of the Independent State of Congo* (Washington, D. C., 1880).

57. In literature Belgians have been overshadowed by greater writers in neighboring countries using the languages spoken in Belgium. What has been produced there, then, is not well known. The works themselves tell their own story, but literature from outside of the country, especially that of France has greatly influenced the thought of that nation.

58. Consult the works of the artists of Belgium. Study especially those of Jordaens and of Rubens.

59. This is the student's problem to determine what the present attitude is by having recourse to the press, current periodical literature, books, and official documents.

60. According to J. L. Monod (*Histoire de l'Afrique Occidentale Française,* p. 147) the Genoese and the Venetians were exploring Africa in the thirteenth century. The contact of the Italian City-States with Africa, however, may be determined by a study of the following: *Cambridge Modern History* (1902), I, chapters iv-viii; *Histoire Générale,* IV, chapters i and ii; H. M. Vernon's *Italy from 1494 to 1700* (1909) ; Pompeo Molmenti's *Venice, its Individual Growth from the Earliest Beginnings to the Fall of the Republic,* translated by H. F. Brown, 6 volumes (1900-1908) ; Edward Armstrong's *Lorenzo de Medici* (1897) in the "Heroes of the Nations" Series. Alessandro de Medici, a Negro, served as Duke of Florence.

61. Othello, the popular play, although borrowed by Shakespeare from the Giraldi Cinthio novel, does not seem to have been popularized in Italy,

IX. THE ATTITUDE OF MODERN ITALY—*Continued*
62. POLICY MODIFIED BY COLONIAL ENTERPRISE—
ABYSSINIA
63. RECENT NOTICES BY AUTHORS
64. THE ATTITUDE IN ART
65. THOUGHT WITH RESPECT TO AFRICAN ART
66. PRESENT-DAY ATTITUDE

X. GERMANY AND THE NEGRO
67. ATTITUDE ILL-DEFINED FOR LACK OF CONTACT

but we are yet to learn that it was an unpopular theme. It might have been taken as a matter of course. No race hate had developed at this time so far as the sources indicate. Moors, Blackamoors or Africans occupied positions of prominence throughout the Mediterranean.

62. It seems that the attitude of Italians toward the Negro or the African did not change until that country entered upon commercial and colonial enterprise in Africa. This, however, requires further study of the sources mentioned above and of the archives of that nation. From the policies of the city-states to that of the nation in dealing with Abyssinia is a rather long step for generalization. Consult Carlton J. H. Hayes, *Political and Social History of Modern Europe,* II, pp. 614-631; H. H. Johnston's *A History of the Colonization of Africa by Alien Races* (1913); *L'Histoire générale,* XII, chapter XXVI, *Le Partage de l'Afrique;* and F. Ernest Work's *Ethiopia, or Abyssinia as a Pawn in European Diplomacy* (New York, 1935).

63. For lack of frequent contact not many Italians have written on the Negro in the sense in which this race has figured in French or English literature. Further study of the Italian literature itself, however, is necessary to learn the actual facts. A few of the productions thus concerned are mentioned on pp. 224-225. See also the *Enciclopedia Moderna Illustrata.*

64. The survey of art works herein suggested is that of the productions peculiarly Italian. There should be no confusion here with the Christian art treated in connection with the Church. Modern Italy is neither Ancient nor Medieval Rome.

65. Some thought with respect to African art has been expressed by Italian artists of today under French influence. See Guillaume and Munro's *Primitive Negro Sculpture* (New York, 1926) chapter iv; and Albert C. Barnes' "Evolution of Contemporary Painting" in *Journal of the Barnes Foundation,* II, pp. 18-27.

66. Consult the present-day magazines and books of literary worth which are now being produced in Italy. The policy of the present government should be noted. The designs of Italy on Africa require interpretation.

67. Germany for lack of contact with Africans had no well-defined attitude toward these people until she participated in the exploitation of Africa. That story is told by Rayford W. Logan in the "German Acquisition of Southwest Africa" in *The Journal of Negro History,* XVIII, pp. 369-395. The atrocities charged to the Germans in that quarter leave the

X. GERMANY AND THE NEGRO—*Continued*

68. FIRST THOUGHT THAT OF THE HOLY ROMAN EMPIRE—ANGELO SOLIMAN

69. THE RECEPTION GIVEN ANTON WILHELM AMO AT WITTENBERG

70. OPINIONS OF GERMAN TRAVELERS RESPECTING THE STATUS OF THE NEGRO IN AMERICA

71. THE INTEREST OF GERMAN HISTORIANS

72. THE NEGRO AS PORTRAYED BY STORM, SEALSFIELD, AUERBACH, SCHIRMER, AND GERSTACKER

impression that they were hard taskmasters for the Africans. Consult the following: Kurt Hassert's *Deutschlands Kolonien* (Leipzig, 1910); Wilhelm Mensching, *Farbige und weisse Rassen, Kolonial und Kulturfragen* (Wernigerode, 1930); Kurd Schwabe's *Mit Schwert und Pflug in Deutsch-Südwest Afrika* (Berlin, 1904); A. Seidel's *Deutschlands Kolonien* (Berlin, 1902; and P. E. Lewin's *The Germans and Africa* (1915).

68. Prior to this participation in colonization the attitude of Germany was mainly the inherited neutral attitude from the Holy Roman Empire, which in turn had the attitude of the Romans. The Negro was to be what he could make himself if he happened to be thrown among them. Consult Abbé Grégoire's sketch of Angelo Soliman in his *De la Littérature des Nègres* (*The Journal of Negro History*, IV, pp. 281-289).

69. See page 95 of *Select Discussions of the Race Problem in the Atlanta University Studies* (Atlanta, 1916); and *The Journal of Race Development*, I, No. 4, pages 482 to 500.

70. Some of these opinions have been collected and published in *The Journal of Negro History*, I, pp. 405-406; II, pp. 177-181. See Paul C. Weber's *America in Imaginative German Literature in the First Half of the Nineteenth Century* (New York, 1926), pp. 104-119. Two of the German travelers, Johan D. Schoepf (*Travels*) and Bernard von Sachsen-Wemar-Eisenach (*Travels*) had anti-slavery views. Gottfried Duden in his *Bericht über eine Reise nach den westlichen Staaten Nordamerikas und einen mehrjährigen aufenthalt am Missouri* (1824-1827), or *Das Leben im Innern der Vereinigten Staaten und dessen Bedeutung für die hausliche und politische Lage der Europäer* had very mild views on slavery and spoke for the slaveholders.

71. Find out from their works themselves whether such writers as Droysen, Treitschke, Schmoller, Lenz, Marcks, Delbruck, Behr-Pinnow, Frobenius, Dietrich, Kayserling, Zimmerman, Herrfurth, Hassert, or Schlieman had any thought with respect to the Negro. Consult the works listed on pp. 447 to 449, in the second volume of Carlton J. H. Hayes' *A Political and Social History of Modern Europe*.

72. See pages 86, 120, 151, 157, 152-158, 216, 219-226, 236, 246 of Paul C. Weber's *America in Imaginative German Literature in the First Half of the Nineteenth Century*. Consult Theodor Storm's *Von Jenseits des Meeres* (1857); Berthold Auerbach's *Das Landhaus am Rheim* (1869);

X. GERMANY AND THE NEGRO—*Continued*
73. The Negro in German Literature after African Colonization
74. The Negro in Recent German Literature

XI. THE RUSSIAN ATTITUDE TOWARD THE NEGRO
75. Little Thought of the Distant Africans and Their Land
76. The Significance of Abram Hannibal, the Grandfather of Pushkin, and of the Father of the Poet
77. The Work of Pushkin in Russia

Adolf Schirmer's *Die Schlavenbarone* (1873) ; and the works of Baldwin Molhausen. Frederick Gerstäcker inveighed against slavery in his *Streifund und Jagdzüge durch die Vereinigten Staaten* (1844). Sealsfield, although condemning slavery in his *Planzerleben,* felt that a brutal race "cannot be civilized in a few years nor be taught in a short space of time to bear the responsibilities of liberty" (127).

73. Writings in which the Germans referred to the Negro up to the World War show all sorts of opinions. Only by extensive reading of the literature of the period can any safe conclusions be reached.

74. The same extensive reading of the German literature from the time of the World War up to the present crisis would hardly be productive of significant results because of volcanic conditions now obtaining in that country. The notices published in the present highly censored press are not reliable.

75. The sources indicate that Russians probably had a little more contact with Africa in the East than was possible for the Germans and Scandinavians. Yet these contacts were not frequent. Russian writers, then, failed to give as much attention to Africans as did the Europeans nearer to the continent across the Mediterranean. It seems that the few Negroes who reached Russia became more of a curiosity than a problem of treatment or attitudes.

76. In the second volume of *The Journal of Negro History,* pp. 359-366, is noted the career of Abram Hannibal or Hannivalov, "The Negro of Peter the Great." His son, the father of Alexander Pushkin, is also discussed therein. All three, of course, are treated in any extensive biography of Alexander Pushkin. See also *The Journal of Race Development,* I, pp. 482-500, and p. 88 of *Select Discussions of the Race Problem* in the *Atlanta University Studies.* Read also the biographies of Pushkin by Clarence A. Manning, D. S. Mirsky, and Alexander L. Nazarov.

77. From a study of Pushkin's career and an evaluation of his works the liberalism of Russia with respect to the Negro race may be estimated. Was Pushkin more to Russia than Alexander Dumas, père, was to France?

XI. THE RUSSIAN ATTITUDE TOWARD THE NEGRO
—*Continued*

78. TOLSTOY AND THE STRUGGLE FOR FREEDOM IN AMERICA
79. OTHER RUSSIAN WRITERS OF THE TIME
80. RUSSIAN LITERATURE AND THE NEGRO SINCE THE WORLD WAR

XII. THE DUTCH AND THE NEGRO

81. EARLY ATTITUDE
82. THE NEGRO IN THE DUTCH COLONIES
83. CHANGES AS A RESULT OF LOSING THEIR COMMERCIAL CONTROL

Russian literature, of course, is not the equal of that of France. This factor must not be overlooked.

78. Study Tolstoy's works. It is said that he had no thought of the Negro as such, although he favored abolition in America as a step toward social reform or regeneration. The study of what he wrote will answer this question.

79. The problem here is to find out the attitude of subsequent writers like Maxim Gorky. Were they neutral with respect to the Negro in other parts? Had they sufficient contact with this race to be concerned about it? Their literary productions are not all translated into English, but some few are thus available.

80. Of the attitude of popular writers since the Russian Revolution there can be no doubt. The study of their works, however, will show whether this is the result of sober thought and literary effort or mere propaganda.

81. The earliest sources on the slave trade show the Dutch as heartless traffickers in human flesh. In this, however, they were the forerunners of others who became more cruel than the Dutch were. The Dutch became the great traders on the high seas in succession to the Portuguese. See Charles de Lannoy and Hermann van der Linden, *Histoire de l'expansion coloniale des peuples européens*, II, *Neerlande et Danemark, dix-septième et dix-huitième siècle;* and Alfred Zimmerman's *Die Europäischen Kolonien,* V. See Stedman's *Narrative of a Five Years' Expedition against the Revolted Negroes of Surinam in Guiana on the Wild Coast of South America* (London, 1806-1813). Consult also Elizabeth Donnan's *Documents Illustrative of the History of the Slave Trade to America.*

82. The attitude as expressed in the treatment of the slaves in Dutch colonies can be traced in the histories of the New Netherlands, of Brazil, and of Dutch Guiana. The sources cited above will suffice for this information. See also P. D. Rinchon's *La Traite et l'esclavage des Congolais par les européens,* Paris, 1929, pp. 70-76.

83. The sources indicate a difference in the attitude of Holland after she lost the lead in European commerce. Is the attitude of the exploiter one

XII. THE DUTCH AND THE NEGRO—*Continued*

84. THE RECEPTION GIVEN NEGROES IN DUTCH CIRCLES—J. E. J. CAPTEIN
85. THE NEGRO AS REFLECTED IN THE LITERATURE OF HOLLAND
86. THE NEGRO AND DUTCH ART

XIII. DENMARK AND THE NEGRO

87. CONTACT RESTRICTED MAINLY TO COLONIES
88. ATTITUDE AS SHOWN IN THE COLONIES
89. IN THE EARLY LITERATURE OF DENMARK
90. AS PORTRAYED BY DANISH ARTISTS
91. THE THOUGHT OF TODAY

and the same regardless of race or place? Do changing attitudes as a result of contacts and occupations indicate this as true?

84. The problem at hand here is whether the people of the home country have an attitude different from that of those sent out to exploit the subjects in colonies. See *Journal of Race Development*, I, pp. 482-500. See also pp. 94 and 95 of *Select Discussions of the Race Problem* in the *Atlanta University Studies*.

85. This thought can be developed only by a survey of Dutch literature. Up to the present no outstanding literary treatment of this country has dealt especially with the Negro. However, from time to time notices have been taken of the Negro as a member of the human family.

86. Dutch art followed the trend of the best literature of the country. The great masters showed much liberalism in the treatments of the entire human family, but they had few occasions to make special productions of Negroes.

87. Little contact with Negroes except in colonies makes the attitude of the Danes mainly neutral. In the colonies themselves the tendencies of a few may be traced. Consult L. A. Pendleton's "The Danish West Indies" in *The Journal of Negro History*, II, pp. 267 to 324; and Charles de Lannoy and Hermann van der Linden, *Histoire de l'Expansion Coloniale des Peuples Européens*, II, *Neerlande et Danemark, dix-septième et dix-huitième siècle*.

88. The sources cited above supply an answer to this question. Briefer accounts may be consulted, but inadequate information often leads to wrong conclusions.

89. The outstanding writers of Denmark should be reviewed for whatever they had to say or did not say about the Negro. The colonial historical literature and the books of travel are cited *in extenso* on pp. 267 and 286 of the second volume of *The Journal of Negro History*.

90. As to what the Danish artists portrayed in their works must be learned from these books themselves. Here it is necessary to note the attitude of the unimportant as well as that of the well known artists, for the former may reflect the popular attitude better than those of higher rank.

91. For the thought of today the current literature must be examined.

XIV. THE ENGLISH IN A VARYING ATTITUDE

92. THE THOUGHT ABOUT THE NEGRO IN EARLY RO-
      MANCES

93. COMMERCIAL EXPANSION—MERCANTILISM

94. LIBERTY NEVERTHELESS A STIMULUS TO A
      STRUGGLE FOR FREEDOM

95. POLITICAL THEORIES OF MILTON, LOCKE, HOBBES,
      BLACKSTONE, FILMER, CLARKSON, WILBER-
      FORCE, BUXTON, CHATHAM, NELSON, AND
      LUSHINGTON

The present policy of Denmark with respect to African problems should be
noted. Consult in connection herewith Karl Kyersmeier's *Negere som Digtere* (Negroes as Poets), in the *Crisis*, XXX, p. 186, August, 1923.

92. The experience of other races in dealing with the "Nordic" is that he
is so subtle that it is difficult to determine his attitude toward others. While
he always thinks of himself as a superior and usually appears in the role
of the exploiter, there is in him an undying sense of justice to which one
may always appeal. Yet the Anglo-Saxon is not considered as liberal as
the Latin. In the sources is an answer. In the "Early Romances" before
there was much contact with the blacks the attitude in England was practically the same as that expressed on the continent in the *Song of Roland*.
The Negro was brought into imaginative literature as a colorful figure. See
The Journal of Negro History, XX, pp. 27-85.

93. The best non-British sources support the conclusion that the English
people as a majority are always swayed by commercial and political interests.
Both sides of this question may be studied in H. H. Johnston's *Backward Peoples and our Relations with Them* (London, 1920); F. Klingberg's *Anti-
Slavery Movement in England* (London, 1926); E. C. Lascelles's *Granville
Sharp and the Freedom of the Slaves in England* (London, 1928); E. C. Martin's "English Slavery and the African Settlements" in the *Cambridge History
of the British Empire*, I, pp. 437-459; W. L. Mathieson's *British Slavery
and its Abolition* (London, 1926); his *Great Britain and the Slave Trade*
(London, 1929); G. G. A. Murray's "Exploitation of Inferior Races in
Ancient and Modern Times" in Hirst's *Liberalism and the Empire* (1900),
pp. 118-157; and *The Journal of Negro History*, IX, pp. 584-568; XVII,
pp. 156-180; XIX, pp. 137-170; XX, pp. 27-85, under "Some Attitudes in
English Literature."

94. It is commonly stated by historians that although most of the early
struggles for liberty in England did not contemplate any such consideration
for others of the lower order, these despised classes nevertheless profited
by the grants of freedom to those above them. Did these victories concern
the Negroes in the British Empire?

95. The extent of the thought of the Negro among the theorists who
formulated the attack on the privileged classes can be understood only by
an extensive study of that literature. Commentaries on political theory do
not give such details. A new point of view is suggested in F. T. H.

XIV. THE ENGLISH IN A VARYING ATTITUDE
—*Continued*

96. IN BRITISH LITERATURE OF THE 17TH AND 18TH CENTURIES
97. NINETEENTH CENTURY WRITERS
98. COLONIAL EXPANSION AT THE EXPENSE OF FREEDOM
99. BRITISH LITERATURE AND THE NEGRO SINCE 1914

Fletcher's "Montesquieu's Influence on Anti-Slavery Opinion in England," *The Journal of Negro History,* XVIII, pp. 414-425.

96. Beginning with the *Cambridge History of English Literature* by A. Ward and A. R. Waller, one may trace the important tendencies in English literature, although parts of this work are decidedly biased with respect to the Negro. The literary works themselves, then, must be examined. Some help may be obtained from Edwin D. Johnson's "Aphra Behn's Oroonoko," *The Journal of Negro History,* X, pp. 334-344. Consult Benjamin Brawley's "Elizabeth Barrett Browning and the Negro," the same periodical, III, pp. 22-28.

97. The same method should be employed here as given under 96. The reader should bear in mind, however, such turning points in history as the commercial expansion, the industrial revolution, the natural-rights-of-man movement, social reform, economic imperialism, and the upheaval of the World War. Consult Joseph H. Park's "Thomas Hughes and Slavery," *The Journal of Negro History,* XII, pp. 590-605. See also Jean Trepp's "The Liverpool Movement for the Abolition of the English Slave Trade," the same periodical, XIII, pp. 265-285; C. G. Woodson's "Some Attitudes in English Literature," the same periodical, XX, pp. 27-85.

98. The problem here is to figure out the extent to which the expansion of England into Africa during the last century has changed the attitude of those people toward the Negro race. This task can be performed by the student himself and by him alone. Consult C. H. Wesley's "The Emancipation of the Free Colored Population in the British Empire," *The Journal of Negro History,* XIX, pp. 137-170; R. L. Jones's "American Opposition to Slavery in Africa," Ben N. Azikiwe's "Ethics of Colonial Imperialism," and R. W. Logan's "The Anglo-Egyptian Sudan," all in the same periodical, XVI, pp. 266-308 and pp. 371-381; R. W. Logan's "The International Status of the Negro," the same magazine, XVIII, pp. 33-38; Lloyd Allen Cook's "Revolt in Africa," the same magazine, XVIII, pp. 396-413. Consult also the works referred to under 96 and 97.

99. In the same way it is advisable to find out also whether there has been any change for better or worse in such attitude since the World War. Much attention has been given the question. With what result? See Woodson's "Some Attitudes in English Literature," *The Journal of Negro History,* XX, pp. 27-85.

XIV. THE ENGLISH IN A VARYING ATTITUDE
—*Continued*

100. THE ATTITUDE IN BRITISH ART
101. IN WORLD MOVEMENTS

100. Whether British artists have taken sufficient interest in the Negro to show an attitude is doubtful, but this requires further study of the painting and sculpture of that country. Products of decorative art must also be studied.

101. The extent to which the British have become broader or narrower from participation in world movements like the League of Nations or the Disarmament Conference should be noted in the study of the methods of participation in such international assemblies. Read W. D. Hambly's "Racial Conflict in Africa," *The Journal of Negro History,* XII, pp. 577-589. Consult also R. W. Logan's "The Operation of the Mandate System in Africa," the same periodical, XIII, pp. 423-477.

CHAPTER XX

THE NEGRO IN AMERICA

SEVERAL authorities believe that Africans discovered America long before the Europeans had any such dreams, for the Occident was all but in a state of savagery until awakened by contacts with the more enlightened Orient during the Crusades. The early European explorers on the Isthmus of Darien found there in caves skulls which were identified as African. Students of ethnology observed also that the religion of the American aborigines is very much like that of the Africans. In the language of the Indians, moreover, are discovered certain words which appear only in the language of the Africans—such as "canoe," "tobacco," and "buckra." These, however, must not be confused with African words like, "goober," "yam," "banjo," and "voodoo," which were later brought from Africa to America. This philological influence is evidence for the claim that Africans on the West Coast rose to such a high level of culture that they early braved the high seas and discovered America thousands of years ago.

We know too that Africans in Europe at the time the Spanish adventurers set out to discover and explore America were brought to the Western Hemisphere in considerable numbers. The Negroes, carried here and there by these adventurers, were not permanently located in all those parts. They became settled largely in the West Indies to cultivate sugar and in Latin America to work the mines and the coffee plantations. Negroes brought later as servants to the English colonies after 1619 to supply cheap labor settled in the southern section of North America adapted mainly to large scale agriculture. The warmer climate in the South, more nearly like that of Africa than that of the Northern colonies, determined to some extent the distribution of the Negroes.

The Negroes brought to this country were in some respects like the Indians. Their life while very interesting was not the least modern like that of the Europeans. In dress, shelter, food, occupations and social organization the Indians and Negroes had much in common. Both the Indians and the Negroes were dislodged and enslaved by the superior force of the European traders and colonists. While both West Africans and Indians had practiced slavery themselves they knew nothing of enslaving a special race to do the drudgery for another.

The relations between these Indians and Negroes were not close in the beginning since for lack of knowledge of the languages in use the one could not communicate with the other. The Negro, moreover, was not acquainted with the country; and it seemed to be more of a howling wilderness than the interior of Africa. As Indians raided the colonial settlements, however, they often carried away Negroes, for in the primitive world one weakens his enemy by taking his useful property. Negroes thus seized by Indians were sometimes enslaved, but the bondage they endured was of a mild order—patriarchal. Such Negroes easily became free and, as a rule, were absorbed among the Indians by inter-marriage. In the beginning the relations between the Negroes and poor whites were similarly cordial even to the point of frequent miscegenation, but in the proportion as the latter became free upon the expiration of the periods of their indenture they tended to rise to a social level above that of the Negroes and Indians.

The Negroes who more easily took over the European culture than did the Indians were a decided help to the Red Men. The Negroes taught them modern methods and the European languages and often served these aborigines as advisors and interpreters. The Europeanization of the Indians, then, as far as it actually took place, was facilitated by Negroes among them. Yet in parts where the Indian died out as a result of the introduction of European culture the Negro survived to possess the land. Whites had to resort to drastic methods to dislodge such Negroes by *ex post facto* proceedings.

While the Indian, the first to be enslaved in America, was not a dependable worker the Negro, a more efficient laborer, was not much more in demand among the Latins except where they exploited the mines or cultivated coffee and sugar. The Latins, as a majority, did not come at first with the intention of remaining in America.

They hoped to become rich quickly by trade and discovery of precious metals and then return to Europe to enjoy their fortunes. The early Latins, then, left their women in Europe and intermingled with squaws and Negro women; but, unlike the English, who often did the same thing, the Latins owned their mulatto children, liberated them, settled property upon them, and recognized them as citizens.

The English who came to establish permanent homes required a dependable labor force to do the drudgery of pioneering. Under them the Negroes and white indentured servants became more like beasts of burden than among the Latins. While the Latins moved from place to place establishing trading posts to secure furs and otherwise bartered with the natives for their raw materials, the English used Negroes to fell the trees, drain the swamps, plow the fields and cultivate the staples of the land. The English settlers built their colonial foundations solidly; the Latins restricted themselves mainly to temporary arrangements. The settlements along the Atlantic, then, offered a new field for exploitation.

Trading corporations organized in Europe under charters from its crowned heads were ever in action to stimulate such enterprise. They supplied the demand for cheap labor by bringing indentured servants from Europe and slaves from Africa; and they transported abroad the productions of their labor. Forts established on the West Coast of Africa received captives in wars driven to the shore to be sold into bondage. They were taken, as a rule, to the West Indies and exchanged there for molasses. This molasses, brought to ports like Philadelphia, New York, Newport and Boston, was manufactured into rum which the ships carried directly to Africa for more slaves. This was the triangular trade with which the navigation laws of England had to deal.

For several reasons the demand for Negroes especially greatly increased toward the end of the seventeenth century, leaving that of other laborers about normal. The Indian, in the first place, was an unprofitable servant. He was not an efficient laborer. The white indentured servants, convicts from European prisons, who were permitted to leave their confinement on the condition of serving here for the development of the colony a few years, were not sufficient to supply the demand. Negroes who were then being captured in large numbers in tribal wars fomented by Europeans and Asiatics could be more easily obtained.

Colonial development along the Atlantic coast made slavery, a new institution, possible. Slavery was unknown to European law in the seventeenth century. At first the Negroes brought into America were received as indentured servants and governed accordingly. They could become free at the expiration of their term of service and take up land as did the white indentured servants. One of the first Negroes brought to Jamestown became free and owned a slave himself. By and by, however, planters and ecclesiastical authorities began to make exceptions in the case of Negro servants. Although they might be converted to Christianity they would not, according to an unwritten law in Christendom, become free; and it was further provided that they should no longer become free at the expiration of a certain number of years but should serve for life. The Negro children, too, should follow the condition of the mother.

Then followed black codes providing for the control of the Negroes as slaves. They had to work from the rising to the setting of the sun. They had to be content with coarse, scant clothing; they lived in rough primitive log huts without comfortable furniture; they had to respect the authority of their owners; they suffered punishment for disobedience to their masters' will. Punishments were such as whipping, branding, hanging, and breaking on the wheel. If the slave tried to escape he was pursued by slave catchers with whips, guns, and bloodhounds. Sometimes he was shot down.

Negroes as slaves were used in various sorts of labor. They figured largely in agricultural production—raising wheat, corn, rice, tobacco, and sugar. When the demand for these so increased as to stimulate the slave trade to supply the rising plantations the lot of the Negro became so hard that he often resorted to flight from bondage and then to insurrections as an ultimate deliverance from this ordeal. The most successful of these insurgents were the Maroons in Jamaica who escaped to the strongholds of that island and for a number of years maintained themselves independently. Likewise did the Maroons of Guatemala. Still more striking were the Maroons of Palmares in the Province of Pernambuco, Brazil, where they resisted attacks on their independent state very much as did the city of Numantia against the Romans. The Bush Negroes of Guiana of today are the descendants of Negroes from Africa who ascended the rapids of the rivers and planted themselves in an independent position which they still hold.

The efforts of Negroes to free themselves from bondage, however, were generally unsuccessful among the English, and the Negroes there settled down to their lot of being the beasts of burden in the New World. Becoming then the best slaves available, the Negroes constituted a great asset from the international point of view. Nations vied with each other, therefore, in the trade which slave labor made possible and in the slave trade itself. The Portuguese, Spanish, and Dutch at first had the lead, but England finally got the upper hand in the *Asiento* of the Treaty of Utrecht in 1713 closing the war of the Spanish Succession.

In this position, however, the Negroes in North America were not a negligible factor. All were not slaves. They not only served as laborers in developing the colonies but as brave soldiers in defence of the land. The Negroes figured in all colonial wars from 1689 to 1763. Both French and English in their conflicts in America were glad to have the cooperation of the blacks. Negroes fought on both land and sea wherever pressure had to be relieved, and they proved to be a determining factor in some of these encounters. For such meritorious services a few Negro soldiers were granted freedom.

Even in the position of the slave the Negro was not altogether hopeless. As the system became more a business of exploitation than a patriarchal arrangement persons interested in humanity began to protest against the institution as an economic evil; and a few thought of it as a sin. The most striking of these were the protest of Alfonso Sandoval, the Spanish Jesuit in Havana, the Germantown Quaker protest in 1688, and the appeal for freedom expressed in Samuel Sewell's *Selling of Joseph* in 1700.

These friends of the Negro could not fail to observe that every element of the population had improved except the Negro. The Indian had been left free to go to the wilderness, the indentured servants, rising to the level of planters, had gradually passed out in a natural process of diminishing numbers, the planters and business men by producing and selling raw materials in Europe had tended to become an aristocratic class lording it over the poor whites. The education of the Negroes was neglected, religion was not thought of as intended for them, since they belonged to an accursed race, according to the interpretation of the Bible at that time. Yet a few Negroes managed to deliver themselves from this lost estate by escaping to parts unknown. Some did extra work for years to earn sufficient money to purchase themselves. Occasionally slaves received their freedom for meritorious services. Such free Negroes, too, were respected as white persons in whatever position they attained. Prejudice at that time was one of caste rather than of race.

Emerging from the colonial period when the international conflict of European nations had finally been decided in favor of the possession of most of North America by the English, the Negro, although he could hardly understand the situation itself, had contributed to his own hard lot in helping to defeat the French. The Latins had treated the Negro as a human being and had thus pointed the way toward a more amicable settlement of the race problem as it has worked out in later years in Latin America. Among the English settlers along the Atlantic Coast the Negro was to be pressed further down in the social order as expressed in that form of slavery which reached its worst stage in this country half a century later.

Before reaching this low ebb in our national life, however, the Negro attained a slightly improved position. The colonies quarrelled with the mother country about the rights of the colonists in America and finally plunged into the American Revolution. In emphasizing natural rights as set forth by John Locke and in idealizing law and liberty as expressed by Milton and Blackstone revolutionary leaders like James Otis, Patrick Henry, Samuel Adams, Alexander Hamilton, and Thomas Jefferson had to concede that the colonies were inconsistent in advocating the natural right of man to be free when they themselves were holding slaves. After the grant of independence this thought was so deeply impressed upon the States where few slaves were found that the emancipation of the bondmen in those sections was provided for either instantly or by gradual methods in the Middle States and New England.

Of no little effect in bringing the country to this position was the fine record of the Negro soldiers during the conflict. Crispus Attucks distinguished himself as the first to shed his blood for independence. Negro minute men braved the dangers at Lexington and Concord. Peter Salem immortalized himself at Bunker Hill, Salem Poor attracted the attention of the Continental Congress by his deeds in the encounter at Charlestown, seven hundred Negro soldiers helped to win the day at Monmouth, the famous black regiment made history by heroism in the battle of Rhode Island, and hundreds of others of this country and the West Indies participated in the closing of the drama at Yorktown.

The Negroes freed in the Middle States and New England, then, were sometimes further provided for. Schools in such areas were established for their education, and an extensive effort was made to proselyte them, especially after religious toleration and later religious freedom which permitted evangelical missionaries to work among the Negroes. From such encouragement developed writers and thinkers like Jupiter Hammon, Phillis Wheatley, and Benjamin Banneker. Andrew Bryan, Richard Allen, James Varick and Lemuel Haynes demonstrated the ability of the Negro to preach and lead the people toward independent effort.

The emancipation of the Negroes in parts where the general liberation of the slaves was not provided for was, nevertheless, stimulated by the grant of freedom for those who usefully served the cause during the American Revolution. In the Ordinance of 1787, moreover, it was provided that slavery in the Northwest Territory should be prohibited. At one time the situation was so promising that persons thought of discouraging the agitation for the abolition of the institution through anti-slavery societies. It was believed that slavery would of itself soon pass away. The main point was to educate and evangelize the Negroes in preparation for this boon which everybody believed would eventually come.

This new day did not dawn, however, in the lower South. In working out government for the states and for the nation after the American Revolution it was soon found advisable not to press the matter of emancipation. Georgia and South Carolina had become so attached to slavery by 1787 when the Federal Constitution was framed and presented to the country that it was deemed unwise to discuss the question in the convention of that year and thus upset plans for forming a more "perfect union." The constitution of the United States, then, was based upon compromises on slavery. The Negro was not to be freed, but in the apportionment of representation in the House of Representatives five Negroes would be counted as three whites. The Negroes escaping from one state to another would be returned to their owners, and the trade in Negroes which had caused much trouble in the Convention of 1787 was not to be forbidden prior to 1808. The anti-slavery effort started during the American Revolution would not easily die, but the petition of the Quakers for the emancipation of certain slaves in 1789 was tabled and given a deaf ear by the Federal Government which thus set a precedent for the consideration of all such matters. This rule obtained until the period of ardent abolition fifty years later.

The reason for this revolution in opinion was the change of the attitudes of the "fathers of the republic" as a result of dealing with practical affairs involved in launching the new nation rather than with doctrines to sustain the right of revolution. Everything which they had advocated, they decided, could not be practically worked out. The main reason was that the whole world was then passing through what was then known as the industrial revolution. The steam engine invented in 1769 was followed in rapid succession by such mechanical appliances as the wool-combing machine, the flying shuttle, the spinning jenny, the power loom, and finally the cotton gin. These appliances revolutionized the making of cloth, lowered the price of it, and thus increased its demand. This meant the demand for more cotton fiber the production of which required additional Negro slaves.

The slave trade, then, became decidedly brisk, the pro-slavery Congress in charge of the Federal Government in 1807 failed to prohibit the traffic according to constitutional requirements, and evaded the issue by law of subterfuge which had no teeth in it. To escape the impending ordeal Negroes, encouraged by the success of Toussaint Louverture and Dessalines in the Haitian Revolution, which made the purchase of Louisiana possible and advisable, again resorted to uprisings. The most daring of these were the organized efforts of Gabriel Prosser in Virginia in 1800, the well-planned Denmark Vesey plot in South Carolina in 1822, and the Southampton Insurrection started by Nat Turner in 1831. These efforts coming at the time the institution of slavery was being fiercely attacked by friends of the Negro on free soil tended to make the lot of the slaves harder, to weaken them as a class in order to maintain the peace of the slave states. Yet the Negroes as defenders of the flag with Jackson on land and with Perry and McDonough on sea helped in the War of 1812 to maintain the honor of the nation to which commercial and industrial development at their expense gave a higher position among the powers. The country still claimed the Negroes as fugitives and demanded indemnity when the British received them in their lines and set them free.

The Negro's status became gradually defined as that of a hard laborer in the production of cotton, and any interference with him in this position was considered an attack on the institutions of the slave-holding element which determined to make cotton king. Although doing well in the production of this raw material, however, the South with its mentally undeveloped slave labor could not compete in industry with the sections using free labor. In spite of themselves, then, the two sections with differing economic interests became politically antagonistic. The struggle to maintain control of the Federal Government so stimulated the rivalry between slave states and free states for occupation of Western territory that it culminated in sectional conflict.

To understand how rapidly the Negroes were losing ground during these years a brief review of their former status is here necessary. That the Negroes were early recognized as citizens with all the rights that others enjoyed there can be no doubt. The first laws of the colonies did not restrict the functions of citizenship with respect to race. Distinctions were made, but they were based on traditions of caste. Persons owning certain amounts of property or paying specified amounts in taxes were permitted to exercise the right of suffrage and to hold office. Such persons, of course, could serve in the militia, sit on the jury, and testify as witnesses in the courts. Biased writers who would now justify restrictions of civic rights to one race say without facts to support such an assertion that, although these early colonial laws permitted Negroes to exercise these functions, there is no evidence that they actually did so. We know, however, that Negroes both voted and had access to public office in certain states in the North where such legislation as the black laws of Ohio and Indiana did not obtain; and they voted until 1834 in both North Carolina and Tennessee. One of the reasons for depriving the free Negroes of suffrage at that time was that in a recent election of a Congressman in Tennessee they had the balance of power and their vote in his favor turned the tide.

The growth of the Southwest during this period especially facilitated the degradation of the Negro as a laborer to be dethroned from any such high position as that of a voter. The progress in that quarter expanded the agricultural area of the South which tended more and more to differ from the North and East with their increasing industries. More territory added to the South as in the purchase of Florida made the proslavery area more hopeful, but a sectional conflict developed out of the debate on the admission of Missouri as a slave or free state. The tariff first championed in 1816 by Calhoun, the leader of the South, was later attacked as legislation in favor of the industrial East at the expense of the agricultural sections. New adjustments were made in 1824 and 1828, but in 1832 South Carolina would nullify the tariff measure so prejudicial to its interests. Nationalism, however, had become too general for any such one-state effort to upset the unionizing program; and the Constitution was finally sustained against South Carolina just as it had been against the New England States which threatened to secede on account of local inconvenience of the embargo policy during the War of 1812. To this end had worked also internal improvements which broke down sectional barriers by connecting distant parts; also the United States Bank which had helped to develop toward a national currency, although both of these were hotly combated by sectional leaders, some of whom, like Andrew Jackson in his antagonistic attitude toward the Second United States Bank, stimulated sectionalism.

The United States had not only grown as a national force able to take care of its internal affairs, but demonstrated by the Monroe doctrine that it was strong enough to prevent Spain and its Holy Allies from subduing the Latin American republics. The country felt strong enough also to press against Great Britain its unsettled claims which had come down from the American Revolution and the War of 1812. Partly for proslavery purposes but also for broad national reasons the country expanded to natural boundaries in the settlement of the Maine boundary, the acquisition of Oregon, the annexation of Texas, and the conquest of additional territory in the Mexican War to maintain the position of Texas as an independent nation with the right to join the Union.

Along with this territory came other questions which accentuated sectional differences. More territory meant greater stimulus to the struggle to keep evenly balanced the slave states with the free. The Wilmot Proviso introduced in Congress in 1846 would prohibit slavery in the territory acquired at that time. Some wanted California admitted as a free state, others would secure for possible slave expansion territory acquired as a result of the Mexican War, still others would prohibit the slave trade under the dome of the Capitol, while the South clamored for a more drastic fugitive slave law to safeguard its human property. Hence, came a measure embodying these five points as the Omnibus Bill which was supposed to please everybody and pleased nobody.

The sectional differences had become too pronounced to be thus adjusted, and the compromises of Henry Clay, supported in the last case by Daniel Webster, failed just as these promoters had failed to keep pace with this rapidly developing country. Harriet Beecher Stowe's *Uncle Tom's Cabin* set people thinking by giving them a dramatization of slavery. Stephen A. Douglas sought to calm the waters with the straddling popular sovereignty of the Kansas-Nebraska Act, but this led only to civil strife in Kansas. The Supreme Court of the United States tried to take the much discussed question out of politics by the Dred Scott decision to the effect that the Negro had no civic rights which that tribunal could respect; but the Lincoln-Douglas Debates showed that the fight was just beginning and would have to end with the country either slave or free. The debates of Seward, Chase, and Sumner further demonstrated that the conflict was irrepressible. Helper's *Impending Crisis,* an economic approach to the question, presented slavery as a national evil which poor whites should endeavor to destroy in the interest of free labor. John Brown's raid in 1859 showed how seriously some persons of both races had thought of slavery and what martyrdom they would undergo for their ideals of freedom.

The division came with the election in 1860 of Abraham Lincoln by the sectional Republican party and by a minority popular vote.

To escape from the control of the imaginary antislavery political party the slaveholding states resorted to secession to destroy the Federal Government whose policy they had dictated for sixty years. Various compromises, the most popular of which was presented by John J. Crittenden, of Kentucky, failed to heal the breach and hold the Union intact. The two sections plunged into the Civil War, and each appealed abroad for sympathy and cooperation. England, dependent upon the South for cotton fibre to supply its mills, gave secretly the most aid and encouragement to the struggle for Southern independence by permitting ships like the *Alabama* for the Confederacy to be built and launched in her ports; but no foreign nation actually intervened. The states had to fight it out among themselves, and the Negro eventually became a factor.

The Negro figured in the drama in various ways. The Confederates used them as laborers in their armies and as mechanics to build fortifications. The Union armies, following the example of Benjamin F. Butler at Fortress Monroe who received Negroes in his camp as contraband of war, began to make similar use of such fugitives. Both the Confederacy and the Federal Government tried to make it appear that slavery was not the issue when it really was. Lincoln, therefore, countermanded the emancipatory orders of Frémont in Missouri and Hunter in South Carolina, but by September 22, 1862 he had to issue the Emancipation Proclamation that if the rebellious States did not return to the Union by the first of the following January he would declare the slaves in that area free; and he did. This put on a different footing numerous Negro fugitives who had flocked to the Union camps and made it possible to enlist them as soldiers. They were much needed at that time since the Union had not carried out all its three objectives of blockading southern ports, getting control of the Mississippi and taking Richmond. McDowell had gone down at Bull Run, Joe Hooker had failed at Chancellorsville, Burnside at Fredericksburg, and McClellan at Malvern Hill. While Grant, Thomas, and Sherman had done well in the West and Farragut in the South there was much to be accomplished. To this finishing of the task in conflicts near the Atlantic the 178,000 Negro soldiers enlisted made a large contribution. The dashing of Stonewall Jackson became ineffective. The morale of the soldiers under Robert E. Lee collapsed even as they began to drill Negro soldiers for the Confederate armies; and the moving spirit of the Lost Cause gave up at Appomattox April 9, 1865.

When the War finally closed reconstruction, which Lincoln had already begun, became the crowning issue. What should be done with the erring states? What should be done for the Negroes? Lincoln had thought of colonizing the freedmen, and with certain Negroes freed by his compensation method in the District of Columbia in 1862 he had tried to settle them on the island of Vache off Haiti. This project, however, failed. With respect to the seceding states Lincoln felt liberal, believing that a state could not actually get out of the Union. He ordered, then, the restoration of the former state governments in the troubled area just as soon as ten per cent of the number of voters functioning as such in 1860 registered as loyal to the Union. Such a plan had been carried out in Tennessee, Arkansas and Louisiana which came under the control of the Union army before the end of the hostilities.

Because of Lincoln's assassination on April 14, 1865, and the accession of Andrew Johnson to the presidency problems of a personal sort developed. Johnson was a hot-headed man, and he had to deal with antagonistic leaders in Congress who were just as much determined as Johnson to have their own way. These were Charles Sumner and Thaddeus Stevens. They disregarded the plans of the President and worked out a Congressional plan of reconstruction. The reasons given for this are various. In the first place, the seceding states, although nominally accepting the Thirteenth Amendment as guaranteeing the Negro his freedom, endeavored to work out a system of control which was virtually the reenslavement of the Negro by drastic vagrancy laws. To secure the Negro in his freedom the new leaders in Congress would grant him the right of franchise and then provide for constitutional conventions on the basis of such suffrage to rehabilitate the state governments while the leading whites suffered from disfranchisement for participating in the rebellion. This was considered "radical," for Lincoln had not thought of the Negro as a voter except in case of being educated and in the possession of property. Yet no one has been able to suggest a better plan which at that time could have been carried out without losing the fruits of the victory of the war.

The leaders of Congress had their way. The President was overridden by a two thirds majority on such measures. The Fourteenth Amendment which was put through as a part of the program made the Negro a citizen and guaranteed him protection in the enjoyment of his rights. The Fifteenth Amendment, coming later was intended to clear up all difficulties not taken care of in the Fourteenth, in preventing states from denying a man the right to vote on account of race, color, or previous condition of servitude. In the meantime the Freedmen's Bureau, already at work as an intermediary for the protection of the freedman, was enlarged and given greater power over Negroes subject to local authorities. The South was next divided into five military districts under officers of the army, and some of the soldiery were Negroes. The states to escape from military rule had to accept the Negro as a voter and an officeholder rather than deal with him as a half-free vagrant subject to the will of his former master.

Some of the states remained for a number of years under the control of the army rather than organize permanent governments with such liberal provisions for the Negroes. Others accepted the terms and proceeded to work out government on free-manhood suffrage basis. Negroes soon began to participate in local, state, and national matters. In this position they inflamed the former ruling class in the South that would recognize them only as a species of property. The Negroes, then, joined the adventurers from the North who followed the armies South; and these with the Southern whites who deemed it wise to cooperate with the enfranchised freedmen thus controlled most of the South. The reclaimed states under the domination of this majority party moved along both the evil and fortunate ways as other state governments of the time. There was corruption everywhere, especially in the East and North where there was sufficient wealth to invite such methods; but merely because Negroes were participants in government at this time writers have told us much about the Southern frauds in the payment of expenses and carrying out contracts for roads, canals and bridges which nobody ever used. Whites handled most of these funds and committed most of these abuses. After the restoration of the former white ruling class to office, moreover, there was as much fraud in two of these states as that under the Negroes and the carpet-baggers, but writers fail to refer to these later abuses.

Negroes concerned in frauds were merely used as a means to an end. In most of the state, local and national offices the majority of Negroes who thus served were honest men like Cardozo, State Treasurer of South Carolina, and Dubuclet, State Treasurer of Louisiana. The former ruling class, however, would not have it so and organized the Ku-Klux Klan, an extra-legal body, a hooded order, which instituted a regime of terrorism and drove the Negroes and their sympathizers out of office—in fact, out of the South, for large numbers of white and black reconstructionists had to flee for danger of losing their lives.

On the whole, the reconstruction was a success. Unfortunately it tended to intensify the feelings of the races against each other, but much good was accomplished. Social reforms which the conservative element had formerly frowned down upon were inaugurated. The whipping post was abolished, branding with irons was discontinued, land monopoly was attacked, education at public expense was provided for, suffrage was extended to poor whites, and representation in the government was based on population rather than on interests. More consideration was given the laboring man. The good things of life under the new regime were treated as belonging to the many rather than to the few. The Negro was later eliminated from the equation, but the good which he helped to accomplish has been retained for the benefit of others who deny him his share merely because he was never an enslaver.

With political reconstruction undone the Negro as a factor diminished in importance. Driven out of one sphere, political leaders had to enter another. Some went into the ministry while others took up education. Many of them had to come to Washington and served in inferior positions until they could readjust themselves. Plunged, too, into such matters as the western lands, transcontinental railroads, the new tariff requirements, and financial reform, the party which had profited by controlling the Negro vote tended to do less and less for the freedmen and finally contented itself with merely a profession of interest in a profusion of phrases in its quadrennial platform. Booker T. Washington then appeared upon the scene, telling the Negroes that although they had tried politics, religion, and classical education to solve their problems, they had failed. They must now begin with the tasks at hand, dignify them by efficient service, and thus become to that extent sufficient unto themselves. Certain others, mainly W. M. Trotter and W. E. B. DuBois, still attached to the idea of meeting the issue by passing resolutions and protesting against their oppression, militantly arrayed themselves against this practical policy.

The next development to receive attention came under Theodore Roosevelt, who both encouraged and discouraged the Negro. Roosevelt believed that one should not shut the door in a man's face because he is black, but Negroes believed that just because the Brownsville Negro soldiers were black he dishonorably discharged those implicated in the riot in that town. Taft condoned segregation of Negroes in the Civil Service, and his administration approved the limitation upon Negroes rising in that sphere.

During these years, however, a few Negroes had made a little progress in the fundamentals of life. They had acquired a billion dollars' worth of property—in homes, farms, churches, schools, banks, and insurance companies. In limited numbers, too, Negroes had figured in practically all professional spheres. The masses, however, had been left to move along as before in drudgery with little hope to override the barriers of the trades unions and rise in the higher pursuits of labor. Their great economic power had never been used, and what political power they had exercised had been parked on one side by the traditions of the Civil War and Reconstruction. The sections hostile to the Negroes undertook further to discriminate against them by special measures for their disfranchisement, by separation in public places and on common carriers. Lynching, moreover, became so general as to establish itself as an American institution for dealing with a despised class.

The Negro struggled against these odds, but could do little to improve his condition even when he again went to the defense of the flag as a brave soldier and acquitted himself with honor in the Spanish American War. Under Woodrow Wilson who would make the world safe for democracy during the World War the Negro was ignored and further segregated, although brave Negro troops shared the sacrifices of the American expeditionary forces in France. The Supreme Court in the meantime while declaring unconstitutional such disfranchising measures as the "Grandfather clause" and ordinances for segregation of property of races in municipalities, abrogated the Civil Rights Law, evaded tests of the laws for separation of passengers on railroads, supported local covenants of whites for segregating Negro residents and virtually annulled the Fifteenth Amendment in supporting the exclusion of Negroes from Democratic primaries. Today the Negroes are still clamoring for social justice.*

I. DISCOVERY AND EXPLORATION OF AMERICA

1. EARLIEST VISITORS TO THE AMERICAN ABORIGINES
2. NEGROES TAKEN TO EUROPE

1. Almost any history of the United States gives an account of the first European visitors to touch the shores of America; but only Leo Wiener in his *Africa and the Discovery of America* gives *in extenso* the earlier discovery of the continent by Africans. The same is briefly stated in the author's *Negro in Our History*, pp. 58-59. In Justin Winsor's *Narrative and Critical History* other evidences are set forth.

2. Most historical works dealing with the beginnings of Portugal, Spain, Southern France, Italy, and Greece mention Negroes in the Mediterranean world, especially in the city-states during the mediaeval period. See W. E. B. Du Bois's *The Negro*, pp. 145-146, *The Journal of Negro History*, XX, pp. 27-31, and A. J. Macdonald's *Trade, Politics, and Christianity in Africa and the East*, p. 111.

---

* In this treatment it will be taken for granted that the student has read or has access to the latest edition of the author's *Negro in Our History* in which all these topics are briefly treated. Sometimes for lack of source material this work will be the only reference available for the development of the topic. For an introductory course as herein outlined this book is sufficient. The references given in this book will be sufficient to expand the treatment of the Negro in America. For more advanced work, of course, the numerous productions herein referred to will lead the student into all the ramifications of the life and history of the Western Hemisphere in which the Negro has been a conspicuous factor. Additional light may be obtained by making use of bibliographical materials given in connection with other courses outlined under education, religion, art, and literature. It is assumed also that the student has access to a complete file of *The Journal of Negro History* which constitutes a veritable encyclopaedia on the Negro.

I. DISCOVERY AND EXPLORATION OF AMERICA
—Continued

3. THE EXPLORATION OF THE WEST COAST OF AFRICA, A PRELUDE

4. EVENTS LEADING THE EUROPEANS TO AMERICA
   (a) COMMERCIAL EXPANSION AND ECONOMIC ENTERPRISE
   (b) ASYLUM FROM RELIGIOUS PERSECUTION
   (c) RELIEF FROM ABSOLUTISM

5. NEGROES WITH THE EXPLORERS—ESTEVANICO, NULFO DE OLANO—ST. AUGUSTINE, SANTA FE, AND JAMESTOWN

II. THE NEW RACES IN A NEW WORLD

6. PHYSICAL FEATURES AND THE DISTRIBUTION OF THE ABORIGINES

3. The exploration of the coast of Africa is told in almost any European or American history touching this period. The contacts with the natives, however, are not presented except from the biased point of view. In J. L. Monod's *Histoire de l'Afrique Occidentale Française* this is briefly done on pp. 146-154. The same is fairly well treated in the second chapter of Sir Charles P. Lucas's *The Partition of Africa*. Consult also J. S. Keltie's *The Partition of Africa* and N. D. Harris's *Intervention and Colonization in Africa*.

4. Commercial expansion, a conspicuous development of the Renaissance, is adequately explained in most European histories; but the discovery of values in Africa which stood in the way of the adventurers to the East is not emphasized in these works. Georges Hardy undertakes to do this briefly in his *Histoire de l'Afrique,* pp. 70-80; and so does Carlton J. H. Hayes in the second chapter of the first volume of his *A Political and Social History of Modern Europe*.

5. The Negroes who accompanied the Spanish explorers are treated by J. F. Rippy in "The Negro and the Spanish Explorers in the New World" in *The Journal of Negro History,* VI, pp. 183-189. Prof. Edward Channing deals with this inadequately in the second and third chapters of the first volume of his *History of the United States*. For other facts see L. P. Jackson's "Elizabethan Seamen and the African Slave Trade," *The Journal of Negro History,* IX, pp. 1-17. The early settlements which followed these explorations and expeditions are described in Woodbury Lowery's *Spanish Settlements in the United States*.

6. The study of any acceptable relief map and the geographic influences thereby resulting will supply the proper foundation for understanding possibilities and developments in the trade along the coast of Africa. The

II. THE NEW RACES IN A NEW WORLD—*Continued*

7. INDIANS, NEGROES, AND WHITES COMPARED
8. EARLY RELATIONS OF NEGROES AND INDIANS
9. THE CONFLICT AND FUSION OF CULTURES
10. FIRST ATTITUDES IN THE NEW WORLD

study of America in like fashion will facilitate the understanding of the engrafting of slavery upon this continent. The distribution of the natives to some extent determined the European settlements and methods of exploiting America. The power of the student to think for himself here in the light of geographic influences is the only hope for understanding the situation in the New World.

7. Most histories compare the Indians with the white settlers, but few project them on the screen in contrast to the Negroes. The customs of the Indians are given *in extenso* in our histories. The customs of the Africans imported, however, are generally ignored in such works. Consult, then, M. Delafosse's *Negroes of Africa*, pp. 141-281, and C. G. Woodson's *Negro in Our History*, pp. 1-36.

8. The contacts possible determined the early relations of these two subordinated groups in the colonies. The sources above cited show that these relations were cordial when well established communication obtained, but during the early years this was not generally possible. See Helps' *Spanish Conquest*, Volume I, pp. 219-220, and II, p. 401; Bryan Edwards's *History of the West Indies*, I, chapter i; and II, chapters ii and iii.

9. Of the triumph of the European culture over that of the Indian and over that of the Negro we learn much from even elementary treatises. The main problem here, however, is to study the conflict of the Negro culture with that of the American aborigines. Consult A. A. Goldenweiser's *Early Civilization*, chapters iii and iv; Joshua R. Gidding's *Exiles of Florida;* S. G. Drake's *Aboriginal Races;* and Benjamin Brawley's *Social History of the American Negro.*

From the Europeanization point of view the question is treated in Robert E. Park's "The Conflict and Fusion of Cultures with Special Reference to the Negro," *The Journal of Negro History*, IV, pp. 111-133. It should be noted, however, that Dr. Park is in error in thinking that the Americanized African retained nothing but his temperament. Consult also G. R. Wilson's "The Religion of the American Slave: His Attitude toward Death," the same magazine, VIII, pp. 41-71. Read Zora Neale Hurston's "Cudjo's Own Story of the Last African Slaver," the same periodical, XII, pp. 648-663; Newell N. Puckett's "Religious Folk Beliefs of Whites and Negroes," the same periodical, XVI, pp. 9-35.

10. The first attitudes were various for the reasons that in a crude country conditions differed widely from place to place and attitudes changed with the rapid exploration and development of the country. In most cases, however, the sources already cited indicate that from the very beginning the Indians and Negroes who understood one another realized that they were the common objects of exploitation by the same masters. Time only could determine whether this attitude would become permanent.

III. DIFFERENT METHODS OF COLONIZATION, 1600-1660

11. CHARACTER AND PURPOSES OF EUROPEAN SETTLERS
12. THE METHODS OF COLONIZATION—LATIN AND ENGLISH
13. TRADING CORPORATIONS AS FACTORS

See C. G. Woodson's *Negro in Our History*, pp. 189-198. The attitude of the whites toward the Negroes brought over to America is set forth in T. R. Davis's "Negro Servitude in the United States," *The Journal of Negro History*, VIII, pp. 247-283. The attitudes of the poor whites toward the Negroes is presented in C. G. Woodson's "Beginnings of the Miscegenation of Whites and Blacks in the United States," the same periodical, III, pp. 335-353.

11. The European background of the colonists supplies an explanation of their character and purposes. These matters are generally treated in the average history of the United States. How the background of these European settlers in America accounts for their different attitudes toward the Negro, however, has not been taken up by such historians. See Joseph Butsch's "Catholics and the Negro," *The Journal of Negro History*, II, pp. 393-410; Hubert B. Alexander's "Brazilian Slavery and United States Slavery Compared," the same magazine, VII, pp. 349-364; Mary Wilhelmine Williams's "The Treatment of Negro Slaves in the Brazilian Empire: A Comparison with the United States of America," the same periodical, XV, pp. 315-336; Jane Elizabeth Adams's "The Abolition of the Brazilian Slave Trade," the same periodical, IX, pp. 607-637; and John T. Gillard's "Lafayette, Friend of the Negro," the same periodical, XIX, pp. 355-371. See also "Some Attitudes in English Literature" and "Attitudes in the Iberian Peninsula," the same magazine, XX, pp. 27-85 and 190-243.

12. The contrast of the Latin methods of colonization with those of the English may be found briefly stated in J. S. Bassett's *A Short History of the United States*, pp. 111-115; and in C. G. Woodson's *The Education of the Negro Prior to 1861*, pp. 20-24. The same information is available in fragmentary form in the sources cited under 11. These facts in their scattered form must be collected and analyzed by the student himself.

13. The trading corporations plying between Africa and America are fully treated in hundreds of works. The most valuable knowledge of the kind, however, has been recently made available in Elizabeth Donan's three volumes of *Documents Illustrative of the History of the Slave Trade to America* (Washington, D. C., 1931-1932). The INTRODUCTION of these volumes is informing, and the contents themselves easily tell their own story. Consult also George F. Zook's "The Company of Royal Adventurers Trading into Africa," *The Journal of Negro History*, IV, pp. 134-231; L. P. Jackson's "Elizabethan Seamen and the African Slave Trade," the same periodical, IX, pp. 1-19. For details the student may consult the works of W. E. B. DuBois, J. R. Spears, Thomas Clarkson, T. K. Ingraham and others.

III. DIFFERENT METHODS OF COLONIZATION, 1600-1660—*Continued*

14. FORCED LABOR OF INDIANS, OF WHITE INDEN-
   TURED SERVANTS, AND OF NEGROES

15. THE SOCIAL ORDER EVOLVED

14. The institution of slavery has been portrayed from the point of view of all the slaveholding states; and such works should be consulted for a detailed exposition of the system as the descendants of the slaveholders have recorded it. As to the slavery of the Indians and the status of the indentured white servants such works are not so informing. This subject is briefly treated in Bolton and Marshall's *The Colonization of North America*, pp. 21-22, 23, 31, 37, 56, 60-61, 72, 75, 270, and 298; and in C. E. Chapman's *Colonial Hispanic America*, pp. 23-28, 110-116, 188-189. For a condensed treatment of this neglected aspect consult Edward Channing's *History of the United States*, II, pp. 372-398. For more information see K. F. Geiser's *Redemptioners and Indentured Servants in the Colony and Commonwealth of Pennsylvania* (New Haven, 1901); J. C. Ballagh's *White Servitude in the Colony of Virginia* (Baltimore, 1895); J. S. Bassett's *Slavery and Servitude in the Colony of North Carolina* (Baltimore, 1896); E. I. McCormac's *White Servitude in Maryland* (Baltimore, 1904); T. R. Davis's "Negro Servitude in the United States," *The Journal of Negro History*, VIII, pp. 247-283; A. B. Ellis's "White Slaves and Bond Servants in the American Colonies," *Popular Science Monthly*, XL, p. 612; W. C. McLeod's "Debtor Slavery and Chattel Slavery in Aboriginal America," *American Anthropology*, XXVII, pp. 370-380; W. R. Riddell's "Notes on the Slave in Nouvelle France," and "Slavery in Canada," *The Journal of Negro History*, V, pp. 261-377; VIII, pp. 316-330; and IX, pp. 26-33; and his "A Tragedy of the Seventeenth Century," same magazine, XIV, pp. 227-236; William Stuart's "White Servitude in New York and New Jersey," *Americana*, XV, pp. 19-37; Marcus W. Jernegan's *Laboring and Dependent Classes in Colonial America, 1607-1783* (Chicago, 1931).

15. For the English colonies Edward Channing's *History of the United States*, II, chapter xix, is satisfactory, if the reader after seeing the picture of the higher strata of the social order will use his imagination and place the free Negroes along with other free elements on a lower level not far below the poor whites. See also "Eighteenth Century Slaves as Advertised by their Masters," *The Journal of Negro History*, I, pp. 163-216; C. G. Woodson's "Beginnings of the Miscegenation of the Whites and Blacks," the same periodical, III, pp. 335-353; the same author's "The Relations of Negroes and Indians in Massachusetts," the same periodical, V, pp. 44-57; Francis L. Hunter's "Slave Society on the Southern Plantation," the same magazine, VII, pp. 1-10; J. H. Johnston's "Documentary Evidence of the Relations of Negroes and Indians," the same periodical, XIV, pp. 21-43; I. A. Wright's "Digest of Documents in the Archives of the Indies, Seville, Spain, bearing on the Negroes in Cuba," the same magazine, XIV, pp. 60-99; "The Convention between Spain and Holland regulating the Return of Deserters and Fugitive Slaves in their American Colonies," the same

III. DIFFERENT METHODS OF COLONIZATION, 1600-
1660—*Continued*
16. The Situation in Latin America

IV. COLONIAL DEVELOPMENT IN VARIOUS
SPHERES, 1660-1763
17. Slavery in the Colonies
18. The Black Codes

magazine, XIV, pp. 342-344; C. H. Wesley's "The Negro in the West Indies," the same magazine, XVII, pp. 51-66. For the West Indies read also T. H. MacDermot's "From a Jamaica Portfolio—Francis Williams," the same magazine, II, pp. 147-159; C. S. S. Higham's "The Negro Policy of Christopher Codrington," the same magazine, X, pp. 150-153; F. W. Pitman's "Slavery on the British West India Plantations in the Eighteenth Century," the same magazine, XI, pp. 584-667.

16. See the sources cited under 11, and consult also Sir Arthur Helps' *Spanish Conquest* (London, 1855-1867), and C. E. Chapman's *Colonial Hispanic America* (New York, 1933), chapter viii. Read also "The Origins of Abolition in Santo Domingo," by George W. Brown, *The Journal of Negro History*, VII, pp. 364-376; Jane Elizabeth Adams's "The Abolition of the Brazilian Slave Trade," the same periodical, X, pp. 607-637.

17. A general discussion of slavery is given in the sixth and seventh chapters of C. G. Woodson's *Negro in Our History*. An interesting discussion of "The Evolution of the Slave Status in American Democracy" by J. M. Mecklin is given in *The Journal of Negro History*, II, pp. 105-125, 229-251. See also Lorenzo J. Greene's "Slaveholding New England and its Awakening," the same periodical, XIII, pp. 492-533; James A. Padgett's "The Status of Slaves in Colonial North Carolina," the same magazine, XIV, pp. 300-327. U. B. Phillips in *American Negro Slavery* and his *Life* and *Labor in the Old South* treats this topic, but these works are spoiled by the bias of a writer who in spite of all his wide experience could not be other than a defender of the slave regime. A scientific treatment of this same aspect of our history is given in M. W. Jernagan's *Laboring and Dependent Classes in Colonial America*, 1607-1783, Chicago, 1931.

18. The law of slavery is stated in the *Code Noir* (Paris, 1745); in William Goodell's *American Slave Code* (New York, 1853); and J. C. Hurd's *Law of Freedom and Bondage* (New York, 1858-62). Consult also W. R. Riddell's "Le Code Noir," *The Journal of Negro History*, X, pp. 321-329; and J. B. Browning's "The North Carolina Black Code," the same periodical, XV, pp. 461-473.

The following works on slavery are helpful in understanding what slavery was from place to place: J. R. Brackett, *The Negro in Maryland* (Baltimore, 1889); N. D. Harris, *The History of Servitude in Illinois* (Chicago, 1904); J. P. Dunn, *Indiana* (New York, 1888); C. T. Hickok, *The Negro in Ohio* (Cleveland, 1896); B. C. Steiner, *Slavery in Connecticut* (Baltimore, 1893);

IV. COLONIAL DEVELOPMENT IN VARIOUS SPHERES, 1660-1763—*Continued*

19. LABOR WITH RESPECT TO TOBACCO, RICE, INDIGO, AND SUGAR

20. FIRST NEGRO INSURRECTIONS—MAROONS, PALMARES, FOLLOWERS OF CUDJO IN JAMAICA, THE BLACK CORSAIR, BUSH NEGROES IN GUIANA

21. THE EARLY PROTESTS AGAINST SLAVERY—ALFONSO SANDOVAL'S ATTACK, "THE SELLING OF JOSEPH," GERMANTOWN QUAKER PROTEST, THE SOMERSET CASE

Mary M. A. Tremain, *Slavery in the District of Columbia* (Lincoln, Nebraska, 1892); J. S. Bassett, *Slavery and Servitude in North Carolina* (Baltimore, 1896); the same author, *Slavery in the State of North Carolina* (Baltimore, 1899); the same author, *Anti-Slavery Leaders of North Carolina* (Baltimore, 1898); J. C. Ballagh, *A History of Slavery in Virginia* (Baltimore, 1902); H. S. Cooley's *A Study of Slavery in New Jersey* (Baltimore, 1896); E. V. Morgan, *Slavery in New York* (Washington, 1891); E. R. Turner, *The Negro in Pennsylvania* (Washington, 1911); P. A. Bruce, *The Economic History of Virginia in the Seventeenth Century* (New York, 1896); Edward McCrady, *The History of South Carolina under Proprietary Government* (New York, 1899); J. A. Saco, *Historia de la Esclavitude de la raza africana en el Nuevo Mundo y en especial en los Paises Americo-Hispanos* (Barcelona, 1879); I. A. McDougle, *Slavery in Kentucky* (Washington, 1918); Edward Channing, *The Narragansett Planters* (Baltimore, 1886); G. H. Moore, *Notes on the History of Slavery in Massachusetts* (New York, 1866). Read also extracts from historians and travelers in the seventeenth century in the *Journal of Negro History,* II, pp. 186-191.

19. Read M. W. Jernagan's *Laboring and Dependent Classes in Colonial America,* and C. E. Chapman's *Colonial Hispanic America.* Consult also Phillips, *Life and Labor in the Old South* and his *American Negro Slavery;* but use these with discretion, for he shows a bias. Chapman also has a Nordic bias.

20. Negro Insurrections are well treated in the following: Levi Coffin's *Account of some of the Principal Slave Insurrections* (New York, 1860); R. C. Dallas's *Maroons* (London, 1803); T. W. Higginson's *Travelers and Outlaws* (Boston, 1889); M. J. and Frances Herskovits's *Rebel Destiny* (New York, 1934); J. Kunst's "Notes on the Negroes of Guatemala during the Seventeenth Century," *The Journal of Negro History,* I, pp. 390-397; Charles E. Chapman's "Palmares: The Negro Numantia," the same magazine, III, pp. 29-32; C. G. Woodson's "The Relations of Negroes and Indians in Massachusetts," the same magazine, IX, 44-57.

21. These are summarized in E. G. Bourne's *Spain in America,* p. 241; Samuel Sewall's *Selling of Joseph* (Boston, 1700); E. R. Turner's *The Negro*

IV. COLONIAL DEVELOPMENT IN VARIOUS SPHERES, 1660-1763—*Continued*

22. INTERNATIONAL CONFLICTS
> (a) TREATIES WITH RESPECT TO AFRICAN TERRITORY
> (b) THE ASIENTO AND THE COLONIES

23. THE NEGRO SOLDIERS AND PRIVATEERS IN THE COLONIAL WARS

V. SOCIAL PROGRESS IN COLONIES AT THE EXPENSE OF THE NEGRO

24. THE CLASSES OF THE COLONIAL POPULATION FURTHER DEVELOPED

25. INDUSTRY, AGRICULTURE AND TRADE WITH RESPECT TO THE NEGRO

in Pennsylvania, pp. 19, 21, 65, 66; and A. B. Hart's *American History told by Contemporaries,* II, section 102, pp. 291-293.

22. Consult the following: T. K. Ingram's *History of Slavery and Serfdom; Encyclopaedia Britannica,* 11th Edition; J. R. Spears's *The American Slave Trade* (New York, 1900); T. H. Clarkson's *History of the Abolition of the African Slave Trade* (London, 1808); B. Mayer's *Captain Canot or Twenty Years of an African Slaver* (London, 1894); W. E. B. Du Bois, *The Suppression of the African Slave Trade* (Boston, 1896). Refer also to G. F. Zook's "The Company of Royal Adventurers Trading into Africa," *The Journal of Negro History,* IV, pp. 134-231; and Elizabeth Donan's *Documents Illustrative of the History of the Slave Trade to America.*

23. George W. Williams has treated this *in extenso* in his *History of the Negro Race in America* (New York, 1882); and in his *History of Negro Troops in War of the Rebellion* (New York, 1887). See "Negro Privateers and Soldiers Prior to the American Revolution," *The Journal of Negro History,* I, pp. 198-200; and W. R. Riddell's "The Privateers and the Negro," the same periodical, XV, pp. 353-364.

24. The various classes constituting the social order are set forth in the references given under 17, especially those of the lower orders in M. W. Jernegan's *Laboring and Dependent Classes in Colonial America.* In the seventh chapter of C. E. Chapman's *Hispanic Colonial America* the same is presented from the point of view of Latin America. These volumes treat also later developments.

25. In M. W. Jernegan *op. cit., passim,* and in Chapman's *op. cit.,* chapter ix, this aspect of colonial history is treated. The treatises on slavery cited under 18 give the details with respect to different parts of the country. Coman's *Industrial History,* Bogart's *Economic History of the United States,* and Cal-

V. SOCIAL PROGRESS IN COLONIES AT THE EXPENSE OF THE NEGRO—*Continued*

26. RELIGION—MISSIONARIES TO NEGROES AND INDIANS
27. THE DENIAL OF EDUCATION TO NEGROES AND POOR WHITES
28. THE INCREASE OF THE FREE NEGROES

lender's *Economic History* are helpful for general reading. Emory O. Hawk's biased and misinforming *Economic History of the South* is not very helpful. Considerable space is given to slave labor in the second volume of Harry J. Carman's *Economic History of the United States*.

26. This phase of the subject is developed in C. E. Pierre's "The Work of the Society for the Propagation of the Gospel in Foreign Parts among the Negroes of the Colonies," *The Journal of Negro History,* II, pp. 347-358; Faith Vibert's "The Society for the Propagation of the Gospel in Foreign Parts: Its Work for the Negroes in North America before 1783," the same periodical, XVIII, pp. 171-212; C. F. Pascoe's *Classified Digest of the Records of the Society for the Propagation of the Gospel in Foreign Parts,* 1701-1892 (London, 1893) ; Margaret T. Hodgen's "The Negro in the Anthropology of John Wesley," *The Journal of Negro History,* XIX, pp. 308-323; C. G. Woodson's "Anthony Benezet," and G. D. Houston's "John Woolman's Efforts in behalf of Freedom," the same magazine, II, pp. 37-50, 126-138, with accompanying documents, pp. 82-96; Rayford W. Logan's "The Attitude of the Church toward Slavery Prior to 1500," the same magazine, XVII, pp. 466-480; John T. Gillard's "Lafayette, Friend of the Negro," the same magazine, XIX, pp. 355-371. See also C. G. Woodson, *History of the Negro Church,* chapters i and ii.

27. The education of the Negro during the colonial period is discussed in detail by C. G. Woodson in first and second chapters of his *Education of the Negro Prior to 1861.* The case of the poor whites is set forth in M. W. Jernegan's *Laboring and Dependent Classes in Colonial America.* The works on white servitude cited under 14 should be consulted also. In most cases these works have covered the various aspects of white servitude including this under consideration.

28. *The Negro in Our History* contains two chapters on the "Free Negro," and there are references to this element throughout the first half of the book. The Free Negro has been discussed in the following: J. H. Russell's *Free Negro in Virginia* (Baltimore, 1913) ; John Daniel's *In Freedom's Birthplace* (Boston, 1914) ; R. H. Taylor's "Free Negro in North Carolina" in *James Sprunt Pub.,* 1920; E. R. Turner's *The Negro in Pennsylvania* (Washington, 1911) ; J. M. Wright's *Free Negro in Maryland* (New York, 1921) ; C. G. Woodson's *Free Negro Heads of Families in the United States in 1830;* and his *Free Negro Owners of Slaves in the United States in 1830; Negro Population in the United States, 1790 to 1915;* and *The Journal of Negro History,* I, pp. 1-68, 99-100, 203-242, 302-317, 361-376; II, pp. 51-78, 164-185; III, pp. 90-91, 196-197, 360-367, 435-441.

VI. THE COLONIES IN THE NEW BRITISH EMPIRE, 1763-1774

29. The Change in Colonial Policy of Great Britain

30. Tax on the Trade in Sugar, Molasses, and Rum, Exchanged for Slaves, Gold and Palm Oil

31. The Protest of the Colonies—Slave Trade

32. The Doctrine that All Men are Created Equal—Samuel Adams, James Otis, Patrick Henry, and Thomas Jefferson

29. The new ideas as to the reconstruction of the empire should be carefully studied from the point of view of their bearing on the Negro. In the first place, when the French were moved from the frontier as a result of the French and Indian War, the Negroes could no longer escape to their settlements across the mountains as had been the case for many years. Now the Negro must serve the new regime or die. The change in the colonial policy of Great Britain with respect to the Negroes lay in the imperial ideas of Grenville, Townsend and North. In the change of the colonial policy the matter of the slave trade was forced to the front by the protests of certain Americans. The slave trade would become more profitable to England and less so to America when carried out according to law. Chatham and Nelson had believed that the slave trade was essential to the prosperity of England. The protest against these undesirable policies led to much talk about freedom which directed attention to the low estate of the Negro. The histories of this period like those of Edward Channing, W. M. Lecky, Otto Trevellyan and C. H. Van Tyne touch these points in a general way only. Read the extracts from Horace Walpole's letters quoted in C. G. Woodson's "Some Attitudes in English Literature," in *The Journal of Negro History*, XX, pp. 57-60.

30. The Navigation Acts themselves set forth in the source books of American History should be examined in order to see that part of the picture since secondary works are often too biased to treat this matter impartially. See the second volume of Channing's *History of the United States,* and G. L. Beer's *British Colonial Policy.*

31. The protest of the colonies against the slave trade as set forth in the first draft of the Declaration of Independence, but omitted from the final draft because of objections, is significant. It tended to make some people think that, if the slave trade was wrong, so was slavery. This made the question more international than it had been. This phase of the question is treated in the works mentioned above, but the detailed treatment may be found in the eighth chapter of Woodson's *Negro in Our History.* Thomas Clarkson's *History of the Slave Trades* shows this attitude. Consult Charles H. Wesley's "The Neglected Period of Emancipation in the West Indies," *The Journal of Negro History*, XVIII, pp. 156-179.

32. The doctrine of the equality of man as taken over from John Locke by the patriots of the American Revolution has been discussed in numerous

VI. THE COLONIES IN THE NEW BRITISH EMPIRE, 1763-1774—*Continued*

33. The Boston Massacre—Crispus Attucks
34. Lexington, Concord, and Bunker Hill, with Negro Minute Men

VII. THE AMERICAN REVOLUTION AS IT CONCERNED THE NEGRO, 1775-1783

35. The Formation of Independent States with and without the Negro
36. The Establishment of a Confederate Government

histories which either ignore its bearing on the Negro or purposely traduce the thought of these patriots. It is necessary then to examine the speeches and writings of Samuel Adams, James Otis, Patrick Henry, and Thomas Jefferson. So many of the comments on their utterances are merely efforts to make history to order. Consult these sources in the *American History Leaflets;* A. B. Hart's *American History Told by Contemporaries,* his *American Patriots and Statesmen,* and W. Macdonald's *Select Statutes,* etc.

33. The Boston Massacre has been minimized and ignored by so-called historians for the reason that the hero was Crispus Attucks, a Negro. This event, however, was considered so significant at that time that it was celebrated as a holiday in New England until the Fourth of July superseded it. The best account is found in W. H. Mazyck's *George Washington and the Negro* (Washington, 1932), pages 150 to 160. This author used original materials to produce this book.

34. See George Washington Williams' *History of the Negro Race in America,* I, pp. 324 to 369, the same author's *The Negro Soldiers in the War of the Rebellion,* chapter i, and W. H. Mazyck's *George Washington and the Negro,* chapters viii and ix.

35. The details of the constitutional provisions with respect to the Negro are given in G. W. Williams' *History of the Negro Race in America,* I, chapter xxviii; in the constitutions and laws themselves of the states, found in F. N. Thorpe's *Federal and State Constitutions;* and in Max Farrand's *Records of the Federal Convention of 1787.* A brief sketch of this period is found in the eighth chapter of C. G. Woodson's *Negro in Our History.*

36. The general outline of this period is given in A. C. McLaughlin's *Confederation and the Constitution* (New York, 1905), and in the third volume of Channing's *History of the United States;* but these authors are not much concerned with problems of those of low estate. The sources given under 35 must be depended upon to tell the other part of this story. McLaughlin has recently published a new book entitled *The Constitutional History of the United States.*

VII. THE AMERICAN REVOLUTION AS IT CONCERNED THE NEGRO, 1775-1783—*Continued*

37. THE NEGRO IN THE DECLARATION OF INDEPENDENCE

38. NEGROES FIRST CALLED TO THE COLORS DISMISSED

39. THE NEGROES APPEALED TO BY THE BRITISH—DUNMORE AND CLINTON

40. THE NEGRO SOLDIERS CALLED BACK TO THE CONTINENTAL ARMY—MONMOUTH, RHODE ISLAND, POINTS BRIDGE, STONY POINT, AND YORKTOWN

41. ANTI-SLAVERY EFFORTS AND GRADUAL EMANCIPATION—LAFAYETTE AND KOSCIUSKO

37. To answer the question as to whether or not Jefferson had the Negro in mind in writing of all men as being created equally free and independent one should have recourse to Jefferson's other writings. Jefferson certainly believed that the Negro should be free. Was Jefferson practical or doctrinaire? Slaveholders said he was the latter. Was Jefferson a theorist as President of the United States? Read John Locke's *Second Essay on Government*. Did John Locke have the Negro in mind?

38. The treatment of the Negro and soldiers during the American Revolution is fully discussed in the sources given under 35. Consult, however, W. B. Hartgrove's "The Negro Soldier in the American Revolution," *The Journal of Negro History*, I, pp. 110-131; Sparks' *Writings of George Washington*, VIII, pp. 322-323; W. H. Mazyck's *George Washington and the Negro*, chapters viii and ix. Read also what is said upon this topic in G. W. Williams's *Negro Troops in the War of the Rebellion*.

39. The references given above treat this approach of the British with promises of freedom to the Negro. Other details are given, however, in Livermore's *An Historical Research*, pp. 114 *et seq;* George H. Moore's *Notes on Slavery in Massachusetts*, New York, 1866; William C. Nell's *Colored Patriots of the American Revolution; Journals of the Provincial Congress of Massachusetts; Journals of the Provincial Congress of South Carolina;* Force's *American Archives*, 4th Series, III; *Journals of Congress,* II; *Rhode Island Colonial Records*, VIII; Sparks's *Correspondence of the American Revolution*.

40. The best account of the Negro soldiers in the Battle of Monmouth is in the seventh volume of George Bancroft's *History of the United States,* p. 421. George W. Williams gives in the first volume of his *History of the Negro Race* on p. 368, the best available account of the Negro soldiers in the Battle of Rhode Island, basing his statement on Arnold's *History of Rhode Island,* II, pp. 427, 428. Williams's accounts in full also for the conflict at Points Bridge and Yorktown.

41. The best records of the early anti-slavery movements may be found in the *Minutes of the Proceeding of the American Convention of Abolition Societies.* Consult "The Appeal of the American Convention of Abolition

VII. THE AMERICAN REVOLUTION AS IT CON-
CERNED THE NEGRO, 1775-1783—*Continued*

42. THE PEACE OF 1783 WITH RESPECT TO THE NEGRO

VIII. THE PROBLEMS OF THE NEW NATION, 1783-1789

43. FREEDOM DURING THE CONFEDERATION

44. CESSION OF WESTERN LANDS—THE ORDINANCE
OF 1787 EMANCIPATORY

45. FAILURE OF GREAT BRITAIN TO CARRY OUT THE
TREATY OF 1783—CLAIMS FOR SLAVES STATED

46. INTERESTS OF ONE STATE OPPOSED TO THOSE OF
OTHERS—DISORDERS

Societies to Anti-Slavery Groups," *The Journal of Negro History*, VI, pp.
200-240, 310-374.   Should this source be inaccessible M. S. Locke's *Anti-
Slavery in America, 1619-1808* (Boston, 1901), will suffice. Read also W. H.
Mazyck's *George Washington and the Negro*, pp. 93-97, 143-149; and "The
Will of Robert Pleasants," *The Journal of Negro History*, II, pp. 429-430.

42. The treaty itself should be examined. A discussion of the question
of the indemnity claimed for slaves escaping to the British has been contributed by A. G. Lindsay in "Diplomatic Relations between the United States
and Great Britain bearing on the Return of Negro Slaves, 1788-1828," *The
Journal of Negro History*, V, pp. 391-419.

43. In addition to what is available in the sources already referred to in
connection with the Negro during the American Revolution, the thirtieth
and thirty-first chapters of the second volume of George Williams's *History
of the Negro Race* will suffice for general purposes. For details state documents must be examined, because this aspect of our history is not treated
scientifically in available books.   Consult such as the *Journal of the Provincial Congress of South Carolina* and the *Journal of the Provincial Congress of Massachusetts, Laws of the State of New York*, John Adams's
Works and Sparks's *Works* of Washington.

44. The cession of the Western lands so far as they concerned the Negro
is discussed in the ninth chapter of J. P. Dunn's *Indiana: A Redemption from
Slavery;* in the chapter on the Ordinance of 1787 in C. T. Hickok's *The
Negro in Ohio;* and in the chapter on the Ordinance of 1787 in N. Dwight
Harris's *Slavery and Servitude in Illinois*.

45. See A. G. Lindsay, *loc. cit., The Journal of Negro History*, V, pp. 391-
419. Additional information on this point may be found below in the discussion of subsequent diplomatic relations.

46. The disorders of the period of the Confederation had no particular
bearing on the Negro except that evidences of anarchy tended to make men
practical rather than doctrinaire—made them believe that man should be
restricted by a stronger government rather than granted more liberty. To
the extent that this thought became widespread the idea of emancipation became less popular.

VIII. THE PROBLEMS OF THE NEW NATION, 1783-
1789—*Continued*

    47. THE NEW CONSTITUTION, EVOLVED WITH COM-
PROMISES ON SLAVERY

    48. THE FREE NEGRO, NEVERTHELESS, A CITIZEN IN
SOME STATES

IX. GOVERNMENT UNDER THE FEDERALISTS—
WASHINGTON AND ADAMS, 1789-1801

    49. ABSORBING PROBLEMS OF PARTIES ELIMINATE THE
NEGRO

See C. G. Woodson's *Negro in Our History,* pp. 161-176. Consult also
the first volume of James Schouler's *History of the United States;* and
Channing's third volume of his *History of the United States.*

47. To answer this question one should read the notes of Yates, McHenry,
and Madison on the Convention of 1787. Where these are not accessible
consult Max Farrand's *Records of the Federal Convention.* If this work is
not available, consult "What the Framers of the Federal Constitution
Thought of the Negro" in the third volume of *The Journal of Negro History,* pp. 381-434. The three compromises on slavery should be carefully
noted.

48. The Free Negro at the close of the eighteenth century is treated in the
second volume of George Washington Williams's *History of the Negro
Race,* pp. 412-441. Consult also R. B. Taney's Dred Scott decision with
respect to Negro citizenship at that time. What is the difference between
citizenship of the state and citizenship of the United States? Which one
takes precedence over the other? Does the one include the other?

Consult J. H. Russell's *Free Negro in Virginia,* J. M. Wright's *Free
Negro in Maryland,* E. R. Turner's *The Negro in Pennsylvania,* J. P. Dunn's
Indiana, and John Daniels's *In Freedom's Birthplace.*

49. It is said that absorbing problems of state made it possible to eliminate
the Negro question or to prevent it from becoming perplexing. Was there
so much else to give attention to or was there a fear to discuss the matter
of slavery and freedom because certain states had already become attached
to the institution? In other words, did the nation begin with a slaveholding
area at that time without an actually free section to array itself in opposition
thereto?

See C. G. Woodson's *Negro in Our History,* pp. 161-176; and his *Free
Negro Heads of Families in the United States in 1830,* the "Introduction."
Consult "Letters of George Washington bearing on the Negro," *The Journal
of Negro History,* II, pp. 411-422; Thomas Jefferson's "Thoughts on the
Negro," same magazine, III, pp. 55-89; "Benjamin Franklin and Freedom,"
the same magazine, II, pp. 41-50; "James Madison's Attitude toward the
Negro," the same magazine, pp. 74-102.

IX. GOVERNMENT UNDER THE FEDERALISTS— WASHINGTON AND ADAMS, 1789-1801—*Continued*

50. FIRST SLAVERY DEBATE, 1789-1790
51. THE INDUSTRIAL REVOLUTION CULMINATING WITH THE INVENTION OF THE COTTON GIN, 1793
52. THE NEGRO IN JAY'S TREATY
53. THE NEGROES SPURRED TO INDEPENDENT ACTION —LIELE, BRYAN, ALLEN, VARICK, HAMMON, WHEATLEY, AND BANNAKER

50. The importance of the debate on slavery in 1789 is not that the question was discussed in detail but that the pigeon-hole disposition of the question at that time set a precedent in Congress. This was tantamount to law for about half a century. Such petitions were to be referred to die a natural death without being brought up for consideration. In the further study of this aspect of our history the student will facilitate his task by bearing this in mind. The matter is mentioned in the general histories of the country, but no details are given as in the other works herein referred to. If accessible the *Annals of Congress* should be consulted for first-hand information in view of the fact that this and other unpopular questions have been neglected by historians.

51. The industrial revolution is treated in all worth while histories of the latter half of the eighteenth and the nineteenth century. See Edward Channing's *History of the United States* (New York, 1917), IV, pp. 430-432; J. S. Bassett's *A Short History of the United States* (New York, 1920), pp. 345-347; Gilbert Slater's *The Making of Modern England* (Boston, 1922), chapter x. Consult also Coman's *Industrial History of the United States,* Bogart's *Economic History of the United States,* Callender's *Economic History,* and Carman's *Economic History of the United States.*

52. This has been freely discussed by the Honorable W. R. Riddell of the Supreme Court of Ontario in "Interesting Notes on Great Britain and Canada with Respect to the Negro—Jay's Treaty and the Negro," *The Journal of Negro History,* XIII, pp. 185-192. Consult also A. G. Lindsay *loc. cit.* Useful also is Edward Channing's *History of the United States,* IV, pp. 136-138, 142-145, 177, 353.

53. The independent movements led by Liele, Bryan, Allen, and Varick are well known. The aim here is to account for them as a sequel of the reaction following the American Revolution. Consult John W. Davis's "George Liele and Andrew Bryan" and the source material in *The Journal of Negro History,* I, pp. 202-205 and III, pp. 119-127. Read the fourth chapter of C. G. Woodson's *History of the Negro Church* (Washington, 1921); and D. A. Payne's *History of the A. M. E. Church.* For the literary and other efforts of Jupiter Hammon, Phillis Wheatley, and Benjamin Banneker see C. G. Woodson's *The Mind of the Negro as Reflected in Letters during the Crisis, 1800-1860,* the "INTRODUCTION." Consult also Vernon Loggins' *The Negro Author.*

IX. GOVERNMENT UNDER THE FEDERALISTS—
WASHINGTON AND ADAMS, 1789-1801—*Continued*

54. THE REVOLUTION OF HAITI AS IT CONCERNED THE
UNITED STATES

X. AFFAIRS UNDER JEFFERSON AND MADISON,
1801-1817

55. THE OVERTHROW OF THE FEDERALISTS, THE EFFECT
OF, ON THE NEGRO

56. REPUBLICAN REFORMS AS THEY CONCERNED THE
NEGRO—STATES' RIGHTS

54. The revolution and the independence of Haiti are discussed in T. G. Steward's *Haitian Revolution;* H. G. Marshall's *Story of Haiti;* Carl Ludwig Lokke's "The Leclerc Instructions," *The Journal of Negro History,* X, pp. 80-98; R. W. Logan's "Education in Haiti," the same periodical, XV, pp. 401-460; and Emily Balch's *Occupied Haiti.* Read also Gragnon LaCoste's *Toussaint Louverture* and Michel Vaucaire's *Toussaint Louverture.* John W. Vandercook's *Black Majesty* (New York, 1927) is a romantic but fairly accurate biography of Christophe. H. P. Davis's *Black Democracy* (New York, 1929) is a good one-volume summary.

55. With the overflow of the Federalists and the rise of the States' Rights Republican or Democratic party the average student is familiar. If not Edward Channing's *Jeffersonian System,* J. S. Bassett's *Federalist System,* Gordy's *Political Parties,* and Babcock's *Rise of American Nationality* will suffice for adequate information in the development of this course.

The problem here is to understand how this revolution in politics influenced the history of the Negro in this country. The Federal Government in spite of all that we have said about democracy has grown at the expense of states' rights. Did the triumph of Jefferson and his party in 1800 delay this development of the central power? And if so what bearing had that on the problems touching the Negro in the United States? Does the Negro have a better chance for freedom under the Federal Government with the national authority strong and that of the states weak, or vice versa? The books available do not answer these questions. Can the student do so?

56. Did the Negro profit in any manner by the changes made under Jefferson and continued by Madison and Monroe? If John Adams could have continued as "His Royal Highness" would the poor devil occupying the lowest rung in the social and economic ladder have suffered? Is the lowest stratum of the social order better off under the control of the upper class or under that of the middle class—commoners, bourgeois or proletarian dictators? What proportion of the population of the United States could vote in 1800? What were the requirements for holding office at that time? Were there any political machines like these we have today?

Read W. B. Munro's *Government of the United States* and Henry Adams' *History of the United States* covering Jefferson's and Madison's administrations. Consult also Beard's and Hart's works on government.

X. AFFAIRS UNDER JEFFERSON AND MADISON, 1801-1817—*Continued*

57. INTERNATIONAL COMPLICATIONS—WAR WITH
    TRIPOLI AND THE PURCHASE OF LOUISIANA

58. THE SECOND WAR WITH ENGLAND—NEGRO SOL-
    DIERS WITH JACKSON, MACDONOUGH, AND PERRY

59. THE TREATY OF GHENT—CLAIMS FOR NEGROES CAR-
    RIED AWAY BY THE BRITISH

60. THE NEGROES WITH THE INDIANS

57. The War with Tripoli and the various troubles with the Barbary states are treated adequately in J. S. Bassett's *Short History of the United States,* pp. 295-296. With the exception of showing the states of North Africa, at that time under Mohammedan domination, the conflict has no such significance as that of the acquisition of Louisiana.

In what way was the Negro a contributor to the purchase of Louisiana? Has the Negro profited thereby? If Louisiana had remained in control of the French would the Negroes in that state be oppressed as they are today? Compare New Orleans with the rural parts of Louisiana.

Read Alice Dunbar Nelson's "People of Color in Louisiana," *The Journal of Negro History,* I, pp. 359-374; and II, 51-78. Consult also the works on Creole Louisiana by George W. Cable, Grace King, and Lafcadio Hearne.

58. In what way did the Negro serve as a cause of the War of 1812? Were Negroes involved in the question of impressment? Strange to say that the request for indemnity for fugitive slaves whom the British had emancipated partly caused the war, and the Negro helped to defeat their benefactors who had been thus appealed to for a reversal of their position.

The Negroes' participation in this war is told in the second volume of George Williams' *History of the Negro Race.* This author's *Negro Troops in the War of the Rebellion* gives in brief the same account. Read especially Andrew Jackson's appeal for the assistance of the people of color in the Battle of New Orleans. These people of color, it must be remembered, did not consider themselves Negroes.

59. The final outcome with respect to the Negro in the War of 1812 may be traced in the reference to A. G. Lindsay's article referred to above. Consult also C. W. A. David's "The Fugitive Slave Law of 1793 and its Antecedents," *The Journal of Negro History,* IX, pp. 18-24.

The amount of money granted to satisfy the United States Government was not so large, but the persistence in pressing such claims for almost half a century shows how proslavery the Federal Government was during those years. Yet this proslavery slant can be exaggerated if one loses sight of the fact that a principle of international law or the honor of the nation was at stake rather than merely the security of a domestic institution. John Quincy Adams, an advocate of free speech, was one of the negotiators of this treaty, and he did his best to enforce this claim.

60. The extent to which the Negroes joined the Indians in the South and Southwest can be best determined by K. W. Porter's "Relations between

X. AFFAIRS UNDER JEFFERSON AND MADISON, 1801-1817—*Continued*

61. COLONIZATION AS A NATIONAL SAFETY-VALVE— FREE NEGRO

Negroes and Indians within the Present Limits of the United States," *The Journal of Negro History*, XVII, pp. 287-367; the same author's "Notes Supplementary to Relations of Negroes and Indians," the same magazine, XVIII, pp. 282-321; E. P. Southall's "The Negro in Florida Prior to the Civil War," the same periodical, XIX, pp. 77-86; Wilton Marion Krogman's "The Racial Composition of the Seminole Indians of Florida and Oklahoma," the same magazine, XIX, pp. 412-430; and Sanford Winston's "Indian Slavery in the Carolina Region," the same magazine, XIX, pp. 431-440. Consult also J. R. Giddings's *Exiles of Florida;* Samuel G. Drake's *Aboriginal Races,* and Benjamin Brawley's *Social History of the American Negro.* The documents in the United States Office of the Indian Affairs in Washington, D. C., may be consulted for advanced study.

61. Colonization was made to mean all things to all men, but it was thus projected to meet the demands of the sections desiring to get rid of the free Negroes while making cotton king and while developing the North and West with foreign laborers immigrating to compete with free Negroes in personal service and drudgery. The attitudes of various sections toward colonization and the history of its development may be studied in the sixteenth and seventeenth chapters of C. G. Woodson's *Negro In Our History* and in the ninth chapter of same author's *Century of Negro Migration.* For details consult the following: William Jay's *An Inquiry into the Character and Tendency of the American Colonization Society;* R. C. F. Maugham's *The Republic of Liberia;* J. H. B. Latrobe's *Liberia, Its Origin, Rise, Progress, and Results;* John H. T. McPherson's *History of Liberia;* Frederick Starr's *Liberia, Description, History, Problems;* the same author's "Liberia after the World War," *The Journal of Negro History*, X, pp. 113-130; L. R. Mehlinger's "The Attitude of the Free Negro toward African Colonization," the same periodical, I, pp. 276-301; "A Typical Colonization Convention," the same periodical, I, pp. 318-338; H. N. Sherwood's "The Formation of the American Colonization Society," the same periodical, II, pp. 209-228; the same author's "Paul Cuffe," the same periodical, VIII, pp. 153-229; M. M. Fisher's "Lott Cary, the Colonizing Missionary," the same periodical, VII, pp. 380-418 together with "Letters of Lott Cary," VII, pp. 427-448; "The Liberian Republic," the same periodical, VIII, pp. 81-84; W. M. Brewer's "John B. Russwurm," the same periodical, XIII, pp. 413-422; N. Andrew N. Cleven's "Some Plans for Colonizing Liberated Negro Slaves in Hispanic America," the same magazine, XI, pp. 35-49; and Ben N. Azikiwe's "In Defence of Liberia," the same periodical, XVII, pp. 30-50.

For the status of the Free Negro see C. G. Woodson's "The Negroes of Cincinnati Prior to the Civil War," *The Journal of Negro History*, I, pp. 1-22; the same author's "The Negro Washerwoman, a Vanishing Figure," the same magazine, XV, pp. 269-277; W. B. Hartgrove's "The Story of Maria Louise Moore and Fannie M. Richards," the same magazine, I,

XI. NATIONAL DEVELOPMENT, MONROE AND J. Q. ADAMS, 1817-1828

62. The Rise of Industries in the East
63. Growth of the West and Southwest

pp. 22-33; J. H. Russell's "Colored Freemen as Slave Owners in Virginia," the same magazine, I, pp. 233-242; "Transplanting Free Negroes to Ohio," the same magazine, I, pp. 302-337; "Banishment of the Free People of Color from Cincinnati," the same periodical, VIII, pp. 331-333; Kelly Miller's "Historic Background of the Negro Physician," the same magazine, Volume I, pp. 99-109; A. G. Lindsay's "The Economic Condition of the Negroes of New York Prior to 1861," the same magazine, XI, pp. 190-199; Alice Dunbar Nelson's "People of Color in Louisiana," the same magazine, I, pp. 359-374; and II, pp. 51-78; "Observations on the Negroes of Louisiana," the same magazine, II, pp. 164-185; L. P. Jackson's "The Free Negroes of Petersburg, Virginia," the same magazine, XII, pp. 365-385; Charles H. Wesley's "The Struggle of Haiti and Liberia for Recognition," the same magazine, II, pp. 369-383; Zita Dyson's "Gerrit Smith's Efforts in Behalf of the Negroes in New York," the same magazine, III, pp. 354-359; Fred Landon's "The Buxton Settlement in Canada," the same volume, pp. 360-367; the same author's "Henry Bibb, A Colonizer," the same magazine, V, pp. 437-447; W. H. Morse's "Lemuel Haynes," the same magazine, IV, pp. 22-32; William Lloyd Imes's "The Legal Status of Free Negroes and Slaves in Tennessee," the same magazine, IV, pp. 254-272; James W. Patton's "The Progress of Emancipation in Tennessee," the same magazine, XVII, pp. 67-102; James Hugo Johnston's "Documentary Evidence of the Relations of Negroes and Indians," the same periodical, XIV, pp. 21-43.

62. The rise of industries in the East is to be noted as a development in an area with little or no Negro population. The Negro then became restricted to the agricultural area requiring unskilled labor. Here then must be noted a tendency which explains the economic status of the Negro today. The South did not feel the need of industrialism as long as cotton was in such demand as it was at that time, and that section once thought that it could not compete with the North in industry with such mentally undeveloped labor. See the first and second chapters of C. G. Woodson and Lorenzo J. Greene's *The Negro Wage Earner* (Washington, 1930).

63. Two volumes devoted to this particular phase of our history are F. J. Turner's *Rise of the New West* and Garrison's *Westward Extension* in the *American Nation* Series. These authors, of course, treat the Negro as purely incidental. The detailed treatment of the movement of the Negro population is in A. A. Taylor's "The Movement of the Negroes from the East to the Gulf States from 1830 to 1850," *The Journal of Negro History*, VIII, pp. 367-384. Some help may be obtained from the brief statement in C. G. Woodson's *Negro in Our History*, pp. 216-222. G. W. Featherstonaugh's *Excursion through the Slave States*, Basil Hall's *Travels in North America*, and Josiah Henson's *Uncle Tom's Story of His Life* are illuminating; but the movement has been scientifically treated in Frederic Bancroft's *Slave Trading in the Old South* (Baltimore, 1932). Consult also "Letters of Governor Edward Coles bearing on the Struggle of Freedom

XI. NATIONAL DEVELOPMENT, MONROE AND J. Q. ADAMS, 1817-1828—*Continued*

64. THE ACQUISITION OF FLORIDA, ONCE REFUGE OF NEGROES—SEMINOLE WARS

65. SLAVERY SECTIONAL

66. THE MISSOURI COMPROMISE

and Slavery in Illinois," *The Journal of Negro History*, III, pp. 158-195; and C. G. Woodson's *A Century of Negro Migration*, chapters i-v.

64. Of the acquisition of Florida much has been written. In the references given under 60 it is brought out that the Negroes there were a factor to be reckoned with. It seems that the relations of the Indians and Negroes were closer in this territory than in any other place along the Atlantic. It must be noted, however, that Negroes had been escaping to Florida ever since they first began to cross over from South Carolina before Georgia was settled and found homes among the Spaniards around St. Augustine. See "Dispatches of Spanish Officials bearing on the Negro Settlement of Gracia Real de Santa Teresa de Mosé," *The Journal of Negro History*, IX, pp. 144-195; and E. P. Southall's "The Negro in Florida Prior to the Civil War," the same periodical, XIX, pp. 77-86 and the article by K. W. Porter cited in note 60. The Seminole wars are treated in the works of Giddings and Drake cited above and in John T. Sprague's *The Florida War*.

65. Slavery made itself sectional in that it was accepted in the South where, although its evils became apparent, that section became permanently attached to the institution. Those who believed in free institutions avoided that section and tried to exclude slavery from the free soil which they settled. What favored agriculture was supposed to be harmful to manufacturing interests. The country had too many and varied interests to have economic cooperation. This was for a long time a question in the United States, and it is one today.

It must be noted, however, not merely that slavery divided the country into sections, but it divided also the South itself. The mountaineers of the western parts of Virginia, North Carolina, and South Carolina had interests differing widely from those of the rich planters of the tidewater. The pasturing of cattle and the production of wheat, oats, and hay did not require so much slave labor as rice, cotton and sugar. Suffrage was therefore safeguarded in the hands of the property owners, and higher offices were restricted mainly to the rich planters of the East by forcing upon the uplanders representation in the legislatures based on interests. This finally led to the disruption of Virginia.

See C. G. Woodson's "Freedom and Slavery in Appalachian America," *The Journal of Negro History*, I, pp. 132-150; I. E. McDougle's "Slavery in Kentucky," the same periodical, III, pp. 211-328; and C. H. Ambler's *Sectionalism in Virginia*.

66. The importance of the Missouri Compromise is that it brought up the questions of the status of the "free" Negro in the "free" and slave states, and also that of the citizenship of the United States in contradistinction to that of the state. Missouri endeavored to become a slave

XI. NATIONAL DEVELOPMENT, MONROE AND J. Q.
ADAMS, 1817-1828—*Continued*

67. THE TARIFF, 1816, 1824, AND 1828

68. THE MONROE DOCTRINE—LATIN AMERICAN RE-
PUBLICS

XII. THE NEGRO AND THE RISE OF A NEW NATION,
1829-1844

69. NATIONALISM A GROWTH, NOT A RESULT OF AN
AGREEMENT

state and in order to secure slaveholding Missouri would exclude free
Negroes coming from other states. Could this be constitutionally done
when these free Negroes enjoyed at that time all the privileges and im-
munities of citizens in certain states? In 1857 Taney said that the Negro
had never been a citizen of the United States. Was he right? Is a Negro
a citizen today?

Read J. W. Burgess's *Middle Period*, pp. 61-107; J. S. Bassett's *A Short
History of the United States*, pp. 371-375; and Edward Channing's *History
of the United States*, V, pp. 323-329.

67. The tariff is treated in F. W. Taussig's *History of the Tariff*. He
is a partisan, but he makes the operations of the tariff clear whereas most
historians merely discuss it from the outside. The sectional tendencies
already explained in other sources cited, however, have prepared the way
up to this point to understand the tariff as a sectional measure. The
southern farmer could buy clothes and the like in England at a low price,
but the tariff for the protection of infant industries was levied upon such
imports to prevent the foreigner from underselling the American manu-
facturers in the East. The South which, handicapped by slavery, could
not easily engage in industry, said this was a tax on one section for the
benefit of the other and, therefore, unconstitutional. Was the South right?

68. The Monroe Doctrine brought the United States to the front as the
defender of the independence of smaller republics on this side of the
Atlantic. It paved the way for the expansion of the United States into
that very area in violation of the independence of the very republics which
this country promulgated the Monroe Doctrine to protect. Was the United
States sincere? Did this country at that time hope that these republics
would fall into its hands? Will the Negroes in these republics be better
off under the United States or under flags of independent Latin nations?
It has been said that this nation has outgrown both the protective tariff
and the Monroe Doctrine. Do you agree with those taking this position?

In J. W. Foster's *American Diplomacy*, A. B. Hart's *Foundations of
American Foreign Policy*, Dexter Perkins' *Monroe Doctrine*, the diplomatic
works of David Jayne Hill, and those of J. B. Moore, the Monroe Doctrine
is discussed in various ways. See also N. Andrew N. Cleven's "The First
Panama Mission and the Congress of the United States," *The Journal of
Negro History*, XIII, pp. 225-254.

69. Did this country agree to become a nation or did it grow into a

XII. THE NEGRO AND THE RISE OF A NEW NATION, 1829-1844—*Continued*

70. SECTIONALISM IN CONFLICT WITH NATIONALISM
71. TARIFF AND NULLIFICATION, THE SEQUEL OF SECTIONALISM
72. INTERNAL IMPROVEMENTS IMPEDED BY SECTIONALISM
73. THE SECOND UNITED STATES BANK ABOLISHED

nation in spite of itself? What evidences of being a nation were apparent in 1832 which had not developed in 1798? Jackson and Jefferson belonged nominally at least to the same party. Did they have similar attitudes toward the Federal Government? Compare the picture in Channing's *Jeffersonian System* in the *American Nation* series with that of Macdonald's *Jacksonian Democracy*.

70. Was sectionalism a modern or medieval manifestation? Is the tendency of modern political organization toward segregation or aggregation? Compare sectionalism in Ancient Greece, in Poland, and in Switzerland, with that in the United States. Was the rift between the North and South actually sectionalism? Should we not speak of sectionalism as existing between the East and the West, a cleavage based upon something other than the presence and exploitation of a despised element? With the loss of interest in the Negro in the North the two divisions of states now tend to agree and cooperate without friction. The so-called sectionalism, then, was partly a divergence in opinion and policy due to traditional attitudes. Between the East and West there are natural differences of greater import, we are told. Read Semple's and Brigham's works on geographic influences.

71. The tariff as a cause of nullification was a mental flareback. It was an unnatural position in which slavery had put South Carolina and those parts of the South which agreed with that state. The episode is discussed fully in Dr. Frederic Bancroft's *Calhoun and Nullification*. The author gives the facts as they were recorded in the light of experience, and he does not try to read into the record theories which "smart historians" have tried to engraft upon the public mind. Von Holst gives the view of the "Constitutionalists." Consult Calhoun's *Works*.

72. A brief treatment of the internal improvement question is found in the eighth chapter of J. W. Burgess's *Middle Period*. The matter is dealt with in detail by Schouler, McMaster and Channing. Throughout the first half of Burgess's work the question is brought up in connection with other national affairs. The explanation of the opposition to the movement is found in sectionalism. Slavery indirectly, it is contended, set the South against internal improvements. This may or may not be true. The whole matter depends on the point of view of the person thus concerned, we are sometimes told. What does the student think about it?

73. It is said that slavery set parts of the South against the Second United States Bank by appealing to its states' rights vanity. It must be noted, however, that Jackson led also part of the West against this institu-

XII. THE NEGRO AND THE RISE OF A NEW NATION,
1829-1844—*Continued*

74. ABOLITION AND ANTI-ABOLITION SENTIMENT—
NEGRO INSURRECTIONS

tion. The United States Bank was popular in certain parts of the South. To a certain extent it must be noted that Jackson's strong personality carried with him a considerable number of persons who would do anything he suggested. Under such circumstances then the play of local and national policies in the drama becomes difficult to understand. See Ralph Catterall's *Second United States Bank.* Von Holst, Schouler and McMaster give the details also in their histories of the United States.

74. Abolition as it broke out during Jackson's administration must be distinguished from the anti-slavery effort organized during the American Revolution. The promoters of that day believed in gradual and compensated emancipation. It was not contemplated to manumit Negroes until they had served apprenticeships at certain occupations and taught to make a living. The fear was that Negroes liberated in large numbers would become a public charge. Now in 1831 under the leadership of the militant William Lloyd Garrison the thing was to be done instantly. Cut the knot now, he insisted. It was necessary to abolish the institution at once because it was not only an economic evil but a sin. Slaveholders, once considered gentlemen, were now dubbed malefactors; and the constitution which permitted them to continue in this sin was "a covenant with death and an agreement with hell." This was conflict.

Compare the *Words of Garrison* (Boston, 1831) with the "Address of the American Convention of Abolition Societies in 1794" (*The Journal of Negro History,* VI, pp. 200-203). Consult the following: Fred Landon's "Anti-Slavery Society in Canada," *The Journal of Negro History,* IV, pp. 33-40; W. R. Riddell's "The Slave in New York," the same periodical, XIII, pp. 53-86; A. H. Gordon's "The Struggle of the Slave for Physical Freedom," the same magazine, XIII, pp. 22-35; W. Sherman Savage's "Abolitionist Literature in the Mails, 1835-1836," the same magazine, XIII, pp. 255-264; E. P. Southall's "Arthur Tappan and the Anti-Slavery Movement," the same magazine, XV, pp. 162-197; J. H. Johnston's "A New Interpretation of the Domestic Slave System," the same magazine, XVIII, pp. 39-45. The study may be carried further with W. P. and F. J. Garrison's *William Lloyd Garrison;* MacDonald's *Select Documents,* 389-437; William Jay's *Miscellaneous Writings;* F. L. Olmsted's *Back Country;* the same author's *Cotton Kingdom,* and *The Seaboard Slave States;* D. R. Goodloe's *Southern Platform;* H. Von Holst's *History of the United States,* III; J. B. McMaster's *History of the United States,* VI, pp. 567-571; A. B. Hart's *Slavery and Abolition;* the same author's *History of the United States told by Contemporaries,* IV, pp. 24, 42, 72-143; C. G. Woodson's *Negro in Our History,* pp. 306-331, and the Appendix; "Documents" in *The Journal of Negro History,* VI, pp. 103-112, 200-240, 310-274; and A. H. Abel and F. J. Klingberg's *Sidelight on Anglo-American Relations.*

For Negro insurrections read the chapter on "Self-Assertion" in C. G.

XII. THE NEGRO AND THE RISE OF A NEW NATION, 1829-1844—*Continued*

75. INTERNATIONAL COMPLICATIONS—SLAVERY ON THE HIGH SEAS—*Creole, Amistad*

Woodson's *Negro in Our History;* J. W. Cromwell's "The Aftermath of Nat Turner's Insurrection," *The Journal of Negro History,* V, pp. 208-234; W. Sherman Savage's "Abolitionist Literature in the Mails, 1835-1856," the same periodical, XIII, pp. 150-184; James Hugo Johnston's "The Participation of White Men in Virginia Negro Insurrections," the same magazine, XVI, pp. 158-167; Joshua Coffin's *Slave Insurrections;* T. W. Higginson's *Travelers and Outlaws;* W. Drewery's *Slave Insurrections in Virginia;* and David Walker's *Appeal.*

75. The best sources for the study of this aspect of United States history are mainly those dealing with the two outstanding cases, the *Amistad* and the *Creole* and with a less important though somewhat significant *Anderson* case. Consult J. Q. Adams, *Argument before the Supreme Court of the Case of the United States, Appellants, vs. Cinque and Others, Africans, Captured in the Schooner "Amistad"* (New York, 1841); *Africans Taken in the "Amistad,"* Document No. *185 of the 1st Session of the 26th Congress, Containing the Correspondence in Relation to the Captured Africans, Reprinted by Anti-Slavery Depository* (New York, 1840); R. S. Baldwin, *Argument before the Supreme Court of the United States, Appellants, vs. Cinque, and Others, Africans, of the "Amistad"* (New York, 1841); William Jay, *A View of the Action of the Federal Government, in behalf of Slavery* (Utica, 1844); De Witt Clinton Leach, *The Amistad Case* (Washington, 1858); *Schooner "Amistad," Message from the President of the United States Transmitting a Report from the Secretary of State Relative to the Schooner "Amistad,"* January 24, 1844; *Trial of the Amistad African Captives* (New York, 1839); J. W. Farewell, *The Anderson Case, Address, Ontario Bar Ass'n,* 1911; *Fugitive Slave Case of Anderson (Law M. and R.* 10:368; 11:42); Fred Landon, "The Anderson Fugitive Case," *The Journal of Negro History,* VII, pp. 233-42; *Correspondence between Mr. Webster and Lord Ashburton: 1. On McLeod's Case; 2. On the Creole Case; 3. On the Subject of Impressment* (Washington, 1842); William Jay, *The Creole Case, and Mr. Webster's Despatch* (New York, 1842); *Message from the President of the United States* (John Tyler) *Communicating Copies of Correspondence in Relation to the Mutiny on Board the Brig "Creole," and the Liberation of the Slaves who were Passengers in the said Vessel,* January 20, 1842 (Washington, 1842); Henry Wheaton, *Examin des questions de jurisdiction qui se sont élévees entre gouvernements anglais et americain dans l'affaire de la Créole* (Paris, 1842).

See text of the resolutions in *House Journal,* 27th Cong., 2nd Sess. For the resolution of censure of J. R. Giddings, *ibid.,* p. 580. For the discussions see the *Cong. Globe,* or Benton's *Abridgement,* XIV. The diplomatic correspondence regarding the *Creole* is in the *House Exec. Doc., 2,* 27th Cong., 3rd Sess., pp. 114-123, and *Senate Doc., 1,* pp. 116-125. See also Von Holst's *United States,* II, 479-486; J. Q. Adams's *Memoirs,* XI, 113-115; Wilson's

XII. THE NEGRO AND THE RISE OF A NEW NATION,
1829-1844—*Continued*

    76. THE SCHISM AND THE NEGRO

XIII. THE SLAVERY QUESTION IN CONGRESS, 1844-
1859

    77. THE SLAVEHOLDING AREA IN A STRUGGLE WITH
      FREE SOIL

        a. THE ANNEXATION OF TEXAS—THE
          MEXICAN WAR

        b. THE WILMOT PROVISO

        c. THE OREGON TERRITORY

        d. THE COMPROMISE OF 1850—FUGITIVE
          SLAVES AND PERSONAL LIBERTY LAWS
          —FREE AND NOT FREE

Rise and Fall of the Slave Power, I, chap. xxxi; Benton's *Thirty Years'
View,* II, chap. xcviii.

The work of Giddings is treated in Byron R. Long's *Joshua R. Giddings,
A Champion of Political Freedom* and in George W. Julian's *Life of Joshua
R. Giddings.* See also J. B. Moore's *International Arbitrations,* I, 417.

76. The schism of the church has been treated in detail in
most of the general histories like those of Schouler, McMaster, and Channing.
A brief statement is found on pages 471 and 477 of Bassett's *Short History
of the United States.* A more extensive treatment of this topic together with
a useful bibliography for advanced study is in the twelfth chapter of W. W.
Sweet's *Methodism in American History.* The same ground is covered in
Woodson's *History of the Negro Church.* The aim here, however, is not
to go into a detailed study of this schism but to understand it as it relates
to the Negro. This has been further developed in this same volume under
the caption of "The Religious Development of the Negro."

77. The history of the United States during this period becomes very
clear if the student can understand the chief issue. This was expansion into
new territory and new fields in our national development within natural
boundaries. The most inviting area was the unclaimed West, and both free
and slave labor or both slaveholding and non-slaveholding states entered
upon a rivalry in competing for control in the new spheres. Since a slave
society cannot move as rapidly as a free society the struggle could have
only the natural outcome; but such a large part of the country had reached
the undesirable stage of thinking to the contrary that the conflict occupied
the stage from 1830 to 1865. Other things of importance took place, but
this conflict of freedom and slavery was the dominating factor of this period.

In addition to what is said hereupon in brief texts of United States History
like those of McLaughlin, Muzzey, Channing, Bassett, Hockett and Schlesinger
the student should read C. G. Woodson's *Negro in Our History,* chapters
xx and xxi; J. W. Burgess' *Middle Period,* pp. 210-474; J. B. McMaster's

XIII. THE SLAVERY QUESTION IN CONGRESS, 1844-1859—*Continued*

History of the United States, VIII, pp. 473-521; James Schouler's *History of the United States*, V, pp. 389-433; T. C. Smith's *Parties and Slavery*, passim; James Ford Rhodes, *History of the United States*, I and II; William McDonald's *Select Statutes*, I, pp. 343, 365-372, 385-390, 397-454; II, pp. 35-38, 42-43, 113; A. B. Hart's *American History Told by Contemporaries*, III, 574-655; IV, pp. 122-192.

Certain phases of this conflict are best treated in special works. Garrison's *Westward Extension* thus deals with the Texan question. A. B. Hart treats in a general way *Slavery and Abolition*. J. Q. Adams's *Memoirs*, Byron R. Long's *Joshua R. Giddings*, Frederic Bancroft's *William H. Seward*, Moorfield Storey's *Charles Sumner*, Von Holst's *John C. Calhoun*, Johnson and Browne's *Alexander H. Stephens*, Alfriend's *Life of Jefferson Davis*, and O. J. Wise's *Henry A. Wise* require careful study to clear up all the ramifications of this question.

For the part the free Negroes were playing at that time one should read E. R. Turner's *The Negro in Pennsylvania;* J. H. Russell's *Free Negroes in Virginia;* J. M. Wright, *Free Negroes in Maryland;* C. T. Hickok, *The Negro in Ohio;* N. D. Harris's *Slavery and Servitude in Illinois;* M. R. Delany's *The Condition of Colored People in the United States* (1852); J. W. Cromwell's *The Negro in American History*, "The Convention Movement Among Negroes;" Frederick Douglass's *The Life and Times of Frederick Douglass;* William Still's *The Underground Railroad;* W. W. Brown's *The Black Man;* C. G. Woodson's *The Education of the Negro Prior to 1861;* W. H. Siebert's *Underground Railroad;* A. G. Lindsay's "The Economic Condition of the Negroes of New York Prior to 1861," *The Journal of Negro History*, VI, pp. 190-199; Leo H. Hirsch's "The Negro in New York from 1783 to 1865," the same magazine, XVI, pp. 382-413; C. W. A. David's "The Fugitive Slave Law of 1793 and its Antecedents," the same magazine, IX, pp. 18-25; Delilah L. Beasley's "Slavery in California" and "California Freedom Papers," the same magazine, III, pp. 33-54; J. H. Paynter's "Fugitives of the Pearl," the same magazine, I, pp. 243-264; M. N. Work's "Life of Charles Bennett Ray," the same magazine, pp. 361-371; W. R. Riddell's "The Slave in Canada," the same magazine, IV, pp. 372-395; Fred Landon's "The Negro Migration to Canada after 1850," the same magazine, V, pp. 22-36; the same author's "The Anderson Fugitive Case," the same magazine, VII, 233-242, the same author's "Canadian Negroes and the Rebellion of 1837," the same magazine, VII, 377-379; and his "Amherstburg, Terminus of the Underground Railroad," the same magazine, X, 1-9; William T. Laprade's "The Domestic Slave Trade in the District of Columbia," the same magazine, XI, pp. 17-34; W. M. Brewer's "Henry Highland Garnett," the same magazine, XIII, pp. 36-52; "Letters of Hiram Wilson to Hannah Gray," the same magazine, XIV, pp. 344-350; E. D. Preston's "The Underground Railroad in Northwest Ohio," the same magazine, XVII, pp. 409-436; the same author's "The Genesis of the Underground Railroad," the same magazine, XVIII, pp. 144-170; William Lloyd Imes's "The Legal Status of Free Negroes and Slaves in Tennessee," the same magazine, IV, pp. 254-272.

XIII. THE SLAVERY QUESTION IN CONGRESS, 1844-1859—*Continued*

78. *Uncle Tom's Cabin* should be read. One cannot understand this period without so doing. The translations of this work into foreign languages and its dramatization in Europe should be noted. See *The Journal of Negro History*, XVIII, pp. 239-240; XX, pp. 42, 43, 44. See also McLean's *Uncle Tom's Cabin in Germany* (New York, 1910).

79. The Kansas-Nebraska debate and the strife which resulted from the passage of that bill are well treated in the sources referred to in 76. A careful study of the theories of Stephen A. Douglas is necessary in order to understand how he complicated matters just as Clay and Webster did in trying to become president by pleasing all sections at the same time. The speeches of these three men show that they had not kept pace with the country.

80. The Dred Scott Decision should be carefully examined and compared with the facts as to the exercise of the functions of citizenship prior to this time. The discussions which came up in connection with the Missouri Compromise and the crisis of 1850 should be connected here to show the trends in public thought and in the interpretation of the laws and the constitution of the United States. Most histories do not bring out this particular phase of the question.

81. Here the debates of Douglas with Lincoln should be read. Commentaries on these utterances will not suffice, for writers of subsequent generations have tried to give them an unwarranted interpretation in remaking the history of the United States to order. This has been done especially in the case of trying to make Abraham Lincoln appear more liberal than he was. He was a "conservative gradual emancipationist," not a radical reformer. The Civil War forced instant emancipation upon him.

82. John Brown's Raid must not be treated in the usual frontier fashion as do many writers who think of him as an insane man who committed a crime in meddling with a problem which was being otherwise worked out. This new attitude is that of the schoolboy, and it is a stronger argument for the insanity of those who write such bias than for that of John Brown. It is unworthy of a man who calls himself an historian. John Brown was the most striking figure in the terrible drama. He was more than a fiery abolitionist. The personal element counted little here. He was an expression of the feeling of thousands of persons who, although they had never seen slavery, had learned to hate the institution to the extent of violating the law to check it. Of course, John Brown was far ahead of the

XIII. THE SLAVERY QUESTION IN CONGRESS, 1844-1859—*Continued*

83. HELPER'S *Impending Crisis*

XIV. THE WAR FOR SOUTHERN INDEPENDENCE, 1861-1865

84. THE ELECTION OF LINCOLN AS IT SEEMED TO THE SOUTH

procession, but in his death he lighted a torch which did not go out until the Negro had been freed. In this he was justified.

The sources for new aspects of John Brown are mainly those which, like the sketch in the *Dictionary of American Biography,* try to make out a case of insanity. In this connection should be read what Edward Channing says of John Brown in the fifth volume of his *History of the United States.* Read also Fred Landon's "Canadian Negroes and the John Brown Raid" in *The Journal of Negro History,* VI, pp. 174-182. F. B. Sanborn's *John Brown* and O. G. Villard's *John Brown* approach the treatments of this career with the attitude of James Redpath.

83. The student should read H. R. Helper's *Impending Crisis.* His production should be considered sympathetically. Certain writers with a decided slant in favor of abolition have carefully pointed out that the author of this book was in no sense a lover of the Negro as he explains in his book called *Nojoque.* While this is true Hinton Rowan Helper in writing this attack on the unsound economic basis of slavery was more than a mere author. He thereby voiced the sentiment of a large number of thinking people, both North and South, who had none of the sentimental attitude of the abolitionists but had sufficient vision to see that this country had outgrown this mediaeval institution. Helper's approach to the question was different from that of Mrs. Stowe, and he reached a smaller but more thoughtful audience. The effect of it in higher circles is best explained by the fact that it caused a great stir in Congress. In trying to elect in 1859 a speaker of the House who had not read or who had not been influenced by this work it required two months before this could be done, and they finally had to decide upon a conservative Republican for that position. It has been said before, and probably truthfully so, that if the Civil War had not broken out as early as it did, Helper's *Impending Crisis* would have done much more than it had the chance to do during the time intervening between its appearance and the sectional clash.

In connection with Helper's work read also A. O. Craven's "Poor Whites and Negroes in the Ante-Bellum South" and W. M. Brewer's "Poor Whites and Negroes in the South since the Civil War," both in the *Journal of Negro History,* XV, pp. 1-37. C. H. Wesley's *Negro Labor in the United States,* chapter i, is enlightening for this period.

84. The election of Lincoln must be seen from two points of view, what it really meant and what his emotional opponents thought that it meant. The slaveholding area was probably insincere in some of the things which they said with respect to Lincoln's plan to abolish slavery immediately, for

XIV. THE WAR FOR SOUTHERN INDEPENDENCE, 1861-1865—*Continued*

85. SECESSION AS A MEANS TO UNDO NATIONALISM
86. COMPROMISES PROPOSED TO SAVE THE UNION

he could not have done so had he so desired. The majority of the members of Congress were not anti-slavery. The pro-slavery leaders, however, had sufficient vision to understand that the safe-guarding of slavery as a dominant factor in the United States was at an end. Free labor had outstripped slave labor in the contest; free institutions had more rapidly expanded than medieval institutions. The slave states, as their protagonists surveyed the situation in 1860, would fall behind the free states thereafter not only in numbers but in wealth and influence both at home and abroad. This being the case the only remedy left was to break up the Union as soon as possible; and it was believed that it could be more easily done in 1860 than at some later date.

As to sources we may be brief. J. K. Hosmer's *The Appeal to Arms* and his *Outcome of the Civil War* do not add very much to the understanding of these matters. John W. Burgess in his anti-Negro and pro-Union attitude does a little better in his *Civil War and the Constitution*. James F. Rhodes in his *History of the United States* deals a little more with the details, especially in the third volume. In the eighth volume of J. B. McMaster's *History of the United States*, and the sixth volume of James Schouler's *History of the United States*, little new ground is covered. Professor Edward Channing has treated the same period in his own style in the sixth volume of his *History of the United States*. Most other sources fall short of these. The history of the Civil War is yet to be written. We are too close to that period to treat it dispassionately.

85. Secession must not be regarded as an invention in the year 1860. Threats to this effect in the Virginia and Kentucky Resolution, in the Hartford Convention, and in the nullification efforts in 1832 must be connected herewith to understand the national drama as it gradually developed. The theory of secession is thoroughly discussed in the third volume of H. W. Wilson's *Rise and Fall of the Slave Power*, and in the first three chapters of J. W. Burgess's *Reconstruction and the Constitution*. Read also A. A. Taylor's "Making West Virginia a Free State," *The Journal of Negro History*, VI, pp. 131-173; and G. W. Brown's "Trends toward a Southern Confederacy," the same magazine, XVIII, pp. 256-282.

86. In the sources already noted the proposed compromises are treated. However, there is a new thought in Clinton E. Knox's "The Possibilities of Compromise in the Senate Committee of Thirteen and the Responsibility for Failure," *The Journal of Negro History*, XVII, pp. 437-465. See also Coleman's *Life of John J. Crittenden*. J. W. Burgess's *Civil War*, cited above, (pp. 151-166) gives also a clear treatment of these proposals for compromise. The main point to observe here is not the details of plans to heal the breach but the evidence of an unconsciously wide estrangement which made such efforts futile. Study also the outcome in a typical border state in W. T. McKinney's "The Defeat of the Secessionists in Kentucky in 1861," *The Journal of Negro History*, I, pp. 375-390.

XIV. THE WAR FOR SOUTHERN INDEPENDENCE, 1861-1865—*Continued*

87. THE WAR WITH NEGRO FUGITIVES AS CONTRABAND AND SOLDIERS
88. THE WAR IN EUROPEAN CIRCLES

87. The conduct of the war with respect to the Negro can be understood only by reviewing the attitudes toward the Negro soldier. It must be remembered that, although the Negro fought freely in the colonial wars and participated in the early battles of the American Revolution, the military chieftains later excluded Negroes from the army on the ground that it was a conflict which concerned only white men. Of course, the Negro was re-admitted to the continental army when the British began to welcome them. Negroes were desired in the critical war of 1812, and were especially appealed to by Jackson at New Orleans, doubtless after learning how bravely they had recently fought with Perry and McDonough on water. By the time of the Mexican War race prejudice had become so rank that few Negroes served in the army except as laborers and mechanics and in menial capacities. There was naturally some fear about having the Negro as a fighter in an army which was said to be on an expedition to acquire slave territory.

In the Union armies of the Civil War there was the fear of the charge of "turning savage Negroes" upon the South rising in the interests of states' rights; and, since the war of subjugation or coercion was "not to free slaves but to save the Union," the presence of Negroes in the Union ranks might give the situation a different aspect. The United States hoped, just as the Confederacy did, to make a good impression abroad; and this sort of a report would work to the contrary.

In the Confederate ranks, of course, there was no thought of using Negro soldiers, for slavery had been justified there on the ground that a Negro could not make a good soldier. In the last extremity just before the collapse of the Confederacy, however, the South reversed itself and accepted Negroes as soldiers. Long before this, after efforts like those of Frémont, Butler and Hunter, Lincoln and his generals had accepted the Negroes as soldiers.

Dr. Charles H. Wesley's *Collapse of the Confederacy* and his "Employment of Negroes as Soldiers in the Confederate Army" (*Journal of Negro History*, IV, 239-253) should be read in the study of the rôle the Negro played during the Civil War. The question of the contrabands is discussed in the sixth chapter of C. G. Woodson's *A Century of Negro Migration*, in "The Federal Government and the Negro Soldier," by Fred A. Shannon, *The Journal of Negro History*, XI, pp. 563-583; in G. K. Eggleston's "The Work of the Relief Societies during the Civil War, the same magazine, XIV, pp. 272-299; and in "The Colloquy," the same magazine, XVI, pp. 88-94.

88. The attitudes of foreign countries toward the combatants during the Civil War were determined mainly by selfish interests. The leading European powers as usual sought to throw their influence where it would count most

XIV. THE WAR FOR SOUTHERN INDEPENDENCE, 1861-1865—*Continued*

89. EMANCIPATION PROCLAMATION
90. LINCOLN'S COLONIZATION PLAN
91. LINCOLN'S PLAN OF RECONSTRUCTION

for them. Dependent upon the supply of cotton from the South, England inclined in that direction and secretly did much to aid that cause. The sentimental groups inheriting the traditions of the anti-slavery and abolition forces in Europe had little effect on the cold-blooded governments.

In this connection, however, one will profit by reading Joseph H. Park's "Thomas Hughes and Slavery," *The Journal of Negro History,* XII, pp. 590-605; and Nelson F. Adkins's "Thomas Hughes and the American Civil War," the same magazine, XVIII, pp. 322-329. A new point of view is presented with much bias by F. D. Owsley in his *King Cotton Diplomacy.* Donaldson Jordan and Edwin J. Pratt in their *Europe and the American Civil War* cover the same ground with more objectivity. The best known work in this field is Ephraim D. Adams's *Great Britain and the American Civil War.*

89. That the Emancipation Proclamation should be carefully read goes without the saying; but at this stage it is necessary to understand the motives underlying this decree. Lincoln was not an abolitionist. He was a "gradual emancipationist" advocating compensation for the slaves and a colonizationist desiring to deport them. Impatient with his dallying with such methods and plans, Greeley, Sumner, Stevens, and Seward had urged Lincoln to change his policies. Why, then, did a man of Lincoln's type issue such a document as the Emancipation Proclamation? He had discouraged such steps made by Frémont in Missouri, by Hunter in South Carolina, and by Butler in Virginia. It is advisable to inquire, too, as to the significance of the Emancipation Proclamation. Was it legal or constitutional? Of what worth would it have been without the Thirteenth Amendment?

The work of Thaddeus Stevens in urging upon Lincoln the policy of instant emancipation should not be overlooked. Stevens was the most influential man in Congress during these years, and what he did to bring Lincoln to this position is a significant contribution to the progress of liberty. Sumner, a great orator of that day, became easily known, but Stevens was the great worker. For the discussion of this neglected aspect of history see Thomas Frederick Woodley's *Thaddeus Stevens* (Harrisburg, Pennsylvania, 1934).

90. Lincoln believed in 1862 that the two races could not dwell together peacefully. Was Lincoln right? When the Negroes of the District of Columbia were freed in 1862 by his compensation methods he undertook to colonize them on the Island of Vache off Haiti. In Charles H. Wesley's "Lincoln's Plan for Colonizing the 'Emancipated Negroes'" in *The Journal of Negro History* (IV, pp. 7-21) and in Harry S. Blackstone's treatment, in the same magazine (VII, pp. 257-277) the details of this story are given.

91. Lincoln's plan of reconstruction as initiated before the end of the Civil War and taken up later by his successor, Andrew Johnson, as he

XIV. THE WAR FOR SOUTHERN INDEPENDENCE,
1861-1865—*Continued*

92. THE THIRTEENTH AMENDMENT RATIFIED

XV. RECONSTRUCTION OF THE SOUTHERN STATES,
1865-1881

93. JOHNSON'S TROUBLES

understood it, is sympathetically treated by J. W. Burgess in the second and third chapters of his *Reconstruction.* Of the short histories covering this topic that of Professor J. S. Bassett (pp. 594-601) is the most satisfactory.

92. The Thirteenth Amendment is clear; but did it abolish slavery? Is the Negro a freeman in the United States? Thomas Carlyle said you can abolish the name of slavery but not slavery itself. Can mere laws change a people's way of doing things? What is law? Is the Thirteenth Amendment Law? How many Negro tenants are actually free from peonage? Can you free a man in body without first freeing him in mind?

93. Certain historians say that Andrew Johnson got into trouble with Congress while trying to carry out Lincoln's plans. It would naturally increase the prestige of Johnson to have as an excuse that even Lincoln would have been humiliated by Thaddeus Stevens and Charles Sumner. There can be little doubt that Johnson followed the letter of the law as he believed Lincoln understood it; but it must be remembered that Lincoln had more common sense than Johnson. Lincoln had the most persistent sort of criticism and opposition throughout the Civil War, which was decidedly more of a perplexing problem than the antagonisms of reconstruction. Yet Lincoln emerged from that ordeal as a hero. Johnson was unfortunately out of place as president at that time. The best case made out for Johnson is in J. W. Burgess's *Reconstruction.* Although pointing out his lack of the qualifications of a political leader Burgess by innuendo gives Andrew Johnson a higher rank than ordinary by belittling from page to page the work of his chief opponents, Stevens and Sumner. Claude Bowers's *Tragic Era,* although favorable to Johnson, is not history. The monographs on the reconstruction in the various states, worked out under W. A. Dunning and elsewhere, are characterized by a still more biased attitude in favor of Johnson and against all who tried to make the Negroes citizens. These particular monographs and other works worse than these, though widely used as scientific productions, constitute merely the *ex parte* history in defense of the section with which these authors sympathized. In some cases these writers were relating the careers of their own relatives and personal friends. These works come about as near the truth as a local account written by a family which for generations had entertained a grudge against another competing with it in the same community. We know that most of the authors of these monographs have been trained in modern historiography; but they have merely prostituted scholarship to sectional bias.

In "Reconstruction and its Benefits" in the *American Historical Review,*

XV. RECONSTRUCTION OF THE SOUTHERN STATES, 1865-1881—*Continued*

94. THE RESTORED GOVERNMENTS OF THE SOUTH—
BLACK CODES AND VAGRANCY LAWS

95. THE FREEDMEN'S BUREAU

XV, No. 4, W. E. B. Du Bois undertook to give a different picture of the drama. The same author's *Black Reconstruction* gives a more detailed account from his point of view. John R. Lynch, a Negro member of Congress from Mississippi during the Reconstruction, has produced in reply to the critics of the reconstructionists a work entitled *Facts of Reconstruction*. Referring especially to the *History of the United States* by James Ford Rhodes and *The Tragic Era* by Claude Bowers as meretricious, John R. Lynch has written several poignant articles, published in *The Journal of Negro History* (II, pp. 345-368; III, 139-157; V, 420-436; XVI, 103-120). Francis Butler Simpkins and Robert Hilliard Woody, although not altogether free from bias, have produced an informing work on *South Carolina during Reconstruction*. In so doing they followed the scheme set up by A. A. Taylor in his *The Negro in South Carolina during the Reconstruction* and *The Negro in the Reconstruction of Virginia*. These last two mentioned works are productions of the Association for the Study of Negro Life and History, which contends that the history of the Reconstruction has not been written.

See Woodburn's *Thaddeus Stevens;* Bancroft's *William H. Seward;* Carl Schurz's *Reminiscences;* Adams's *Charles Francis Adams;* Moorfield Storey's *Charles Sumner;* Carl M. Frasures's "Charles Sumner and the Rights of the Negro," *The Journal of Negro History,* XIII, pp. 126-147; Sterling A. Brown's "Unhistoric History," the same magazine, XV, pp. 134-161; Bertram W. Doyle's "Some Progress in Race Relations," the same magazine, XVIII, pp. 12-32; Thomas Frederick Woodley's *Thaddeus Stevens* (Harrisburg, Pennsylvania, 1934).

94. That the restored state governments went back to the *status quo ante bellum* with the exception of granting the nominal freedom of the Negro is clear from the Black Codes themselves. These laws are not treated *in extenso* in the reconstruction works defending the old régime. The codes themselves should be read by every student of this period of our history. Without such knowledge he cannot understand the Reconstruction at all. According to these codes, the Negroes were to be less free than the free people of color were before the War. The Negroes not only would have no civil or political rights; but, although nominally free, they could be forced to work and for such wages as the employing class saw fit to pay. If they refused to work they were adjudged vagrants and punished as criminals.

95. The Freedmen's Bureau set up to protect the freedmen became the object of all sorts of attacks because it prevented the carrying out of the program for the Negro based upon the Black Codes. As shown by G. K. Eggleston's "Work of the Relief Societies during the War," *Journal of Negro History,* XIV, pp. 272-299, voluntary efforts were not sufficient. The Freedmen's Bureau made some mistakes in its administration, but this does not prove that the reenslavement of the Negro would have been wise. Read the

XV. RECONSTRUCTION OF THE SOUTHERN STATES, 1865-1881—*Continued*

96. THE FOURTEENTH AMENDMENT
97. CONGRESSIONAL RECONSTRUCTION AUTHORIZED—JOHNSON IMPEACHED
98. WHITE DISFRANCHISEMENT AND CORRUPTION

statutes organizing the Freedmen's Bureau and enlarging its powers in order to know all the facts. If there were abuses in the administration such were in keeping with the spirit of those parlous times.

96. The Fourteenth Amendment was intended to make the Negro a citizen. The whole country or rather all states had to accept the Negroes as citizens exercising the right of suffrage, and if they did not, their representation in Congress would be proportionately reduced. This has never been done. Although these hostile states have disfranchised the Negro, Congress has never had the courage to enforce the law. Some Negroes themselves object to the cutting down of the representation in the South, for that would concede the fight as having been won. Is this position sound? Was the Fifteenth Amendment necessary?

In connection with this new aspect of citizenship should come up again the question of citizenship of the state and citizenship of the United States as it developed in the debate of the Missouri Compromise. Read what is said in C. G. Woodson's "Fifty Years of Negro Citizenship as qualified by the United States Supreme Court," (*The Journal of Negro History*, XI, pp. 1-53). J. W. Burgess, more interested in legal history than in other aspects, frequently refers to citizenship in his *Middle Period* and *Reconstruction,* but, being of slave-holding antecedents, he did not feel that the Negro is qualified for citizenship.

97. The Congressional plan worked out in opposition to Johnson, who was later impeached for going too fast to the contrary, was based on free manhood suffrage without regard to race. The states had to accept the Fourteenth Amendment. In other words, this country was to be a democracy. Every man regardless of race was to be the political equal of every other man. There is nothing faulty in this ideal; but it was hardly natural for slave-holding people to accept it without a prolonged fight. Up to that time poor ignorant white men had not been permitted to vote in the South.

The plan to enfranchise the Negroes had to be enforced by dividing the South into military districts and placing in each an army which with the state militia would enforce the new law. Was this wise? Could this have been accomplished in some other way? The more peaceful method had been tried, but by the Black Codes the Negro's reenslavement had been actually begun.

98. Read the United States laws with respect to those who had rebelled. Were these measures too drastic in disfranchising the leaders of the South when the Negroes were exercising the right of suffrage? What other remedy could have saved the victory of the war without stirring up so much racial feeling? Was this the beginning of the racial feeling? Has any one ever discovered a better remedy than Congressional reconstruction for a similar

XV. RECONSTRUCTION OF THE SOUTHERN STATES, 1865-1881—*Continued*

99. THE FIFTEENTH AMENDMENT AND THE NEGRO IN POLITICS

100. POLITICAL RECONSTRUCTION UNDONE—KU KLUX KLAN

crisis? What is corruption? How much of it actually existed in the South as compared with that in the East and West? Were the Negroes the corruptionists? Seek the facts.

99. The Fifteenth Amendment forbids the disfranchisement of male voters on account of race, color or previous condition of servitude. Did it actually make the Negro a voter? Was it intended to supplement the Fourteenth Amendment because the South had refused to honor the Negro as a voter? What has the Fifteenth Amendment accomplished in the light of the present day situation?

For reference the following may be cited: N. P. Andrew's "The Negro in Politics," *The Journal of Negro History*, X, pp. 420-436; A. A. Taylor's "Negro Congressmen a Generation After," the same magazine, VI, pp. 127-171, G. D. Houston's "A Negro Senator," the same magazine, VII, pp. 243-250; W. A. Russ' "The Negro and White Disfranchisement during Radical Reconstruction," the same magazine, XIX, pp. 171-192; "Some Negro Members of Reconstruction Conventions and Legislatures and of Congress," the same periodical V, pp. 63-124, 235-254, VII, pp. 311-340; "Extracts from Newspapers and Magazines," the same periodical, VIII, pp. 84-91; Irving Dillard's "James Milton Turner: A Little Known Benefactor of His People," the same magazine, XIX, pp. 372-411.

100. The Negro was eliminated from politics in the South by illegal methods, the most drastic of which was the work of the mob. Why? Was it due to the lack of courage among Negro leaders or a lack of knowledge as to how to manœuver in a trying situation? In the final analysis can any force from without be depended upon to defend and protect the Negro in the enjoyment of his rights? Is not this a local problem which he must work out for himself? Has politics an economic foundation?

Practically all studies of the Reconstruction mention the Ku Klux Klan. The history of the movement however, has not yet been written. It must be done from new sources. The Congressional report on the investigation of the Ku Klux Klan is voluminous, but it is more confusing than helpful. See Lester and Wilson's *The Ku Klux Klan; Its Origin;* Louis F. Post's "A Carpet-Bagger in South Carolina," *The Journal of Negro History*, IX, pp. 10-79; Francis B. Simpkins's "The Ku Klux Klan in South Carolina, 1868-1871," the same magazine, XII, pp. 606-647; Fred Landon's "The Kidnapping of Dr. Rufus Bratton," the same periodical, X, pp. 330-333; James Hugo Johnston's "The Participation of Negroes in the Government of Virginia," the same magazine, XIV, pp. 251-271; Sophia Walker's "Carpet-Baggers," the same magazine, XIV, pp. 44-59; R. W. Woody's "Jonathan Jasper Wright," the same magazine, XVIII, pp. 114-131; W. E. B. Du Bois's *Black Reconstruction.*

XV. RECONSTRUCTION OF THE SOUTHERN STATES, 1865-1881—*Continued*

101. SOCIAL REFORM BENEFICIAL TO THE SOUTH
102. RESTORED RULE WITH FRAUDS
103. THE EXODUS TO THE WEST IN 1879 AND AFTER
104. THE TARIFF AND MONETARY REFORM, SECTIONAL ISSUES WITH THE NEGRO VOTE AS A BALANCE OF POWER

101. Was the Reconstruction undone? Outline the social reforms made by the reconstructionists. Compare the conditions of the South in 1876 with those obtaining in 1860. Compare the Negro-Carpet-Bagger constitutions with those of the Southern States today. See C. G. Woodson's *Negro in Our History*, pp. 423-424. Consult also John R. Lynch's "Historical Errors of James Ford Rhodes," *The Journal of Negro History*, II, pp. 345-368, III, pp. 139-157, and Du Bois's *Black Reconstruction*.

As to education examine the following: C. G. Woodson's *The Negro in Our History*, chapter xxiii; A. A. Taylor's *The Negro in South Carolina during the Reconstruction*, chapters vi and vii; the same author's, *The Negro in the Reconstruction of Virginia*, chapters viii-xi; F. B. Simpkins' and R. H. Woody's *South Carolina during Reconstruction*, pp. 47, 100, 103, 415-443; L. P. Jackson's "The Educational Efforts of the Freedmen's Bureau and Freedmen's Aid Societies in South Carolina, 1862-1872," *The Journal of Negro History*, VIII, pp. 1-41; the same author's "The Origin of Hampton Institute," the same periodical, X, pp. 131-149; W. Sherman Savage's "Legal Provision for Negro Schools in Missouri, 1865-1890," the same periodical, XVI, pp. 309-321; G. Smith Wormley's "Educators of the First Half Century of the Public Schools of the District of Columbia," the same periodical, XVII, pp. 124-140.

102. Examine the government frauds of the Southern States during the first ten years of the restored governments of the whites and compare these with the much advertised frauds of the reconstructionists. Read John R. Lynch's "Some Historical Errors of James Ford Rhodes," *The Journal of Negro History*, II, pp. 345-367; III, pp. 139-157; and a letter from Lynch on Claude Bowers's *Tragic Era*, in the same magazine, XVI, pp. 103-120.

103. The Exodus to the West in 1879 is discussed in the seventh chapter of C. G. Woodson's *A Century of Migration* (Washington, 1918). The following works should also be consulted: George W. Williams's *History of the Negro Race*, II, p. 374 *et seq.*; *Atlantic Monthly*, LXIV, p. 222; *The Nation*, XXVIII, pp. 242, 386 and LXVIII, p. 279; *American Journal of Social Science*, XI, pp. 1-34; *Spectator*, LXVII, p. 571; *Dublin Review*, CV, p. 187; *Cosmopolitan*, VII, p. 460; *Congressional Record*, 46th Congress, 2d Session, X, p. 104; *The Vicksburg Daily Commercial*, May 6, 1879; W. O. Scroggs's "Fifty Years of Negro Migration," *American Journal of Political Economy*, 1917.

104. It is fashionable now in certain circles to charge that the enfranchisement of the Negro during reconstruction was not to grant the freedmen what was believed to be their rights, not to prevent their re-

XVI. THE NEW NATION AND THE NEGRO, 1882-1914

105. Economic Progress of the Race Along with National Development

106. Classical Education and Industrial Training

enslavement and assure them protection before the law, but to keep the Republican party in power. Thus assured of the reins of government for a long while, it is said, the Republicans used the tariff and manipulated the money of the country to enrich the victorious North and the rising West. The Negro voter with the balance of power, then, is held responsible for all the actual and imaginary evils charged to the party for which he voted.

Is this sound reasoning? Furthermore, is the tariff an evil? Did those who developed the great industries of the East and conquered the Western frontier make mistakes and mistakes only? Was the financial system of the United States during the years before the Civil War as creditable as it was after that conflict? Trace the development unto that of today.

Read William A. Russ' "The Negro and White Disfranchisement during Radical Reconstruction," *The Journal of Negro History*, XIX, pp. 171-192; F. W. Woodley, *op. cit.;* and John G. Van Deusen's "Did the Republicans 'Colonize' Indiana in 1879?" the December issue of the *Indiana Magazine of History*, 1934. Almost all the monographs on reconstruction go into the details of this question with their sectional and racial bias.

105. The records of the United States Bureau of the Census show that the Negroes have made at least a little progress since 1865, especially after 1890. Has the progress of the Negro been proportionate to the economic advancement of the entire country? If not how do you account for the difference? Lack of initiative? Lack of opportunity? Is there any thing inherent in the Negro to cause him to lag behind the procession? Has background or environment any thing to do with it? Consult C. G. Woodson's *Negro in Our History*, his *Mis-Education of the Negro*, chapter xxvi; Henry E. Baker's "The Negro in the Field of Invention," *The Journal of Negro History*, II, pp. 21-36; Monroe N. Work's Negro Year Book; and Booker T. Washington's *Story of the Negro*. Read also James S. Russell's "Rural Economic Progress of the Negro in Virginia," *The Journal of Negro History*, XI, pp. 547-555; Charles S. Johnson's "The Rise of the Negro Magazine," the same periodical, XIII, pp. 7-21; J. H. Harmon's "The Negro as a Local Business Man," A. G. Lindsay's "The Negro in Banking," and C. G. Woodson's "Insurance Business among Negroes," all three of the last mentioned in the same magazine, XIV, pp. 109-226; A. G. Paschal's "The Paradox of Negro Progress," in the same magazine, XVI, pp. 251-264; A. B. Jackson's "A Criticism of the Negro Professional," J. B. Blayton's "Are Negroes now in Business, Business Men?" and C. C. Spaulding's "Is the Negro Meeting the Test in Business?" all three in the same magazine, XVIII, pp. 46-70.

106. What is industrial education? Is there any such thing as a people being entirely without facilities for industrial education? Who were the forerunners of Booker T. Washington? What did Booker T. Washington

XVI. THE NEW NATION AND THE NEGRO, 1882-1914
—*Continued*

107. LABOR MOVEMENT AND THE NEGRO
108. CIVIL SERVICE AND THE NEGRO

mean in putting new emphasis upon this sort of education at that time? Has the program of industrial education succeeded or failed? Was the program as outlined at that time suitable for that epoch only or for all time and for all people? Did Booker T. Washington emphasize industrial education as much as he did the practical things of life in general? Is this philosophy sound?

For further study see C. G. Woodson's and L. J. Greene's *The Negro Wage Earner*, the chapter on industry; W. E. B. Du Bois' *The Gift of Black Folk*, the chapter on labor. See also *The Negro Artisan* and *The Negro American Artisan* in the *Atlanta University Studies*. Consult the works of Booker T. Washington and those dealing with Hampton.

107. In Abram Harris and S. D. Spero's *The Black Worker;* and in C. H. Wesley's *Negro Labor in the United States*, the story of Negro Labor is well told. It is summarized in C. G. Woodson's *Negro in Our History*, pp. 535-539, and in Greene and Woodson's *The Negro Wage Earner*. Consult also L. Hollingsworth Wood's "The Urban League Movement," *The Journal of Negro History*, IX, pp. 117-126.

Would the Negroes have more standing as laborers than they have today if they had devoted at least as much attention to this problem of industrial efficiency as they have to politics and religion? In what ways have the politicians interfered with the labor movement among Negroes? The trade unions often give as an excuse that Negroes will not unionize. Can this charge be supported? What is the present status of the Negro with respect to the American Federation of Labor?

108. Not long after emancipation it seemed that the Negroes had a knack of getting into the United States Civil Service. The number increased as a result of the elimination of Negroes from politics in the South. Many of the dethroned Negro leaders came to Washington to serve as clerks. At one time there were seven or eight thousand Negroes thus serving. Now they have dwindled down to a few hundred. How has it happened that at the time the Civil Service was developing so that a man thus employed would be assured of permanent tenure regardless of his politics, the Negroes who are qualified have been gradually eliminated? The various treatises on Civil Service do not account for this. The Negroes thus eliminated say it was done on account of politics and race prejudice requiring segregation. What are the facts in this case? Talk with men who have long served in this capacity. Find out what their experiences have been. Printed materials will not help much.

Some of the general works in this field are C. R. Fish's *Civil Service and Patronage*, Tyler's *Parties and Patronage;* G. W. Curtis's *Orations and Addresses;* and D. B. Eaton's *Government of Municipalities*. A brief statement with respect to the Negro is found in A. B. Hart's *Southern*

XVI. THE NEW NATION AND THE NEGRO, 1882-1914
—Continued

109. INTERPRETING THE WAR AMENDMENTS—COLONIZATION REVIVED

110. THE NEGRO IN THE SPANISH AMERICAN WAR

South. Consult the roster of United States Government employees for several decades. Figure out the inferior position of Negroes. See Lorenzo J. Greene and Myra Colson Callis's *The Employment of Negroes in the District of Columbia* (Washington, 1931), chapter vii.

109. The Fourteenth Amendment, intended to help the Negro, has been used chiefly to prevent courts and agencies from depriving our gigantic corporations of their property "without due process of law." As a rule the highest court of the United States has evaded the interpretation of these amendments with respect to the rights of the Negro thereby guaranteed. Make a list of the cases involving the rights of the Negro coming before the United States Supreme Court and note the number of cases in which the issue has been dodged. Usually the excuse is lack of jurisdiction. Is this due to the determination of this tribunal to leave the Negro at the mercy of hostile state courts or a failure to bring these cases properly before that body? How many lawyers out of a thousand can be depended upon to pilot an important case through the inferior tribunals to the United States Supreme Court?

To answer these questions the cases themselves must be studied. A brief account, however, may be found in C. G. Woodson's *Negro in Our History*, pp. 485-487, 554-558. See also L. E. Murphy's "The Civil Rights Law of 1875," *The Journal of Negro History*, XII, pp. 110-127; I. C. Mollinson's "Negro Lawyers in Mississippi," same magazine, XV, pp. 38-71; C. G. Woodson's "Fifty Years of Negro Citizenship as Qualified by the United States Supreme Court," the same periodical, VI, pp. 1-53; R. H. Hainsworth's "The Negro in the Texas Primaries," the same magazine, XVIII, pp. 426-450.

The revival of the African colonization scheme, because of the Negro's losing ground in the United States, is set forth in the addresses of Bishop H. M. Turner and Senator Morgan of Alabama. See C. G. Woodson's *A Century of Negro Migration* (Washington, 1917), chapter xiii; *The Spectator*, LXVI, p. 313, *Public Opinion*, XVIII; J. Fred Rippy's "A Colonization Project in Mexico in 1895," *The Journal of Negro History*, VI, p. 60-73.

110. The Negro in the Spanish American War is told by E. A. Johnson in a special volume bearing this title and with the same published as the appendix of this author's *History of the Negro Race*. John Edward Bruce, an historian of that day, has told the same story of the *Negro Soldier in the Spanish American War*. The record of these soldiers, as attested by men like Joe Wheeler under whom they fought, was creditable. Theodore Roosevelt, whom they saved from destruction at San Juan Hill, made statements both ways. What was his opinion of the Negro?

XVI. THE NEW NATION AND THE NEGRO, 1882-1914
—*Continued*

111. ROOSEVELT'S OPEN DOOR POLICY
112. THE BROWNSVILLE AFFAIR
113. TAFT'S ELIMINATION OF THE NEGRO FROM FEDERAL SERVICE
114. THE INCREASE IN SEGREGATION AND LYNCHING

111. Several students of history charge Theodore Roosevelt with being inconsistent. Defending himself against attacks of the narrow-minded who objected to his entertaining a Negro at the White House, he took the high ground that he would not shut the door of opportunity in the face of any man because he is black. Yet he dismissed the Negro soldiers in the Brownsville riot without proof of guilt. Was this consistency? In what way was Theodore Roosevelt like Andrew Jackson in being an aggregation of self-contradictions and inconsistencies?

112. James B. Foraker fanned among the Negroes the flame of hatred for Theodore Roosevelt in playing up in Congress by speeches and investigations the unconstitutional methods resorted to in the dismissal of the Brownsville soldiers. Was this sincerity or political effort to defeat the wing of his party in control? It soon became known that Foraker, like Haskell of Oklahoma, had questionable connections which lowered him in public esteem. Should there be a distinction between public and private morals? Can politicians be depended upon to advance human rights? One man has said that a political party is an organization without principle but accepting a principle to get into office. Does our history support or refute this statement?

113. When William H. Taft came into the presidency he tried to please the political foes of Negroes by saying that he would not appoint Negroes to office in any place where they were not desired thus to function. Carried to the extreme, this would mean the elimination of the Negroes from the Federal Government altogether. With the promotion of race hate, the Negro has become generally unacceptable to the public in all higher spheres. Was Taft's position constitutional? Is a man of this type qualified to be the chief executive of a nation? Was Taft President of the United States or President of certain people in the United States?

Norman P. Andrews, in his "The Negro in Politics" in *The Journal of Negro History* (V, pp. 420-436) has discussed this and other problems and so has C. G. Woodson in his *Negro in Our History*.

114. To what extent did Roosevelt's action and Taft's position with respect to the Negro stimulate segregation? Did segregation increase rapidly because the Negro had become less desirable or more desirable? Is segregation legal? Is it constitutional? If, according to the constitution of the United States, a state cannot deprive a man of the rights pertaining to citizenship, what sort of construction of the law is that which permits groups of individuals here and there to covenant to do so? What is the state of a country which cannot protect its own citizens? What is the difference between forced segregation and voluntary segregation like that set forth in

XVII. MAKING THE WORLD SAFE FOR DEMOCRACY, 1914-1936

115. THE RISE OF NEGRO NATIONAL ORGANIZATIONS
116. THE DIVISION OF THE NEGRO VOTE
117. THE PURCHASE OF THE VIRGIN ISLANDS—HAITI
IN THE GREATER CANAL ZONE

J. E. Moorland's "The Young Men's Christian Association among Negroes," *The Journal of Negro History*, IX, pp. 127-138?

Consult for lynching Roland G. Usher's "Primitive Law and the Negro," *The Journal of Negro History*, IV, pp. 1-6; the *Report on Lynching* published by the National Association for the Advancement of Colored People; and other data published in Monroe N. Work's *Negro Yearbook* and Arthur Raper's *The Tragedy of Lynching*.

115. Did the Negro agitative organizations spring up before the segregation scare or after? Did such action show foresight? Has the Negro been sufficiently vigilant in watching and understanding the trends of the times? Does the Negro rely upon prevention or cure? With what achievements do you credit the various propaganda organizations which have operated among Negroes since 1865? What mistakes do you charge to their account?

For organizations among Negroes see M. W. Ovington's "The National Association for the Advancement of Colored People," L. Hollingsworth Wood's "The Urban League Movement," and J. E. Moorland's "The Young Men's Christian Association among Negroes," all in *The Journal of Negro History*, IX, pp. 107-138. Consult also M. W. Ovington's *Half a Man*.

116. The Negro voters as a large majority have voted to keep the Republican party in power for the reason that practically all they have gained in this sphere has been due to the initiative and defence of these partisans of days ago. Is such an attitude on the part of Negroes to be expected? Is it wise? In recent years the same political party, in name at least, that "once stood by the Negroes" has carefully avoided them in crises and has done nothing but to retain office with the help of Negroes thus ignored; but the Negroes have been loyal, like him who said, "Though he slay me, yet will I trust him." At the present the Negroes, at last awakened to realize the meaning of things, have begun to divide their votes. Is this wise? Can a minority group solve its problems by politics? What instances in history support such a conclusion?

117. Of what value to this country are the Virgin Islands? How do you connect the purchase of these islands with the Panama Canal? Hoover referred to them as a poor house. The country has immensely suffered in recent years. Did the natives, ninety-five percent of whom are Negroes, gain by being taken over by the United States? Do any people of African blood gain or lose by becoming subjected to the jurisdiction of the United States? Why do so many West Indians come to the United States to live permanently? Is England more liberal than our country? Why do they not go to England?

With Cuba and Panama under our influence and Puerto Rico in our pos-

XVII. MAKING THE WORLD SAFE FOR DEMOCRACY,
1914-1936—*Continued*

118. THE NEGRO LEFT OUT OF WOODROW WILSON'S
"NEW FREEDOM"

119. THE DEMAND FOR NEGRO LABOR IN INDUSTRY—
THE MIGRATION

session the Virgin Islands helped to complete our sphere of influence in the Greater Canal Zone. Read George W. Brown's, "Haiti and the United States," *The Journal of Negro History,* VIII, pp. 134-152. Consult also L. A. Pendleton's "Our New Possessions—The Danish West Indies," the same magazine, II, pp. 267-288, and accompanying documents, pp. 289-324, 423-428.

118. Read Woodrow Wilson's *New Freedom.* Not long after he began to show an attitude of indifference toward the Negro when serving as President of the United States, some one asked him how he harmonized his deeds with his theories. He promptly replied that he did not have the Negro in mind when he was writing those thoughts. In other words, the Negro was a negligible factor in the mind of this man who had become the head of the nation. To what extent was Wilson's attitude typical? Has the Negro become a negligible factor in the thought of the world?

119. The World War came. Before we plunged into it, we had become immensely wealthy in supplying the food and munitions of war for one nation to destroy the other. Labor became inadequate, and the crude Negro laborers were called from the agricultural section to the industries of the East. Even Negro women, the last to be employed, were called upon, as brought out by Mrs. E. R. Haynes in her "Negroes in Domestic Service in the United States," *The Journal of Negro History,* VIII, pp. 384-442. For a time, as shown by G. E. Haynes, H. H. Donald, Abram Epstein, and Emmett J. Scott, the Negroes were shown great deference while being used as a means to an end.

The Negro mistook this for a permanent attitude, and when deflation followed inflation his sorrows multiplied as fast as his joys had during the World War. Was this an economic gain or loss? Had the Negro remained on the farms what would have been the result? Less farm labor is required today than a generation ago. In fact, machines have done the same for the farms as for the industries. Does it make any difference now as to where the Negro remains?

For the study of the migration various sources are now available. Among the important are "Letters of Negro Migrants of 1916-1918," *The Journal of Negro History,* IV, pp. 290-340 and 412-465; and other such letters of Migrants in the Carter G. Woodson Manuscript Collection in the Library of Congress. Consult H. H. Donald's "The Negro Migration of 1916-1918," *The Journal of Negro History,* VI, pp. 382-498; G. E. Haynes's *The Negro Migration in Pittsburgh;* E. J. Scott's *The Migration of the Negro during the World War;* Charles S. Johnson, *The Negro in American Civilization,* and L. V. Kennedy's *The Negro Peasant Turns Cityward.*

XVII. MAKING THE WORLD SAFE FOR DEMOCRACY, 1914-1936—*Continued*

120. THE INCREASE IN NEGRO ORGANIZATIONS FOR AGITATION

121. EFFORTS TO DEFAME THE NEGRO BY TESTS AND MEASUREMENTS

122. EDUCATIONAL DEVELOPMENT AMONG NEGROES

123. EFFORTS TOWARD ECONOMIC AND INDUSTRIAL EFFICIENCY

124. THE HARDSHIPS OF THE DEPRESSION

120. The most striking militant organization among those adding to the number already active was the Back-to-Africa-Movement led by Marcus Garvey. He was ridiculed by W. E. B. Du Bois, who organized the Pan African Congress, and by Kelly Miller who started the Negro Sanhedrin, both of which showed less vitality than Garvey's idea. Garvey, however, did something which no Negro had hitherto accomplished. He made himself a national leader and all but developed into one of international proportions. Was Garvey's idea reasonable? Was he sincere? Consult M. W. Ovington's "The National Association for the Advancement of Colored People," *The Journal of Negro History*, IX, pp. 107-116. Read J. A. Bailey's "Perspective in Teaching Negro History," the same periodical, XX, p. 25. See also G. Cecil Weimar's "Christianity and the Race Problem" and Newell L. Sims's "Techniques of Race Adjustment," both in the same periodical, XVI, pp. 67-87.

121. This is briefly treated in C. G. Woodson's *Negro in Our History*, pp. 549 to 550. The details as to these efforts and their failure to discredit the Negro are found in the October, 1934 issue of *The Journal of Negro Education*. Consult also T. Wingate Todd's "An Anthropologist's Study of Negro Life," Nathaniel Cantor's "Crime and the Negro" and W. O. Brown's "Racial Inequality; Fact or Myth," *The Journal of Negro History*, XVI, pp. 36-66; L. D. Reddick's "Racial Attitudes in American History Textbooks," the same magazine, XIX, pp. 225-265.

122. The recent developments in Negro education are summarized in C. G. Woodson's *Negro in Our History*, chapter xxxii. Consult, however, the works of Dr. Ambrose Caliver, such as *A Background Study of the Negro College Student*, and *Secondary Education for Negroes*. Some help may be obtained also from D. O. W. Holmes' *Evolution of the Negro College*, from T. E. McKinney's *Higher Education Among Negroes;* and from Max Bond's *The Education of the Negro in the American Social Order.* For a new point of view read C. G. Woodson's *Mis-Education of the Negro.*

123. The efforts of the Negro toward economic efficiency are presented in C. H. Wesley's *Negro Labor in the United States*, in Abram Harris and S. D. Spero's *Black Worker*, in L. J. Greene and C. G. Woodson's *Negro Wage-Earner*, and in C. G. Woodson's *Rural Negro.*

124. Of the depression no satisfactory picture has been drawn. We have many, but they are colored by local influences and a rapidly changing order.

XVII. MAKING THE WORLD SAFE FOR DEMOCRACY,
1914-1936—*Continued*

125. THE NEGROES DIVIDE THEIR VOTE

The student here must think for himself. What was the status of the Negro during these hardships? Did they forebode evil or serve as a blessing in disguise?

125. Consult George F. Robinson's "The Negro in Politics in Chicago," *The Journal of Negro History,* XVII, pp. 180-229; Nowlin's *The Negro in Politics;* Paul Lewinson's *Race, Class and Party;* and H. F. Gosnell's *The Rise of the Negro in Politics in Chicago* (Chicago, 1935).

CHAPTER XXI

THE EDUCATION OF THE NEGRO

THE education of the Negro prior to the Civil War once sounded like historical fiction. The whole country was largely in a frontier state. Public schools were not common. It was thought that since a rich man was in a position to have his children educated privately the support of the system would be a tax on the man of means to provide for the enlightenment of the poor. Yet difficult as it was for the Negro to provide for such facilities there was always a chance for a few of this element to acquire the fundamentals. This opportunity was afforded sometimes not only in the free states in which dwelt most of the one-half million Negroes already free but sometimes by clandestine methods in the South where it was generally proscribed even in the case of the free people of color. The education of the Negro in all but three states of the South was legally prohibited. This step had been taken because of numerous efforts to escape from bondage and uprisings for liberation mainly between 1800 and 1835. Public opinion, moreover, was sometimes stronger than law.

The first opportunity for the education of the Negro came as a natural outcome of his status in the New World. He was brought thither to be used in the exploitation of the country. Sometimes, then, in the interest of efficiency it was necessary to educate the bondman. In a crude country where a knowledge of the mechanic arts was a great advantage many of the desirable Negroes were educated practically by being apprenticed to trades. This was provided especially for Negro orphans and illegitimate children of whites and Negroes in order that they might not become a public charge.

The larger opportunity for education during this period, however, came from the religious element. One of the excuses given to justify the enslavement of the African was that he would thereby become Christianized. To Christianize the Bushman with whom one could not communicate was not a problem to be easily solved. The clergy interested in the evangelization of the Negro, then, had as their first task to teach him at least enough English to read the Bible and religious literature. This was not so much of a concern for the colonial clergy of the regularly established church of England, but the missionaries sent to America by the Society for the Propagation of the Gospel in Foreign Parts engaged in this as their first duty. The Catholics and Quakers similarly interested in the Negro had the same attitude. Doubtless much more would have been accomplished by these sects than was actually achieved, but the Quaker ideas and the ritualistic methods of the Catholics did not evoke much of a response from the Negroes. These Quaker and Catholic workers, moreover, did not always have access to large numbers of the blacks inasmuch as their masters with respect to religious matters were otherwise concerned. The rise of the Methodists and Baptists after the grant of toleration and later religious freedom did not have much effect on the actual education. The appeal of these new sects to which Negroes flocked in large numbers was emotional rather than intellectual. The effort to educate the Negro was further stimulated during these years, but the impetus came from another source.

The struggle for the rights of man on this side decidedly advanced education. Education was referred to as one of the rights of man. The movement to free the country from the British yoke had the effect of encouraging the emancipation of the Negroes in most parts of the country either by instant or gradual methods. The thought that it was necessary to prepare these freedmen to live as citizens forced upon such promoters a program of education. Of course, this was done privately. Negroes provided special schools themselves when able so to do; and sympathetic white persons came to their assistance. The rural Negroes of that day, however, profited little by the movement, but in almost every urban center an enterprising Negro had some opportunity to acquire the fundamentals. The Negro had access to New England schools in certain places; and sometimes studied in those of New York and Pennsylvania.

The education of the Negro was further advanced by the movements to educate the poor. The Old Field Schools, those resulting from the Lancastrian Movement, the academies established mainly by lotteries about a hundred years ago, and the Manual Labor Schools of that day influenced the education of the Negro. These movements stimulated education in the sense of popularizing it and thus served as forerunners of education at public expense. When the public schools came, however, a reaction had set in; and the Negro had to fight to enter although he was taxed to support the system. Only here and there was any such provision made for the education of the Negro. Finally a few states like Pennsylvania, New York, Massachusetts and Connecticut began to make such provision not long before the Civil War. Ohio and Illinois long delayed action on educating the Negro at public expense. Indiana actually prohibited it by law.

Additional stimulus came from two other sources, the colonization movement and abolition. Although it was embarrassing to the colonizationists to point out their inconsistency in educating Negroes to function as builders of a nation in Africa when they denied that the Negro would ever be able to develop thus here, they nevertheless educated a number of Negroes with the understanding that they would go to Liberia. Several additional schools for Negroes were then established, but it was not always possible to determine beforehand what use the students would make of such education. Some of these graduates emigrated to Africa and afterward returned to the United States. Others never undertook the much-dreaded trip.

The abolition movement with respect to education was practical. Many of these people not only served as lecturers denouncing the institution of slavery, but toiled among Negroes at the same time to remove the curse of ignorance which that system entailed. A larger number of abolitionists would have thus functioned, but they could not always reach the illiterate Negroes, and it was not generally popular to establish such schools even on so-called free soil. The main objection expressed was that such places in the North might be sought for refuge by so many free Negroes that they might become a public charge. By the Irish and German elements immigrating to compete with Negroes in drudgery and menial service the free blacks were generally branded as ignorant, shiftless undesirables who should be driven out of any community. For these reasons the Negroes of the North were not allowed to establish their proposed manual labor school in New Haven, the Canaan Academy in New Hampshire was promptly destroyed for admitting Negro students, and Prudence Crandall, of Canterbury, Connecticut, was imprisoned for violating an all but *ex post facto* law which anticipated her admitting Negro girls to her private academy. Wilberforce and Lincoln, however, took form during these days, and the Negro was given meager facilities for education at public expense in a few centers in the North. During that generation, however, the Negro, as a rule, obtained his education in spite of opposition. Clandestine schools, moreover, were in operation in most of the large cities and towns of the South where such enlightenment of the Negroes was prohibited by law.

A revolution in such attitudes, of course, came as one outcome of the Civil War. The new movement for the actual education of the Negro, however, was characterized more by spontaneous efforts to uplift the lowly than by a systematic procedure in the light of the actual needs of the people to be taught. The movement was not a sustained effort toward definite ends. Even before the union armies left the area where the emancipated Negroes had their day soldiers had begun teaching the many fugitives to the army. In the camps where these "contrabands" were housed for special care education was a conspicuous part of the program. Relief agencies taking form about the same time supported these early efforts, and the United States Freedmen's Bureau, charged by the Government to protect, defend, and prepare the freedmen for life as citizens, cooperated in these enterprises. This agency expanded further the educational program with not only elementary schools but with colleges and universities as the capstone of the new structure. States under the control of Negroes, scalawags and carpetbaggers during the Reconstruction provided liberally in letter for schools and colleges at public expense in order to assure certain support which could not be expected from philanthropy.

In the establishment and direction of these schools the main thought was to provide for the Negroes the same facilities of education which others had enjoyed. These opportunities once withheld begrudgingly were now to be taken without asking. In our frontier condition at that time, however, education had never been scientifically worked out. We referred occasionally to the Prussian system which showed a beginning in this direction, but we had not put such theories into practice. We had never depended upon education for success in America. On this frontier where land was abundant and raw materials cheap we could waste what would support another nation and in hit-or-miss fashion still pile up fabulous fortunes. It was not until we began to think that these resources were not inexhaustible that we finally saw the necessity for training men to eliminate waste and develop efficiency.

Even when we reached this stage in our thinking we still failed to give any particular thought to the education of the Negro. The Negro himself was the last to give his own situation serious consideration. He had recently been made a citizen of the country. In some of the states he attended the schools without any discrimination as to race, and he was determined to break down the remaining barriers to make educational systems throughout the country cosmopolitan and democratic. By and by, however, the Negro was eliminated from the advanced guard of politics, and his restrictions were increased rather than diminished. Even from the beginning of his freedom the Negro remained mainly a menial or common laborer. Socially he was kept in the ghetto with others exploiting him while yielding in return little for what he did for them.

In spite of this untoward condition the Negro continued with his educational system unchanged and positively opposed to innovations. He objected especially to industrial education, which, rising in the nineties, under the preachments of Booker T. Washington marked a new epoch in the development of education among Negroes. Whites in control of Negro institutions, however, seized upon the idea to change Negro schools to an industrial basis and thus be able to make a distinction in education to harmonize with discriminations as to races elsewhere. Very soon, however, the whites began to see that this practical educational program offered many valuable suggestions for reform in their own schools; and it was not long before the principles developed around the new idea were incorporated into their systems. Fiery Negro leaders, blinded by the very thought of racial distinction, continued nevertheless in their antagonistic attitude.

The country, however, developed more and more industrially and trades unions easily eliminated Negroes from the higher pursuits of labor. There remained comparatively few Negro mechanics and artisans inasmuch as these skilled workers as a whole became gradually reduced, and these were all but eliminated by mechanization which forced such formerly highly paid laborers to take over the Negro's menial service and drudgery. The Negroes, then, began to realize that in spite of all their education the world had changed against them without their knowing it. All of the educational experience which they had undergone failed to lead them to think. The education of the Negro had not been connected with life. He had been trained to conform to a general pattern and had been denied the opportunity thus to function. He had been trained to render the service required of the large majority of American citizens but by segregation and social repression he had been doomed to lead the life delimited as that of the pauper.

It became clear, too, that unfortunately the Negro had been educated in school and by tradition to think of himself as an undesirable whose only salvation is to associate with or profit by contact with and help from others at the very time that others were doing all they could to remove themselves farther from the Negro. The educated Negro, then, was at his best in the controversial sphere, showing why he with his knowledge of the best in culture should enjoy the best in life, but manifesting at the same time his inability to secure to himself the enjoyment of these things. Lamentations and abuses only aggravated a deplorable situation when there was a lack of wisdom for meeting the exigencies of the hour.

A few Negroes, recovering from this education sufficiently to see the error of their ways, urged that the point of view in the education of the Negro be changed, that the Negro be educated to his race rather than away from it. In other words, in the education of the Negro we should begin with the race itself. We should first acquaint the Negro child with his own background regardless of what that may be. If the past shows achievements which may stimulate and inspire the youth, by all means penetrate that background. If the past of the Negro shows a succession of dismal failures, it is equally important to know those facts, for only by knowing wherein one has failed can he easily learn by experience how to succeed. A race that has no history to draw upon or fails thus to use its past must grope in the dark and make thousands of mistakes to achieve little.

This new point of view in education is not to teach less of what has been taught the Negro before, not to concentrate altogether on his status and history. Such a tendency would mean the continuation of the same biased attitude of the Negro made to despise himself and that of the white man likewise not only hating the Negro but oppressing and exterminating him in keeping with the program of the subordination which has brought us all to the present chaotic and self-exterminating state throughout the modern world. The new thought is to make the history and status of the Negro the nucleus of a new program of teaching the Negro about himself and about others in relation to himself. The aim is to bring the Negro into the drama not as the sole performer, not necessarily as the star actor, but playing his part in the great drama of life just as the unbiased history of the world shows that he did in ancient and medieval times.

With the Negro thus developed, it is believed, he will cease to despise himself and his race. He will see among the people with whom he has to do opportunities for social and economic improvements which will eventually lift the Negro above charity and dependence and equip him as a factor in the making of the nation. The Negro under this process of transformation will tend more and more to become not a beggar seeking what others may do for him but an efficient and inspired citizen seeking what he may do for others.[1]

[1] An introductory treatment of the facts herein summarized may be obtained from the use of the author's *Education of the Negro Prior to 1861;* his *Mis-Education of the Negro;* his *History of the Negro Church;* the sixth and seventh chapters of A. A. Taylor's *Negro in South Carolina during the Reconstruction;* the eighth, ninth, and tenth chapters of his *The Negro in the Reconstruction of Virginia;* Arthur J. Klein's *Survey of Negro Colleges and Universities;* T. E. McKinney's *Higher Education of Negroes;* Ambrose Caliver's *Secondary Education of Negroes;* his *Background Study of Negro College Students;* Horace Mann Bond's *Education of the Negro in the American Social Order;* John W. Davis's *Negro Land-Grant Colleges;* and D. O. W. Holmes, *Evolution of the Negro College.* Advanced work requires carrying out the suggestions for further study in the bibliographical footnotes accompanying the outline.

I. FIRST EDUCATION OF THE NEGRO IN THE NEW WORLD

1. AFRICAN TRADITIONS
2. "BREAKING IN"

1. The first force at work in the education of the Negro in the New World was the traditional training transplanted from Africa to America. No people can exist without some system of education. The Africans, as pointed out by Leo Frobenius in his *Voice of Africa* greatly emphasized the training of the youth. Frobenius said that he had never visited a country where education was more generally emphasized or more thoroughly carried out. The work was done, of course, not through schools of the European or American order but by thoroughly training the boys and girls first under their parents at home and then in certain "Age Classes" and other such circles directed for the girls by matrons of purity, and for the boys by elderly men of wisdom.

In the West Indies where Negroes were sometimes brought into the Western Hemisphere in sufficiently large numbers to keep up their tribal customs this system of training of the youth continued for some time. Only in a few cases in the colonies along the Atlantic, however, could this be done, for there were, comparatively, only a few Negroes in the various settlements in these parts until late in the Eighteenth Century, and often these descended from different tribes. Instead of being brought directly to the British colonies along the Atlantic, moreover, they were picked up here and there at different points in the West Indies. In the process of these two transplantations not very much of the traditional education of the African actually reached what we now call the United States. In the West Indies, Central America and in South America, however, it was very much in evidence. Traces of these customs may be found there today in British Guiana as has been brought out by Melville and Frances Herskovits in their recent book called *Rebel Destiny*. J. J. Williams, although biased, shows these influences in his *Hebrewisms of West Africa, from Nile to Niger with the Jews*. The observation of the same custom in these parts is noted also in Admiral Vernon's *History of Jamaica*, R. C. Dallas's *Maroons*, and Bryan Edwards' *History of the West Indies*, cited above.

2. The first systematic education of the Negro in the Western Hemisphere, that sort of education of the Negro in which participated the enslavers of the African, is what is commonly known as "breaking in." We sometimes forget the fact that slavery itself was a process of training the Negro to do what was required of him. His social, economic and industrial background in Africa was decidedly different from what he faced in America. He had to be trained to perform certain duties. The first of these was the arduous tasks of working in the mines and on plantations. In the beginning the Africans imported were taught by white men how to do this work, and after these had become well trained or "broken in" the new slaves imported were trained by attaching a certain number to each one of the gangs of the slaves already trained. In this way they learned to do by observing the efforts of others.

I. FIRST EDUCATION OF THE NEGRO IN THE NEW WORLD—*Continued*

3. APPLICATIONS OF MECHANICAL SKILL
4. APPRENTICESHIP

This process is discussed in the books of Dallas, Vernon and Bryan Edwards as mentioned above, but it is thoroughly explained in the more accessible work, Frank Wesley Pitman's "Slavery on the British West India Plantations in the Eighteenth Century" (*The Journal of Negro History*, XI, pp. 584 to 668). More detailed information along this line may be found in histories of the various West Indies like Ligon's *History of the Barbadoes*, W. P. Livingstone's *Black Jamaica*, Hans Sloanes's *Voyage to Jamaica*, M. J. Lewis's *Journal*, George Fox's *Journal*, E. A. Long's *Jamaica*, Edward Lyttleton's *Groans of the Plantations*, and Auberteuil's *Considérations sur l'état présent de la colonie française de Saint-Domingue* (Paris, 1776), I, pp. 130-146.

3. The ordeal of slavery also enabled the Negro to take a new step in his training or to rise to the higher ground which he had occupied in Africa. On all of these plantations there was a need for mechanics and artisans. The Negroes even in Africa had made a reputation of being great metal workers. Africans were the first people to learn the use of iron, and they learned it so early, it is said, that the Africans passed from the stone-age directly to the iron age without groping in the dark through what is called the bronze age. All of these Africans, however, were not artisans. Those who were thus found employment, and others underwent training to function in this capacity on plantations and in mines. One may go today to the West Indies, Central America, South America, or even to certain parts of the United States like Charleston and New Orleans and see numerous buildings showing the brick masonry, the stone cutting, and the iron work of slaves who were thus employed during the early days.

The point to be noted is that the employment of slaves in such capacities necessitated some knowledge of mathematics and science. This offered opportunities for the development of the mind of such slaves; and because of the increase in worth which they thereby showed they were often treated with more respect than those who were kept down on the level of meniality and drudgery. In some cases slaves thus occupied were permitted to go from plantation to plantation and make contracts for work themselves. Sometimes they were not seen by their actual owners more than twice or three times a year when it was necessary to check up on what they were doing. Carter Woodson, the grandfather of Carter G. Woodson functioned in this capacity in Fluvanna and Buckingham counties in Virginia.

4. This use of the Negro in the mechanic arts constituted the beginning of industry in the slaveholding colonies of what we now call the South. The occupation of the Negro as such became so important that it was considered desirable for one to be thus elevated and function in this capacity. Whenever the colonists found that they had to take charge of Negro waifs and orphans they usually provided that they should be apprenticed to some

I. FIRST EDUCATION OF THE NEGRO IN THE NEW WORLD—*Continued*

5. PERSONAL CONTACTS

trade in order to be sure that they would be useful to the community. Apprenticeship in the slaveholding colonies, then, often meant the binding out of young Negroes to the older mechanics and artisans.

When as a result of miscegenation, which took place between white indentured servants and Negroes, public opinion had begun to set itself against the custom, laws were passed dealing with the mulatto offspring of such unions. The laws prohibiting miscegenation, therefore, usually provided that those children be apprenticed to some trade. Lemuel Haynes, the son of a white woman by a Negro in New England, was thus apprenticed to a Puritan family in Vermont. With respect to Virginia which may be considered typical in that it was an influential colony, we may cite Hening's *Statutes at Large* (I, pp. 146, 552; II, p. 170; III, pp. 86-88, 252; VI, pp. 360-362). The situation in Maryland is presented in the *Archives of Maryland, Proceedings of the General Assembly, 1637-1664* (pp. 553-554); and also in the *General Public Statute Law and Public Law of the State of Maryland from 1692-1839* (p. 79). This matter of apprenticeship is mentioned in C. G. Woodson's "The Beginnings of the Miscegenation of the Whites and Blacks" (*The Journal of Negro History*, III, pp. 335-353). The point to be noted here is not the matter of miscegenation but that the mulatto children of the whites and blacks were sometimes taken from them and thus provided for through apprenticeship according to law.

5. It must be noted also that the Negro in the New World was being educated by personal contacts in spite of himself. This was a very unsatisfactory method in the case of large plantations where the Negroes were naturally far removed from their owners and came into contact with the overseers and slave drivers only to receive orders, obtain their supplies, or to undergo punishment for some offence. The brogue with which the Negroes learned to speak under such circumstances is the best evidence of the inefficiency of this particular method of education. It was largely imitation from afar.

In the case of those Negroes who were made house servants and attendants of their owners, however, the situation was decidedly different. They learned to speak the English language as correctly as their owners did and also imitated them in their habits and general way of living. To function in these close contacts, too, it was necessary to teach such Negroes the fundamentals of education that they might give assistance in doing any thing in which their owners participated. Sometimes as attendants of those owners who traveled in foreign countries these Negroes learned to speak as many as three or four modern languages. The best evidence of this is supplied in a collection of documents entitled "Eighteenth Century Slaves as Advertised by their Masters" (*The Journal of Negro History*, I, pp. 163-216). In order to identify these Negroes who had thus escaped their owners gave in detail their attainments to convince the public that Negroes thus mentally developed could easily tell plausible stories or write passes and escape.

II. RELIGION TAUGHT WITH LETTERS

6. Slavery Justified by Enlightenment
7. Reaching the Negro Mind by Education

6. Another stage was reached in the education of the Negro not long after slavery became engrafted upon the colonies. After it became a settled fact that the church and state would agree to the enslavement of the Negroes the antislavery religious elements were silenced by the ingenious explanation that the slaves in America in contact with Christianized Europeans would be much better off than remaining in a heathen state in Africa. To save its good name, then, the church had to insist that the Africans be trained in the principles of Christianity. Petitions, memorials and decrees to this effect are found all through the papers of Azurara, Bartolemé de las Casas, and the distinguished priests and bishops, who figured in the evangelization of the Negroes and Indians in the New World. The same concern appears in the decrees of the crowned heads of Spain and in the *Code Noir* of France. The Catholics insisted upon this much more so than the Protestants, most of whom came from England. When masters failed to provide for the enlightenment of their slaves, complaints against such indifference or dereliction of duty found their way to the public as the papers cited above will show.

7. The first difficulty which the church observed was that the Negroes had not been sufficiently Europeanized to understand the religion which they desired to teach them. It quickly dawned upon them, then, that in order to· enlighten the Negroes, it would be necessary to educate them, at least, in the fundamentals. What mental development they had undergone as a result of contact with their owners and their employment in industries was insufficient. The large masses of the slaves were worked in gangs and kept far removed from helpful contacts. The teaching of such modern languages as Spanish, French or English, according to the colonies in which the effort was undertaken, was the first task of the clergymen undertaking to impart to the imported Africans the principles of Christianity. In fact, this was the teaching of religion with letters. It did not go along so smoothly, for such thorough training required too much of the time of the slaves who were to spend the day and sometimes a part of the night in the service of their owners. But, during the first years, clergymen had won the point of finding access to the slaves although their efforts were not as successful as they had hoped.

The method of attack in this evangelical work is well set forth in the sources already cited herein, but still better in C. F. Pascoe's *Digest of the Records of the Society for the Propagation of the Gospel in Foreign Parts,* Dalcho's *An Historical Account of the Protestant Episcopal Church in South Carolina,* William Meade's *Old Families and Churches in Virginia,* the *Works* of Bishop Secker, the *Works* of Bishop Porteus, and the *Works* of Bishop Gibson. A sketch is given also in the second chapter of Carter G. Woodson's *Education of the Negro Prior to 1861* (New York, 1915). *The Jesuit Relations* gives some facts with respect to efforts in Louisiana.

II. RELIGION TAUGHT WITH LETTERS—*Continued*

8. WORK OF SPECIAL MISSIONARIES—ANGLICANS AND PURITANS
9. THE QUAKERS
10. THE CATHOLICS

8. The churchmen in Europe who were instrumental in advocating the enlightenment of the slaves soon realized that the thing could not be done with the inadequate number of clergymen stationed to serve the colonies. Special efforts, therefore, had to be made for the religious education of these Negroes thus situated. For this special work of dealing with Negroes and Indians, Dr. Thomas Bray, a distinguished Englishman of a religious bent, organized what was known as the "Associates of Dr. Thomas Bray," who made special efforts here and there to stimulate the enlightenment of the slaves. The more serious efforts from the English speaking people, however, were those of the "Society for the Propagation of the Gospel in Foreign Parts," organized in London in 1701. Immediately after launching the movement they sent one or more missionaries to each one of the colonies where they taught the Negroes to read the Bible and to learn the principles of Christianity. The Puritans supported only a few of such missionaries, but they were liberal in the religious instruction of the slaves among them in New England.

9. The Quakers did not have as much contact with the Negroes as did the Anglicans, because the Quakers as dissenters did not have standing in some of the colonies, and they were sometimes persecuted. Whenever possible, however, the Quakers usually trained the Negroes systematically. They took the Negroes into their fold, carried them to their meetings, and permitted them to pursue whatever they studied and to embrace whatever principles they espoused. The Negroes among the Quakers were educated, then, both by contact and by special effort in their behalf. These facts are set forth in the works of the Quaker Fathers such as the *Journal of John Woolman, Observations* of Anthony Benezet, *Southern Quakers* by S. B. Weeks, the *Quaker Pamphlet, A Brief Statement of the Rise and Progress of the Quakers,* and Levi Coffin's *Reminiscences.*

10. Catholics were probably second to no other force in the education of the Negroes. They covered as much territory as any other religious element in America although they did not have as much contact with as many Negroes as did the others. Their religious teaching is such that a man must be trained in order to understand their church doctrine and strictly conform to its tenets. Since the ignorant man cannot develop very far as an orthodox Catholic, it was necessary for the Catholic clergy to undertake the education of the Negroes. An examination of the *Jesuit Relations* will show that as these priests came down the Mississippi valley into Louisiana and began to instruct the people they undertook also the instruction of the Negroes. They regarded them as brethren and, therefore, entitled to the same revelation of God as provided for the other people in the Western Hemisphere. These missionaries did not need any special instructions from headquarters. These priests insisted that ample time should

III. ENLIGHTENMENT POPULARIZED BY THE AMER-
ICAN REVOLUTION

11. EDUCATION AS A PREPARATION FOR FREEDOM

be given for the development of the mind and the enlightenment of the slaves.

In addition to the *Jesuit Relations* such sources as the *Special Report of the United States Commissioner of Education, 1869* may be consulted. In this volume are numerous reports from those parts in which the Catholic clergy were situated and accounts of what they accomplished among these people. Facts along this line are also available in Herrera's *Historia General* and in Oviedo's *Historia General.* The matter may be further studied by consulting the records in the Municipal Archives of New Orleans and records in the St. Louis Cathedral of that city. These show that the instruction of slaves was an important concern there throughout the eighteenth century.

11. The third stage in the education of the Negro in the Western Hemisphere was reached during the revolutionary movement which resulted in the independence of the United States and within a few generations thereafter the independence of the Latin-American republics. Because of more efforts to educate the Negroes in Latin-America from the very beginning, however, the change was not so sudden or noticeable in those parts as it was in the United States where less had been undertaken to develop the mind of the Negro. The sudden change along the Atlantic was due to the unusual emphasis placed upon the natural rights of man. One of the complaints against the mother country was the restriction shown in the lack of toleration and the lack of religious freedom. The evangelical denominations coming into the United States at that time were the chief promoters of the movement in this respect; and along with the advocacy of the freedom of the individual they included that of the Negro to be free and to develop as a man. When toleration and later religious freedom gained ground and finally became recognized and provided for by law one of the first uses these new sects made of their freedom was to proselyte the Negroes. To do this, as had been demonstrated before, required actual education, and in the proportion as this movement gained ground it meant additional opportunities for the enlightenment of the Negroes. They had to learn to search the scriptures.

The claims of the Negroes to such a bounty are set forth in the works of all of the early Methodist and Baptist missionaries, in the records of the Quakers, and in those of the Puritans of New England who felt the same way, although they did not come into contact with the large body of Negroes farther South where such efforts were much in need. This particular phase of the movement is briefly sketched by C. G. Woodson in *The Education of the Negro Prior to 1861,* chapter iii. The matter may be studied further, however, by consulting such works as M. S. Locke's *Anti-Slavery in America, from the Introduction of the African Slaves to the Prohibition of the Slave Trade 1619-1808;* John Woolman's *Journal;* Jonathan Boucher's *A View of the Cause and Consequences of the American Revolution;* Brissot de Warville's *New Travels;* Johann Schoepf's *Travels in the Confederation;* John Wesley's *Thoughts on Slavery;* Abbé Gregoire, *La Littérature des*

III. ENLIGHTENMENT POPULARIZED BY THE AMER-
ICAN REVOLUTION—*Continued*

12. EDUCATION FOR SERVICE
13. SPECIAL SCHOOLS

Nègres; "Othello," and "An Essay by a Free Negro" in the *American Museum* (IV, pp. 415, 511). The works of Thomas Jefferson, John Adams, George Washington, and James Madison contain letters and other observations bearing upon the same topic.

12. The Negro, then, was declared entitled to freedom and was to be educated as a preparation for citizenship. The sort of antislavery movement popular at that time was a slow process. In fact, these reformers should be referred to as gradual emancipationists. They did not believe that the Negro slaves in their crude form should be liberated and turned loose upon society without first having been trained in the fundamentals and in the duties of citizenship. This policy, therefore, as pointed out in the second chapter of *The Education of the Negro Prior to 1861,* made education a correlative of emancipation. Owners of slaves were induced to join the general movement for the emancipation of slaves on the condition that they would be thus prepared and, therefore, would not become a public charge. They were to be educated, too, not only to work at occupations but also to administer a household, to teach their less fortunate fellows, to organize churches for further religious instruction and spiritual salvation. This education, then, was of a higher order than that which was intended merely to render efficient service in the employ of a master class.

The actual plan for this education is best set forth in the records of the meetings of the Society of Friends or Quakers—the accounts of the steps taken to carry out this very program. These plans are also given in the records of the American Convention of Abolition Societies which began to meet as a national assembly as early as 1775 and continued such meetings until about 1830. These friends organized committees to take charge of Negroes who had just been liberated or who were free men in prospect. A course of study consisting of the fundamentals of reading, writing and cyphering and special training in agriculture and industrial arts together with the instruction in administration incident thereto, was drawn up and published abroad among such workers as a guide for the education of the Negro. The proceedings of local organizations like that of the Pennsylvania Society for the Abolition of Slavery, the New York Manumission Society, and the Massachusetts Anti-Slavery Society, are also informing.

13. Special schools for the Negroes were established. This effort, however, must not be understood as that of segregation which the Negroes face today. In some of these cases the Negroes to be thus trained were adults. They could begin with the same studies assigned children, but because of their experience in life they could proceed more rapidly and complete the required course in less time. Furthermore, as pointed out in *The Education of the Negro Prior to 1861,* chapters ii and iii, there were certain things which the Negroes had not been permitted to learn as slaves whereas other persons in school had mastered such by experiences earlier in their careers. In addition, the Negro in his peculiar situation had to learn to work efficiently at the occupations open to him.

III. ENLIGHTENMENT POPULARIZED BY THE AMER-
ICAN REVOLUTION—*Continued*

14. DEMOCRATIC EDUCATION
15. MISSIONARY EDUCATION ABROAD

Such special schools were established in all of the cities along the Atlantic, especially in Boston, New York, Philadelphia, Baltimore, Charleston, and Savannah. Very little was offered the Negro in the rural districts, then, except in parts where the Quakers and Catholics came into contact with them. Here and there missionaries for the Society for the Propagation of the Gospel in Foreign Parts accomplished something among the Negroes in the rural sections. An effort of this sort had been undertaken in South Carolina by these very missionaries as early as 1744. At that time they established there a special school for training young men who would go out to give instruction to their own people. The first two young men thus trained were Harry and Andrew. One proved to be a success and the other a failure. The school continued for about a generation, but the effort failed for various reasons. What education the Negro received in the rural districts was restricted thereafter largely to what the clergy moving from place to place could carry out.

14. It must be borne in mind that in those days education was much more democratic than it is today. Black and white often studied together. As stated above, the main reason for the special schools for Negroes was to minister to peculiar needs. In those days Negroes were trained even to teach whites themselves. The profession of education had not been dignified. The task of teaching at that time was despised. Men in good health and able to render efficient service in some more useful sphere were required to function accordingly. Only the maimed, with one limb, with a withered arm or the like were permitted to throw away time at teaching. Cotton Mather at one time drew up a system of rules for the instruction of servants and he even advocated that intelligent servants be used in the teaching of children.

Some of the most highly educated people in the colonies at that time were the felons and convicts brought over from England as indentured servants. Inasmuch as some of these men were educated persons who had been imprisoned merely because they could not pay their debts they were made school teachers on reaching America. Jonathan Boucher said that in 1773 two-thirds of the school teachers in Maryland were such felons and convicts. These despised poor white teachers associated with Negroes, taught them and thus equipped the blacks also to teach.

15. This education of the Negro assumed a sort of missionary aspect. The Negroes were not only to be trained in this country to function efficiently, but they were to think also of those who did not have the opportunities here. In training the Negroes to serve as teachers and ministers in those days it was believed that Africa could be redeemed by bringing over certain captives, to be instructed in principles of Christianity and afterward returned to Africa to serve at various posts in the evangeliza- tion of the people in the so-called Dark Continent. The Quakers were the foremost advocates of such a plan, and in 1774 actually carried out the

IV. THE REACTIONARY FORCES, AN IMPEDIMENT TO EDUCATION

16. CONCENTRATION ON THE PRACTICAL
17. CHANGE OF ATTITUDE WITH THE INDUSTRIAL REVOLUTION

experiment of stationing such Negroes on African soil. Throughout the records of the meetings of the Quakers from time to time reference is made to this noble experiment, but because of the sentimental attitude of those people toward their task it is difficult to determine whether these accounts showed what was accomplished in those parts or whether such achievement was due more to efforts made by other agencies which later participated in the Europeanization of Africa.

It may not be out of place to add that the Maroons in Jamaica who finally became so troublesome to the people that they had to be deported from Jamaica to Nova Scotia and from there to Sierra Leone were provided with such Negroes who had been trained to function among them as leaders. Dallas's *Maroons* gives a full account of this particular transplantation. Bryan Edwards in his *History of the West Indies* does likewise with the earlier aspects. The early histories of Sierra Leone, as a rule, fail to go into such details, but the facts are briefly stated in W. E. B. Du Bois's *The Negro,* on pp. 68 and 69. The matter with respect to Sierra Leone may be studied further in Sir Harry Johnston's *Opening up of Africa* and in E. D. Morrell's *Affairs of West Africa.*

16. The early effort in the more systematic education of the Negro did not get well on its way before reactionary forces tended to bring these endeavors to an end. As already mentioned elsewhere, the fathers of the American Revolution later thought less of freedom in the abstract and began to deal with practical matters. The idea of emancipating the Negro, then, and the movement to prepare him· for the enjoyment of life as a citizen in the United States, received from them less thought during the last decade of the eighteenth century and practically none during the first quarter of the nineteenth century. The writers who. have enlarged upon the theories underlying the revolution directed their attention thereafter to other matters. The thought of helping the Negro in particular concerned fewer and fewer persons as the years passed by.

This is well set forth in the debate of the Continental Congress, in which the question of slavery and the status of the Negro came up during the years of the Confederation. This attitude is made very clear, also, in the way that the framers of the Federal Constitution in the Convention of 1787 referred to the matter of dealing with the Negroes or silenced or suppressed the debate with respect to this element of the population. The compromises on slavery in the Constitution itself indicate exactly how far away the fathers of the revolution were from their attitude in 1775 and 1776, when many of them believed that the Negroes should be trained as a preparation for emancipation and for the duties of citizenship in the new republic.

17. Of these continued reactions, however. there was another effective force at work throughout the modern world. This was the industrial revolution. This changed materially the system of producing cloth and

IV. THE REACTIONARY FORCES, AN IMPEDIMENT TO EDUCATION—*Continued*

18. NEGLECTED SCHOOLS

lifted the world out of discomfort into ease.   This particular part of the story is related in the seventh chapter of Carter G. Woodson's *Education of the Negro Prior to 1861* and in the fourth chapter of the same author's *History of the Negro Church*.   The change in the situation may be further studied by contrasting what was said about the Negro during the early period and general silence on this question which obtained thereafter.

Both Kosciusko and Lafayette, who assisted in winning the independence of the United States, became horrified at the very thought of fighting for establishing on this side a republic which would perpetuate slavery.   These liberal-minded men addressed communications to Thomas Jefferson, James Madison and George Washington, endeavoring to secure their support in promoting rapidly the emancipation of the slaves and their elevation to citizenship.   The most important feature of these plans was education.   The will of Kosciusko is given in the appendix of the *Education of the Negro Prior to 1861,* also in the appendix of W. H. Mazyck's *George Washington and the Negro.*   The plan of Lafayette will show how greatly the educational feature figured in the program, and, above all, it will disclose (the main fact with which we are interested here) how Jefferson, Madison and Washington, in their correspondence with their friends of freedom, grew colder and colder with respect to such plans.   In giving their reasons in such correspondence, these fathers of the country reflected the change in attitude of Americans toward the Negro.

18. As a result of this reaction the schools which had been opened for the education of the Negro during the first years of the revolutionary period were neglected by the whites.   Fortunately the Negroes, who themselves had become sufficiently interested in the movement to appreciate its worth to themselves, were sometimes in a position to support such efforts on their own resources.   Stimulated, too, by the thought of being deprived of a forbidden fruit, they struggled more earnestly to keep alive such institutions.   In their poverty-stricken state they could not accomplish all which they had undertaken, but the spirit of the oppressed struggling for liberation, made up to some extent for what they lacked in resources.   The actual education of the Negro, then, continued in spite of the failure to retain all of the support that the Negro schools had once received.

The schools thus organized and supported were scattered—one here and there.   They could not be systematized, and therefore did little better than to ground the students in the fundamentals and certain practical vocations.   This applies, however, to the states in the South rather than the extreme East.   In cities like New York, Boston, Philadelphia and Providence where slavery had been abolished before the reactionary forces became effective, more support of such institutions could be found.   The reaction had its blighting effect in the states of Maryland, Virginia and North Carolina.   South Carolina and Georgia, being ardently attached to slavery from the very beginning of the United States as a nation, were generally antagonistic.   No education of the Negro slaves continued there except what could be done clandestinely in cities like Charleston and Savannah.

IV. THE REACTIONARY FORCES, AN IMPEDIMENT TO EDUCATION—*Continued*

19. EDUCATION PROHIBITED
20. CLANDESTINE SCHOOLS

19. The time had come in the South when the education of the Negro openly was proscribed by law. In the first place, as a result of the industrial revolution which debased the Negro to the plane of a beast and deprived him of all human rights to improve himself and enjoy life, the Negroes had begun to solve their problem militantly. It was deemed wise, then, to prohibit the training of the Negro altogether. Even religious instruction, in so far as it could be given orally, was prohibited except so far as it could be done in the presence of a certain number of the "wisest and discreetest men." Negro preachers were silenced and had to give place to white pastors for Negro churches in the South. By 1835 it was almost impossible for a Negro to attend school below the Mason and Dixon Line except when disguised.

The insurrections which so terrorized the slave-holding class were so easily crushed that little was heard of them a few years thereafter. The chief ones were the plot of Gabriel Prosser in Richmond in 1800, that of Denmark Vesey in 1822, and that of Nat Turner in Southampton, Virginia in 1831. The *Appeal* published in 1828 by David Walker, an educated Negro of Boston who hoped thereby to stir up the slaves against their masters, did have the effect of frightening slaveholders.

The extent of these reactionary steps are summarized in the *Education of the Negro prior to 1861*, already referred to above, and in the *History of the Negro Church;* however, the details are given in the laws of the various States. These should be studied to show certain phases of the movement which have never been developed in secondary works. The preambles of these laws are especially informing. They state the reason for the enactment of these measures and thereby give the history of the education of the Negro at that time.

20. In referring above to clandestine schools, it should be borne in mind that these establishments were not merely those of Negroes. Some few Negroes had participated in this effort, but inasmuch as it was a violation of the law, most Negroes were afraid thus to operate such institutions. A study of these schools clearly shows that the majority of them were conducted by sympathetic whites rather than by the Negroes themselves. They were usually in some secluded spot in a narrow street or a building in a back yard; the adults attending went late at night and the children who frequented them in the day time disguised themselves as bearers of bundles of clothing in which they had their books concealed.

In spite of the law to the contrary, however, there were some masters who maintained schools for the imparting of useful information to their slaves, and there were communities like Norfolk, Charleston, Savannah, and especially New Orleans, where the free Negroes had sufficient influence to maintain their schools and to do other things in spite of the law. These schools are mentioned here and there in the study of schools for the Education of the Negro published in the *Special Report of the United States*

IV. THE REACTIONARY FORCES, AN IMPEDIMENT TO EDUCATION—*Continued*

21. TRANSPLANTED SCHOOLS

Commissioner of Education, 1869. These schools are referred to also in books of travel written by men who touched some of the Southern cities such as Brissot de Warville's *New Travels in the United States of America,* Johann David Schoepf's *Travels Through North America,* C. D. Arfwedson's *The United States and Canada in 1833 and 1834,* Frederika Bremer's *The Homes of the New World, Impressions of America,* and J. S. Buckingham's *Travels in the United States.*

21. There were some schools which catered to the education of the Negro in the North. These schools, to a certain extent, were transplanted institutions. The Quakers in North Carolina and Virginia resented the restriction upon their effort in enlightening the Negroes. About 1815, therefore, they began to transplant their efforts to the Northwest territory. The movement was kept up until about 1835 and even thereafter with diminishing numbers. These Quakers, carrying their slaves with them, settled in Southern Ohio, Southern Indiana, and Southern Illinois. There the Negroes were settled upon thousands and thousands of acres of land and taught to farm. They, of course, had the opportunity to attend schools in that section established by the Quakers, for the local schools thus made possible, would not always admit them.

Two of these outstanding efforts made an impression upon the time. One was the Union and Literary Institute in Spartanburg, Indiana; and another was the Emlen Institute in Mercer County in Ohio. These institutions were established on the manual labor basis, and the Negroes were permitted to attend along with other persons. Oberlin itself was established as a manual labor school, and because of its antislavery beginning it welcomed Negro students in 1835. In certain settlements of the Negroes in the East the same tendency developed. Gerrit Smith, who followed the methods of the Quakers, settled a number of Negroes in the southeastern counties of New York, and provided schools also in the same fashion. Oneida Institute owed some of its support to such an effort.

Another educational effort, not exactly that of the transplanted order, was the establishment of schools at certain points in the free states for the education of those Negroes who had been emancipated in the South with the understanding that they would participate in the enlightenment of Africans in Liberia. Of course, all free Negroes in the North who desired thus to cooperate were provided for in the same schools.

These facts are set forth in H. N. Sherwood's "Formation of American Colonization Society" (*The Journal of Negro History,* II, pp. 209-227). References to these schools are found in various issues of the *African Repository,* the organ of the *American Colonization Society.* An account is also given in R. G. Boone's *History of Education in Indiana.* The best story of Emlen Institute is presented in Howe's *Historical Collections of Ohio,* under "Mercer County." The efforts of Gerrit Smith are given in Zita Dyson's "The Philanthropic Efforts of Gerrit Smith" (*The Journal of Negro History,* III, pp. 354-359). Other facts with respect to the operation of these institu-

V. EDUCATION ON FREE SOIL

22. EXCLUSION FROM RISING PUBLIC SCHOOLS
23. SCHOOLS FOR AFRICAN COLONIZATION

tions in the Northwest are recorded in C. T. Hickok's *Negro in Ohio*, N. D. Harris' *Slavery and Servitude in Illinois* and J. P. Dunn's *Indiana*.

22. The education of the Negro on free soil during these years was not a very encouraging development. Before the middle of the nineteenth century, some effort had been made to establish schools at the expense of the state. It had been a long struggle because the well-to-do people, in a position to educate their children privately, did not feel that their property should be taxed to provide for the education of the poor. They were finally converted to the position of seeing the necessity of thus providing for the education of all people through public schools; but the Negroes had a special battle of their own in trying to convince the public that they, too, should be thus provided for. This request was flatly refused in some of the Northern states, but later they reversed their position in states like Pennsylvania, New York, Massachusetts, and Connecticut and provided for separate public schools for Negroes. Massachusetts abolished caste in education by 1855. The idea of separation elsewhere was opposed by a large number of people and by the forward-looking Negroes themselves. This was another battle which had to be continued even until the close of the Civil War.

In the West the education of the Negro at public expense was also an issue. The state of Ohio refused to make any such provision, and any education which the Negro received in that area was by subscriptions or grants from philanthropic persons and Negroes themselves. The state of Indiana specifically provided for the exclusion of the Negroes from the benefits of the public schools, while refusing at the same time to collect the state tax from Negroes. The question did not cause quite as much trouble in Illinois.

23. In the case of schools established for preparing Negroes to participate in the African Colonization, there was less opposition. It was made clear that these Negroes were to be trained for service in their native land and would not remain here in competition with the whites. A school of the sort was at Parsippany, New Jersey. Such schools did not develop very far, since a number of those already in existence admitted Negroes preparing for colonization in Africa. Several were trained in medicine at Dartmouth and at the Berkshire Medical School. Where prejudice was so strong that they could not be admitted to the regular schools, there were professors who taught them privately. This, however, was being done even in the South among whites who were promoting colonization. However, most Negroes there requiring education for work in Africa made their way first to the North to undergo adequate preparation before sailing.

This story is told in the eleventh chapter in the *Education of the Negro prior to 1861*. The steps taken by the colonizationists for the education of their wards from time to time is well set forth in their official organ *The African Repository*. Thomas H. Hodgkins's *Inquiry into the Merits of the American Colonization Society* and William Jay's *Inquiry* give further

V. EDUCATION ON FREE SOIL—*Continued*

24. DISCOURAGED AND PROHIBITED FROM ESTABLISHING SCHOOLS OF THEIR OWN

details. Jay, however, must be understood, as the chief opponent of colonization. He believed it was useless for the Negro to undergo expatriation in order to be elevated. He insisted that they be trained to live as citizens in the United States. The best of all sources as to the actual operation of the educational department of the American Colonization Society, is its collection of letters which have recently been made available in the Library of Congress.

24. In view of these difficulties which the Negroes experienced in securing education at various points in the country, they undertook to establish colleges of their own. It was not only a matter of necessity, but self-respect which impelled them to take this action. They had been taught by their abolition friends not to send their children to the public schools, but to educate them privately. To send them to such charity establishments, would be merely robbing the poor of what was provided for them. That the Negroes might not have attached to them this stigma, they undertook to provide in some way for their own education.

The most promising effort toward this end was that made by the National Convention of the Free People of Color which began to meet annually in cities like Philadelphia and New York as early as 1831 and continued thus to assemble every year until the Civil War. One of the chief objectives was to establish somewhere in the North a college of their own that would be the same to the Negroes that Harvard or Yale was to the white people. These Negroes passed a resolution to this effect and appointed a committee to work out plans for the founding of such an institution in New Haven, Connecticut. On hearing this, however, the local whites arose in protest, and the program failed. The Negroes were advised that they would not be permitted to establish any such college in that city. This action was similar to that of the people of Canterbury, Connecticut, who some years later broke up the school of Prudence Crandall because she decided to admit Negro girls to her academy; and the same spirit was shown in Canaan, New Hampshire, where another academy was broken up because it admitted Alexander Crummell and Henry Highland Garrett, two students from New York City.

In Ohio Negroes had started a school, which they intended to develop into a college. It was first established by Bishop J. M. Brown in the basement of his church in Columbus, but it was later moved about twenty miles out of Columbus on a farm where it was conducted as a manual labor school on the basis of agriculture. It continued as such until it was merged with Wilberforce when purchased by Bishop Daniel A. Payne of the A. M. E. Church. It must be borne in mind that Wilberforce was first established by Methodists who desired to provide on free soil for the education of the well-to-do mulatto children of aristocratic white men in the South. When the Civil War came both their students and funds were cut off, and the crisis thus facing the management necessitated the sale. These matters are briefly discussed in the *Education of the Negro Prior*

V. EDUCATION ON FREE SOIL—*Continued*

25. THE ENDURING SCHOOLS AT CERTAIN CENTERS

to *1861* and the *Special Report of the United States Commissioner of Education, 1869*. The story of the efforts of the Negroes is set forth in the chapter on the "Convention Movement" in J. W. Cromwell's *Negro in American History*. The account of Prudence Crandall is available in several sources. Among them one may consult G. Smith Wormley's "Prudence Crandall and the People of Canterbury" (*The Journal of Negro History*, VIII, pp. 72-80) and his "Myrtilla Miner" (the same magazine, X, pp. 448-457) ; Alfred Thurston Child's "Prudence Crandall and the Canterbury Experiment" (*Bulletin of the Friends' Historical Association, 1934*) ; Samuel J. May's *The Right of the Colored People to Education* (Brooklyn, 1833) ; the sketch of Henry Highland Garnett in W. J. Simmons's *Men of Mark* (Cleveland, 1887).

25. In spite of all these difficulties, however, schools for the Negroes in cities like Baltimore, Philadelphia, New York, Boston, Pittsburgh, Cincinnati, Columbus, Cleveland, and Chicago continued. While there were commercially connected with the South persons who denounced the abolitionists and their efforts to help the Negroes, there were also an increasing number of friends who made sacrifices to educate them. The Negroes themselves, impoverished by competition with the poor Irish and German elements coming to the United States to do menial service, did not have large incomes ; but a sufficient number of friends came to their rescue to keep these schools going throughout the period of slavery. In New York it was largely the work of the New York Manumission Society organized there in 1787 with a membership of distinguished men, among whom were John Jay and Alexander Hamilton.

Some of these sources should be carefully noted. An account of the schools in Cincinnati, Ohio, is given in J. P. Foote's *The Schools of Cincinnati and its Vicinity* (1855). A brief sketch of the schools in the District of Columbia is given in W. S. Montgomery's *Historical Sketch of the Education of the Colored Race in the District of Columbia* (Washington, 1907). The situation in Philadelphia is well covered in reports on the condition of the colored people in that particular city: *The Present State and Condition of the Free People of Color of the City of Philadelphia and adjoining Districts as Exhibited by the Report of a Committee of the Pennsylvania Society for Promoting the Abolition of Slavery,* (1838) ; *Trades of the Colored People* (1838) ; *Report of a Committee of the Pennsylvania Society of Abolition on Present Condition of the Colored People,* etc. (1838) ; *Statistical Inquiry into the Condition of the People of Color of the City and Districts of Philadelphia* (1849) ; and *Statistics of the Colored People of Philadelphia in 1859,* by Benjamin C. Bacon. Some information with respect to such schools in Baltimore may be obtained from Charles Varle's *A Complete View of Baltimore* (1833). Other facts bearing on that city are given in the biography of Noah Davis, a Baptist minister who toiled there. C. W. Birnie's "The Education of the Negro in Charleston before the Civil War" (*The Journal of Negro History*, XII, pp. 13-22), is also illuminating.

V. EDUCATION ON FREE SOIL—*Continued*

26. THE STRUGGLE FOR DEMOCRACY IN EDUCATION
27. EDUCATION OF AMERICAN NEGROES ABROAD—CANADA, EUROPE

26. The struggle for democracy in education on free soil is set forth in the works cited above, also in *The Triumph for Equal School Rights in Boston*. This contains the addresses of representatives of the abolition element in that city. In these discourses they review the situation with respect to the schools for Negroes in various parts of the country and especially in New England. In this way we obtain valuable information concerning the status of the schools as well as the movement to open the public schools proper to the Negroes.

This same question was kept for a long time before the people of the state of New York, and it is given in detail in Thomas Boese's *Public Education in the City of New York* (1869). Some of these facts are also set forth in C. C. Andrews' *History of the New York African Free Schools from their Establishment in 1787 to the present time* (1830); Thomas B. Stockner's *History of Education in Rhode Island from 1636 to 1836*. Touching also on this point is J. B. Wickersham's *History of Education in Pennsylvania* (Lancaster, 1886). Useful also are the *Minutes of the Annual National Convention of the Free People of Color of the United States*. Only a few of these reports are now available.

The movement for democratic education connected with the agitation for increasing the facilities of education. Sometimes the matter was tabled without action; in most cases the Negroes were flatly refused any consideration. In cities like Columbus, Philadelphia, and New York, although the Negroes were not permitted to attend the schools with the whites, some portion of the school fund was turned over to them. In New York City developed a number of schools with all elementary grades, some high school work and teacher training, all of which made it resemble a complete system set apart for the Negroes.

27. During these years of caste in the education of the Negroes in the United States, there were those in a position to solve their own problems without appealing to those who might not grant their request. There were free Negroes who were doing well as mechanics and artisans in cities like Charleston, Savannah and New Orleans. They sent their children to Northern centers to be educated in private schools. Some of them went to Canada and settled permanently because of the chances there for education in the Negro communities which had been established in that country as an asylum for fugitive slaves from the United States. Josiah Henson, a slave from Kentucky, the prototype of *Uncle Tom's Cabin,* participated in the establishment of one of the schools which provided for the education of the Negroes in Canada. In the case of Louisiana lived a number of rich mulattoes, some of them owning thousands of acres of land. They educated their children in Paris. A smaller number of Negroes in Charleston and other such cities educated their children in England.

This story is told in such works as C. W. Birnie's "Education of the Negro in South Carolina before the Civil War" (*The Journal of Negro*

VI. ORAL EDUCATION OR RELIGIOUS INSTRUCTION

28. TEACHING NEGROES IN THE HOMES
29. PREACHING TO NEGROES

History, XII, pp. 13-22) and Margaret C. Douglass' *Educational Laws of Virginia* (Cleveland, Ohio, 1854). This shows that one of the laws of Virginia provided that a Negro leaving the state for education could not return. The sketch of F. L. Cardoza in Wm. J. Simmons's *Men of Mark* shows that he left Charleston to attend school in Glasgow, Scotland. A similar sketch of Robert B. Elliott in the same book says that he was educated at Eton College in England. As to New Orleans the books of Grace King, George W. Cable, and Alice Dunbar Nelson's "People of Color in Louisiana" (*The Journal of Negro History*, I, pp. 359-374 and II, pp. 51-78) are useful. See also W. B. Hartgrove's "Maria Louise Moore and Fannie M. Richards" (*The Journal of Negro History*, I, pp. 23-34).

28. Oral education or religious instruction of the Negro in the South in spite of the laws to the contrary may be styled "Religion without Letters." It must be understood, however, that the laws against the Negroes in the South were passed in emotional fashion to deal with unpleasant developments and in some cases they were not rigidly enforced. The Southern planter, moreover, was a law unto himself. If he decided to have his slaves taught he did so. The actual picture of the South, then, cannot be seen through a detailed study of its laws. It must be grasped from a study of a good many sources which have not yet been made available. In certain homes in the South the teaching of the Negroes continued among sympathetic persons, especially in ministers' families. The wives or children of most ministers taught slaves to read the Bible although it was prohibited by law. Certain masters, too, like Joseph Davis, brother of Jefferson Davis, had slaves trained to be used for special business purposes on the plantation. If these slaves could not read and write it was difficult to use them to run errands unless the employer or overseer would take the time to write a note for what he wanted. This liberal Mississippi planter, therefore, had Isaiah T. Montgomery trained to be the accountant of his plantation. Bishop Polk in Louisiana taught his slaves to read the Bible. Olmsted in his *Cotton Kingdom* mentions a slave owner in Alabama doing the same thing for all of the slaves on his plantation when he himself could not read. Susan Dabney Smedes in her *Memoirs of a Southern Planter* refers to this benevolence of certain masters who had their slaves taught in spite of the laws to the contrary.

29. In the case of white preachers in the service of Negro churches after the reaction, however, not so much enlightenment was made possible. Public utterances had to be safeguarded. Preachers usually spoke from texts such as "Servants, Obey your masters for it is right in the Lord." To justify the institution of slavery they enlarged upon that passage of scripture which they believed accounts for the curse of Ham, namely, "Cursed be Canaan" or "Japheth shall dwell in the land of Shem and Canaan shall be his servant." The Negroes in these meetings, however, were not permitted to learn to read the Bible. They were to be given such instruction as could be presented orally. This preaching from intelligent white men was never-

VI. ORAL EDUCATION OR RELIGIOUS INSTRUCTION
—*Continued*

30. MISSIONS FOR NEGROES
31. MISSIONARY SOCIETIES

theless informing, for while the Negroes were not taught the fundamentals they acquired much other information, and sometimes by dint of energy and secret instruction they learned to read and write.

This is well set forth in *The Education of the Negro Prior to 1861*, chapter vii, entitled "Religion without Letters." For further treatment one may read C. C. Jones's *Religious Instruction*, F. L. Olmsted's *Cotton Kingdom*, and R. R. Wright's *Negro Education in Georgia*.

30. Another stimulus to such education as was permitted in the South was that of establishing missions. Southerners argued that such little education as the Negroes were receiving in the North did not facilitate their Christianization. They said as Chancellor Harper had set forth in J. R. D. Debow's *Industrial Resources of the South* that those Negroes who knew how to read seldom read anything but the Bible and that was a very unsatisfactory sort of religious instruction. To remove from their record the stigma of preventing the Negro from receiving the revelation of God in the Bible these Southerners provided more generally for oral instruction of the Negroes in the principles of religion. This was worked out by committees from Southern conferences and conventions which ordered that special textbooks be produced for this purpose, and numerous appeals were made for funds to have such literature printed for free distribution and to employ catechists and ministers to toil among the Negroes.

The books which they were to use in this work were the following: Dr. Capers's *Short Catechism for the Use of Colored Members on Trial in the Methodist Episcopal Church in South Carolina; A Catechism to be Used by Teachers in the Religious Instruction of Persons of Color in the Episcopal Church of South Carolina;* Dr. Palmer's *Catechism;* Rev. John Mine's *Catechism;* and C. C. Jones's *Catechism of Scripture, Doctrine and Practice Designed for the Original Instruction of Colored People.*

31. During these years there were churches of consequence maintained especially for Negroes in the South. These churches had large memberships; in some cases more than one thousand persons were thus attached. Some of these members, too, were in comfortable circumstances; a few were free and worked in the higher pursuits. Others were slaves known to be trustworthy and functioned in the same capacities with almost the same privileges as those granted the free people of color. As a result, then, when appeals were made for funds to help extend the church work to parts where the Negroes were not so circumstanced considerable sums were thereby raised. One of the most successful of these appeals was usually for their funds to maintain foreign as well as home missions. The missionary societies of these large Negro churches in the cities like Baltimore, Norfolk, Charleston, Savannah, Mobile, Louisville, and the like raised sufficient money to assist Negroes who desired to settle in Liberia or other parts of Africa as missionaries. Lott Cary, sent as missionary to Africa, was supported partly by the Missionary Society of the First Baptist Church in Richmond. Har-

VI. ORAL EDUCATION OR RELIGIOUS INSTRUCTION
—*Continued*

32. AGITATION AGAINST RESTRICTIONS

rison Ellis in Alabama was thus assisted by a white missionary society in that part, but the Negroes gave some assistance.

This is treated in the seventh chapter of C. G. Woodson's *History of the Negro Church*. Further information may be found in such sources as the "Life of Lott Cary" by Miles Mark Fisher (*The Journal of Negro History*, VII, pp. 380-418) ; and in Daniel A. Payne's *History of the A. M. E. Church*.

32. During these years, too, not only the Negroes facing such difficulties demanded a change but other persons in sympathy took this position in their behalf. This appeared both in the North and in the South. While the friends agitating in behalf of the education of the Negro in the North approached the matter on sentimental grounds those who took up this question in the South were actuated by economic motives. The South was running behind the North in that the latter was being industrialized; and it was argued that with slave labor, which had to be kept in its mentally undeveloped state to maintain slavery, the South could not compete with the North and must continue forever the economic inferior to that section. There were, then, those who advocated the repeal of the laws of the South prohibiting the education of the Negro. It was urged that the Negro be educated at least to the extent of learning to read, write, and cypher.

This proposal was approved by agricultural conventions in several states, especially those in North Carolina and in Georgia. Bills were introduced to repeal hostile legislation. Such a measure was all but enacted in North Carolina, and it received considerable consideration in the legislature in Georgia. It is said that the ardent abolition agitation during the forties and fifties stopped this movement which otherwise might have been successful.

Some of the most prominent persons in the South had discussed this matter. Among these were Chancellor William Harper and Judge J. B. O'Neall of South Carolina. Other persons entered upon the discussion as set forth in the first three volumes of Debow's *Industrial Resources of the South*. In these appear essays from various parts of the country by some of the greatest thinkers of that time, and the matter is discussed in much detail. The debates by others as reported in the proceedings of the legislatures of Georgia and North Carolina when this question was discussed are further informing.

The connection of this topic with industrialism in the South is well set forth in Charles H. Wesley's *Negro Labor in the United States*. It is also given in the proceedings of these agricultural conventions which met annually throughout the South in such cities as Charleston, Nashville, Memphis, Birmingham, New Orleans and St. Louis. These proceedings were usually given in full in newspapers of the cities where these conventions met. It should be noted that these conventions represented the best element in the South, and in bringing together leaders of this type they served as forerunners of the Confederacy.

VI. ORAL EDUCATION OR RELIGIOUS INSTRUCTION
—Continued
33. WINKING AT VIOLATIONS OF THE LAW

VII. THE EDUCATION OF THE NEGRO DURING THE CIVIL WAR
34. REFUGEES IN THE ARMY AND CAMPS

33. As a result of this belief in the necessity for the education of the Negro there were here and there certain persons who continued to wink at violations of the law. This is treated in detail in C. G. Woodson's *Education of the Negro Prior to 1861* in the chapter entitled "Education in Spite of Opposition." There was hardly a city in the South where secret schools were not maintained for the education of the Negroes.

The teachers thus employed were usually white. When caught they were called in, given a lecture, and told to desist. Sometimes they were compelled to leave the city. It was made so unpleasant for Margaret Douglass in Norfolk, Virginia, where she was found teaching such a school for the Negroes in 1856 that she finally left that city. J. C. Napier, an octogenarian still living, often relates how when as a boy in 1858 he was attending school in Nashville one day a policeman knocked on the door and said to the Scotch-Irishman in charge, "What are you doing here?" "You are violating the laws of the state." "Close up this school and leave the city within twenty-four hours." This he did without protest.

The reason for enforcing the laws spasmodically on such occasions was that something unusual had happened, and persons in the fever of excitement demanded that something unusual be done. The laws which had almost fallen into desuetude were renewed and enforced. This matter is well set forth in the books of travel referred to above and in the sources given under 25 and 26.

34. To the freedmen education was a forbidden fruit which they eagerly sought as soon as released from bondage. Their white friends readily provided such opportunities, believing that education was the only barrier which separated the races. As soon as the Negro had his mind enlightened, it was believed, he would measure up to the standard of other Americans. With this thought in mind even the soldiers in the Union armies began at once to teach the fugitive slaves who escaped from the plantations to the lines of the invaders of the South. For those freedmen who congregated in large numbers near the District of Columbia, in the region of Fortress Monroe, and around Port Royal, South Carolina, were established schools which functioned so efficiently that some of them continued and became the nucleus of permanent institutions.

This is discussed in detail in connection with "Confusing Movements During the Civil War" in C. G. Woodson's *A Century of Negro Migration.* The topic is further treated in G. W. Williams's *History of the Negro Troops in the War of the Rebellion,* pp. 66 *et seq.;* John Eaton's *Grant, Lincoln and the Freedmen;* E. W. Pearson's *Letters from Port Royal;* E. H. Botume's *First Days Among the Contrabands;* E. L. Pierce's *Freed-*

VII. THE EDUCATION OF THE NEGRO DURING THE CIVIL WAR—*Continued*

35. SCHOOLS ESTABLISHED BY SOLDIERS
36. ELEMENTARY SCHOOLS ESTABLISHED BY NEGROES

men of Port Royal, South Carolina; Mary Ames's *From a New England Woman's Diary in 1865;* Levi Coffin's *Reminiscences; Special Report of the United States Commissioner of Education, 1869,* chapter on the "Legal Status of Colored Schools in the District of Columbia"; *Atlantic Monthly,* XII, pp. 308 *et seq.*

35. A study of the early history of some of the most popular and useful schools today will reveal the startling fact that many of them were established by soldiers. Hampton developed out of such a nucleus of schools. Howard University was indirectly influenced thereby from the very beginning. Fisk was established by a man who had just emerged from the army; and such a soldier had much to do with the working out of Lincoln University in Missouri. In addressing themselves to these larger tasks these military educators were not functioning in connection with the United States Army, but with the Freedmen's Bureau which had begun to establish schools for Negroes before the Civil War closed. Former soldiers remained in the South to serve as agents of this organization which was to protect the Negroes and prepare them for citizenship.

The best sources for this information are the local histories of those schools themselves. The reports of the Freedmen's Bureau will also supply such data. Brief sketches of these schools are given in the second volume of Thomas Jesse Jones's biased *Negro Education* (Washington, 1917); D. O. W. Holmes's *The Evolution of the Negro College;* the same author's "Fifty Years of Howard University" (*The Journal of Negro History,* III, pp. 128-138, 368-380); and L. P. Jackson's "The Origin of Hampton Institute" (the same magazine, X, pp. 131-149). Benjamin Brawley has produced a history of Morehouse, several have written on the history of Hampton and Tuskegee, and F. A. McKenzie has written on the *Ideals of Fisk.*

36. Negroes themselves, ever active in their own behalf, established in the South local schools of their own as soon as the power of the old régime had been overthrown or weakened too much to question what the Negroes might do. Many child-like, pseudo-historians assert that the Negroes themselves were unacquainted with the issues of the war and did not know that their own freedom was at stake. The author has talked with thousands of ex-slaves and has on file the testimonials of hundreds of them, and he has never yet found an ex-slave who did not know what the war was about. These Negroes as a majority knew in some way long before the thing happened that they were going to be emancipated and began to prepare themselves accordingly. Getting "a little schooling," as they called it, was one of the first steps in such preparation; and they sought literate Negroes and intelligent, sympathetic whites for such assistance in private schools.

The best evidence of this acquisition of knowledge is found in the sketches of prominent Negroes who had no education in 1864 or 1865 and who before the time of the Congressional reconstruction of the states began in 1867 and 1868 had acquired the fundamentals. Only about one-tenth of the male

VII. THE EDUCATION OF THE NEGRO DURING THE CIVIL WAR—*Continued*

37. THE FREEDMEN'S BUREAU
38. EDUCATION ON FREE SOIL

Negroes of the United States were literate in 1860, but by 1870 one-fifth of all were literate. They had doubled their knowledge mainly by private enterprise during these years. Southern contemporary writers say that the Negroes were more anxious to obtain an education than were the poor whites who were also illiterate. See A. A. Taylor's *The Negro in the Reconstruction of Virginia*, pp. 148-149, and the same author's *The Negro in South Carolina during the Reconstruction*, p. 98.

37. The Freedmen's Bureau is often thought of as an agency created after the Civil War to meddle with affairs in the South. All who could foresee the outcome of the Civil War saw that something had to be done to supply for the freedmen the oversight, protection, and guidance which had once lodged in the ruling classes of the South. Persons who had been thus held down and suddenly released from bondage could not easily take care of themselves. The experience with Negroes who had crowded the Union camps before the war was far advanced convinced the Union authorities that such provision was necessary, and the Federal Government so provided long before the conflict closed. Of course, as the conflict advanced and the question of providing for additional fugitives became urgent it was necessary to enlarge the powers of the Freedmen's Bureau. One of the features of these enlarged powers was the new provision for education. In fact, during the closing days of the Civil War the Freedmen's Bureau bore practically the whole burden of Negro education. The devastated Southern States had not been rehabilitated; and, even if so, they had no inclination to take on the burden of educating the freedmen. The philanthropic agencies which later came to the rescue had not been organized and brought in to play their part at this early stage.

The reports of the Freedmen's Bureau support these claims. The set-up of the Freedmen's Bureau is found in the United States statutes providing for this agency. These provisions have been exaggerated in J. W. Burgess's *Reconstruction*, W. A. Dumming's *Reconstruction*, and the long series of reconstruction studies worked out under such professors by defenders of the prostrate South, posing as men trained in modern historiography. A different point of view is given in W. E. B. Du Bois's "Freedmen's Bureau" (*Atlantic Monthly*, XXXVII, p. 354), in the same author's "Reconstruction and its Benefits" (*American Historical Review*, XV, pp. 781 to 799), and his *Black Reconstruction* (New York, 1935).

38. While the Negroes were thus acquiring education in the South the same was taking place in the North, especially where refugees had gone during the Civil War. Some few Negroes who came within the Union lines during the conflict were permitted to go on to certain places on free soil where friends undertook to provide for them the facilities of education. The Negroes already in the North, moreover, began to prepare to return South when near the end of the struggle they realized that slavery would be abolished. The chief preparation was education to serve as teachers and

VIII. EDUCATION DURING RECONSTRUCTION
39. FREEDMEN'S AID SOCIETIES
40. THE PHILANTHROPISTS

ministers. Many of these who returned, of course, went into politics, but it was not known for some years after the Civil War how the Negro would figure in that sphere.

The local but mainly unwritten history of the Negroes in Philadelphia, Columbia, Pittsburgh, Cincinnati, and the St. Louis area across the Mississippi River in Illinois is replete with instances of teaching the refugees. Most of such history, however, is buried in personal sketches, in such as W. J. Simmons's *Men of Mark*, I. Garland Penn's *Afro-American Press;* the *Biography* of A. H. Binga; C. L. Forten's "Freedmen, Life on the Sea Islands" (*Atlantic Monthly*, XIII, pp. 587, 666, in 1864) ; and C. Kassel's "Education of the Slave: a Forgotten Chapter of Civil War History" (*Open Court*, XLI, pp. 239-256).

39. Between 1865 and 1875 the chief agents cooperating with the Freedmen's Bureau in the education of the Negroes were the Freedmen's Aid Societies. Prior to 1865 most of such work had been carried on through the Freedmen's Bureau. After 1875 the public school system and private institutions supported by especially interested philanthropists had come into the picture. The list of these important Freedmen's Aid Societies may be consulted on pp. 206, 207, and 208 of C. G. Woodson's *History of the Negro Church*. The details as to the headquarters of these organizations and the personnel may be studied further in *Negro Education, A Study of the Private and Higher Schools for Colored People in the United States, Bulletin, 1916, No. 38,* of the United States Bureau of Education. The distribution of the supporters of these efforts will be informing as to what type of Americans were thus interested in the uplift of the Negro and the sections of the country in which they lived. Likewise are presented the centers of foreign countries thus interested and the extent to which they cooperated.

40. The first relief obtained for the Negroes set adrift by emancipation was obtained in all but spasmodic fashion. Persons throughout the loyal area of the country were appealed to for relief from these direful conditions just as the Red Cross appeals today in time of disaster. To carry forward this work these agencies had to reach the stage of permanent organization and impress favorably the rich element in a position to finance this undertaking as a sustained effort. Gradually there came to the rescue a few philanthropists to assure the future of the education of a considerable number of Negroes, and this number of friends continued to increase with the years.

The names and donations of these philanthropists and the sketches of the schools which they founded are given in the records of these agencies. For the outstanding ones the sources already given will be adequate. Additional facts may be obtained from J. L. M. Curry's *Education of the Negroes since 1860* (Baltimore, 1894) ; H. P. Douglass's *Christian Reconstruction in the South* (Boston, 1909) ; L. P. Jackson's "The Educational Efforts of the Freedmen's Bureau and Freedmen's Aid Societies in South Carolina 1862-1872" (*The Journal of Negro History*, VIII, pp. 1-40) ; R. S. Rust's *The Freedmen's Aid Society of the Methodist Episcopal Church* (Cincinnati,

VIII. EDUCATION DURING RECONSTRUCTION—*Continued*

41. The Reconstructed States
42. Higher Institutions Established by Negroes

1882) ; R. R. Wright's *A Brief Historical Sketch of Negro Education in Georgia* (Savannah, 1894) ; J. P. Wickersham's "Education as an Element in Reconstruction" (*The American Journal of Education*, XVI, p. 283) ; D. H. Strother's "Education of the Freedmen" (Harpers, XLIV, p. 457, 1874) ; D. O. W. Holmes' "Fifty Years of Howard University" (*The Journal of Negro History*, III, pp. 128-138, 367-380) ; and the same author's *Evolution of the Negro College* (New York, 1934).

41. The seceding states were reconstructed on the basis of free manhood suffrage, including the Negro and poor whites who had been disfranchised by the slaveholders before the war. At the same time Federal laws disfranchised the former ruling class for participation in the war for the independence of the South. Being in the large majority, then, these poor elements established in such states the first system of education at public expense. This was one of the outstanding achievements of the Reconstruction. Defenders of the old régime are now busy writing books to "prove" that the South had established public schools before the Civil War, but they do not tell us where these schools were and whom they educated. It is true that practically all the states from time to time provided by law meager sums for the education of the poor and passed measures which established a fund for such a purpose. In some cases these gradually increased; but these funds in the various Southern States were kept inadequate, too small to finance a system of schools for all children; and in some of these states, as in Virginia, the fund provided for these schools for the indigent children was often diverted to the support of colleges and professional work of the upper classes. The aristocracy of the South could not overcome the belief that, since the rich were able to educate their children privately, they should not be taxed to educate those of the poor. Such few free schools as were provided for the poor prior to the Civil War were intended as a charity system to which was attached the same stigma as that of today to the bread line. Even the Negroes in the North about a century ago were told not to send their children to the public schools but to have them taught privately lest the Negroes might be charged with unjustly profiting by what was provided for the poverty-stricken element.

For the facts in this case see A. A. Taylor's *The Negro in South Carolina during the Reconstruction*, two chapters on education, and the same author's *The Negro in the Reconstruction of Virginia*, two chapters on education. The attitude of the Negro toward education at that time is set forth also in the speeches of Negroes in the proceedings of the conventions which framed the constitutions of the states during the Reconstruction. The addresses on education delivered in the Congress of the United States by B. K. Bruce and Joseph H. Rainey are also enlightening. These are available in the author's *Negro Orators and Their Orations*.

42. The public school system, although provided for by law, had to develop with time. The Reconstruction governments in the South were not

VIII. EDUCATION DURING RECONSTRUCTION—*Continued*

43. THE PARTICIPATION OF THE SOUTH

in a position to finance the sort of school system stipulated in these measures. The terms of the schools were rather short and the number inadequate. Even what the white philanthropists were doing was not adequate to supply these deficiencies. Negroes, then, generous to a fault, established, in spite of their poverty, a number of schools of their own. Some of these were never properly equipped, were poorly supplied with teachers, and inefficiently managed; but they were inspirational in that they showed that the Negro was not altogether dependent upon others. Some of the educated Negro leaders of today would not have obtained any education at all had it not been for these institutions.

Inasmuch as most of these Negro institutions were established by churches and churchmen, their history is interwoven with that of the religious development of the Negro in the United States. These are mentioned in the ninth chapter of C. G. Woodson's *History of the Negro Church*, but more details are given in such works as Daniel A. Payne's *History of the A. M. E. Church*, B. T. Tanner's *Outlines of the History of the A. M. E. Church*, J. W. Hood's *One Hundred Years of the A. M. E. Zion Church*, C. H. Phillip's *History of the C. M. E. Church*, Miles Mark Fisher's *Short History of the Baptists*, and L. G. Jordan's *History of the Baptists*.

43. The participation of the South in the education of the Negro has been underestimated. In the first place, the poor whites in the state Legislatures should be given credit for joining with the Negroes to establish actual public school systems. Outstanding men like Ruffner, Curry, and Haygood stood out for education. Many of the best educated southern men and women taught in the Negro public schools while the Negroes were trying to prepare themselves thus to function, for the supply of teachers from the North was inadequate. Some of those Southern whites teaching the Negroes, of course, were impoverished and went into it for a livelihood. Some of them were hopelessly inefficient, but not a few of them were conscientious and thorough. Maggie L. Walker had such a teacher in Richmond. The older brothers of C. G. Woodson had for their teacher in Buckingham County, Virginia, the son of Colonel Joseph Fuqua, of the Confederate Army; and he was actually interested in helping the Negro to develop mentally. Dr. E. E. Smith of North Carolina, was thus assisted privately by a distinguished man in that state. A chaplain in Robert E. Lee's army established a school for Negroes in Petersburg.

The sources on this point are not very numerous because the cooperation of the Southern white man in the education of the Negro is a neglected aspect of our history. The two works of A. A. Taylor on the reconstruction contain some of these instances. The lives of prominent Negroes sometimes carry such references. The more recent works on reconstruction are concerned with the polemics of the situation. It should be noted, too, that some of these public schools for Negroes are still under white principals. Until a few years ago teaching positions were also held by whites. The whites recently occupying these posts are not representatives of the higher

VIII. EDUCATION DURING RECONSTRUCTION—*Continued*

44. At Northern Centers

IX. THE WAVE OF INDUSTRIAL EDUCATION

45. The Rise of Booker T. Washington

type employed during the Reconstruction days, and Negroes are repeatedly trying to get rid of them.

44. At certain Northern centers Negroes were undergoing education under much more favorable conditions than those obtaining in the South. In the first place, the Northern schools had advanced far ahead of the Southern, and education had been popularized there to the extent that by the middle of the Nineteenth Century public schools were very well established. This had enabled the colleges and universities of the North to develop along their special line. Fortunately, too, a few of these institutions felt obligated to participate in the education of the freedmen. Some of the institutions themselves offered promising young Negroes scholarships or connected them with philanthropists who were sufficiently interested to finance their education. In this way by the middle seventies such Negroes as R. T. Greener, the first graduate of Harvard College, and Inman Page, the first graduate of Brown University, completed their education; and one or more of such Negroes appeared thereafter in the graduating classes of practically all of the leading institutions of the North. These men supplied the urgent demand for teachers of thorough training and also administered certain schools which were in need of direction from within the race. The number of such graduates has never been compiled, and their distribution has not been worked out. By a study of the sketches of the lives of such persons in books like Simmons's *Men of Mark,* and I. Garland Penn's *Afro-American Press* many useful facts may be thus obtained.

It should be added also that some of these Northern institutions were not only educating Negroes but assumed the obligation of stimulating through their influential Northern alumni the work which some of these graduates undertook when they returned to the South. In that way certain centers of the education of the Negro came under the influence of these Northern institutions. It was a sort of assistance which was much needed at that time, and without it the story of the education of the Negro today would be decidedly different from what it is. In the course of time these connections grew weaker; and very little evidence of it now appears in Negro education. For this reason persons of today may miss this very important development in the unwritten history of the education of the Negro.

45. After the elimination of the Negroes from politics it seemed to be difficult for them to readjust themselves. The schools and churches were overrun with former politicians, and the desirable results of education promised to the Negroes who rushed in large numbers into the school at the close of the Civil War did not materialize. The Negro had acquired information but had not learned to deal with life as he found it. Booker T.

IX. THE WAVE OF INDUSTRIAL EDUCATION—*Continued*

46. THE HAMPTON AND TUSKEGEE IDEA POPULARIZED

Washington thereupon appeared, preaching the doctrine of practical education. He contended that education, religion and politics had been tried by the Negro and he still found himself about as badly off as he was at first. It was now necessary for the Negro to devote himself to doing efficiently the practical things in life and thus lay an economic foundation for the progress of the generations to come. This, he believed, could be done by mastering the trades, to tighten the grip of the Negro on certain mechanical pursuits which were rapidly slipping away from the race, and by developing business enterprises to make the Negro sufficient unto himself.

The highly trained Negroes led by such men as W. E. B. Du Bois, William Monroe Trotter, Bishop C. S. Smith, and William Pickens, fearlessly combated this idea and insisted that the Negroes be trained along the lines found to be proper for the training of any other people. It looked to them like a surrender of the Negroes' struggle for his civic rights should he direct his attention solely to one special kind of education and the development of economic enterprises. This battle continued for many years and ended only in our day when we have realized that, although the doctrine of practical education at the time it was brought forward by its chief advocate, was timely and desirable, the world has since then undergone such a revolution by mechanization that this program is no longer as feasible as it was when presented.

For review of this new development in Negro education read the treatment given in fifteenth chapter of *The Negro in Our History* entitled "Finding a Way of Escape." It is treated from a more recent point of view in the same author's *Mis-Education of the Negro*. Reference to this idea of practical education is made also in almost any work treating the education of the Negro since the Civil War. Kelly Miller in his *Race Adjustment* and *Out of the House of Bondage* refers to these ideas but unfortunately this author never takes a decided stand on any question.

46. The story of the popularization of industrial education, now an uninteresting one, may be traced in Du Bois's *Soul of Black Folk,* in the files of the *Boston Guardian*, edited by William Monroe Trotter, and in early speeches delivered by William Pickens and Bishop C. S. Smith. The matter is further treated in productions of white men who were serving as presidents of Negro schools. Unfortunately, however, few of these addresses have been made available other than by private publication.

The defense of the position taken by the advocates of practical education is well set forth in such works of Booker T. Washington as his *Up From Slavery, Character Building, My Larger Education, The Man Farthest Down, Sowing and Reaping, Working with Hands,* and *Tuskegee and Its People*. Some of the important addresses and contributions of Booker T. Washington appear also in various magazines like that of "Education for the Man Behind the Plow" (*The Independent*, LXIV, pp. 918-920); "Industrial Education for Negroes" (*Our Day*, XVI, p. 79); "Industrial Education, Public Schools and the Negroes" (*Annals of American Academy*,

IX. THE WAVE OF INDUSTRIAL EDUCATION—*Continued*

47. THE EXTENSION TO FOREIGN LANDS
48. THE STRUGGLE OF THE NEGRO COLLEGE

XLIX, pp. 219-232); "Relations of Industrial Education to National Progress" (the same magazine, XXXIII, pp. 1-12); "Some Results of the Armstrong Idea" (*Southern Workman*, XXXVIII, p. 170); "Extracts and Letters collected by R. E. Park and Booker T. Washington" (*The Journal of Negro History*, VII, pp. 206-222); "What I am Trying to Do" (*World's Work*, XXVII, pp. 101-107); Robert Russa Moton's *Finding a Way Out* (New York, 1920); Scott and Stowe's *Booker T. Washington, the Builder of a Civilization* (New York, 1916). In this connection should be read also books which deal primarily with Hampton Institute such as E. A. Talbot's *Samuel Chapman Armstrong* (New York, 1904); Francis G. Peabody's *Education for Life* (New York, 1918); *Hampton Virginia Normal and Agricultural Institute* (Hampton, 1893).

47. So much literature produced to popularize industrial education shows that it must have gripped the public mind and secured support. It not only thus affected the Negroes in the United States but touched also foreign lands where Negroes were being elevated or where efforts were being made to educate other persons whose condition paralleled that of the Negroes. Teachers who had been trained by Tuskegee and Hampton were called for by some of the mission stations in Africa, and the idea of industrial training was applied in the Philippine Islands when its educational system was being built by the Government of the United States following the occupation of that country at the close of the Spanish-American War.

Among books which give some thought as to the extent to which this practical education was used are the following: *Achimota, Education at the Prince of Wales College, at Achimota, Gold Coast;* Pierre Bovet, *Education as viewed by the Phelps-Stokes Commission;* Fred R. Bunker, "Hampton in Africa—Shall it Be?" (*Southern Workman*, LVI, pp. 213-223); F. W. Cobb, "An Experiment in African Education" (*Mis. R.*, X, pp. 755-756); James Hardy Dillard, "Continent of Great Misunderstandings" (*Southern Workman*, LII, pp. 70-79); J. Henderson, "Industrial Training in Africa: the Situation in South Africa" (*Int. R. Missions*, III, pp. 336-43); "Industrial Training for the African," (*Biblical World*, LIV, p. 61, July, 1914); "Industrial Education in Africa (*Independent*, LX, pp. 616-619, March 15, 1906); Mather, "Industrial Education in Uganda" (*Southern Workman*, LIV, pp. 70-74); Rowling, "Industrial Training in Africa" (*Int. R. Missions*, VII, pp. 492-500); "Industrial Training in Africa (*Southern Workman*, XLVIII, pp. 405-10); Saunders, "The Training of Girls in Missionary Schools" (*So. African Outl.*, LVI, pp. 232-234); Wilkie, "Industrial Training in Africa, in Calabar" (*Int. R. Missions*, III, pp. 742-787).

48. In view of the fact that the education of the Negro in the mechanic arts was thus popularized it naturally follows that the Negro college promoted along the purely classical line was having a hard time during these years. At first these schools maintained a hostile attitude toward the new industrial program of education. Seeing that this was fatal, a considerable

IX. THE WAVE OF INDUSTRIAL EDUCATION—*Continued*

49. INDUSTRIAL EDUCATION MADE ANTIQUATED

number of them compromised by adding industrial departments to their institutions. They were not in the movement heart and soul. They were merely stooping to conquer. They thereby continued to raise sufficient money to keep their doors open, although it was a terribly trying struggle. Negro colleges which had not been efficiently managed and were poorly equipped went out of existence. Those which did live to tell the story now welcome the day when all outstanding schools devoted to industrial education have veered around to their point of advocating the necessity for a thorough college training regardless of what practical education may be insisted upon as a necessary concomitant.

This story is best told by comparing the incomes of leading Negro colleges like Howard Fisk, and Atlanta with the incomes of Hampton and Tuskegee a generation ago. The majority of the philanthropists of this country had been converted to the practical program and gave their money, as a rule, to the industrial schools. This aspect of the educational history of the Negro is still fresh in the minds of the older educators, but it has never been scientifically treated in any dissertation. The books which have been written thereupon have merely advocated the cause of the impoverished Negro colleges of that day or that of the flourishing industrial schools. In D. O. W. Holmes's *The Evolution of the Negro College* there is ample discussion of the college from its very beginning after the Civil War, its stimulus under the direction of philanthropists and boards of denominations, and its development unto efficient service. But this aspect of the educational history is not dealt with in detail. Some of these facts are set forth in Klein's *Survey of Negro Colleges*. Certain information is available also in Thomas Jesse Jones's report on *Negro Higher Education* (published by the United States Bureau of Education in 1917); but this report is biased in favor of industrial schools. It is not worked out along scientific lines.

49. The advocates of the thorough training of the Negroes have boldly proclaimed the failure of industrial education. What they have in mind is that even the industrial schools have been forced by the new development to the position of providing a college education for their students. They have observed also that many of the trades given in the training which was emphasized by the advocates of industrial education a generation ago have passed almost into oblivion because of the multiplication of machines which have taken the place of mechanics and artisans. These people point out, too, that such training as the industrial schools gave failed to equip students for competition with those trained in the factories of the great industrial centers.

In this respect the defenders of the classical system of education make the mistake of charging to these educators the lack of vision. It is doubtful that Booker T. Washington, if he were living today, would not see the wisdom of modifying his program just as others of vision have since done. We must not fail to note also that what he advocated was not so much the preparation for any particular trade or occupation but to deal with life

IX. THE WAVE OF INDUSTRIAL EDUCATION—*Continued*

50. The Struggle of the Public Schools

as it is rather than as you would have it. This theory is a fundamental principle of education which cannot be controverted.

This change with respect to industrial education is amply discussed in Lorenzo J. Greene and C. G. Woodson's *The Negro Wage Earner*, chapter ix, and also prophesied as well as discussed in W. E. B. Du Bois's *The Negro Artisan* (*Atlantic University Publications*, Number 7, 1902) and W. E. B. Du Bois and A. G. Dill's *The Negro American Artisan* (*Atlanta University Publications*, Number 17, 1912). Numerous works bearing upon the same topic are listed in the bibliography of *The Negro Wage Earner*, pp. 374-379.

50. The struggle of the Negro colleges was indicative also of another struggle in the public schools. Since the philanthropists believed that the education of the Negro should be restricted to industrial education, the public authorities were influenced thereby and accordingly failed to provide for the education of the Negro beyond the fundamentals. During these years seldom could a Negro obtain in the southern public schools an education beyond the eighth grade. High schools which had been provided were permitted to decay or were disestablished, sometimes only remaining in name, their courses being so changed as to force them to function on a lower level. For an education, then, most of the Negroes in the South had to attend private institutions which opened after the Civil War and maintained high school departments. Beyond meager facilities for learning to read and write fairly well the Negro public schools of the South up to the time of the World War were largely a make-shift.

Fortunately, since that world conflict southern leaders as a result of the preachments of their own intelligent men and the operations of such organizations as the Sociological Congress and the Interracial Commission, have reconstructed the Negro public schools in most parts and provided in some cases almost as adequately as they do for whites. Because of the unwritten law that Negroes must not expect as much as white men it is still difficult to provide comfortable buildings, modern equipment, and equally prepared teachers, with the same salaries, but the standards have been raised tremendously during recent years. In a few cities of the South like Baltimore, Washington, and St. Louis has been worked out a nominal equality in the schools for the races.

The present status of the public schools as well as the problems which they face have been well discussed in such works as Dr. Ambrose Caliver's *Secondary Education for Negroes*, and *National Survey of the Education of Teachers;* Charles Lee Coon's *Public Taxation and Negro Schools* (Cheyney Pennsylvania, 1909); Horace Mann Bond's *The Education of the Negro in the American Social Order;* "The Negro Common School in Oklahoma" (*The Crisis*, XXXV, 1928); "The Negro Common School in North Carolina" (*The Crisis*, XXXIV, pp. 79-90); Annie Tolman Smith's "The Support of Colored Public Schools" (*Independent*, XLII, p. 7); W. T. B. Williams's "Colored Public Schools of Texas" and "Public

X. TENDENCIES TOWARD EQUALIZATION AFTER SOCIAL UPHEAVAL OF THE WORLD WAR

51. The Justification of the Negro College

Schools in the Southern States" (*Southern Workman*, XXXIV, p. 615, and LIII, p. 445); Mary Church Terrell's "History of the High School for Negroes in Washington, D. C." (*The Journal of Negro History*, II, pp. 252-266); Henry S. Williams's "The Development of the Negro Public School System in Missouri" (the same periodical, V, pp. 137-165); C. G. Woodson's *Early Education of the Negro in West Virginia.*

51. The appalling illiteracy disclosed during the World War and the liberal-mindedness developed out of that social upheaval brightened the future of both the college and the public schools for Negroes. Makeshifts and distinctions in education they believed, should cease. The Negro college was justified by its promoters on the ground that training without college education is inadequate for the demands of efficiency. Instead of using education, then, as a means to equip oneself for the vocations of life, it is necessary to use these vocations as the first application of the thought emerging from a well-developed mind. The extent to which this so-called justification has gone is measured by the increased support which has come for the colleges in recent years. The promoters of Negro education, the North and South, white and black, have changed their attitude toward the Negro colleges.

The increased support of these institutions is accounted for in Klein's *Survey of Negro Colleges;* in D. O. W. Holmes, *Evolution of the Negro College,* and in more detail in the *state reports* of the departments of education and in the reports of the United States Office of Education. This financial aid of the present day compared with that of former years indicates that there must be something in the Negro colleges which has been considered compensating for the amount of money thus invested. Read also Loretta Funk's "The Negro in Education" (*The Journal of Negro History,* V, pp. 1-21).

In C. G. Woodson's *The Mis-Education of the Negro,* however, there is expressed the point of view that although we have produced a large number of graduates of colleges, we have not produced men that can think and do. Not that they do not become good mechanics and artisans, but they have not become leaders and makers of men. The Negro of today is in the bread-line because he has not developed a producing class. His knowledge of chemistry has not led to the establishment of chemical industries; his knowledge of printing has not led to the establishment of printing plants of large production; his knowledge of economics has not enabled him to establish financial enterprises. In other words, what the Negro has learned has been largely memorizing history and developments of other people. Until he can learn to do something for himself, it cannot be said that such college education as he has received has amounted to very much.

The extent to which the Negroes still believe in the great achievements of these colleges, however, is very well expressed in recent publications of the Negro like Horace Mann Bond's *Education of the Negro in the American Social Order; The Background of Negro College Students,* by Dr. Ambrose Caliver, and the addresses of various persons in T. E. McKinney's *Higher*

X. TENDENCIES TOWARD EQUALIZATION AFTER SOCIAL UPHEAVAL OF THE WORLD WAR—*Continued*

52. THE DEVELOPMENT OF THE LAND GRANT COLLEGES
53. THE NEW PROGRAM OF ADVANCED EDUCATION

Education Among Negroes. In the recent productions of Kelly Miller on education the treatment has been pro and con in straddling fashion.

52. The greatest achievement in Negro education since the rise of Booker T. Washington, is undoubtedly the development of the Land Grant Colleges. Up to the World War they existed in some fashion with the small allowances due them from the Morrill Fund together with such meager appropriations as the states provided. Since that time the boards engaged in education have appropriated larger sums of money, not only to aid the outstanding private colleges in the South, but also to aid the Land Grant Colleges. These funds matched by state appropriations have enabled the Land Grant Colleges to provide their institutions with up-to-date modern equipment. This applies to all of the fourteen states of the South. Some have accomplished more than others, but all have felt this impulse and have found funds with which to carry out their program of reconstruction during recent years.

This story is given in detail in D. O. W. Holmes' *The Evolution of the Negro Colleges,* chapter xi. Some help may be obtained, also, from Ford McCuiston's *Higher Education of Negroes* and from a monograph on the Land Grant Colleges recently published by President John W. Davis of West Virginia State College.

It is wise to note, however, that the program of the Land Grant Colleges during this period has been largely that of increasing their equipment and training their teachers. The buildings came first, and next followed certain scholarships to have their unprepared teachers trained in the best universities of the North. They have not, as yet, had time to finish these two tasks. Many of these teachers are still in training, trying to acquire in a short while a knowledge of the advanced phases of education as they are now understood and carried out in the greatest universities of this country and Europe. The few who have undergone this training have not been back in the work long enough to register an important effect on the minds of the students in training. We are still to see, therefore, the real results from this reconstruction of education through the Land Grant College program. This, however, does not apply merely to the Land Grant Colleges. The same must be understood here as the actual situation in schools like Hampton and Tuskegee. These schools cannot be remade over night, by persons who have been trained in mushroom fashion. A great institution is made largely by developing educational traditions.

53. The new program of education for the Negro has been worked out altogether outside of the Negro race. There are a number of Negroes at the head of institutions of learning, but they are subjects of boards and foundations which direct them in the way the donors desire them to go. These agencies determine how this money shall be spent for equipment, teachers, and the like. At present it has been agreed among the foundations thus interested

X. TENDENCIES TOWARD EQUALIZATION AFTER SOCIAL UPHEAVAL OF THE WORLD WAR—*Continued*

54. THE DEVELOPMENT OF THE RURAL SCHOOLS

to establish four universities in the South, namely, Howard, Fisk, Atlanta, and Dillard. It seems that along with these there will be a number of smaller colleges which will feed these larger institutions. Exactly how many these will be, in addition to the Land Grant Colleges, has not been clearly defined.

The whites in control of these centers of higher education say that they hope to provide in the South facilities for professional and specialized education by Negroes themselves inasmuch as Negroes are not permitted to teach in the other universities. Certain persons, however, see only segregation in this effort which will divert Southern Negroes from Northern institutions where they are becoming less and less acceptable as race hate increases. Southern white men, it is said, have been made to see the wisdom of the new program of higher education, for if the Negro is to undergo such training it is better for him to do so in the South where he will not be spoiled by social equality as he would be as a student in the North.

Whether or not this attitude explains the increasing appropriations for Negro state colleges in the South is not clear, but some insist that this is just as great a motive as the tendency to provide more liberally for the Negroes as a matter of justice. The extension work of such institutions as the University of Georgia and that of Kentucky can hardly be fully explained by such an attitude, for some of the Southern States which exclude Negroes from their universities have grown liberal enough to pay the cost of educating such students elsewhere. The branches of municipal colleges and universities set apart for Negroes in Louisville and Houston may be another effort to solve the same problem. At present the Negroes are staging a legal fight in the courts for admission to state universities to undergo training which such states do not provide for Negroes elsewhere. As a result of this effort one Negro has already been admitted by mandamus to the Law School of the University of Maryland.

Up to our time, however, we must regard the present condition of the Negro in the world as evidence that his education has little bearing on his problems. He has been educated from himself rather than to himself. He is learning to plan for others but not to plan for himself. He has learned to understand others, but not the people with whom he has to do. He is studying the possibilities of others but not the possibilities of the Negro. The longer the Negro is thus educated, therefore, the worse off he is. He is like the man travelling through a strange country and at the fork of the road he takes the wrong way. The longer he travels, then, the worse off he is.

54. During these years it is fortunate that much has been done for the development of the rural schools. There have been few questions as to the way in which these schools have been built and in which the work in them has been administered. A few were established under the direction of the John F. Slater Fund and the Jeanes Fund, given to industrial training,

X. TENDENCIES TOWARD EQUALIZATION AFTER SOCIAL UPHEAVAL OF THE WORLD WAR—*Continued*

55. THE DIFFICULTIES OF SCHOOLS CONTROLLED BY NEGROES

which at the present time is not emphasized so much. However, there was no evidence of neglect of the fundamentals. The rural schools have always paid attention to these things and the work recently done among them has tended to emphasize the importance of learning to read, write and speak the English language correctly while grasping the essentials of history, mathematics and science.

The unusual impetus given to the rural school movement came from Booker T. Washington, who saw the need of helping the man in the remote districts of the country and planned early to do extensive work among the people in the backwoods of Alabama. From H. H. Rogers and W. H. Baldwin he obtained small sums to enable him to demonstrate that the work could be accomplished. This impressed Julius Rosenwald who financed it in cooperation with the state departments of education, the Negroes in these communities, and the whites who lived among them. In this way the donors spent about five million dollars and built five thousand rural schools. The story is told in the chapter on "Rural Schools" in C. G. Woodson's *The Rural Negro,* in the same author's *The Negro in Our History* (pp. 563-565), and in the reports of the Julius Rosenwald Fund. The earlier accounts of the rural school movement appear in the reports of Tuskegee of about a generation ago.

55. During these years of the new development in Negro education the special schools established and promoted by the Negroes themselves became decidedly impoverished. For a long time this impoverishment was comparatively so only. The Negro denominations supporting these schools continued to raise the same amount of money they had been accustomed to collecting, but they made a very poor showing compared with the larger incomes of other institutions in the same sections of the country. The best prepared teachers went to the institutions with the larger incomes and the reputation of such colleges for doing more efficient work than was being done in the Negro schools attracted to them the largest bodies of students. In the Negro denominational schools, therefore, remained mainly those students who were children of the clergy particularly interested in such institutions and the poorer types of students unable to meet the requirements or to pay the expenses in the other Negro colleges. During recent years, moreover, these Negro colleges have been unable to raise what they formerly obtained for these purposes. The depression through which the country has gone has made it difficult for many of them to eke out an existence. The local churches cannot finance education, for they have been unable to reduce their debts and pay their pastors compensations adequate to keep them above want. Because of such small funds raised for education during these years some of these schools have reached the point of bankruptcy and have ceased to operate. In a few cases, when convenient, some have been enabled to

X. TENDENCIES TOWARD EQUALIZATION AFTER SOCIAL UPHEAVAL OF THE WORLD WAR—*Continued*

56. PRESENT STATUS OF NEGRO EDUCATION

continue by merging with other institutions. This unfortunate situation, however, applies not only to the Negro denominational schools but to other schools supported by boards from the North. These, too, have faced the same problems and have had to deal likewise as did the institutions maintained by Negroes in the South. The daily papers and magazines report these circumstances and changes from day to day. The actual data can be obtained only by consulting the records of the schools themselves. These, of course, at the present time are not always available.

56. Of the present status of Negro education we may speak briefly. At the present time the schools controlled by Negroes are too heavily indebted to project anything far into the future with any constructive program. The schools controlled by whites working for the Negroes are sometimes not much better off, and we do not know what their future will be. The larger institutions recently constructed by philanthropists also face the problem of diminished income because of the crash of the stock market and the unproductive endowment which yields less than was expected. Further mergers and disestablishments may be necessary before it can be determined exactly what will be the status of the Negro schools in the United States. The whole program of education, too, is also in a chaotic state. The educators and the teachers working through this transition period when the world is being remade, are not meeting the test of dealing with the world as it is and, therefore, may be doing harm rather than good. The present day situation is characterized, then, by a mere marking of time. It does not yet appear what useful things the Negro can learn in the schools established for his education.

CHAPTER XXII

THE RELIGIOUS DEVELOPMENT OF THE NEGRO

THE religious development of the Negro in the New World in its beginning was a structure based upon the experiences of the natives in Africa. The Negro brought from the African wilds in his untutored state, from the modern point of view, had to grope in the dark to find the modern God in ascendancy in this new sphere. In Africa the Negro had learned that there is in Heaven the God that made everything; but, diverging from the Europeanized creed of the Orient, the Negro believed that this God after creating things went so far off and became so unmindful of man that there was no necessity for man to concern himself about his divinity. What man needed to do, as the African understood it, was to appease the spirits of the millions of things organic and inorganic in which the spirit of this divinity is manifested. Such Christianity as the Negro conceived in his beginning in America was influenced by this African animism.

This African creed, however, was not to be despised. While it is "pagan," from the point of view of the so-called Christian, it is not more unreasonable than many of the superstitions which have been handed down as interpretations of Christianity. The African animism expresses itself apparently in many ways, but a study of it shows unity. There is a variation with respect to place. The African in the plains would see that great stretch of land animated with the spirit of the supreme divinity. One living in the forests would find this animation in the trees. The native dwelling near the streams would discern this power in the beneficent developments of this river or a manifestation of evil in the damage which might result from its overflow. Rain in one region is a blessing when it makes crops grow and an evil in another where floods destroy life and property.

The African brought over to America, then, lived first in this world of spirits. Ghosts still walked. The souls of the dead returned to dwell with the living. Ancestors remained in spirit to guide those from whom they had departed. Dreams were realistic manifestations from spirit land revealing the will of those from whom they were separated in body. Dreams, too, were merely the wandering of one of man's two souls while he is sleeping. The other soul left the body when it perished. Man, then, was considered to be immortal.

Unfortunately, the enthusiastic promoters of Christianity among the first Negroes brought to America took no account of this background, although observers marveled at the readiness with which Negroes accepted the new faith. This, however, could have been easily explained. Christianity is an Oriental product. The Negro has an Oriental mind suitable for that faith. Yet it worked among Negroes a manifestation decidedly different from that of the whites, but no one spared the time to find out why. The Orthodox Anglican Church of the colonies paid little attention to the poor whites. Certainly its hierarchy would not give slaves serious thought. Negroes were abandoned, then, to respond in their African manner when occasionally evangelized. While it was easy for the Negro to accept a faith which differed little from the one he had in Africa he faced the more difficult task of giving it an intelligent interpretation. A few who undertook the religious instruction of Negroes of that period sometimes tried to develop their minds by systematic instruction, since only an intelligent man can appreciate this religion. This was the more arduous task of teaching letters as a preparation for religion or religion with letters; but all did not take the time required for such systematic effort. This thorough method appealed especially, however, to the Catholics both in North and South America.

Taking the task a little more seriously than the permanently stationed Anglican priests had, the representatives of the Society for the Propagation of the Gospel in Foreign Parts, beginning in 1701, invaded the Negro domain with missionaries and catechumens. This effort brought that connection many new proselytes of greater understanding of this ecclesiastical order, but the Negroes went in large numbers to the Baptists and Methodists. Proscribed during their first years in the New World, these popular sects had gained toleration and religious freedom during the American Revolution. These new workers finally won the ear of the Negroes not only by their emotional preaching but by their bold stand for the abolition of slavery. Catholics, Quakers, and Presbyterians, equally as interested in the liberation of the bondmen as others, failed for various reasons to obtain a following among those whom they continued to befriend. Their religious expression was too cold or ritualistic for the imported Africans.

The new freedom of the American Revolution stimulated not only the proselyting of the Negroes by these popular orders, but also the elevation of Negroes to the position of preaching and organizing churches themselves; and they often functioned thus among the Baptist and Methodist adherents without regard to race. The time came, of course, when with the passing of the revolutionary spirit men began to lose their liberal attitude and no longer welcomed the Negro in the forefront of the popular religious movement. They began to subject the Negro to restrictions which had not marked their first acceptance in the churches of their choice; and Negroes led by Andrew Bryan in Georgia set the example of an independent religious movement in organizing and directing their own congregations. This effort, however, cost them humiliation and the privations of imprisonment with cruel bodily torture. Carrying this independent effort still further, men like Richard Allen and James Varick not only established local churches, but set up their own national religious bodies which have increased with time and now constitute two of the most important national organizations of the Negro race.

The independent church movement, however, was restricted to the North where only a few Negroes lived. There was once an effort to extend it to the South; but because of the supposed connection of Negro churchmen with the Denmark Vesey insurrection in 1822 and the widespread notion that Nat Turner, the promoter of the formidable insurrection in Virginia in 1831, was a fanatical preacher, the function of the Negro clergy was proscribed in most of the slave states. Thereafter Negroes could not preach at all in most parts of that region, and they could assemble for religious purposes only in the presence of a specified number of the "wisest and discreetest men of the community." White ministers were assigned to Negro churches.

This gave the whites the chance to formulate a doctrine which had been considered essential in all teaching of the Negroes on the slave plantations. From their point of view the Bible justified slavery, for the Noachian curse was an established fact. Descendants of the unfortunate son of Noah, then, were to be visited with the afflictions of their fathers. The prophecy was that the Lord would enlarge Japheth. He would dwell in the land of Shem, and Canaan should be his servant. Now since Negroes are Hamites, the descendants of Canaan, they succeeded to this curse manifested in that day in the form of slavery. In other words, God is a respecter of persons. He arrays himself on the side of one branch of the human family. He brings it to pass that all the good things of the world shall go to that highly favored branch while the unfortunate group plays the rôle of hewers of wood and drawers of water. Slavery was necessary that one branch of the human family might be left free to participate in politics and promote literature, philosophy, and science. Servants, then, be obedient to your masters, for it is right in the Lord.

In protest against such theories the Negro, subordinated as a slave, dared not say anything lest he might lose his life in the midst of the terrorism by which the institution was maintained. The Negro, however, was thinking and indirectly through his folk songs he expressed himself as being highly displeased with the system which nominally regarded him as a Christian but refused to treat him as a brother. Often the Negro sang, "Nobody knows the trouble I see. Nobody knows but Jesus." Sometimes he dared to sing, "Everybody talking about Heaven ain't going there," referring, of course, to the hypocrisy of the enslaver.

After Nat Turner's insurrection in 1831 the Negro preachers were silenced; but, invited to the pulpits occasionally by the white pastors then in charge of Negro churches, these former preachers were called on to pray after the white advisers had preached. There was no law to prevent Negroes from praying in public. In these prayers thus offered the Negro preachers often served to break the silence of a suppressed leadership in working a sermon into their prayers. They thanked God for what they had, and they prayed for many other things which only a larger freedom could bring.

Such protest, however, could not go very far toward the solution of the problem. The white man in question was not usually present, and the Negroes could not reenforce these silent protests with any outward manifestations without bringing upon themselves ills which they considered worse than slavery itself. Gabriel's plot in Virginia had failed in 1800; Denmark Vesey had met a similar fate in South Carolina in 1822; and Nat Turner had done no more than to make himself a renowned martyr in the Virginia uprising in 1831. Negro preachers, then, resorted to moral suasion only.

Within the churches themselves, however, another force was at work in that conscience was branding hypocrisy as cowardice. For years the churches in tyrannical fashion had endeavored to evade the question. The Catholic church, the Anglican sect, and its successor, the Protestant Episcopal Church in America, refused to make slavery a matter of discipline; but the Presbyterian, Methodist and Baptist churches which had once attacked slavery and then tried to compromise on the question after so many of their members had become rich slaveholders themselves, finally had to take a stand on the matter. The agitation became intense and so disturbed the national councils annually that these denominations divided about 1844. This made it possible for some of their constituents to seek their way to glory while promoting slavery when others were accepting as a Christian duty the task of boldly attacking the institution as a sin.

In this all but "lost condition" of the Negro, however, some hope came out of the very controversy itself. The North and the South had gradually become divided in politics; and the abolitionists, playing up slavery as a sin when others would regard it only as an economic evil, added fuel to the flames. At the same time the churches of the North, having washed their hands of the stain of slavery, pointed the finger of scorn at the South, saying, "Shame upon you! You call yourselves Christians, and by laws prohibiting the enlightenment of the slaves you have closed up the Bible to the Negro, the only revelation man has of God."

To this charge the Southern churches replied in vitriolic language; but they felt the sting of truth, for at the same time they endeavored to remove the cause of such censure. They therefore worked out a new scheme of religion without letters. The Negro was to be taught the Christian religion orally, but he was not to be permitted to learn to read and write. White persons enlisted in the cause would not only preach to them, but would become the teachers in their Sunday Schools where they imparted the principles of Christianity in catechetical fashion. Stonewall Jackson taught Negroes in such a Sunday School in Lexington, Virginia. Increasing vigor pushed these efforts even into remote parts of the South under the direction of devotees like Bishop Leonidas Polk, of Louisiana; Josiah Law and C. C. Jones, of Georgia; Bishop William Meade, of Virginia; and especially William Dwight Capers, of South Carolina. He became widely known for his effective enlightenment of neglected slaves in those parts. For them he established as many as thirty missions in ten years at the expense of $15,000.00 annually.

This, however, did not satisfy other denominations in the North. The people of the nation had drifted too far apart in their religion to cooperate nationally, and less than a generation later they had diverged too far in politics. The secession of the churches was the forerunner of the secession of the states. The Civil War came as a natural result. The outcome was to free the Negroes and give them the opportunity to develop in churches of their own. Their pride would not sanction any longer their going to the gallery, to the "Black Pew," the "Court of the Gentiles outside of the Temple of Jehovah." Thus came in 1870 the establishment of the Colored Methodist Episcopal Church which assumed an independent existence as had done the African Methodist Episcopal and African Methodist Episcopal Zion churches in 1816 and 1821 respectively.

One of the greatest achievements of the Negro church immediately after the Civil War was not religious work but education. The church could not accomplish its aims without an educated ministry. Uneducated freedmen ambitious to preach had to be trained. The white religious and philanthropic organizations did most of this work, but gradually the Negro church bodies invaded the field and assumed a fair share of the burden. In their all but impoverished condition the Negro organizations could not establish all the schools that they needed, and those that they founded were so poorly equipped that they never reached the status of standardized institutions. Yet in spite of their lack of equipment and poor support they trained in a way a number of Negroes who would not have obtained any education at all if they had not had access to these institutions.

The Negro churches operated by themselves functioned more efficiently in the social order. Attachment to the whites meant no social contact with that snobbish element. It was merely serving under the supervision of those who believed that they were ordained to direct others. With more freedom the Negro church became Negro. It offered outlets which it could not supply under its former subjection. The Negroes, cut off from theatres, clubs, and parks by the process of segregation, had to use his church for almost every sort of activity. The only other agencies supplying such a social outlet were the lodges, or fraternal orders, but these embraced a much smaller percentage of the people than did the churches.

The Negro Baptist churches, although apparently independent, were until 1886 subjected unnecessarily to the white Baptist national organizations. These had established the first Negro schools after the Civil War, had trained most of their preachers, and had supplied them with religious literature. When the Negro later began to ask for consideration as leaders in these movements, these white "benefactors" repeatedly contended that the time was not ripe for such initiative. The Negro Baptists, however, felt that they had passed the fledgling stage and set up their own National Baptist Convention. This body established a publishing house to produce its own literature. The movement from the very beginning was a success, but unfortunately on account of a misunderstanding as to ownership and control of the establishment this group split in 1915 into two national bodies which have developed in different directions with the one duplicating unnecessarily the work of the other.

Such duplication in this and other denominations was further aggravated by a new factor injected into the equation. When the Negro became a nonentity in politics as a result of the undoing of reconstruction, the church had to assume another rôle. While some of the Negro politicians went into business and education a much larger number took up preaching. They were ambitious to lead and the church at that time supplied the best opportunity for reaching this end. It is a simple task to point out even today a large number of ministers who began life in politics but now occupy conspicuous positions in the churches. Recently, too, since we have had a return of the Negro to politics many ministers who started out as preachers are now devoting much of their time to politics and use the pulpit as a political platform. At the same time the Negro church has suffered from an infiltration of corrupting agencies which have led to such scandals of pecculation and immorality as to cause the institution to lose ground.

As it stands today, however, the Negro church is the only institution which the race has developed and now controls. In business the Negro has hardly made a beginning. In politics he is used mainly as a tool because he does not divide his vote. In education the Negro is subject almost altogether to the will of others. The Negro teaching corps is used not to set up a program of education which experience shows that the Negro needs but is hired to carry out the program drawn up for the Negro. In the church, however, the Negro has things his own way; and it is probably because of the opportunity for leadership offered by the institution that selfish persons unprepared for religious work have gone into it to use it as a means to an end.*

I. TRANSPLANTED RELIGION

1. ANIMISM AND HEBRAISM

1. The religion of the Negro in Africa prior to the transplantation of the Africans to the New World must be studied in order to understand the development of the religion of the Negro in America. As is pointed out above in chapter xv of this work the religion of the Negro resembles very much that of the Hebrews. In fact, it is believed that the Hebrews who were polytheists during the early period of their history got the idea of Jehovah as one God when they were in captivity in Egypt. Certain Egyptians, it is said, had learned the theory from the Africans of the interior who, as a rule, believe in the unity of God. They differ somewhat from the Hebrews in the dualism of good and evil. The African theory of creation and the like, however, resembles very much that of the Hebrews. The Supreme God sent the elder son to create the world and when he failed to do so the younger son was sent to redeem the other. The main difference between the Hebrew religion and that of the Africans is that the Africans believe that God, after

---

* These and other facts are treated in more detail in the author's *History of the Negro Church,* which will suffice as the basis for an introductory treatment of this aspect of the past of the Negro in America. Along with such a general treatment should be frequently used the denominational histories like those of Robert Pius, L. G. Jordan, and M. M. Fisher for the Baptists; those of Bishop D. A. Payne, Bishop B. T. Tanner, Bishop W. J. Gaines and J. T. Jenifer for the African Methodists; those of Bishop C. Rush and Bishop J. W. Hood for the African Methodist Episcopal Zion connection; that of Bishop C. H. Phillips for the Colored Methodist Episcopal Church; and that of I. L. Thomas for the Methodists. Of the other communicants connected with white denominations there are various accounts like those of George F. Bragg for the Episcopalians, M. W. Anderson for the Presbyterians, and J. T. Gillard for the Catholics.

I. TRANSPLANTED RELIGION—*Continued*

2. ANIMISM IN AMERICA
3. OBJECTIONS TO EVANGELIZATION

creating the world, absented himself from the scene of human activity and is no longer concerned with man, or with what man does. For that reason the African should not be concerned about Him and, therefore, does not worship God. He worships the numerous spirits which God has animated in order to please the good spirits and appease the evil ones. Most of the works of Europeans and Americans writing on Africa are misinforming with respect to the religion of the African and everything else.

2. Being unable to speak the language of the Europeans settling in the New World, the Negroes among them remained for a long while just as they were when they arrived from Africa. They were used as beasts of burden, and no one had any particular thought about their religious or moral improvement. Religion among the whites themselves was largely a reminiscence, for they did not always bring their clergymen with them, certainly not in the number adequate to all the colonies. Referring to the religion of the Negroes in such an abandoned state Vice-Admiral Vernon said on pages 306 to 308 in his *History of Jamaica* in 1740.

"Their Notions of Religion are very inconsistent, and vary according to the different Countries they come from: But they have a kind of occasional Conformity and join without Distinction in their solemn Sacrifices and Gambols. They generally believe there are Two Gods, a good and a bad one; the First they call Naskew in the Papaw Language, and the other Timnew: The good God, they tell you, lives in the Clouds; is very kind, and favours Men; 'twas he that taught their Fathers to till the Ground, and to hunt for their subsistence. The evil God sends Storms, Earthquakes and all kinds of Mischief. They love the one dearly, and fear the other as much. Their Notions are extremely dark; they have no Idea of Heaven, further than the Pleasures of returning to their native Country, whither they believe every Negro goes after Death: This thought is so agreeable, that it cheers the poor Creatures, and makes the Burden of Life easy, which otherwise would be quite intolerable. They look on Death as a Blessing: 'Tis indeed surprising to see with what Courage and Intrepidity some of them will meet their Fate, and be merry in their last Moments; they are quite transported to think their Slavery is near an End, and that they shall revisit their happy native Shores, and see their old Friends and Acquaintance. When a Negro is about to expire, his Fellow-slaves kiss him, wish him a good journey, and send their hearty Recommendations to their Relations in Guiney. They make no Lamentations but with a great deal of Joy interr his Body, firmly believing he is gone home, and happy."

3. When the Negroes reached America, as already stated, there were no clergymen to proselyte them. The Anglican priests were few and, being of the aristocratic type, had no time to spend with hopeless heathen. When, however, there had arrived others of the faith sufficiently interested in the slaves to try to save their souls, their efforts were seriously objected to for several reasons. In the first place, it was regarded as a futile effort because it was not believed that the Negroes had souls; and, if they had souls,

I. TRANSPLANTED RELIGION—*Continued*

4. EVANGELIZATION—CONFLICT AND FUSION OF RELIGIOUS IDEAS

5. DIFFICULTIES IN EVANGELIZATION

the whites were not anxious to meet them in heaven. Eliza Lucas, of Charleston, found the very thought revolting. In the second place, there was an unwritten law that only individuals captured in just wars could be enslaved. Christians were entitled to freedom. Negroes brought from Africa had been captured in such wars. They were, therefore, enslaved in accordance with the supposed will of God. Now, if the Negro made a profession of the Christian religion, he automatically became free. Masters, therefore, prevented sympathizing clergy from approaching their slaves until it was decided by the church and state that, although the Negro might become a Christian, his conversion would not thereby work manumission. This matter is thoroughly treated by Carter G. Woodson in *The Education of the Negro Prior to 1861,* chapter ii, and by M. W. Jernegan in his "Slavery and Conversion in the Colonies" in the *American Historical Review,* Volume xxii, p. 353.

4. When the way was opened for evangelizing the Negro further difficulty was experienced in trying to uproot certain ideas which did not harmonize with Christianity. While the Africans may have had fundamental religious views like those of the Hebrews they had never heard mention of "Jesus of Nazareth" and the more modern interpretation of the Christian religion. Furthermore, a considerable number of the Negroes brought to America had been Mohammedanized. This presented another difficulty as pointed out by Bryan Edwards in his *History of the West Indies,* Book iv, chapters iii, iv, and v. When these Negroes had accepted the faith and really intended to live as Christians were required, they had difficulty in abandoning immediately the customs and practices of their religion brought from Africa, and some of their descendants have not even done so today. In some aspects of the new religion there was so much parallelism with that of the religion of the imported African that about the only change he made was to label as Christian what he had practiced in Africa. Negroes are said to be Episcopalians, Catholics, Methodists, Baptists or Presbyterians, but they still have their own way of manifesting their religious feeling and worshiping God.

These differences are pointed out in such works of the early church as Nathan Bangs' *A History of the Methodist Episcopal Church,* four volumes (New York, 1845); David Benedict's *A General History of the Baptist Denomination in America and in Other Parts of the World* (Boston, 1813); Rev. Robert Davidson's *History of the Presbyterian Church in the State of Kentucky with a Preliminary Sketch of the Churches in the Valley of Virginia;* Lucius Matlack's *The History of American Slavery and Methodism from 1780 to 1849,* and *History of the Wesleyan Methodist Connection of America,* in two parts, with an appendix (New York, 1849); Holland N. McTyeire's *A History of Methodism* (Nashville, Tenn., 1884); and R. B. Semple's *History of the Rise and Progress of the Baptists in Virginia.*

5. There were also additional difficulties in the evangelization of the

I. TRANSPLANTED RELIGION—*Continued*

    6. SPECIAL EFFORTS

II. TOLERATION AND RELIGIOUS FREEDOM

    7. THE PROSCRIPTION OF DISSENTERS

Negroes. Their very life did not facilitate the promotion of religion among them. In the first place, they had to live as slaves; most of their time had to be given to hard work. Their masters were unwilling to release them from arduous duties for such a trifle as religious instruction. The time spent at preaching or with the catechist was not adequate, and they forgot the teachings almost as fast as they were imparted. The chief difficulty was that the Negro did not understand the language of the clergymen first sent to work among them. The task, therefore, was to teach the Negroes to speak and read the English language before the principles of religion could be taught. This is well covered in the second chapter of *The Education of the Negro Prior to 1861* by Carter G. Woodson. This may be carried further in the fourth chapter of *The History of the Negro Church* by the same author.

    6. Because of these unusual difficulties special efforts were made for the evangelization of the Negroes. A larger number of Catholic priests were sent out from the home countries as a result of interest manifested by sovereigns and by the Negroes themselves. Their aim was not only to reach the Negroes but also the Indians. These special provisions were set forth in the decrees of Ferdinand and Isabella of Spain and in the *Code Noir* of France.

    The most systematic effort made by the English was the organization of the Society for the Propagation of the Gospel in Foreign Parts, in London in 1701. The aim of this organization was to do missionary work especially among Negroes and Indians. Certain missionaries were sent out for this purpose. The missionaries to Negroes were to restrict themselves to these under-privileged people. Their work is well set forth in Dalcho's *An Historical Account of the Protestant Episcopal Church in South Carolina, from the First Settlement of the Province to the War of the Revolution;* Bishop Meade's *Old Families and Churches in Virginia;* C. F. Pascoe's *Digest of the Records of the Society for the Propagation of the Gospel in Foreign Parts;* C. E. Pierre's "The Work of the Society for the Propagation of the Gospel in Foreign Parts among Negroes of the Colonies" (*The Journal of Negro History*, I, pp. 347-358) ; and Faith Vibert's "Society for the Propagation of the Gospel in Foreign Parts, Its Work for the Negroes in North America before 1783" (the same periodical, XVIII, pp. 171-212).

    7. The religious development of the Negro in America was handicapped by the proscription of dissenters. The laws of England extended to America with the same interpretation; and Quakers, Baptists, Methodists, and sometimes Catholics, suffered as much in the colonies as they had in England. The point here is that these sects were much more interested in the man far down than were the aristocratic slaveholders who belonged to the Anglican Church, the forerunner of the Protestant Episcopal Church. The latter, moreover, did not encourage the religious instruction of Negroes

II. TOLERATION AND RELIGIOUS FREEDOM—*Continued*

8. RELIGIOUS LIBERTY AND CIVIL LIBERTY MADE COMMON
9. THE VICTORY OF THE POPULAR DENOMINATIONS
10. RELIGION CONNECTED WITH EMANCIPATION

even when it had been decided by the majority of the planters that it might be done without working manumission. Those who were most interested in the religious uplift of the Negroes could not reach them under these restrictions.

This aspect of this history is well set forth in the laws of the various colonies themselves. Consult Hening's *Statutes of Virginia,* an especially informing source. However, the laws of all of the colonies carry practically the same provisions as shown by Cooper's *Statutes of South Carolina,* Iredell's *Laws of the State of South Carolina, North Carolina Records,* and the *Massachusetts Historical Society Collection,* 3rd series.

8. In proportion as a larger number of persons who did not believe in the principles advanced by the Anglican Church reached the colonies the rise of such popular sects as the Methodists or Baptists was facilitated. Although suffering from such a disability as imprisonment for preaching, they struggled on in spite of persecution. This became a live issue after the close of the Seven Years' War and the reconstruction of the British Empire following the settlement of 1763. The result of the effort was to make the colonists believe in themselves and to develop a desire for more freedom. This attitude facilitated the struggle of the underprivileged religious bodies and made toleration and religious freedom one of the issues between the colonies and the mother country. The American Revolution brought toleration and soon thereafter came religious freedom.

This question is treated in the *Anglo-American Episcopate,* a serious study which was made by C. H. Mason at Harvard University. It is treated also in Channing's *History of the United States,* Vol. III, pp. 560-566. Some help may be obtained also from W. S. Perry's *History of the American Episcopal Church,* II, and from Byrd Wilson's *Memoir of William White, Bishop of Pennsylvania.*

9. The victory of the popular denominations was not merely the enactment of laws which allowed them to worship according to their own conscience and relieved them from contributing to the support of the church which they opposed. With this victory followed an unusual popularity among the poor whites and Negroes who were convinced that these liberal sects were interested not only in their spiritual salvation but in their earthly welfare. This tended further to force the Anglican or Protestant Episcopal Church to the position of an aristocratic religious body which took little thought of the man far down.

This thought is brought out in Matlack's *History of Methodism,* Semple's *History of the Baptists,* and Benedict's *History of the Baptists.* A summary of this is presented in the first chapter of C. G. Woodson's *History of the Negro Church.*

10. The chief reason for the favorable impression which the Baptists and

II. TOLERATION AND RELIGIOUS FREEDOM—*Continued*

11. THE NEGRO ACCEPTED AS A BROTHER
12. THE NEGRO DENIED EQUALITY IN THE CHURCH

Methodists made upon the Negroes was not only that they were interested in the welfare of the poor but they attacked slavery, the institution which had handicapped the progress of the Negro in the New World. Practically all of these early preachers of these two denominations were sound on this question. They considered it hypocrisy in a man to call himself a Christian and hold his fellowman in slavery. This was set forth not only in sermons which they preached here and there but reproduced in their literature. In 1784 the National Conference of the Methodist Church came out in an official declaration against the institution, and so did the Baptists in their national body in 1789. When conditions in Virginia seemed unfavorable to the group of emancipating Baptists in that state after the American Revolution they migrated to the mountains of Kentucky where they could carry forward their effort with more freedom.

This topic is briefly discussed in the *History of the Negro Church,* pp. 25-29. The details are given in Matlack's *History of the Methodists,* McTyeire's *History of Methodism,* Semple's *History of the Baptists,* and Benedict's *History of the Baptists.*

11. The Negro, then, was received in the Methodist and Baptist Churches as a brother. It was the highest level reached by the Negro in the social order up to that time. Brought into the church, he was educated in the fundamentals that his enlightened mind might facilitate his spiritual growth. Schools connected with churches were opened here and there, and sympathetic persons established private institutions for the education of Negroes. Negroes, moreover, were permitted to preach to mixed memberships in the various churches as did Gowan Pamphlet and Josiah Jacob in Virginia, and Harry Hosier and Richard Allen with Watcoat, Coke, and Asbury on their preaching tours.

Daniel A. Payne in his *History of the African Methodist Episcopal Church* briefly treats this situation, and so do Benedict and Semple in the introductory statements of their histories of the Baptists. A brief statement is given also in the second chapter of the *History of the Negro Church.* For the work of the Catholics consult Joseph Butsch's "Catholics and the Negro" in *The Journal of Negro History,* II, pp. 393-410; and for the Quakers see S. B. Week's *Southern Quakers and the Negro.* See also W. H. Morse's "Lemuel Haynes," *The Journal of Negro History,* IV, pp. 22-33.

12. This equality of the Negro in the church did not continue longer than a generation. The rights of man theory on the basis of which the American Revolution was begun and the independence of this country maintained diminished in popularity. The leaders in facing practical problems began to think of restricting man in the interest of safe government rather than to enlarge his liberties. Furthermore, with the increase of slaves during the first generation of the republic as a result of the industrial revolution came an increase of slaveholders among the poor, many of whom belonged to the popular Methodist and Baptist Churches. Such persons

III. THE INDEPENDENT CHURCH MOVEMENT
13. THE RISE OF LOCAL NEGRO CHURCHES
14. THE ORGANIZATION OF NATIONAL RELIGIOUS BODIES

began, then, to advocate restrictions and to withdraw from the Negro rather than to treat him as a brother. The most striking evidence of this is found in the actual documents themselves in *The Journal of Negro History,* I, pp. 202-205. Several cases are given of Negroes who, after having been accepted as equals among these parishioners and after having been permitted to preach, resented the practice of inequality and escaped from the country in protest. The result, then, was to blight the hope of the Negro in the church and to force him to look for some other solution of this problem. The details of this situation are set forth in the histories of the Methodist and Baptist Churches already cited.

This change may be studied from the recent point of view also in William Warren Sweet's *Methodism in America,* chapter xii; H. B. Bascomb's *Methodism and Slavery;* Charles Elliot's *History of the Great Secession from the Methodist Episcopal Church;* J. N. Norwood's *The Schism in the M. E. Church;* C. B. Swaney, *Episcopal Methodism and Slavery;* A. H. Redford's *History of the Organization of the M. E. Church, South;* Gross Alexander's *History of the Methodist Church;* James M. Buckley, *History of the Methodists in the United States.*

13. The rise of local Negro churches on the independent basis was the direct result of the denial of brotherhood in the regularly established churches in this country after the fever of the American Revolution had subsided. The first of these were Baptist churches not because the Negroes of such churches were more revolutionary than others, but the democracy of the Baptist Church facilitated the establishment of these independent units. A local Baptist church or any considerable number of Baptists associating as a church is a legally constituted Baptist organization and a law unto itself. Sympathetic whites and enterprising Negroes, therefore, easily entered upon this undertaking.

The early Baptist churches are sketched by John W. Davis in his "George Liele and Andrew Bryan, Pioneer Negro Baptist Preachers," (*The Journal of Negro History,* III, pp. 119-127). The documents, the original sources for the study of these efforts, appeared in the same magazine, (I, pp. 69-92) as "Letters showing the Rise and Progress of the Early Negro Church in Georgia and West Indies." Read also Walter H. Brooks' "Priority of the Silver Bluff Church" (the same periodical, VII, pp. 172-196). Accounts of the independent Negro Methodist churches are given in Bishop Daniel A. Payne's *History of the A. M. E. Church,* B. T. Tanner's *History of the A. M. E. Church,* Christopher Rush's *History of the A. M. E. Zion Church,* and J. W. Hood's *One Hundred Years of the A. M. E. Zion Church.*

14. These same sources show various steps taken to organize local churches as national bodies. There was no such possibility in the case of the Baptists because of their loose organization or lack of organization beyond that of the local church. Some of them did unite to form associa-

III. THE INDEPENDENT CHURCH MOVEMENT—*Continued*

15. The Handicaps and Obstacles of the Effort

tions and conventions several generations later, but these did not develop very far before the Civil War.

In the case of the Methodist Churches, however, the story was decidedly different. Their scheme of things requires episcopacy which means local organization brought under the supervision of higher authorities in the church. To function as Methodists not only local conferences but quadrennial conferences of the entire church were necessary. Under the leadership of Richard Allen, as set forth in sources given above, a national organization was effected in 1816 by the African Methodist Episcopal Church, and a similar national body of the Zionites was established in 1821 with James Varick as the moving spirit.

Connected with these organizations of the two national bodies should be considered the continuous effort made to bring these duplicating branches of Methodists together as one strong aggregation. About one hundred years ago it seemed that this was about to be done, but because of denominational jealousies and their own peculiar pride in the past of these respective bodies the merger was never effected. This question has been brought up repeatedly since then, and is a very important matter today before these two national bodies.

15. One reason for the suggestion that the two Methodist organizations be merged is that they were weak. They were handicapped by serious obstacles in the very beginning. They had to seek from whites the ordination of their bishops or they had to ordain them "schismatically" themselves. Their problem was finally solved in a way satisfactory to the adherents and their attention could be given thereafter to other difficulties. Chief among these new problems was that of the stigma of being a Negro church without prestige and without standing. Negroes embracing Christianity were told that it was more honorable to sit in the gallery or in the black pew of the white church than to support such questionable Negro churches of their own. Some Negroes believed, too, that the influential white church offered the only way to glory. This made the extension of these churches into parts of the country extremely difficult. The matter of financing, too, was another difficulty. It was not an easy problem to support local pastors, and few of them had sufficient funds to finance the expansion of the national body. That the Negro church was an independent organization, moreover, made it appear to the whites as an agency beyond the law inasmuch as Negroes were supposed to be controlled in the same fashion always by the so-called superior whites.

This particular aspect of the story is best told by Richard Allen in his own writings and by Bishop Daniel A. Payne in his *History of the A. M. E. Church* and his *Recollections of the Last Seventy Years. The History of the A. M. E. Zion Church* by Christopher Rush contains also some references to these difficulties. Read also "Letters of Richard Allen and Absalom Jones" in *The Journal of Negro History*, I, pp. 436-443 and XIV, pp. 237-238, and Charles H. Wesley's *Richard Allen* (Washington, 1935).

III. THE INDEPENDENT CHURCH MOVEMENT—*Continued*

16. THE NEGRO CHURCH PROSCRIBED
17. RELIGION ACCORDING TO ORDER
18. THE NEGRO IN THE ANTISLAVERY CHURCHES

16. These problems herein set forth faced the independent Negro church in the South, and in addition thereto was the difficulty resulting from being always under the suspicion that the Negro church might in some way stir up the slaves against their masters. The Denmark Vesey insurrection of Charleston, South Carolina, in 1822, was considered a case in evidence. Certain members there under the leadership of Morris Brown, were charged with participation in working out the plan. His church as such was proscribed, and he and his coworkers had to leave Charleston for Northern parts. Negro churches were unpopular in South Carolina thereafter; and because of Nat Turner's insurrection, supposed to be the plot of a Negro preacher himself to stir up the whole South against slavery, Negro ministers were proscribed in most parts.

The hostile laws of the South enacted in 1831, 1832, 1833, 1834, and 1835 best explain exactly what this proscription of the Negro Church meant. Negroes no longer preached. Their pastors had to be supplied from the white ministry. They could not assemble even for prayer meetings without having a certain number of the "wisest and discreetest men" present. Worship, then, was largely passive, the Negroes being allowed to participate only in singing and praying. This is sketched in *The History of the Negro Church*, pp. 52 and 69. It is also treated in John W. Cromwell's "Aftermath of Nat Turner's Insurrection" (*Journal of Negro History*, V, pp. 208-234).

17. After this reign of terror even the doctrine in the Negro churches of the South had to be changed. The Negro was not to be taught religion as a white man received it. Special books had to be produced "for his benefit," and a prescribed interpretation of the scripture and of religious literature had to be given. Preachers were required to select certain texts which emphasized the obedience of slaves to their masters and "justified" the régime by which one man's will was made subordinate to another.

This thought is discussed in C. G. Woodson's *History of the Negro Church*, chapter vii. Details may be found in C. C. Jones's *Religious Institution of the Negroes*, the same author's *Catechism of Scripture, Doctrine and Practice Designed for the Original Instruction of Colored People*, Robert Ryland's *Pilgrim Progress, The African Preacher, The Life of Samuel Pierce*, the same author's *The Scripture Catechism for Colored People*, the *Church Members Guide*, Dr. Capers's *Short Catechism for the Use of Colored Members on Trial in the Methodist Episcopal Church in South Carolina, A Catechism to be Used by Teachers in the Religious Instruction of Persons of Color in the Episcopal Church of South Carolina*, John Mines's *Catechism*, and E. T. Winkler's *Notes and Questions for the Oral Instruction of Colored People with Appropriate Texts and Hymns*.

18. Northern Negroes, unwilling to connect themselves with the African Methodist Episcopal Church, the Zionites, and Negro independent Baptist Churches, remained under the control of the white denominations. In most

IV. ANTISLAVERY AGAINST PROSLAVERY ELEMENTS IN THE WHITE CHURCHES

19. REACTIONARY AND PROGRESSIVE FORCES IN THE RANKS

20. THE EFFORT TO IGNORE THE SLAVERY QUESTION

cases they were segregated, but since there were no large numbers of them in most of the churches the segregation did not look painful. They had no function in such churches except to worship passively. In the course of time there were a few churches which encouraged Negroes to establish congregations of their own rather than to keep up the hypocritical policy of segregation. Some few acted accordingly, and others, losing interest in religious efforts altogether, thereby suffered for lack of such protection as Christian teaching might offer. This is briefly sketched in Thomas's *Methodism and the Negro,* and in the works of Daniel A. Payne and Christopher Rush already cited.

19. In spite of the effort to get rid of the Negro in the various churches, it could not be easily done. Some relief of this sort came in the voluntary establishment of separate churches for Negroes, but the slavery question remained as a disturbing factor. Can a man be a Christian and hold another as a slave? Can a man be a Christian and fraternize with a slaveholder? Should a slaveholder be considered a member of a church in good standing? These questions disturbed all of the churches of the country except the Catholic and Episcopal churches which ignored them. The Methodists, Baptists and Presbyterians could not thus dispose of it; and the antislavery Quakers, especially interested in the Negro, did not have a large slaveholding element in their connection.

This matter is briefly discussed in the author's *History of the Negro Church,* chapter vii. It is presented also in C. B. Swaney's *Episcopal Methodism and Slavery,* Lucius Matlack's *The History of American Slavery and Methodism from 1780 to 1849;* his *History of the Wesleyan Methodist Connection of America;* and E. Channing's *History of the United States,* V, pp. 204-241.

20. In most places slavery was accepted as an institution of a certain part of the country, and it was believed that one section should not meddle in the affairs of another. Furthermore, as contended by numerous ministers of the South, the Bible justified slavery, and everybody should be contented to live up to such teachings. To advocate a program to the contrary was not Christian. But there were those in these churches who did not feel this way about it, and repeatedly brought up the question of preventing the extension of slavery or of destroying the institution altogether. The large majority, however, voted to the contrary and succeeded in continuing the policy of silence.

This attitude is traced in the works cited above. The main point here is to understand the means by which silence was maintained and at the same time to understand that these discussions with members from sections of widely different opinions made the quadrennial conference and national religious meetings smouldering volcanoes. A study of the topic in connection with the political history of the time will be found in the fifth volume

IV. ANTISLAVERY AGAINST PROSLAVERY ELEMENTS IN THE WHITE CHURCHES—*Continued*

21. THE ATTEMPTS AT COMPROMISE
22. THE SCHISM
23. THE BATTLE OF SEPARATED DIVISIONS

of Edward Channing's *History of the United States* and in Bassett's *History of the United States*, pp. 468-472. Other histories give the same facts.

21. It was finally made clear to men of vision in the church that this matter could not be adjusted by ignoring it. Something had to be done. Both factions in the church asked for satisfaction. In some way they had to be appeased. The details of the attempts to compromise in this conflict appear in Bishop's *History of the Baptists*, J. N. Norwood's *Schism in the Methodist Episcopal Church*, and in McTyeire's *History of Methodism*. Brief discussions are given in William E. Dodd's *Cotton Kingdom*, and in A. B. Hart's *Slavery and Abolition*. The space devoted to this in James Schouler's *History of the United States* and in J. B. McMaster's *History of the United States* will show how important this question was at that time.

22. The schism itself is treated in the sources given above. The steps taken and the way that the separation from the national church was effected by the secessionists should be carefully noted. The student cannot escape the fact that each faction had given its own interpretation of the question, and had set up its own particular genius as their God. The people in the two sections did not worship the same God. The doctrines formulated were the same, but each reserved the right in considering themselves creatures of God and to create their own God. In other words, God did not make man, but man made God. Here we have God made to order or religion made to order, and environment becomes a great factor in the making of God or in the making of religion. The section that believed in slavery could not think of God as being opposed to the institution. The section which believed in freedom could not think of God as countenancing involuntary servitude except as punishment for crime.

23. When the divisions separated the national churches engaged in a moral battle. This is an interesting study in the social development of the United States from 1844 to 1860. The old faction had to convince the new faction that justification was on its side. The Northern division of these churches redoubled the effort to portray the evils of slavery and to show how slaveholders could not be accepted as clergymen and, therefore, awaited damnation with fire and brimstone. The Southern division of these churches endeavored to prove that the slaves were better off and more kindly treated than were the socially oppressed laboring classes of the North. The records will show, however, that both sections exaggerated as reformers always do. There were not as many cruelties practiced in the South as often said, although they were numerous; and the Southern Christians treated their slaves kindly only from the point of view of their own interpretation of kindness. The facts as to whether or not the slaves were dealt with in cruel fashion in the South are set forth in the three volumes of Mrs. H.

IV. ANTISLAVERY   AGAINST   PROSLAVERY   ELE-
MENTS IN THE WHITE CHURCHES—*Continued*

24. MISSIONARY EFFORTS IN THE SOUTH—THE BLACK
PEW

V. THE NEGRO CHURCH IN THE CRISIS, 1830-1865

25. COWED BY PROSLAVERY ELEMENT

26. ANTISLAVERY EFFORTS

T. Catterall's *Judicial Cases Concerning American Slavery and the Negro.*
The records here establish the facts beyond a shadow of a doubt that
Negroes were being poorly fed while being hard worked and that they
were subjected to cruel treatments which would have been considered crimes
if applied to white men.   Families were broken up by the slave trade, young
children were sold from their mothers, the wife from the husband, and the
husband from the wife.   These same facts are further corroborated by Dr.
Frederic Bancroft's *Slave Trading in the Old South.*

24. This effort is set forth in Carter G. Woodson's *Education of the Negro
Prior to 1861,* the chapter entitled "Religion Without Letters"; in L. P.
Jackson's "Religious Development of the Negro in Virginia from 1760-1860"
(*The Journal of Negro History,* XVI, pp. 168-239), and his "Religious
Instruction of Negroes, 1830-1866, with Special Reference to South Caro-
lina" (the same magazine, XV, pp. 72-114) ; E. P. Southall's "The Attitude
of the Methodist Episcopal Church, South, toward the Negro from 1844 to
1870," (the same periodical, XVI, pp. 359-370).

25. The Negro church during the critical period from 1830 to 1865 was
independent in name only.   Their own ministers were in charge, but many
things which they would like to do were not done for the reason that these
people were dependent upon the community and had to conform in the main
to local standards.   Those churches which were afraid to fight the institution of slavery sometimes cooperated with the American Colonization Society which, being all things to all men, had the cooperation of a few Negro
churches, especially those emphasizing missionary work in Africa.   Such
churches are noted from time to time in the *African Repository,* the organ of
the American Colonization Society.   Those of the more militant type are
referred to in the histories of Bishop B. T. Tanner, Bishop Daniel A. Payne,
and Bishop Christopher Rush.

26. The reason for the disinclination of Negro churches to go very far
with the antislavery effort was that throughout the North there were proslavery sympathizers—those who had been disgusted by the poverty and
undesirable aspects of Negro communities in the North and others who had
commercial connections with the South and thereby opposed any effort
which might cause a loss of business by attacking the institutions of that
section.   Negro churches were sometimes burned because they were used for
antislavery meetings.   The late John W. Cromwell tells a story of how one
day when he was a boy sitting in the Sunday School of a Negro church in

V. THE NEGRO CHURCH IN THE CRISIS, 1830-1865—
Continued

27. RELIEF WORK FOR FUGITIVE SLAVES
28. EDUCATIONAL EFFORTS

Philadelphia Frederick Douglass was called upon by the pastor to make a few remarks to the children; but he was cautioned in being introduced not to utter in that church one word against slavery. Lewis Woodson, a teacher and minister in the A. M. E. Church in Pittsburgh, was once proclaimed far and wide as a Judas of his race because he refused to permit the anti-slavery people of Pittsburgh to hold a meeting in his church. It might have been immediately burned down by proslavery elements in the city if such a thing had been done.

This part of the history of the Negro church in the United States is unwritten. Only now and then we find in the sources some mention of these conditions which obtained in many parts of the North and border states where the half million free Negroes had numbers of churches of their own. Examine in this connection C. T. Hickok's *The Negro in Ohio*, N. D. Harris's *Slavery and Servitude in Illinois*, J. P. Dunn's *Indiana*, and E. R. Turner's *Negro in Pennsylvania*.

27. These Negro churches which openly refused to permit public anti-slavery meetings detested nevertheless the institution of slavery and the proslavery element which dominated the government of the United States during these years. The refusal was a matter of policy and not one of conviction. In their hearts the managers of these churches longed for the power to destroy the institution of slavery, but they did not care to destroy their churches in this effort. Secretly during these years these same churches did much to help out in a different way. They aided the fugitive that knocked at the door of the pastor at night or appeared in the church and secretly communicated his needs to his friends. In a good many cases the poverty stricken Negro church had little with which to aid the Negro fugitive, but they usually had some contact with well-to-do white congregations which cooperated with them.

In this way Charles Bennett Ray, Samuel Cornish, and Theodore Wright aided numbers of fugitives by bringing them into contact with Henry Ward Beecher. He found some solution of the problem among his well-to-do parishioners. Read the papers of Charles Bennett Ray (*The Journal of Negro History*, IV, pp. 361-372); the *Autobiography of Samuel Ringgold Ward; the History of the A. M. E. Zion Church*, by Christopher Rush; and *As a Freeman and a Slave*, by J. W. Loguen. These show how those problems were secretly solved sometimes with the aid of the Negro church.

28. The educational work of the Negro churches did not have to be carried out secretly. Almost every Negro church was both a school and a church. The pastor preached on Sunday but taught during the week or hired somebody else to conduct such a school in connection with the church. The element antagonistic to the agitation of the slavery question did not generally object to the teaching of the Negroes. It was believed that this would materially elevate them socially and economically and make of them a more desirable element.

V. THE NEGRO CHURCH IN THE CRISIS, 1830-1865—
Continued

29. An Avenue for Leadership—Social Center
30. Represented by Secret Efforts in the South

VI. THE RECONSTRUCTION OF THE NEGRO CHURCH

31. Religious Reconstruction

These educational efforts of the churches are set forth by C. G. Woodson in *The Education of the Negro Prior to 1861* in the chapter entitled "Educating the Urban Negro." The special work of the A. M. E. Church is treated in the two works of Bishop Daniel A. Payne, already cited. The life of Bishop J. M. Brown in the *Dictionary of American Biography* shows how he, while pastoring a church in Columbus, Ohio, organized in its basement a school.

29. In spite of handicaps the number of Negro churches in the North continued to increase, and those already established gradually added a membership sufficient to be effective. The main reason, of course, was that the Negro church was then and even today is the only agency which the race controls and through which something can be done to work with the Negroes and work for them. It was at the same time a social center independent of other agencies which the Negroes in their impoverished condition could not supply. This becomes evident when we glance at the career of the outstanding Negroes before the Civil War. We find at least sixty-five percent of them were ministers, and most of the others who did not function as ministers had once been thus trained or had had such aspirations. On this point no documentation except the record of the men themselves is necessary. The author has examined the various sketches of their lives.

30. Religious life of the Negro in the South was not exclusively in the hands of the churches which had been brought under the control of the white management. At several points in the border states of Maryland, Virginia, Kentucky, and Missouri, the independent Negro churches were permitted to go on without interruption. This kept alive the spirit of the Negro independent communicants who were silenced during the thirties. In spite of the fact that they were often punished they held secret meetings and connected with such independent organizations that endured even down to the Civil War.

The Negroes had accepted their oppressor's religion or his interpretation of Christianity, but, as a majority, the Negroes never believed that the enslaver was the best administrator of such in the premises. Secretly they had to find their own outlet in the woods and rural retreats, where they hung up wet blankets and turned upside down pots and pans to diminish the sound from their fervent prayers and soul-stirring hymns.

31. Immediately after the Civil War the Negro church had to be remade to supply the needs of a "free people." The former restrictions were removed incidentally with the abolition of slavery and with the grant of

VI. THE RECONSTRUCTION OF THE NEGRO CHURCH
—Continued
32. Religious Education
33. General Education

social and economic rights by the states; but the program of the church had to be modified to suit new conditions. How this was done is told in the biographies and church histories written by and about the early workers. Among these we find W. E. Hatcher's *John Jasper;* E. A. Randolph's *Life of John Jasper;* A. W. Wayman's *My Recollections of A. M. E. Ministers;* I. L. Butt's *History of African Methodism in Virginia;* W. J. Gaines's *African Methodism in the South;* William Hick's *History of Louisiana Negro Baptists;* L. G. Jordan's *History of Negro Baptists;* C. H. Phillip's *History of the Colored Methodist Episcopal Church;* Patrick H. Thompson's *History of Negro Baptists in Mississippi;* W. H. Sweet's "Negro Churches in the South; A Phase of Reconstruction" (*Methodist Review*, CIV, pp. 405-418); J. W. Hood's *One Hundred Years of the A. M. E. Zion Church;* Walter H. Brook's "Evolution of the Negro Baptist Church" (*Journal of Negro History*, VII, pp. 11-22); J. W. Cromwell's "First Negro Churches in the District of Columbia" (the same periodical, VII, pp. 64-106); J. C. Hartzell's "Methodism and the Negro in the United States" (the same periodical, VIII, pp. 301-315).

32. Religious education was serious instruction in the principles of religion. It was much more serious than the work of the Sunday Schools of our day where children are entertained rather than taught. The literature used was worked out primarily at first for adults who had never had the chance to study religion independently and at that time anxiously awaited the opportunity. Knowing that the freedmen attending those churches and Sunday Schools needed first to learn to read, their friends freely supplied them with teachers who taught them on Sunday the same fundamentals which were emphasized in the day schools during the week. Some Negroes who thereby learned to read and write never had any other opportunities for education. Religious instruction, then, was actual education as a preparation to understand principles of faith and to improve oneself further by self education. This story is told by a glance at some of the literature distributed among the Negro churches at that time—primers, readers, catechisms, brief stories of the patriarchs, sketches of the apostles, and copies of the life of Christ, simplified. Consult David H. Sims's "Religious Education in Negro Colleges and Universities" (*The Journal of Negro History*, V, pp. 166-207) and L. W. Kyles's "The Contribution of the Negro to the Religious Life of America" (the same periodical, XI, pp. 8-16).

33. While the Negro churches assumed this burden of religious education it added another of general education of the youth. In places where public schools for Negroes had not been provided or, if made legal, could not function for lack of funds, the Negro churches came to the rescue. Where the public schools were actually supported by public taxation the amount provided was not adequate for the building of school houses. The churches, therefore, were used to shelter schools. Most of the Negro schools during the Reconstruction period were taught in Negro churches for which no rent at all or

VI. THE RECONSTRUCTION OF THE NEGRO CHURCH
—Continued

34. FURTHER INDEPENDENCE
35. FURTHER EXPANSION

only a small pittance was paid. Compare the number of school houses for Negroes with the number of schools provided and note the small amount paid for rent of buildings, when no school buildings for Negroes had been constructed. Until about a generation ago there were still practically no rural school houses for Negroes in Louisiana, according to a statement made by Mr. W. H. Harris, the State Superintendent of Schools of Louisiana, speaking before an educational Conference in Washington, D. C., in 1917. The reason for the rural school building program of Julius Rosenwald was to lift the schools from the level of renting churches and dilapidated halls.

In the case of a short term of the Negro school, cut down to three or four months, the Negro churches sometimes raised funds by subscription to extend the term. In addition to this, moreover, these churches contributed annually to school funds raised to found new colleges for Negroes as well as supported those already established. In recent years the amount of money thus raised among Negroes for education has amounted to more than a million a year; including the amount for missions the sum today is between three and four million. See the *Census of Religious Bodies.* Consult R. E. Clement's "The Church School as a Factor in Negro Life" (*The Journal of Negro History,* XII, pp. 6-12).

34. For details consult C. H. Phillips's *History of the C. M. E. Church,* Miles Mark Fisher's *Short History of the Negro Baptists,* and L. G. Jordan's *History of the Negro Baptists.* The Negroes in the Episcopal, the Presbyterian, the Catholic, and other churches, with one exception, were too small in numbers to enforce their claims to such consideration.

35. The Negro churches soon realized that their duties were not restricted altogether to the needy in the United States. The churches as a whole, then, assumed the responsibility of extending their Christian ministrations to foreign lands. Sometimes, however, these efforts were unfortunate duplications. Some of these endeavors were projected on the basis that one converted to Methodism was nevertheless lost from the Baptist point of view, since he did not believe in immersion; and large numbers of Negroes felt it was their duty to maintain missionaries in Catholic countries to convert the people to Protestantism. The unusual emphasis placed at that time on what was called doctrinal preaching was the bolstering up of one's own denomination and the attacking of the other in all but pugnacious fashion. The frequent recurrence of this today will indicate the effect which such teaching must have had on those mentally undeveloped communicants. This is briefly discussed in the seventh chapter of the author's *Mis-Education of the Negro.*

In spite of this struggle, however, the churches have accomplished much in establishing successful stations in the West Indies, Central America, South America, and Africa. *The Census of Religious Bodies of 1926* indicated the extent of these efforts in that more than three million dollars was being spent for missions at that time by Negro churches. Because of the recent de-

VI. THE RECONSTRUCTION OF THE NEGRO CHURCH
—*Continued*
36. DIFFICULTIES IN PROSELYTING ABROAD

VII. CONSERVATIVE AND PROGRESSIVE FORCES
37. MISSIONARY WHITE TEACHERS FOR INTELLIGENT WORSHIP
38. SPIRITUAL LEADERSHIP DIVIDED BEFORE ILLITERATE MASSES

pression, however, this income has diminished, and some of the stations formerly maintained thereby have been abandoned.

36. One reason why the Negro churches have not expanded more than they have is that these organizations have not always found it easy to station their missionaries in parts of the world dominated by Europeans oppressing the blacks. Having subdued the natives in those parts, the controllers of these territories do not desire to have matters further complicated by the importation of strange teachers whose doctrines may stir up the blacks. Missionaries of the white race may easily reach those points, but only those Negroes who may be certified as harmless will be permitted to land on those shores. The religion taught most of the so-called heathen, then, is made to order just as it has been in the United States. The last chapter in the *History of the Negro Church* shows how this recently worked out. The files of the missionary boards of Negro churches yield ample information as to these operations with respect to Africans in particular. Unfortunately no printed materials have been produced from these documents.

37. The missionary white teachers brought to the South for the Negroes the same ideals of education and religion which had been developed in the North. The Freedmen in their illiterate condition could not always appreciate what they were trying to do and for that reason often misunderstood their efforts as unsympathetic and uncooperative. The whites did not realize that they were engaged in a task in which they would have to make haste slowly only. This may be easily traced by reading such records of that period as Mary Ames's *From a New England Woman's Diary in 1865*, E. W. Pearson's *Letters from Port Royal*, E. L. Pierce's *Freedmen of Port Royal, South Carolina*, Charles Ward's *Contrabands*, John Eaton's *Grant, Lincoln, and the Freedman*, E. Botume's *First Days among the Contrabands*, A. F. Beard's *The Crusade of Brotherhood*, and C. H. Corey's *A History of the Richmond Theological Seminary*.

38. This effort of the white teachers of the Negroes to emphasize the necessity for intelligent worship naturally divided the Negro spiritual leaders. All listened carefully to the exhortations to be up to date, but some were too diplomatic to introduce innovations which might alienate the people. Knowing that their success depended upon remaining with the masses, they decided so to do. When they appeared before their congregations the education which they had undergone did not always show immediate results.

VII. CONSERVATIVE AND PROGRESSIVE FORCES— *Continued*

39. METHODISTS THROUGH EPISCOPACY FOLLOW THE GOLDEN MEAN
40. BAPTIST CHURCHES DEVELOP TWO ORDERS, PROGRESSIVE AND CONSERVATIVE

For a discussion of this in case of the African Methodist Episcopal Church before the Civil War the two works of Bishop Daniel A. Payne herein cited are very useful. *The History of the A. M. E. Zion Church,* by Christopher Rush, adds further information on this point. See also John W. Cromwell's "First Negro Churches in the District of Columbia" (*The Journal of Negro History,* Vol. VII, pp. 64-106). Of the Baptists little is in print except in the case of local church history which does not teem with facts on this point. For this situation after the Civil War the sources are scant. Useful, however, are the observations in the twelfth chapter of the author's *History of the Negro Church* and in sixth and seventh chapters of the same author's *Mis-Education of the Negro.*

39. History of the various Methodist churches herein cited lead to the conclusion that the Methodists followed the golden mean. They so conducted their worship as to offer something stimulating to every one who attended their churches. The minister usually selected a certain text, stuck thereto until near the end of the exposition when he took occasion to say certain things in such a way as to arouse the emotions of the common people and to evoke expressions of their joy. While most of the music was of the higher order there was no serious objection in a good many of these churches to some one's starting a hymn which might mean a shout. Furthermore, when a pastor failed to please his audience some one more diplomatic could be easily sent to that charge by the bishop of the diocese. This enabled the congregation to hold together and permitted the churches to accomplish a great deal more than would have been possible in the case of divisions in local bodies.

40. In the case of the Baptists it worked out often to the contrary. Only by comparing the data in the United States Bureau of the Census reports dealing with the number of Negro Baptist churches for the decades from 1890 to 1930 can one see a disproportionate multiplication of the churches of this denomination in spite of the fact that one half of the Negro communicants of this country belong to the Baptist Church. This unnecessarily large number of churches has resulted from division in the ranks, factional struggles which have ended with the separation of certain elements in order to establish new churches. The data of the United States Bureau of Census, however, do not give the full story in these observations. These churches are of all gradations from those having the lowest form of worship like that of the store-front holy rollers to that of the most refined type of worship found in up-to-date white churches of this denomination. In the case of the Baptist, then, the problem was solved by separation so that there would be a larger number of churches from which to choose, and Baptists of whatever stamp in a large city would always find a church

VII. CONSERVATIVE AND PROGRESSIVE FORCES—
   Continued
   41. NEGROES IN WHITE CHURCHES FOLLOW THEIR
         LEADERS
   42. NEW FAITHS—THEIR OPPORTUNITY

VIII. SOCIAL AND ECONOMIC ASPECTS
   43. SECRET SOCIETIES OUT OF THE CHURCH

to suit their attitude. In the case of the people living in the rural districts such a development was impossible, and lack of progress has often been the most striking aspect which one witnesses in these parts.

41. In the case of the Negroes in the white churches their ministers could only take orders from their superiors of another race. Since the latter do not tolerate ignorance or superstition there was no other course to follow but to develop as intelligently as possible and conform the best they could to the standards observed among the whites. The following of such ministers, as the data of the United States Bureau of the Census report will show, even today, is not very large; and in some cases their support has been so meager as to call for help from without the community. Investigation shows, however, that this is not due to the fact that there was not a sufficient number of progressive Negroes in the communities where such churches have a poor following but that the Negroes prefer their own independent churches, some of which are just as progressive as those of the white denominations. This is discussed in the sixth chapter of Woodson's *Mis-Education of the Negro*. A briefer discussion of it is found in the seventh chapter of his *History of the Negro Church*.

42. In communities where the Negro churches moved forward too rapidly and became assimilated to the standards of the white churches more quickly than some of the illiterate members believe that this should have been done some of their followers were left behind to find other connections. They have therefore become the prey for new faiths which make the strictly emotional appeal to Negroes. Several other denominations have come to the Negroes from emotional whites. The *Religious Bodies of the United States of 1926* shows that there are thousands of Negroes who belong to these organizations. The distribution indicates, too, that they are not restricted to the South where it is often thought that the masses of the Negroes are not as well advanced as are those who have come into contact with the more intelligent people in the North. The following of this type is very large in the cities of the East, especially in the large industrial centers. This, of course, can be understood by the study of the census records themselves and by the reports of these various churches which indicate their following in the various sections.

43. All but out of the Negro churches developed a number of social and economic forces which must be understood to appreciate the institution in its new order. Among these was the secret society. Long the observers

VIII. SOCIAL AND ECONOMIC ASPECTS—*Continued*
44. RELIGIOUS LEADERS IN POLITICS
45. POLITICS IN THE CHURCH

only of the display made by whites in this sphere, Negroes in freedom resolved that they would delve deeply into these mysteries. A few orders, mainly the Masons and Odd Fellows, had been introduced among the free Negroes of the North prior to the Civil War; but the Negroes in the South had been prohibited by custom and law from indulging in such efforts. Picking up these as forbidden fruit immediately after emancipation, the Negroes established throughout their populous area all such lodges as existed at that time and in addition a number of others of their own invention. Most of these leaders were ministers, and they organized these fraternities from their churches.

The story of this as well as that of the excursion movement which was also worked out mainly through the churches is told in A. A. Taylor's *The Negro in the Reconstruction of Virginia* (pp. 64-65); William H. Benderson's *A Brief History of the Most Worshipful Grand Lodge of Free and Accepted Ancient York Masons* (Baltimore, 1920); A. E. Bush's *History of the Mosaic Templars* (Little Rock, 1924); C. H. Brooks' *The Official History and Manual of the Grand United Order of Odd Fellows* (Philadelphia, 1902); S. M. Brown's *The History of the Order of the Eastern Star* (Des Moines, Iowa, 1925); G. W. Crawford's *Prince Hall and His Followers* (New York, 1914); W. H. Gibson's *History of the United Brothers of Friendship* (Louisville, 1897); W. H. Grimshaw's *Official History of Free Masonry among Colored People* (New York, 1902); Lewis Hayden's *Caste Among Masons* (Boston, 1866); and W. W. Browne's *The True Reformers.*

44. The Negro preacher was a prominent figure in politics from the very beginning of the reconstruction. It was not that the Negro preacher desired to abandon or neglect his religious work but that often because he was the most intelligent man in the community the people set him up as a leader also in the other sphere. He responded as a matter of duty. This, of course, does not apply to some of the ministers who took up almost anything new for exploitation. The best evidence of this division of interests may be obtained by examining the sketches of prominent Negro politicians of that time to determine how many of them were ministers. W. J. Simmons' *Men of Mark* supplies many of these accounts. The matter is briefly treated in C. G. Woodson's *Negro Professional Man and the Community,* chapter iii. Some of such information may be obtained by glancing at the list of Negroes who served in the State Legislatures of the South during the Reconstruction, published in the *Journal of Negro History* (V, pp. 63-120, 235-248). Interviews with aged ministers now living will also throw light on this tendency among the clergy of those days.

45. The study of this period shows that the church in politics was not so harmful as politics in the church. When large numbers of political leaders were dethroned and they could find nothing else to do they took up preaching for a livelihood. Unfortunately, then, they brought into the church the

VIII. SOCIAL AND ECONOMIC ASPECTS—*Continued*

46. THE BUSINESS INTERESTS
47. AVENUE FOR PROFESSIONAL SERVICE

methods which they had used in politics. Baptist conventions and Methodist conferences thereafter assumed the aspect of political conventions. Instead of giving attention exclusively to such matters as education, evangelization, and missions, they devoted too much time to determining who should be the next chairman of a committee, president of a convention or bishop of a diocese. In this respect the Negroes proved that they were apt scholars of the whites, and with the new pressure from politics they added some other features of competition and strife which may have increased the numbers of communicants, but did not elevate the tone of the church. The respect which other people once had for the Negro ministry was not thereby increased, and certain Negroes themselves manifested some disgust.

The thought is presented in G. W. Alexander's *The Kind of Preacher and the Preaching* (Atlanta, 1924) ; J. E. Moorland's *The Demand and Supply of Increased Efficiency in the Negro Ministry* (Washington, 1909) ; E. T. Clark's *The Negro and His Religion* (Nashville, 1924) ; and A. A. Taylor's works on the Reconstruction cited above. See also R. A. Carter's "What the Negro Church has Done" (*The Journal of Negro History,* XI, pp. 1-7).

46. The church received also the summons to help the Negro economically. Among the first business men developed in the race after emancipation were ministers. Not because they were trained in business but because they usually had more education than others except the teachers; and, above all, the preachers had a large following which assured success when properly exploited.

This story is best told in Booker T. Washington's *The Negro in Business* and in Harmon, Lindsay and Woodson's *The Negro as a Business Man* (Washington, 1928). Details may be obtained by an examination of the sketches of distinguished Negroes already referred to herein. It has been said that W. W. Browne, a Methodist minister, in organizing and developing the True Reformers as a fraternal insurance enterprise started the Negro in this direction. Most of the Negro insurance organizations organized by Negroes since that time had promoters who had enjoyed some contact with this religious leader in a business sphere.

47. As in the case of business so was it sometimes in the professions. The community often needed a lawyer or a teacher and could do no better than to call upon the minister who had been trained a little along these lines. Sometimes, when possible, ministers seeing these needs took courses in the professions while serving churches. Some few found it apparently profitable to abandon the ministry altogether, but others rendered the additional service while laboring for the higher cause to which they remained loyal.

This story is briefly sketched in the twelfth chapter of the author's *History of the Negro Church* and it is given in more detail in his *The Negro Professional Man and the Community.* These aspects are noted here and there in B. E. Mays and Joseph W. Nicholson's *The Negro's Church* (New York, 1933).

VIII. SOCIAL AND ECONOMIC ASPECTS—*Continued*
48. NEGLECT OF SOCIAL WELFARE

IX. CRITICISM AND ANTAGONISM
49. OBJECTIONS TO UNSPIRITUAL LEADERSHIP
50. CRITICISM AS TO UNBUSINESS-LIKE METHODS

48. During these years, as indicated by the sources examined, the Negro Church paid little attention to social welfare. In this respect the Negro Church was no exception to the rule. Social uplift had not been taken up by other churches. The poverty-stricken and under-privileged Negroes, however, were much more in need of such welfare work than those better circumstanced. The failure of the churches in this case offered the outside agencies an opportunity. The chief movements of the sort were the Young Men's Christian Association and the Young Women's Christian Association. They shut their doors in the face of the Negroes, but so great was the need among the Negroes that they accepted the program of segregation in the name of God and gave these establishments financial support and community cooperation. For a few years certain Negro churches were lukewarm or failed to cooperate; but, finally convinced by the national agencies that segregation is God's will, the Negroes yielded. The account of this development is found in J. E. Moorland's "The Young Men's Christian Association among Negroes" (*The Journal of Negro History,* IX, pp. 127-138) and in George R. Arthur's *Life on the Negro Frontier* (New York, 1934).

49. The Negro church, made to render this sort of service to the community, naturally wandered somewhat from its standards of strictly orthodox religious work and, therefore, became an object of criticism by persons who wanted to see the church play a purely religious rôle in the life of the race. The most pronounced criticism of the time was that of the lack of spirituality among its leaders. In picking up almost everybody through the Reconstruction and subsequent periods the church net had caught and dragged into its fold the rather large number of politicians, business men, and professionals who were using the institution as a last resort. These criticisms, however, were seldom printed or proclaimed from the rostrum for the reason that it was unpopular to criticize the church. Those Negroes who had sufficient vision to see the undesirable drift of things often lacked the courage to take a position which meant economic loss in the community where such conditions obtained; for, in spite of all that was said about the Negro preacher, he was at that time and is today in most parts of the Negro area the most influential person in the community. To incur his displeasure or ill will was suicidal in most communities.

These conditions are hinted at by W. E. B. Du Bois in *The Negro Church,* (*Atlantic University Publications*); in the second chapter of C. G. Woodson's *History of the Negro Church;* in the seventh chapter of the same author's *Mis-Education of the Negro;* and in the fifth chapter of his *Negro Professional Man and the Community.*

50. Another general criticism of the Negro church is that of management. It is claimed that Negro ministers are too ambitious to build costly churches

IX. CRITICISM AND ANTAGONISM—*Continued*

51. COMPLAINTS OF CORRUPTION
52. FAILURE TO GRIP THE YOUTH

that the race may apparently have "a heaven on earth to go to heaven in." Before having the required funds or any considerable amount on hand they make with the contractors outside of their own circles agreements which are so drawn up that when carried out they work to the disadvantage of the Negro church, and in so doing to the disadvantage of the community. The church thereby becomes a drain on the net income of the people in requiring large sums of their earnings to discharge these unnecessarily high obligations. The same mistake, it is said, is made also by the unwise Negroes who take over churches abandoned by white congregations which because of race prejudice have moved away from Negro residents penetrating their communities. These churches have been in many cases sold at exorbitant prices with which these white congregations have built elaborate temples in their other communities. In the details of the church administration, too, it is observed that they have not kept proper accounts of funds received and paid out; and both pastors and church officials have been charged with stealing the funds of these institutions. These criticisms have tended to discredit their churches in these communities, and with certain elements of the race, throughout the United States.

This is discussed in the twelfth and thirteenth chapters of the author's *History of the Negro Church;* in the seventh chapter of his *Mis-Education of the Negro,* and in the fifth chapter of his *The Negro Professional Man and the Community.*

51. The chief argument given as to the corruption in the church is not so much that funds are sometimes stolen from its treasury; most fair-minded persons concede that such a thing may happen in almost any institution. It is also conceded that unbusinesslike agreements may be made and the institution may suffer thereby just as it happens sometimes among persons who are devoting their attention exclusively to business. The biting criticism is that in order to secure a commanding position in the church and to exploit the institution thereby in receiving a large salary and in purloining what monies may be passed through the hands of officers these functionaries actually buy these positions in the conventions and conferences where they are elected. It is known that campaigns for such offices are conducted in the same way as the political campaigns are, and the natural conclusion is that these unusual means thus employed can be justified only in the way that they would be justified in strictly political campaigns.

These matters are briefly discussed in the references given above. Certain details of such charges may be found in the proceedings of the National Baptist Convention for 1915, 1930, 1931, 1932, 1933, and the proceedings of the quadrennial conference of the A. M. E. Church in Cleveland in 1932. The local verbal histories of the same churches in practically all of the large cities of the United States teem with statements of this kind.

52. Another criticism of the Negro Church is its failure to grip the youth. Persons complain that the old people in these churches who still follow the pastors slavishly will soon die out, and then the institution will

IX. CRITICISM AND ANTAGONISM—*Continued*

53. MODERNISM AND FUNDAMENTALISM
54. INVESTMENT OF TIME AND MEANS WITHOUT ADEQUATE RETURNS

weaken for lack of accessions from the youth. It is noted, too, that the young men of today do not readily go into the ministry. The call of business which has increased among Negroes during recent years, and the increase in the income from teaching have tended to divert from the ministry numbers of young men who might otherwise become interested. The youth making an explanation as to why they do not manifest more interest in the church mention such as uninteresting sermons, rather long services, poor music, lack of interest in matters pertaining to young people, opposition to amusements for the youth, and too much effort to raise money.

The most recent discussion of this is found in the fifth chapter of the author's *Negro Professional Man and the Community*. In connection with this should be studied also B. E. Mays and J. W. Nicholson's *The Negro's Church*. Some help may be obtained also from W. A. Daniel's *The Education of Negro Ministers*. This last mentioned work, however, is chiefly concerned with other matters.

53. The troublesome struggle between the modernists and fundamentalists has not yet made much of a stir among religious Negroes. The investigations recently made by persons who have studied the Negro church show that there is not very much of this agitation among the Negroes who actually attend church. Such radical doctrines together with that of communism have gripped more tightly those Negroes who drifted away from the church years ago or who have never been church-going. There have been very few cases of churches forcing their pastors to resign because of their being radical or conservative. The questions stirring the body of Negro communicants are of a different kind. Among all Negro churches, of course, there are a few members who have such ideas and inclinations, but the number of those who have recently claimed connection with the church has not been sufficient to cause as much trouble as has been experienced in the white churches.

This thought has been discussed in the references already given in the author's *Negro Professional Man and the Community* and Mays Nicholson's *The Negro's Church*. The indications at present, however, according to the prominence given to editorials and articles spreading such alarm are that these inroads are imminent. A complete picture of the church in this respect at the present time, therefore, is difficult.

54. The most striking criticism leveled at the Negro church is that the time and means invested in the establishment and in the promotion of these churches do not bring adequate returns. In thus attacking the church these critics point out the fact that Negroes have invested in church property more than a billion dollars. In fact, the public property of Negroes in the United States is largely church property. The title to most of their school property is in white boards and agencies. Inasmuch as the Negroes have spent more for churches and for church work than for any other institution, the critics believe that the church should have given a better account

X. THE PRESENT STATE OF THE CHURCH

55. HEAVILY INDEBTED BY AN AMBITIOUS PROGRAM
56. UNABLE TO FINANCE EDUCATION ACCORDING TO LATEST STANDARDS
57. THE DIFFICULTY OF FACING INCREASING VICES

of its stewardship in producing better results than are evident. In this case the youth thus criticising the church have in mind the social level to which Negroes are depressed, the lack of economic resources, the want of industrial organization—the general failure of the Negro to become sufficient unto himself. The Negro church replies emphatically that the mission of the church is not to do those things but to save men's souls. If the church maintains this position and the Negro becomes modernized in his religious belief it will lose the only grip which it has in the community. This is a matter which is giving great concern to many of its functionaries.

55. The present state of the church is worth noting. However, the complete picture of it should be obtained from facts rather than from sentimental statements. Looking at the data presented by the *Religious Bodies* in 1926, published by the United States Bureau of the Census, we find that the most appalling thing with respect to the Negro church is the handicap of being in debt. These data are not up to date, of course, for during the lean years following 1926 the churches have not been able to reduce their obligations rapidly, and this particular aspect of their situation has become more and more appalling. The reason for these debts do not concern us particularly here inasmuch as that is discussed elsewhere. It is sufficient to note that the Negro churches of the country faced this generation with twenty-three and five tenths percent of them thus handicapped in 1926, and according to observations made since that time a much larger percentage should now be reported. In 1926 the debts of 3,961 Negro city churches aggregated $19,642,007 or the amount of $4,959 for each one in the country. Of the 4,923 rural churches the total debt was $2,536,574 or $515 for each church, whereas the figures for all churches both Negro and white were larger, $15,846 for the city, but in the case of the rural churches a smaller amount of $2,764. The greater ability of the white community to pay these debts than in the case of the unemployed impoverished Negro element makes the situation seem more alarming.

56. The two difficulties of the church are that because of these debts and its inability to discharge such obligations they are unable to finance their educational program according to the latest standards. By the recent raising of the standards requiring more commodious buildings, up-to-date equipment, and well-trained faculties, the problem of financial support has been made more difficult. The church schools have, therefore, lost ground in seeing their better trained teachers going to institutions which can pay them higher salaries and also in losing their brightest students to the adequately supported institutions where they believe they may be properly trained. Some of the church schools, therefore, are being merged while others with no chance for existence have been temporarily suspended or disestablished.

57. The Negro church is facing also the problem of increasing vices of recent years. The tendency of a large number of people of both races to

X. THE PRESENT STATE OF THE CHURCH—*Continued*

58. COMPETITION WITH OTHER SOCIAL CENTERS
59. DIFFICULTY OF JUSTIFYING "CHRISTIANITY"

engage in bootlegging, number-playing, and racketeering has weakened the church considerably. Large numbers of church-going people still attend church or maintain connection with it while searing their conscience with the thought that these vices are not necessarily evils inasmuch as one thereby earns a livelihood. Others in the churches observing the silence of the institution or the straddling position which some have undertaken to assume have tended to drift away or to lose their faith in the institution. There are preachers who take the position that number-playing, bootlegging, and racketeering are simple operations on a small scale which have been applied in big business from time immemorial. If this advanced business man is regarded as honest and upright what then can we hope for from the poor devil who does the same thing in a restricted quarter?

58. The Negro church also has the competition of the other social centers. Years ago when the Negroes were not theatre-going as they are today the church was used to a very great extent to supply this need. It also functioned in the same way as the municipal community center, Y. M. C. A., and Y. W. C. A. establishments. Theatres have been established in the Negro communities now as a business proposition financed by rich men who look upon it as the same sort of investment as they did when using theatres for the other elements of the population. The facilities are such now, then, that in almost every city and town the Negro may go to the movies every day during the week. This diverts a good many from the churches. The social welfare centers supported by philanthropists and also by funds from the community chest in the various cities offer the Negroes also much greater recreational and amusement facilities than do the churches and at the same time keep up the semblance of being Christian organizations. These have also attracted some portion of the church membership although the exercises of these social agencies may be so worked out as not to interfere with attendance at church services at eleven o'clock and eight in the evening on Sunday. What they have at these centers serves as a satisfactory substitute for what these people might enjoy at church.

59. Probably the greatest difficulty of the Negro church today is that of justifying Christianity as practiced by the whites. Race prejudice has increased tremendously during recent years not only in the United States but throughout the world. It has become so terrible that some Negroes often fear that they will soon be exterminated. When such Negroes think of the fact that the religion of the Negro in this country and in many portions of Africa is the oppressor's interpretation of Christianity he becomes indignant and fearlessly attacks it on the grounds of being sham and hypocrisy. The argument of the Negro to the effect that Christianity is all right, although the oppressor may not be living up to it, does not satisfy these critics for the reason that the Negro has no other interpretation of Christianity than that which he received from the American or European. The situation, therefore, has become more critical as the days go by and no one at the present time seems to be able to figure out what will be the attitude of the youth toward the church of tomorrow.

X. THE PRESENT STATE OF THE CHURCH—*Continued*
60. Inroads by Communism

60. These people thus assuming this attitude toward the church are the ones who are gradually turning toward Communism, and their minds are open to almost anything which the dissatisfied elements may desire to offer. The most striking thing in the appeal of the Negro radical element is that Communism offers everything which the church does not offer. Communism is intended to save humanity. If humanity can be saved the churches will be unnecessary. There are even some preachers who concede this as true, but nevertheless doubt that Communism will save humanity as it claims that it will.

CHAPTER XXIII

THE NEGRO AND AMERICAN LITERATURE

THE Negro in America has influenced its literature both as a subject treated and as a participant in the expression of the best thought of our mature minds. The chief participation of the race in this contribution, of course, was subsequent to the projection of the discussion of the race into our literary productions. It must be noted, however, that Americans of the pioneer period, both lord and serf, were not at once interested in things literary. That the oppressed Negro had a special reason to express himself, probably much more so than any other element in the country, may account for the development of his literary talent not long after other Americans more fortunately circumstanced began to give their best thought to the world.

In one respect the Negro made the first contribution to American literature. While the white American long continued with ideas brought from Europe and only slowly diverged therefrom, the African culture of the Negro merging here with that brought over from Europe produced something new. This new aspect of literary production first appeared in the folksong and in the oral expression of thought thereby evoked—Negro folklore, the myths and fables remembered from Africa. We are informed that there were such foreign influences as that of the Arabs and probably that of few others in African folklore prior to the importation of those natives as servants in the New World; but scientists have recently studied African and American folklore sufficiently to trace to native Africans a large number of folktales of which Europeans and Asiatics had never heard.

Of the Negro folksongs, the spirituals and the jubilee airs which came out of the life of the Negroes in America, we think as rather recent productions; and for lack of proper records it is almost impossible to figure out how early these developed. We learn from

392

the earliest explorers and colonists, however, that the Negroes were mirthful in spite of their status and that they sang their own songs in their own peculiar way. When others were noted as being cold and inexpressive in this respect the Negro was recorded as active and jubilant in thus giving vent to thought. Such music as the crude whites pioneering in this country retained or developed was influenced by the African music; and in later years when the Negroes were evangelized the hymns taught them had some influence on the Negro religious songs. In the very beginning no attempts were made in America to engraft the culture of Europe upon the imported African mind. The Indians and Negroes were generally neglected.

In like manner the native comedy of the African survived and finally became the plantation dance. The earliest Negroes not only danced freely, but with a strange crooning they continued to reproduce the African drama. With a peculiar action or movement while reciting some account of ancestors or family history dramatizing a hero or heroine they danced around in the center of those assembled while these things of the past were thus rehearsed. This comedy from Africa as such could not live for the reason that the imported Africans were brought from so many different parts that their traditions were not common, but the dance connected therewith remained and became known later as the plantation breakdown. The Negroes thereafter adopted slowly the method of literary expression developed or imported from Europe. In the West Indies and Latin America where larger numbers of Negroes were brought from the same tribe in Africa and settled in the New World with less dispersion their native customs tended to endure much longer than in the settlements along the North Atlantic.

Our first recorded American literature was chiefly of Puritan and Quaker traditions. Examining these early contributions, we find the appeal of the religious element with respect to the Negro, mainly interested in the salvation of the souls of Negroes and therefore championing the freedom of revelation as a divine right. These first echoes came in sermons and addresses from missionaries like Samuel Thomas, Thomas Bray, Hugh Neill, and clergymen like Benjamin Fawcett, John Elliot, Cotton Mather, and Jonathan Edwards; but Judge Samuel Sewall, viewing the untoward condition of the bondmen as unjustifiable also on moral grounds, attacked slavery in his "The Selling of Joseph." Quaker leaders like George Keith, John Hepburn, Ralph Sandiford, Benjamin Lay, John Woolman and Anthony Benezet gave the race and its problems still more space in their discourses. In a mainly frontier country where the loftier things of life gave way to the more practical concerns of the American pioneers, however, the literature thus developed did not impress many people of that day.

With the increase of literature of the American Revolution resulting from the social and political upheaval apparent after 1763, the thought of the Negro was carried to a larger audience. Unable to escape from the conviction that the freedom desired of Great Britain should mean on this side also the liberation of the bondmen, writers of this bold antislavery spirit did not fail to write accordingly. Thus expressing themselves were Enos Hitchcock, Jonathan Trumbull, Benjamin Franklin, Sara Wentworth Morton, Timothy Dwight, Thomas Paine, Philip Freneau, Joel Barlow, Patrick Henry, and Thomas Jefferson. John Murdock, Henry Sherbrune, Robert Mumford, and Thomas Brannagan joined the issue. Jupiter Hammon, John Marrant, and Britton Hammon, Negroes, published verse and prose in the style of their day. Phillis Wheatley, lamenting her own fate in Alexander Pope's style, appeared in the same picture. Benjamin Bannaker, the astronomer and mathematician, said not much about the race but advocated universal peace and democratic education in which all elements should be given equal opportunity. Essays on slavery by a "Free Negro" and by "Othello" in the *American Museum* in 1788 had similar import.

Others to follow these writers had reasons for more silence. First, the matter of practical government drove from men's minds the political theories as to freedom by which the American Revolution had been effected. Next the industrial revolution, ushered in by the multiplication of mechanical appliances, made cloth abundant and cheaper and increased the demand for slaves to supply the required cotton. Since a larger number of Americans in the East and South became commercially interested in the trading and exploiting of African slaves there were few to listen to the more outspoken writers of the earlier period. In the production of works reflecting the social order of that day the Negro came in for consideration, but not frequently as the dominant factor in many literary productions. From the beginning of the nineteenth century to the time of the ardent slavery agitation of the thirties the Negro was a negligible factor in the American mind. The diminishing number of anti-slavery writers of that time reached only a small audience.

Those few writers who did refer to the Negro during that period deserve more than passing notice. With the exception of Ralph W. Emerson's observations on slavery in 1822, however, most of these productions are not highly literary. Anne Royall attacked slavery fearlessly; and so did David Walker, a Boston Negro, who, in his *Appeal,* stirred the country in 1828 with a summons to all Negroes to rise up and kill off their masters to make themselves free. Lemuel Haynes, a Negro preacher to whites in New England, wrote on the current theological disputes without saying much about the Negro or his plight at that time. In unattractive style James Raymond of Maryland pointed out the social and economic evils of slavery in an essay in 1828. Mathew Carey made similar observations on the system about that time when much interested in African colonization. William Dunlap and James K. Paulding saw and expressed the same errors of our policy in *Letters from the South.* William Cullen Bryant published in 1826 a poem entitled "The African Chief." A play, "The Gladiator," by Robert Montgomery Bird showed further interest. Near the end of the period George M. Horton, a Negro poet of North Carolina, began the publication of his poems on slavery and liberty.

During the thirties William Lloyd Garrison as the editor of *The Liberator,* ushered in a new period of antislavery and proslavery literature. Most writings against slavery up to this time had not been generally noticed, but Garrison, one of the most forceful editors in the history of the United States, so influenced the minds of both factions that representative writers began to speak out. While the writings of this period are more inflammatory than formerly, they are nevertheless more literary, for the talented of both factions reached the conclusion that the opposing arguments had to be intelligently answered. As long as the agitation was a mild moral attack no one needed to pay any particular attention thereto, but when a newspaper, circulating as an organ of abolitionists who would instantly emancipate the slaves so rapidly gained ground, men of all elements had to express themselves on one side or the other.

To these writings the proslavery interests replied not only with laws proscribing the circulation of such literature but with treatments to the contrary. Letters were addressed to inquirers in order to give the South-side view of the much-questioned institution. The life on the plantation was described in all its favorable aspects. The ideals of the master class were brilliantly presented. The Negroes were portrayed as indulged children under the care of benevolent masters. Everybody in the South was reported as being content. Why disturb peace and happiness? "Let well enough alone."

In the same period belongs the literature resulting from making the slave question an issue in politics and the subject of debate in Congress. There appeared the speeches of John Quincy Adams on the freedom of the press, and the right of petition. Next we hear the addresses of John P. Hale, the first United States Senator to take up the question in Congress after it was tabled by a vote on antislavery petitions presented in 1789. Then followed the speeches of the fearless Joshua R. Gidding and Charles Sumner on the cases involving the status of slavery on the high seas.

The proslavery argument in literature was a dominant factor in the slave states as was the antislavery argument in literature elsewhere. While Garrison and his adherents had with them Ralph W. Emerson, William Jay, Samuel J. May, William E. Channing, Richard Hildreth, John G. Whittier, Theodore Parker, Sophia Little, Daniel S. Whitney, William Cullen Bryant, and James Russell Lowell, the cause of abolition was combated by William Harper, Thomas R. Dew, Robert D. Rhett, A. H. Smith, Nehemiah Adams, John Van Evrie, and J. D. B. DeBow. The proslavery literature was just as voluminous and forceful as the antislavery, but it did not have the merit of the productions of more experienced men of the East.

A still more inflammatory period was reached about the middle of the nineteenth century. The abolition element not only redoubled its efforts and further stirred up the country in playing up the mistakes resulting from the passage and enforcement of the Fugitive Slave Law of 1850, but divided among themselves, leaving one branch led by Garrison with a less militant and smaller number following Arthur and Lewis Tappan, rich antislavery merchants of New York. The condition of the slave poetically described already in the works of Bryant, Lowell, and Whittier was dramatized by Mrs. Harriet Beecher Stowe in her *Uncle Tom's Cabin*. This work was so extensively circulated that it had to be translated into twenty-three foreign languages to be read and dramatized abroad. It moved the country to repentance and helped to doom slavery.

Other writers took their cue from this successful effort. William Wells Brown, a Negro lecturer and historian, did something of the same sort in his *Clotel or The President's Daughter*. Two of his plays, the most widely read of which was *The Escape, or A Leap for Freedom,* soon followed. Frances Ellen Watkins Harper, the next Negro woman poet after Phillis Wheatley, appeared also with her productions, the most significant one of which was "Bury Me in a Free Land." Harriet H. Bigelow tried her hand with *The Curse Entailed*. Hattie M'Kechan did likewise with *Liberty or Death;* and so did Elizabeth D. Livermore, in her *Zoe or the Quadroon's Triumph,* J. T. Trowbridge in his play called *Neighbor Jackwood,* and Dion Boucicault in another play, the *Octoroon.* Frederick Douglass, the outstanding Negro antislavery editor and lecturer, had joined these with his *Narrative* and *My Bondage and Freedom.* Hinton Rowan Helper's *Impending Crisis,* appeared a little later to show by economic argument that slavery prevented the rise of industrialism in the South and that it was prejudicial to the interests of the poor whites. This work proved to be almost as successful in stirring up opposition to the institution of slavery as was *Uncle Tom's Cabin.*

Numerous anti-slavery orators took the platform in the North and some of them elected to Congress opened the debate there. Among these were Benjamin F. Wade, Salmon P. Chase, W. H. Seward, and Charles Sumner. In opposition to the stand taken by the friends of freedom should be noted also the proslavery statesmen who spoke to the same question. These were the successors to Calhoun and Hayne—Henry A. Wise, Howell Cobb, Alexander H. Stephens, Reverdy C. Johnson, and Jefferson Davis. While the utterances of the last mentioned lack historical truth in that they spoke for a lost cause, these orators taken together from both sections produced the most stylistic oratorical literature hitherto developed in America. The anti-slavery speeches of the 1850 crisis had the advantage of having all the essentials of great orations. They were delivered not only in a great crisis on a great occasion but also expressed a great truth which time has justified.

The Civil War itself made further contributions especially in the field of oratory, in the speeches of men who spoke for liberty and for the ideal of a united nation. The debates of Abraham Lincoln and Stephen A. Douglas set the stage for the closing of the drama. The additional speeches of statesmen already referred to require comment and especially the war speeches of Abraham Lincoln. Other efforts purely literary are hardly noticed now. The moral issue is raised again in Stephen C. Bulfinch's *Honor or The Slave Dealer's Daughter,* M. B. Smith's *My Uncle's Family or Ten Months at the South,* and Epes Sargent's *Peculiar: A Tale of the Great Transition.* Socially the question was taken up by the author of *Down in Tennessee.* Louise M. Alcott joined the ranks in 1863 with "M. L." the brand on the hero of her story. William Cullen Bryant became more active. Whittier increased in his fire. Walt Whitman projected the Negro into his war poems. H. W. Longfellow had been writing, but he was never sufficiently fired to be effective. Oliver Wendell Holmes, who thought that the Negro was better off subordinated to the white man, nevertheless expressed in one of his poems the desire that the freedman might go forth in his new status and be a man.

After the Civil War the chief contributions embodying the thought of the Negro appeared in books of travel by Americans like Edward King, Sidney Andrews, Whitelaw Reid, and J. T. Trowbridge; and in those of distinguished foreigners like David McCrae, Robert Somers, and Sir George Campbell. American and foreign writers, too, began to produce novels idealizing the Negro and giving him a setting in world brotherhood. In some of these the Negro is again made a saint as he was sometimes in the abolition literature. There were others in the political sphere making speeches and working out reports which presented the situation in the other extreme. Subsequently there followed the purely propaganda productions to undermine the sentiment favorable to the

Negro and to deprive him of the rights recently granted. In this sphere belong the speeches of Henry Grady, the novels of Thomas Dixon, the more literary productions of Thomas Nelson Page, and the social, economic and political essays of Thomas Pearce Bailey and Edgar J. Murphy. The historical productions on slavery and reconstruction written by men of the South trained in modern historiography in Northern universities had the same purpose. They prostituted science to propaganda.

After the Civil War, Negro writers no longer had for their inspiration the motive of lamenting their condition. The works of Frederick Douglass, Bishop Daniel A. Payne, and William Wells Brown continued the same. Charles L. Reason, Ellen Watkins Harper, and James Madison Bell added poems of freedom. Other Negro writers had mainly the eulogistic and exulting oratory of the reconstruction period for their contribution. Those like Robert Brown Elliott, eulogizing the distinguished white statesmen who had befriended the race or upholding the rights of freedmen, became also a popular form of literary expression. In the South at the same time the white writers were publishing their lamentations on the Negro-carpet-bagger rule, but they were generally too biased and vitriolic to be considered literary. This sort of literature did not diminish even after the Negroes and their cooperating constituents had been overthrown and the Southern States had been turned over to the former ruling class. The production of this very literature, however, had its desired effect. It tended to discourage the Negro and silence him in the literary field; the other part of the country was then giving an ear to the other side of the story.

The Negro, however, finally reached the real literary period in his development. The thinking element of the race began to manifest a sense of humor. The Negro learned to know himself, to appreciate his strength and to laugh at his misdirecting leadership from without. He finally saw also how utterly the white authors had failed in portraying the Negro by regarding him from the outside. The new Negro writer would paint the picture from within. A large number of Negroes, of course, never appreciated this point of view and refused to read the works of writers thus influenced.

The first of these writers was James Edwin Campbell of Middleport, Ohio. He was educated in the public schools of that place and later served as the first president of the West Virginia Institute. Campbell found a great theme in his own environment and undertook to depict Negro life in dialect. Carrying this still further, Dunbar penetrated the innermost life of the Negro and unfolded to the world what he saw. Unlike most persons who had written about the Negro, Dunbar did not approach this task with a problem to solve. He succeeded, then, in expressing lyrically the life of these lowly people, and the world acclaimed him as a poet to be ranked with Whittier and Burns.

Hundreds of other Negro writers have tried verse, but with the race problem ever before them they have alienated the public without securing a hearing. Later writers have undertaken Negro dialect, but for their bias and failure to interpret the Negro's philosophy of life they have never attained any such distinction as that of Dunbar. Joel Chandler Harris with his "Brer Rabbit" stories, however, made himself immortal by doing well what the Negro did not consider worthwhile.

Later the treatment of the Negro in literature assumed the form of polemic writing in which members of both races have participated. Most of the white writers of this class, however, have also missed the mark in playing up unduly in propaganda fashion the weaknesses of the Negro to leave him before the world branded as an undesirable or misfit in the social order. Negroes undertaking to counteract the influence of such literature have written much matter presenting facts to the contrary, but they also have shown too much racial bias and little literary merit. About a score of writers of verse of the people of color of Louisiana, protesting against the Jim Crow system imposed upon them after the Civil War, belong to this class. Charles Waddell Chesnutt, dominated somewhat with the same purposes, reached a higher level with his short stories and novels.

Viewing the Negro more dispassionately, a number of white writers have almost reached the high level of treating the life of the Negro in novels as did Dunbar in poetry, but there are still striking reasons for not thus classifying *Old Man Adam*, *Birthright*, *Scarlet Sister Mary*, *Black April*, *Green Thursday*, *Mamba's Daughters*, *Porgy*, and *Nigger Heaven*. Negro writers, apparently similarly motivated have undertaken the same sort of productions as Jean Toomer's *Cane,* Rudolph Fisher's *Walls of Jericho,* Zora Neale Hurston's *Jonah's Gourd Vine,* and Langston Hughes's *Not Without Laughter.* The novels of Jessie R. Fauset, *There is Confusion, Plum Bun* and *Chinaberry Tree* are of a different order in portraying the virtues of the talented tenth, but they are not great interpretations. The novels of Walter White, *Fire in the Flint, Flight,* and his other work, *Rope and Fagot,* have their chief claim in the propaganda which they have served in advancing the cause of the Negro. *Black No More,* a satire, by George Schuyler did not impress the public favorably.

Up to the present, then, it may be said that in literature the chief production of the Negro has been in poetry. James Weldon Johnson, Langston Hughes, Countee Cullen and Sterling A. Brown are recognized as poets almost universally; and Georgia Douglass Johnson, Angelina W. Grimké, Joseph Seaman Cotter, long active, the race cannot be discounted on the score of poetry. Speakers like R. C. Ransom, William Pickens, Booker T. Washington, and W. Monroe Trotter have made a favorable impression with their oratory. W. E. B. Du Bois has achieved fame as an essayist. Kelly Miller has developed into a successful pamphleteer and columnist. W. S. Braithwaite has established a claim of his own as a literary critic. But these have not brought the race as much literary prestige as the productions of the poets.

The recent interest in the Negro as an object of literary effort has been expressed also by a different type of white writer of the present day. These are scandal-mongers, and debunkers who feel that the North with its ideals of freedom and justice has been idealized in exaggerated fashion; and now the tale of the South must be told anew. Following the historians of the South who have written for the same purpose, these gentlemen have painted that section as a sort of paradise with slavery as a desirable institution and the Reconstruction as an affliction. The masters were ideal landlords of a chivalrous age, the poor whites were supernumeraries, and the slaves were the pampered pets who were ever happy in bondage. Abolitionists, then, were liars and meddlers with an ideal state, and legislators trying to elevate the Negro to citizenship were visionary and doctrinaire. Such are writers like Joseph Hergesheimer, Allen Tate, Robert Penn Warren, Stark Young, and Claude Bowers.*

I. FIRST LITERARY EXPRESSION TO 1700

    1. IN THE ACCOUNTS OF AFRICAN EXPLORATION OF AMERICA
    2. IN THE NARRATIVES OF EUROPEAN EXPLORERS

1. Of the earliest explorations of Negroes in America there are no written or printed accounts produced by the Negroes themselves. There are, however, persons who say that the Negroes touched the shores of America before the Europeans discovered it. Several well-known scholars believe that more than a thousand years ago there existed on the West Coast of Africa a highly civilized seafaring nation which sent its ships to American shores. Peter Martyr, a learned historian and an acquaintance of Columbus, mentions a region, not two days' journey from Quarequa's territory in the Darien district of South America, where Balboa found a race of black men. He thought they had come from Africa and had been shipwrecked on this coast.

This claim that the African first discovered America has been held by men of distinction of our times. Justin Winsor believed it for the reason that "skulls found in the caves in the Bahamas seemed to be very like those in the early burial places of the Canaries," which are really a part of Africa. A report of the Bureau of Ethnology finds support for this claim in the early American pottery with faces very much like Africans. Leo Wiener, a professor of Harvard University, has written several volumes to prove this early coming of the Africans by showing how they made an impression on the life and customs of the Indians. He sees evidences of it in the resemblance of the Indian's religion to the fetishism of Africa, and in such borrowed African words as *buckra, canoe,* and *tobacco.*

See the *American Journal of Anthropology* (XX, 233), Justin Winsor's *Narrative and Critical History of America* (X, 333), and Leo Wiener's *Africa and the Discovery of America* (Philadelphia, 1919).

2. The accounts of explorers are numerous, but only a few deal with the

---

* For an introductory treatment of these facts there is no single volume which deals critically with the Negro in American literature. Benjamin Brawley's inadequate *Negro in Literature and Art* merely skims the surface uncritically with mainly biographical sketches of a few well known writers and artists. Vernon Loggins' widely known *Negro Author* has been referred to as such a history, but the work is neither a history of the Negro in American literature nor a critical bibliography. At best the book is a check list of works in this field with very little discrimination as to the relative value of the productions mentioned or as to their historical significance. Loggins' work, however, is the only production of the sort now available, and, used together with L. D. Turner's *Anti-Slavery Sentiment in American Literature,* it renders possible an introductory treatment of this course. Of value also in this connection is Benjamin Brawley's *Early Negro Writers* (Chapel Hill, 1935). The study of the advanced phases of the course is possible only by following the footnotes and bibliographical suggestions herein given.

I. FIRST LITERARY EXPRESSION TO 1700—*Continued*

3. NEGRO FOLKLORE
4. FOLK MUSIC OF THE NEGRO

African himself. These narratives are primarily concerned with the business aspects of the sea-rovers and their sea-roving, e.g., Peter Martyr's *De Orbe Novo.* These records were not intended to portray the Negro, but so many of the race were brought over from Europe by the early explorers that references to the customs and feats of these sable companions appear in practically all these narratives. These explorers were Spanish rather than English. The latter had little contact with the Africans prior to the discovery of America.

In the *Historia General* by Oviedo, and the *Historia General* by Herrera such accounts in brief are given. A good index to the study of these early accounts of exploration is Professor J. F. Rippy's "The Negro with the Spanish Explorers" (*The Journal of Negro History,* VI, pp. 183-189).

3. Of the first Negro folklore in America we have collected very little, although it is frequently referred to in the earliest narratives of America. For the study of Negro folklore, then, we are dependent upon Europeans and Americans of our day whose chief aim has been to try to prove that Africans learned these tales from Asiatics or Europeans. They have failed to find adequate evidence for such a position. Dr. Elsie Clews Parsons, who inclines too much toward the theory of foreign influence in her "Provenience of Certain Negro Folk Tales" (*Folklore,* XXX, No. 3) admits in a letter to the author that the imported Negroes brought to America folklore which was peculiarly African.

These aspects of our literary history may be further studied in numerous contributions to the *Journal of American Folklore* and in *Folklore* edited in London. In Joel Chandler Harris's *Uncle Remus,* in A. M. H. Christensen's *Afro-American Folklore,* in C. C. Jones's *Negro Myths from the Georgia Coast,* and in many other such treatises this literary contribution may be studied from the American point of view. Along with these should be considered the works mentioned in the bibliographical note on the literature of Africa in Chapter XVI of this work. Consult also Kenneth B. M. Crooks' "Forty Jamaican Proverbs: Interpretations and Inferences" (*The Journal of Negro History,* XVIII, pp. 132-143).

4. Of the folkmusic, the words and history of which have enriched our literature, we know practically no more than in the case of other such manifestations. These songs, however, are noted in the earliest records which show the African contribution to America. The best accounts come from the West Indies where Negroes from the same tribe first appeared in large numbers in the New World. The slave population along the Atlantic did not reach large proportions until the latter part of the eighteenth century, and there were not often in any place sufficient Negroes from the same place to preserve their traditions. Referring to this situation in Jamaica prior to 1740 Admiral Vernon said:

"They have a great many other remarkable customs, which you may see very curiously described in the INTRODUCTION to Sir Hans Sloane's *Natural History of Jamaica.* Sunday Afternoon the Generality of them dance or wrestle, Men and Women promiscuously together. They have two musical

I. FIRST LITERARY EXPRESSION TO 1700—*Continued*
5. History—Drama—Dance

instruments, like Kettle-Drums, for each Company of Dancers, with which they make a very barbarous Melody. They have other musical instruments, as a Bangil, not much unlike our Lute in anything but the Musick; the Rookaw, which is Two Sticks jagged; and a Jenkgoving, which is a way of clapping their Hands on the Mouth of Two Jars: These are all played together, accompanied with voices, which make a very terrible kind of harmony."—Admiral Vernon's *History of Jamaica*, p. 310 (London, 1740).

Later another observer in referring to this same West Indian situation said:

"Their songs are commonly impromptu, and there are among them individuals who resemble the improvisatore, or extempore bards of Italy; but I cannot say much for their poetry. Their tunes in general are characteristic of their national manners; those of the Eboes being soft and languishing; of the Koromantyns heroic and martial. At the same time, there is observable, in most of them, a predominant melancholy, which to a man of feeling, is sometimes very affecting."—Bryan Edwards's *History of the West Indies*, IV, p. 293.

5. In this folklore and folkmusic, as already noted, there were also history, drama and poetry. The observers of that day generally failed to see these things. Only now and then one of these narrators penetrated the life of the Negro sufficiently to understand these manifestations. The Negroes when in sufficiently large numbers brought from Africa the traditions of the professional story-tellers, the *griots,* who confusing fiction with fact rehearsed daily the tales of their beginning and the heroes and heroines of their people. These narratives were given in a peculiar crooning, with the music of drums and banjos and with dancing of various characters, sometimes in imitation of war scenes, sometimes portraying events in time of peace. Having observed these exhibitions, the same author wrote:

"In general, they prefer a loud and long continued noise to the finest harmony, and frequently consume the whole night in beating on a board with a stick. This is in fact one of their chief musical instruments; besides which, they have the Banja or Merriwang, the Dundo, and the Goombay; all of African origin. The first is an imperfect kind of violoncello; except that it is played on by the finger like the guitar; producing a dismal monotony of four notes. The Dundo is precisely a tabor; and the Goombay is a rustic drum; being formed of the trunk of a hollow tree, one end of which is covered with a sheep's skin. From such instruments nothing like a regular tune can be expected, nor is it attempted.

"At their merry meetings, and midnight festivals, they are not without ballads of another kind, adapted to such occasions; and here they give full scope to a talent for ridicule and derision which is exercised not only against each other, but also not infrequently, at the expense of their owner or employer; but most part of their songs at these places are fraught with obscene ribaldry, and accompanied with dances in the highest degree licentious and wanton."—Bryan Edwards's *History of the West Indies*, IV, p. 292-293.

Bryan Edwards regards as licentious the African dance which we today

II. TRENDS DURING THE COLONIAL PERIOD
6. Appeals in Behalf of Negroes
7. Sermons Preached to Negroes

find interesting. Edwards was from cold-blooded and Puritanic England which prohibited the dance and popular music as sinful indulgences. The Americans with the same attitude crushed much of this art in the Negro in trying to Europeanize him.

Certain works written by the Negroes themselves show this African culture enduring in the New World. Among these should be mentioned the *Letters* of Ignatius Sancho. One of the most informing of productions of this sort is *Thoughts and Sentiments on the Evil and Wicked Traffic of Slavery and Commerce of the Human Species,* by Ottabah Cugoana, published in 1787. Of like import is *The Interesting Narrative of the Life of Olaudah Equiano, or Gustavus Vassa, The African,* published in 1789. In this treatise the author undertook to relate his childhood, capture, enslavement, and sufferings. It is then the portraiture of the African mind in its reaction to things European and American. The experiences of a slave of Michael Denton in Maryland (*The African Repository,* XIII, 204) of Lahmen Kebby from Futa (*Methodist Review,* XLVI, 77-90) and of Omar Ibn Said from the same area (*The American Historical Review,* XXX, 787-795), support this conclusion.

6. These appeals in behalf of the Negroes, like most productions of that day concerned with the underprivileged and the oppressed, belonged to our early religious literature. While not very literary these utterances reflected the best thought of the time. The well-known entreaties of this sort were those of the Spanish Jesuit, Alfonso Sandoval, of the two Capuchin monks imprisoned on this account in Havana, and that of the Germantown Quakers in 1688. Other appeals more forceful and elaborated followed from time to time and are noted in the records of the religious organizations.

The accounts of such endeavors kept in the Vatican Archives must be consulted to make available such literature with respect to Catholic missionaries among the Negroes in America. The *Digest of the Records of the Society for the Propagation of the Gospel in Foreign Parts,* by C. F. Pascoe, gives only the substance of these appeals from the Anglican missionaries. The documents themselves in the office in London must be sought. Of such appeals from the Methodists, Moravians, Presbyterians, and Baptists we have little of the earliest period because of the lack of toleration and religious freedom which impeded their circulation. Although not the productions of a churchman, *The Selling of Joseph* (1701) and the *Athenian Oracle* (1705) by Judge Samuel Sewall well represent the attitude of the Puritan of Massachusetts toward the Negro at that time.

7. Among these sermons one finds John Woolman's *Some Considerations on the Keeping of Negroes Recommended to the Professors of Christianity of every Denomination* (Philadelphia, 1754); Benjamin Fawcett's *A Compassionate Address to the Christian Negroes in Virginia and other British Colonists in North America* (1755); Cotton Mather's *Resolutions on the Instruction of Negroes;* and Bishop William Meade's *Sermons of the Rev. Thomas Bacon* (Winchester, Virginia, 1805).

It should be noted that sermons found in the following, although delivered

II. TRENDS DURING THE COLONIAL PERIOD—*Continued*

8. ACCOUNTS OF TRAVELERS OBSERVING NEGROES IN THE
       NEW WORLD
9. THE JESUIT RELATIONS
10. EARLY ACCOUNTS OF PLANTATION LIFE

in England, belong to the same class of literature circulated on this side of the Atlantic: Bishop Beilby Porteus, *Works* (London 1816); Bishop Thomas Secker, *Works* (London, 1811); the same author, *A Sermon Preached before the Incorporated Society for the Propagation of the Gospel in Foreign Parts* (London, 1741); Bishop Gibson, *Pastoral Letter* in Dalcho's *Historical Account of the Protestant Episcopal Church;* Bishop William Warburton, *A Sermon Preached before the Incorporated Society for the Propagation of the Gospel in Foreign Parts* (London, 1766).

8. Few fulsome accounts of European visitors to America during the colonial period prior to 1760 are available. An exception is the work of Andrew Burnaby, an Englishman, in 1743. Few Americans outside of the slaveholding area left any vivid accounts of what they saw along the Atlantic, for prior to the rise of industrialism the Negro's condition was about the same as that of the poor whites and did not always interest those from the parts where Negroes were not generally found. In the records of the Quakers, the Catholic missionaries, and those sent out by the Society for the Propagation of the Gospel in Foreign Parts such impressions are available and should be studied. A typical account is the Rev. James Mac-Sparran's *Diary;* and another of this sort is that of the Reverend Mr. Davies who toiled among the Negroes in the Middle Colonies and Virginia during the second quarter of the Eighteenth Century. This in abridged form is found in C. G. Woodson's *Education of the Negro Prior to 1861*, pp. 353-357. Several such accounts appear in John Woolman's *Journal, passim;* and in Anthony Benezet's *Observations on the Enslaving, Importing and Purchasing of Negroes* (Philadelphia, 1760). The journals of Wesley, Asbury, and Coke, although chiefly concerned with religion and recorded during a later period, give impressions of conditions which had long obtained among the Negroes in America.

9. In this connection should be read some of the most interesting accounts embodied in the *Jesuit Relations*, especially those of Paul Le Jenne, Le Petit, and François Philibert Watrum (V, 62-63; LXVII, 259, 343; LXVIII, 201; LXIX, 31; LXX, 245). In the Saint Louis Cathedral Archives in New Orleans and in the Municipal Archives of that city are other interesting and informing unpublished accounts of the observations and early experiences of the Catholic clergy with the Negroes in the New World. These productions are not only as literary as others of that day but still more so because of the thorough training of many of these Catholic missionaries. These accounts reflect the thought taken of the Negro of that time and at the same time connect it with considerations shown other elements of the population.

10. Of the early accounts of plantation life we have little in print. In

III. LITERATURE OF THE REVOLUTIONARY PERIOD, 1760-1800

11. THE NEW THOUGHT UNDER THE NEW BRITISH EMPIRE—JONATHAN BOUCHER AND BENJAMIN RUSH

12. IN THE LITERATURE OF TOLERATION AND RELIGIOUS FREEDOM

local records in cities like Savannah and Charleston such accounts of a later period have been preserved. These records so far as they are unconscious give a living picture of conditions at that time and must be taken into account in any study of the literature of America. They are just as important to the understanding of the past of America as the Domesday Book is to that of England. The aim here, however, is not merely to see the picture of the Negro at that time but to understand the Negro in his relation to other forces in the life of the colonies.

While we have not the earliest accounts we get a glimpse of the situation through the diaries of George Washington. See Fitzpatrick's *Washington's Diaries;* W. H. Mazyck's *George Washington and the Negro,* chapter ii. Read also *A New Description of Virginia* (London, 1649) ; *Journal and Letters of Eliza Lucas* (Wormesloe, Georgia, 1850).

11. Almost any of the great patriots of the American Revolution who happened to be active throughout the Seven Years' War and saw the British Empire "reconstructed" under Grenville and broken up under Townsend and North had a new thought with respect to the social order and at times thought seriously of the enslaved Negroes. This was true of James Otis, Samuel Adams, Patrick Henry, George Washington, Benjamin Franklin, and Thomas Jefferson, although, with the exception of the last two mentioned, they did not enlarge upon this topic as they did upon matters which more vitally concerned them. The new thought was forcefully expressed by Jonathan Boucher in a discourse delivered in 1763 as an address on "American Education." A renewed appeal in behalf of the Negro is recorded in his *A View of the Causes and Consequences of the American Revolution.* The book gives this discourse among twelve others delivered in North America between the years 1763 and 1775. Comparing what Boucher said with what others were uttering on this point at that time, the student is forced to the conclusion that he represented the most advanced thought concerning the Negro after the world upheaval of the Seven Years' War. In connection herewith should be studied also Dr. Benjamin Rush's *An Address to Inhabitants of the British Settlements in America on Slave Keeping,* delivered not long after the utterances of Jonathan Boucher but not published until much later.

12. The position of these two distinguished Americans was not in advance of that of the popular evangelical sects seeking toleration and religious freedom; but speaking as a member of the Anglican Church, Boucher had more force in official circles than those who as dissenters were considered all but outlaws and therefore handicapped in their efforts for the

III. LITERATURE OF THE REVOLUTIONARY PERIOD,
1760-1800—*Continued*

13. In the Political Philosophy of the American Revolution

14. The Addresses of Abolition Societies

uplift of the Negroes. Benjamin Rush, who was not a clergyman but distinguished in medicine, also had influence. When the despised sects obtained both toleration and religious freedom they set forth in their sermons and addresses to the laity similar thought with respect to freedom and opportunity for the oppressed. The declaration of the Methodist Quadrennial Conference against slavery in 1784 and that of a similar national body of the Baptists in 1789 should be noted.

Among these utterances may be cited also Samuel Webster's *A Sermon Preached before the Honorable Council* and his *Earnest Address to My Countrymen on Slavery;* James Swan's *A Dissuasion to Great Britain and the Colonies;* Samuel Hopkins's *Dialogue Concerning Slavery;* Dr. Alexander McLeod's *Negro Slavery* (1802) ; David Rice's *Speech in the Constitutional Convention of Kentucky* (Philadelphia, 1792, and London, 1793). While Rice's speech was delivered after the American Revolution he showed what had been working in the minds of the mountaineers for two generations.

13. In addition to infrequent mention of the Negro in their communications during the period from 1760 to 1775 it is necessary to study in connection therewith the more mature thought of the fathers of the American Revolution when they were actually engaged in trying to maintain the independence of the nation. Read the Declaration of Independence, as it was first drafted. Did Jefferson, who therein followed John Locke's "Second Essay on Government," have the Negro in mind? Did Patrick Henry think of the Negro in his speeches on liberty and freedom? To what extent did the Negro figure in the *Debates* of the Federal Convention of 1787 which framed the Constitution of the United States? Did the writers in the *Federalist* in advocating the adoption of the constitution have the Negro in mind? What was George Washington's best thought with respect to the Negro? The will of Kosciusko and the plans of Lafayette for the emancipation of the slaves in the United States should be borne in mind in studying their lives and letters. Thomas Paine's "African Slavery in America" (in his *Works* edited by Conway, I, 6-7) should be examined.

14. The annual addresses of the American Convention of Abolition Societies with representatives from various parts of the country except the extreme South are just as well written and much more so than many works of that day now regarded as standard. These reformers represented the best thought in America not merely because they were fighting slavery but because they espoused this cause along with such others as the opposition to land monopoly, the rights of the laboring man, prison reform, temperance, and woman's rights. At this time were active our "distinguished Americans" who were beginning to direct the destinies of the nation toward things material. These materialists expressed little thought with respect to humanity. The reformers, however, kept these fires burning in the temple,

III. LITERATURE OF THE REVOLUTIONARY PERIOD, 1760-1800—*Continued*

15. The Self-Expression of Jupiter Hammon, Phillis Wheatley, and Benjamin Bannaker

IV. NATIONAL DEVELOPMENT, 1795-1830

16. The Negro a Negligible Factor

dedicated eternally to equality and justice. Their thoughts reflect the best in America at that time.

15. Well should one note here not merely that John Marrant, Britton Hammon, Jupiter Hammon, Phillis Wheatley and Benjamin Bannaker produced creditable poetry and prose but that as Negroes observing the reaction after the American Revolution they were impelled to express themselves on liberty and freedom. The essays on Freedom by "Othello" and by a "Free Negro" in 1788 (American Museum V, 415, 511 and *The Journal of Negro History*, I, pp. 49-65) require study in this connection.

What the white contemporaries of these writers thought of them should not be ignored. Jefferson's *Works*, Washington Edition, V, p. 429, and W. H. Mazyck's *George Washington and the Negro* will be useful toward this end. The important works of Jupiter Hammon, Phillis Wheatley, and Benjamin Bannaker are given in the INTRODUCTION of C. G. Woodson's *Mind of the Negro as Reflected in Letters Written during the Crisis, 1800-1860*. Consult "The Learned Negro," *The Journal of Negro History*, XIV, pp. 238-242. Mrs. Sara W. Morton's novel, *The Power of Sympathy*, her poem, "Beacon Hill," John Murdock's comedy, *The Triumph of Love*, Henry Sherburne's novel, *The Oriental Philanthropist*, and Royall Tyler's *Narrative*, *The Algerine Captive*, should be noted. Hugh H. Breckinridge's novel, *Modern Chivalry* (1792) and Theodore Dwight's *An Oration Delivered in 1794 before The Connecticut Society for the Promotion of Freedom and the Relief of Persons Unlawfully Held in Bondage*, should be carefully studied together with the essay by Thomas Paine. They were the most significant of this period.

16. The Negro, a negligible factor in the thought of American politicians after the industrial revolution, is nevertheless a factor in the reform literature. American writers of the liberal tendencies of Thomas Paine and Thomas Jefferson diminished, but some thought had to be given occasionally to the rapidly increasing element of the population. In the milder tone in which Thomas Jefferson began also to express himself Thomas Brannagan revived Anthony Benezet's idea of settling the Negroes on the Western lands in producing in 1804 *A Preliminary Essay on the oppression of the Exiled Sons of Africa, Consisting of Animadversions on the Impolicy and Barbarity of the Deleterious Commerce and Subsequent Slavery of the Human species*. *Serious Remonstrances* followed this. In 1805 Brannagan published two epics entitled *Avenia; or a Tragical Poem* and *The Penitential Tyrant; or Slave Trader Reformed*. These works should be given special attention.

IV. NATIONAL DEVELOPMENT, 1795-1830—*Continued*

17. The Literature of the Independent Negro
    Movement
18. The Negro Mildly Treated in New Produc-
    tions
19. Literature of the Colonizationists

17. The literature produced by Negroes after the time of Jupiter Hammon and Phillis Wheatley and Benjamin Bannaker was mainly religious
and less significant from the literary point of view. Independent Negro
preachers like George Liele, Andrew Bryan, James Varick, Harry Hosier,
John Stewart, and John Gloucester were delivering sermons to the people
who failed to preserve them. From Richard Allen, the founder of the
African Methodist Episcopal Church, and Absalom Jones, the founder of
the African Protestant Episcopal Church in Philadelphia, and from William
Miller, a Methodist minister of New York, more letters and sermons have
been preserved. Lemuel Haynes, a successful preacher to whites in New
England, plunged into the theological discussion of the first quarter of the
nineteenth century and left us several sermons among which we find *Ye
Shall not Surely Die*. The proslavery régime as a result of the rise of
cotton was dominant in this country by 1825. Negroes were pushed lower
down in the social order, and those who had a thought dared not express it.
David Walker in faraway Boston did produce in 1828 his *Appeal* in which
he called upon the slaves to rise against their masters. Anne Royall, a
white woman, had shown the same attitude in mild form.

18. The writers of the white race daring to be liberal were few, and
they had the tone of the moral and religious. William Dunlap appeared
with a mild play, *Africans,* in 1811. James K. Paulding attracted attention
with *Letters from the South* in 1816; and William Cullen Bryant with a
poem *The African Chief* in 1825. The most outstanding was Ralph W.
Emerson who produced the *Vision of Slavery* in 1822. Matthew Carey and
James Raymond advanced economic arguments without much literary em-
bellishment. *The Free Press* at Newburyport, *The National Philanthropist*
of Boston, *The Journal of the Times* at Bennington, the *Genius of Universal
Emancipation,* edited by Benjamin Lundy, and the *Emancipator,* by Elihu
Embree, should be noted for their essays and editorials.

19. The literature of colonization is so voluminous that the best productions have been lost in the mass of works, most of which had little weight
when produced, and they have not a literary finish. A brief history of the
organization is given in H. N. Sherwood's "The Formation of the American
Colonization Society" (*Journal of Negro History,* II, 209-228). The best
case for colonization was probably made by J. H. B. Latrobe in his *Liberia*
and by A. Alexander in his *History of Colonization on the Western Continent of Africa*. The best written attack on colonization was doubtless William Jay's *An Inquiry into the Character and Tendencies of the American
Colonization and Anti-Slavery Societies* (New York, 1835). W. L. Garrison's *Thoughts on African Colonization* is well written. C. H. Stebbins'
work of the same theme is not so carefully worked out. The cause of de-

IV. NATIONAL DEVELOPMENT, 1795-1830—*Continued*
20. In Indian Legends and Romances

V. THE MILITANT ABOLITION PERIOD, 1830-1852
21. Abolition Literature

portation is forcefully set forth and ably defended by whites and blacks in some of the contributions appearing in the *African Repository,* the official organ of the American Colonization Society. Some letters on colonization have been published in C. G. Woodson's *Mind of the Negro as Reflected in Letters.* In this connection should be examined the letters of Frances Wright who corresponded with James Madison and others with respect to plans for establishing a self-supporting Negro settlement in Tennessee. Consult James Madison's *Works.*

20. The relations of Negroes and Indians have never been treated *in extenso* in literature. The Negroes who have ventured to live among them have been, as a rule, fugitives using this as a means of escape. Men of this type usually lack literary ability; and the Indians themselves have not risen to higher levels in this sphere. Some of these Negro fugitives, like Negro Abraham, however, became interpreters and spokesmen for the Indians.

The general facts are recorded without much literary finish in John T. Sprague's *The Florida War,* Samuel G. Drake's *Aboriginal Races,* and Joshua R. Giddings's *Exiles of Florida.* Consult C. G. Woodson's *Negro in Our History,* the chapter on "Self-Assertion," and Benjamin Brawley's *Social History of the American Negro,* the chapter on the Indian and the Negro. The United States Office of Indian Affairs in Washington, D. C., contains valuable unpublished materials which may be examined by persons in and near this city. Useful also are two articles by Kenneth W. Porter, "Relations between Negroes and Indians within the Present Limits of the United States" (*Journal of Negro History,* XXVII, 241-286) and "Notes Supplementary to 'Relations between Negroes and Indians'" (the same magazine, XVIII, 281-321).

21. During the militant abolition period of the agitation for instant emancipation the chief contributor to abolition lterature was William Lloyd Garrison through the *Liberator.* He had most of the stage until about 1850 when he had alienated the other wing of these reformers led by the rich Tappans of New York City, who were no match for Garrison on the rostrum or through the press. Garrison was one of the most forceful editors developed in modern times.

In the field of such journalism should be noted also the *National Anti-Slavery Standard,* of New York, and *The Philanthropist,* of Cincinnati. *The North Star* edited by Frederick Douglass at Rochester, later changed to *Frederick Douglass's Paper,* must also be taken into account. There were about twenty Negro abolition papers started between 1830 and 1860 but they did not endure a long while, and their files have not been preserved. One finds today only a few copies of *Freedom's Journal, The Colored American,* and the *Anglo-African,* a magazine which appeared in New York only one

V. THE MILITANT ABOLITION PERIOD, 1830-1852—
Continued

22. PRO-SLAVERY LITERATURE
23. ADDRESSES, SERMONS, LETTERS AND EDITORIALS OF
NEGROES THEMSELVES

year, 1859. For polished eloquence wielded in behalf of the slave Wendell Phillips, one of the greatest orators of his day should be carefully studied. Edmund Quincy and William Burleigh's orations also ranked high; and so did the antislavery addresses of Lucretia Mott, William Ellery Channing, and Susan B. Anthony.

Among the strictly literary productions of the time should be noted the anti-slavery novel, *The Slave or Memoirs of Archy Moore* (1836), by Richard Hildreth; the play, *The Branded Hand* (1845), by Mrs. Sophia L. Little; *Warren: A Tragedy* (1850), by Daniel S. Whitney. There were appearing, too, such antislavery productions as Whittier's "Massachusetts to Virginia" in 1843; and James Russell Lowell's antislavery poems. The speeches of John Quincy Adams in behalf of free speech and the antislavery addresses of John P. Hale in the United States Senate belong to this same body of literature.

22. That one may not have a lopsided picture of the literary efforts of the time it is necessary not only to understand the institution of slavery itself but to know the arguments by which slavery was justified. The social aspects as a key to proper interpretation of this point of view are given in Frances L. Hunter's "Slave Society on the Southern Plantation" in *The Journal of Negro History* (VII, 1-10). Both arguments are summarized in Caroline L. Shank's "The Biblical Anti-Slavery Argument of the Decade 1830-1840" in the same magazine (XVI, pp. 132-157). Calhoun's papers in the six volumes of his *Works* should be consulted for one or more of his letters and addresses on slavery. He was the greatest exponent of this idea. The essays appearing in J. D. B. De Bow's *Industrial Resources of the United States,* especially those of Chancellor Harper and Judge J. B. O'Neall should be noted. These views are summarized in the *Pro-Slavery Argument* which gives the opinions long held in the slaveholding section. The most literary of the productions in this collection are J. H. Hammond's "Letters on Slavery," William Harper's "Memoir on Slavery," Thornton Stringfellow's "A Brief Examination of Scripture Testimony on the Institution of Slavery," and Thomas R. Dew's article.

23. Negroes like Nathaniel Paul, Charles Lenox Remond, Theodore Wright, Peter Williams, Charles Bennett Ray, Samuel Cornish, James McCune Smith, J. W. C. Pennington, Samuel R. Ward, Alexander Crummell, Henry Highland Garnett, David Ruggles and Frederick Douglass left on record addresses which require examination to complete the picture of the thought of that day.

Most of these writers published their works, and excerpts therefrom may be found in L. D. Turner's *Anti-Slavery Sentiment in American Literature.* Few of the Negro orators published their discourses, but extracts from the best of their productions may be found in C. G. Woodson's *Negro Orators and their Orations.*

V. THE MILITANT ABOLITION PERIOD, 1830-1852—
Continued

24. SLAVERY IN POLITICS
25. PLANTATION LITERATURE
26. WORKS OF TRAVELERS
27. EARLY HISTORIANS

24. Slavery in politics stimulated literary production. Men of greater influence near the middle of the nineteenth century began to speak in state legislatures and in Congress on slavery. The addresses of men like Clay, Calhoun, and Webster of the passing regime should be noted. New statesmen of different points of view were delivering themselves of a new thought which later received a hearing but Clay, Webster, and Calhoun reflected the thought of the majority of the American people up to the time that they passed from the stage. To ignore this particular sort and style of oratory would be unwise. So many Americans are wont to do this because of the subsequent rise to a higher level of thought. The debates on the compromise of 1850, especially Calhoun's death-bed utterance, Clay's last word, and Webster's Seventh of March speech should be thoroughly studied. The address delivered by W. H. Seward about this time indicates a new point of view. The nation was beginning to have a new vision.

25. The plantation situation is well presented by Fanny Kemble in her *Residence on a Georgia Plantation.* Mrs. Smedes' *Memorial of a Southern Plantation* is also readable. A. E. Grimke's *Letters to Catherine E. Beecher* likewise illuminates the picture. *Letters of Theodore Dwight Weld, Angelina Grimké Weld, and Sara Grimké, 1822-1844,* edited by Gilbert H. Barnes and Dwight L. Dumond (New York, 1934), sheds additional light. J. C. Hurd's *Law of Freedom and Bondage;* Stroud's *Slave Code,* and Goodell's *Slave Code* give the legal aspects without any literary pretension; but they may be used to check up on the works which are colored by feeling.

26. There were produced many books of travel in the South at that time, but the most readable are those of Frederick Law Olmsted: namely, *A Journey in the Seaboard Slave States; Texas, The Black Country,* and *The Cotton Kingdom.* Harriet Martineau's *Society in America,* De Tocqueville's *Democracy in America,* J. S. Buckingham's *Travels in the United States,* and Fredrika Bremer's *Homes in the New World* should also be studied.

27. The historians like Sparks, Hildreth, and Redpath, gave more space to the Negro than the minor historians, but, as a rule, they mentioned the Negro only incidentally in their general histories. Long before the Civil War William C. Nell had produced a creditable work known as the *Colored Patriots of the American Revolution.* Following Nell appeared Martin R. Delany with his *Condition of the Colored People in the United States* (1852). William Wells Brown four years later brought out *The Black Man,* followed after the Civil War by *The Rising Son.* To such histories came as supplements the autobiographies of Frederick Douglass (1845) and (1854), the *Autobiography of Samuel Ringgold Ward* (1852), J. W. Loguen's *As a Slave and a Free Man;* Christopher Rush's *History of the African*

VI. THE STORMY PERIOD, 1852-1865
28. THE DEBATES IN CONGRESS
29. *Uncle Tom's Cabin*

Methodist Episcopal Zion Church; and later Daniel A. Payne's *Recollections of the Last Seventy Years* and his *History of the African Methodist Episcopal Church.*

28. The Compromise of 1850 intended to silence David Wilmot with his proviso and to "repeal" the Missouri Compromise lighted a flame which the Kansas-Nebraska adjustment of squatter sovereignty origin failed to extinguish. Franklin Pierce, the most popular man in the country when elected in 1852, had been shunted aside politically by 1856; and things changed so rapidly during that decade that James Buchanan was equally unpopular by 1860. The crisis had resulted in sectional conflict which had actually begun in Kansas. During these years, then, all statesmen had to reverse their position of silence on the slavery question and speak out whether they would or not. The speeches of these leaders of the North and South of that day, therefore, represented the highest level reached in American oratory. Joshua R. Giddings, Benjamin F. Wade, Salmon P. Chase, and Charles Sumner had to be answered by Reverdy C. Johnson, Henry A. Wise, Robert Tombs, Alexander H. Stephens and Jefferson Davis. The "Irrepressible Conflict" and the "Higher Law" of William H. Seward lodged in the minds of the friends of freedom; and the Lincoln-Douglas Debate as a forensic effort as well as a political contribution cleared the atmosphere for the drama of civil strife.

29. This outburst of expression had been made possible by movements outside of Congress. In the west free labor was outstripping slave labor, and the justice of freedom had been sentimentally portrayed by Harriet Beecher Stowe in *Uncle Tom's Cabin.* In spite of all that has been said to detract therefrom this was the greatest purpose work after Jean Jacques Rousseau's *Contrat Social.* It not only made Americans feel ashamed of their pet institution of slavery but, translated into a score of modern languages, the book made the civilized world feel ashamed of the United States. Lincoln referred to it as the book that caused the war. *Dred* and *The Minister's Wooing* by Mrs. Stowe should be noted along with the *Key to Uncle Tom's Cabin.*

Detractors of Mrs. Stowe in trying to make out against her a case of exaggeration say that no single slave ever experienced all of those hardships, but no one of the least literary capacity or appreciation would argue for discrediting the book on such grounds. The author did not label the work a history of slavery in the United States. It is a fact, however, that numerous slaves had experiences which in the main parallel those of Uncle Tom. Josiah Henson in *Father Henson's Own Story* claims that he was the prototype of Uncle Tom; W. B. Hartgrove presents the same claim in condensed form in "The Story of Josiah Henson" (*The Journal of Negro History,* I, pp. 1-21). George Woodson, the uncle of Carter G. Woodson, experienced practically the same as a slave. He was beaten, bled, washed down in salt and water, and sold to the South from Fluvanna County, Virginia; and relatives and friends never heard of him again.

VI. THE STORMY PERIOD, 1852-1865—*Continued*

    30. HELPER's *Impending Crisis*

    31. THE LITERATURE ON JOHN BROWN

    32. THE POETS OF THE CIVIL WAR

        (a) NORTHERN

        (b) SOUTHERN

Wishing to strengthen the case made by Mrs. Stowe appeared William Wells Brown publishing in 1853 the anti-slavery novel, *Clotel or the President's Daughter* and *The Escape or A Leap for Freedom* (1858) ; Sara J. Hale, *Northward or Life North and South* (1852) ; Elizabeth A. Roe, *Aunt Leanna* (1855) ; Harriet H. Bigelow, *The Curse Entailed* (1857) ; Elizabeth D. Livermore, *Zoe or the Quadroon's Triumph* (1855) ; J. Trowbridge, *Neighborhood Jackwood* (1857) ; Dion Boucicault, *The Octoroon,* a play based upon Mayme Reid's *Quadroon* (1856) ; Frank J. Webb, *The Garies and Their Friends* (1857) ; Mattie Griffith, *Madge Vertner,* John Jolliffe, *Chattanooga; J. C. Swayze, *Ossawattomie Brown or the Insurrection at Harpers Ferry.*

30. Helper's *Impending Crisis,* though not so well written as *Uncle Tom's Cabin,* was another attack on slavery but from the economic rather than from the sentimental point of view. This book was not widely read among the common people, and it had no extensive circulation abroad. It was read, however, by the leaders in the political life of the nation, and they were thereby stirred to the very depths. The ardent abolitionists had been attacked on the ground that they were a sentimental group whom the thinking people would never follow; but Helper, a North Carolinian, drawing upon the argument of those who had contended that slavery was an economic evil which would forever keep the South inferior to the North had successfully dramatized this idea. The thinking people in the South knew that this was true; but, like the man stricken with an incurable malady, that section did not care for this prophecy of its untimely death. If a Southern white man thought this about slavery what could the public expect from the advocates of free soil, free speech and free men, who as a national political party tried as early as 1840 to elect one of their opinion to the presidency of the United States?

31. The poets like Lowell, Whittier, and Bryant became more active. Longfellow began to mention slavery more frequently. Walt Whitman developed an attitude toward freedom and the Union which dominated his writings throughout the Civil War. Charles L. Reason, a Negro, had long written on freedom; and now appeared two other Negro poets, J. M. Whitfield with *America and Other Poems* and Frances Ellen Watkins Harper with her poem *Bury Me in a Free Land.* George M. Horton, a Negro in North Carolina, gained even there recognition for his verses some of which advocated freedom. James Madison Bell, of Ohio, figured also in this same circle.

32. While the Civil War was raging a number of Northern and Southern writers entered upon literary efforts under the impulse of sectional feeling, but their hurried productions with the exception of a story by Louisa M.

VI. THE STORMY PERIOD, 1852-1865—*Continued*

33. The Speeches and Papers of Lincoln, Stevens and Sumner

VII. THE RECONSTRUCTION PERIOD

34. Exulting in Freedom—Novels, and Poems

Alcott did not meet the test of literature. Novels of this order were such as Stephen C. Bullfinch's *Honor or The Slave-Dealer's Daughter;* M. B. Smith's *My Uncle's Family or Ten Months at the South;* Epes Sargent's *Peculiar: A Tale of the Great Transition.* There were such poets too as Stedman, H. H. Brownell, Henry Baker, Herman Melville, Bayard Taylor, Thomas Buchanan Read, Weir Mitchell, John Burns, and Bret Harte; but these were more concerned with the war for the Union than with freedom.

The Southern writers of the Civil War period showed a preference for poetry. Prominent among these were W. G. Simms, A. B. Meek, Theodore O'Hara, John R. Thompson, Henry Timrod, W. G. McCabe, and Paul Hamilton Haynes. Not many of the productions of these are classified today as literary treasures.

33. A special study should be made of Lincoln's two inaugural addresses, and his Gettysburg address. Some of his papers, most of which show literary excellence, may be likewise examined. Of the other statesmen who figured in the closing of the Civil War the most highly literary was Charles Sumner. He was a well educated man and prepared his addresses carefully. Thaddeus Stevens was more of a man of action than an orator. Stevens all but forced Lincoln to issue the Emancipation Proclamation; and the "Old Commoner" from Pennsylvania fathered Congressional Reconstruction.

34. Immediately after the Civil War, the South, prostrated with devastation and fired with race hate because of its Lost Cause and the ascendancy of the freedman in politics, was too bitter for literary effort. Writers like B. H. Hill, R. B. Wilson, Carlyle McKinley, J. B. Tabb, and R. B. Wilson, manifested sufficient ability to show possibilities, but Sidney Lanier was the only real poet discovered in that circle. The race problem-solving political oratory of L. Q. C. Lamar, J. B. Gordon and Henry Grady became popular and left on their people a more lasting impression than the poetry of that time.

The Negroes, on the other hand, no longer handicapped by the slavery of their bodies, did not supply a large audience for the poems of oppression and sonnets to freedom produced in former years by George M. Horton, Charles L. Reason, Frances Ellen Watkins Harper, and James Madison Bell. The freedmen also took to oratory. The exultation over their new status and due tribute to their benefactors who had wrought the change became the first order of the day. In politics, too, the freedmen had to be told eloquently how to rally around the standard of the political party which had championed their cause. Frederick Douglass, whose oratory during the Civil War served to stimulate the Negroes to fight on the Union side for freedom, easily found a place as a political leader during the Reconstruction. He was followed by scores of others, some of whom served in Congress—mainly

VII. THE RECONSTRUCTION PERIOD—*Continued*
35. Books Vindicating the Lost Cause
36. Observations on the South After the War
37. The Negro Preacher Enlightened

Hiram Revels, B. K. Bruce, John R. Lynch, Joseph H. Rainey, John M. Langston and Robert Brown Elliott. Their most interesting speeches have been made available in C. G. Woodson's *Negro Orators and Their Orations*. Their discourses in Congress are given in full in the *Congressional Globe*.

35. Lacking the training and experience in the production of books, the Negroes of this period left little to interest the public. The Southern whites in justification of the Lost Cause, however, presented their case to the world in numerous productions eulogistic and laudatory of the fallen leaders of their section. The most widely read of these were E. A. Pollard's *Lost Cause*, Alexander H. Stephen's *Constitutional View of the Late War between the States*, and Jefferson Davis's *Rise and Fall of the Confederate Government*. These works were forerunners of productions of Southern men trained in modern historiography in the large universities, especially Johns Hopkins and Columbia, a generation after reconstruction—men who used science to justify terrorism and bloodshed required to debase the Negroes to the status of peons and serfs. J. G. de Roulhac Hamilton and W. L. Fleming were representative of this school. Literary works of this type appearing at a later date are summarized by Sterling A. Brown in his "Unhistoric History" in *The Journal of Negro History*, XV, pp. 134-162.

36. Books showing the conditions in the South at that time were sometimes readable. We may not say much for U. S. Grant's or Carl Schurz's hurried reports on conditions immediately following the Civil War, but Whitelaw Reid's *The South After the War*, Sidney Andrew's *The South Since the War*, and Edward King's *The Great South* may be read with interest and profit. These compare favorably with such books of travel by foreigners as Robert Somers's *The Southern States since the War*, Sir George Campbell's *White and Black in the South*, and David Macrae's *The Americans at Home*.

37. The Negro preacher next became the literary figure. The Negro church was under the control of the race and supplied the only forum available for the depressed freedmen. The Negro newspaper, moreover, had not developed at that time; and the church had to be used as a means for communicating the best thought of the Negro community. There were few libraries, and most Negroes of the first years after emancipation were not sufficiently literate to use them, if they had been accessible. Negroes as a large majority, then, learned to depend upon their pastors for information. Notices regarding everything pertaining to the Negro were read in the churches every Sunday or short speeches concerning such matters were made; and the pastors took occasion to work into their sermons everything social, economic or political which they believed the Negroes should know. Of such sermons we have only a few recorded, but this must be kept in mind in order to understand the intellectual development of the Negro in the United States.

VII. THE RECONSTRUCTION PERIOD—*Continued*
38. THE NEGRO TEACHER AS A SPOKESMAN

Some of these sermons may be noted as Alexander Crummell's *The Greatness of Christ and Other Sermons* (New York, 1882) ; J. W. Hood's *The Negro in the Christian Pulpit* (Raleigh, N. C., 1884) ; T. G. Steward's *Genesis Reread* (Philadelphia, 1885) ; J. H. Caldwell's *Negroes and the Methodist Episcopal Church* (1886). In a much later period came R. A. Carter's *Feeding Among the Lilies;* S. T. Jones's *Sermons and Addresses;* F. J. Grimké's *Sermons;* G. W. Alexander's *The Kind of Preacher and Preaching for Negroes;* George C. Clement's *Boards of Life's Building;* M. C. B. Mason's *Solving the Problem;* R. C. Ransom's *The Spirit of Freedom and Justice.*

38. In the course of time the Negro teacher or educator became the spokesman or orator of the race. Of their productions we have only a few in print, but one should note Richard T. Greener's *The Missionary Work of Education among the Colored People of the South* (Baltimore, 1877) ; his *The Academic Life* (Washington, D. C., 1879) ; his *The Educational and Industrial Progress of the Colored People* (Philadelphia, 1881) ; W. S. Scarborough's *Our Civil Status,* and his "The Birds of Aristophanes," in the publications of the American Philological Association of 1884. It may not be out of place to note that Scarborough produced in 1883 *First Lessons in Greek.*

Because of a required silence on the rights of the Negro some teachers could not always be considered actual leaders, but they gained ascendancy by being better trained than their competitors. Although restricting themselves to things mainly pedagogic they could deal with so many practical things that they too became interpreters of the will of the oppressor with respect to the oppressed and served as means to convey to their watchful protectors the "program best adapted" to their people. These men, doing more writing than most others of the Negro race, produced a literature which must be considered here in the effort to understand the literary forces at work at that time.

Consult W. E. B. Du Bois's "The Burden of Negro Schooling" (*Independent,* LIII, 1667, July 18, 1901) ; his "Of the Training of Black Men" (*Atlantic Monthly,* XC, 289-97, September, 1902) ; and his "Possibilities of the Negro" (*Book. M.* II, 3, 1903) ; Isaac Fisher's "School Problems of the Southern Negro" (*Fisk University News,* October, 1922) ; Kelly Miller's "Education of the City Negro" (*Southern Workman,* XXXII, 10, January, 1903) ; "Education of the Negro in the North" (*Educational Review,* LXII, 323, October, 1921) ; "Forty Years of Negro Education" (*Educational Review,* XXXVI, 484, December, 1909) ; "National Responsibility for the Education of the Negro" (*Educational Review,* LVIII, 31, June, 1919;) "The Negro and Education" (*Forum,* XXX, 693, February, 1901) ; J. C. Price's *Education and the Race Problem* (*National Education Association Proceedings,* 1890, pp. 267-85) ; W. T. B. Williams's "Financial Contributions to Negro Schools in Virginia" (*Southern Workman,* XXXV, 550, October, 1904) ; "The South's Changing Attitude toward Negro Education" (*Southern Workman,* LIV, 398-400, September, 1925) ; M. N. Work's "Educational

VII. THE RECONSTRUCTION PERIOD—*Continued*
39. THE NEGRO AND THE AMERICAN PRESS

VIII. ACTUAL LITERARY CONTRIBUTIONS
40. THE IDEALIST IN POETRY

Problems" (*Southern Workman,* XXXIX, 520, October, 1910); R. R. Wright's *Self-help in Negro Education* (Cheyney, Pa., 1901); Booker T. Washington's "Education and Suffrage of Negroes" (*Education,* XIX, 49-50, September, 1898); "Education of the Southern Negro" (*National Education Association Proceedings,* 1904, pp. 128-34); "Education Will Solve the Race Problem" (*North American Review* CLXXI, 221-32, August, 1900); "Negro Education and the Nation" (*National Educational Association Proceedings,* 1908, 87-93); "Value of Educating the Negro" (*Southern Workman* XXXIII, 558, October, 1904); *Education of the Negro* (Albany, 1900).

39. That the Negro press was in a struggle throughout the period is evident. The Negro of that day clamored mainly for a hearing through the regular press. While it was advisable to publish worth while materials in the Negro newspapers and magazines, one did not thereby reach many Negroes and very few others. Negroes occasionally, then, served as regular contributors on the editorial staffs of the metropolitan dailies. Such were T. T. Fortune, J. Edward Bruce, and later Lester Walton. By and by, however, when the readers of these dailies increased among those antagonistic to the Negroes such correspondents were discontinued and seldom could any Negro have an article published in one of these journals. What these Negro staff writers produced during that day, however, is a part of American literature. The newspapers of that time and these journals only contain these productions. These articles have never been reproduced for further use.

40. After emerging from the chaos of the reconstruction period and becoming adjusted to serfdom and peonage to which the Negroes were thereafter reduced, a larger number of Negro writers began to focus their attention upon their own life. The first of these writers, like most of their predecessors, however, were bitter because of the loss of what they thought they had gained through "emancipation." They failed to find a large audience for the reasons that their lamentations were not comforting to the Negroes themselves, the people of the North were not interested, and the South laughed at the effort. There was not very much poetry, but a number of books did appear. Among these productions were *The Life and Times of Frederick Douglass,* William Wells Brown's *Rising Son,* Frances Ellen Watkins Harper's *Iola Leroy,* and *Moses,* a story of the Nile. The most outstanding of the new negro poets, in the opinion of Benjamin Brawley was A. A. Whitman, an imitator of Sir Walter Scott. Then there were some books like *Black and White,* by T. Thomas Fortune, in 1884, and *A Voice from the South* by Anna Julia Cooper in 1892. Further effort was made to preserve the traditions of the Negro in the publication of J. T. Wilson's *Black Phalanx,* in William J. S. Simmons's *Men of Mark,* in George W. Williams's *Negro Troops in the War of the Rebellion* and his *History of the Negro Race,* and in I. Garland Penn's *Afro-American Press.*

VIII. ACTUAL LITERARY CONTRIBUTIONS—*Continued*

41. THE POETS OF OBJECTIVITY—CAMPBELL AND DUNBAR

42. THE NEGRO ON THE STAGE

41. The first case of the Negro poet to regard his race with objectivity was James Edwin Campbell, a native of Middleport, Ohio. He became a writer of verse in dialect after having served as the principal of the West Virginia Institute. Campbell died in Chicago before he became widely known. Then came a master in this sphere—Paul Laurence Dunbar. He made his way by struggles during the nineties and finally attained fame about the end of the century. He was not the first Negro to sense the philosophy expressed in the brogue of the Negro, but he was the first to popularize it. Like Joel Chandler Harris, famous with his stories of Uncle Remus, Dunbar also chose to write much in dialect. In this case he was following the advice of Hamlet to the players, "Suit the word to the action and the action to the word." Dunbar differed from his predecessors who had undertaken to write polished poetry based on the life of the Negro. He approached the Negro with an open mind; he studied the Negro's setting and learned his attitude toward life. Forgetting the race problem which so many Negro writers had hoped to solve, Dunbar merely portrayed the particular manifestations which immensely interested him. He thus won a large audience and never alienated it by introducing prematurely the race problem. His works were eagerly sought by editors of magazines and by publishers. His productions appeared serially, and from time to time in such form as the *Lyrics of Lowly Life,* and *Poems of the Cabin and Field*. These, of course, are available today in his complete works; and some of them as they originally appeared. See Edward F. Arnold's "Some Personal Reminiscences of Paul Laurence Dunbar" (*The Journal of Negro History*, XVII, pp. 400-408).

Following Dunbar came Charles W. Chesnutt, a novelist born in Ohio and transplanted to North Carolina to engage in the education of the freedmen. With his *House Behind the Cedars* and *Conjure Woman* Chesnutt easily took rank as one of the best producers of fiction in his day. During the last years of his career Chesnutt ceased to write.

42. The Negro was also making a contribution on the stage. This, however, was mainly through minstrelsy, which was more histrionic than literary. However, it must not be thought that there was not a preservation of literary traditions in giving free play to the Negro minstrels after the Civil War. Developed on the plantation during the days of bondage, these efforts rehearsed the story of bondage and gave a more graphic picture than had ever appeared in books. *Uncle Tom's Cabin,* which was popular as a play outside of the South for years after the Civil War, became unpopular a generation thereafter, because it apparently tended to keep alive the sores left by sectional conflict; but the Negro minstrel groups which were able to continue some time thereafter tended to extend in a very much modified form the effort which had been thereby brought to an end. It was unfortunate, however, that the minstrel did not always give the Negro on the stage a chance to express the best in him or to portray what he considered the most significant manifestations of the culture of his race. The race was received

VIII. ACTUAL LITERARY CONTRIBUTIONS—*Continued*
43. THE ESSAYISTS
44. THE PROPAGANDISTS
45. THE UTILITARIANS

only as a clown, and even today only a small American audience can be found to witness presentations of the Negro in other capacities. This is well brought out by James Weldon Johnson in his *Black Manhattan,* which gives a very good brief history of the Negro on the stage. The introduction to Locke and Gregory's *Plays of Negro Life* likewise account for this attitude.

43. After the Negro had been silenced in the state legislatures and in Congress, he had very little chance to reach white audiences of consequence. The Negro orator, as an interpreter to the oppressors of the Negro the wishes of the oppressed, ceased to function. White men were designated to serve in this capacity. There appeared upon the scene, therefore, essayists or Negro orators turned essayists. More frequent use than formerly was made of the printed page. Even when a man made a speech he would have it printed in order to reach a larger audience. This was a new movement, for the Negro press had not yet developed. This new effort stimulated such newspapers as were then being conducted by Negroes. It gave them a higher function when there appeared in their columns numerous articles bearing on the race. Prominent among these contributions were those of T. Thomas Fortune, John Edward Bruce, Richard T. Greener, and I. Garland Penn. These men were working through such rising Negro newspapers as the *Illinois Conservator* in Chicago; the *Freeman* in Indianapolis, the *Afro-American* in Baltimore; the *Tribune* in Philadelphia; *The Age* in New York City, and the *Planet* in Richmond.

44. In the course of time, however, some of these writers lost their audience as a result of the rise of contributors to newspapers, who were more militant as propagandists. What they wrote was chiefly to expose the oppressors of the race and to clamor for recognition of the Negro as a citizen. Among these should be mentioned William Pickens, who for a number of years served as a teacher; William Monroe Trotter, editor of the *Guardian* in Boston; James H. Hayes, of Richmond, and later of Washington, D. C., and W. E. B. Du Bois of varying fortune. These propagandists directed the attention of the Negro to the gradual lowering of his status in the social and political sphere. They gave little or no thought to the Negroes' economic status. This is well observed in the study or articles produced in the *Guardian,* of William Pickens's *New Negro,* and of Du Bois's *Soul of Black Folk* and *Darkwater.* Du Bois has been commended most highly and justly for his excellent literary style; and, regardless of his lack of vision as to the situation of his people and how to deal with it, his works must be regarded as significant contributions to American literature.

45. These writers just referred to devoted their talent to propaganda in behalf of the oppressed people. They objected to the program of practical education and to the thought that the Negro should restrict himself to that particular effort only. They had sufficient judgment to understand that no one particular effort could be worked out as a panacea for all evils from

IX. THE NEW LITERATURE
46. More Realistic Poets
47. Rise of Negro Novelists

which the race was suffering. The utilitarian idea of Booker T. Washington was projected on the basis that religion, politics, and classical education had failed to solve the problem of the Negro, and now it was time for the Negro to prepare himself to deal with the practical things of life. Without such foundation in things material there would be no hope for the race to rise to a higher level. This thought was set forth in the famous address of Booker T. Washington at Atlanta in 1895 and in such of his works as *Up From Slavery, My Larger Education, Working with Hands, Character Building, Tuskegee and Its People, The Man Farthest Down,* and *The Future of the Negro.*

46. The rise of a "New Negro Literature" dates from the period of the World War. The universe was in a chaotic state. One nation was flying at the throat of another to force it to grant certain considerations, and the attack on one was carried throughout the whole family of nations. Men and materials became scarce, and those in need turned to the Negro. The Negro who since emancipation had been reduced to serfdom and peonage and passed by as a negligible factor in the thought of the world, then, believed that the time had come for him to state his case to this country at least and, if possible, enforce his claims. His soul was bitter, and he welcomed the opportunity to treat for more favorable terms when he was asked to labor in the industries and to don the uniform "to make the world safe for democracy."

The poets were the first to take up the story. Almost in the language of Jeremiah they poured out the lamentations of an oppressed people. They sang of liberty which they idealized as the boon which they hoped to attain before going too far in righting the wrongs of others. This tone was not pleasing to those now in need of the services of the Negroes; and there were those of their own race who cautioned these new thinkers against taking such a position when every one was being called upon to stand by his country right or wrong.

These same expressions of protests which had appeared in the Negro press were published by Robert T. Kerlin, a sympathetic white author, as a book entitled *The Voice of the Negro,* and those of the poetic order were produced later by the same author as *Negro Poets and Their Poems.* James Weldon Johnson brought out a similar anthology known as *The Book of American Negro Poetry,* and Countee Cullen, one of the poets himself, another anthology called *Color.* White and Jackson, two white professors making a study of this new literature, produced about the same time *Poetry by American Negroes.* Whether the world was well pleased or not Negro writers at last began to get a hearing; and some of their protests of the so-called radical import alarmed public functionaries.

47. The Negro authors were told that this was not the proper approach, that they should write dispassionately of what they saw in need of interpretation, that they should not alienate their audience before they find it. Accordingly a larger number of these writers became more objective. James

IX. THE NEW LITERATURE—*Continued*

48. NEGRO WRITERS SCIENTIFICALLY TRAINED

Weldon Johnson, for years a poet recognized by both races for his *Autobiography of an Ex-Colored Man* and *Fifty Years and Other Poems*, brought out as *God's Trombones* a caricature as well as an interpretation of the pioneer Negro preacher's philosophy. Countee Cullen attracted attention with his well written interesting verse in his *Caroling Dusk, Copper Sun*, and *Tears of Christ*. Langston Hughes, dealing with the average Negro as a theme, further penetrated the life of the Negro in *Weary Blues* and *Fine Clothes to the Jew* with his new blank verse. While numbers of others have since that time won recognition, these three have been ranked higher than any other writers of the kind since the days of Dunbar.

More and more, too, the purely literary attitude has dominated the circle of Negro writers. Sterling A. Brown in his *Southern Road* has shown how the woes of the race may be sung even in dialect and without affront to any class or race. The purely objective attitude in Rudolph Fisher's *Walls of Jericho*, in Claude McKay's *Banjo* and *Home to Harlem*, and in Zora Near Hurston's *Jonah's Gourd Vine* and her *Mules and Men* is not generally appreciated by the people whom these works portray. The Negro public has received more gladly *Passing* and *Quicksand* by Nella Larsen, *There is Confusion, Plum Bun*, and *Chinaberry Tree*, by Jesse Fauset. *Flight, Rope and Faggot*, and *Fire in the Flint*, by Walter White, had their run as propaganda productions exposing lynching, and then yielded to publications dealing with different themes. The *Dark Princess*, like the *Quest of the Silver Fleece* of an earlier period, by W. E. B. Du Bois, is an unsuccessful effort of an excellent essayist to go beyond his sphere in writing a purpose novel.

48. With an increasing number of men scientifically trained in modern methods of research there has resulted a considerable output of works with the stamp of scholarship. While most of these are in the field of social science the natural sciences have not been neglected. Charles H. Turner of St. Louis made a record in his study of animal behavior. Ernest Just has achieved national standing as an investigator of marine biology. George W. Carver, an agricultural chemist at Tuskegee, has become internationally known by his hundreds of unheard-of products which he has made from the sweet potato and the peanut. The largest number of productions in the field of social science bearing on the Negro have come from the press of the Association for the Study of Negro Life and History, organized in 1915. Other works of value are Charles S. Johnson's *The Negro in the American Civilization* and his *Shadow of the Plantation*, W. E. B. Du Bois's *Suppression of the African Slave Trade, The Gift of Black Folk*, and *Black Reconstruction*, and James Weldon Johnson's *Black Manhattan* and *Along This Way*. In our day the works of history have been enriched by certain monographs in J. W. Cromwell's *Negro in American History*, and by E. A. Johnson's *History of the Negro Soldiers in the Spanish American War*. We have also the *History of the Negro in the World War*, by Emmett J. Scott, and *A Short History of the Negro* and *A Social History of the American Negro*, by Benjamin Brawley.

IX. THE NEW LITERATURE—*Continued*

49. NEGRO ARTISTS IN CORRELATION
50. THE NEGRO THEATRE
51. THE OPERA

49. During this period there has been a recrudescence of interest in the background of the Negro, especially in Negro art. This has been too recent to require a special treatment, but notice has been taken of the movement in Alain Locke's *New Negro* and in the histories by C. G. Woodson. Benjamin Brawley has written *The Negro in Literature and Art,* but the book deals mainly with biographical materials available. It is not an adequate interpretation.

50. On the drama of the background of the Negro a number of play-wrights have focussed their attention. Some of these plays have appeared on the stage, and others have served as scenarios for moving pictures. For lack of capital the firms undertaking this new venture have not pushed this effort as far as it seems destined to go. The Negroes on the stage are being better trained, however; and there is an increasing clientele for the productions which they can best present. The present status and outlook has been summarized by George C. Grant in "The Negro in Dramatic Art" (*The Journal of Negro History,* XVII, p. 19). "Shuffle Along" "Smart Set," "Bandanaland," and the like, caricaturing the Negro, have given place to "Green Pastures" with Richard B. Harrison's dramatization of the backward Negro's religion as seen by Roark Bradford in *Old Man Adam.* Du Bose Heyward's "Porgy" and Green's "In Abraham's Bosom," other dramatizations by white men, have not run so well. Yet these have been so much more successful than Torrence's plays, "Grand Maumee" and "The Rider of Dreams." Eugene O'Neill's "Emperor Jones" has succeeded with both Charles S. Gilpin and Paul Robeson as stars. The latter has risen to a higher level in "Othello" in England.

A number of less known plays which have been tried out in restricted circles have been published in Locke and Gregory's *Plays of Negro Life.* Simpler plays which have been extensively used in the Negro public schools have been published as Willis Richardson's *Plays and Pageants from the Life of the Negro.* One of the most popular of these in the schools is J. W. McCoo's "Ethiopia at the Bar of Justice." The development of this movement is traced in the introduction of Locke and Gregory's work and also in that of Richardson. Recently Willis Richardson and Mae Miller have produced *Negro History in Thirteen Plays.*

51. Likewise interest has been shown in several attempts to present the history of the Negro in grand opera. This was undertaken some years ago by Will Marion Cook; but he, like a few other predecessors in this effort, failed. Clarence Cameron White has undertaken the same in a recent composition of *Ouanga* based upon Haitian history, but he has not yet had a hearing in the exclusive circles. Frequently the Negro is portrayed by the movies but not often in the rôle in which the race would like to appear. An effort is now being made to interest the great moving picture corporations in working out a picture depicting the rise of the Negro from the lower levels unto usefulness and recognition.

CHAPTER XXIV

THE NEGRO IN ART

DURING the scramble for African territory European nations thus concerned gave little thought to the natives. The first thought of the interlopers was of the vast area which had not been developed according to modern methods of exploitation. Let us go forth, then, they said, and possess it. The Africans settled upon this land must be dislodged and driven to the swamps to make the best soil available for the conquerors. That they may have no hope of returning destroy their present habitations. So went African works of art—the images so readily destroyed by the missionaries as obstacles to their inculcating upon the natives the doctrine of that divinity that made the conqueror the lord of the universe.

Up to about thirty years ago, the fetish sculptures, ritualistic masks, and carvings of the Africans were laughed at as poor efforts compared with modern art; and the early explorers and travelers in Africa considered these images of persons and things as evidence of backwardness. These observers regarded them, too, as childish attempts to imitate European art even when the selfsame persons reaching such conclusions were convinced that these people had had no contact with Europe. These pieces of art, however, it was later discovered, were not copied from foreign productions, but were worked out according to images in the African mind—something decidedly different from works produced in Europe and on a new pattern. By and by, moreover, the observers concluded that not in all cases does differentness mean inferiority. After closer examination the students of that continent reached the conclusion that the African had risen to a much higher level than the modern world had believed that he was capable of attaining.

To understand the art of these people the foreigner needed first to know their mind, their way of thinking, their conception of the

425

world, of the past, of the present, of the future, of the life beyond, the rôle of their ancestors in that distant sphere, and the relations of the living to their worshipped dead. Regarding African art from this point of view, the investigator saw that these misshapen, disproportioned figures were skilfully executed to express thought peculiar to the African. The Greek pattern of beauty was unknown to the African and was not desired in his sphere. This, however, only a few learned to see; for, still unable to understand this point of view, numerous writers even today refer to these figures as grotesque, comic, repellent and bizarre, because they do not resemble human beings and animals as they normally are. This is an unscientific attitude. The African artists in producing these strange figures had no more thought of imitation than did the Gothic artists who adorned cathedrals of Europe with gargoyles and dragons. Some of these African statues and statuettes of persons, moreover, may be the actual representations of the "Negrilles," a short, small-bodied, big-headed race "known" to have dwelt in Africa before the coming of the Negroes.

An epoch was marked in the study of African art, however, about a generation ago. Modern art had reached a non-productive stage; and the adventurous in this field, in looking for a new stimulus, started what became known as the much-talked-of Cubist movement. They were soon informed that they had produced nothing new, for the Africans had used this sort of esthetic expression centuries before that time. There sprang up, then, so many enthusiastic followers of these liberal artists that they could be spoken of as the African school. The French art circles were especially enthusiastic, and mainly through their interpretations the works of African art became so highly prized as to make imitations of them a source of revenue. The cold-blooded British with their usual conservatism and disinclination to see anything of worth beyond the confines of the Nordic, however, did not respond in this fashion. Yet large exhibits of these relics have found their way to the museums in England.

The whole modern world with any appreciation of art nevertheless conceded that the African contributions to culture had been very much underrated, and this art at least must be taken as a justification for a revision of the customary estimate of African civilization. The esthetic strength and simplicity of these statues, masks, carving and craft weaving, at last revealed to the uninformed European, have become values eagerly sought for by the greatest art galleries of the world. Studied scientifically, these objects showed symmetry, harmony, and propriety of taste. Guillaume and Munro in their *Primitive Negro Sculpture* took the position that the key to the understanding of African art is to appreciate it through its distinguishing characteristic, sculptural design. French, German, and Italian artists since these discoveries have been greatly influenced thereby and acknowledge their indebtedness to this art. Among these are Cézanne, Picasso, Matisse and Soutine in painting; Lipchitz, Modigliani, Archipenko, Brancusi, Epstein, and Lembruch in sculpture.

The scientific study of the African art, however, has hardly begun. Yet we are giving more attention to this aspect of the past than to others for the reason that we have recently learned much about the despised African through his art. The Negro mind when penetrated does not reveal the African as a filthy cannibal, a dull child, or a simpleton as seen through the eyes of biased explorers in Africa in search of something to exaggerate in order to make money off a gullible public. The Negro may not have the European's power of analysis, but he can analyze. He may not organize to the point of destruction as his conqueror does, but he can organize. He may not feel the impulses which others experience, and it may be fortunate that he does not, but he can nevertheless feel. The African musical rhythms show unusual subtlety. The folklore of that continent is full of vivid imagery. African sculpture reveals the very nature of the oft-misunderstood fetishism which inspires striking creations.

Speaking of art in Africa as it has been revealed up to the present, however, one must not think of the entire continent. Not of that part which has been thoroughly Islamized; not even of all native Africa. Africa is a large continent. Art in one part is manifested in one way; in another region in an entirely different manner. Bearing in mind, however, the Sudan, Guinea, Chad, the West Coast, Cameroon, Benin, Dahomey, Gabun, Congo, and Angola, one may speak of numerous works of native art which, although differing much from one another, nevertheless show a tendency toward a general pattern. This may serve as the basis for carefully guarded generalization for a layman's information.

Going into more detail, we may add that certain tribes have shown special aptitude in art. The most prominent of these are the Baule, Bobo, Agni, Mossi, Guro, and Dan to the northwest; the M'Fang and M'Pongwe in Gabun; and the Bushongo, Baluba, Sibiti, Sangha, Bambalu, Gwembi, Bakelele, Yungu, and Bangongo to the south and east. To speak of the art of the French Congo or of the Egyptian Sudan does not mean anything since these political divisions of European claims in Africa are not delimited according to the tribal areas, and their social organizations. The differences in art from the point of view of the dwellers in the desert in contradistinction to the pastoral and cultivating element of the plain or to those hunting and fishing in the forest should be noted in the scientific approach to this study. Wherever art has highly developed in Africa it has found expression mainly through religion—the belief in one supreme God who created the world and before leaving it forever animated things with thousands of spirits which man must appease in the effort toward earthly welfare and spiritual salvation.

Explaining African art as a religious production, Georges Hardy notes the distinctions not only as to the abstract of the plain and the realism of the art of the forest but also an *art libre* at points along the coast. In other words what distinguishes the art of the forest from that of the open plain is realism. This is explained by the stifling rôle of the forest which accounts for the nations' lack of creative imagination when thus dominated by nature and forced to lead the life of hunters and fishermen. The people in the open plain are joyous, nonchalant, and gay shepherds and farmers. The objects of art produced by those in the plain, as a rule, do not resemble so much the personages and things which they are supposed to honor and they are not so abundant. However, wherever the forest in its might dominates the individual and modifies his customs and temperament works of art are more abundant and more realistic. Those living in the region of Benin and the Gulf of Guinea are said to inhabit *Afrique adoucie*. These people are different from those of the forest. They are open-minded, brave, restless, inquisitive, and very skilful, as in the case of the natives of Benin, Yoruba, Dahomey, and Togo. In addition to a religious art they have a princely and domestic art, represented not only by statues and sacred objects but by a veritable architecture of wood and clay, by very important and ornate industrial objects. Religious obsession has ceased to be the dominating fact of their moral and social life.

Among the most striking manifestations of such art are often pointed out the excellent small sculptures in stone, wood, ivory, or modeling in wax, clay or metals. In all these the Negroes have shown themselves to be "ingenious workers, powerfully helped by inspiration, a sharp sense of detail and a very profound conception of the form to be given to their ideas," says Delafosse. "At the side of religious art or art for art's sake there is another domain in which the Negroes are pastmasters: it is that of the industrial arts, represented by work in clay, wood, iron, copper, gold, leather, and textiles. Ornamented and glazed pottery of all forms and dimensions, finely carved spoons, gongs, staffs of command, low or high stools each one of which is a masterpiece of patience and elegant execution; harmoniously slender paddles, straight or curved knives having handles made of wood incrusted with metal, lances with multiple blades of graceful contours, axes for war or parade, small objects in molded or hammered copper; golden jewelry of filigree or made in a mold, rings and bracelets with delicately wrought openwork, cushions, saddles, boots and sheaths in supple leather diversely colored; curious boxes of oryx skin, trays and mats of colored reeds, fabrics of cotton, wool or raffia that are veritable tapestries with motifs as sober as they are varied and of a very sure taste in coloring, silk or cotton embroideries of a singular richness and happy design."

In architecture, however, the African has not made a record equal to that in the industrial arts. In such structures for homes as generally abound in the least advanced regions the materials are of clay, wood, straw, bark and leaves which do not assure anything grand and enduring in the bee-hive like or ant-hill shaped huts. The Negroes of Africa, however, deserve credit for another contribution to architecture in a style of building which may or may not have been influenced by Islam. These structures are built of bricks held together by a mortar or white clay. The outstanding characteristics are trapezoidal porticos and decorations upon walls with holes and an ornamental arrangement of battlements on the terraces. To this class belong the mosques with pyramidal or conical minarets and horizontal decorations at the extremes jutting beyond the beams of the timber work. This style, it is said, was introduced in 1325 by an Arab architect from Granada, Es-Saheli, brought to the Sudan by Gonga Musa on his return from a pious pilgrimage to Mecca, and it was followed in the decoration of Jenne, Gao, and Timbuctoo. This modification of style, however, must not be understood as the beginning of the construction of enduring buildings in that part of West Africa.

At a very ancient epoch, not yet known when, the African did reach a high level in this sphere with varying constructions of stone. An example of this ancient architecture is the ruins of the stone walls found in the region of Gao of the Upper Volta with all but perfect masonry. Such also are the cylindrical monoliths in circular lines seen at several points in the Gambia basin. These look much like broken cylindrical sacred stones still in use among the Dogon or Habé of the slopes of the Bandiagara and of Homburi of the Bend of the Niger and among various tribes of Southern Nigeria.

There have been found, however, constructions of still greater magnitude and splendor in the area along the southern fringe of the Sahara, and in Rhodesia around Zimbabwe. In the case of the latter still stand parts of massive walls of forts or citadels in concentric circles which indicate a center of great political organization and social development requiring the contribution of an architecture harmonizing with the splendor of that people. Unfortunately, however, the public has been confused by pseudo-European archaeologists who just as soon as the discovery of the ruins was announced set to work to manufacture "evidence" to prove that some other race more ancient than the Negro left these ruins of imposing structures. Some protagonist of this group in a "learned circle" in London, Paris, or Berlin read a paper to this effect. It was transmitted to other parts, and others thus interested took up the distortion of the truth in glad refrain of the traducer and exploiter.

In similar fashion "scholarly" Europeans without any trustworthy evidence have assigned to some prehistoric race of "modern manufacture" the credit for the Bushman painting and sculpture in South Africa. It appears that the cave-dwellers among the Bushmen produced the paintings and the Kopje-dwellers the sculptures. This art, it is said, belongs to three distinct periods: namely, the first of a crude effort, the second of more mature art, and a third of decadence due to the harrying of other peoples coming to break up the social order of the Bushmen. Beginning with a patination of the surfaces of rocks to produce simple figures, then, these Bushmen finally ventured to portray in better fashion designs of animals, symbolic dances, and tribal emblems. These natives produced also paintings remarkable for their realism and for freedom from the limitation to delineation in profile so characteristic of the drawings of so-called primitive people. These efforts showed some knowledge of the perspective. In painting the "colours were laid on uniformly over the surface which they individually covered, but a shading off is sometimes exhibited."

In the art of music, too, the achievements of the African must not be despised. In this sphere the African ranks high. His claims must not be confused with jazz which is not African except in the sense that jazz shows a resemblance to the "tom-tom." But the "tom-tom" is not music; it is only the instrument of the dance. Those who play merely the drum and the fife are not considered musicians in Europe. The instruments used in the production of African music are xylophones, violins, guitars, zithers, harps, and flageolets. The xylophone, the most extensively used, is a sort of piano, many players of which sometimes become real virtuosos.

"Music is accompanied by singing, the words and the air being composed at the same time by the musician," says Delafosse. "Women often sing without the accompaniment of an instrument, but men unless they belong to the caste of singers seldom thus indulge for pleasure or recreation since they must preserve their voices for religious or war ceremonies. Their voices and ears are remarkable for their true pitch. Seldom does one hear a false note. Whether the choruses are executed in unison or in parts, the harmony is generally impeccable. As for the melodies themselves, many are mediocre, but the majority have a charm to which European ears are as sensitive as African, a charm imprinted with

sweetness and melancholy much oftener than with gayety, sometimes with force and with pride in the war-songs and the odes
praising a famous hero."

"The only reproach that could be made of these melodies," says
Delafosse further, "is that they are too short; each one is generally
composed of a very brief musical phrase which is repeated over
and over, twenty or thirty times. The phrase is often delightful,
but we are quickly satiated with the most exquisite things. The
Negroes, on the contrary, seem to experience a real pleasure in end-
lessly repeating or hearing the same air."

The histrionic art is well developed in Africa. The European
looking for the modern theatre in Africa, however, never sees the
drama there as it is. As we have noticed that the life of the
African is infinitely complex, with government in religion and
religion in art, so does one find the African theatre connected with
other manifestations. The dance around the fire in the village or
camp at night is often a comedy staged to divert those who after
the toil of the day require this form of recreation. The war dance
is often a recital of the deeds of a hero whose example the present
generation is thereby stimulated to emulate. These performances
are often accompanied by a crooning recital of professional story-
tellers, who in thus rehearsing the history of the people serve not
only as actors but as walking encyclopædias for the nation. The
function of such artists in Africa is so general that we may speak
even of the African as a natural born actor. This, however, is
possible only from the point of view of objectivity, for the modern
theatre in its general ramifications has hardly had a beginning in
Africa except where the European ideas have penetrated the life
of the natives.

No extensive comment is necessary here to show the connection
between African art and the achievements of American Negroes
in this sphere. Buildings, utensils, and ornaments made by Negro
slaves in America during the early colonial period can still be
pointed out in cities like Charleston, Savannah, and New Orleans
as evidences of the perpetuation of the work in the industrial arts.
Some Negro-American folklore is an importation from Africa
without much modification. The religion of many Negroes in spite
of its Protestant or Catholic label still carries a few African marks

which appear as influences in Negro-American art. The folk music of the American Negro, the outstanding contribution to art in the Western Hemisphere, is all but an African survival in America. Submerged in the social order of the New World, the Negroes have been unequal to other manifestations, but that the influence of African art did endure is clear.

In art as in religion and other manifestations, however, all Negroes have not been deeply influenced by African traditions. About one-fourth of the so-called Negroes of the United States are ethnologically more Caucasian than African, and some of those with a preponderance of African blood have nevertheless been Caucasianized. Their whole life proceeds along the line of imitation. Africa means no more to them than it does to the white Americans. By scientists who have given thought to the culture of the American Negro, however, the achievements influenced by African traditions have been highly evaluated as worthwhile whereas the uninteresting fitting into the mold of what others have produced has not been given much consideration. The thought is that man at his best must not merely imitate. He must give the world something new. While the American Negro may not by imitation gain all he desires, with the passing of time and the higher elevation of the African to the level of the European, there must come a recognition of this despised Oriental as a colaborer with others in the making of civilization.

The extent to which the American Negroes have developed in the fine arts may be determined by a sketch of those who have figured in these spheres. The large majority of such contributors have distinguished themselves in the emotional arts, chiefly music and dance. In decorative art, sculpture, design, and craft work the American Negroes' development was stifled in the very beginning by slavery. Mimicry, song, and dance endured in spite of the ordeal to which the Africans imported had to undergo. It is snap judgment, then, to conclude that the American Negro has not the capacity for art in its broadest ramifications. Even before the Civil War Edmonia Lewis and Edmund Bannister had made an impression in sculpture and painting respectively. H. O. Tanner has distinguished himself in painting after going abroad. The recent achievements of Aaron Douglass, Hale Woodruff, Archibald

Motley, and James Lesesne Wells, painters of African bent, and of Sargent Johnson, Richmond Barthé, Elizabeth Prophet, and Augusta Savage, sculptors, likewise influenced, show evidence of recovering this ground lost in the transition from Africa to America. And yet these artists with this new vision are at the same time profiting by what they know of the skill of their American and European contemporaries. To such workers the American public is learning to look for creative efforts and esthetic contributions.

In music the American Negro has risen higher than his musicians, although Clarence C. White, Harry T. Burleigh, Nathaniel Dett, and Roland Hayes deserve honorable mention among the best of the time. On the stage continues the effort to hold the Negro down to the rôle of the clown or minstrelsy, a Negro creation of ante bellum days; but Gilpin and Robeson, following the example set by Ira Aldridge, have taken higher ground. The chief handicap to the Negro on the stage has been that he has not been interested in dramatizing his own life and history, and the white man has not welcomed the Negro as his assistant in dramatizing that of the Caucasian. A proper study of the past of the Negro may lead artists of both races to see a new theme in that drama; and the Negro with a natural insight into it may find an opportunity to excel.[1]

[1] For an introductory treatment of the Negro in art there is no text available as in developing some other aspects of Negro culture. The subject must be treated from the point of view of the investigator. In 1920 Paul Guillaume and Thomas Munro summarized most of the recent thought with respect to *Primitive Negro Sculpture.* Later in *Opportunity* in May, 1928, Albert C. Barnes elaborated such thought further as he and his coworkers had already done in the first and second numbers of the second volume of the *Journal of the Barnes Foundation.* The chapter on art in Alain Locke's *New Negro* added some other thought. Numerous magazines and books since the first efforts in this sphere about two generations ago have carried chapters and articles bearing upon various discoveries of African esthetic creations and interpretations of these works. Much later appeared also James Johnson Sweeney's *African Negro Art,* published in New York in 1935. These considered together with Georges Hardy's *L'Art Nègre,* an effort to interpret the art of the Negro philosophically, may be sufficient to give the layman an intelligent grasp of these contributions. The special contributions of Negro artists in the United States have been noted in several brochures recently published by the Harmon Foundation in New York City with the title *Negro Artists* in 1933 and with that of *Negro Artists, An Illustrated Review of Their Achievements* in 1935. For music M. C. Hare's *Negro Musicians* is helpful.

I. FINE ART MISUNDERSTOOD

    1. ART AS A RACIAL OR NATIONAL EXPRESSION
    2. ART FROM ITS OWN POINT OF VIEW
    3. ART IN ISOLATION

1. Art, as the layman ordinarily understands it, is the application of skill and taste to production according to esthetic principles or such application to the production of beauty in plastic materials by imitation or design as in painting and sculpture commonly observed in Europe and America. In this attitude, however, there is a misconception in regarding art as imitation. Considered thus, as is usual among the unscientific and uninformed, art is usually misunderstood or unknown to the average man. In the study of art we seek the beautiful, but the beautiful is purely relative. One's conception of beauty is determined altogether by his own standard. It is almost impossible, then, for one people to evaluate accurately the esthetic contributions of another as is well brought out in the book, *Primitive Negro Sculpture,* by Guillaume and Thomas Munro. This point of view enables us to understand that art must be studied as a racial or national expression. Approached otherwise, this particular contribution, like all others, will be misunderstood. Georges Hardy in his *L'Art Nègre* tries to explain thus the African effort in this sphere.

2. Studying art from the point of view of people themselves, the student must know who these people are, where they live, and the age to which they belong. He must know also what their occupations have been, the ideals which they have followed, the contacts which they have made with other parts of the world, and outside influences which have affected their life. In other words, people must be studied scientifically. Their contributions must not be contrasted with those of races or nations otherwise circumstanced under different influences at a different time and with different contacts. Unless this is borne in mind, instead of arriving at an appreciation of the progress of a people one's efforts result in the worst sort of misunderstanding. This tends to engender excessive self-estimation or unjustifiable high evaluation of present day achievement which may be relatively inferior to that which we despise. This sort of procedure has been an enduring handicap in the so-called scientific circles in both Europe and in America.

3. Art, then, is sometimes isolated as well as under foreign influence. While perfect isolation is practically impossible the influence from contacts within a large area of peoples very much alike may not result in such changes as those of migrations of cultures from afar. Where art is reached by forces from without one may find a change for the better but change may often mean decadence and finally destruction. People, when isolated, usually develop certain patterns for doing almost everything which their social order requires. Left to themselves, they do not readily change. In the various parts of the world, therefore, we do find in countries which have not been brought under modern influences this isolated art which is often referred to as "primitive." There is not, however, any such thing as "primitive art" or a "primitive people." No word has been more extensively misused than the word "primitive." People are not "primitive," and their art is not "primitive." Art is art whether it was produced yesterday or six

I. FINE ART MISUNDERSTOOD—*Continued*
    4. Art under Foreign Influence
    5. The Destruction of Art by the Ignorant

II. AN AWAKENING AS TO AFRICAN ART
    6. Developing Scientific Standards

thousand years ago. If art is the expression of the beautiful, the workman in his isolated sphere could have just as accurately produced the image of the beautiful in the mind of the ancient as the artist of today may express the beautiful as it is now conceived. The task well done at that remote period is just as significant and deserves an estimate just as high as one performed today with equal care and observance of the standards required.

4. Art under foreign influence is another mischievous thought which leads astray so many investigators of the so-called ancient civilization. In Australia is found something that resembles a similar production found in Syria, and the unscientific observer sets out immediately to find out when some one from Syria carried this idea into Australia. Finding no facts to support his conclusion that there was such a migration of culture, he falls back on theories which have no more significance than an ordinary yarn told by drinkers in a modern café. The chief difficulty in this case is that men are thus misled in not understanding that people, although far apart may be subjected to practically the same stimuli; and science has shown that, under such circumstances, regardless of race, they will respond very much in the same way. Grief is but grief, and joy is but joy whether experienced by the Hottentot or the Anglo-Saxon; and the reactions under these circumstances do not differ widely.

5. For failure to study art from this point of view the esthetic creations of some of the peoples of the world, especially of those who have not come into close contact with Americans and Europeans until recently, have been thrown aside as worthless. So many of us have not even the intelligence of the Roman general who in completing the conquest of Greece destroyed Corinth. He finally decided to ship to Rome certain works of art which happened to impress him but cautioned the subordinate in command not to lose them; for if he did, he would have to supply others of equal value. In most cases of conquests practically all the works of people thus humiliated have been destroyed. With the aid of archaeology, however, we can unearth these ruins today and with their relics reconstruct the picture of the various peoples who have left one civilization buried upon another. Valuable service has been rendered in this field by persons like Heinrich Schelieman, Sir Arthur Evans and others who have thereby changed our notions with respect to the ancients around the Mediterranean sea. Considerable excavations in Asia have had similar profitable results. Africa, however, is just beginning to attract the attention of scientists. With the exception of a score or so of productions bearing thereupon, therefore, the books supposedly presenting the picture of ancient and medieval Africa have no scientific value.

6. In the proportion as a nation becomes educated it tends to broaden. One of the results in the development of education in Europe during the last century has been an increase in the study of foreign civilization. During

II. AN AWAKENING AS TO AFRICAN ART—*Continued*
7. A NEW EVALUATION OF THINGS
8. THE QUEST OF THE NEW IN ART CIRCLES

this period of expansion of European nations both into Asia and into Africa this opportunity for such investigation has been facilitated. Scientific commissions have been organized and sent to various parts of the Orient for special surveys, scholars have undertaken such on their own initiative, and some persons of scientific preparation while engaged in government or missionary effort have also availed themselves of the opportunity to penetrate the background of the ancients. The works of various scholars which have been produced as the results from such efforts are too numerous to mention here where the concern is chiefly to note the promising sign of the scientific approach to matters which had been taken for granted.

7. It has been fortunate, too, that these findings of investigators who have given attention to these ancient achievements have not been restricted to their own particular circle. Noticed by the press and on the platform, these ideas have tended to percolate through the entire masses of the social order to the extent that the thinking element has developed a new standard for the evaluation of things. There has been a tendency to broaden one's mind so that he may take himself and his nation less seriously and think of all humanity as a common family to the preservation and welfare of which various members have made their respective contributions. The whole world, to be sure, has not been brought to this way of thinking; but the right way has been indicated, and from year to year the number of persons thus inclined has gradually increased. The main battle has been against those who see and will not believe, and who believe and will not order their doing along the channels which science has determined to be wise. In the case of the works of these scholars specializing in the study of the progress of foreign nations, especially of the ancient, there have arisen a number of voices to the contrary, those who are still trying to bolster up a false nationalism, economic imperialism, and racial snobbishness which are still dominant among those manipulating the masses of the exploited races.

8. This new appreciation of values has grown stronger and at the same time has tended to soften the attitudes of self-admiration, "scholarly circles" that refuse to hear the voice of science. The chief reason for such a change in spite of efforts to the contrary, has been in the unproductiveness of both European and American artists during the last two or three generations. Art has been facing stagnation. Although these sculptors and painters have extensively copied the ancient art started by Africa, embellished by Greece, and passed on to them by Rome, they have not been able to add very much thereto. Surfeited with the material things supplied by the wealth resulting from modern appliances, the esthetically inclined element on a level above this vulgar plane has gone in search of greater values. In this quest for something new the academicians changed their ideals, as discussed by Guillaume and Munro in their *Primitive Negro Sculpture* and by A. C. Barnes and his coworkers in their articles on Negro art (*The Journal of the Barnes Foundation*, I, Numbers 1 and 2, and *Opportunity*, May, 1924, May, 1926, and May, 1928).

II. AN AWAKENING AS TO AFRICAN ART—*Continued*

9. The Discovery of Works of Art in Africa

    a. Painting

    b. Sculptures

    c. Decorations

9. It was fortunate at this time that Africa, penetrated to the interior by 1870 and opened up to European exploiters before the close of the century, began to interest men who were thus esthetically inclined. Agents of governments, explorers, and travelers who touched those innermost parts occasionally brought back unusual relics which were different from anything that they had seen. These may be classified under paintings, sculptures, and decorations. The painting could not be easily carried to Europe because it had not been divorced from personal decorations or architecture, but there were reports as to the uses that the natives had made of colors and representations which they had left in their homes and even on the walls of the caves in which the most ancient peoples of Africa had once lived. A considerable number of fetish statuettes, masks, and other images were collected. Small utensils, implements, and weapons with all sorts of designs, abounded.

Reports about these findings were set forth in numerous works among which the following may be noted: Marius de Zayas, *African Negro Art* (New York, 1916); Maurice Delafosse, *Negroes of Africa* (Washington, 1931); Clive Bell, *Since Cezanne* (New York, 1922); Georges Hardy, *L'Art Nègre* (Paris, 1927); Harmon Foundation, *Exhibition of Productions by Negro Artists* (New York, 1933); Sheldon Cheney, *Primer of Modern Art* (New York, 1932); Herbert Kuhn, *Die Kunst der Primitiven* (Munich, 1923); H. Clouzot and A. Level, *L'Art nègre et l'art océanien* (Paris, 1920); the same authors, *Sculptures Africaines* (Paris, 1920); Carl Einstein, *La Sculpture africaine* (Paris, 1920); the same author, *Negerplastik* (Munich, 1920); P. C. Lepage, *La Decoration primitive* (Paris, 1925); E. Merwart, *L'Art dahoméen* (Marseille, 1922); Leo Frobenius, "Die Bildende Kunst der Afrikaner," *Anthropol. Gesell. in Wien Mitt.*, XXVII, pp. 1-17; same author, *The Voice of Africa*, translation by Rudolf Blind (London, 1913); G. S. Perier, *L'Art nègre de Congo belge* (Brussels, 1925); Pitt Rivers, *Antique Works of Art from Benin* (London, 1900); Felix von Luschan, *Die Altertümer von Benin* (Berlin, 1912); F. de Zeltner, *Notes sur quelques industries du Soudan français*, in the *Bulletin de la Société d'Anthropologie* (1915); Ernst Wasmuth and A. G. Berlin, *Orbis Pictus, Band 7, Afrikanische Plastik* (Leipzig, 1920); Alain Locke, *The New Negro*, the chapter on Negro art (New York, 1925); Stephen Chauvet, *Les arts indigènes* (Paris, 1919); Daniel Real, "Basreliefs of Dahomey," *Opportunity* (May, 1927); G. Daniel, "L'art Nègre au Congo belge," *La Nature*, LI, pp. 37-40; Martin Heydrich, *Afrikanische Ornamentik* (Leiden, 1914); R. S. Rattray, "Arts and Crafts of Ashanti," *Journal of the African Society*, XIII, pp. 265-270; *Religion and Art in Ashanti* (Oxford, 1927); George W. Stow, *The Native Races of South Africa* (New York, 1905). Other books and articles treating of the Negro in art may be cited, but most of them are based secondarily on the authorities herein cited.

II. AN AWAKENING AS TO AFRICAN ART—*Continued*

10. A Thought as to Imitation of Others
11. A Revised Estimate of African Culture
12. The African School

10. In the beginning, as the works cited above will show, the first thought after the discovery of these works of art was that of imitation. The observers had not considered the African capable of any such efforts in a high sphere. Yet inasmuch as many of these statuettes apparently represented animals but poorly, they seemed grotesque, comic and bizarre. Some Europeans considered these as evidences of backwardness. At the same time these works of art which resembled those of Europe were considered imitation in spite of the fact that the natives apparently had had no opportunity to be influenced from that quarter. Scientific investigation of these findings, however, soon revealed the fact that these productions were more ancient than most of the arts by which they thought the Africans had been influenced. Works of African art produced at a later period, moreover, support generally the claim of originality. Instead of feeling that the art of Africa has been worked out in imitation of that of other nations the tendency in scientific circles today is to think of the art of other parts as having been influenced by that of Africa. This is the position taken by Guillaume and Munro, by A. C. Barnes, and indirectly by Sheldon Cheney, Maurius de Zayas, and Clive Bell.

11. With the new point of view as to the originality of African art, then, there was awakened a new interest in the African not only in his art but in all manifestations of his life. The best scholars of the time easily saw that if the African had been original in art he might have had the capacity for originality in some other sphere. The attitude thereafter was that the whole life of these aborigines when properly investigated and understood would force the snobbish world to revise its estimate of the African natives. The result has been especially to investigate the contributions of the native to science. His knowledge of diseases and application of cures extracted from nature, the mixing of colors, the poisoning of arrows, and the refinement of metals. The whole picture had to be reconstructed. We have learned not only to appreciate the African art and to classify it among other such productions but to think of the natives as men along with other members of the human family with the same capacity.

12. The inevitable result of this unusual interest in Africa at the time that the artists were in quest of something new to lift the world above the low level in materialism was a sort of idealization of African art. Workers in Europe. and later a few in America, have begun to follow African models. This has appeared in the paintings of a number of artists chief among whom are Cézanne, Picasso, Matisse, and Soutine; and in the sculptures of Lipchitz, Modigliani, Archipenko, Brancussi, Epstein, and Lembruch. These may be considered a sort of African school. It must be admitted, however, that their works are not so popular today as they were when the discovery of African art values was first made; and these works never enjoyed the vogue in Great Britain that they experienced in France and Germany. In the United States, however, among Negro painters like Aaron Douglass, A. J. Motley, and J. L. Wells, and among sculptors like Sargent Johnson,

III. INFLUENCES DETERMINING ART IN AFRICA

13. Environment and Art—Religion
(a) The Plain
(b) The Forest
(c) In Advanced Areas
14. Generalizations, the Difficulty of
15. Sculptural Design, Key to African Art

Richmond Barthé, and Augusta Savage this African pattern is still popular and is regarded in circles interested in the study of the background of the Negro as a helpful sign that the race is thus becoming interested in its past.

13. There are hundreds of books mentioning African art. Most of them, however, are mainly descriptive, devoted to details as to what the author saw or heard and efforts to compare these discoveries with what the observer believes he knows to be art. Georges Hardy is the only one who has undertaken to penetrate the African's philosophy of life underlying his art. One will hardly agree with everything this author says, but it must be conceded that these findings cannot be explained by our usual methods of comparison.

Hardy believes (*L'Art Nègre*, p. 33) that the key to the understanding of Africa is to see it as dominated by religion. Captain R. S. Rattray takes up the religious theme in Ashanti; but Hardy, looking at all Africa, sees a difference in the esthetic expression of the dwellers in various parts. The gay cheerful shepherds and farmers of the open plain do not express themselves as do the hunters and fishermen who are overwhelmed by the tyrannical nature of the forest; and neither of these show the finer art of those in *Afrique Adoucie*—Dahomey, Togo, Benin and the like. The art last mentioned becomes domestic and princely and even reaches the heights of architecture where it is not dominated by religion.

Without going into the details of the influence of religion on art, we may raise here the question as to whether this category is sufficiently embracing to account for all in the life of the natives circumscribed even on the plains or in the forests. It leaves the impression that the Negro is by nature religious, for this motive above all others figures prominently in what he does. Hardy's theory should not be dismissed because it may not sound pleasing. He has made a commendable effort to clarify African art, and what he says must be taken into account.

14. Generalizations are always dangerous. Science does not proceed in such fashion. Because of the difficulty involved in reaching Africans and the paucity of materials for examination, moreover, still greater care is required in this particular case. Africa is a large continent, so large that the natives in distant parts show no more resemblance to each other than do Europeans to Africans. Under the circumstances, then, can we speak of *African art?* Is art *African* or *European?* Is there a distinction between *art in Africa* and *African art?* Is such a thing as *Negro art* possible? What is a Negro? Do any two persons give the same answer to such a question?

15. While Hardy finds religion the explanation or the key to the interpretation of African art, Guillaume and Munro, having in mind that part of

III. INFLUENCES DETERMINING ART IN AFRICA—
Continued

    16. Tribes Especially Gifted
    17. The Decadence of African Art

IV. ARCHITECTURE IN AFRICA

    18. Types of African Homes
        a. Straw
        b. Clay
        c. Stone

Africa where religion is no longer an obsession, consider sculptural design the key to the understanding of these creations. From this point of view the African design of a structure is inspired by the thing designed and in harmony with the purpose of the object decorated. Few things can be designed exactly alike, and unity or uniformity is lacking. Yet there are those who refer to design as not a prominent feature in art in Africa. What is design from the African point of view? What have these authors in mind in speaking of *sculptural design?* In other words, what seems to have been the dominating factor in the thought of the native when he set to work to produce these pieces of art? By what was he guided? Was he guided at all?

16. The works of art from Africa found in the British Museum, in the Trocadero, and in the Belgian Congo Museum especially show more esthetic creations among some Africans than among others. Is there any way to account for the special gifts of these particular tribes? How can one explain that the Romans, with the exception of the Roman arch stumbled upon in their great building program, did little more than to copy what the Greeks produced? Have we any satisfactory answer for these differences in achievement in the Mediterranean world? Does this offer any explanation for Africa?

17. It is evident that with the harrying and the pressing of one stock or tribe upon the other in Africa the social organization of the aborigines has been destroyed and what they had been accustomed to produce has tended to decay. Certainly within the memory of Europeans now living in Africa there has disappeared native art along with other evidences of progress, and what has not disappeared is in a state of decay. The culture of the native has been destroyed and that of the European has not been introduced. The Mohammedan religion in one area and the Christian faith in another have supplanted the religion of the native and along with it the art which it once inspired. The life to which the native is consigned in the economic imperialistic order does not enable him to rise to a high level. Is this progress?

18. According to Delafosse, Negroes of Africa have not done as much in architecture as they have in the arts in other forms. Hardy does not give the Negro on the plain and in the forest very much credit for accomplishment in this sphere. In the more accessible, mild portions of Africa, in such areas as Togo, Dahomey, Benin, and neighboring districts, there

IV. ARCHITECTURE IN AFRICA—*Continued*

19. ISLAMIC INFLUENCE
20. BUILDINGS IN CITIES OF GAO, JENNE, TIMBUCTOO
21. GREAT RUINS

has been a development of architecture among Negroes of which he takes notice. In other words, the Negroes in the other parts of Africa have not learned to separate art from architecture, and art has appeared mainly in small statues and in the ornamentation of ordinary things like tools, jewelry, and utensils. The homes of the natives in such areas are built of straw and clay, and they have left few monuments in stone. Monuments are found in parts which have long been inhabited, but Europeans have not ceased to try to give credit for them to foreigners immigrating into Africa.

19. One of the chief forces from a foreign sphere operating to stimulate architecture in Africa was Islam. The extent to which the homes and monuments of certain parts of Africa invaded by Mohammedans resemble the homes which they left in Asia and in North Africa is considered the measure of the influence of Islam on the architecture of the Negroes of Africa. As yet, however, little effort has been made to construct the picture of architecture in Africa below the Sahara before the immigration of large numbers of Mohammedans into the country about the year 1,000. Very little has been done to study this prehistoric period, and much of what has been actually revealed has been ignored by the biased writers. The impression which they leave as to their methods is that they have sought the line of least resistance in giving a stereotype explanation of foreign influence as well as to conform to the bias which most modern authors are not able to escape.

20. The striking evidences of architecture in the cities of Gao, Jenne, and Timbuctoo were not considered by authors in discussing the progress of the African Negro. The mere fact that Gonga Musa persuaded Es-Saheli to come with him to the Sudan on his return from his pious pilgrimage to Mecca that he might direct the beautification of these three cities should not deprive the Negro of all credit for such architecture. While the foreign influence is present here, native ideas were not altogether thrown aside as the very buildings and monuments thus constructed testify. It is evidently more like the truth to conclude that there one sees the architecture of the native African modified by this foreign influence in this conflict and fusion of Eastern ideas; for the buildings thus resulting, as well as other manifestations, are neither replicas of what was found in North Africa or Asia nor of the constructions which ruins in other parts of Africa indicate that the natives had learned to build in ancient times.

21. Equal to the occasion of explaining things by foreign influence as the key to understanding most of these creations, Europeans writing on the great ruins found along the Southern fringe of the Sahara, in the region of Gambia, and around Zimbabwe in Rhodesia, have had to resort to another theory. These ruins in some cases were built so far in the interior where no foreign contact with the European or Asiatics of the last millennium was possible that the theorists manufactured all but mythical peoples of geological ages who they claim once inhabited Africa. These ruins consist

IV. ARCHITECTURE IN AFRICA—*Continued*
22. Theories as to Origins

V. AFRICAN MUSIC
23. Distinguished from Jazz—Tom-Tom

of unusual figures in stone, great mounds of kings, foundations of large temples, and walls of great fortresses that probably once guarded the confines of kingdoms and empires. That these were discovered sometimes in parts where very "backward" natives now live, the authors thus inclined, have regarded as extra evidence that such achievements of architecture should not be accredited to the black Africans, as seems to be the inclination of David Randall-Maciver in his *Medieval Rhodesia.*

22. These theories as to origin, however, do not rest on any scientific foundation. They do not even show regard for investigation. It is evident to any one who has observed conditions in Africa even during the last two or three generations that in the disorganization of the social order of the tribes they easily decline and sometimes undergo extermination. Records of the past are destroyed, traditions are upset, generations far removed from others return less and less to the past of their forebears and finally reach the level of living mainly in the present. What these commentators consider as having happened because of numerous migrations in Africa and immigrations into that continent may have happened as a result of ordinary upheavals of tribes of local kingdoms and empires a few hundred or a thousand or so miles apart. In all these cases, moreover, it is unfortunate that these persons undertake to make distinction with respect to black Africa and white Africa, referring to every person who has even one per cent of white blood as a white person and to only the purely black types of isolated areas as Negroes. At the same time other authors, using the facts and conclusions therein set forth, approach the same question from the American race-hate point of view in referring to every person as a Negro if he happens not to have one hundred per cent of white blood. Theories worked out in such confused fashion, therefore, have no significance and must be disregarded in estimating the architecture and everything else in Africa.

23. Music in Africa has been better preserved than some other arts. Although intangible, this creation of the African has been handed down from generation to generation in more enduring fashion than in the case of relics, monuments, statues, and masks which have suffered from inroads and upheavals from time immemorial. Melodies may be carried along with the dislodged natives when other creations have to be left behind to undergo decay or destruction. Professional musicians or persons almost of this order function more generally in Africa than other artists.

Delafosse points out, however, that African music (p. 262) must not be confused with that of the jazz band so common today in Europe and America. The tom-tom which is the instrument of dance rather than of music is the only manifestation in Africa resembling jazz. Even the jubilee and the spiritual in America must be considered modifications or adaptations of African music to the peculiar slavery environment of the Negro in America.

V. AFRICAN MUSIC—*Continued*

24. INSTRUMENTS IN USE
25. METHODS OF PRODUCTION OF MUSIC
26. COMPARISON WITH THE MUSIC OF OTHERS
27. MUSIC AND THE OTHER ARTS

Is American Negro music African music or European music modified by the African temperament of the Negro? It is well to consult in connection herewith Stephen Chauvet's *La Musique Nègre,* Delafosse's chapter on music in his *Negroes of Africa* and M. C. Hare's *Negro Musicians and Their Music.*

24. Another approach to African music is to list the instruments which have been used by the natives from time immemorial. Among these are xylophones, violins, zithers, harps, flutes, and flageolets. Dr. Nathaniel Cantor, of the University of Buffalo, says that Africans were the first to use stringed instruments. Yet we find that some of these instruments were in use elsewhere among the most ancient people. Does it necessarily follow that the Africans had to borrow from others? Is it unreasonable to think that others may have borrowed from the Africans? While the ancient European contacts with Africa may have been infrequent the Asiatics even as far away as Japan and China had early contacts with the east coast of the so-called Dark Continent thousands of years ago. Numbers of Africans found their way into India, China, and Japan just as adventurers from those lands reached Africa. With the exception of North Africa, however, we have no evidence of the egress or ingress of sufficient numbers in either direction to uproot a culture altogether and introduce customs entirely new.

25. The methods of producing music as shown by Delafosse (pp. 262-263) may enable the observer to penetrate further the mind of the African as it reacted to such stimuli. Singing and performance on instruments are both spontaneous and professional. African women, like those of other nations, more frequently indulge in music than men who must preserve their voices for demonstrations in war. All sorts of instruments are employed in supplementing the frequently used human voice; and in crude style practically all phases of musical reproduction are thereby made possible. Does this mean that the African knew little of other things while all but perfect in music?

26. Many writers estimate the Africans' achievements in music more highly than in the case of other so-called primitive peoples. Taking into consideration this capacity of the American Negro, there are those who indulge in the superlative and place the Negro in music on the topmost round among modern peoples. Do the facts justify such conclusions? In thus estimating the Negroes' accomplishments few writers on Africa think of this music as a result of the migration of ideas. Asiatics or Europeans, however, are considered contributors of other creations in Africa. Does it not seem, then, that wherever the evidence is not preponderatingly in favor of the African, the foreigner seeks to discredit him? Can the African ever be scientifically presented by those who have always approached him in the distorted attitude of the superior lording it over the inferior or that of the conqueror subduing the victim?

27. To what extent do the sources examined indicate a correlation of the

VI. THE AFRICAN DRAMA
28. Manifested in its Own Peculiar Way
29. The Position of Drama in the Life of the People

arts, the interdependence of one upon the other? Recently we have learned much about the fine arts, but they have been emphasized so generally as being separate and distinct when they all spring from a common motif. In Africa, as among other ancients, there is apparently more evidence of this interplay than in the highly developed social order of modern nations. Among the ancients we find things nearer their sources. Do these relationships and interrelationships of that early period help us to understand better the connections of these things today? In other words, is the ancient always the pupil of the modern man? Can he not also at times assume the rôle of teacher? What progress have we made in this sphere? Is there any such thing as progress? Do we go forward or around in a circle?

28. Going to Africa in quest of the drama as revealed to the ancient Greeks would prove to be a fruitless effort. The African is an actor by nature. His unusual emotion seeking expression could not permit his development otherwise. The drama in Africa, however, is not manifested in European but in African fashion. Comments on this aspect of African culture, therefore, are scarce. Few observers have sufficient penetration to note its correlation with other things or that of other things with it. The African theatre does not exist in the "backward" parts as a center of the community. It does exist, however, in the inner life of the people. There it is an effort to supply an ever recurring need for amusement and for reminding the people of the best in the past—a sort of rehearsal of history as the monitor to the future.

Of books bearing on this topic we have only a few dignifying the African stage with even so much as a paragraph. The most interesting production bearing hereupon is Maurice Delafosse's "Contribution à l'Étude du theatre chez les Nègres" (*Annuaire et Memoires du Comité d'Études historiques et scientifiques,* Goree, 1914). A short reference to the African drama is made in the same author's *Negroes of Africa* (p. 272) but the thought is not fully developed there. This author does not find the theatre in Africa well defined from the modern point of view, but in spite of all that is said the facts presented show its rôle in the life of the people.

29. Drama in Africa is a natural consequence as it is among almost all other people. Story-telling is a dominating factor in the amusement and education of Africans. The drama developed from the telling of the story by actions. Another source of the drama was in the religious festivals and imitative dances in connection with which such recitals are required. Into such plays, of course, came the elements of mystery, miracle and morality. These performances assumed, too, the phases of the farce, the burletta, the opera, the melodrama, the comedy, the tragi-comedy, and the tragedy. The professional story-tellers, the "griots," who are the walking encyclopaedias are also the actors on this African stage. Others less professional are often called in to assist.

Authorities discussing in detail these origins have not yet appeared upon

VI. THE AFRICAN DRAMA—*Continued*

30. DRAMA AND RELIGION
31. IN MEMORY OF HEROES
32. CONNECTION WITH OTHER ARTS

the scene. Yet all writers on Africa delving in folklore, religion and the like give the picture of the African theatre along with other manifestations. Consult especially the folklore collections of Blaise Cendrars, Charles Monteil and Franz de Zeltner. Note also the works cited herein under literature on pp. 393, 403, and 404.

30. The reading of almost any of the works on religion herein cited will show how the drama would naturally take root in the religious feasts where actions are staged to impress the people with morality or to strike terror to their hearts by staging the miraculous. The man in the ancient world lived in an atmosphere of mysticism, and the drama was often resorted to as a most impressive way to exhibit one's power or to recall that of some important personage once conspicuous in that community. Thereby so to speak were revealed sometimes mysteries which had been kept from the ordinary people and only occasionally manifested through certain characters with unusual power or in communication with the great spirits of the world in which the African lived.

31. The drama, too, like fine art, had a princely as well as a religious function. In the well developed parts of Africa distinguished by political organizations like kingdoms and empires there arose great rulers who impressed their worth on large areas as conquering and governing heroes. In the absence of a written literature the story-tellers recited their parts in dramatic fashion to perpetuate the memories of these heroes. Thus were celebrated in such drama rulers like Gonga Musa, Sonni Ali, and Askia Mohammed. Later the "griots" thus honored El-Hadj Omar and Samori. Such dramatization took place in the camps, in towns, and almost anywhere on the occasion of great festivals. Sometimes these performances were connected with war.

32. The drama here as already noted was correlated with other arts. Masks which are generally ritualistic were sometimes brought into such dramatizations. The dance was conspicuous, for it was drama itself. Music was an important feature. In pantomime the story could be told in honoring some hero or in appropriately observing some development vital to the people. Architecture, so conspicuous in the modern theatre, was the chief element lacking here among the people who lived mainly out of doors. As the groves in most cases were the only temples of the gods, in Africa likewise were they the theatres. We cannot from the ruins of such imaginary "structures" figure out the staging of the African drama. Literature, oral tradition, is our chief source.

Of this Delafosse bears witness (p. 272) and others discussing this aspect of the life of the African write accordingly. Collectors of African folklore and commentators on their customs also cover this ground inadvertently. Few of them with the exception of Delafosse would dignify African life with the function of the theatre. Delafosse, however, lived among the Africans on the West Coast for more than a generation and therefore saw more than the casual observer or the student from afar could understand.

VI. THE AFRICAN DRAMA—*Continued*
33. MINSTRELSY

VII. AFRICAN INDUSTRIAL ARTS TRANSPLANTED
34. INDUSTRIAL ARTS AMONG SLAVES
a. MECHANICS ON PLANTATIONS
b. LOCAL MANUFACTURING IN TOWNS

33. In these performances as described especially in the comedies there was much mimicry. Actors disguised themselves in grotesque fashion and thus imitated characters to excite laughter or to entertain the public. In some parts of Africa not only the faces of such participants but even their bodies were painted in bewildering colors to have the desired effect. The use of various sorts of materials for disguise of the whole body and the apparent transformation of it into something like the person or thing mimicked facilitated the performance. This custom like other practices varied according to the temperament of the people. Not much evidence of it was found among the submerged people of the forest. It developed to better effect among the gayer and more astute shepherds and farmers of the plains and the still more highly developed Africans near the West Coast. The extent to which this obtained, however, is not yet known. We do not yet know much of what went on in the interior. We are beginning to learn that the East Coast is more interesting than we first thought.

34. There are in our universities professors of national and international standing who in writing and speaking on Africa like one having authority are nevertheless so ignorant of our background as to say that the African imported into America retained nothing but his temperament. This assertion by itself if we had no other grounds for estimating our knowledge is sufficient to show the utter lack of scholarship with respect to the past of the so-called Dark Continent. One would conclude from such misinformation that much of the darkness is on our side of the Atlantic.

The misleading thought is that because the imported Africans did lose their language, as others here have, and underwent a sort of external Europeanization as other Orientals have done, the Negroes dropped everything else on reaching the American shore. But the American Negro is not a European. He is an American product resulting from the conflict and fusion of Western and Eastern cultures. The American white man is merely the European carried backward to the frontier conditions of the tribes in the northwestern part of Germany and, therefore, developed into the agent of such barbarous methods as racial exploitation, social repression, and lynching. The Negro, therefore, in spite of the lack of opportunity for development has shown more evidence of contributing to the esthetic side of life by continuing in America African creations.

One of the most striking of things transplanted was the African skill in industrial arts. The Africans first discovered iron and early learned to work in other metals. Fairminded writers concede that Africans took the lead as the greatest metal workers of the ancient world. Some of their productions developed so far in the direction of things ornate that they are

VII. AFRICAN INDUSTRIAL ARTS TRANSPLANTED—
Continued

35. PRODUCTIONS IN THE WEST INDIES
36. IN LATIN AMERICA
37. ALONG THE ATLANTIC—CHARLESTON, SAVANNAH,
     MOBILE, AND NEW ORLEANS

referred to as pieces of fine art. The work of Negro mechanics among the first imported Africans may be observed today in several of the oldest parts of America. Occasionally are found implements and utensils made by Negroes of these areas to which they brought their peculiar style of carving and weaving. The author has a dipper thus fashioned for lifting butter from the churn, made by Pompey, a slave in the family of Louis F. Post's grandparents in New Jersey, about one hundred and thirty years ago. This dipper shows the usual lines, angles, and form characteristic of African workmanship.

35. Some evidences of this transplantation are found in the West Indies. It must be noted, however, that in that warm climate house construction was not much of a necessity, for both the European and the imported Africans lived in a crude condition as testified by Admiral Vernon in 1740 and Bryan Edwards in 1806. The natives, as a rule, were confined to the drudgery of producing sugar at which the landlords would quickly grow rich and return to Europe to live thereafter in luxury and ease. The beautification of homes, then, was not much of a necessity in that quarter during the early years. In some few homes of the officials and the well-to-do who finally settled permanently there the imprint of the skill of the Negro-African mechanic is observed. A few articles carried from the West Indies to European museums show this African influence in America.

36. In Latin America where the imported Africans, taking the place of the unprofitable Indian slaves, worked in mines and on coffee plantations as well as on areas producing sugar, the situation in the beginning was not very different from the conditions obtaining on the islands. In the course of time, however, things became more settled as dreams of fabulous wealth were shattered and imported Africans were given the opportunity to rise above drudgery and follow the pursuits of mechanics and artisans. In the churches and cathedrals which slavishly followed European patterns in that Latin atmosphere, as was also the case in certain parts of the West Indies, there was not sufficient freedom in the construction of edifices to permit much engrafting of foreign ideas. In a few structures not thus dominated by fixed standards some evidences of African skill and art may still be traced. In objects of local manufacture during the earliest colonial period this African influence is more apparent. One may examine these in museums.

37. In what is now the United States settled by British, less dominated in this sphere by home ideals, the Negro mechanics and artisans had more liberty to draw upon their originality in the case of house decoration. The actual construction, however, was European; and the Negro worker had no such function as to determine general outlines. If he could add anything to the beauty of the establishment there was no serious objection as long as

VII. AFRICAN INDUSTRIAL ARTS TRANSPLANTED—
Continued

38. LOST GROUND SINCE EMANCIPATION

VIII. CONTRIBUTION TO MUSIC IN AMERICA

39. FOLKSONGS WITH FOLKLORE

a. SPIRITUALS
b. JUBILEE
c. JAZZ

these structures provided comfort and showed the capacity for endurance. Such decorations are still observed in some of the oldest colonial mansions; and homes built by Negroes in cities like Charleston, Savannah, Mobile, and New Orleans have some of these same characteristics. While trying to follow European models the imported African artisan could not throw aside what he had brought with him from Africa.

38. With the rise of the white mechanics and artisans coming from Europe and developing in this country the Negroes working in these spheres began to lose ground, and the influence of Africa in the industrial arts in America tended to pass out. Negro workers about a hundred years ago began to face the rising tide of trades-unionism which has tended to eliminate them from this sphere. Even before the Civil War the Negro workers ceased to make the tools, the furniture, the shoes, and the clothes used on the plantations; and these former workers were not accepted in the factories which began to supply such products. Since emancipation these forces have operated to diminish still further the number of Negroes thus employed, and mechanization in the modern world has about closed this chapter of the story.

39. That the folk music, like folk literature of the imported Africans, should be transplanted to America was a natural result. The folk music of other nations and races has undergone transplantation. That the African music would thus endure was rendered still more necessary by the isolation of the Negroes on the plantations where only a few out of a hundred had any close contact with the pioneering Americans. As far as the endurance of the folksongs of these Negroes did not prove prejudicial to the interests of their exploiters there could be no reason for stamping out these manifestations. Finding no serious objections to singing when other avenues of expression were closed, the Negro in conformity to the law of economy in the social world, made this form of expression do the work of others. Concentrating thus on musical expression, the Negroes harking back to the melancholy manifestations of the African shores, could easily portray in song the ills of slavery. Rising occasionally to the heights where they could see a ray of hope, they had reason to rejoice in jubilee chants as well as to pour forth lamentations of the deep spirituals while groping in darkness through an unfriendly sphere. These "canticles of love and woe" are more than songs, for they trace the history of the Negro from Africa to America and depict his past and present status in the New World. Functioning as such then in the life of a people, this music has taken its place in esthetic history

VIII. CONTRIBUTION TO MUSIC IN AMERICA—*Continued*

40. NEGLECTED BY NEGROES
41. POPULAR AS COMIC MANIFESTATIONS

as one of the most remarkable contributions of modern times. Negro folk music is the only great contribution which America has made to art.

Care should be taken here, however, not to confuse the spiritual and the jubilee with what is commonly referred to as jazz, a post bellum production of Negro musicians in the United States. Jazz, as pointed out above, has no connection with African music except in its resemblance to the tom-tom which is an instrument of dance rather than of music. Jazz at its worst is Negro music broken down. At its best jazz is an effort of a few Negro composers who would like to imitate that barbaric melody found among the Africans in the depths of the forest. For lack of contact with that land these composers working with an insufficient knowledge of the African background have produced some horrible melodies which intelligent Negroes deplore, but a few like Duke Ellington have composed certain strains which have evoked the admiration of the best musical circles. What jazz is and what it will become, however, the modern world does not yet know. At present it cannot be scientifically evaluated.

40. When the Negroes of the United States became free and studied European music made popular through their churches and schools, they took great pride in getting away from the plantation music to which in their mentally undeveloped stage they were restricted. Even those Negroes who could not attend school and acquire this appreciation of European music believed nevertheless that these folksongs composed in the humiliation of slavery should be neglected and thrown aside. The uneducated Negroes of the early post bellum years, those above singing folksongs and not sufficiently advanced for European music, composed a new kind of song, commonly referred to as the "shouting hymn." They were thus designated for the reason that in the churches on Sunday after the choir had surfeited the audience with excellent European music which the majority of the congregation could not appreciate, the pastor, out of deference to those who had not thus been spiritually fed, would permit some one to start from the floor one of these soul-stirring tunes which usually ended in a triumphant shout "on the way to glory."

When Fisk, Hampton, and Tuskegee took up the plantation music and staged productions of it throughout the country the most highly educated Negroes threw up their hands in holy horror; and some of this class dislike these institutions today on this account. The singing of such songs caused a strike of the student body at Howard University. For years Wilberforce would not have folksong singing on its campus. Negroes well trained in the rudiments of music and serving in the conservatories of these institutions would not for a moment raise one of these folk tunes.

41. One reason for this attitude, however, was that the entire American public, lacking in appreciation of the beautiful, misunderstood the Negro folksong. The American people of that day saw only the comic and festive side of this music. And it was appalling to see groups of students from our

VIII. CONTRIBUTION TO MUSIC IN AMERICA—*Continued*

42. DIGNIFIED BY J. W. WORK
43. CLAIMED BY WHITES

best institutions going through the back doors of halls and hotels to sing to clubs of ignorant, drunken, rich white men and women who, for being thus entertained a few moments, would give small sums to the support of the institutions which these youths represented. These revellers were looking for a thrill; and some of them developed since slavery, or outside of that area where this system obtained, found the music new and interesting but could not appreciate its meaning.

This tendency of the liberated Negro to forget this remnant of slavery days was not peculiar to this art. The Negro had the same attitude toward everything connected with his past. He did not care to hear anything about his African background. Africa was the "Dark Continent," and the American Negro desired to feel that he had no connection with that benighted land. He readily agreed with those "scholars" who said that the Negro retained nothing that he brought from Africa but his temperament. The break was complete. Negroes also made a desperate effort to forget that they had been slaves. Some Negroes tried to forget that they were Negroes and seriously objected to being thus designated. To refer to one as being black was an insult. Under such circumstances this important contribution of the Negro to art could not be appreciated.

42. Fortunately John W. Work, long a professor at Fisk University, gave the Negro folk song a new hearing. He published a book, *Folk Songs of the American Negro,* containing not only a collection of these "canticles of love and woe," but a classification and comment as to their origin and purpose. This small but epoch-making volume awakened new interest in the Negroes' musical background and served as the key to a new interpretation of the soul of the race. All other worthwhile commentaries on the Negro folk music like those of White, Fisher, Johnson, Odum, Jesseye, and Dett have followed the standard set by John W. Work. Unfortunately, however, some of these writers do not give this pioneer musical philosopher credit for the valuable service which he thereby rendered.

Divested of this comic and festive aspect chiefly apparent to the mentally undeveloped, the Negro folk song began to enter circles of Negroes formerly closed. Churches gradually took them up in connection with their services, concert managers found it profitable to have their stars render at least a few of these numbers, and theatres permitted the staging of efforts of composers to bring these fragments together with the theme of a grand opera. For lack of sufficient capital and the still inadequate audience for such performances these ambitious undertakings have not succeeded. The Negro folk songs, however, have won their way both in Europe and America. A number of composers on both sides of the Atlantic, like Dvorak, have been influenced by this Negro music.

43. It is to be hoped that the American Negro has not become thus interested in his background too late. The American whites, in keeping with their custom of making history to order in fiat fashion, are now writing

IX. THE AMERICAN NEGRO IN DRAMA

44. RESTRICTION TO MIMICRY AND DANCE
45. MINSTRELSY FROM THE PLANTATION

books to prove that this valuable contribution to art was not made by the Negroes. In their earlier days in America the whites developed this music, they say, and the Negroes merely copied it. Of course, if we follow the usual order of things in the United States that settles the matter. If the traducer of the race says that it is a fact, for his following it is a fact. George Pullen Jackson who has written one of these works for this purpose, *White Spirituals in the Southern Uplands,* elaborates this claim; but he adduces no facts in support of this position except that Negroes did take over certain church hymns from the whites, a thing which no one doubts, for the whites also took over hymns from Negroes as would be perfectly natural in case of such close contacts. See Maud Cuney Hare's *Negro Musicians and Their Music* (Washington, 1936).

The Negro spirituals, however, developed out of the sufferings of African souls, out of experiences which the whites in America never had. Among people passing through an ordeal art develops. The Greeks never had much art until they saw their beautiful country overrun by Orientals who killed their leaders and trampled upon them. So when the Negro saw blood lashed from his back, he sang, "Nobody Knows the Trouble I See; Nobody Knows but Jesus." When in the midst of his trials he could find no one to comfort him he sang, "Steal Away to Jesus; I Ain't Got Long To Stay Here." When he saw that there was no escape from his oppressor he had some consolation in the thought of final deliverance and sang, "I'm So Glad Trouble Don't Last Always." When in old age the burdens accumulated to the point of being unbearable, he sang, "Swing Low Sweet Chariot, Coming to Carry Me Home." When the Negro saw at worship the hypocrite who so cruelly abused the slave he sang, "Everybody Talking About Heaven Ain't Going There." These are spirituals.

44. In his *Black Manhattan* James Weldon Johnson has well established the fact that the American theatre has not permitted the Negro actor to rise above the level of the clown. There have been numerous attempts of Negroes to break into a higher histrionic sphere, but for lack of capital to provide for their own amusements and education while lacking at the same time a sufficiently large appreciative audience, these undertakings have failed. Attempts of this sort made since 1865 have not been much more encouraging than those efforts in this sphere prior to the general emancipation. Yet both the American and European have conceded the unusual histrionic ability of the Negro, many of them estimating him more highly than they do the Caucasian. The difficulty seems to be due to the fact that in spite of the Negro's ability in this sphere the Caucasian does not welcome his black compeer as a competitor on the stage.

45. Inasmuch as the other actor believes that he can do everything satisfactorily except the mimicry, the dance, or breakdown developed in the depths of slavery the Negro on the stage has been used only to perpetuate these traditions. Here again the highly trained Negro, assimilated to

IX. THE AMERICAN NEGRO IN DRAMA—*Continued*

46. THE ENDURANCE OF THE CLOWN ON THE STAGE
47. MORE RECOGNITION ABROAD

modern standards, seriously objects. He wants to see the Negro figure in Shakespeare and vie with the best on the stage in America and Europe. The Negro, according to this point of view, should not cooperate with the traducers of his race in thus caricaturing his people.

In this attitude, however, both Negro actors and their impresarios contend that they are thus justified in dramatizing the race. The picture which they present is that of the average Negro, the representative of the large majority of the race. The highly developed Negro as a significant factor has not yet arrived. He is of the small minority; and to center the portrayal of the whole race around him would be a distortion of facts. While all the truth may not be on the side of the minstrel and the clown the fastidious Negroes do not seem to realize that the greatest possibility for dramatizations in their history is slavery. That ordeal was a great tragedy which may supply hundreds of themes for the stage. Since emancipation the race has made an encouraging step forward, but the masses have not yet worked their way through any great crisis to heights from which they may look back upon glorious achievement. The Negroes in the United States have had many troubles to encounter, but the world is not interested in the troubles of particular groups. These are matters to be taken care of on the inside.

46. The Negro clown on the stage, then, has endured. Actors like Sam Lucas, Billy Kersands had their day with the minstrels when *Uncle Tom's Cabin* was being shoved aside to avoid sectional feeling. Ernest Hogan, Robert Cole, Ada Overton Walker, Egbert A. Williams, George Walker, and S. H. Dudley, did not rise to higher ground. Rosamond Johnson as a composer with his brother James Weldon Johnson, collaborating as a writer, gave a little more dignity to the Negro song; but we still saw on the stage the Southern breakdown with "coon songs" and "new coon songs." A little progress was shown in that these actors and singers, although restricted still to mimicry and dance, sometimes selected their themes from the life of the Negro since the Civil War. One Negro dared to go so far as to show the progress of the race in composing the song, "I've Got a White Man Working for Me." After all, however, the portraiture was that of the Negro on the lowest level. A struggling race did not like this representation, for it seemed to be subtle propaganda to hold the Negro down to that level.

47. A little hope remained with the Negro, however, when he received some recognition abroad. Just as Ira Aldridge had gone to Europe to distinguish himself as a Shakespearean actor, other Negroes thus inclined have penetrated that sphere. Unfortunately, however, most of such Negroes who have thus attempted to impress Europe have not been properly trained for the stage and have lacked knowledge of foreign languages in which they might have better presented their case on that side of the Atlantic. Restricted mainly to England, dominated by race distinctions chiefly of American importation, some of these adventurers abroad have had a rather

IX. THE AMERICAN NEGRO IN DRAMA—*Continued*
48. ADMIRATION FROM AFAR IN AMERICA
49. THE NEGLECT OF THE LIFE OF THE NEGRO

narrow sphere. The large majority of them, therefore, have been engaged only for musical and dance performances which can be interpreted visually; and unfortunately too many of these have been in aggregations known as jazz bands. Representing the lower type of the Negro musicians rather than the more highly developed jazz organizations permanent in the United States, these performers have not lived up to the high level they reached when they set Europe wild with jazz immediately after the World War. It is fortunate for the Negro, however, that the race has recently received recognition in the highest spheres which have welcomed Roland Hayes as a singer and Paul Robeson both in this rôle and that of an actor. Many regret that the late Richard B. Harrison who immortalized himself as the star of "Green Pastures" did not have the opportunity to see how Europe would have received him in this drama.

48. It is clear that recently the public in the United States has been inclined to accept the Negro restrictedly in the higher histrionic spheres; but in the two most striking cases, those of Hayes and Robeson, they had to win their spurs abroad. The Negro actor in America, then, is still admired only from afar. The forces militating against the race in other spheres appear also in this. The Negro actor like Richard B. Harrison, finds an opportunity by accident only; after toiling unsuccessfully almost to the end of his career he finally did well something which the public accepted. There can be little wonder, then, that the richer traditions of the African in the drama have had to be restricted to expression through mimicry and breakdown. With the broadening of the mind of all people in America, the Negro may some day find full opportunity on the stage.

49. Many students of Negro life and history believe that the Negro has made a mistake in neglecting to dramatize his own life and history as it should be rather than participate in the distortion of it by the traducers of the race. The excuse made is that the other people are not thus interested, and the majority of Negroes are not theatre-going people, as noted in the chapter on actors and showmen in the author's *Negro Professional Man and the Community*. Most Negroes have developed under strictly primitive church indoctrination which brands the theatre as an evil.

The most plausible explanation of this neglect, however, is that the Negro has not been interested in his background. What he has known of it has been revealed through the traducer who has painted both the African and the American Negro in a distorted attitude. With an increasing interest in the scientific study of the Negro during recent years the minds of the people have been disabused of some of these false ideas. The intelligent Negro no longer feels that he is disgraced by not being white, and he himself has begun to evaluate his own contributions. Plays are being written to dramatize various aspects of the history of the Negro, and actors well trained in schools of dramatics are staging them, as shown by Willis Richardson and Mae Miller's *Negro History in Thirteen Plays* (Washington, 1935).

X. IN PAINTING AND SCULPTURE

50. Brought from Africa into America to be forced into the mold of slavery where conditions with respect to art and architecture were not much more conducive to creative work than were those obtaining in Africa, little achievement in this sphere followed. The Negro had not the opportunity for such creative work as painting to the extent that he was called upon to apply himself in the industrial arts. Shuffling off the shackles of slavery, however, the Negro as a free man easily developed in that direction. Negro children brought into private and public schools were often scolded or punished because they were too eager to draw pictures when they should be trying to read, write and cipher. The Negro is still being punished for dancing too much. The American people in the frontier stage could not understand these propensities of the Negro toward fine arts. This was lacking even in the first educators who had charge of training the Negroes immediately after their emancipation.

Yet before the Civil War there were Negroes who distinguished themselves in the fine arts in spite of the discouragement of being denied helpful associations and the opportunity to undergo training for such work. Among those noted were Edmund Bannister in painting and Edmonia Lewis in sculpture. The struggle during the first years of freedom for the possession of the material things of life overshadowed other interests and precluded the possibility of rapid development toward the esthetic ideal among people whose latent powers indicated possibility.

51. Henry O. Tanner complains that he could not grow in this stifling atmosphere and had to transplant himself to France for that more congenial circle in which he has developed unto full stature. May Howard Jackson and Meta Vaux Warrick Fuller in sculpture and William E. Scott, William A. Harper, and Laura Wheeler Waring in painting have tried to show the ability of the Negro to conform to academic standards. These, however, have not reached Tanner's level.

52. Because of the increase in interest of the Negro in his background the world has become much more interested in sculptors like Sargent Johnson, Richmond Barthé, and Augusta Savage, and in painters like Aaron Douglass, Alexander Motley, and James Lesesne Wells than in the work of academicians. These new workers have been given honorable mention and much publicity through the publications of art brought out by the Harmon Foundation of New York City. It is interesting to observe in the careers of most of these persons that they have been better trained than workers of former years. Their minds have been broadened by more knowledge of history and literature as well as by study of the fine arts. Their productions consequently have shown broader conceptions of the task and keener powers of execution. Numerous other students in the field of fine arts now in process of development in the educational centers of this country will doubtless measure up to the status of those who have been recently recognized. It is unfortunate that many of these workers are not financially situated to finish their studies

X. IN PAINTING AND SCULPTURE—*Continued*
53. An Increasing Number of Artists
54. Interest in the African Background

abroad, for they do not have here all of the opportunities which America might afford.

53. The increase in the number of artists now operating in this sphere is not spasmodic but results from proper emphasis. It impresses one as a sort of spontaneous evolution resulting from a general awakening of the Negro to an appreciation of his own capacity and development of a will power to apply himself to that in which he happens to be interested regardless of forces which may try to divert him to the contrary. While there has been a desirable tendency toward placing more emphasis upon esthetic education this has not become general. The majority of the schools now engaged in the education of the Negro are emphasizing those things in which history reveals that he has not shown any greater aptitude than the average man. In American education the special gifts of the Negro have been generally ignored. When he finishes his education he has to go out in life and struggle in the hit-or-miss fashion; and if he succeeds it is usually by accident. Only recently have large Negro universities established departments of fine arts; and recently under the dictation of persons of another race, one of these departments was scheduled for disestablishment.

54. The present tendency to concentrate more generally on the study of the African background has been very helpful to the development of the Negro in the fine arts in the United States. Here it is not only a matter of aptitude in this particular line but also the position of portraying greater situations and themes of which we have never heard. With increased power, new insight, and broader vision, the Negro artist has a great future in spite of all the discouragements which may be listed as now facing him.

IMPORTANT EVENTS AND DATES IN
NEGRO HISTORY

January 1. Emancipation Proclamation issued by Abraham Lincoln, 1863. *The Liberator* first issued by William Lloyd Garrison, 1831. Haiti declared its Independence, 1804.

January 1. Kumbi (Ghana) discovered to be in its apogee, 990.

January 3. Lucretia Mott, Pennsylvania abolitionist, born, 1793.

January 4. Benjamin Lundy, colonizationist, born, 1789.

January 6. Charles Sumner, fearless advocate of equality and justice, born, 1811.

January 17. Benjamin Franklin, a supporter of the Anti-slavery movement, born, 1706.

January 17. The Virgin Islands purchased by the United States, 1917.

January 17. Paul Cuffe, a Negro business man, first actual colonizationist, born, 1759.

January 21. Osai Tutu Kwamina defeated the British under Sir Charles McCarthy at Assamako, Ashanti, 1824.

January 23. Lott Carey, Negro minister and pioneer leader in Liberia, sailed for that country in 1821.

January 26. Bishop William Capers, founder of missions for Negroes in South Carolina, born, 1790.

January 28. George S. Boutwell, author of the Thirteenth Amendment, born, 1818.

January 29. Thomas Paine, an advocate of freedom, born, 1737.

January 31. Anthony Benezet, a teacher of Negroes and promoter of the anti-slavery cause in Pennsylvania, born, 1713.

February 1. Charles Lenox Remond, Negro abolitionist, born, 1810.

February 4. James G. Birney, Free Soil candidate for President, born, 1792.

February 10. Joseph C. Price, Negro orator and educator, born, 1854.

February 12. Abraham Lincoln, born, 1809.

February 14. Frederick Douglass's Birthday.

February 15. Senator B. K. Bruce presided over the United States Senate.

February 16. Henry Wilson, abolitionist, born, 1812.

February 20. Angelina E. Grimké, South Carolina abolitionist, born, 1805.

February 22. George Washington, the liberator of his slaves, born, 1732.

February 22. James Russell Lowell, liberal poet, born, 1819.

February 24. Bishop Daniel A. Payne, reformer and educator of the A. M. E. Church, born, 1811.

February 25. Hiram R. Revels, first Negro United States Senator, took the oath of office, 1870.

February 27. Dominican Republic established, 1844.

February 27. Henry W. Longfellow, liberal poet, born, 1807.

February 28. Phillis Wheatley, Negro writer of verse, invited by George Washington to visit him, 1776.

March 1. The Abyssinians defeated the Italians at Adowa, 1896.

March 1. B. K. Bruce, United States Senator, born, 1841.

March 1. Cudjoe, leader of the Maroons in Jamaica brings the Jamaican Government to terms in 1738.

March 5. Crispus Attucks, a Negro seaman, fell in the Boston Massacre, 1770.

March 7. Little Stephen, a Negro, sets out to explore the Southwestern part of the United States, 1539.

March 10. El-Hadj Omar, Tukulor Conqueror, started his empire with the capture of Segu, 1861.

March 12. Benjamin Bannaker with L'Enfant to lay out Washington in the District of Columbia, 1791.

March 14. Menelik became ruler of Abyssinia, 1889.

March 17. The Republic of Texas prohibited the slave trade, 1836.

March 18. Gabriel de la Concepción Valdes (Placido), poet, born in Havana, Cuba, 1809.

March 23. Slavery abolished in Porto Rico, 1873.

March 25. British Parliament abolished slave trade, 1807.

March 25. Samori, the builder of the Wasulu Empire, signed with the French the Treaty of Bisandugu, 1887.

March 28. Samuel Sewall, anti-slavery author, born, 1652.

March 30. Thomas Clarkson, English abolitionist, born, 1760.

March 30. Promulgation of the Fifteenth Amendment, 1870.

April 1. Thomas Fowell Buxton, British Emancipationist, born, 1786.

April 2. Thomas Jefferson, advocate of freedom, born, 1743.

April 3. Edward Everett Hale, anti-slavery writer, born, 1822.

April 3. James Madison Bell, Negro poet, born, 1826.

April 4. Thaddeus Stevens, distinguished reconstructionist, born, 1792.

April 9. Surrender of Robert E. Lee, 1865.

April 10. Judge John Belton O'Neal, of South Carolina, advocate of the enlightenment of the Slaves, born, 1793.

April 12. Battle of Fort Pillow during the Civil War, 1864.

April 14. First Abolition Society in the United States organized, 1775.

April 16. Emancipation in the District of Columbia, 1862.

April 17. Francis Williams, first Negro college graduate in the Western Hemisphere, published Latin poem in 1758.

April 18. Booker T. Washington, born, 1856.

May 5. The Will of Thaddeus Kosciusko, providing for the education of Negroes, 1798.

May 6. Martin R. Delany, Negro army officer and author, born, 1812.

May 9. John Brown, the Martyr, born, 1800.

May 10. Elizabeth Taylor Greenfield, a Negro woman, invited to sing before Queen Victoria, 1854.

May 10. P. B. S. Pinchback, Negro reconstruction statesman, born, 1837.

May 13. Robert Smalls, of South Carolina, dared to take the *Planter* to the Union Fleet, 1862.

May 14. Abolition of slavery in Brazil, 1888.

May 20. Toussaint Louverture, Haitian liberator, born, 1743.

May 22. Arthur Tappan, abolitionist, born, 1786.

May 23. Assault on Port Hudson, 1863.

May 23. Lewis Tappan, abolitionist, born, 1788.

May 25. Ralph W. Emerson, advocate of freedom, born, 1803.
May 28. Daniel Reaves Goodloe, North Carolina emancipationist, born, 1814.
May 31. Walt Whitman, open-minded poet, born, 1819.
June 3. The United States recognized Hayti and Liberia as nations, 1846.
June 10. Richard Allen started independent African Methodist movement, 1794.
June 10. Antonio Candido Goncales Crespo, Portuguese poet, born, 1883.
June 14. Harriet Beecher Stowe, born, 1811.
June 16. Dessalines became emperor of Hayti, 1804.
June 20. Charles Waddell Chesnutt, Negro novelist, born, 1858.
June 21. Henry Ossawa Tanner, famous Negro-American painter transplanted to France, born, 1859.
June 21. James Varick elected first bishop of the A. M. E. Z. Church, 1821.
June 22. Lord Mansfield's decision in the Somerset case, 1772.
June 24. Henry Ward Beecher, promoter of equal rights, born, 1813.
June 27. Paul Laurence Dunbar, born, 1872.
July 1. Slavery abolished in the Dutch West Indies, 1863.
July 4. Booker T. Washington opened school at Tuskegee, 1881.
July 4. E. M. Bannister, painter of African blood, exhibited "Under the Oaks" at the Centennial Exposition in Philadelphia which was awarded first prize, 1876.
July 16. Pompey at Stoney Point with Anthony Wayne, 1779.
July 17. The arming of Negroes approved by Congress, 1862.
July 18. Lemuel Haynes, Negro preacher to whites, born, 1753.
July 21. Charles L. Reason, Negro teacher and poet, born, 1818.
July 24. Alexandre Dumas, père, the great French novelist, born, 1803.
July 24. Ira Aldridge, Shakespearean actor acknowledged in Europe, born, 1804.
July 25. Maria Weston Chapman, abolitionist, born, 1806.
July 28. Fourteenth Amendment declared ratified, 1868.
July 29. Alexandre Dumas, fils, French author, born, 1824.
July 31. Europeans get their first glimpse of Chaka, the distinguished chieftain of the Zulus, 1824.
August 1. Slavery finally abolished in British dependencies, 1834.
August 3. Edward W. Blyden, scholar and diplomat, born, 1832.
August 4. Robert Purvis, Negro abolitionist, born, 1810.
August 20. Twenty Negroes brought as slaves to Jamestown, 1619.
August 21. Nat Turner's Insurrection, 1831.
August 23. Jean Baptiste Lislet-Geoffroy, a distinguished French geographer, grandson of Touca Niama, King of Galam, born, 1755.
August 23. African Methodist Episcopal Church incorporated, 1796.
August 24. Theodore Parker, liberal-minded minister, born, 1810.
August 24. Independence of Liberia proclaimed, 1847.
August 31. Gonga Musa (Mansa Musa), the most famous of the rulers of the Manding, went on a pious pilgrimage to Mecca, 1324.
September 1. Hiram R. Revels, first Negro United States Senator, born, 1822.
September 1. Bishop Charles Betts Galloway, of Mississippi, promoter of interracial goodwill, born, 1849.
September 6. Marquis de Lafayette, friend of the Negro, born, 1757.

September 9. John Gregg Fee, Kentucky abolitionist and founder of Berea College, born, 1816.

September 11. Angelo Solimann (Mmadi-Maké) Warrior under Joseph II, of the Holy Roman Empire, born, 1721.

September 11. Samuel J. May, abolitionist, born, 1797.

September 18. Second Fugitive Slave Act passed, 1850.

September 22. Lincoln gave notice of his intention to proclaim the emancipation of the slaves, 1862.

September 24. Jupiter Hammon published his Address to the Negroes of New York, 1786.

September 28. David Walker, author of the "Appeal" against slavery, born 1785.

October 7. William Still, Negro anti-slavery worker and agent of the Underground Railroad, born, 1821.

Juan Latino, Spanish Negro poet, writes Latin poem in celebration of the Battle of Lepanto, 1571.

October 10. Robert Gould Shaw, colonel of the Fifty-Fourth Massachusetts Regiment, born, 1837.

October 16. John Brown's attack on Harper's Ferry, 1859.

October 19. Cassius Marcellus Clay, Kentucky emancipationist, born, 1810.

October 19. John Woolman, anti-slavery worker, born, 1720.

October 25. William Goodell, abolitionist and author of the *American Slave Code,* born, 1792.

October 28. Levi Coffin, organizer of the "Underground Railroad," born, 1798.

November 1. Elijah P. Lovejoy, the abolitionist killed by a pro-slavery mob at Alton, Illinois, 1837.

November 3. William Cullen Bryant, liberal-minded poet, born, 1794.

November 9. Benjamin Bannaker, Negro inventor and astronomer, born, 1731.

November 11. Elihu Embree, Tennessee emancipationist, born, 1782.

November 11. Bishop William Meade, preacher to Negroes in Virginia, born, 1789.

November 17. Behanzin, King of Dahomey, made his last stand against the French in defense of his native land, 1892.

November 17. Henrique Dias, distinguished Negro general, won a decisive battle against the Dutch in Brazil, 1636.

November 17. Stephen S. Foster, abolitionist, born, 1809.

November 25. Andrew Carnegie, philanthropist, born, 1835.

November 26. Sara Grimké, South Carolina anti-slavery worker, born, 1792.

November 29. Wendell Phillips, orator of the abolition cause, born, 1811. Edmonia Lewis, a sculptor of African blood, presents medallion portrait of Wendell Phillips.

November 29. Louisa May Alcott, anti-slavery sympathizer, born, 1832.

November 30. Askia the Great claimed the throne vacated by the death of Sonni Ali, 1492.

December 2. John Brown executed at Charleston, West Virginia, 1859.

December 4. Bishop Henri Grégoire, anti-slavery worker in France, born, 1750.

December 6. Christopher Columbus discovered the Island of Haiti, 1496.

December 7. Antonio Maceo, the martyr, died in battle for the liberty of Cuba, 1896.

December 10. William Lloyd Garrison, born, 1805.

December 12. Joseph H. Rainey takes his seat as the first Negro member of the House of Representatives, 1870.

December 14. John M. Langston, Negro Representative in Congress, born, 1829.

December 15. Colored Methodist Episcopal Church established, 1870.

December 15. Frank Sanborn, anti-slavery author, born, 1831.

December 17. John G. Whittier, the anti-slavery poet, born, 1807.

December 18. Thirteenth Amendment declared ratified, 1865.

December 20. Charles Colcock Jones, missionary to Negroes in Georgia, born, 1804.

December 20. Moshesh, the builder of the Basuto nation, defeated the Boers in the Battle of Berea Mountain, 1852.

December 22. Thomas Wentworth Higginson, commander of Negro soldiers in Civil War, born, 1823.

December 23. Henry Highland Garnet, Negro minister and reformer, born, 1815.

December 25. Le Chevalier de Saint Georges, distinguished French musician and soldier of African blood, born, 1745.

December 28. The American Colonization Society organized, 1816.

INDEX

A

Aahmes, 26
Abdallah, 122
Abdallah-ben-Yassine, 49
Abdelkader, 122
Abdelkerim, 122
Abderrahman Gaurang, 122
Abderrahmin I, 124
Abdulkader Torodo, 104
Abdullah, 126
Abel el-Hakem, 86
Abolition, 294, 318, 319, 411-412
Abou el-Hacen, 30, 57
Abron, the, 117
Abu-Dardai, 50
Abu Ishak, 57
Abubakari, 56, 81
Abubakari II, 56
Abubekr, 49, 53, 124, 125
Abubekr-ben-Omar, 50
Abubekr Guerbei, 122
Abu-Sekkine, a ruler, 122
Abyssinia, 25, 126, 127, 140, 248
Adams, John Quincy, 396
Adams, Nehemiah, 396
Adams, Samuel, 261, 281, 282
Adanzan, a ruler, 118
Addresses, 408, 412
Adja, the, 118
Administration in ancient Africa, 68-69
Adowa, the battle of, 29, 140
Adrar, 49
Advanced education, 354
Aeschylus, references of, to Africa, 4, 217, 236
Afar, the, 127
Afno (Hausa) States, 82-88, 120, 198, 199
Africa, physical features, of, 1, 2, 3, 4, 5, 6
African background, the summary of, 179-187; outlined, 198-216
African natives under Europeans, 143-148; culture, 149-156; survivals in America, 168-175; school of art, 439; traditions, 323

Agitation, the increase of, 120; against educational restrictions, 341
Agni, the, 117, 428
Agonglo, a ruler, 118
Agriculture, 150, 213, 259, 277, 278, 279-280
Ahl-Massine, the, 41
Ahmadu, 107
Aïr, 88, 121
Akaba, 118
Akil, 60
Alawine, 122
Alcott, Louisa M., 398
Ali, a ruler, 121, 124
Ali Buri, 102
Ali Folen, 69
Ali Ghajideni, 87
Ali Kolon, 64-65
Allada, the, 118
Allakoi, 54
Allen, Richard, 286, 360
Almohades, the, 30
Al-Morabetin, the, 49
Almoravides, 49, 50, 90-96, 193, 194, 200
Aloama or Idris III, of Bornu, 88
Alphonso VI, 49-50
Amadi N'Gone N'Della Cumba, a ruler, 103
Amari-Sonko, 55
Ambrose, 219
Amenemhat I and III, the statues of, 26
America, African survivals in, 168-175; the Negro in, 256-315
American Colonization Society, 114
American literature, the Negro in, 392-424
American Revolution, the Negro in, 114, 282-284, 359, 360
Amo, Anton Wilhelm, 228, 249
Amozighs, 8
Amusements, 214
Ancients, their knowledge of Africa, 1-19
Andrews, Sidney, 398
Anglicans, 327

463